MAKING THE UNIPOLAR MOMENT

MAKING THE UNIPOLAR MOMENT

U.S. FOREIGN POLICY AND THE RISE OF THE POST–COLD WAR ORDER

HAL BRANDS

CORNELL UNIVERSITY PRESS

Ithaca and London

First published 2016 by Cornell University Press

Printed in the United States of America

Library of Congress Cataloging-in-Publication Data

Names: Brands, Hal, 1983– author.
Title: Making the unipolar moment : U.S. foreign policy
    and the rise of the post-Cold War order / Hal Brands.
Description: Ithaca : Cornell University Press, 2016. |
    Includes bibliographical references and index.
Identifiers: LCCN 2015048539
ISBN 9781501702723 (cloth : alk. paper)
Subjects: LCSH: United States—Foreign relations—
    1977–1981. | United States—Foreign relations—
    1981–1989. | United States—Foreign
    relations—1989–1993.
Classification: LCC E872 .B73 2016 |
    DDC 327.73009/04—dc23
LC record available at http://lccn.loc.gov/2015048539

Cornell University Press strives to use environmentally responsible suppliers and materials to the fullest extent possible in the publishing of its books. Such materials include vegetable-based, low-VOC inks and acid-free papers that are recycled, totally chlorine-free, or partly composed of nonwood fibers. For further information, visit our website at www.cornellpress.cornell.edu.

Cloth printing   10 9 8 7 6 5 4 3 2 1

Contents

Acknowledgments

A book's acknowledgments are rarely sufficient to convey the extent of an author's debts. I have become ever more conscious of that fact in writing this book. This book draws on research done as far back as 2004–2005, and on ideas that I have been mulling over for several years. It follows that I have racked up a daunting list of intellectual, professional, and personal debts along the way.

I have benefited from the assistance and guidance of archivists far too many to mention, and from the support and wonderful intellectual climate provided by my home institution, the Duke Sanford School of Public Policy. I have equally benefitted from my interaction with individuals who helped me formulate, reconsider, and refine some of the key ideas in this book. An undoubtedly incomplete list includes Colin Dueck, Charles Edel, Eric Edelman, Jeffrey Engel, John Gaddis, Peter Feaver, Bruce Jentleson, Judith Kelley, Bruce Kuniholm, Melvyn Leffler, Peter Mansoor, John Maurer, Williamson Murray, Joshua Rovner, Daniel Sargent, Josh Shifrinson, and James Wilson. I am particularly grateful to Frank Gavin, James Goldgeier, Robert McMahon, and Jeremi Suri, all of whom read the complete manuscript and offered invaluable comments. At Cornell University Press, Michael McGandy offered support along with insightful advice and was, as always, a pleasure to work with.

My greatest debts by far, of course, are owed to my family. Emily, Henry, Annabelle, and Dolly put up with a lot of long hours and authorial absent-mindedness as I was researching and composing the book. But they were always unfailingly loving and supportive, and having them in my life has been the greatest inspiration I can imagine. They did more than anyone else to make this book possible. And so it is dedicated, with great love, to them.

Introduction
Structure, Strategy, and American Resurgence

1979 was a bad year for U.S. foreign policy. At home, the country was being battered by stagflation and high oil prices, developments that raised fundamental questions about the economic underpinnings of American power. Abroad, the United States was suffering a seemingly unending train of setbacks and humiliations. From the overthrow of longtime allies in Iran and Nicaragua, to the seizing of U.S. hostages in Tehran, to the Soviet invasion of Afghanistan and the final collapse of détente, signs of American impotence and geopolitical decay abounded. *Malaise* was the watchword in foreign and domestic affairs alike; all around the world, it seemed, the United States no longer controlled events but was at their mercy. "The principal developments of 1979 registered the continued decline in the nation's international position," wrote one observer in *Foreign Affairs*. "The impact of the events which have brought this decade to a close has been such as to make the fact of America's decline very nearly a commonplace."[1]

This perception of American decline was not simply a product of what had happened in 1979, but of what had happened in the entire decade before that. In many ways, the 1970s had seemed to represent the final passing of the international predominance that Washington had wielded after World War II. In the wake of that conflict, the United States had used its unmatched power to erect a postwar order that carried the distinctive mark of American supremacy. By the 1970s, however, that postwar order—and the supremacy on which it rested—were coming under serious doubt.

The Cold War was frequently feared to be tilting in Moscow's direction, amid a major Soviet military buildup and a string of Kremlin advances— and American defeats—in the Third World. U.S. economic hegemony looked equally imperiled, due to fierce competition from Western Europe and Japan, and the massive vulnerabilities exposed by the oil shocks. Across the developing regions, an increasingly restive global south seemed to be in revolt against U.S. authority. And throughout the decade, from the collapse of Bretton Woods to the fall of Saigon and beyond, the United States had been buffeted by crises that ruthlessly revealed its weaknesses and suggested that its global influence was receding. Against this backdrop, it was hardly surprising that so many informed observers doubted U.S. staying power. During the mid-1970s, no less a figure than Henry Kissinger often deplored the erosion of America's position and the "paralysis" of its diplomacy.[2] By the end of the decade, the warnings were starker still. "The retreat of American power" could "become a rout," former Secretary of Defense and Secretary of Energy James Schlesinger wrote in 1979. "The trend could well become irreversible in many respects."[3] The American century, Schlesinger and like-minded commentators worried, might be dying a premature death.

As we now know, of course, such predictions turned out to be inaccurate. The United States was not destined to see its global leadership slip inescapably away. On the contrary, by the early 1990s the country was enjoying an international supremacy so pronounced that it required an entirely new nomenclature: *unipolarity*.[4] The world had become indisputably unipolar in a geopolitical and military sense, with the Cold War ending on U.S. and Western terms, the opposing Eastern bloc disintegrating, and America's longtime global rival—the Soviet Union—in the process of outright dissolution. No longer were international affairs defined by a bipolar standoff between hostile strategic heavyweights. The new order, rather, had America as the world's sole superpower—the only international actor with truly global reach, and a country whose unmatched military, economic, and diplomatic capabilities gave it a vast margin of power and influence over any competitor. If anything, that influence was poised to expand even further with the Cold War's end, and the events of recent years had generally underscored, rather than undermined, U.S. authority in world affairs. The United States, National Security Adviser Brent Scowcroft wrote, was now "in a unique position, without experience, without precedent, and standing alone at the height of power."[5]

The world had become unipolar in an ideological sense, as well. The values and practices that Washington preferred were experiencing an unprecedented global ascendancy, as democracy and free-market economics spread far and wide. These liberal institutions were flourishing in areas where they had been weak or even absent only years earlier, sweeping across much of the Third World and broad swaths of the former "Second World." Competing ideological models, by contrast, seemed to be in wholesale retreat before this relentless advance. "The end of history" had arrived, one U.S. policymaker memorably declared: the triumph of economic and political liberalism was so complete as to bring mankind's ideological evolution to a close.[6] Hyperbole aside, the preeminence of the U.S.-backed liberal model was striking, and the international system as a whole now appeared to be remaking itself in America's image and to America's advantage. It was, altogether, a remarkable and even stunning turnaround. In just over a decade, the United States had gone from the apparent decline of the late 1970s to the reinvigorated and multidimensional primacy of the post–Cold War era. "Now is the unipolar moment," conservative pundit Charles Krauthammer wrote in 1991; the core feature of global politics was U.S. dominance.[7]

In this book, I examine U.S. foreign policy from the late 1970s to the early 1990s, focusing on two fundamental questions about the arc of American power. First, how did the United States make this transition from malaise to renewed primacy in such a relatively modest amount of time? How, in other words, did a unipolar, post–Cold War order take form following the traumas and travails of the 1970s, and what role did U.S. policy play in forming it? Second, and more generally, what is the relationship between structure and strategy in shaping the global environment? To what extent are major changes in the international order driven by deep structural forces over which policymakers have little direct control, and to what extent are those changes driven by concrete strategy—the deliberate and coordinated use of national power to achieve major objectives—pursued by countries such as the United States? In essence, this book seeks to make sense of a crucial period of transformation and renewal in U.S. foreign policy; it also explores the broader issue of how American power affects, and is affected by, the larger global milieu.

To be clear at the outset, this book is *not* simply another study of the end of the Cold War, the subject that has heretofore dominated the scholarly literature on the period. The trajectory of the late Cold War does certainly play a central role in the story, and one that is informed by the new archival materials and secondary works that are continually enriching our understanding of that issue. This volume, however, opens the analytical aperture wider. It weaves the late superpower struggle into a broader story about the interplay of global change and U.S. policy in the making of the post–Cold War order, one that also gives prominence to subjects like international political economy, processes of democratization and political transformation in the developing world, and the rise of new global challenges such as terrorism and Islamic fundamentalism. As I argue, these and other issues were all integral to crafting the contours of the unipolar order that emerged in the early 1990s. Taking this more holistic view is therefore indispensable to assembling the key pieces of the historical puzzle, and to grappling with the extraordinary changes under consideration here.

This more holistic approach is also what most distinguishes this book from the existing scholarship on the period. As the voluminous and fast-growing literature on the end of the Cold War indicates, historians and other analysts have begun to assess parts of U.S. foreign relations during the 1980s and the years immediately surrounding that decade.[8] What has not yet been done, however, is to draw these various parts together, into the larger whole that is necessary to really make sense of the U.S. resurgence. The relaunching of American primacy from the late 1970s to the early 1990s was one of the most momentous global developments of the late twentieth century, and it can only be understood by examining international events and U.S. policy across a number of key dimensions. To the best of my knowledge, this book is the first to provide such a perspective.[9]

This book is further distinguished by the fact that it draws heavily on relevant archival material, much of which has only recently become available. Admittedly, the archival record on the years from the late 1970s to the early 1990s is not what it should be, and full declassification will not occur for some time. But the frontiers of declassification have progressed far enough that scholars can now use archival materials to study, in considerable detail, American policy on subjects from U.S.-Soviet relations to Persian Gulf security, and on episodes from the Jimmy Carter years through the presidencies of Ronald Reagan and George H. W. Bush. This book relies heavily on such documentation, gathered from presidential libraries and other U.S.-based collections and repositories. It also uses oral histories and interviews, the records of multilateral organizations such as the International Monetary Fund (IMF) and the World Bank, and a smaller number of foreign records relating to the policies of key countries with which U.S. officials interacted. Taken together, these records yield new insights on U.S. policy in a pivotal era, and they shed light on the relationship between volition and circumstance—between American strategy and broader global currents. By aggressively mining the emerging archival and primary-source record, this book offers a fuller picture of its subject than has heretofore been possible.[10]

At the same time, however, this book is necessarily limited and focused in what it seeks to achieve, and two disclaimers regarding scope and method may be useful here. First, this volume is not a full international history of world affairs during this period, but rather emphasizes how U.S. leaders perceived, responded to, and ultimately shaped global change. Telling this story, of course, requires appreciating the international environment in which American initiatives were situated and the policies of the countries with which U.S. officials dealt. Without such analysis, it is impossible really to grasp either the sources or impacts of U.S. behavior. Nonetheless, a complete global history of this period—one that examines in great detail the perspectives of all key nations and participants—is beyond the scope of this project, which remains essentially a study of American policy and strategy in a dynamic international context.

Second, although this book offers a broad perspective on American statecraft in the run-up to the unipolar moment, it is by no means a fully comprehensive account of U.S. policy. My approach here is meant to be more interpretive than encyclopedic—I focus less on covering *all* aspects of U.S. diplomacy than on emphasizing those aspects and themes that were *most critical* to the rise of the unipolar order. The result is an account that is necessarily somewhat selective in what it stresses and what it minimizes or ignores. But it is one that is thereby intended to keep the interpretation and argument relatively clean and clear, and to ensure that the analysis and evidence presented go straight to the heart of the story.[11]

To relate that story, I focus on three principal stages of U.S. renewal. First, I begin by reexamining the 1970s, a period when several deep structural trends were starting to rework the international landscape in America's favor, even as short-term events made it appear decidedly otherwise. Second, I follow the story through the 1980s. This was the crucial decade when U.S. officials—particularly the Reagan administration—increasingly perceived these structural trends, and exploited them through forward-leaning policies that restored American momentum and accentuated the positive forces at work. Third, I conclude by analyzing the climactic period between 1989 and 1992, when George H. W. Bush and his advisers wrestled with the final crises of the bipolar era, while also taking advantage of those crises to forge a post–Cold War order based on U.S. primacy.[12] Throughout this volume, my analysis is therefore on the way that underlying global shifts interacted with specific U.S. initiatives to foster far-reaching changes in the international system. Indeed, a core thesis is that the emergence of the unipolar era reflected a synergistic interaction between structure, on the one hand, and deliberate and proactive strategy, on the other.

I trace this process across six substantive chapters, organized according to the periodization and analytical approach just sketched. As I explain in chapter 1, the American renewal actually began in the 1970s, a decade whose history was far more paradoxical than it initially looked. The difficulties that Washington encountered during that decade were hardly imaginary, and they created pervasive anxiety about U.S. prospects. In doing so, however, they masked the emergence of three profound global trends that were beginning to shift the international environment to longer-term U.S. advantage. The Soviet Union was slipping into irreversible systemic decline, leaving it ill-suited for prolonged geopolitical competition and highly vulnerable to the Western counteroffensive that was gradually taking shape. Meanwhile, the onset of modern-day globalization was rejuvenating U.S. economic power, and setting the stage for the proliferation of free-market practices and ideas. Not least of all, the rise of a transnational human rights consciousness and third-wave democratization were starting to alter world politics in ways that would eventually prove quite beneficial to U.S. ideological proclivities and strategic interests. Amid the day-to-day crises of the 1970s, great historical forces were moving strongly in America's direction, and laying the structural basis for a very different post–Cold War order.

To some extent, U.S. policymakers were even beginning to develop the approaches needed to make the most of those trends. The story of the 1970s was definitely not one of masterful strategy, and as chapter 1 makes clear, U.S. officials from Kissinger to Jimmy Carter often found themselves tossed about by challenges that were hard enough to comprehend, let alone control. What can be said for those officials—in the Gerald Ford and particularly the Carter administrations—is that they did progressively come to understand the more fundamental changes occurring in the world, and to start piecing together initiatives meant to adapt U.S. policy accordingly. The near-term record of those initiatives was not always impressive—Carter's most significant efforts to promote human rights and democracy were catastrophic failures, for instance, and no administration could conquer global economic upheaval. But from the Cold War struggle, to the human rights and democratic revolutions, to the major issues of globalization and international economic relations, the initial components of more effective strategy were slowly, fitfully, and sometimes ironically coming into place. In this sense, the policymakers of the 1970s, although often frustrated in their own time, helped lay the foundations on which their successors would so fruitfully build.

In chapters 2–5, I take the story through the 1980s. This was the period when U.S. leaders truly began to harness the structural forces at work, so as to reassert national power and shape the international environment in highly advantageous ways. The Cold War, for example, was utterly transformed during Ronald Reagan's presidency, and in chapter 2 I contend that perceptive U.S. statecraft was a vital reason why. Even before taking office, Reagan had identified the weaknesses of the Soviet position and the possibilities for a concerted U.S. counterattack. During the early 1980s, his administration built on Carter-era programs to launch a multipronged campaign that pounced on those weaknesses and reclaimed the geopolitical high ground. From mid-decade onward, Reagan and Secretary of State George Shultz then deftly intertwined pressure and diplomacy to elicit a dramatic easing of tensions on remarkably favorable terms. To be sure, U.S. policy toward Moscow was hardly seamless under Reagan, and his eventual successes were assisted enormously by factors such as the worsening crisis of the Soviet system and the innovative leadership of Mikhail Gorbachev. But even so, the course of U.S.-Soviet relations showed that American strategy had become highly attuned to underlying international shifts, and that it was moving energetically to reap the rewards. The result was to help fundamentally alter the trajectory of the Cold War, and to advance that conflict markedly toward its triumphant conclusion.

The Cold War was not the only area in which structural opportunity evoked productive strategy during the 1980s. In chapter 3, I explore how U.S. policy capitalized upon another historic opening by empowering the democratic revolution. As early as the Carter years, American officials had argued that a more democratic, rights-conscious world would be one in which Washington was ideologically and geopolitically ascendant, and they had started more intensively (if not always effectively) to apply U.S. power in the service of liberalization abroad. Despite some significant early backtracking, the Reagan administration ultimately embraced the logic of democracy promotion with even greater fervor, and with far better results. Reagan, Shultz, and other officials pursued a strategy meant to seize upon and extend the moment of democratic opportunity. That strategy mixed long-term efforts to strengthen the building blocks of democracy, with nearer-term initiatives to bolster reformers and move authoritarian regimes toward political openings. Admittedly, the strategy was sometimes applied haltingly, and its implementation entailed unavoidable costs and compromises. But in case after case, from Latin America to East Asia and beyond, U.S. influence became a critical factor in assisting democratic breakthroughs, preventing authoritarian backsliding, and fostering a global climate in which American values and institutions were ever more preponderant. "History is on freedom's side," Shultz said; America had the initiative in the struggle to influence the world's political future.[13]

It also had the initiative in the struggle to shape the global political economy, as I discuss in chapter 4. During the 1970s, major tectonic shifts had begun to create a more integrated world economy in which market principles were advancing and the United States was well situated to prosper. During the 1980s, U.S. strategy helped affirm those shifts and drive the neoliberal advance forward. The Reagan administration had always been committed to fostering a more open, market-oriented order, and over the course of the decade, that administration and the next one would develop the concrete policies and leverage needed to make it happen. After some first-term diffidence, Reagan and his second-term treasury secretary, James Baker, gradually built on the steps taken by their 1970s-era predecessors to renew international cooperation among the major developed countries and thereby smooth the frictions caused by globalization. The administration also managed a fraught relationship with Japan in ways that brought that country more deeply into the global financial system, and it catalyzed a new round of multilateral trade talks that would eventually deliver a far-reaching liberalization of world commerce.

If anything, the gains were more dramatic in the developing regions. Here, U.S. investment, technology, and policy figured centrally in the astonishing economic liberalization undertaken by China from the late 1970s onward. Moreover, in cooperation with the IMF and the World Bank, the Reagan and later the George H. W. Bush administrations used the Third World debt crisis as an aperture to encourage free-market reforms and push globalization into the global south. By the end of the 1980s, the neoliberal order was becoming more firmly entrenched from the First World to the Third, and the international economy was becoming progressively more reflective of U.S. interests. From geopolitics to geoeconomics, American statecraft was accelerating the pace of positive change, and moving the global system in a more unipolar direction.

This imposing record was a testament to the strategic acumen of U.S. officials, and especially to that shown by the Reagan administration across an array of surpassingly consequential international matters. Not everywhere were the trends working America's way, however, and as I argue in chapter 5, events in one region offered an essential counterpoint to the favorable flow of world affairs and U.S. policy. In the greater Middle East, the late 1970s had seen the rise of three key countercurrents that generally cut against U.S. interests: chronic and growing instability in the oil-rich Persian Gulf, the emergence of often-radical forms of political Islam, and a surge in international terrorism emanating from the region. All these trends had deep roots in regional politics and society, all were simultaneously dramatized and invigorated by the Iranian revolution of 1979, and all posed severe difficulties for U.S. officials concerned with maintaining access and influence in a crucial area. Elsewhere, the United States could ride the wave of history; here, it was coming face to face with the intractable issues that would plague U.S.–Middle Eastern relations for decades.

In this more adverse climate, both the Carter and Reagan administrations struggled mightily to overcome the challenges they confronted. In some instances, as with the conflict against Middle Eastern terrorism, the problem simply proved resistant to the decisive application of U.S. power. In others, such as the struggle to stabilize the Gulf amid the Iran-Iraq War, progress on one front led to dilemmas and conflicts anew. Finally, in the case of Washington's support for the anti-Soviet jihad in Afghanistan, U.S. policies purchased short-term gains at the price of inflaming the underlying dangers. When the 1980s ended, then, lasting victories of the type won elsewhere in the world remained elusive, and Washington's troubles in the Middle East were only escalating. As the unipolar era was gradually taking shape, then, so were some of the most persistent and perilous threats that would preoccupy U.S. officials in the years ahead.

These threats notwithstanding, by the late 1980s a mix of profound global trends and conscious U.S. policies had moved the world to the brink of an epochal shift in the international order. The consummation of that shift, which I examine in chapter 6, came between 1989 and 1992. During these years, the George H. W. Bush administration faced a series of epic strategic shocks that shattered the creaking Cold War structure and marked the transition to the post–Cold War era. And in each case, the administration responded in ways that established U.S. primacy as the foundation of the new global system. As the Soviet empire in Eastern Europe crumbled, Bush used U.S. influence to facilitate the reunification of Germany on terms that gutted the Warsaw Pact, and replaced a bifurcated European order with one in which Washington, its allies, and their values were clearly dominant. In responding to the Persian Gulf crisis of 1990–1991, the administration showcased America's unrivaled military and diplomatic muscle, and demonstrated that U.S. leadership would remain the essential guarantor of stability in the post-bipolar era. Finally, amid the decay and downfall of the Soviet Union, the Bush team laid the groundwork for a post–Cold War strategy aimed at preserving and exploiting U.S. primacy into the future. At a series of critical junctures in global politics, an administration that was often scored for lacking vision and purpose pursued policies that were both purposeful and visionary indeed.[14]

By the early 1990s, the United States had thus completed its impressive international revival, and the outlines of the unipolar order were coming plainly into view. American power had proven far more durable and resilient than so many observers had only fairly recently predicted; the crisis of U.S. primacy in the 1970s had been followed not by an inexorable decline into mediocrity but by the ascent to a new era of international preeminence. The key strategic questions that now confronted the United States were how long its unipolar moment would last, and how rewarding it would actually be.

Several interpretive themes run through this book; five are of primary importance. First, as noted previously, the post–Cold War unipolarity that the United States enjoyed was not defined solely by an abundance of material capabilities and the absence of a "peer competitor"—the metrics that international relations scholars generally use to characterize unipolar systems.[15] Rather, American preeminence reflected a broader set of international arrangements and power dynamics. U.S. superiority in the military, economic, and strategic realms was reinforced by organic alliance and diplomatic relationships that enhanced America's strength and extended its global influence. More important, that superiority was complemented by a soft-power ideological hegemony embodied in the breathtaking advance of free markets, free trade, and free political institutions. As discussed in the following chapters, Washington's geopolitical triumph in the Cold War was intertwined with the increasing pervasiveness of its vision for how societies should be run and international interchange should be organized. The post–Cold War global imbalance in capabilities was thus equaled by the imbalance between the U.S.-supported liberal model and any of its rivals. The unipolar order was one in which the United States possessed multiple and mutually reinforcing dimensions of dominance, and it was this compound character that made America's post–Cold War perch seem so formidable.

This first theme is closely related to a second, which has to do with the manner in which that order emerged in the first place. Contrary to what numerous authors have argued, the rise of the unipolar moment and America's post–Cold War dominance was not a mere accident of history, or something that simply "happened" with the unexpected opening of the Berlin Wall in 1989 or the Soviet collapse two years later.[16] In reality, it was something that had much deeper, and broader, historical origins. This transformation traced back to a whole collection of deeply rooted international phenomena affecting issues ranging from superpower relations, to trends in the world's political complexion, to the nature of the global economy. These were phenomena that began to unfold in earnest during the 1970s, that received an essential impetus from U.S. policy in the 1980s and after, and that thereby culminated in the astonishing historical rupture of the Bush era. In this sense, the global turn toward unipolarity was an episode that played out over a period of years, and it involved a broad range of issues, initiatives, and interventions that all interacted to produce the eventual outcome. The unipolar turn, in other words, was not a discrete *event* but rather a historical *process,* one that drew on long-term structural change as well as calculated U.S. strategy.

This second theme leads, in turn, to a third, which is that understanding the changes in the global environment during this period requires looking not solely to structure, on the one hand, or strategy, on the other, but to the symbiotic interaction between the two. Historians and other analysts have long argued the merits of "individual agency" versus "structural forces" interpretations of the past, a debate that has been vigorously renewed in recent scholarship on the end of the Cold War.[17] What I argue in this book is that neither of these approaches is, by itself, adequate. The American resurgence would not have been possible without the tectonic shifts that commenced in the 1970s, which helped rejuvenate a sagging superpower and created tremendous opportunities for U.S. policymakers to exploit. Yet it is nearly inconceivable that events would have unfolded as they did had not U.S. policymakers so adroitly exploited those opportunities—by recognizing the trends in play and deploying American power to accentuate them, and by acting decisively at points of great fluidity in world affairs. The rise of the unipolar moment occurred at the nexus of impersonal historical forces and conscious policy choices; good strategy allowed the United States to make the most of its good fortune.

This statement holds true as a general proposition regarding the period under consideration in this book; it also pertains particularly to the two administrations that receive most extended treatment here. The Reagan and Bush administrations did not engender epochal global departures from scratch, and objective observers must recognize that both teams were exceptionally fortunate to wield power at a time when so much was breaking Washington's way. But across a wide assortment of issues, both administrations proved highly adept at identifying the critical contingencies and conjunctures, and thereby leveraging U.S. influence to deliver outsized results. If a core task of strategy resides in determining the structural propensity of things and positioning one's nation to profit, then American strategy in the Reagan and Bush years was historically potent and perceptive.[18]

This third theme, however, touches on a fourth, which is that the *making* of good strategy was itself a process, one that could be as iterative and messy as it was far-sighted and inspired. Strategy is too commonly thought of as a panacea that allows policymakers to transcend the challenges of the international environment, or as a roadmap that plots out all the twists and turns of policy in advance. But strategy is actually something quite different. Strategy is inherently iterative—it requires combining a long-range vision of where one wants to go with a degree of trial-and-error adaptation in devising the concrete policies that will get one there. Strategy is also inherently messy—it is an imperfect discipline in which missteps and trade-offs are unavoidable.[19] American strategy during this period underscores these innate characteristics. It generally took time for U.S. policymakers to fully grasp the global trends that emerged during the 1970s, and to integrate those trends into long-range visions for national renewal. It often took even more time and effort, along with a substantial amount of learning and recalibration, to turn those visions into the effective policies that so improved the U.S. posture during the 1980s. Whether in U.S.-Soviet relations, democracy promotion, or efforts to spread market-oriented reforms, the road to success was bumpy and tortuous. In each case, American strategy would eventually get the country to the desired destination—but not without detours and course corrections along the way.

Even then, the legacy of U.S. strategy and resurgence was not without ambiguities; this is a fifth and final theme. On the whole, America's international position improved greatly over the years covered in this book, and the record of U.S. policy could reasonably be called one of historic achievement. By the early 1990s, the United States had attained a level of international superiority and reach that empires past could only have dreamed of. From the early 1990s onward, Washington would then manage to sustain its unipolar status for longer than many international-relations experts had initially predicted, while also using its prerogatives to continue influencing global outcomes in unparalleled—and often very constructive—ways. By virtually any reasonable standard—and certainly compared to what so many informed observers had expected in the late 1970s—these outcomes were enviable indeed.

Yet we must avoid the triumphalism that can be so tempting in recounting this history, because there was a debit side of the ledger as well.[20] The global forces unleashed in the 1970s were not uniformly beneficial for America, for they included challenges—such as Islamic radicalism and Middle Eastern terrorism—that would bedevil U.S. policymakers for decades. Nor were even the positive changes unalloyed in their effects. As we will see, the strategic successes of the 1980s frequently came at a cost, whether in moral, financial, or even geopolitical terms, and in some cases they helped foster the very problems that U.S. strategy would confront in the unipolar era. Similarly, phenomena such as globalization and neoliberalism would ultimately prove to be something of a double-edged sword. Not least of all, the U.S. determination to maintain the primacy it had won by the early 1990s had its own downsides. It would leave the country engaged in a costly and taxing global mission, while also courting the hubris that came with unrivaled strength—and the enmity of those whom U.S. power and policies seemed to threaten. For all the benefits it bestowed, the unipolar moment would therefore not be a time of peace or repose for America. It would simply introduce the country to a new set of dangers and problems.

CHAPTER 1

Roots of Resurgence

Unipolarity is a rare and valuable commodity in international affairs. It refers not simply to a situation in which a leading country has marginally more power than its competitors, but to one in which the leader has a clear and overwhelming superiority. A country that enjoys unipolarity has no near-term challengers for the status of preeminent actor in the international system; it can also do far more than any other country to shape that system to its own benefit. For a country to have unipolarity, then, is to have more than great influence over its own destiny. It is to have an unmatched say in how the broader world works.[1]

The deepest origins of America's post–Cold War unipolarity lie not in the close of the superpower conflict in 1989, or in the end of World War II a half-century earlier. They lie in the very opening of U.S. history, generations before. From its birth as a republic, the United States possessed attributes that would enable a meteoric geopolitical rise. It boasted uniquely favorable geography that offered cheap security and abundant chances for territorial enlargement, and a natural resource base that provided the foundations of awesome economic power. It was equally blessed with an energetic and fecund population, a national ideology that both impelled and rationalized American assertiveness, and a political system that generally performed well enough to let the country make the most of its other advantages. From the late 1700s to the mid-twentieth century, these characteristics permitted not just a steady accretion of U.S. power and influence; they underwrote a record of expansion and national aggrandizement that had few historical peers.

This was the long-term backdrop to what might be thought of as America's first unipolar moment—the period after World War II. By the time the guns fell silent in 1945, the United States was preeminent in virtually all key measures of national might. In economic terms, U.S. output roughly equaled that of the rest of the world combined. In military terms, America accounted for three-quarters of great-power defense spending, and it alone possessed the atomic bomb, an air force with global striking power, and a navy that dominated the maritime commons. In diplomatic and ideological terms, no country emerged from the war with greater influence or prestige. As Melvyn Leffler has written, the United States possessed a preponderance of power.[2] In the postwar decades, that power enabled a sustained global activism meant to craft world affairs. America's Cold War statecraft, said Henry Kissinger, was premised on "the notion of a predominant United States, as the only stable country, the richest country, the country without whose leadership and physical contribution nothing was possible, and which had to make all the difference for defense and progress everywhere in the world."[3]

The results of this approach were impressive by any standard, and as Daniel Sargent has written, U.S. policies erected a veritable "Pax Americana."[4] The relatively liberal international economy that emerged in the noncommunist world after World War II was certainly an American project. U.S. money and technology helped rebuild shattered societies in Western Europe and East Asia, and revive them as thriving hubs of capitalist prosperity. The Bretton Woods institutions promoted reconstruction, development, and economic stability within a generally pro-market framework. Washington likewise gave impetus to postwar trade liberalization through its role in the General Agreement on Tariffs and Trade (GATT) and by opening its own market to foreign goods, while the dollar sat at the center of world commerce and finance. In sum, the United States spearheaded the creation of a vibrant Western economy from the wreckage left by global war, and served as the leader of the international trade and monetary order. This postwar economic system, Jonathan Kirshner writes, was "successful beyond its most optimistic hopes, ushering in a quarter-century known as the golden age of capitalism, of unprecedented global economic growth and prosperity."[5]

The U.S.-led economic order was intertwined with a geopolitical and security order that was equally Washington-centric. Had the Cold War not erupted, America's postwar geopolitical presence would not have been so extensive; the fact that the Cold War did erupt ensured that this presence soon became nearly global. The United States headed a network of military alliances that provided security and locked in American influence in key regions of the world. The country also maintained unprecedented peacetime military forces meant to provide leverage vis-à-vis Moscow and to substantiate these global commitments. Not least, U.S. officials used their country's wealth and influence to affect the fate of developing nations from Latin America to Southeast Asia and beyond, in hopes of keeping them beyond the Kremlin's reach and integrating them into the Western economic and political orbit. From the Marshall Plan to the Alliance for Progress, from the North Atlantic Treaty Organization (NATO) to the nuclear arms race, the outlines of the postwar world bore the imprint of American primacy.

The problem with being on top, however, is that one can only go down from there. America's postwar dominance was based not only on its own strengths, but on the weaknesses of a world laid prone by wartime devastation. So even as Washington put its power to such productive use after World War II, that power was in relative decline. The economic recovery of U.S. allies in Europe and Asia, the gradual rise of the Kremlin as a full-fledged military and diplomatic rival, and the emergence of a growing and more assertive Third World: these trends meant that, while America's absolute wealth and capabilities grew following the war, its comparative standing was steadily receding from the imposing heights of 1945. By the late 1960s, Richard Nixon would write that "the postwar period in international relations has ended." America's superiority had become less overwhelming; its advantages were not what they had been.[6]

This theme of decline was particularly pervasive during the 1970s—the decade I analyze in this chapter, and one that constituted a critical inflection point in the trajectory of U.S. power. At the time, the 1970s often appeared to mark the last, dying breath of U.S. primacy. From Vietnam to Afghanistan, from the collapse of Bretton Woods to the oil shocks, American leaders confronted crises that laid bare the limits of U.S. influence and showed a superpower in retreat. More broadly, the decade produced a seeming abundance of evidence to suggest that the underlying strategic currents were unfavorable, and that Washington was inexorably losing its capacity to shape global affairs. No longer did the United States appear to be the colossus of the early postwar years; no longer did its arc seem to point upward. As one Ford-era official said, "it was clear that we were in a new world" in which U.S. supremacy was fading fast.[7]

This was the impression many informed observers took away from the 1970s, and one that was often echoed in leading scholarly assessments that emerged in that decade and even after.[8] With the distance of time, however, we can now see that the history of the 1970s was neither so straightforward nor discouraging as it initially looked. To be sure, the United States was battered by crises during this period, and policymakers often seemed at a loss to deal with those challenges. But even amid such travails, the global system was undergoing profound tectonic changes that would prove immensely beneficial to the United States. The onset of the terminal decline of the Soviet empire, the emergence of a transnational human rights movement and third-wave democratization, and the rise of globalization and other economic transformations—these trends were laying the groundwork for reinvigorated statecraft and a renewed geopolitical ascent. Appearances to the contrary, the 1970s did not represent the twilight of the American age. They were the prologue to America's post–Cold War unipolar moment.

The 1970s and the Crisis of American Power

Perceptions of U.S. decline were ubiquitous during the 1970s. At home and abroad, the conventional wisdom was that America had passed its apex of global power. Intelligence and diplomatic reports regularly brought news of allies' decreasing confidence in U.S. authority; adversaries gloated about Washington's weakness. "The United States is presently seen as suffering setbacks and defeats—giving ground on several fronts," noted one National Security Council (NSC) appraisal in 1975.[9] The shah of Iran privately predicted that the United States might become "a fifth or even a tenth-rate power," and Marxist guerrilla groups asserted that "the imperialist tiger has begun to show signs of weakness and fatigue."[10] Even top U.S. officials worried about the country's prospects. Henry Kissinger lamented that "never has America been weaker," and Richard Nixon mused that the nation might be treading a well-worn path of decadence and downfall. "I think of what happened to Greece and to Rome," he said; "what is left—only the pillars."[11] This analogy was quite common; observers inside and outside government saw the United States as an empire in decay.[12]

It is not hard to understand why so many were so bearish about America's future, for the 1970s were a decade when Washington's international position often looked to be crumbling. Setbacks and crises were legion, indicators of lost preeminence were all too easy to find. America had hit its "years of middle age and decline," one observer wrote even as the decade began: wherever one looked, there were signs of how far U.S. influence had fallen.[13]

Nowhere did that decline seem starker than in the economic realm. Throughout the postwar era, U.S. power had rested on a foundation of

economic hegemony. In 1945, America possessed half of the world's manufacturing capacity and an economy perhaps five times larger than its nearest
competitor. It produced half of the world's steel and oil, controlled the bulk
of international financial reserves, and dominated the competition for export
markets. "We are the giant of the economic world," Harry Truman declared
in 1947. "Whether we like it or not, the future pattern of economic relations
depends on us."[14] In the years that followed, this economic might underwrote
the reconstruction of Western Europe and Japan, enabled the provision of
foreign aid to countries around the world, and financed the military power
that undergirded a global containment policy. In myriad ways, economic
primacy was the bedrock of U.S. influence.

By the early 1970s, however, that primacy had eroded significantly. As
Japan, West Germany, and other countries rebounded from the devastation
of World War II—using U.S. aid and support to do so—the balance of economic power swung dramatically. Whereas Washington had bestrode the
world economy in 1945 and commanded 27.3 percent of global GDP in
1950, by 1970 its share had fallen to 22.4 percent.[15] America's share of oil and
steel production, international reserves, and world exports declined sharply, as
did its trade and payments balances. Meanwhile, Japan's GDP rose by around
11 percent annually during the 1960s, its portion of world GDP roughly quadrupled between 1950 and 1970, and its manufactures increasingly competed
with U.S. products for market share. The European Economic Community
also grew rapidly, coming to rival the U.S. economy in size, and West Germany
became an economic juggernaut in its own right.[16] "While the U.S. continues
to be the world's most advanced economy," wrote White House adviser Peter
Peterson in 1971, "the gap between ourselves and the rest of the developed
world has been narrowing." Treasury Secretary John Connally was blunter:
"No longer does the U.S. economy dominate the free world."[17]

The collapse of the Bretton Woods international monetary system in
1971 was a symptom of this relative decline. In simplified form, Bretton
Woods was a system of fixed but adjustable exchange rates in which countries tied the value of their currencies to the dollar, while the dollar was tied
to gold. Since its advent at the close of World War II, this system had been a
mechanism for preserving monetary stability within a pro-growth and pro-
trade framework. It was no less a symbol of American leadership and power.
Bretton Woods represented the U.S. commitment to managing a prosperous
and comparatively open world order after the chaos of depression and war.
More tangibly, it enshrined the dollar as the preeminent national currency,
the primary medium of global exchange, and the anchor of international
trade and finance.

This status gave the United States prestige and important benefits, namely the ability to run deficits that would otherwise have been unsustainable. Yet it also carried significant costs. Bretton Woods required the United States to stabilize international monetary relations by pegging its currency to gold at $35/ounce, while also lubricating the system by providing a steady outflow of dollars to foreign countries—all while sending still more dollars abroad via overseas troop deployments and foreign aid. This was the famous Triffin dilemma—that Bretton Woods essentially forced Washington to run a payments deficit to facilitate world growth and liquidity, but that in doing so it ensured that the real value of the dollar would eventually fall out of alignment with its nominal value. In other words, Bretton Woods imposed heavy and conflicting burdens on its leader, burdens that accumulated over time. It was a system that could be maintained only by a truly hegemonic power, and the impressive postwar performance of the Western economy was tribute to America's ability to play this role.[18]

As U.S. economic hegemony diminished after 1945, however, the costs of Bretton Woods gradually became too much to bear. By the late 1960s, the outflow of dollars had made the U.S. payments imbalance look dangerously unsustainable, and the system was plagued by chronic instability. Monetary crises were becoming more frequent and severe; Bretton Woods was being held together only through emergency interventions and the use of capital controls in the United States and other countries. Most troubling of all, the threat of a run on the dollar—in which foreign banks cashed in their devalued greenbacks against the limited U.S. supply of gold—hovered ominously. Richard Nixon's decision to suspend dollar-gold convertibility in August 1971, thereby abandoning the core of the Bretton Woods system, thus represented nothing so much as an admission of American financial overstretch. As IMF officials noted, "The changes in relative economic position among the major countries during the past 25 years have meant that the United States is no longer in a position . . . to assume ultimate and virtually sole responsibility for the functioning of the system."[19]

Although the abandonment of Bretton Woods would ultimately benefit the United States, the short-term aftermath merely compounded doubts about its leadership and power. The Western world was in disarray, as Washington and its allies grappled inconclusively—and contentiously—over what should replace the now-defunct system. "European leaders want to 'screw' us and we want to 'screw' them in the economic area," Nixon said.[20] The leading Western powers eventually and rather fitfully settled on a more flexible system of floating exchange rates, but the cost of this shift, writes Harold James, was "a fair measure of anarchy."[21] The demise of Bretton Woods and its fixed parities threw the world into a period of monetary disorder, fueling inflation and exposing currencies to sharp, destabilizing swings. The dollar was particularly vulnerable, losing 43 percent of its value against the deutschmark and 36 percent against the yen from late 1972 to late 1978. "The dollar is regarded all over the world as a sick currency," wrote one observer.[22] With the dollar in decline and the West careening from one monetary crisis to another, it was natural to wonder if the end of the U.S. era had arrived.

This was certainly the impression given by the oil shocks. The postwar Western economic boom had been fueled by cheap and plentiful oil, and America had held great sway in the global energy equation as the world's largest producer. By the early 1970s, however, these permissive conditions were gone. The United States was no longer the world's swing producer—its share of global production had fallen, and it lacked spare capacity to tap in times of crisis. Meanwhile, skyrocketing overall demand during the 1950s and 1960s had tightened the world market, leaving the West more vulnerable to fluctuations in price or supply, and giving the major exporters—many of which had banded together in the Organization of Petroleum Exporting Countries (OPEC)—greater leverage. At the instigation of key Middle Eastern producers such as Libya and Iran, prices rose by 45 percent from early 1970 to mid-1973, and close observers warned that a full-blown crisis was nigh. "This time," the top State Department energy expert wrote, "the wolf is here."[23]

The reckoning came in late 1973. The October War led the Arab producers to impose temporary—but punishing—cutbacks on production and an embargo on shipments to the United States that lasted into the next year. More important from a long-term perspective, OPEC approved price hikes leading to a quadrupling of the cost of oil (from $2.90 to $11.65 per barrel) between mid-1973 and early 1974.[24] The resulting crisis was a geoeconomic event of the first order. It caused a massive resource transfer from consumers to producers, giving OPEC leaders such as Venezuela, Saudi Arabia, and Iran unprecedented wealth and influence. It underscored the reliance of the West on resources possessed by others, and the fact that the First World was therefore captive to the whims of a few desert states in the Third. Efforts to redress this weakness by forging greater consumer unity produced only middling results, and U.S. officials were soon reduced to imploring Persian Gulf autocrats not to raise prices further, lest disaster result.[25] In short, the oil crisis upended global power dynamics and inverted assumptions about influence and dependency. "We are now living in a never-never land," Kissinger said, "in which tiny, poor and weak nations can hold up for ransom some of the industrialized world."[26]

Indeed, the traumatic effects of the oil shock were profound and far-reaching, and they shook the very pillars of the Western order. Inflation surpassed 20 percent in some industrial countries, while growth plunged and unemployment skyrocketed. Oil importers scrambled to cover rising energy bills, and several NATO allies seemed close to financial catastrophe. One suddenly plausible nightmare scenario was a cascade of defaults that might throw the world economy into chaos; another was that economic turmoil might drag countries such as France, Spain, and Italy hard to the left. European leaders such as Helmut Schmidt invoked the specter of the 1930s in warning of depression and unrest. U.S. officials feared for the future of the global economy, and the stability of the noncommunist world. "I'm convinced that the biggest problem we face now is possible economic collapse," Kissinger said: "fall of the western world."[27]

Although these worst-case contingencies never came to pass, the oil crisis still cast grave doubts on U.S. staying power. Coming as postwar growth rates had already begun to decline, soaring energy prices ruthlessly exposed inefficiency and weakness. U.S. gross national product (GNP) fell 6 percent between 1973 and 1975, unemployment doubled to nearly 9 percent, and inflation hit 13.5 percent by decade's end. Entire sectors of manufacturing were hollowed out, with the auto industry shedding over one-third of its workforce in three years. Real wages slumped, and poverty began to rise.[28] Most troubling of all, policymakers had no solutions for these problems. "I had a depressing breakfast with economic advisors, who don't know what to do about inflation or energy," Carter wrote in 1979.[29] By this point, the Iranian revolution had set off a second oil shock, further battering the economy and accentuating the "crisis of the American spirit" that Carter identified in his July 1979 address.[30] Relief would come only when overproduction and new supplies drove down prices in the early 1980s. All told, it was an intensely demoralizing state of affairs, one that raised fundamental questions about America's future as a global power. As one official with the State Department Policy Planning Staff warned in 1980, "the U.S. is not in a strong economic position to pursue an activist foreign policy" in the years to come.[31]

Nor did the broader U.S. geopolitical position seem particularly robust during the 1970s. The twenty-five years prior to that decade had seen a dramatic expansion of U.S. presence and influence overseas. From the construction of an alliance system that nearly spanned the globe, to Washington's economic statecraft and its interventions in the Third World, America had energetically used its power to mold the development of other societies and construct a sphere of influence as vast as that of any empire past. By the 1960s, there was hardly an area of the noncommunist world in which the country was not involved in critical issues of politics, security, and economics. In many ways, the escalating U.S. intervention in South Vietnam in the latter half of that decade represented the apogee of this remarkable geopolitical project. The fact that Lyndon Johnson could devote 500,000 troops, and copious treasure, to a war in a small country far from the world's central strategic theaters was a marker of just how powerful and ambitious postwar America really was. By the 1970s, however, ambition and power alike were coming under doubt. A world that was increasingly assertive in its own right no longer seemed so receptive to U.S. guidance, and along the global perimeter, Washington often appeared to be in ignominious retreat.

The shifting of the tide was signaled, appropriately, by events in Southeast Asia. As early as 1968, the long U.S. campaign to preserve a noncommunist South Vietnam had been stalemated by revolutionary nationalism. The 1970s saw the final failure of that campaign, with the evacuation from Saigon in 1975 a humiliating coda to the whole sad saga. Kissinger had earlier vowed that America would "not be confounded by a fifth rate agricultural power," but in the end, this was just what happened.[32] Along the way, the war caused major cleavages in U.S. politics and society; it also exposed the limits of both America's military power and its ability to sustain accumulated global commitments indefinitely. No longer would the country "pay any price, bear any burden" to "assure the survival and the success of liberty." The new reality, as Nixon wrote, was that "America cannot—and will not—conceive all the plans, design all the programs, execute all the decisions and undertake all the defense of the free nations of the world."[33] Not surprisingly, the war bred doubt and alarm among those who depended on U.S. power, while invigorating those who sought radical change. "Our allies have been disturbed, and our adversaries heightened," said CIA Director William Colby.[34]

Other setbacks soon followed. During the late 1970s, Washington was forced to surrender ownership of the Panama Canal—a key symbol of America's rise to global power—after being outmaneuvered by a crafty dictator who mobilized anti-U.S. and anticolonial sentiment to generate irresistible diplomatic pressure. "The world we live in today is not the world of Teddy Roosevelt," one U.S. official lamented.[35] Then, in 1979, the Carter administration watched helplessly as the pro-U.S. regime in Nicaragua was overthrown by Marxist rebels, presaging a decade of war—and increased Soviet and Cuban influence—in Central America. That same year, Carter saw another longtime ally, the shah of Iran, toppled by a revolt that shattered the U.S. position in the Persian Gulf and empowered virulently anti-American

Islamist revolutionaries. The subsequent hostage crisis underscored how willing those revolutionaries were to challenge Washington, while Carter's inability to respond effectively exacerbated perceptions of U.S. debility. As Carter acknowledged, he felt "the same kind of impotence that a powerful person feels when his child is kidnapped."[36] In place after place, the superpower was on the defensive, losing long-held positions and its ability to influence events.

U.S. authority was certainly under attack throughout much of the Third World. Since World War II, American leaders had sought to direct the political and economic development of the global south, even trying to reshape entire regions in the U.S. image. By the 1970s, however, these hopes had come in for a hard landing. The failures of programs such as the Alliance for Progress had dispelled what Nixon called "the illusion that we alone could remake continents."[37] More worrying still, the Third World often appeared quite hostile to U.S. policy. From Latin America to the Middle East, Washington confronted a rising tide of nationalism, anti-U.S. sentiment, and ideological radicalism. The growing body of developing nations often took neutralist or pro-Soviet positions in the United Nations, and organizations such as the Group of 77 (G-77) and Non-Aligned Movement (NAM) used anti-Americanism as a least-common denominator among their diverse memberships. It was "a world where more and more don't like us," said Daniel Moynihan, U.S. ambassador to the United Nations, in 1975. "For the last decade and for the next generation, the U.S. will be a beleaguered garrison in international forums."[38]

Nothing made this clearer than the Third World economic challenge. It was not just OPEC that sought to reshape global economic relations; by the early 1970s, much of the Third World was rebelling against the liberal postwar order. Empowered by the apparent weakness and disarray of the industrial West, and conscious of the massive disparities between rich and poor nations, the lesser-developed countries (LDCs) condemned Washington as the defender of an unjust status quo and sought to fundamentally alter the balance of international economic power. There were 336 expropriations of U.S.- and foreign-owned companies between 1970 and 1975, as LDCs aimed to weaken outside economic influence and assert control over their own resources. Expropriation, one observer noted, had become the "Damoclean sword" for investors overseas.[39]

More broadly, the LDCs pushed for sweeping changes in the basic structure of global economics. The G-77 and NAM championed programs such as the New International Economic Order (NIEO) and the Charter of Economic Rights and Duties of States, using their numerical superiority to pass these items through the UN General Assembly. Among other things, these initiatives envisioned one-way tariff preferences for the LDCs, price supports for LDC commodity exports, the freedom to nationalize or expropriate foreign property on highly favorable conditions, increased (and unconditional) aid and technology transfer from rich countries to poor, the payment of reparations for past economic injustices, and dramatically increased LDC influence over the World Bank and the IMF. In essence, the Third World was demanding the socialization of global wealth and a radical reformulation of international exchange.[40] It was an agenda, moreover, often pursued in highly confrontational fashion. LDC statesmen embraced dependency theory, which depicted world economic relations as a predatory system in which the weak were exploited by the strong, and they inveighed against Western "neo-colonialism" and "economic totalitarianism."[41] Far from charting the path of the LDCs, the United States was now struggling to prevent them from overturning the world economic order. If Washington did not defuse the radicalism, warned Deputy Secretary of State Charles Robinson, "We . . . risk seeing the democratic-free enterprise-market system become the dinosaur of the 20th century."[42]

As U.S. influence frayed at the periphery of the global system, it also looked to be declining at the core. The forging of alliances with Western Europe and Japan was the crowning achievement of postwar U.S. diplomacy, and a testament to American power in the Cold War order. By the mid-1960s, however, the departure of France from the NATO military command had signaled that alliance cohesion was declining, and throughout the 1970s, those coalitions were in disarray. Relations with NATO and Japan were wracked by an unending train of contretemps—over trade and monetary issues, the oil shocks and the Arab-Israeli dispute, *ostpolitik* and East-West relations, the "year of Europe" and the neutron bomb. These disagreements stemmed from various sources, from personality clashes to simple divergences of national interest. But taken together, they indicated that Western solidarity was slipping, and that American allies—now economic powers in their own right—were no longer so inclined to follow the U.S. lead. It is notable that Carter referred to a summit *among allies* as "one of the worst days of my diplomatic life."[43] The problem, argued a CIA assessment in 1979, was that "American influence is declining . . . in all phases of the alliance relationship." "The United States is losing its leadership position within the OECD arena."[44]

Then there was the Cold War competition with Moscow. Containment was in crisis in the 1970s. That policy had always rested on two key premises: that the United States and its allies would outperform the Soviet system over the long term, and that they had the power to restrain Kremlin expansion in the meantime. These ideas had informed George Kennan's original call to embark "with reasonable confidence upon a policy of firm containment," and for two decades thereafter, they were well reflected in the state of the superpower contest.[45] During the 1950s and 1960s, Western democratic capitalism provided prosperity and living standards that far outstripped anything the communist world could offer. And in military terms, there was no doubting overall U.S. superiority. As late as 1962, the United States had a more than a seven-to-one edge over Moscow in strategic nuclear weapons, and enjoyed utter dominance in the power-projection capabilities that allowed it to sustain alliances and influence events around the world. As William Odom, a military aide to Carter's NSC, noted, the early postwar era had been more unipolar than bipolar, and that unipolarity had backstopped global containment.[46]

By the 1970s, however, the situation had changed, and the twin pillars of containment looked shakier than ever before. The West was beset by internal squabbles and economic crises, whereas Moscow—a major oil exporter— was reaping unprecedented financial gains. The value of Soviet oil exports to the West soared from $781 million in 1972 to over $14 billion in 1980, financing foreign policy initiatives as well as imports of technology, food, and other goods.[47] The contrast in performance led to a widespread questioning of how superior the capitalist model really was: Soviet leaders touted the "magnetic force of socialism," while a group of seven Nobel Prize winners called for "an intensive search for alternatives to the prevailing Western economy."[48] Meanwhile, the Kremlin was conducting a massive military buildup intended to negate long-standing U.S. strategic advantages, while the Vietnam War had left America demoralized and overextended. The future of containment was now increasingly cloudy; it was hardly assured that Washington could hold the line.

This was the backdrop to détente, the policy pursued (with important variations) by three administrations during the 1970s. Particularly under Nixon and Ford, détente was based on the idea that America no longer had the raw power to keep containment in place and that it must bound Soviet influence through subtler means. By negotiating arms-control agreements and expanding East-West trade, the United States would lower superpower tensions and draw Moscow into a more stable relationship. By pursuing an opening to China and empowering Third World allies, Washington would simultaneously keep the Kremlin off balance and limit the prospects for Soviet adventurism, all while shedding U.S. burdens in the bargain. The goal, Kissinger said, was to lead Moscow "to a realization of the limitations of both its physical strength and of the limits of its ideological fervor"—to tame Soviet power even as that power grew.[49]

Détente was a creative response to a difficult problem. Maneuvers such as the rapprochement with China undoubtedly mitigated the erosion of America's strategic position, and as discussed subsequently, détente fostered momentous long-term changes in the communist bloc. What détente could *not* do, however, was arrest the near-term geopolitical trends that seemed so alarming. In particular, the military balance continued shifting in adverse ways. Already approaching rough strategic nuclear parity by the early 1970s (a status enshrined in the Strategic Arms Limitation Treaty, or SALT, of 1972), Moscow outproduced Washington in land- and sea-based intercontinental ballistic missiles (ICBMs) by more than four to one in the decade that followed. "The current Soviet programs for development of intercontinental attack weapons are unprecedented in scope," said Colby in 1974.[50] Soviet force designers also dramatically increased the accuracy and lethality of their ICBMs, and they modernized their theater nuclear forces by deploying mobile, high-speed SS-20 missiles that could target all of Western Europe. At the same time, the Kremlin poured resources into conventional forces, including the naval, air, and logistical capabilities needed to project power afar. Looking at this massive accretion of Soviet arms, American observers worried that the era of U.S. military supremacy was over, and that the balance was tipping dangerously toward Moscow. "The Soviet Union has broken the containment policy through a steady and long-term buildup and projection of military power," Odom wrote.[51]

Nor did détente produce Soviet restraint in the Third World. Marxist revolutionaries or leaders seized power in a spate of countries in the mid- and late 1970s—South Vietnam, Laos, Cambodia, Angola, Ethiopia, Mozambique, South Yemen, Afghanistan, Nicaragua, and Grenada—and hopes were high for further gains. "The world was turning in our direction," one Kremlin official recalled said.[52] Moscow actively supported this process, making unprecedented arms deliveries to its Third World clients, supporting Marxist guerrillas in southern Africa and elsewhere, and increasing its intelligence and military presence from Vietnam to Peru to Ethiopia. More ominously, the Soviets used their growing power-projection capabilities to intervene decisively in Third World conflicts. Airlifts of Cuban troops and Soviet weaponry sealed the outcomes of the Angolan civil war in 1975–1976 and the Ogaden War between Somalia and Ethiopia in 1977–1978, and the Kremlin used 80,000 of its own soldiers to invade Afghanistan in 1979. In all three cases, Soviet officials ignored U.S. warnings or calls for restraint, exhibiting what NSC staffer Fritz Ermarth termed "strategic contempt" for American power.[53] At a time when the global balance appeared to be shifting in their favor, Soviet officials felt less inhibited about using military tools for geopolitical purposes. Said KGB chairman Yuri Andropov, "The Soviet Union is not merely talking about world revolution but is actually assisting it."[54]

As Moscow was becoming more assertive, Washington looked downright paralyzed. The 1970s were a time of dissent and dissonance in U.S. policy. A perfect storm of factors—economic crisis, the traumas of Vietnam and Watergate, revelations of Central Intelligence Agency (CIA) misdeeds in countries from the Congo to Chile—ruptured the Cold War consensus and caused a backlash against executive authority. Public support for an activist global posture tumbled, and by 1975, just 36 percent of Americans felt "it was important for the United States to make and keep commitments to other nations."[55] For its part, Congress reacted to previous presidential excesses by passing a slew of measures, from the War Powers Act to new restrictions on covert action and arms sales, to constrain executive action in foreign affairs. What was happening, wrote the State Department's Charles Robinson, was

> the breakdown of the 'American political contract': that unwritten arrangement which has existed more or less intact since at least World War II under which the Executive was given considerable flexibility in the implementation of foreign policy. . . . Today, it is becoming increasingly difficult to develop any consistent coalition or consensus. . . . There is a *growing feeling of concern, frustration and doubt* throughout the nation which, in itself, compounds the problem of marshaling the consensus without which no policy—foreign or domestic—can succeed.[56]

This political climate had significant geopolitical effects. For one thing, it meant that, as the Soviet Union built up in the 1970s, the United States built down. Constant-dollar defense outlays shrank by nearly 40 percent from 1968 to 1976, and military manpower fell from 3.547 million to 2.086 million. The number of U.S. aviation squadrons and ships decreased by 46 and 47 percent, respectively, between 1964 and 1974, and the number of divisions fell by 16 percent. What forces remained—particularly in the army—were plagued by low morale, indiscipline, and poor readiness resulting from Vietnam. "The Soviets have a strong momentum, while we have a strong downward momentum," noted Secretary of Defense Donald Rumsfeld in 1976.[57]

Moreover, this political environment made it harder to use what tools remained to resist communist advances abroad. This effect became painfully evident in 1975. In the spring, Congress prevented the Ford administration from providing a massive aid package to South Vietnam or using other measures to avert the final collapse. Months later, that body terminated a covert effort to influence the Angolan civil war, just as the conflict was entering its decisive phase. "We are living in a nihilistic nightmare," Kissinger said; the Soviets were gaining momentum, and Washington was ceding the field.[58]

Ironically, it was the Soviet invasion of Afghanistan in December 1979 that seemed best to encapsulate America's declining Cold War fortunes. While we now know that the invasion was a catastrophic blunder by Moscow, this was not how it first appeared. The invasion was the largest and most aggressive Soviet military operation outside of the Warsaw Pact area since World War II. It brought Soviet forces within striking distance of the Persian Gulf, and threatened to exacerbate instability throughout the region. Most of all, following a string of Soviet successes in the Third World, this "naked display of Soviet military strength" (as CIA officials termed it) seemed confirmation that the Kremlin was on the march.[59] National Security Adviser Zbigniew Brzezinski summed up the prevailing view in a memo to Carter:

> The Soviet occupation of Afghanistan is the first time since 1945 that the Soviet Union used its military forces directly to expand its power. This took place even though we warned the Soviet Union of adverse consequences. Moreover, Afghanistan is the seventh state since 1975 in which communist parties have come to power with Soviet tanks and guns, with Soviet military power and assistance. . . . I think it is clear that the Soviets have discounted our likely reaction and that they have concluded that our previous expressions of concern need not be heeded.

"I believe that a major historical turning point has been reached," Brzezinski concluded. If America did not respond to Moscow's global challenge, its geopolitical position might deteriorate irreparably.[60]

This fear may seem extreme in retrospect. Yet it was not an isolated opinion in the mid- and late 1970s. Among many observers, there was a sense that containment was unraveling. Singapore's Lee Kwan Yew asked Carter about "U.S. resolve to frustrate the Soviet's relentless drive for domination," while China's Deng Xiaoping warned that "the United States is in a defensive position and the Soviet Union is in an aggressive position."[61] Key European allies voiced similar concerns. Within the Kremlin, by contrast, there was much confidence—a belief, as Defense Minister Dmitri Ustinov said, that there had occurred a "fundamental alteration in the correlation of forces in the world in favor of socialism."[62] In the Cold War as elsewhere, American power looked to be in eclipse.

The United States, *Business Week* observed, was "entering the decade of the 1980s as a wounded, demoralized colossus."[63] Indeed, America hardly looked poised for a new era of primacy as the 1970s ended. The crises and setbacks, the challenges and humiliations—these were the issues that most observers fixated on as they considered the arc of American power, and that led many analysts to conclude that U.S. postwar preeminence was draining away. Yet as we can now see in retrospect, the United States was much stronger than it seemed at the time. For even amid the turmoil of the 1970s, a series of longer-range global processes were starting to alter the nature of the international system, and quietly setting the stage for a dramatic American renewal.

The Paradoxical Cold War

One of these trends was the onset of terminal Soviet decline. There was no little irony in this, because events in the 1970s had convinced so many observers that it was Washington on the downslope and Moscow on the make. The world was witnessing "the growing strength of the force and position of socialism," Leonid Brezhnev told Warsaw Pact leaders in 1978; "imperialism is not able to face the crises."[64] Likewise, Yuri Andropov (Brezhnev's successor) would later look back on this period as "a time of further growth in the power and influence of the socialist commonwealth."[65] In essence, Soviet leaders believed that the historical tides were running irreversibly in their favor. The reality, however, was just the opposite. The 1970s were when history began to catch up to the Soviet Union, fostering the conditions for a decisive U.S. victory in the Cold War.

In some sense, this shift was probably bound to happen eventually. Amid the ups and downs of the Cold War, it was easy to forget that the superpowers had never really been equally super. Even at its post-Vietnam nadir, the United States commanded a range of essential medium- and long-term strengths: a flexible and legitimate political system, the world's largest economy, organic alliances with economic powerhouses in Europe and Asia, massive (if somewhat reduced) military muscle, and diplomatic influence around the world. Even at its strongest, by contrast, the Soviet Union was plagued by fundamental long-term weaknesses: a rigid and inefficient economy that was far smaller than its U.S. counterpart, a brittle and authoritarian political system, a decidedly *in*organic relationship with many of its chief "allies," and an ideology that often proved repulsive to capitalists and communists alike.[66] The Soviet offensive of the 1970s obscured these realities, but it could not erase them. For this was actually the period when Moscow's deep-seated vulnerabilities started to work their way to the surface, presaging profound geopolitical changes in future years.

This was certainly true in the economic sphere. Even as high oil prices brought the Kremlin a temporary financial bonanza, the Soviet economy had begun its slow but inexorable grind to a halt. Soviet GDP peaked relative to U.S. GDP sometime around 1970, and declined in comparative terms there-after.[67] Annual growth in industrial production slowed dramatically during the 1970s, and overall productivity growth turned negative between 1976 and 1982. By 1978–1979, Soviet economic performance was worse than at any time since World War II, and by the early 1980s, real growth was near zero.[68] Most problematic of all, this poor performance owed less to temporary adversities than to the inescapable and accumulating deficiencies of the command economy. "These problems are chronic," reported CIA analysts in 1977; they were "expected to worsen during the next half-dozen years."[69] Sure enough, as the West shifted toward a post-industrial, information-age model during the 1970s and 1980s, the very nature of the Soviet system thwarted the spontaneity and creativity necessary to make that leap. It was, in some ways, a cruel irony: just as Moscow was reaching the peak of its global influence, it was losing the economic wherewithal to sustain that influence over the long term.

It was also losing the political vitality needed to adapt to changing circumstances. The Brezhnev era saw an unprecedented stability in government, a welcome departure from the purges and terror of earlier eras. But the by-product of stasis was stagnation. The 1970s were "the golden age of the Soviet bureaucrat," as aging *apparatchiks* clung to their positions and privileges, carving out corrupt fiefdoms and eliminating opportunities to rejuvenate the governmental machinery. This problem was particularly severe at the top. By assiduously sidelining potential challengers, Brezhnev and his cronies entrenched a group of sclerotic, corrupt, and sometimes downright decrepit leaders in power. Brezhnev himself personified this pathology; by the late 1970s, his health was so bad that U.S. officials termed him "a genuinely pitiful figure." More broadly, the lack of turnover and imagination within the leadership rendered the Kremlin less capable of exploring economic and social reforms, while also creating a growing body of disaffected younger party members. Behind a façade of strength and solidity, the Soviet system was choking on its own dysfunction.[70]

In fact, even as Soviet leaders touted the prospects of socialism, Soviet society was slipping into pervasive malaise. Life expectancy actually dropped, by 3.75 years for men and 1.74 years for women, between 1966 and 1980. Fertility declined and alcoholism soared. Shortages of milk, meat, and other goods were widespread; cynicism and disillusion, conversely, were plentiful.[71] The youth had "nothing of the ideology and romanticism of the 1930s," lamented one Kremlin official. The public was "sick of the official theme of 'Social Heroism' and the like."[72] What dynamism existed was increasingly oriented *against* the state, as a diverse group of dissidents—religious believers, political activists, nationalists who sought greater autonomy for their respective republics, and others—became more assertive in critiquing the regime. "This is dangerous," warned Andropov; the system was under fire from its own population.[73]

As the foundations of Soviet power were eroding at home, so was the stability of the empire in Eastern Europe. Although the invasion of Czechoslovakia in 1968 had restored Kremlin dominance in the region, it had not headed off the growth of several alarming, longer-range trends: intensifying resentment against Soviet hegemony, rising popular restiveness vis-à-vis politically repressive and economically incompetent regimes, and not least of all, the region's headlong rush toward the financial abyss. Partly due to the oil shocks, and partly through bad policy, East European countries accrued massive debts, which rose from $6 billion in 1970 to $56 billion in 1980. And because these governments were loath to risk greater unrest by letting living standards drop, austerity was often politically impossible. This dynamic surfaced with a vengeance in Poland in 1976, when an attempt to raise prices of basic staples produced widespread strikes and protests, forcing the regime into a humiliating retreat. Communist Eastern Europe—the keystone of Moscow's presence abroad—was becoming an ideological hollow shell and an economic deadweight, the source of more burdens than benefits. "All it will take to bring the entire house down is just one spark," one Soviet general warned.[74]

What was only dimly apparent at the time was that détente was actually compounding these Soviet-bloc vulnerabilities. Critics such as Ronald Reagan viewed détente as a geopolitical walkover for Moscow, in that it allowed the Soviets to make strategic gains while reaping greater trade with the West. "Détente—isn't that what a farmer has with his Turkey—until Thanksgiving day?" Reagan quipped.[75] Yet whatever its liabilities, détente encouraged long-term changes that would profoundly corrode communist authority. Imports of Western goods, decreased Soviet jamming of Radio Free Europe (RFE) and the Voice of America (VOA), expanded human contacts, and freedom to travel—all these developments flowed from the more relaxed diplomatic climate of détente, and all eventually helped reveal just how backward and repressive the Soviet bloc was.[76] Moreover, although the bloc exploited Western loans, credits, and imports to mask its economic decline, by the end of the decade this approach had fostered a dangerous dependency on the enemy. The East European regimes were particularly exposed, owing vast sums to Western banks. In economic terms, noted a 1977 CIA report, détente had shown that "the Communist countries need the West more than the West needs the Communist countries."[77]

Détente was a double-edged sword in other ways, too. Soviet leaders counted the Helsinki Final Act of 1975—the culmination of years of East-West negotiations—as a great victory, because the agreements conferred diplomatic legitimacy on Moscow's European sphere of influence. Yet in a way that neither Soviet nor U.S. officials had foreseen, Helsinki boomeranged on the Kremlin. Due largely to the efforts of America's Canadian and West European allies, the accords contained provisions that highlighted precisely those political and human rights that the Eastern-bloc governments systematically denied their citizens. The Brezhnev Politburo had agreed to these conditions only because it doubted that they would have any impact: "We are masters in our own house," Foreign Minister Andrei Gromyko declared. The aftermath of Helsinki, however, told a different tale. The accords, Anatoly Dobrynin, Soviet ambassador to the United States, later wrote, "became a manifesto of the dissident and liberal movement, a development totally beyond the imagination of the Soviet leadership." The late 1970s saw blossoming dissent and popular assertiveness throughout the Soviet empire, as citizens seized on the Helsinki principles, and protested their governments' failure to honor them. And as the Soviet-bloc regimes worked frantically to quash this activity, they merely underscored, in the eyes of their own populations, how ideologically and morally impoverished communist rule had become.[78]

The explosive tendencies within the Soviet bloc were demonstrated by the Polish crisis of 1980–1981. That crisis drew on the political, economic, and ideological decay of the 1970s. It was catalyzed by the 1979 visit of Pope John Paul II, a native Pole who exhorted his countrymen not to accept the evils of communist rule. And it unfolded in earnest in mid- and late 1980, with the formation of Solidarity, an independent, nongovernment-controlled trade union that quickly gained 10 million members, and whose popularity demonstrated the breadth of popular repudiation of the regime. Solidarity, a CIA analyst wrote, "represents a massive emotional rejection of the way the party has managed the country."[79] As protests swept the nation, it became clear that communism had failed in Poland. It was in that country, KGB official Vasili Mitrokhin wrote, that communist authorities began to realize "that the ideological battle had been lost."[80]

The crisis put Moscow in an agonizing bind. "Poland is on the brink of a catastrophe," said Marshal Viktor Kulikov—socialist rule was in jeopardy.[81]

Yet the threat of military intervention, the core of the infamous Brezhnev Doctrine, was no longer credible. The use of force would probably elicit open resistance from the Poles, force Moscow to assume the financial burden of stabilizing the country, and provoke Western sanctions that would disrupt the economic ties on which the Soviet bloc had become dependent. In essence, intervention would impose costs that the Kremlin could no longer afford. "If troops are introduced, that will mean a catastrophe," one Soviet official said.[82] The Kremlin skirted this dilemma, and avoided an embarrassing display of weakness, by inducing Polish authorities to declare martial law and restore internal order themselves. Nonetheless, Poland remained a point of vulnerability for Moscow, and the entire bloc was becoming more fragile.

As we have seen, Moscow's geopolitical gains of the 1970s often cloaked these internal weaknesses. Yet in the international sphere, too, Soviet victories proved evanescent or even illusory. The Soviets may have been advancing in Southwest Asia and sub-Saharan Africa, for instance, but they were losing influence with important Third World actors such as Egypt and India. And although U.S. alliances were strained, international communism was tearing itself apart. The Sino-Soviet split reached its apex with the border conflict of 1969, which forced the Kremlin to devote greater military resources to its Eastern flank in subsequent years and paved the way for the Sino-American rapprochement. This latter development was a signal grand strategic setback for Moscow: the Soviets now had to fear a partnership between their two greatest foes, whereas the United States, reported Dobrynin in 1972, had the opportunity of "building a new strategic alignment of forces in Asia and in the world as a whole."[83] Mao Zedong agreed, telling Kissinger that Beijing and Washington should cooperate to "commonly deal with a bastard." They increasingly did just that, through intelligence exchanges, mutual support for anti-Soviet groups in Angola and later Afghanistan, and eventually direct military-to-military ties. Compounding the injury was the Chinese turn toward a market-oriented economy from the late 1970s onward, which reinforced the tacit Sino-U.S. partnership and underscored just how bankrupt the Soviet command model had become.[84]

In these circumstances, not even the U.S. defeat in Vietnam was as unambiguous a victory for Moscow as it seemed. That episode was certainly humiliating for Washington, and acted as a stimulant to the geopolitical optimism in the Kremlin during the 1970s.[85] But the end of the war also liquidated America's greatest strategic liability, and removed the most divisive issue from the U.S. foreign policy agenda. Conceding defeat in Vietnam was therefore a precondition to the revitalized U.S. statecraft of the 1980s.

For Moscow, by contrast, the fall of Saigon shattered the façade of unity that the conflict had imposed on the various communist powers in Southeast Asia, exposing the poisonous vitriol among them. The U.S. withdrawal from the region cleared the way for an intracommunist military clash between Soviet-aligned Vietnam and Chinese-backed Cambodia, followed by China's own intervention into northern Vietnam. The end of the Vietnam War may have been painful for the United States, but it unleashed civil war in the communist world.[86]

The Soviet Union, meanwhile, was pushing its geopolitical luck by ignoring the rapidly approaching limits of its capabilities. The expansion of the 1970s was driven by feelings of power and opportunity so strong that they created a sort of "irrational exuberance" in Soviet policy. "As soon as a leader in Mozambique, Angola, Ethiopia, or Somalia mentioned the word 'socialism,'" General Anatoly Gribkov recalled, "our leaders immediately picked up on it up and decided that this particular country would become socialist."[87] This attitude produced short-term advances in areas such as sub-Saharan Africa, but it also courted disastrous long-term overstretch. For it caused the Soviets to pile up new responsibilities in the Third World just as the economy entered terminal decline. Although "we were at the peak of our power in 1979," one official said, "it was the period when the country's back began breaking."[88] Moreover, while these "successes" created a perception of Soviet momentum, they also left the Kremlin backing repressive Marxist governments that were incapable of generating prosperity for—or consent from—their citizens. Moscow would soon encounter signs of what became a key geopolitical trend of the 1980s: the rise of dogged insurgencies against its Third World clients. The Soviets, Dobrynin lamented, had gotten "caught up in patters of imperial overextension like those that had begun to afflict the United States a generation earlier."[89] Karen Brutents of the Central Committee International Department was blunter: "Certain things were done very incorrectly, if not in a suicidal way."[90]

The invasion of Afghanistan exemplified this perverse dynamic. For all the alarm that invasion provoked, we now know that it was actually an expression of Soviet weakness and an invitation to strategic disaster. Soviet leaders were impelled to intervene not by dreams of reaching the Persian Gulf, but because they were desperate to save a communist regime that was destroying itself through factional infighting and misguided attempts to communize a traditional Muslim society. "There is no active support on the part of the population," the Afghan prime minister admitted.[91] And when Soviet forces entered Afghanistan, the results were indeed "suicidal." The Kremlin earned near-universal opprobrium, as its forces were stalemated in a guerrilla war that became a cause célèbre for Muslim fighters from Afghanistan to Saudi Arabia—and a gift-wrapped opportunity for Soviet enemies to exploit. As one Soviet observer wrote in 1980, "With the introduction of troops into Afghanistan our policy . . . crossed the permissible bounds of confrontation in the 'Third World.'"[92] Moscow had stumbled into a quagmire, and it would never recover from the blunder.

The Soviet military buildup had similarly Pyrrhic results. Soviet leaders hoped that the buildup would provide greater security and leverage vis-à-vis the United States, just as U.S. officials feared that it would tilt the strategic balance toward Moscow.[93] And the shifting nuclear balance in particular did cause growing fears of an opening "window of vulnerability" in the United States. Yet the ultimate effects of the buildup were still more dangerous to Moscow than Washington. Because the Soviet defense industry was so inefficient, and because Moscow was seeking to outpace a much richer adversary, the Kremlin spent truly vast sums on its military power. The defense budget consumed perhaps 15 percent of GDP in the late 1970s—a huge burden for a staggering economy—and diverted resources that might have been invested more productively. "We were enthusiastically arming ourselves, like binging drunks," Soviet adviser Georgi Arbatov recalled. And through this self-destructive behavior, the Soviet Union was backing itself into a corner. It was tempting the United States, with its stronger economic and technological base, to respond with a buildup of its own. By pushing the boundaries of the arms race, Arbatov later noted, Moscow was risking "economic exhaustion in a hopeless military rivalry."[94]

By the end of the decade, the potential for such blowback was becoming apparent. The deployment of the SS-20s temporarily improved Moscow's position in Europe, and sowed consternation in the West. But it also shook NATO out of its disarray—no small favor to Washington—and elicited plans for a counterdeployment of Tomahawk cruise missiles and Pershing-II intermediate-range ballistic missiles (IRBMs). The Pershing-II was a deadly, mobile weapon that was both faster and more accurate than the Soviet missiles it was meant to offset, meaning that Moscow had, as General Dmitri Volkogonov later lamented, "handed the Americans a knife to put at the Soviet throat."[95]

More broadly, Soviet aggressiveness in the arms race eventually produced a drastic shift of opinion in the United States. By the late 1970s, the Cold War consensus, seemingly so discredited after Vietnam, was making a comeback. Whereas Congress had consistently exerted downward pressure on defense during the early and mid-1970s, at the end of the decade the hawks were again flying high. Arms control had fallen into disrepute, with SALT II facing strong opposition even before the Soviet invasion of Afghanistan killed that accord altogether, and in general, legislative sentiment was now pushing the executive to be more assertive vis-à-vis Moscow. The same trends were present in the public at large. Domestic opinion gravitated toward hardliners such as Reagan and the Committee on the Present Danger, who warned that the deteriorating geopolitical balance demanded a vigorous response. In 1974, just 17 percent of Americans thought defense spending was too low; by 1980, the number was 56 percent. "The continuous Soviet military buildup," Defense Secretary Harold Brown noted, "has finally sunk into American consciousness as an important fact."[96]

The resulting counteroffensive would fully take shape under Ronald Reagan, but key elements traced back to the Carter presidency. Contrary to the more polemical broadsides launched against his administration at the time and after, Carter occupies an ambiguous place in the history of the Cold War and America's rise to unipolarity.[97] In one sense, Carter and his aides were prophets of revival. They understood, far better than Nixon and Kissinger, that the United States was actually stronger than it looked during the 1970s, and that it was really the Soviets who faced profound problems ahead. Internal planning documents regularly stressed the need to take a holistic view of global power, and to understand that the Soviet buildup was veiling "serious problems caused by unfavorable demographic trends, economic slowdown, and inefficiencies in the agricultural sector, nationality aspirations, and intellectual dissidence." PRM/NSC-10, a net assessment of the East-West rivalry, put it bluntly: "No detached observer from another planet would today harbor any reasonable doubt as to which is the most powerful nation in the world."[98] Carter himself had an abiding faith in long-term U.S. prospects. "If we can buy at least five or six years' time in getting along with the Soviets," he wrote, "the trends will be in our favor."[99]

What good this insight did Carter is another question, for his administration perpetually struggled to devise a comprehensive, effective strategy for waging Cold War. For most of Carter's presidency, he and his advisers had enormous difficulty resolving bureaucratic clashes, determining what mix of détente and confrontation should characterize superpower ties, deciding how seriously to take the Soviet military buildup and advances in the Third World, and reconciling issues such as human rights with other priorities like arms control. Even in 1980, Secretary of State Cyrus Vance acknowledged, there were widespread doubts as to "whether the Carter administration had a coherent view of the international situation, a sense of global strategy, and consistent policies and objectives."[100] In consequence, for all his prescience about the future, Carter often seemed at a loss to contain Soviet power in the present. "The Soviets are feeling their oats," one NSC official wrote in 1979, "and are projecting a mood of almost disdain for the U.S."[101] And as one internal review concluded, during Carter's early years in office it may have been his sanguinity about the long term that inhibited him from reacting more sharply or successfully to Soviet assertiveness in areas such as the Horn of Africa: "The Carter Administration began with the assumption that our political and strategic competition with the Soviet Union was inexorably resolving itself in our favor. . . . We thought we had pretty clear sailing. This estimate regrettably turned out to be wrong."[102]

Yet while Carter's Cold War confusion has been amply documented, the thirty-ninth president did begin to lay the foundations for a reassertion of U.S. power versus Moscow. In the realm of human rights, Carter took numerous actions that undermined communist authority within the Soviet bloc. His administration expanded U.S. radio broadcasting into the bloc, disseminated subversive publications in Eastern Europe and the Soviet Union, and expressed strong support for dissidents such as Aleksandr Solzhenitsyn and Andrei Sakharov. The administration also used the follow-on conferences resulting from Helsinki as a forum for criticizing Soviet abuses, while Carter personally pressed the issue with Kremlin officials. The rationale for doing so drew on Carter's strong moral attachment to human rights, but there was geopolitical logic as well. "Human rights has placed great strains on the Soviet system," he told aides in 1980. "If we can get by the next five years without war, we will win the peaceful competition."[103] Indeed, while Carter's pressure initially made the Soviets less cooperative on human rights and other issues, it underscored their ideological vulnerabilities and opened up new lines of assault for his successors. Whenever Carter talked about human rights, Gromyko admitted, "the Soviet leadership reacted with a conditioned reflex . . . waiting for the arrow that would be launched in the direction of the Soviet Union."[104]

Looking beyond human rights, as Soviet advances and American setbacks mounted in the late 1970s, the Carter administration began to develop many other initiatives that figured prominently in U.S. policy during the decade to come. The "Reagan buildup" truly began under Carter, as constant-dollar military outlays rose from $216.4 billion in 1977 to $229.4 billion in 1980.[105] The administration invested in strategic programs such as the MX missile, the B-2 Stealth bomber, and the upgrading of the existing ICBM force; it also approved a more aggressive nuclear doctrine premised on targeting Soviet command, control, and communications assets— including leadership targets and the "political control system"—in event

of war. Said Harold Brown in 1980, "We are . . . appropriately strengthening our strategic nuclear capabilities across the board."[106] These strategic improvements complemented important conventional programs under
development, such as precision-guided munitions, the Apache and Black-
hawk helicopters, the M-1 Abrams tank, the F-117 Stealth fighter, and the
Patriot missile. Many of these programs were specifically intended to exploit
American technological advantages over the Soviet Union, and they would
ultimately produce dramatic improvements in the accuracy and lethality of
U.S. military power.[107]

By the end of the Carter era, the U.S. posture was stiffening in other
ways, as well. The president showed increased determination to prevent further Kremlin moves in the Third World in 1979–1980, and established a
"strategic partnership"—including full diplomatic relations and limited military sales—with China.[108] At the same time, Carter's team laid the foundations for the Reagan Doctrine by initiating covert support for anticommunist
movements and governments in countries such as Nicaragua, El Salvador, and
the Yemeni Arab Republic. "Through political pressure and covert action,"
Brzezinski wrote, the administration must "make life as difficult as possible
for the Soviets." And following the invasion of Afghanistan, the United States
imposed economic sanctions on Moscow, while also initiating covert support
for the mujahedin. "Our hope is to keep the Soviets beleaguered in Afghanistan itself and too off-balance to take advantage of the grave weaknesses of
our present position," Brzezinski wrote.[109] For his part, Carter was no longer
the president who had once chastised Americans for an unhealthy obses-
sion with anticommunism. It was "essential," he told British prime minister
Margaret Thatcher, "that we make this action as politically costly as possible to the Soviet Union."[110] When Reagan took power, these Carter-era
initiatives would be building blocks for his broad geopolitical assault on a
weakened Soviet Union.

In sum, the 1970s were a paradoxical decade in the Cold War. On the
surface, the preponderance of evidence suggested that America was declining and the Soviet Union was surging ahead. Yet at a deeper level, it was the
Soviets who came out of the 1970s hobbled, overextended, and heading into
an irreversible slide. The internal weaknesses of the Soviet bloc were intensifying and becoming harder to conceal; the geopolitical gains of the decade
were transient or even counterproductive. And by the end of the Carter
years, Soviet assertiveness had begun to elicit a counterattack that would
ultimately have devastating effects. To be sure, Washington did not yet have
a fully articulated strategy for exploiting Soviet decline, and the full extent
of Soviet weakness was still becoming apparent. But neither of these key

elements would be missing for long. As the 1970s ended, the United States was surprisingly well positioned for a geopolitical comeback, and the Cold War was on the verge of a dramatic turn.

Human Rights and the Democratic Revolution

If the 1970s saw key tectonic shifts in geopolitics, they were also a time of profound ideological transformations. "The world's population is experiencing a political awakening on a scale without precedent in its history," said Brzezinski in 1978: people around the globe were challenging the institutions and orthodoxies that structured their lives, and embracing new concepts that channeled their energies in provocative and disruptive ways.[111] The ideological crisis of communism and the growth of Third World nationalism were part of this phenomenon, as were trends such as the movement for greater social equality in the West and the revival of Islamist politics in the Middle East. As we will see in chapter 5, some of these forces would be quite challenging for U.S. officials, posing more threats than opportunities. Yet amid this upheaval, there were also ideological currents that proved central to the reassertion of U.S. prestige and influence. Prominent among these were two trends that formed key parts of the global explosion of political consciousness during the 1970s: the rise of a transnational human rights movement focused primarily on protecting individuals from physical abuse or political repression, and the onset of a democratic revolution destined to spread liberal institutions more widely than ever before.

Both trends were transformative in their impact, and both originated in an array of influences that were beyond the control of any single statesman. Regarding human rights, the global movement of the 1970s represented the rebirth of an earlier movement that traced back to Enlightenment ideas about fundamental rights and liberties, and whose history ran through the French and American revolutions and the antislavery campaigns of the nineteenth century. That movement had briefly reached the top of the international agenda in the mid-twentieth century, with the drafting of the Universal Declaration of Human Rights following the Holocaust and the horrors of World War II. For most of the Cold War, however, universal human rights were more honored in the breach than the observance. This was surely true in the Soviet bloc, where paper guarantees were mocked by suffocating governmental repression. Yet it was also true in many quarters of the noncommunist world, where concerns of geopolitics, empire, and sovereignty often led governments to reject the idea of universal rights, or at least to sacrifice their practical observance.[112]

It was only in the 1960s and 1970s that a newer, more powerful human rights movement took hold, impelled by a diverse set of trends that coalesced during this period. In the West, desegregation and decolonization were now easing the issues that had earlier made U.S. and European officials resist the rights paradigm. In the Soviet bloc, the post-Stalin thaw was opening slightly more space for dissidents to declaim governmental transgressions, and the publication of subversive literature was shedding greater light on the everyday horrors of communist rule. Meanwhile, in Third World regions such as Latin America, the spreading influence of liberation theology was creating a religious framework in which human rights could be situated, and encouraging the sense of individual dignity at the core of the rights ideal. Finally, and above all else, the burgeoning rights movement was being driven by the proliferation of commercial satellites and other communications technologies. These advances made the abuse of innocents half a world away far harder to obscure or ignore—it was no longer possible, Brzezinski had written in 1970, to maintain "moral immunity to 'foreign' events" amid "the electronic intrusion of global events into the home." Technological improvements equally facilitated the astonishing growth of a veritable army of nongovernmental organizations (NGOs) dedicated to publicizing and contesting rights violations abroad. Together, these factors merged to forge a global human rights consciousness that would influence world politics for decades to come.[113]

The rise of that consciousness was both illustrated and sharpened by a series of man-made humanitarian catastrophes. When the Nigerian civil war that resulted from the attempted secession of Biafra threatened to cause famine for millions between late 1967 and early 1970, for instance, an ad hoc coalition of humanitarian groups swung into action to raise awareness of the atrocities and provide desperately needed aid. Religious relief groups instituted a makeshift airlift to feed the Biafran population, while assorted activists lobbied Washington and other governments to intervene. These efforts failed to win foreign governmental support for the Biafran rebels, but they elicited widespread global sympathy and presaged similar episodes to follow.[114] In particular, the quasi-genocidal atrocities committed by East Pakistani authorities against the Bengali population in 1971, and the brutal repression undertaken by South American governments in Argentina and Chile during the mid- and late 1970s, invigorated the emerging movement. These events stimulated international efforts to protect vulnerable individuals and groups from deliberate victimization, and led to concerted campaigns to influence global opinion and isolate murderous regimes. They fostered partnerships between rights-oriented groups and individuals across borders, and gave human rights issues a higher profile—albeit at terrible cost—than before.

Indeed, whereas earlier postwar efforts to promote universal human rights had been predominantly legalist in focus, this newer movement had an activist bent. The courageous protests of South American and Soviet-bloc dissidents; the activities of advocacy groups such as Amnesty International and Freedom House; the involvement of churches and campus groups in promoting humanitarian causes; the efforts of European statesmen and citizens to make human rights central to the Helsinki Accords; and the actions of doctors, lawyers, and relief groups that aided the oppressed or helped innocents caught in the crossfire—all these things testified to the growing salience and mobilizing power of rights issues. More notable still, the development of communication and cooperation among these actors forged a truly transnational human rights network, through which disparate groups and individuals joined forces in support of common goals. Local dissident communities interacted with human rights NGOs, feeding them information on abuses and receiving solidarity and support. NGOs established relationships with officials and opinion leaders in the United States and elsewhere, serving as sources of information and sometimes helping to craft human rights legislation and other policy measures. As Samuel Moyn has observed, human rights was becoming an organizing principle and overarching ideological framework for a wide assortment of actors seeking to bring about a more just status quo.[115]

Human rights certainly made strange bedfellows in the U.S. Congress. From the early 1970s, conservatives and neoconservatives such as Senator Henry Jackson (D-Washington) took up the issue as a bludgeon against the Soviet Union, and a way of escaping the moral relativism they associated with détente. Urged on by Soviet dissidents such as Solzhenitsyn and Sakharov, who rejected the norms of state sovereignty and pleaded for more interference in Moscow's affairs, Jackson and his allies thrust human rights into superpower diplomacy by demanding that the Kremlin liberalize its treatment of Soviet Jews and other groups in exchange for expanded East-West relations. The goal, Jackson said, was to "promote human rights in the Soviet Union"; détente must not be "a formula between governments for capitulation on the issue of human rights." The high point of this campaign was passage of Jackson-Vanik amendment, which explicitly tied most favored nation (MFN) status for Moscow to the easing of restrictions on Jewish emigration—and which killed a central economic plank of détente when Brezhnev refused to yield.[116]

Liberals such as Edward Kennedy (D-Massachusetts) and Donald Fraser (D-Minnesota), meanwhile, were mounting a parallel campaign from the left. They were concerned less with waging Cold War than with moderating its excesses, and they sought particularly to ease the moral anguish induced by Vietnam and U.S. partnerships with ugly Third World regimes. "Basically we feel it's very difficult to continue to support foreign assistance programs to governments which oppress their own people," Fraser told Kissinger.[117] Fraser's House subcommittee issued an influential 1974 report that critiqued the perceived moral obtuseness of Washington's Cold War policies, and he and his allies—supported by Amnesty International and other NGOs—began adding human rights amendments to foreign aid bills. By the mid-1970s, the Ford administration confronted what Deputy National Security Adviser Brent Scowcroft called an "unholy alliance" of left and right.[118] Human rights, agreed a State Department report, was "no longer a bleeding heart issue presided [over] by fairies in Geneva."[119] Rather, that issue was shaping the global agenda, and its influence would grow with time.

The explosion of human rights activism was also closely related to a broader phenomenon of the 1970s: the emerging global crisis of authoritarianism, and the start of an unprecedented onrush of electoral democracy. Scholars generally define electoral democracy as a system in which the "most powerful collective decision makers are selected through fair, honest, and periodic elections in which candidates freely compete for votes and in which virtually all the adult population is eligible to vote."[120] By this standard, the world had seen alternating waves of democratic and authoritarian advance since the early nineteenth century, and at first glance, there was little to suggest that the former system was presently on the upswing. The years since 1960 had seen an erosion of democratic hopes worldwide, punctuated by endemic coup-making in Latin America, the crushing of the Prague Spring, the rise of post-colonial autocracy in much of sub-Saharan Africa, and the momentum of Marxist-Leninist movements in Southeast Asia and elsewhere. Prominent intellectuals even wondered whether Western democracies could handle the strains imposed by the crises of the 1970s. As one expert writes, midway through the decade it seemed that "authoritarianism, not democracy, was the way of the world."[121] The reverse was true, however, because by 1975 democracy was on the verge of a dramatic global expansion.

Like the human rights revolution, this democratic revolution reflected many factors and took many forms. Some of the democratic transitions from the mid-1970s onward were initiated from above by authoritarian elites, while others were the product of popular pressure from below. Sometimes democratic change came rapidly, unexpectedly, or even via bloodshed; at other times it was peaceful, consensual, and deliberate. Moreover, just as forms of democratization varied widely, the precipitating causes of transitions were diverse and often idiosyncratic. The death of a long-time authoritarian ruler, the defeat of a military regime in a poorly chosen foreign war, the splintering of an autocratic coalition, and other mechanisms all played critical roles in triggering political transformations, and there was so single pattern or formula that explained the advance of democracy. When one looked beyond the inevitable variations and idiosyncrasies, however, it was possible to identify several broad, underlying themes that did much to move the world in a more democratic direction.[122]

To a large extent, these structural factors revolved around economics. In countries across several continents, the comparatively rapid growth of the early postwar era had given dictatorships a claim to legitimacy. Yet that growth had also undermined the socioeconomic base of authoritarianism, by producing more complex economies that were harder for dictators to manage, and by generating a broader, better educated, and more political middle class. In many countries, that middle class was increasingly concentrated in urban areas, where mass mobilization was easier, and its members were bound to grow restive in systems in which educational and economic attainment brought them few meaningful political opportunities. By the late 1960s and 1970s, these conditions were already starting to pull more countries—particularly in Latin America, East Asia, and southern Europe—into a "transition zone" in which democratization was more likely. Counterintuitively enough, the economic crises of the 1970s and 1980s only increased the pressure. Whereas the economic expansion of earlier decades had afforded authoritarian regimes some prestige and popularity, economic turmoil now left dictators from Poland to Peru discredited and struggling to meet basic societal needs. In doing so, that turmoil often fostered acute civil discontent, and created openings in which a more active and engaged populace could begin pushing for liberalization.

This liberalizing impetus was simultaneously drawing strength from a host of other factors. In the Latin American and Iberian worlds, for instance, the shifts of the Catholic Church were crucial. The Church itself had become more politically liberal and anti-authoritarian following doctrinal reforms of the mid-1960s, creating a strong ideological challenge to dictatorial governments, and in many cases turning local Catholic leaders and institutions into sources of opposition to undemocratic rule. More broadly, the spreading of a global human rights consciousness naturally contributed to greater popular assertiveness vis-à-vis oppressive regimes, while the mobilization of international groups and networks committed to denouncing rights abuses ensured deepening international legitimacy problems for such governments.

Outside actors such as the European Community further reinforced the impetus to democratization from the mid-1970s onward by offering to admit new members—and confer the economic benefits that membership entailed—as long as they were democracies. And finally, once underway, democratization could be something of a self-reinforcing process. A successful transition in one country further isolated remaining authoritarian regimes; it also created new sources of support and inspiration for would-be liberalizers in other nations. Together, these forces combined to put dictators on the defensive and create the conditions for a rapid and sustained democratic advance.[123]

Even as democratic pessimism lingered during the 1970s, in fact, that advance was getting underway. The phenomenon started with democratic transitions in European countries such as Portugal, Greece, and Spain in the mid- and late 1970s. It soon made inroads in South and East Asia, and would sweep nearly all of Latin America in the decade and a half after 1977. By the end of the 1980s, it would even take hold in the communist world, via the political reforms initiated by Gorbachev in the Soviet Union, and the dramatic transitions that occurred across Eastern Europe. And by the 1990s and early 2000s, democratic change was afoot in sub-Saharan Africa, with openings in South Africa, Kenya, and other key countries. Admittedly, many of these democratic transitions were halting or incomplete, and many new democracies still contained lingering elements of authoritarianism. Questions of how *effectively* democratic governments could actually govern also remained to be answered.[124] But overall, there was no question that democracy was enjoying a remarkable renaissance, one that was carrying it far beyond its traditional homes in the Anglophone countries and the developed West and into other areas around the world.

The cumulative results of the democratic surge that began in the 1970s were therefore momentous. By one count, the number of electoral democracies nearly doubled from 1974 to 1990, rising from thirty-nine to seventy-six.[125] The momentum persisted into the 1990s, and by the end of that decade, there were 120 electoral democracies, constituting nearly two-thirds of all countries.[126] "Nothing like this continuous growth in democracy had ever been seen before in the history of the world," one expert wrote.[127] Indeed, whereas the two previous waves of liberalization in the nineteenth and twentieth centuries had both been followed by strong reverse waves of authoritarian resurgence, this "third wave" proved to be the most powerful and farthest-reaching yet. Its full effects would only be evident with time, but even at the outset, a few sharp-eyed analysts could see that the political complexion of the world was beginning to change markedly. "The world itself is now dominated by a new spirit," observed Jimmy Carter in 1977. "Peoples more numerous and more politically aware are craving, and now demanding, their place in the sun."[128]

What the human rights and democratic revolutions meant for U.S. power, however, was not immediately clear. Although these trends would eventually make opportunities for constructive statecraft, at the outset U.S. policymakers were often disoriented by the profound shifts in train, or were simply unable to fashion effective policies in response. Henry Kissinger, for one, was ill-suited to grappling with these forces. For all his geopolitical acumen, Kissinger had a backward-looking approach to international affairs. His worldview was rooted in nineteenth-century European realpolitik, and he saw efforts to alter the internal nature of states—whether friendly or hostile—as dangerous distractions from the core task of preserving international order. Like Nixon, he was deeply skeptical that the United States *could* promote democracy or human rights in foreign societies, and he thought it irresponsible to suggest that Washington *should* attempt such feats amid great geopolitical turmoil. "Anyone who wants to join a missionary organization should wait for the next Secretary of State," Kissinger said. "That's not what we're doing foreign policy for."[129]

As a result, Kissinger was generally indifferent—even hostile—to the political and ideological changes afoot. He deplored the Jackson-Vanik amendment for undermining diplomacy with Moscow, and he disdained efforts by U.S. allies to bring human rights into the Helsinki accords. "The Soviet Union won't be overthrown without noticing it, and certainly not because of things like increased circulation of newspapers and so on," he said.[130] And in his efforts to uphold containment amid U.S. retrenchment, Kissinger saw no alternative to leaning on friendly—if murderous—autocrats from Indonesia to Argentina to Iran. "Any differences we have are 'in the family,'" he told Brazil's Emílio Médici. "Our fundamental relationship is of paramount importance."[131] Kissinger even collaborated with those autocrats in seeking antidemocratic change abroad, as when the United States and Brazil pursued parallel endeavors to overthrow Salvador Allende's socialist (but elected) government in Chile. "However unpleasant they act," he said of the brutal junta that followed, "the government is better for us than Allende was."[132]

To protect these initiatives, Kissinger implacably opposed the growing emphasis on human rights and political reform. He blocked State Department efforts to criticize Chile or other friendly regimes for their abhorrent human rights practices, and obliquely encouraged those governments to crack down on their opposition. "We are sympathetic with what you are trying to do here," he told Augusto Pinochet in 1976.[133] Similarly, Kissinger had subordinates withhold information on the rights abuses of allies from Congress. "I have an old-fashioned view that friends ought to be supported," he said.[134] Human rights, from this view, represented more of a threat than an opportunity for U.S. statecraft.

This approach was understandable at a time when containment seemed to be in serious trouble, and Kissinger's methods purchased some short- and medium-term stability in key regions. The problem, however, was that Kissinger's initiatives also put him at odds with the longer-term trends in the international system, and with the proponents of those trends in the United States. His approach tied Washington to regimes that would soon come under assault from within, as became piercingly clear when two key allies— the shah of Iran and the Somoza dynasty in Nicaragua—were overthrown in 1979. Even before that, his policy had become politically unsustainable. Kissinger's obstructionism failed to thwart the human rights advocates in Congress; it only provoked them to take more punitive steps. Fraser and his allies used their influence to mandate annual reports on the practices of countries receiving U.S. aid, to reduce or terminate assistance to egregious violators such as Chile and Argentina, and to strengthen the previously mar- ginalized State Department office on human rights issues.[135] When Kissinger left office, the human rights lobby was thus all the more ascendant. Kissinger, by contrast, was seen by critics on both the left and right as a retrograde fig- ure, one who grasped neither the significance of issues such as human rights and democratization, nor the need for a more morally grounded foreign policy after Vietnam. In 1976, State Department soundings of public opin- ion showed "a deep-seated yearning that the moral aspect of foreign policy issues should be a significant factor in policy decisions," the implication being that Kissinger's stance had not cleared this bar.[136]

The Carter administration was more attuned to the importance of the dem- ocratic and human rights revolutions, and to the ethical—and geopolitical— imperatives of supporting them. Washington faced "a new world that calls for a new American foreign policy," the president asserted in a speech at Notre Dame in May 1977—"a policy based on constant decency in its values and on optimism in our historical vision."[137] From the start, Carter and aides like Brzezinski believed that a policy of promoting human rights and democratic reform could serve several important ends. It could regenerate domestic support for an assertive internationalism by reconnecting American policy to American ideals.[138] It could also ease the repression and alienation that caused Third World instability, while improving the U.S. image around the globe. "The moral heart of our international appeal," Brzezinski had written in a speech drafted for Carter, was "as a country which stands for self-determination and free choice."[139]

Carter fundamentally agreed. From his perspective, Cold War concerns had too long prevented U.S. officials from honoring these basic moral principles. As he put it at Notre Dame, the United States must reject "that inordinate fear of communism which once led us to embrace any dictator who joined us in that fear."[140] At the same time, however, there was a strong belief within the administration that human rights and democratization could actually be powerful weapons of Cold War and geopolitical renewal. Focusing on these issues would allow the United States to cut a sharp contrast to Soviet totalitarianism, while harnessing dynamic global forces to foster an international environment that would be more reflective of American values, and more conducive to U.S. interests. An early administration review of human rights issues noted that U.S. policy "promotes the fundamental long-term American interest in a world of nations whose systems of government and societies reflect individual freedom and dignity and thus reject totalitarianism," while assisting "in the philosophical debate with the Soviet Union as to the type of society worth developing."[141] Carter himself captured the sense of moral and geopolitical opportunity driving this policy in his inaugural address. Around the world, he argued, "The passion for freedom is on the rise. Tapping this new spirit, there can be no nobler nor more ambitious task for America to undertake on this day of a new beginning than to help shape a just and peaceful world that is truly humane." Americans, Carter believed, must "take on those moral duties which, when assumed, seem invariably to be in our own best interests."[142]

These ideas infused U.S. statecraft under Carter. The administration committed to protecting three essential categories of rights—"integrity of the person," "basic economic and social rights," and "civil and political liberties."[143] To an unprecedented extent, U.S. officials used numerous tools—moral suasion and quiet diplomacy, the manipulation of military and economic aid, and others—to advance these ends in countries from the Soviet bloc to South America. Human rights, noted Anthony Lake, director of the Policy Planning Staff (PPS), was the "cardinal tenet" of Carter's statecraft.[144] And although the administration nodded to the need "for caution to avoid giving our policy a parochial cast that appears to export American-style democracy," there was also great emphasis on encouraging democratic reform and consolidation.[145] Carter would intervene on behalf of democratic forces in several Latin American countries, and internal documents asserted that human rights and democracy went hand in hand. "To stop the torture of one person or to alleviate hunger in one family is important," noted one assessment. "To build institutions that safeguard against torture and promote an equitable distribution of resources is, in the long run, more important."[146] As NSC aide Robert Pastor would write in 1980, "We have tried to use every opportunity to show that democracy pays, and the trend is clearly in a positive direction."[147]

This was a bold and visionary agenda—one that sought to accommodate and exploit global change, and one that presaged key aspects of U.S. statecraft for decades to come. But as was often true with Carter, prescient ideas did not ensure coherent or effective policy. Perhaps unavoidably, his stance invited charges of double standards, as officials condemned the abuses of some tyrannical regimes while downplaying those of others. (In Carter's dealings with China, for instance, issues of human rights and democracy were conspicuously absent.)[148] U.S. policy also occasioned continual infighting. Carter's advisers may have agreed on the basic importance of encouraging human rights and political reform, but they incessantly clashed over how vigorously to do so, causing mixed signals and muddled messages. There were, one Chilean diplomat wrote, "two currents in battle" in Washington.[149] Partly in consequence, Carter never wielded as much leverage as he had expected, and efforts to spur real improvements in "hard cases" such as South Africa, El Salvador, and Guatemala were often exercises in futility.[150]

More problematic still was the damage that Carter's policy inflicted on other U.S. interests. Human rights advocacy underscored Soviet ideological weaknesses, for instance, but it also complicated arms control and undermined Carter's hopes for preserving what remained of détente. As Dobrynin recalled, "Sometimes Carter behaved as if he were deliberately trying to disprove the truth of the aphorism that politics is the art of the possible."[151] Carter's policies also alienated numerous allies from Brazil to the Middle East, straining key relationships just as Moscow was making gains in the Third World. Filipino officials condemned Carter's stance as "moral imperialism," while Pinochet deemed human rights "an international conspiracy . . . orchestrated by Marxism."[152] In Latin American, several governments renounced U.S. military aid rather than accept human rights conditions, effectively terminating long-standing defense ties. "Our influence has diminished," George Brown, chairman of the Joint Chiefs of Staff (JCS), reported. "Our policies have left bad feeling in their wake."[153] The long-range benefits of promoting human rights and democratization seemed clear enough; whether Carter could do so at tolerable near-term cost was open to question.

Ultimately, it was the Iranian and Nicaraguan revolutions that served as acid tests for U.S. policy—and mercilessly exposed its flaws. In both cases,

Carter was handed a very delicate situation: a longtime ally was reaping the whirlwind caused by decades of brutality and corruption, leading to rising dissatisfaction, upheaval, and eventually revolt. And in both cases, Carter's proposed solution fit squarely with the logic of his broader statecraft. The United States would not precipitously withdraw support from these regimes, but it would push them to make internal reforms, show greater respect for human rights, and gradually transition toward more democratic institutions. Carter's philosophy, he wrote, was "to combine support for our more authoritarian allies and friends with the effective promotion of human rights within their countries. By inducing them to change their repressive policies, we would be enhancing freedom and democracy, and helping to remove the reasons for revolution that often erupt among those who suffer from persecution." Reform would be the antidote to instability.[154]

In Iran and Nicaragua alike, the administration made earnest efforts at liberalization. In the former country, Carter continued selling arms to the shah, but also encouraged him to release political prisoners, relax emergency measures, and engage the opposition. Well into 1978, U.S. officials urged the regime not to use force against mounting protests, and to keep opening the political system. And as the chaos climaxed late that year, the same concerns prevented Carter from unambiguously endorsing a crackdown. "The Shah was never explicitly urged to be tough," Brzezinski wrote; "U.S. assurances of support were watered down by simultaneous reminders of the need to do more about progress toward genuine democracy."[155] In Nicaragua, meanwhile, the administration pushed Anastasio Somoza to loosen political controls, negotiate with the moderate opposition, and refrain from fully unleashing the praetorian National Guard. Over the longer term, U.S. representatives argued, Somoza must hold elections and permit a democratic transition. "What is needed in Nicaragua is true reform to allow for democratic participation and avoid escalating conflict," said U.S. ambassador Mauricio Solaún.[156] To reinforce the point, Carter restricted U.S. arms sales and military aid. Carter did not openly disavow the dictator in 1977–1978, but the pressure was sufficient for Somoza to say that he faced a "rebellion encouraged by functionaries in Washington."[157]

Somoza was onto something, for while Carter's approach made sense in theory, in practice the results were perverse. In Iran, the shah did take steps that the administration had urged as part of a broader program of liberalization. "The Shah has been changing under foreign criticism of the government's handling of security-related cases," CIA officials wrote.[158] The problem, however, was that because the Shah had so thoroughly infuriated the population by this point, limited reforms could not assuage public anger.

But coming just as the foundations of the regime were cracking open, those reforms *did* send signals of weakness that exacerbated the upheaval. International observers were "impressed by the degree of which the Carter policies seemed to be giving encouragement to the opposition groups chafing under the Pahlavi yoke."[159] Or as U.S. diplomat Stanley Escudero noted, "The Shah's absolute rule had established clearly defined parameters of dissent. His liberalizing moves and the impact of our human rights statements altered these parameters without establishing new ones. Unwilling to believe that the regime would lessen its controls except through weakness, the Iranian people began pushing in all directions, attempting to determine the new limits of individual political behavior."[160] And as the crisis came to a head, conflicting signals from Washington left the shah unsure whether Carter would back full-on repression, contributing to the paralysis that sealed his fate.[161] U.S. policy had not lessened the danger of revolution; it had *encouraged* that very result.

In Nicaragua, Carter's approach was equally counterproductive. U.S. pressure did cause Somoza to refrain from an all-out crackdown during the crucial early days of the revolution, to show a surprising tolerance for opposition and exile groups that were openly seeking his ouster, and to take very modest steps toward reform—all of which emboldened the antigovernment forces.[162] Yet U.S. policy failed to induce Somoza to leave power, and Carter blanched at the heavy-handed methods—an explicit call for his resignation, backed by credible threat of military intervention—that might have sufficed. The administration thereby ended up with a worst-of-both-worlds policy that undermined Somoza without doing anything to staunch the polarization that was tearing the country apart.[163] In late 1978 and early 1979, Carter watched helplessly as moderates swung into alliance with Sandinista radicals, precipitating the extremist triumph he had hoped to avert. "Human rights," Deputy Secretary of State Warren Christopher acknowledged, "was perhaps the principal engine that brought about the downfall of Somoza."[164]

The Iranian and Nicaraguan revolutions fueled perceptions of U.S. decline during the 1970s, and gave succor to the idea that trying to remake authoritarian regimes was but a fool's errand. In her famous essay "Dictatorships and Double Standards," Jeane Kirkpatrick alleged that Carter's policy reflected "the pervasive and mistaken assumption that one can easily locate and impose democratic alternatives to incumbent autocracies," and the "equally pervasive and equally flawed belief that change *per se* in such autocracies is inevitable, desirable, and in the American interest."[165] Even Carter's aides admitted that aspiration had exceeded strategic acumen—that the administration had underestimated the difficulties of reforming polarized societies, and that efforts to produce stability had encouraged catastrophic instability instead. "By the time a friendly despot has lost his legitimacy by destroying the trust between his regime and politically significant segments of society," Lake wrote, "efforts to plug in the liberal formula of reformism are exercises either in irrelevance or destabilization."[166] Brzezinski put it more pithily: "If you emphasize liberalization without a counterbalancing emphasis on authority, liberalization can become a departure point for anarchy."[167] Carter had lost sight of this reality, and his well-intentioned policies had contributed to severe strategic setbacks.

At the end of the 1970s, then, it hardly seemed that promotion of democracy and human rights would soon become pillars of a highly effective foreign policy.[168] But if one looked closely, there were encouraging signs. Broadly speaking, the mere fact of the democratic and human rights revolutions was good for America, as Carter and his advisers understood. The United States was, after all, the world's foremost democratic state and a country whose closest allies were themselves liberal democracies. It followed that an increasingly democratic, rights-conscious world was likely to be a world that was moving in Washington's direction ideologically and geopolitically, and one in which America would be far more comfortable and influential than its authoritarian rivals. It also followed that the spread of democratic values and institutions offered a long-term opportunity— provided it could be handled correctly—to align the United States with some of the strongest global forces for change. "The growth in democracy—not because we forced it, but because of its inherent appeal—should be cause for American confidence," Vice President Walter Mondale wrote in 1979. "I believe we should start from the assumption that our long-term interests are best served by democratic change and seek ways to help our friends, within the limits of our influence, along that road."[169]

To be sure, Iran and Nicaragua had shown the pitfalls of such a policy. Yet the balance sheet on Carter's efforts to encourage democracy and human rights was not entirely negative. At home, Carter's policy began to restore a belief in the basic morality of U.S. internationalism, no small issue after Vietnam. "We re-identified America with a certain basic aspiration . . . namely that of freedom—and I think that was good for America," Brzezinski recalled.[170] Abroad, human rights initiatives had a similar effect. They distanced Washington from several widely reviled pariah states, and earned favorable comment from observers around the world. "The administration's stand on human rights has spearheaded efforts to re-exert U.S. moral leadership in world affairs," CIA analysts reported; Carter's policies had "been heartening to many of those who feel oppressed by tyrannies of either the right or left."[171] Long afterward, in fact, anti-authoritarian dissidents recalled that Carter's solidarity helped sustain them in their struggle against dictatorial regimes. "In those years of dictatorship, those of us in the opposition had to struggle practically in the dark," said Julio Sanguinetti, who would become the democratically elected president of Uruguay in 1985. "One of the few significant sources of support we had was the policy of the U.S. government, which was constantly looking for human rights violations."[172]

In this sense, Carter's policies contributed to preserving and strengthening pro-reform forces that would later burst forth. And even at the time, his diplomacy had some concrete, positive impacts. Although Carter's human rights campaign often ran up against determined resistance, it still encouraged incremental gains in numerous countries. The grossest abuses, such as torture and extra-judicial killings, declined in several Latin American nations. In East Asia, dictatorships released political prisoners, eased states of exception or emergency, and generally lowered the intensity of repression. U.S. policy was not solely responsible for these developments, but as one NSC review concluded, it had "helped to create a climate in which such changes are more likely."[173]

Although hardly anyone noticed it, Carter also helped save several fragile democratic transitions. In at least three cases, he used U.S. leverage with economically vulnerable Latin American governments to strengthen democratic reformers and deter challenges to electoral processes. In the Dominican Republic in 1978, Carter sprang into action when the military and incumbent president sought to steal national elections from the rightful winner. U.S. military officials warned Dominican officers that the bilateral aid and defense relationship was at stake, and Carter announced that "the degree of our country's support for the Dominican Government will depend upon the integrity of the election process."[174] Intelligence reports confirmed that this statement was "the decisive factor" in keeping the electoral process on track.[175] In Ecuador that same year and Peru in 1977–1978, the administration employed a similar mix of pressures and inducements to discourage ruling militaries from overturning plans for a return to elections and civilian rule. Carter's intervention, Ecuadorian leaders acknowledged, "played a crucial role."[176] In some sense, these were "easy cases," because there was already strong, pro-democracy sentiment in each country, and because the domestic balance was such that minimal U.S. interference could tip the scales. But even so, these episodes presaged an essential tactic of the 1980s: the targeted use of U.S. power, in key times and places, to throw the outcome to the forces of democracy and reform.

Just as quietly, Carter had prepared the U.S. government to embrace the challenges of human rights and democracy promotion in the decade ahead. "Human rights," wrote Brzezinski, "has been woven into the bureaucracy."[177] At the State Department, the human rights office became a full-fledged bureau that was stronger and better funded than before. That bureau, in turn, established lasting ties to the relevant congressional committees, NGOs, and refugees and dissidents abroad. In the field, U.S. ambassadors were now required to make human rights a priority in their reporting, and embassies had to have a dedicated human rights officer. As one official noted, human rights had been "injected into the State Department's bloodstream."[178] Likewise, the Carter administration mooted ideas for the sort of quasi-governmental, democracy- and human rights–promotion endeavors that would fully take hold in the 1980s.[179] Once Ronald Reagan dedicated his administration to pursuing these same issues, he was able to build on the foundations Carter had laid.

When it came to human rights and democratization, the 1970s thus left a better legacy than contemporary observers might have guessed. The international shifts of the period were creating opportunities for constructive statecraft and the reassertion of U.S. influence, even if the short-term crises often made it appear otherwise. And while Carter's highest-profile efforts in this regard had proved disappointing or worse, his administration had nonetheless achieved some positive results, and had begun to position the country to better exploit these trends in the years to come. As Iran, Nicaragua, and other setbacks had shown, doing so would require not just the long-range vision that the president and his advisers possessed, but the coherent and discerning strategy that too often eluded them. Yet if Carter's successors could provide such an approach, then the prospects for U.S. resurgence would be promising indeed.

Globalization and Economic Renewal

Of course, the United States could hardly exploit this or other openings if its underlying economic vitality was in irreversible decay. As noted, this prospect seemed frighteningly real in the 1970s. The oil shocks and stagflation, the collapse of Bretton Woods and the resultant monetary instability— these problems created a generalized impression that America was in steep decline and that capitalism itself was perhaps coming unhinged. "Can Capitalism Survive?" *Time* magazine asked in 1975.[180] These concerns lingered; as Carter's presidency waned, domestic policy adviser Stuart Eizenstat warned that "we truly are on the verge of an economic crisis." "There is a growing national sense," Eizenstat wrote, "that things are out of control."[181] Yet just as in the ideological and geopolitical realms, there was another side to the story of world economic affairs in the 1970s. The crises of this period were real enough, but they shrouded deeper and far more positive long-range trends: the revitalization of the global market economy, and of U.S. economic power as well.

At root of this counterintuitive outcome was the basic resilience of the free-market system. As we have seen, the Soviet Union initially looked to be a major beneficiary of the economic shocks of the 1970s, but in fact its command economy was slipping into stagnation and obsolescence. In the West, by contrast, policymakers were often at a loss to deal with the disruptions of that decade, but the greater flexibility inherent in the capitalist system left these countries better positioned to cope with changing conditions over the long term. Precisely because the Western economies were more exposed to market forces, they ultimately proved more effective at reallocating resources, incentivizing adaptation, and catalyzing the entrepreneurial and technological creativity necessary for renewed growth. As a result, this period was not just one of adversity for the West, but one of intense creative destruction, too.

Indeed, in hindsight it is clear that the economic traumas of the 1970s—particularly the oil shocks—had double-sided effects. In the short and medium term, they took a severe toll on the Western economies, battering a Fordist industrial model that was already suffering from declining growth rates and other signs of wear. But in doing so, they accelerated the ongoing shift to a post-industrial model driven less by mass manufacturing than by rapid-fire, high-tech innovation and the productivity of a decentralized services sector. This restructuring was wrenching for every country that experienced it, in economic, political, and social terms. Yet from a macro perspective, this process was also rejuvenating; it catalyzed innovation and efficiency, reinvigorated the advanced economies, and set the stage for a new period of dynamism lasting from the 1980s into the early twenty-first century. The 1970s were not the end of the road for the developed West; they marked a "transitional pivot" from one economic era to another.[182]

This was true in another sense as well, in that the 1970s marked a hinge point in the emergence of an increasingly integrated global economy. As with the human rights and democratic revolutions, the rise of late-twentieth-century globalization was driven less by any single decision or individual than by deep-seated structural trends.[183] Foremost among these was technological innovation. Just as the advent of railways, telegraphs, and steamships had spurred an earlier era of globalization in the late nineteenth century, the rebirth of that phenomenon a century later was rooted in what Charles

Robinson termed "a techno-commercial revolution which created an accelerating global interdependence."[184] The advent of supertankers and standardized shipping containers led to dramatic reductions in shipping times and costs, for example, while improvements in refrigeration broadened the range of goods that could profitably be traded overseas. Advances in air freight and commercial aviation, symbolized by the debuts of the Boeing 747 and the Concorde, were simultaneously shrinking distances between countries. Most important, the 1960s and 1970s saw the emergence—or proliferation—of numerous advanced information technologies, many of them offshoots of Cold War military research and development (R&D). The development of microprocessors and fiber optics; the invention of email, the Internet, and personal computers; and the spread and increasing power of commercial satellites—these advances heralded the dawn of the information age and a quantum leap in interconnectedness. Together, these tools tore down barriers to the movement of goods, people, capital, and information, enabling huge strides in global interchange.[185]

Technological change dovetailed with another defining feature of globalization: the increasing international mobility of capital. This trend had been evident as early as the 1950s and 1960s, when enterprising bankers created offshore currency markets as a way of evading Bretton Woods–era capital controls, and multinational corporations (MNCs) increasingly used those markets as vehicles for investing profits and avoiding exchange constraints. The resulting growth of largely unregulated cross-border monetary flows, in turn, badly undermined exchange-range stability and the fixed parities of the Bretton Woods system. Yet if this phenomenon thus helped cause the economic upheavals of the 1970s, it also received a decisive thrust forward from them. For even though the collapse of Bretton Woods and fixed exchange rates certainly injected greater uncertainty into international finance, it permitted far greater fluidity as well. In particular, the breakdown of that system and the shift to floating rates made possible the gradual removal of the national capital controls that had been instituted in the vain hope of stabilizing the old order as its imbalances accumulated. The upshot was powerfully to accentuate the trend toward freer monetary flows in the years and decades thereafter.

Ironically, this financial globalization also received a critical impetus from the oil shocks. Despite fears that unprecedented oil prices might wreck the world economy and cause a return to protectionism, this phenomenon amplified global capital flows tremendously. Soaring export revenues created huge pools of money that petro-states could neither spend on imports nor invest productively at home. (By one estimate, the current-account surplus of the oil exporters was $70 billion in 1974, rising to $114 billion in 1980.)

Accordingly, this money went abroad in search of higher returns. It flowed into major international banks in Europe and the United States, which subsequently lent these funds to countries that were now borrowing heavily to finance energy costs. This process of petrodollar "recycling" was hardly seamless, in that massive capital movements held the potential for cross-border economic instability. Nonetheless, petrodollar recycling fed a surge of capital in the international banking system and a phenomenal growth in extraterritorial currency markets. Here too, then, the crises had counterintuitive results: "The macro-shocks of the 1970s did not bring an end to global finance; on the contrary, they provided a fillip."[186]

In consequence, this decade saw not the implosion of global capitalism, but the beginnings of a veritable explosion thereof. World trade roughly tripled between 1973 and 1979 in nominal terms, even as the West struggled with inflation and low growth. International finance and investment grew even more impressively. The value of international financial markets rose from $160 billion to $3 trillion from 1973 to 1985, and global lending went from $25 billion per year in the early 1970s to around $300 billion annually a decade later. New foreign investments by MNCs increased more than sixfold (from $15 billion to nearly $100 billion annually) during this period, and the overall number of MNCs began a spectacular rise that would take it from 7,000 in 1970, to 63,000 parent companies (with another 690,000 foreign affiliates) by the end of the century.[187] By virtually any measure, the 1970s witnessed a rapid, dramatic move toward global integration. As Theodore Levitt wrote in his seminal 1983 essay, "the sweeping gale of globalization" was revolutionizing the international economy.[188]

This was no exaggeration, because the globalization of the late twentieth century was qualitatively different than earlier waves of that same phenomenon. In those earlier waves, international trade had boomed, but production had remained organized largely on a national basis. In the current wave, by contrast, production itself was becoming globalized. Sophisticated MNCs were able to exploit improved technology, along with the easier movement of goods and capital, to divide their production activities into multiple pieces, and to situate each piece where efficiencies were highest and costs lowest. R&D might be located in one country, manufacturing in others, and assembly in yet another, while the entire process was overseen by corporate management in still another country. "The strategy of the vertically integrated multinational is to place the various stages of production in different locations throughout the globe," Robert Gilpin would write, so as to maximize competitive advantages and wring maximum value out of the process.[189]

This disaggregation of production quickly became a defining characteristic of the globalized economy, and a symbol of the deep changes that were making such globalization possible.

From the 1970s onward, moreover, these transformative economic processes were reinforced by a parallel transformation in the realm of ideas. The crises of that decade may not have destroyed the global economy, but they did batter the dominant economic paradigm of the postwar era. "The rules of economics," remarked Federal Reserve Chairman Arthur Burns, "are not working quite the way they used to."[190] The failure of Keynesian remedies to redress the persistence of high inflation and low growth created an intellectual vacuum, soon to be filled by a more laissez faire, "neoliberal" approach that was predicated on rolling back the state and seeking greater dynamism and efficiency by freeing market forces at home and abroad. This "intellectual counterrevolution" was symbolized by the awarding of Nobel prizes to Friedrich A. Hayek and Milton Friedman. More tangibly, it was reflected in far-reaching policy shifts that began in this period: the removal or relaxation of capital controls, the move toward deregulation and privatization in the United States and other Western countries, and the decisive turn to market solutions in countries such as Pinochet's Chile and Thatcher's United Kingdom. Similar tendencies were even at work in China, where by 1978–1979 Deng Xiaoping had broken with Marxist orthodoxy through liberal reforms that would usher in breathtaking growth. The market now had the momentum; the rise of globalization would go hand in hand with the neoliberal ascent.[191]

Global capitalism thus proved more resilient than many observers had expected. So did the economic power of the United States. Although fears of American comparative decline abounded during the 1970s (and for years thereafter), we can now see that in macroeconomic terms the decline had mostly ended by the time the decade began. It was during the 1950s and 1960s when the U.S. share of world and Western GDP fell most sharply, as Western Europe and Japan bounced back from World War II and achieved sky-high growth. This phenomenon was less problematic than was sometimes thought, because the revitalization of these countries was a signal success of U.S. policy and a major victory vis-à-vis the Soviet bloc. But in any event, by the early 1970s the postwar rebound was over, a more organic balance of economic power had been reached within the West, and U.S. relative decline had roughly bottomed out. "The U.S. economic position within the industrial world stabilized during the 1970s after declining for two decades," one CIA analyst concluded, "and there is every expectation that it can sustain its present position through the 1980s."[192] Sure enough, over the next three decades, America would maintain upward of 20 percent of world GDP and around 40 percent of Western output—a share much reduced from 1945 but still far greater than any other country.[193]

Meanwhile, the international economy was evolving in ways that accentuated long-term U.S. advantages. The collapse of Bretton Woods, for example, was jarring at first, and it fed the general sense of economic chaos and U.S. decline. Yet just as the demise of that system and the subsequent shift to floating rates had helped liberate global finance, they also ended up enhancing America's position. By closing the gold window and floating its currency, Washington shed the burden of stabilizing the global monetary system single-handedly, while also letting the dollar fall to a level that, although alarming to some observers, made U.S. exports far more competitive in the world market. In addition, despite predictions that the end of Bretton Woods would mean the end of the dollar's reign, just the reverse happened. Because there were no other plausible candidates to become the medium of international trade and finance, the dollar persisted as the de facto global reserve currency. The United States could thus enjoy the benefits of this status—the ability to borrow cheaply, and to finance deficits by increasing the money supply—with fewer of the burdens. The end of Bretton Woods, in other words, marked a new beginning for U.S. economic power.[194]

The same was true of the broader structural shifts at work. The United States was hardly spared the dislocations inherent in the transition to a post-industrial economy. By the close of the decade, two analysts note, "every newscast seemed to contain a story about a plant shutting down, another thousand jobs disappearing from a community, or the frustration of workers unable to find full-time jobs utilizing their skills and providing enough income to support their families."[195] On the whole, though, this transition was one that played to America's long-run strengths: its advantages in sectors such as computers, information technology, and professional services; its relatively skilled and educated workforce; its deep reserves of capital; and its prodigious investments in research and development. Additionally, the fact that the United States had one of the Western world's more agile economies—one that benefitted from flexible labor markets and was generally responsive to market pressures—meant that the country was well placed to spur creativity, purge inefficiency, and otherwise adapt in changing times. In fact, Washington was an early mover in the broader trend toward economic deregulation, beginning with reforms in the transportation and financial sectors from the late 1970s onward, and then accelerating and expanding thereafter. Overall, one U.S. intelligence analysis concluded, the United States was "particularly well equipped to adjust" to global economic shifts.[196]

Nothing showed the truth of that assessment like the extraordinary trajectory of Silicon Valley. Having emerged as a hub of high-tech industry in the early postwar decades, Silicon Valley represented in microcosm many of America's enduring advantages. It benefited from proximity to world-class scientific and technological education, flexible state labor laws that stimulated entrepreneurship, a regional culture that emphasized innovation and risk-taking, and an enormous R&D capacity funded by private investment and federal defense spending. In this setting, the 1970s were not a time of malaise, but a halcyon era of high-tech development. Silicon Valley experienced awesome growth: a new firm was created every two weeks in the 1970s, and high-tech employment in the region went from 51,951 in 1970 to 179,113 in 1980. Breakthroughs in microprocessors and semiconductors by companies such as Intel enabled revolutionary advances in computer technology; agile start-ups like Apple grabbed hold of that revolution to begin making personal computers available on a heretofore unimaginable scale. These firms would become major MNCs and symbols of America's information-age leadership; Silicon Valley itself came to be "hailed worldwide as an heroic model of innovation in the service of dynamic economic growth."[197]

If the United States was thus well-positioned to succeed in a post-industrial age, it was equally well-placed to profit from a more fluid global economy. As numerous scholars have noted, of course, the rise of globalization had mixed and contradictory effects for America. In certain respects, the phenomenon actually underscored the weaknesses and tensions that the crises of the 1970s had laid bare. The fiercer international competition that globalization entailed accelerated the hollowing out of vulnerable sectors of manufacturing, as the growing mobility of capital helped decimate entire swaths of the working class by giving management cheaper production options overseas. Global integration also exacerbated the cleavages between those with the skills and resources to profit from openness and those without, providing a goad to rising income inequality in the 1970s and after. Finally, and from a broader perspective, the intertwining of national economies necessarily decreased the sovereignty even of superpowers, rendering them more exposed to forces they could not control. The world was "condemned by technological and economic progress to still more complex relationships," noted a Trilateral Commission report in 1973; "new forms of common management" were needed. Over the succeeding decades, U.S. officials would have little respite from the insecurities and challenges that globalization wrought.[198]

Yet if globalization was hardly an unmixed blessing, it still did more than perhaps any other factor to give the country what Charles Maier aptly terms its economic "second wind."[199] Because the United States had the world's largest and most advanced economy, it was uniquely situated to benefit from greater openness of the international system. U.S. direct investment abroad began a meteoric rise that took its overall value from $86.2 billion in 1971 to $2.4 trillion in 2006, as firms exploited the greater mobility of capital to achieve new efficiencies in production and otherwise increase their operations and profits overseas.[200] McDonald's established a truly international presence in the 1970s, and by the early 1980s, Ford was building more cars in foreign countries than in the United States. Countless other corporations reaped the benefits of the lower wages and production costs that could be found in foreign countries, a factor crucial to reviving U.S. corporate profitability in later years.[201] Meanwhile, globalization was also creating new openings for the export of both goods and services, particularly in key areas such as computers and information technology, biotechnology and pharmaceuticals, and professional and financial services—those emerging sectors that were increasingly driving the international economy, and in which America boasted significant advantages. As one perceptive contemporary assessment noted, "The spectacular increase in income from overseas investments (double the corresponding payments to foreigners investing in the United States) and the crucial role that services now play in balancing the U.S. current account constitute a widely underappreciated area of U.S. competitive strength."[202]

Perhaps most important, in a globalized world the United States, with its deep and sophisticated financial markets, immediately emerged as a beacon for the massive flows of money coursing through the international financial system. As William Eberle, head of Nixon's Council on International Economic Policy, had correctly predicted of the OPEC surplus in 1974, "The United States, with the world's largest capital market and economy, will inevitably attract the largest portion of these investments."[203] Foreign capital subsequently surged into U.S. financial markets and government securities. Note two analysts, "In 1970 foreign private investors already held almost 10 percent of U.S. Treasury securities. . . . By 1980 foreigners held over 21 percent of U.S. Treasuries, and over the previous decade their aggregate value had increased seven-fold." This influx of funds helped reenergize the domestic economy from the 1970s onward while allowing Washington the luxury of living beyond its means. As long as America could attract massive quantities of funds from abroad at comparatively low rates of interest, it could effectively tap the savings of foreigners to finance its own deficit spending—on a global military and diplomatic presence, among other things.[204] In all these respects, globalization allowed the United States to leverage its immense power in the world economy to find new sources of dynamism and advantage.

Over time, some observers would even come to see the rise of globalization as part of a deliberate program for perpetuating American economic hegemony. This interpretation is testament to the benefits that the United States derived from the economic shifts of the 1970s onward, but it would be a mistake to think that Washington had masterminded those changes from the beginning. As one expert writes, seen from historical perspective globalization "appears more as the consequence of exogenous structural changes than as the achievement of specific policy choices," and the United States "found itself as bereft of long-range strategic vision as any other country."[205] Amid myriad shocks, U.S. officials generally did not see themselves as implementing a coherent, far-sighted strategy for remaking the global economy; more often, they felt that they were reacting to trends that they did not control or even fully comprehend. Robert Hormats, an economic aide to Kissinger, put it bluntly prior to one Western summit: "The essential *dilemma of the summit* is that it will try to project publicly that Western leaders are able to manage current problems at a time when they do not fully understand the nature of the new types of problems they confront."[206]

The reshaping of international monetary affairs amply demonstrates this dynamic. As noted, the end of Bretton Woods and the move to floating rates were key steps toward liberating global capital and strengthening the U.S. position. Yet if the outcomes of this process were beneficial and transformative, the process itself was halting and confused. The Nixon administration had not fully understood where it would end up when it first broke with Bretton Woods in August 1971. Then and for some time thereafter, the dominant preference in Washington was not for the floating rates that would eventually emerge, but for the reconstitution of fixed rates at different levels. What torpedoed this plan was less a clear, unified vision of the future shared broadly within the administration, than the fact that the turbulence of the early 1970s made any system of fixed rates impossible to sustain. "The resort to floating in early 1973 was not taken out of any general conviction that it was a preferred system," writes Paul Volcker, a leading Treasury official at the time. "It was simply a last resort when . . . the effort to maintain par values or central rates seemed too difficult in the face of speculative movements of capital across the world's exchanges."[207]

U.S. policy, then, was initially less trenchant than is sometimes assumed. But as the 1970s went on, U.S. officials did gradually perceive—and seek to exploit—the benefits of globalization. Amid the turmoil of the oil shocks, the Nixon administration vetoed proposals to channel petrodollar recycling through the IMF, encouraged commercial banks to become the principal intermediaries of this process, and thereby facilitated the explosion of capital flows. At the same time, the administration made the United States the first major power to lift its capital controls, incentivizing other countries to do likewise and putting America in pole position to reap the rewards of recycling. That step, one Treasury official wrote, constituted a vital contribution toward "reviving the United States as an international financial center." From the mid-1970s onward, the government further encouraged this outcome via the deregulation of financial and equities markets. The ethos of U.S. policy, William Simon, Ford's treasury secretary, observed, was that "market forces must not be treated as enemies to be resisted at all costs, but as the necessary and helpful reflections of changing conditions in a highly integrated world economy with wide freedom for international trade and capital flows."[208]

U.S. policy also facilitated international cooperation to channel globalization in productive directions. Once it became clear that a "floating world" was unavoidable—and that such a world had real advantages—U.S. officials worked to gain formal acceptance of that system by other Western countries.[209] Washington was also a driving force behind the Tokyo Round of multilateral trade negotiations, which involved roughly one hundred nations and concluded in 1979. These talks made only limited progress in decreasing trade barriers, but they did defuse protectionist pressures aroused by the economic turbulence of the period and keep the path clear for longer-term integrative trends. The Tokyo Round, Carter said, was "an antidote to protectionist sentiments around the world."[210] Similarly, under Ford and then Carter, the United States played a key role in institutionalizing annual summits among the major Western powers as a way of encouraging the multilateral coordination needed to provide some stability in an interdependent global economy. Despite their sometimes contentious character, these summits began to produce a greater synchronization of macroeconomic policies by the late 1970s, and they would remain a fixture of Western diplomacy into the 1980s and beyond.[211]

The 1978 Bonn Summit was noteworthy in this regard. Prior to and during the summit, intensive negotiations produced what U.S. official Henry Owen called a "three-way deal."[212] Under Carter's leadership, the United States pledged to attack excessive oil consumption and domestic inflation. Despite their own fears of inflation, Bonn and Tokyo reciprocated by promising additional stimulus to reinvigorate both their domestic and the broader global economies. This U.S.-German-Japanese bargain, in turn, facilitated commitments by the remaining summit countries to resolve lingering disputes in the Tokyo Round. "We feel like members of a fraternity," Carter wrote; "we share problems and political analyses, try to understand different national perspectives, and cooperate."[213] To be sure, the Bonn agreements were no silver bullet, and they hardly eliminated friction within the West. But they did show that intensified cooperation was possible, and they set a precedent for managing a more globalized world.

Finally, although the Carter administration never fully mastered the economic challenges it faced, in the waning years of the decade it did take two further—and essential—steps toward fortifying the U.S. position at home and abroad. First, the administration moved to halt the continuing slide of the dollar, a decline that, even as it enhanced export competitiveness, had become so pronounced that it threatened the currency's global position. "For as long as the United States is concerned to keep the dollar at the center of the international financial system, the United States must maintain the credibility of the dollar and not allow its position to deteriorate too significantly," wrote one Council of Economic Advisers (CEA) official.[214] In late 1978, the administration unveiled a dollar-defense package featuring intervention in the foreign exchange markets and an increase in the discount rate (the interest rate on loans from the Federal Reserve to commercial banks). These measures compounded the existing pressures on the domestic economy, much to Carter's political misfortune. But they also helped keep the dollar at an internationally acceptable level and avoided alternative solutions—such as the reimposition of capital controls—that would have met the crisis only by choking off progress toward financial globalization.[215]

The following year, Carter made a second and equally fundamental decision in appointing Volcker as Federal Reserve chairman and giving him the political leeway to launch a full-on attack on inflation. Interest rates soon rose to nearly 20 percent, as credit controls and other measures squeezed the money supply. This "Volcker shock" induced a painful recession, with unemployment reaching double digits by the early 1980s. In the long term, however, this program—which was later adopted and supported by Reagan— was vital to wringing inflation out of the economy and positioning the United States to exploit its advantages.[216]

These advantages were already having an impact in the 1970s. Predictions of doom to the contrary, the United States weathered the shocks of that decade quite well compared to other leading economies. Domestic inflation, although high by postwar standards, was held under 8 percent for the 1973–1981 period, far better than in many European countries. Similarly,

U.S. unemployment—although higher in absolute terms than in most of the West—increased at a much lower rate than in many of these countries. And even though American growth averaged just 2.3 percent between 1973 and 1981, this record was still more impressive than that of any other major economy save Japan. (Even here, the gap between U.S. and Japanese growth was much narrower than during the 1960s.) The 1970s were not exactly boom years, analysts from the National Intelligence Council (NIC) noted, but "a more careful look at the historic record reveals a relatively robust U.S. performance in the past decade and a more favorable prospect for the mid-1980s than is generally assumed."[217]

This was a prophetic insight, because as the 1970s ended the United States was on the verge not of a precipitous decline, but of a prolonged economic expansion that was ultimately one of the most impressive in its history. After a sharp contraction between 1979 and 1982, strong and sustained growth resumed, hitting 7.2 percent in 1984 and settling into a pattern of 3–4 percent for the rest of the decade. Inflation dropped to roughly 3 percent in the early 1980s and stayed low through the close of the millennium, and the Dow Jones index soared from 777 to 11,000 between 1982 and 1999.[218] As a result, the United States was able to roughly maintain its share of world GDP between 1973 and 2001 (22.1 vs. 21.4 percent), and America's position vis-à-vis its major economic rivals actually improved. Average annual U.S. GDP growth during this period was 2.94 percent, versus 2.71 percent for Japan, 2.21 for Western Europe, and 1.75 for Germany.[219] Declinist forecasts notwithstanding, the United States would remain the world's economic leader into the twenty-first century, giving it a strong base from which to influence international affairs.

If the economic pillars of U.S. power were thus far stronger than they appeared coming out of the 1970s, so was Washington's ability to shape the contours of the global economic environment. This was not necessarily what analysts would have predicted at the time, because as discussed earlier, that decade had seen a broad Third World challenge to the U.S.-led economic order, featuring a preference for statist, redistributive approaches. That revolt was premised not simply on the anger of the have-nots at persistent global inequality, but also on the sense that the oil shocks and other economic crises had fundamentally altered the balance of power between the West and the rest. "Irreversible changes in the relationship of forces in the world," wrote the authors of the NIEO, enabled a radical revision of international economic arrangements.[220] The Economic Commission for Latin America, a leading repository of Third World thought, argued that the oil crisis showed "the vulnerability of the powerful and the strengthened position of the weak."[221] What U.S. officials termed the "strategy of confrontation" pursued by the LDCs was rooted in a pronounced feeling of Third World ascendancy.[222]

In the event, however, the Third World challenge never achieved its desired results. This was partly a function of shrewd U.S. diplomacy. During the mid-1970s, Kissinger pursued a divide-and-conquer strategy, offering tactical concessions so as to split LDC moderates from radicals and defuse pressures for more extreme solutions. The Nixon and Ford administrations agreed to initiatives such as increased IMF lending to cash-strapped Third World countries, the holding of a World Food Conference in Rome in 1974, the extension of trade preferences to LDCs, and the creation of a North-South economic dialogue. "Obviously we can't accept the new economic order, but I would like to pull its teeth and divide these countries up, not solidify them," Kissinger said.[223] This strategy was well suited to playing upon the ideological, political, and economic differences among Third World countries, and it gradually undercut the momentum of the NIEO movement. LDC behavior, the CIA reported in 1977, was becoming "relatively non-confrontational," characterized less by angry denunciations than "a searching for pragmatic solutions through give-and-take bargaining."[224]

More important than Kissinger's diplomacy, however, was fact that the LDC empowerment of the 1970s soon proved illusory. The oil shocks provided an ideological fillip for the Third World as a whole, but for all those LDCs save the petro-states, they were really an economic disaster. Soaring oil prices meant that import costs dwarfed export earnings, leading to a massive accrual of debt. (High commodity prices in the early 1970s had temporarily shielded many LDCs from this reality, but as those prices fell, the extent of the problem became inescapable.) As early as 1974, IMF officials reported that many LDCs would see "a very large deterioration in the current accounts of their balance of payments."[225] If anything, this understated the problem: the debt of non-oil LDCs quadrupled from $73.1 billion in 1973 to $281.8 billion in 1980, and debt service rose similarly.[226] The oil shocks did not strengthen the Third World; they left it far more vulnerable and exposed.

Throughout the 1970s, most LDCs were able to meet their borrowing needs without excessive difficulty, given the surge of liquidity created by petrodollar recycling and expanded lending by the international financial institutions. Yet even so, rising LDC debt was creating points of leverage for the United States and other advocates of the global market economy. As the LDCs grew more indebted, they became more dependent on the goodwill of their creditors, which increasingly included Western-dominated institutions like the IMF. IMF lending packages proliferated due to the oil shocks, with the institution approving over one hundred balance-of-payments loans (known as "stand-by arrangements") between 1972 and 1978.[227] Before long, the major capital subscribers of that institution—notably the United States—would be primed to push for liberal economic reforms as the price of their support. As Undersecretary of the Treasury Anthony Solomon said in 1977, LDCs "must be encouraged, and permitted, to adjust their economies in ways that are compatible with our liberal trade and payments objectives, in ways that avoid discrimination against others and disruption of the world economy."[228] Spiraling LDC debt, in other words, could be used to bring Third World nations into the more open system taking shape.

The full impact of these dynamics would not become evident until the collapse of private lending in the early 1980s turned the Third World debt problem into a full-fledged debt crisis. But even before this, there were signs of what was coming. In 1976, IMF officials, with backing from the U.S. Treasury and Federal Reserve, demanded severe austerity and other liberalizing measures as the price of a rescue package for Great Britain, which was in desperate financial straits.[229] This particular crisis was unusual in that the borrower was a member of the developed West, but the same pattern was emerging in dealings with Third World countries such as Peru and Mexico. Both countries had been at the forefront of the NIEO movement, and in 1976–1977, both had to begin cutting spending, rolling back state control, and otherwise opening their economies to receive U.S.- and IMF-brokered loan packages. "We know it will be difficult for you," Carter told the Peruvians, but there was no alternative save insolvency.[230] In neither case would the reforms fully take hold for some time, but even so, these episodes foreshadowed key characteristics of U.S.–Third World relations during the 1980s. By 1979, one observer was already alleging that the IMF represented "the newest and finest expression of imperialism": a vehicle through which Washington could promote market institutions and perpetuate its own ideological and economic influence.[231]

As we will see in chapter 4, the advance of market-oriented reform in the Third World during the 1980s was not solely a function of U.S. pressure—the story was more complicated. Still, the fact that this charge was being made testified to the ways in which recent economic trends had left the United States far better off than it sometimes seemed. "The overall picture that emerges," concluded one NIC assessment, "is considerably more encouraging than the gloomy perceptions now gaining wide currency even among well-informed observers."[232] The 1970s had witnessed the emergence of a more globalized economy that played to key U.S. strengths. It had also seen the rise of trends that would soon help American officials integrate Third World countries into that very system. The effort to achieve this particular goal would become a core feature of U.S. policy during the 1980s, and a key element in the rise of a unipolar, post–Cold War order.

Conclusion

The Bosporus is the narrow body of water that divides Turkey and constitutes part of the boundary between Europe and Asia. Among its defining features are its complex, multilayered currents. On the surface, the water runs powerfully from north to south, from the Black Sea to the Sea of Marmara. Deeper down, however, there is another strong current, flowing in the opposite direction. The question of which way the water is moving in the Bosporus is therefore not an entirely straightforward one. Simply observing what is happening on the surface can give a misleading impression about what is going on below.

The same point holds true regarding U.S. foreign policy during the 1970s. The story of American power during that decade was paradoxical. On the surface, the United States was a battered, disoriented giant that looked to be getting weaker and more vulnerable with time. America's margin of superiority had diminished considerably since World War II, and around the world, its authority seemed to be under near-constant attack. "As a nation," observed the *New York Post* in 1979, "we appear to have become steadily more dependent on forces seemingly beyond our control, losing confidence in our ability to master events, uncertain of our direction."[233] Given all the crises and challenges, it is hardly surprising that so many saw the United States as a superpower in decline.

But although the difficulties that the country endured during the 1970s were not illusory, they concealed profound longer-term advantages. Beneath the surface of day-to-day events—at a deeper level of historical change—the currents were running strongly in America's favor. The growing debility and overstretch of the Soviet empire, the spread of democracy and a broad-based human rights movement, the revitalization of the market economy and American economic power—these structural trends were opening doors for dynamic statecraft and putting the United States in position to reinvigorate its international primacy. As the 1970s ended, U.S. officials had only begun to grapple with, and exploit, the transformative potential of these underlying shifts. In the decade that followed, they would do so to great effect.

CHAPTER 2

The Reagan Offensive and the Transformation of the Cold War

The 1980s were a crucial period in the renewal of U.S. primacy and the making of the unipolar moment. During the 1970s, the structural context of world affairs had begun to offer significant opportunities for the reassertion of national power and influence. In the decade after, U.S. policymakers fully began to seize those opportunities to advance American interests and reshape the international environment in highly advantageous ways. They pursued forward-leaning policies for capitalizing on Soviet vulnerabilities and reestablishing U.S. ascendancy in the Cold War, for spreading democratic governance in countries from Latin America to East Asia, and for aggressively encouraging the advance of global capitalism. The subsequent rise of the unipolar post–Cold War order was undoubtedly a function of deep tectonic forces that had started to make themselves felt in the 1970s; it was also a result of concrete U.S. initiatives in the 1980s and after.

In each of the chapters that follow, I focus on a key aspect of U.S. statecraft during this pivotal decade, beginning with the Cold War. The course of that contest was ambiguous when Carter left office: the United States had undoubtedly been on the defensive during the 1970s, but the longer-range trends were far more favorable. In the space of Ronald Reagan's presidency, the ambiguity lifted entirely, and the Cold War moved markedly toward its ultimate resolution. By early 1989, it was the Soviet Union that was conducting a broad-gauged retreat from bipolar competition, and bilateral relations had improved so drastically that leaders on both sides were concluding that the superpower confrontation was reaching an end.[1] It would be hard to imagine a more dramatic or consequential turnaround. A decade earlier, the dominant view had been that the United States was losing ground in the Cold War. Now it was on the verge of winning that struggle altogether.

The question of how and why all this occurred has inspired heated controversy.[2] In retrospect, there is no question that the intensifying crisis of Soviet power provided the essential backdrop to the astonishing turn in the Cold War during the 1980s, or that the rise of Mikhail Gorbachev was indispensable to easing East-West tensions after 1985. Yet as the available source material manifestly demonstrates, the policies of the Reagan administration—and the role of Reagan himself—were also central to this outcome. Even before he took power, Reagan understood that the Kremlin confronted massive and growing difficulties. He also believed that the United States could exploit those weaknesses to restore American advantage, compel Moscow to behave with greater moderation, and ultimately begin *easing* Cold War tensions on highly favorable terms. Beginning in the early 1980s, his administration thus mounted a multipronged offensive that regained the geopolitical initiative and ratcheted up the pressure on a weakened Soviet empire. From mid-decade onward, he worked diligently and successfully to maintain this pressure while also engaging Gorbachev in productive diplomacy. In sum, Reagan took hold of the opportunities afforded by structural change, and in doing so, he facilitated a remarkable transformation of the Cold War and America's international position.

There are, however, important caveats to this story. For all of Reagan's eventual gains vis-à-vis Moscow, the history of his Cold War statecraft was more complicated and tortuous than is sometimes made out. Reagan's first-term initiatives very effectively exacerbated the strains on the Kremlin and reestablished U.S. strength in the bilateral relationship. In the process, however, those initiatives also *raised* Cold War tensions to alarming levels. What permitted the diplomatic advances of the second term was therefore not simply Reagan's vision and determination in waging Cold War, but also his willingness to learn and adapt. Beginning in late 1983 and early 1984, Reagan made a significant recalibration of U.S. strategy. He toned down his confrontational rhetoric, stressed the need for dialogue and communication, and generally worked to fuse the power and pressure he had built with the reassurance and trust that were necessary to permit fruitful diplomacy.[3] This shift would prove essential to engaging Gorbachev from 1985 onward, and it showed that the process of forging successful strategy in the 1980s was often a complex and iterative one.

When it came to U.S.-Soviet relations, that process also entailed adverse consequences along the way. On the whole, Reagan's Cold War record was one of historic achievement on an issue of tremendous geopolitical salience. There were notable drawbacks, however, from morally problematic partnerships with Third World allies, to military expenditures that figured in an explosion of national deficits and debt, to measures that ultimately encouraged dangers such as Islamic fundamentalism and nuclear proliferation. The United States may have been resurgent during the 1980s, but in the Cold War as in other areas, that resurgence had its costs.

Reagan, American Prospects, and the Cold War

Ronald Reagan became president at a critical juncture in U.S. foreign policy. As we have seen, America had absorbed blow after blow to its global position during the 1970s, fostering a widespread sense that the country was in inexorable decline. Amid the tumult and pessimism, however, several key trends were converging to create new sources of U.S. advantage and new openings for perceptive statecraft. The question of the 1980s, then, was whether American officials could turn structural opportunity into successful strategy—whether they could devise policies that would harness the positive trends, reverse recent setbacks, and mold the global environment in ways that accentuated U.S. influence and power.

The answer was hardly obvious when Reagan took office. Although he had deftly exploited Carter's failings during the 1980 campaign, Reagan was not generally regarded as an incisive strategist when he arrived in Washington. Rather, Reagan's apparent inattention to detail, his ideological and even Manichean rhetoric, and his attraction to simple solutions for complicated problems all caused many critics to view him as unsophisticated at best and downright dangerous at worst. Throw in his advanced age and his Hollywood background, and some of Reagan's own advisers were initially skeptical. "When I first met Reagan," said Paul Nitze, a top arms-control official during the 1980s, "I thought he was just a born loser." One historian of this period has rendered an equally severe judgment, calling Reagan a "ceremonial monarch" with "limited knowledge of what was going on in the outside world."[4]

Appearances can deceive, however, and Reagan was actually well equipped for the challenges he faced. The president had good strategic instincts, in that he possessed an intuitive ability to get to the heart of difficult issues, and a keen sense of how individual policies related to broader designs. Reagan, one adviser recalled, had "this marvelous ability to work the whole while everybody else is working the parts."[5] He also had the confidence to think big—to challenge prevailing orthodoxies and chart potentially ground-breaking courses of action. Reagan's "strongest qualities," George Shultz later wrote, included "an ability to break through the entrenched thinking of the moment to support his vision of a better future, a spontaneous, natural ability to articulate the nation's most deeply rooted values and aspirations, and a readiness to stand by his vision regardless of pressure, scorn, or setback."[6] Moreover, while Reagan was no master of detail, he had spent nearly two decades prior to 1980 speaking and thinking about the central problems of U.S. diplomacy. This sustained intellectual engagement allowed Reagan to develop many core principles of his foreign policy before becoming president; it also gave him a firmer grasp of key geopolitical issues than many of his contemporaries realized.

Most important of all, Reagan possessed an unshakable faith in America's national potential. To be sure, Reagan had frequently deplored the state of the country during the 1970s, and he was alarmed by many of the threats at hand. "Our nation is in danger, and the danger grows greater with each passing day," he declared in 1976.[7] Yet at a deeper level, Reagan firmly believed that the United States possessed immense and enduring strengths, from the dynamism of its economy, to the resilience of its political system, to the force of its ideological example. "It is important every once in a while to remind ourselves of our accomplishments lest we let someone talk us into throwing out the baby with the bathwater," he said. Throughout the 1970s, Reagan thus took issue with those "who think we are over the hill & headed for the dustbin of history," arguing that the country's best days and greatest glories were ahead of it.[8] This essential optimism pervaded his later conduct as president, and it left him well suited to pursue the sort of ambitious—even transformational—endeavors that ongoing global changes were now making possible. "Let us begin an era of national renewal," he declared in his inaugural address. "We have every right to dream heroic dreams."[9]

Nowhere, in Reagan's view, was the imperative of such renewal greater than in superpower relations. Reagan had long seen the Cold War as an all-encompassing conflict between freedom and darkness, and he was as worried as anyone about the course of that contest in the 1970s. "If present trends continue," he said in 1978, "the United States will be assigned a role of permanent military inferiority vis-à-vis the Soviet Union."[10] Reagan feared that adverse trends in the nuclear balance would soon give Moscow the chance to coerce and intimidate the West; he was equally troubled by recent Marxist victories in the Third World and by America's apparent inability to respond effectively. The Soviets were becoming bolder by the day, he believed, and

U.S. passivity would invite disaster. "The Soviets have spoken as plainly as Hitler did in 'Mein Kampf,'" he said shortly becoming president. "They have spoken world domination—at what point do we dig in our heels?"[11]

Reagan, then, believed that the Cold War was reaching a crisis point. But as someone who had long expounded on the pathologies of the Soviet system, he was also perceptive of emerging strategic opportunities. The flip side of Reagan's faith in democratic capitalism had always been a deep skepticism that communism could permanently endure. "Communism is neither an economic nor political system—it is a form of insanity—a temporary aberration which will one day disappear from the earth because it is contrary to human nature," he observed.[12] Throughout the 1970s, Reagan was thus keenly aware that it was not Washington but Moscow that faced the more intractable long-term problems, from growing dissidence, to an increasingly brittle political system, to a command economy that was becoming less competitive by the year. "Nothing proves the *failure of Marxism more* than the Soviet Unions [*sic*] inability to produce weapons *for its mil. ambitions and at the same time provide* for their peoples [*sic*] everyday needs," he wrote.[13] Even when things seemed darkest during the Carter years, Reagan could still say that his theory of the Cold War was simple: "We win, they lose."[14] So long as the United States could tap into its fundamental advantages—and Moscow's fundamental weaknesses—it would triumph in the end.

Doing so presupposed sound policy, however, and here Reagan believed that the country had taken a detour. Like many conservatives, Reagan saw détente as a strategic blunder, one that had "increased the tempo of Communist efforts to undermine Western security, while at the same time inhibiting the West from making appropriate responses to defend our security interests."[15] Détente had led America to slash defense outlays, he alleged, while doing nothing to prevent Moscow from raising its military budget or seeking advantage in the Third World. Likewise, it had allowed the Soviet bloc to profit from increased East-West trade and financial linkages, while causing leaders like Kissinger to mute their criticism of communist repression at home. Relaxing international tensions was a worthy goal, Reagan believed, but the particular characteristics of détente had helped Moscow increase its influence and hide its internal decay. "I don't know about you," he said in 1977, "but I [don't] exactly tear my hair and go into a panic at the possibility of losing détente."[16]

These attacks on détente were not entirely fair, because they ignored the constraints that U.S. policymakers faced, and because they slighted the fact that expanded East-West contacts were actually compounding Soviet-bloc weaknesses. But Reagan's critique nonetheless informed his calls for a more assertive approach, one that would use all aspects of national power to meet the Soviet threat, exacerbate Moscow's debilities, and regain the edge in the Cold War. "The essential elements of any successful strategy," he said in 1979, "include political, economic, military and psychological measures."[17] In particular, Reagan advocated more determined steps to halt Kremlin encroachment in the Third World, and efforts to punish Soviet overextension by aiding anticommunist rebels in countries such as Afghanistan. More vocally still, he argued for a major military buildup to reverse the trends of the past two decades and provide greater leverage vis-à-vis Moscow. Military power was not "the only measure of national power," he commented, but it was "the cement which makes national power effective in the diplomatic arena."[18]

Perhaps most provocatively of all, Reagan contended that Washington should intensify the strains on the Soviet system itself. He called for stricter curbs on East-West commerce, and a public diplomacy campaign to support Eastern-bloc dissidents and highlight the worst aspects of communist rule. "A little less détente with the politburo and more encouragement to the dissenters might be worth a lot of armored divisions," he predicted. In the short term, these measures would accentuate the ideological and economic bankruptcy of the system; over time, they might help foster internal reforms that would make Moscow a less authoritarian and threatening rival. "The more we focus attention on internal Soviet repression, and focus our demands in this area," Reagan wrote, "the better chance that over the years Soviet society will lose its cruelty and secrecy. Peace could then be insured, not only because the Soviets fear our deterrent, but because they no longer wish to blot out all who oppose them at home and abroad."[19] The United States could turn the tide of the Cold War, Reagan believed, if it were willing to hit Moscow at its most vulnerable points.

During Reagan's run for the White House, these proposals invited criticism that he was a reckless ideologue. The charges were misleading, however, for they mischaracterized Reagan's long-term objectives. "Our goal is a stable peace," he had said in 1978. "Who has ever met an American who favored war with the Soviet U.?"[20] Reagan himself was appalled by the prospect and worried that an indefinite nuclear standoff might end in catastrophe. It was unacceptable, he said in 1980, that current strategic doctrine required holding "tens of millions of people hostage to annihilation in order to maintain a deterrent."[21] Accordingly, Reagan actually favored the eventual elimination of nuclear weapons, and he coupled his calls for a military buildup with reminders that true security lay not in the growth but in the ultimate reduction of superpower arsenals. "The nuclear threat is a terrible beast," he declared, and the survival of civilization required that it be tamed.[22]

Reagan's strategic goal, then, was not simply to wage Cold War more effectively. What he sought was leverage that would allow him to *wind down* that conflict on advantageous terms. Reagan calculated that by retaking the geopolitical offensive and maximizing the pressure on an ailing Soviet empire, the United States could compel real changes in Moscow's behavior. It could force the Kremlin to act with greater restraint and to accept that cooperation—not confrontation—was the only feasible course. Reagan's underlying concept, he had once written, was that "in an all out race our system is stronger, and eventually the enemy gives up the race as a hopeless cause. Then a noble nation believing in peace extends the hand of friendship and says there is room in the world for both of us."[23] This idea often resurfaced during Reagan's pre-presidential years, and after he had taken office, as well. "There was no miracle weapon available with which to deal with the Soviets," he said in 1981, but "we could threaten the Soviets with our ability to outbuild them, which the Soviets knew we could do if we chose. Once we had established this, we could invite the Soviets to join us in lowering the level of weapons on both sides."[24] If the United States acted with vision and purpose, Reagan believed, the 1980s might be a transformative decade in the Cold War.

Taking the Offensive

The basic challenge of Reagan's first term was to turn this aspiration into a concrete set of policies. When he took office, the political climate for doing so was more propitious than at any time since the Lyndon Johnson years. The Soviet overreach of the 1970s had shaken America out of its strategic malaise, creating greater domestic receptivity to assertive statecraft. "The U.S. has recovered from the traumas of the 1960's and 70's and is prepared to move beyond its passive post-Vietnam foreign policy to deal decisively with the realities of the 1980's," Secretary of State Alexander Haig told Chinese officials.[25] This did not mean that Reagan had an entirely free hand politically, because certain types of endeavors (such as the use of U.S. troops in combat) remained very sensitive, and the administration constantly had to gauge the limits of domestic backing for its initiatives.[26] On the whole, though, public and congressional support for strong Cold War policies was far greater than it had been for recent presidents, giving Reagan an opening to begin turning rhetoric into reality.

This new atmosphere pertained most clearly to the defense budget. The downward pressure on defense had already been halted and reversed under Carter, and by Reagan's presidency, the balance of power in Congress lay indisputably with the hawks. "Let's face the realities," one Democratic representative said in 1980. "There's overwhelming support in this Congress for defense."[27] The appropriations process remained highly contested, of course, and debates over particular weapons systems and policies would rage throughout Reagan's tenure. But there was nonetheless strong backing for significant overall defense increases, which created room for the multiyear buildup the administration sought. "The Congress granted the President virtually everything he asked" in his crucial first defense budget, Secretary of Defense Caspar Weinberger later wrote, and Reagan would generally have his way with Pentagon appropriations through mid-decade.[28]

Politically, then, the administration was well positioned for a fast start in Cold War strategy. The bureaucratic climate often appeared more problematic. While virtually all the president's advisers favored a more vigorous policy toward Moscow, "hardliners" clashed bitterly with "moderates" over the modalities and long-range aims of such an approach.[29] "We had gobs of infighting on everything," one official recalled. Reagan generally remained above the fray rather than tackling these disputes head on, a tendency that preserved good relations with his advisers but allowed the internal brawling to persist.[30] The policy process could get very messy in consequence: end runs and other intrigues were commonplace, leaking was rampant, and American allies—and even U.S. officials—sometimes struggled to decipher the mixed messages emanating from Washington. "There is genuine bewilderment here and abroad," wrote NSC staffer Richard Pipes in mid-1981, "whether we really have any ideas about the Soviet Union, or merely gut feelings and rhetoric."[31] The first year of Reagan's presidency was particularly chaotic. Haig himself called the administration "a sort of Babel," and his departure after just eighteen months fueled perceptions of a foreign policy adrift.[32]

Historians have echoed this judgment, characterizing Reagan's management style as disorganized and even disastrous. Yet even though that approach had real—and sometimes very costly—liabilities,[33] Reagan's statecraft was never rudderless. The president, Pipes later reflected, "held a few strong convictions and they guided all his policies."[34] Reagan's pre-presidential writings certainly demonstrate that he knew where he wanted to go in U.S.-Soviet relations, and his reluctance to resolve the internal conflicts on this subject was influenced by the fact that he simply did not fully agree with either side. Looking back on this period, no less an observer than Henry Kissinger concluded that Reagan "was the quintessential loner," and that his style stemmed from a determination that "no one would have a special claim on him."[35] After all, the president's vision of Cold War strategy was a nuanced one that incorporated hardline and moderate concepts. Between 1981 and 1983, he would work with representatives of both factions to set a multipronged geo-political offensive in motion.

Reagan's man at the Pentagon was Weinberger, and his role in that offensive was to oversee a major expansion of U.S. military power. The Carter administration had laid the foundations by increasing defense spending and investing in advanced technologies and weapons programs; Weinberger and Reagan now built on those foundations and accelerated the buildup dramatically. The Pentagon poured resources into conventional and nuclear programs, including B-1B and B-2 bombers, MX intercontinental missiles, air- and ground-launched cruise missiles, Trident nuclear submarines and Trident II SLBMs, F-117 Stealth fighters and Apache attack helicopters, and precision-guided munitions. The constant-dollar defense budget surged over 40 percent from 1980 to 1986, with slower growth through the end of Reagan's presidency.[36] Despite strong criticism from peace activists, the administration also affirmed the 1979 NATO decision to deploy a new generation of cruise missiles and Pershing-II IRBMs to Western Europe. "The Soviets have a great fear of the Pershing," Weinberger said; it was highly accurate and could reach East-bloc targets in under ten minutes.[37] These and other improvements were deemed vital to bolstering U.S. credibility and deterrence and restoring American geopolitical advantage. "We must first make America strong again," Weinberger commented.[38]

The urgency with which Weinberger and Reagan approached this task sometimes encouraged a scatter-shot approach to accumulating military capabilities.[39] Yet although the administration was certainly plugging gaps wherever it found them in the early 1980s, key aspects of the buildup were very targeted and strategic in nature. The United States must "capitalize on our advantages and exploit our adversaries' weaknesses," Weinberger wrote. "It is essential that we . . . emphasize our specific comparative advantages."[40] The Pentagon invested, for instance, in the intelligence, surveillance, and reconnaissance (ISR) and deep-strike capabilities needed to defeat numerically superior Warsaw Pact forces by hitting them at geographical and logistical chokepoints far in the enemy's rear. These capabilities drew on U.S. technological advantages in areas such as sensors and guidance systems, and they would be incorporated into doctrinal concepts—the Army's AirLand Battle and NATO's Follow-on Forces Attack—that explicitly stressed the application of U.S. strengths against Soviet soft spots.[41] The Navy was on the same wavelength. Its Reagan-era buildup was accompanied by adoption of a bold Maritime Strategy that threatened to counter aggression in one theater by utilizing superior naval striking power to hit exposed Soviet territories, lines of communication, and client-states in others. "The Maritime Strategy is a mobile, forward, *flanking strategy of options,*" Navy officials wrote; it would "carry the fight to the enemy" and attack his weakest points.[42]

A similar ethos prevailed in the nuclear realm, as well. Reagan had been particularly concerned by the shifting strategic balance in the 1970s, because he believed that the ability to dominate the escalatory process conveyed significant coercive leverage. "The nuclear weapon," he commented in 1978, "was always a decisive factor in the background."[43] In the 1980s, Reagan's defense program emphasized exploiting superior U.S. technology to swing the balance back in America's favor. Building on programs initiated during the 1970s, Reagan's strategic modernization program prioritized the development and deployment of more accurate SLBMs, bombers (such as the B-2) that could penetrate Soviet air defenses, ICBMs (namely the MX) that could carry multiple warheads and strike their targets with great precision, and reconnaissance systems that would provide better damage assessment in real time.[44] As in previous years, these programs were complemented by aggressive intelligence efforts to map Soviet nuclear forces—including ballistic missile submarines and mobile missile-launchers—to allow their effective targeting in case of war.[45] And, again following in the footsteps of late Carter-era doctrine, the administration outlined a nuclear employment policy that envisioned using improved U.S. weapons and targeting capabilities to conduct crippling counterforce strikes, decapitate the Soviet "military and political power structure through attacks on political/military leadership and associated control facilities," and achieve an "overall warfighting capability" that would allow Washington to prevail in any type of nuclear conflict.[46] That capability would significantly strengthen deterrence vis-à-vis Moscow, administration officials believed; it would also strengthen U.S. leverage by ensuring that it was the Soviet Union—and indeed the Soviet leadership itself—that was most vulnerable in any crisis.

The vulnerability that Reagan was most interested in targeting, of course, was the Soviet economy, and here, too, the military buildup had tremendous implications. Dating back to the early and mid-1970s, defense intellectuals such as Andrew Marshall had predicted that the Pentagon could better shape the superpower rivalry through well-aimed military expenditures that would drive the Soviets into counterproductive, self-defeating responses. By investing in programs—particularly high-tech programs—in which the United States had major competitive advantages, Marshall believed, the Pentagon could tilt the strategic competition in America's favor while also forcing the Soviets to expend disproportionate sums in a futile effort to keep pace.

Marshall laid out this framework for long-term competition in a seminal 1972 study. The goals, he wrote, were "to induce Soviet costs to rise" and "to complicate Soviet problems in maintaining its competitive position." The key to success was "seeking areas of U.S. comparative advantage, and . . . steering the strategic arms competition into these areas."[47]

This concept of a cost-imposing strategy had already begun to influence U.S. weapons procurement during the Ford and Carter eras. It was even more closely matched to Reagan's emphasis on taking advantage of Soviet frailties. "The Soviet Union is more vulnerable than ever," he said in 1982. "They are literally starving their people to keep this up."[48] Drawing on recommendations from Marshall and other officials, Reagan endorsed the idea that sustained increases in U.S. spending, especially in areas such as Stealth technology and nuclear modernization, could force the pace of the competition and exacerbate Moscow's military-economic dilemmas. A Pentagon review completed in 1982 integrated this concept into force development plans, emphasizing programs that would be "difficult for the Soviets to counter, impose disproportionate costs, open up new areas of major military competition and obsolesce previous Soviet investment."[49] Weinberger affirmed the same ethos with respect to nuclear issues specifically, writing that the United States would modernize its strategic forces in ways "that will force the Soviets into an expensive program of research, development and deployment to overcome it."[50] In effect, the United States would compel Moscow to choose between falling behind militarily, and courting still greater economic dangers by trying to match the pace. "If they want an arms race," Reagan said in 1983, the Soviets would have to "break their backs to keep up."[51]

The decision to pursue an antiballistic missile shield, the Strategic Defense Initiative (SDI), represented the apotheosis of this approach. SDI demonstrated that Reagan was the one setting the policy agenda—he announced that initiative without consulting several prominent advisers—and it showed the peculiar mix of romanticism and realism that infused his worldview. On one level, SDI was a manifestation of Reagan's repulsion at the stark logic of mutual assured destruction, and of his near-religious faith that strategic defenses could incentivize arms reductions by making ballistic missiles "impotent and obsolete." It was "his personal hope," Reagan commented, "that SDI could bring an end to nuclear war."[52] It was also Reagan's hope, however, that SDI would throw the Kremlin badly off balance. Missile defense was "cost-imposing strategy" par excellence: it was an area in which America's immense wealth, and its superiority in computers, sensors, and high-tech innovation, gave it all the advantages. Moscow, by contrast, would find it hard to respond, through either a major offensive buildup or development of a defensive shield of its own, without putting unbearable pressure on its rigid economy. Robert McFarlane, the NSC official who was deeply involved with SDI, repeatedly touted these advantages, and Reagan had the same idea. The Soviets had "great respect for our technology" and "must be concerned about our economic strength," he said in one conversation on SDI. "It will be especially difficult for them to keep spending such vast sums on defense."[53]

Reagan's military policies were meant to reassert U.S. strength, exploit Soviet vulnerabilities, and allow Washington rather than Moscow to set the course of the superpower relationship. His Third World policies had the same objectives. Reagan had long warned that the struggle for the global south was reaching a critical stage; he now found kindred spirits in advisers such as CIA Director William Casey. "Nations which control key choke points are under severe threat," Casey warned the NSC; the United States had to respond.[54] Accordingly, the administration took several early steps to fortify the global perimeter. It endeavored to repair relations with estranged allies—and human rights violators—such as Chile, Argentina, and South Korea, with Reagan assuring their leaders that "there would be no public scoldings and lectures."[55] The president also affirmed U.S. support for China's role in tying down Soviet troops and checking Kremlin influence in Asia, despite his earlier criticism of that country's brutal communist regime. Washington and Beijing cooperated to support the Afghan resistance, and despite a serious dispute over Taiwan in 1982, the administration permitted greater sales of civilian and military technology to Deng Xiaoping's government. "A strong, stable China can be an increasing force for peace, both in Asia and in the world," a classified national security decision directive (NSDD) stated.[56]

More important still, the administration resolved to do whatever was possible to prevent additional Third World allies from falling prey to Marxist insurgencies. It was in El Salvador, of all places, where this determination to hold the line was most pronounced. A powerful guerrilla movement seemed poised to overthrow an unstable but pro-Western government when Reagan took office; the president feared that this outcome would further open the Western Hemisphere to Soviet influence and reinforce perceptions of U.S. impotence worldwide. Building on an initiative from the last days of Carter's presidency, Reagan approved an infusion of emergency military aid to defeat a rebel "final offensive" in early 1981. His administration subsequently provided billions of dollars in economic and security assistance, along with training and intelligence support, to stave off a collapse, while also engaging in intensive diplomacy to stabilize El Salvador politically. "We must not let Central America become another Cuba on the mainland," Reagan said. "It cannot happen."[57]

The counterpart to these defensive efforts was an aggressive campaign to contest and roll back Moscow's own sphere of influence in the Third World. The Kremlin was like "an overanxious chess player," NIC analysts wrote: by expanding so eagerly during the 1970s, it had "exposed lines of attack to its adversary, placed advanced pawns in jeopardy, and acquired positions that it must defend at high cost."[58] At Reagan's urging, Casey's CIA sought to make those costs as high as possible. It provided arms, training, and funding to anticommunist insurgents, first mainly in Afghanistan and Nicaragua, and later in countries such as Angola and Cambodia. Opinions differed internally as to whether these groups could actually overthrow the regimes they confronted; what was not disputed was that the United States was now attacking Moscow's overseas empire at its most exposed points. Washington would "do to the Soviets what they have been doing to us," Pipes said. "At a very low cost, without a big investment on our part, we can make it very hard for them in these places."[59]

Afghanistan was the centerpiece of this emerging Reagan Doctrine and the place where it would obtain greatest results. "Russia has fallen into a hornet's nest in Afghanistan," Casey declared in 1981.[60] Again following Carter's lead, the CIA built a covert partnership with Pakistan, Saudi Arabia, and other countries to provide the anti-Soviet *mujahedin* with tools to sustain the resistance. The level of foreign support was modest at first but would grow substantially with time, culminating in the provision of Stinger anti-aircraft missiles and up to $650 million in annual aid by the latter half of the 1980s. Even before that, however, the administration was determined to make Afghanistan a Vietnam-type quagmire for the Soviets, and to demonstrate that Moscow would not be allowed to consolidate its recent expansion. "The U.S. should not accept the notion that, once a Communist or pro-Soviet regime has come to power in a state, this situation is irreversible," an NSC study concluded.[61]

To be clear, there were limits to Reagan's assertiveness in the Third World. The president brushed away an ill-conceived proposal to blockade or perhaps attack Cuba in 1981, and because he was wary of courting "another Vietnam," he generally viewed the use of U.S. troops as an inappropriate means of rollback.[62] But even so, the administration did overthrow one pro-Soviet government by force of arms, by invading Grenada in October 1983. That intervention was truly a spur-of-the-moment affair; a radical coup had stoked fears about the safety of U.S. citizens, while also intensifying Reagan's concerns that extremist elements were taking that small but strategically placed island more firmly into the Soviet-Cuban orbit.[63] The expected low costs of military action against such a weak opponent sealed the case for intervention, which turned out to be a sloppier affair than U.S. commanders had predicted. All the same, the invasion succeeded in rescuing the American citizens, depriving Moscow and Havana of a potential client astride the Caribbean sea lanes, and underscoring Reagan's harder and more opportunistic line toward the Soviet sphere of influence. "Now it is their dominos that are toppling," wrote one U.S. intelligence official.[64]

As the administration contested Kremlin positions along the periphery, it also put pressure on the core of Moscow's empire in Eastern Europe and on the Soviet Union itself. The intelligence that Reagan received once president only confirmed his long-standing belief that Kremlin authority was in advanced erosion throughout the bloc, and that communist regimes had no good answers to the internal problems they faced. It was becoming impossible to ignore just "how tenuous was the Soviet hold on the people in its empire," Reagan said in 1981.[65] Numerous administration assessments echoed this conclusion, and contended that it was in America's interest to exploit this distress and amplify pressures for internal change. "It makes little sense to seek to stop Soviet imperialism externally while helping to strengthen the regime internally," wrote National Security Adviser William Clark; the task was to "weaken Moscow's hold on its empire" though various means.[66]

One such means was a campaign of ideological warfare led by Reagan himself. From his earliest days in office, the president minced few words in his public statements on the Soviet bloc. He condemned Kremlin leaders as purveyors of "totalitarian darkness" and the "focus of evil in the modern world," and he denounced communism as "some bizarre chapter in human history whose last pages are even now being written."[67] "The cult of the state is dying," he pointedly declared in 1981; all Marxism had provided humanity was "a gaggle of bogus prophecies and petty superstitions."[68] This rhetoric was ideologically charged and even incendiary, but it was rooted in cold geopolitical logic. Reagan was seeking to lend encouragement to Soviet-bloc dissidents; to further discredit bloc governments at home and abroad; and to hammer home the fact that communism was a repressive, inhumane, and unproductive system that had little organic legitimacy with those it ruled. The idea, as one internal study put it, was that that "the long-term weaknesses of the Soviet system can be encouraged in part simply by telling the truth about the USSR."[69]

Reagan's rhetoric was only one part of this effort. The administration launched what VOA director Charles Wick called a "coalesced massive assault of truth" to illuminate the most repugnant aspects of communist rule via radio broadcasts, print media, and other outlets.[70] Reagan also quietly repudiated his earlier criticism of the Helsinki accords, instead building on Carter's example by using follow-on meetings of the Conference on Security and Cooperation in Europe (CSCE) to publicize Eastern-bloc repression. At CSCE meetings in Madrid and later Vienna, U.S. representatives expressed solidarity with persecuted groups and individuals behind the Iron Curtain, and called bloc regimes to account for violating their Helsinki obligations. They linked improved performance on human rights to a broader warming of East-West relations, and made clear that the Kremlin would not enjoy real international legitimacy absent domestic reform. The Soviets were "seriously vulnerable to a counter-ideological attack by us," lead U.S. diplomat Max Kampelman wrote; public criticism could isolate Moscow and empower dissidents within the bloc.[71]

At the outset, Reagan was especially optimistic about encouraging ferment in Poland. "This is a revolution started against this 'damned force,'" he said; the rise of Solidarity showed just how fragile the bloc had become.[72] Throughout 1981, Reagan's goal was to create political space so the revolution could proceed. The administration communicated its support to Solidarity's leaders; Reagan also attempted to deter Soviet military intervention by informing Leonid Brezhnev that an invasion would have "very serious" consequences in East-West relations.[73] The imposition of martial law by the *Polish* government in December 1981 confounded this aspect of Reagan's policy, but the administration still mounted a response. "We can't let this revolution against Communism fail without our offering a hand," Reagan wrote. "We may never have an opportunity like this in our lifetime."[74] The administration imposed economic sanctions on Moscow and Warsaw, and increased U.S. radio broadcasting into Poland and the bloc. And with help from various intermediaries, the CIA covertly provided funding and aid to Solidarity, helping to sustain that organization despite intense repression.[75]

This last initiative highlighted the tacit partnership taking shape between the United States and the Catholic Church. "It was a quite holy alliance," Weinberger said. The pope's visit to Poland in 1979 had helped spark the fire in that country, and demonstrated the power of religion as a fount of opposition to communist rule. Even before the crackdown, Reagan had therefore observed that "the Vatican and the Pope had a key role to play in events in Poland," and the White House and Vatican had exchanged intelligence on the crisis.[76] After the crackdown, the president and the pontiff undertook parallel efforts to keep Polish political resistance alive. The Church in Poland offered its facilities as protected "free space for independent, non-regime controlled educational and cultural activities" amid the repression that had driven Solidarity underground. The CIA began (indirectly) to provide Solidarity with printing materials, communications gear, organizational assistance, and other aid, geared, as one official wrote, toward "waging underground political warfare." These mutually reinforcing programs (as well as another sponsored by the American Federation of Labor and Congress of Industrial Organizations, AFL-CIO) were deliberately kept separate at the operational level, but there was plenty of information sharing and high-level strategic coordination among Reagan, John Paul II, and their aides. The president aimed to harness the moral authority of the Vatican "and make them an ally" against the Kremlin; the Polish crisis helped cement that partnership.[77]

The crisis also catalyzed Reagan's efforts to wage economic warfare against the Soviet bloc. "The Soviet Union is economically on the ropes—they are selling rat meat on the market," he told advisers. "This is the time to punish them."[78] Beyond emplacing sanctions—such as suspension of export licenses for electronics technology and oil and gas equipment—on Moscow, Reagan took several extra steps to force the Kremlin to foot the bill for reviving the battered Polish economy. The administration vetoed Warsaw's membership in the IMF and obstructed debt-rescheduling proceedings for Poland. Although avoiding the extreme measure of declaring Poland to be in default on its debts, administration officials also aimed to limit commercial lending to Warsaw, by working privately with potential lenders and by declaring publicly that Eastern Europe—and the Soviet Union itself—had become risky bets for bankers. "Private sources of long-term credit to the Bloc have largely dried up," the NIC reported in April 1982.[79]

In the aftermath of the Polish crackdown, Reagan's initial impulse had been to act even more aggressively. "We would quarantine the Soviets & Poland with no trade, or communications across their borders," he wrote in his diary. "Also tell our NATO allies & others to join us in such sanctions or risk an estrangement from us."[80] Urged on by hardliners such as Casey and Weinberger, the president gave vent to this impulse by forbidding U.S. firms from participating in construction of a long-planned Soviet gas pipeline connecting Siberia to Western Europe, and then—over Haig's heated objections—extending the reach of the sanctions to cover U.S. subsidiaries and licensees overseas. This latter measure was aimed primarily at Western Europe, where such licensees and subsidiaries were heavily involved in the pipeline project. The immediate goal of the sanctions was to derail a project that was vital to Moscow's energy exports; a broader objective was to signal that NATO, under U.S. leadership, would no longer be subsidizing the Kremlin economy. "One of the key foreign policy objectives of the Reagan administration," an internal discussion paper noted, "has been to achieve a fundamental shift in the way in which our Allies view their relationship with the Soviet Union."[81]

The pipeline sanctions were certainly punishing. The problem, as Haig had warned, was that they seemed to punish U.S. allies as severely as its adversaries. Margaret Thatcher and other leaders cried foul after the sanctions were applied extra-territorially in mid-1982, complaining that the restrictions were exacerbating economic pressures at a time when Western Europe was already in recession. "Naturally we feel particularly deeply wounded by a friend," Thatcher said in a rare public censure of U.S. policy. In private, the message was the same. "She had a serious problem with unemployment and bankruptcies," she told Weinberger, "and she didn't want her closest friend, the United States, to be blamed by her people."[82] The pipeline sanctions were soon threatening an open rupture within NATO, and the crisis underscored, as the CIA wrote, that there remained significant "differences between the United States and our Western European allies."[83] It was left to Shultz, newly installed as secretary of state, to salvage the situation by finding a compromise. This he successfully did, via painstaking negotiations that eventually obtained an intra-alliance accord to place curbs on strategic trade and credit provision to Moscow in exchange for lifting the pipeline sanctions. The end result was a policy that was less sharp-edged than Reagan and some key advisers might have desired, but one that preserved alliance cohesion and, in conjunction with the other measures already described, represented the most sustained effort in decades to pressure the Soviet economy.[84]

That pressure was simultaneously being accentuated by Casey's CIA, which was prosecuting a quieter, but potentially more damaging, campaign of its own. During the early 1980s, U.S. intelligence operatives reportedly sabotaged a branch of the Siberian gas pipeline by covertly providing Moscow with faulty computer software. When activated, that software caused malfunctions resulting in "the most monumental non-nuclear explosion and fire ever seen from space." Casey was, meanwhile, trying something even more ambitious, waging a personal crusade to eviscerate Soviet hard-currency earnings by inducing Saudi officials to flood the market with cheap oil. And in 1984–1985, the CIA cooperated with NATO intelligence agencies as part of a counterespionage initiative that rolled up KGB programs to steal or illicitly purchase Western technologies. That initiative, one insider later wrote, "effectively extinguished the KGB's technology collection capabilities" at a very inconvenient time.[85] Reagan had long advocated a determined attempt to compound Soviet economic weaknesses. Within the confines of alliance politics, his administration was now doing just that.

All these policies added up to a wide-ranging assault on Moscow's geopolitical position, and to an intensive effort to put Washington back in control of the Cold War. Internal planning documents spoke of "shaping the Soviet environment" and "maximizing our restraining leverage over Soviet behavior."[86] Following Clark's appointment as national security adviser in early 1982, the NSC staff began to formalize these concepts through a series of presidential directives. NSDD-32, a major study approved by Reagan in May, laid out the objectives of American policy in blunt and ambitious tones: to "strengthen the influence of the U.S. throughout the world"; "to contain and reverse the expansion of Soviet control and military presence throughout the world"; "to foster . . . restraint in Soviet military spending, discourage Soviet adventurism, and weaken the Soviet alliance system by forcing the USSR to bear the brunt of its economic shortcomings"; and "to encourage long-term liberalizing and nationalist tendencies within the Soviet Union and allied countries." The end goal was to achieve "a fundamentally different East-West relationship by the end of this decade"—or, as Clark put it in a report to Reagan, to "re-establish American ascendancy" in the global arena.[87]

Even as Reagan pursued this program, however, he was also seeking to lay the groundwork for productive diplomacy. "The West has a historic opportunity, using a carrot and stick approach, to create a more stable relationship with the USSR," he told West German officials; pressuring Moscow now could ultimately induce greater Soviet circumspection and facilitate bilateral breakthroughs. The Soviets might soon find themselves "in a desperate plight," he predicted on another occasion, "and we might be able to say to them: 'Have you learned your lesson?'"[88] No adviser did more to support Reagan in this regard than Shultz. After replacing Haig in mid-1982, Shultz regularly affirmed the desirability of diplomatic engagement with the Kremlin once the proper conditions had been set. "While recognizing the adversarial nature of our relationship with Moscow," he wrote to Reagan, "we must not rule out the possibility that firm U.S. policies could help induce the kind of changes in Soviet behavior that would make an improvement in relations possible."[89]

This was precisely what Reagan aimed to accomplish in arms control. Little noticed amid Reagan's emphasis on rearmament during the early 1980s was that his negotiators were simultaneously advancing some of the boldest *dis*armament proposals in decades. "Let us agree to do more than simply begin where . . . previous efforts left off," the president declared. "We can and should attempt major qualitative and quantitative progress."[90] This ethos informed the administration's "zero option" proposal, which called for not just reducing but eliminating all intermediate-range nuclear forces (INF) in Europe. It also drove Reagan's decision to discard the concept of strategic arms limitation in favor of more aggressive Strategic Arms Reduction Talks (START) focused on slashing strategic ballistic missile arsenals by at least one-third (which would later become one-half). The U.S. buildup, Reagan believed, would make these dramatic advances more rather than less likely. "For us to be successful in arms control," he said in 1981, "the Russians have to see that the alternative is a buildup to match theirs."[91] This was a theme that the president consistently underscored. As he explained to Thatcher, "The main reason why the Russians were at the negotiating table in Geneva was the build-up of American defences. The Russians would not be influenced by sweet reason. If they saw that the United States had the will and the determination to build-up its defences as far as necessary, the Soviet attitude might change because they knew that they could not keep pace."[92]

Admittedly, this emphasis on negotiating from strength could give U.S. diplomacy a fairly standoffish character. At home, Reagan opposed calls for a "nuclear freeze," arguing that it would undercut the buildup needed to restore U.S. diplomatic leverage. The Soviets "are neither unilateralists nor philanthropists" with respect to arms control, he told congressional leaders; a freeze would "send precisely the wrong signal" to Moscow.[93] Abroad, his negotiators took a hard line in START and the INF negotiations, making proposals that required asymmetrical Soviet reductions and signaling that they would rather forgo agreement than cut deals that fell short of U.S. goals. In 1982, the administration declined a potential breakthrough in the INF talks, made possible by informal contacts between Nitze and his Soviet counterpart, on these grounds. The decision pleased Pentagon hawks—who may have thought that a maximalist posture would scuttle prospects for arms control altogether—but, when it inevitably leaked, led many U.S. and European observers to worry that Reagan's diplomacy was insincere.[94]

That critique might have applied to officials such as Weinberger and Casey, but it misunderstood Reagan's position. In his diary, the president criticized those who "don't think any approach should be made to the Soviets. I think I'm hard-line & will never appease but I do want to try & let them see there is a better world if they'll show *by deed* they want to get along with the free world." Even during 1981–1982, Reagan was working to establish lines of communication that might make such eventual progress possible. It was important, he told his NSC, not "to compromise our chance of exercising quiet diplomacy."[95] Reagan composed hand-written letters to

Brezhnev and his successors during the early 1980s, stressing the need for dialogue and cooperation. "Is it possible that we have permitted ideology, political and economic philosophies, and governmental policies to keep us from considering the very real everyday problems of our peoples?" he wrote in 1981. "Should we not be concerned with eliminating the obstacles which prevent our people—those we represent—from achieving their most cherished goals?"[96] Reagan also lifted the Carter-era grain embargo on the Soviet Union, and following Brezhnev's death in 1982, he expressed interest in meeting with Yuri Andropov and with Konstantin Chernenko after him. The United States was not seeking an "open-ended, sterile confrontation with Moscow," an administration directive stated, but a more "stable and constructive long-term basis for U.S.-Soviet relations."[97]

This was indeed the essential thrust of Reagan's policy: to bring all of America's strengths to bear against an overextended Soviet Union, and thereby to accumulate diplomatic leverage that could be used to foster a longer-range improvement of relations on U.S. terms. NSDD-75, the single most important directive of Reagan's presidency, made this program unmistakable. Signed by Reagan in January 1983, NSDD-75 described the key pillars of his Soviet policy:

1. To contain and over time reverse Soviet expansion by competing effectively on a sustained basis with the Soviet Union in all international arenas—particularly in the overall military balance and in geographical regions of priority concern to the United States. . . .
2. To promote, within the narrow limits available to us, the process of change in the Soviet Union toward a more pluralistic political and economic system in which the power of the privileged ruling elite is gradually reduced. . . .
3. To engage in the Soviet Union in negotiations to attempt to reach agreements which protect and enhance U.S. interests and which are consistent with the principle of strict reciprocity and mutual interest.

This approach was explicitly framed as a carrot-and-stick strategy, meant to maneuver Moscow toward the eventual recognition that competition was hopeless, and that accommodation was the better path. "The U.S. must convey clearly to Moscow that unacceptable behavior will incur costs that would outweigh any gains," the directive stated. "At the same time, the U.S. must make clear to the Soviets that genuine restraint in their behavior would create the possibility of an East-West relationship that might bring important benefits for the Soviet Union." This process would take time, and it would involve risks. But if it could be carried through successfully, the result would be a very different U.S.-Soviet relationship—and an immense payoff for America's global position.[98]

Success, Failure, and Adaptation

So could it be carried through effectively? During the early 1980s, the record was one of success, failure, and adaptation. Reagan's policies succeeded in harnessing the global currents at work and reasserting U.S. ascendancy over the Soviet Union. They failed, however, to produce more restrained Soviet behavior or reduce superpower tensions, and they actually contributed to a dramatic and potentially dangerous escalation of the Cold War. That failure, in turn, led to adaptation. During late 1983 and 1984, Reagan began to marry the strength he had built with a more conciliatory posture better suited to negotiation. It was less than a full-fledged "reversal" of policy, but this shift was nonetheless vital to preparing him to deal with the more flexible Soviet leadership that would soon emerge.

A key reason why Reagan was able to execute that mid-course correction effectively was that he was doing so from a position of great strength. If the president's top priority was to restore U.S. power and confidence vis-à-vis the Soviet Union, the outcome of his first term could hardly have been better. By 1983–1984, there was a pervasive sense—in Washington and Moscow alike—that the trajectory of the superpower competition had changed remarkably. U.S. officials evinced great confidence that their country was again on the march. "We have shown," noted one NIC analyst, "that history is not on their side, but on ours."[99] In the Soviet Union, by contrast, the self-assuredness of the 1970s had given way to geopolitical pessimism bordering on despondency. "We are facing one of imperialism's most massive attempts to . . . stop the advance of socialism or even to push it back in some places," Andropov told Warsaw Pact leaders in 1983, and it was not clear how long Moscow could sustain the fight.[100] As both U.S. and Soviet officials understood, the "correlation of forces" had shifted, and Washington was reaping the advantages.

This reversal of fortunes demonstrated what could happen at the intersection of good timing and good policy. The early 1980s were an opportune moment to press the Soviets, as it was then that the underlying structural trends of the prior decade began fully to burst into the open. The United States and the West were starting to recover from the recent economic shocks, whereas the Soviet Union was being exposed as a "crippled giant" in stark decline. "It is crippled in having only a military dimension," a U.S.

intelligence officer wrote in 1983. "It has not been able to deliver economic, political, or cultural benefits at home or abroad."[101] The economic stagnation, the social and ideological malaise, the ossification of the bureaucracy and the political system, the inability of a geriatric leadership to respond creatively to such challenges—all these fundamental debilities were getting progressively worse, leaving Moscow in an ever-weaker competitive position. Herbert Meyer, Casey's close adviser at the CIA, put it squarely in a 1985 memo: "The tectonic plates of global power have broken loose." "We are probably heading toward a major shift in the balance of global power, of a magnitude that happens only once or twice in a century."[102]

Reagan had anticipated the possibility of such a shift, and his policies put Washington in position to leverage its effects. At every turn during the early 1980s, Soviet officials were confronted with aggressive U.S. initiatives that compounded Moscow's problems and exploited its weaknesses. In the military realm, the U.S. buildup dramatically altered the dynamics of East-West rivalry. By this point, Soviet officials were coming to realize that improvements in the accuracy of U.S. ICBMs over the past decade had multiplied the lethality of the American nuclear arsenal by as much as a factor of three.[103] The particular programs emphasized from the late 1970s onward, and especially under Reagan, accentuated the resulting disquiet. Kremlin planners now faced serious threats and vulnerabilities, from Pershing-II missiles that—they feared—were ideally suited to decapitating Soviet command-and-control targets, to precision-guided munitions that might vitiate Moscow's conventional edge in Europe, to the looming deployment of MX missiles that would be the deadliest American ICBMs yet.[104] The U.S. buildup thereby shattered Soviet confidence that the strategic balance was moving in Moscow's favor; the new reality, said Defense Minister Dmitri Ustinov, was that America and its allies were building military strength "with unprecedented means and speed."[105] Moreover, the Reagan buildup showed that the United States was using its dominance in information technology to make qualitative leaps in the arms race, and to intensify that competition in ways the Soviets could not match. "We cannot equal the quality of United States arms for a generation or two," Chief of General Staff Nikolai Ogarkov admitted. The United States had made "an incredible breakthrough of modern technology," another Soviet official said, which would be "unthinkably expensive" to emulate.[106]

No aspect of the U.S. buildup was more effective in this regard than SDI. Although U.S. officials knew that the system was years or even decades away from deployment, for the Soviets it had an immediate psychological impact. Missile defense threatened to negate Moscow's chief military achievement of the post-Stalin era—the building of the world's largest ICBM force—and thereby, one Kremlin official later admitted, "to negate the essence of Soviet power in the international arena."[107] Nor was there any good recourse in prospect. Soviet military officials understood that the economy would have great difficulty supporting an equivalent investment in missile defense, or a major offensive buildup to overwhelm the prospective U.S. shield. "We will never be able to catch up with you in modern arms," Ogarkov said, "until we have an economic revolution."[108] The Kremlin had spent a generation—and taxed the system severely—in a quest for strategic parity and advantage; now those gains were evaporating and a new period of inferiority loomed.

The tables were turning just as markedly in the Third World, where the Soviet optimism of the 1970s had become a fading memory. In part, this was due to structural factors, in that Soviet economic stagnation—and the dismal performance of Moscow's Third World clients—was badly undercutting the appeal of socialism in the global south.[109] Yet it also reflected the concrete impact of U.S. policy. During the early 1980s, American intervention blunted the progress of the Farabundo Martí National Liberation Front (FMLN) insurgency in El Salvador and prevented an outright government collapse. In Nicaragua, the U.S.-backed Contras did not seriously threaten the survival of the Sandinista regime, but they did inflict rising punishment and keep it in a perpetual state of insecurity. "The guerrillas," Shultz noted in 1983, "are now making the Sandinistas pay a price."[110] In Grenada, U.S. intervention destroyed socialism altogether. And in Afghanistan, U.S. aid helped sustain and gradually strengthen the insurgents, enabling them to become better-armed, more tactically proficient, and better able to raise the costs of a strength-sapping Soviet endeavor.[111] All told, this renewed U.S. activism left a deep impression on Soviet policymakers. "Never before has the aggressiveness of American imperialism been so apparent," Ustinov said. The cumulative effect of these endeavors was to limit prospects for additional Soviet advances, and to call into question whether Moscow could hold what it had. "There are trouble spots on every continent," Ogarkov lamented.[112]

There were also trouble spots closer to home, and Reagan's policies were having an impact here as well. Covert aid to Solidarity helped preserve that group as the core of political resistance to communism in Poland, and as a glaring example of Moscow's inability to extinguish dissent within the bloc. And even though the U.S. economic warfare campaign was never as decisive as some officials had hoped, it did take a toll. The sabotage of the Siberian pipeline, the imposition of tougher NATO curbs on credit and strategic trade, the constriction of KGB technology-acquisition programs—these initiatives imposed additional costs on an economy in distress.[113] Efforts to deny foreign lending to Poland had a similar effect. By early 1982, Western observers noted that Moscow and other Eastern-bloc governments were "digging into their pockets" to help Poland avoid default, and that the Kremlin had been forced to increase aid "at a time of considerable economic woe for the Soviet Union itself."[114] The total cost of all this is hard to quantify, but Moscow was feeling the squeeze. The West was exploiting "the growth of foreign debts, the food situation, our technological lag in certain areas and a series of other bottlenecks," Andropov said in 1983. "For as long as these problems exist, our class enemies will try to turn them to their benefit."[115]

Reagan's rhetoric was proving just as discomfiting to Kremlin officials. "By drawing attention to the fact that in all the world there is not a single communist success story," wrote Meyer, "we have at long last launched an offensive for which the Soviets have no defense at all."[116] This was no exaggeration—Soviet officials felt just these anxieties about Reagan's verbal assault. As early as 1981, Chernenko had worried that this "especially strong anti-Soviet agitation" was catalyzing dissatisfaction with Moscow's internal practices and inciting demands for reform. By 1983, Ustinov was saying that Reagan and NATO had "launched a limitless psychological offensive against the USSR and the countries of the socialist community," maligning the Kremlin image at home and abroad.[117] In this as in other areas, the well-timed and well-targeted use of U.S. power was making Moscow pay for its weaknesses, and contributing to a striking change in the trend lines of the Cold War.

Unfortunately, those policies were leading to a tenser and more dangerous Cold War in the process. Reagan had long believed that a successful geopolitical offensive could force the Soviets to accept the necessity of restraint and thereby enable a thoroughgoing reduction of tensions. For most of his first term, however, this was not what was happening. In Geneva, the START and INF talks seemed hopelessly stalemated. Soviet leaders dismissed U.S. proposals as "a mockery of reason," and suspended arms-control negotiations altogether following the deployment of the first Pershing-II missiles in West Germany in late 1983.[118] That decision severed the most substantive ongoing diplomatic process between East and West, and caused the *Bulletin of the Atomic Scientists* to move the hands of its "Doomsday clock" to just three minutes from midnight. "As the arms race . . . has intensified," that publication stated, "other forms of discourse between the superpowers have all but ceased."[119]

Relations were simultaneously deteriorating in other areas. Soviet involvement in Afghanistan hardly slackened, indicating that Moscow did not intend a near-term retrenchment in the Third World. And within the Soviet Union, the security services responded to growing international concern with human rights by repressing political dissent more severely than at any time since the Stalin years.[120] Meanwhile, Soviet officials reciprocated Reagan's confrontational rhetoric, likening the president to Hitler and charging him with "fanning the flames of war."[121] The overall diplomatic climate was abysmal, and the CIA deemed it "highly unlikely" that Moscow would "shift to a policy of genuine and far-reaching accommodation" anytime soon.[122] Reagan might have turned the tide of the Cold War, but an end to that conflict—or even the moderation thereof—was nowhere in sight.

In retrospect, there were two reasons why Reagan's success in achieving the former objective did not produce progress toward the latter. The first was simply age, in the sense that the enfeebled Kremlin leadership was probably incapable of executing fundamental policy changes of the sort Reagan sought.[123] The second and perhaps more troubling factor, however, was the perception created by Reagan's initiatives. From the Soviet perspective, Reagan's offensive did not look like the prelude to diplomacy; it looked like an all-out crusade to destroy socialism, force Moscow into abject geopolitical capitulation, and maybe even prepare the conditions for war. Kremlin officials alleged that U.S. strategy aimed at "the annihilation of socialism as a socio-political system," and Andropov warned that a "first strategic strike" could not be ruled out. "The Reagan administration has inaugurated open preparations for war," Ogarkov said. "In several fields, the battle is already going on."[124]

This attitude was perhaps the inevitable by-product of Reagan's Cold War assault, and it is hard to see how he could have achieved such strength and advantage without also producing fear and hostility in the Kremlin. The trouble, of course, was that Reagan's strategy rested on the idea that he could ultimately cut through that hostility to find accommodation, and yet the very nature of his policies made Soviet leaders view that prospect as absurd. Reagan was the "bearer and creator of all anti-Soviet ideas," Andropov said; he wanted "a Soviet unilateral laying down of its arms."[125] Making concessions to such a zealot would be appeasement and a recipe for catastrophe. As one well-placed Soviet observer told NSC staffer Jack Matlock, "The leadership is convinced that the Reagan Administration is out to bring their system down and will give no quarter; therefore they have no choice but to hunker down and fight back."[126]

This effect was probably exacerbated by the disorder within Reagan's team. Throughout the early 1980s, administration hardliners consistently sought to short-circuit any move toward diplomacy, and made comments

that could only have intensified Kremlin apprehensions. Pipes once insinu-
ated that negotiations were fruitless and that conflict was inevitable as long
as the Soviet Union was run by a Marxist-Leninist regime. Weinberger and
other Pentagon officials made statements indicating that the administration
sought a capacity not just to deter the Soviets but to "win" a nuclear war.
One adviser even suggested that Americans build backyard bomb shelters to
prepare for that conflict: "If there are enough shovels to go around, everybody's going to make it." Reagan's preference for collegiality over discipline
allowed this loose talk to go on for far too long, and fostered a climate in
which it was even more difficult to signal his commitment to the eventual
reduction of tensions.[127]

Just how cornered the Soviet leadership felt became clear in 1983, which
marked the tensest period in superpower relations since the Cuban Missile Crisis. That year represented the peak of the Reagan offensive, punctuated by the "evil empire" speech and the announcement of SDI in March,
aggressive naval maneuvers near the Soviet Far East in April, the invasion of
Grenada in October, and the deployment of Pershing-II missiles in November. Throughout this period, Soviet nerves were frayed and the potential for
miscalculation was severe. That fact became tragically evident in September,
when an overanxious air defense command ordered the downing of a South
Korean airliner that had accidentally strayed into Soviet airspace, killing all
269 people aboard—including a U.S. congressman. At the United Nations,
U.S. diplomats accused the Kremlin of "wanton, calculated, deliberate murder." For their part, Soviet leaders believed that the incident was a CIA provocation, and the international denunciations that followed only added to their
anxieties. "Fear of war seemed to affect the elite as well as the man on the
street," reported a U.S. observer in Moscow. "A degree of paranoia seemed
rampant among high officials, and the danger of irrational elements in Soviet
decision making seems higher."[128]

It was an acute observation, given what came next. In November 1983,
NATO held a major military exercise known as Able Archer 83. The exercise
took place in locations across Western Europe, and was meant to simulate
the escalation to general war and the launching of a full-scale nuclear attack.
Unlike previous exercises, Able Archer was even initially slated to feature the
participation of Reagan and other top Western officials, and it involved the
use of new, highly encrypted communications codes.

For Moscow, Able Archer could not have come at a more alarming
time. Soviet officials had long worried that Reagan might launch a surprise
nuclear strike, and in fall 1983, malfunctioning radar systems had at least
once reported that an attack was in progress.[129] In this context, the elaborate

procedures surrounding Able Archer looked suspiciously like an effort to mask preparations for war. Just how frightened the Kremlin leadership was remains debated, but high-ranking military officials may briefly have believed that war was likely, and Soviet conventional and nuclear forces went on higher alert. The mounting peril subsided when the exercise came to an end, but revelations about the Soviet view of Able Archer—soon provided by a British double-agent within the KGB—were hardly reassuring. As Deputy Director for Intelligence Robert Gates later wrote, "A genuine belief had taken root within the leadership of the Pact that a NATO preemptive strike was possible."[130] Reagan had intended to throw the Soviets on the defensive, but this was something else entirely.

As a result, the events of late 1983 and early 1984 marked an inflection point in U.S. policy. By this juncture, Reagan was already concluding that America's Cold War prospects were trending upward, and that the moment was approaching to place greater emphasis on diplomacy. The United States, one classified directive stated, could now "deal with the Soviet Union from more of a position of strength than in previous years."[131] At the same time, Reagan was feeling domestic pressure to adopt a less hostile stance. While the renewed Cold War consensus of the early 1980s was strong enough to sustain the U.S. buildup and other key measures, the escalating superpower tensions had produced concerns that Reagan's policies might be *too* aggressive. There remained a strong antinuclear movement nationally and at the state and local levels; there were also widespread anxieties about the Cold War turning hot. Up to three-quarters of Americans thought nuclear war "likely" within the next few years, and nearly half thought that Reagan's policies were "increasing the chances of war." With a presidential election looming in 1984, such perceptions could prove politically fatal. The president had to counter the impression, wrote one adviser, that "Ronald Reagan would push us too close to the brink of war. . . . We must strongly position the President on the 'peace' side of the formula—'peace through strength.'"[132]

The administration faced a similar imperative in U.S. alliance relations. Key NATO partners such as West Germany, the Netherlands, and the United Kingdom had faced vociferous domestic criticism over INF deployments. Demonstrations, sometimes featuring upward of 200,000 people, had become regular occurrences, and the political temperature had risen steadily as the first INF deployments approached. In October 1983, U.S. intelligence had warned of likely mass protests and sit-ins at U.S. military installations in West Germany, and that left-wing groups might employ "violence and terrorist acts" to impede the deployments.[133] More broadly, it had become clear that

Reagan's policies were causing growing fears among NATO publics about the prospect of a superpower showdown that would leave Western Europe as its first and deadest victim. "European opposition to [INF] extends far beyond relatively insignificant traditional neutralist groups," State Department Bureau of Intelligence and Research (INR) analysts had reported. "It stems from a deep-seated European anxiety that the U.S. may embark on a confrontational course with the Soviets."[134]

Such concerns and agitation did not ultimately derail the NATO INF deployments. But they had already led the United States to inject some flexibility into its INF-negotiation position in early 1983, by announcing that it would accept an interim agreement that would merely reduce permitted deployments by the Soviets and NATO en route to the desired "total elimination of weapons of this class."[135] Moreover, these European sensitivities ensured that NATO leaders would continue to urge Washington to lean forward diplomatically as the alliance's strategic position improved. "While the Federal Government would not be deflected from stationing," West German officials stated, "the scale of the demonstrations and of the internal political problems caused by stationing would be far greater if the Americans were not seen to be negotiating really seriously." In early 1984, West Germany's Helmut Kohl recommended a Reagan-Chernenko summit to "probe" Moscow's intentions. By that point, even Thatcher, the strongest supporter Reagan had in Europe, was reminding the president that "we all had to live in the same planet." "We needed to ask ourselves how we could influence Soviet thinking," she said. "It was clear that we could not do so unless we had a reasonable relationship."[136]

As the crisis of late 1983 subsided, Reagan too was increasingly ready to move in this direction. Able Archer had underscored the president's fears of nuclear war and his sensitivity to the prospect of tragic miscalculation. More generally, it gave him increased empathy for his Soviet counterparts. Reagan now grasped, he later wrote, that "many Soviet officials feared us not only as adversaries but as potential aggressors who might hurl nuclear weapons at them in a first strike."[137] It was thus necessary to blend strength with reassurance: to convince the Soviets, as he told French president François Mitterrand, in early 1984, that "no one meant them harm," and that they might actually benefit if they "joined the family of nations."[138] Advisers such as Shultz and Matlock echoed this conclusion, arguing that Reagan could only translate his position of advantage into successful diplomacy if he gained a "minimal level of trust" with Soviet leaders. If Reagan's policy appeared geared toward war or "forcing collapse of the Soviet system," the Kremlin hierarchy would not make the accommodations that would lead to a more stable relationship.[139]

What resulted from these various influences has been described as a dramatic "Reagan reversal." It was really more of a calculated Reagan recalibration. The president remained convinced that firmness and pressure were essential to making Moscow cooperate, and through the end of his presidency, he would work to maintain and even increase U.S. leverage.[140] Beginning in late 1983 and early 1984, however, he also made overtures designed to moderate the most aggressive aspects of his rhetoric, convince Kremlin leaders that he was genuinely interested in diplomacy, and thereby begin working toward an improved relationship.

Reagan made this case in public and in private. On January 16, 1984, he gave a major address in which he reiterated the need for "strength" and "realism," but also stressed the dangers of unrestrained competition and the corresponding imperative of "dialogue." "We will never retreat from negotiations," he pledged. "Our commitment to dialogue is firm and unshakeable."[141] In his State of the Union address days later, Reagan declared that "a nuclear war cannot be won and must never be fought," and promised the Soviet people that "if your government wants peace, there will be peace."[142] Meanwhile, the president was seeking a personal connection with Chernenko following Andropov's death in February. In letters to the general secretary, Reagan acknowledged "the tragedy and scale of Soviet losses in warfare through the ages," and averred that "our common and urgent purpose must be . . . a lasting reduction of tensions between us."[143] He continued this diplomatic offensive in a meeting with Andrei Gromyko in September. Reagan reiterated that "we live in one world and we must handle our competition in peace," and suggested opening a high-level, private channel to Moscow.[144]

All this was very good news for George Shultz. For much of the first term, Shultz had been undercut by bureaucratic rivals—Casey and Weinberger chief among them—who seemed determined to obstruct substantive negotiations. There was an attitude among Reagan's more hawkish aides, Shultz's aide Charles Hill recalled, that "you could never do any kind of work" with the Soviets, and that "Shultz should be brought to his senses and locked up in a closet."[145] Reagan never fully clamped down on the infighting, which subsided only when Casey and Weinberger resigned in 1987. As the president corrected course from late 1983 onward, though, he did make it plain that he sided with Shultz on the need to match pressure with diplomacy. "George is carrying out my policy," Reagan wrote in 1984. "I'm going to meet with Cap & Bill & lay it out to them." Shultz's star was ascendant, and he would soon emerge as the president's most influential adviser. The secretary of state "would not win all the bureaucratic battles over Soviet policy" in the years to come, Gates later wrote, "but he would win increasingly often and he would win nearly all of the important struggles."[146]

In the short term, these changes were mainly useful in preventing U.S.-Soviet relations from deteriorating further, and in aiding a very modest thaw in the second half of 1984. In July, the two governments concluded minor agreements on consular relations, trade, and improvement of emergency communication links. Soviet officials also confided that the Kremlin had decided to "unfreeze" the bilateral relationship, and following his long meeting with Reagan in September, Gromyko agreed to restart the arms-control talks.[147] The prospects for more substantive change remained limited while the "old men" ruled in Moscow.[148] But the longer-term effect of the Reagan recalibration was to better poise the administration to exploit the broader generational shift that was now approaching. By mid-1984, the fact that each recent Soviet leader had been more senescent than the last made it seem likely that the torch would soon be passed to a new cohort—"younger men," Shultz wrote, "who might have a significantly different outlook." When that shift did occur in March 1985, Reagan and Shultz were ready. In Moscow for Chernenko's funeral, Shultz conveyed a special message to the new general secretary, Mikhail Gorbachev. He said, "President Reagan told me to look you squarely in the eyes and tell you: 'Ronald Reagan believes that this is a very special moment in the history of mankind.'"[149]

Reagan and Gorbachev

It was a special moment indeed. The period between early 1985 and early 1989 marked a great change in the Cold War and in international relations. The dangerous hostility of the early 1980s gave way to intensive diplomacy, punctuated by five Reagan-Gorbachev summits, an unprecedented arms-control agreement that eliminated an entire class of nuclear weapons, and a singular improvement in the tenor of East-West affairs. The Soviet Union, meanwhile, had begun to moderate its conduct virtually across the board, by initiating a withdrawal from Afghanistan and the Third World, making asymmetric or even unilateral military reductions, renouncing its long-standing claim to historical infallibility and ideological supremacy, and allowing remarkable liberalization at home. These changes represented an extraordinary deescalation of bipolar tensions, and the onset of a decisive Soviet retreat from the Cold War. The superpower contest was moving toward a conclusion when Reagan left office, and one that was eminently favorable to U.S. and Western interests.

Although the causes of this change are still subject to vigorous debate, there is no denying that Gorbachev's ascension was absolutely indispensable to the process. If Reagan had been looking for a more flexible and forthcoming interlocutor in Moscow—someone who was actually willing to alter long-standing policies in the face of reality—then he could hardly have designed a better partner than Gorbachev. For as the president would soon realize, the new general secretary was a "somewhat different breed" of Kremlin ruler, far better suited than his predecessors to engagement with the West. He was younger and more vibrant than the men who had come before him, and was willing—as they were not—to confront outdated shibboleths and strike out in new directions. The new general secretary was "a real find of a leader," adviser Anatoly Chernyaev wrote, "intelligent, well-educated, dynamic, honest, with ideas and imagination. . . . Myths and taboos (including ideological ones) are nothing for him. He could flatten any of them."[150]

Most important, Gorbachev grasped that the Kremlin had maneuvered itself into a dire and deteriorating predicament, both at home and abroad. He often referred to the Afghan war as a "bleeding wound" for the Soviets. He also spoke eloquently of the unsustainable costs and dangers of the nuclear arms race, and he was keenly aware of just how onerous controlling Eastern Europe had become for the Kremlin. More broadly still, he understood from the outset that Moscow needed a period of international calm if it were to find the time, money, and focus necessary to address the metastasizing cancers of the system. "We had to understand," Gorbachev believed, "that 'we couldn't go on living like this,' both inside our country and in world politics." This sense that the Soviets must "alleviate the pressure that had borne down on us due to our involvement in conflicts all over the world and in the debilitating arms race" continually influenced Gorbachev's thinking, and it provided a powerful impetus to his policy departures.[151]

It was also, in some ways, a testament to the impact of Reagan's first-term offensive. Although the general secretary would undoubtedly have had to confront the problems of internal stagnation and decline in any event, U.S. policies badly exacerbated the strains that so preoccupied Gorbachev when he took power. Even in 1985, he referenced the "very dangerous shift" the Cold War had taken under Reagan, and admonished Soviet officials to grapple with "the changes in the correlation of forces that are occurring."[152] More specifically, Gorbachev viewed the Pershing-IIs as a grave threat, and he worried that the Reagan buildup might soon force Moscow to choose between strategic vulnerability and economic disaster. The Soviets were faced with "'Tridents,' 'Minutemen,' arms in space," he lamented in 1986, a new arms race that threatened "the deterioration of our ecological, strategic and political security, the loss everywhere, but above all exhausting our economy." If Gorbachev wanted détente, in other words, Reagan's policies were a key reason why.[153]

Unfortunately, none of this meant that Gorbachev pursued a broad-gauged retrenchment immediately upon taking power. From the start, the general secretary did genuinely want a relaxation of tensions. Yet he still had to contend with a strong faction of hawks in the Kremlin, and he remained uncertain whether Reagan would reciprocate or merely exploit conciliatory behavior. "You want to take advantage of the Soviet Union," he charged during their first meeting.[154] Moreover, as CIA officials correctly assessed, Gorbachev still believed that crafty maneuvering could permit him to secure a favorable détente—one that restored expanded East-West commerce and provided a more relaxed international environment—"on the cheap."[155] As a result, Gorbachev's early appeals for rapprochement were matched with few concrete policy changes on Afghanistan, human rights, or arms control. "The USSR cannot simply reduce and will not reduce nuclear weapons to the detriment of its security, when the SDI program is being implemented in the U.S.," he informed Reagan. What diplomatic overtures Gorbachev did broach during this period—his proposal for a superpower military withdrawal from Central Europe or an INF "freeze"—were slanted toward Soviet advantage, and were advanced as much to wrong-foot Reagan as to elicit serious negotiations. "However much Gorbachev represents the 'new Soviet man,'" Shultz wrote in late 1985, "he and his colleagues are not about the squander the legacy of Soviet power and influence bequeathed to them by Brezhnev, Andropov, and the old guard."[156]

The evolution of Gorbachev's policies was thus gradual, and it was spurred by three principal factors. The first and most essential was the intensifying crisis of Soviet power. The Soviet domestic situation continued to worsen in the late 1980s, driven partially by plummeting oil revenues, and partially by blowback from Gorbachev's own initiatives. The general secretary was determined to reinvigorate the Soviet system, but—in a recurring theme of his leadership—his solutions tended to make the underlying problems worse. Gorbachev's early response to the deepening economic crisis, for instance, was an "acceleration" program that emphasized doubling down on investment in heavy industry in a quixotic quest to revive the moribund Soviet growth model. These investments, financed largely through deficit spending, could not restart an economy with fatal structural flaws. They did, however, intensify a fiscal crisis that became progressively more crippling. Similarly, Gorbachev's anti-alcohol campaign did little to alleviate the societal pathologies that were driving Soviet citizens to drink, but it did deprive the Kremlin treasury of perhaps $100 billion in proceeds from alcohol sales, and thereby compounded the budgetary problems all the more.

Gorbachev's political reforms, which began in earnest in 1987, would prove even more corrosive to the stability of the state. These reforms, which would ultimately include competitive elections and a real separation of powers, were intended to breathe life into a socialist project that had grown stale, and to create the political space necessary to pursue more thoroughgoing economic *perestroika* after Gorbachev's initial quick fixes failed. In practice, however, political *glasnost* began to destabilize the Soviet system by venting long-repressed conflicts and grievances, and by unleashing criticism from hardliners and more radical liberalizers alike. In the end, these worsening domestic crises—political and economic—would destroy the union. Even before that, they made Gorbachev increasingly dependent on good relations with Washington, so as to gain greater access to Western trade and technology, transfer resources from military spending to domestic endeavors, and stabilize the international front amid domestic upheaval. "No matter where we turned," Foreign Minister Eduard Shevardnadze later recalled, "we came up against the fact that we would achieve nothing without normalization of Soviet-American relations."[157]

That realization, in turn, interacted with a second factor, which was the radicalization of Gorbachev's thinking. Even before he took power, Gorbachev had been a fairly unconventional thinker, one who drew on humanistic concepts, Western ideas about social democracy, and a deep revulsion at the Cold War arms race. As he subsequently gained authority and cooperated with liberal aides such as Chernyaev and Shevardnadze, Gorbachev fashioned these and other ideas into what he termed the New Political Thinking. The New Political Thinking stressed the impracticality of autarchy and isolation in the modern world, the imperative of avoiding war and reducing international tensions, and the need to promote global welfare rather than solely national interests. Whether these ideas reflected sincerity or an expediency born of desperation is still debated even among experts. What is clear is that these concepts loosened the grip of traditional Cold War thinking in the Kremlin and provided an ideological rationale for Gorbachev's move toward accommodation with the West.[158]

These first two factors did not exist in a geopolitical vacuum, however; they were intertwined with a third, external factor, which was Reagan's second-term diplomacy. From 1985 onward, the president was determined to seize the opportunities afforded by Gorbachev's rise. He invited Gorbachev to a summit shortly after the Soviet statesman took power, and stressed that "our differences can and must be resolved through discussion and negotiation."[159] At this point, Reagan remained prudently suspicious of Gorbachev's intentions, and he did not expect immediate breakthroughs. He did believe, however, that the pressures were building such that Soviet leaders could not indefinitely stand pat, and that Gorbachev was sufficiently different from his predecessors that he might be induced to initiate those changes and "make some practical agreements." The key, Reagan told the NATO allies, was not to treat an early summit "as a watershed event in and of itself," but as a way of drawing Moscow into "a vital long-term process" of diplomacy.[160]

The president's confidence that such a process could be successful, in turn, was reinforced by reports he had received from many of those same allies. Just as leading NATO members had sometimes sought to take the sharper edges off of Reagan's offensive, they were, in many cases, quick to perceive the possibilities presented by Gorbachev's rise. Both Thatcher and Mitterrand had separately met with Gorbachev in 1984, when he was evidently a rising star in the Kremlin, and both had been struck by the contrast with the dour bureaucrats of the Brezhnev era. Mitterrand took note of Gorbachev's willingness to speak frankly about Soviet economic difficulties, and his seeming openness to meaningful dialogue. Thatcher took a similar impression. "I like Mr. Gorbachev," she memorably commented. "We can do business together."[161] Thatcher would subsequently tell Reagan that "she had the impression Gorbachev . . . was an advocate of economic reform and was willing to slacken government control over the Soviet economy," and that prudent engagement might pay dividends.[162]

The question was how to structure such engagement, and here the administration had begun to set the parameters of the process well before Gorbachev took office. As Reagan started to recalibrate his policies in 1983–1984, State Department and NSC officials had laid out a four-pronged approach to diplomacy with Moscow, emphasizing superpower arms control, Third World issues, human rights and political reform within the Soviet Union, and bilateral economic and cultural ties. This approach was based on the idea that U.S.-Soviet negotiations could not be confined to arms control and trade, or otherwise compartmentalized to suit Soviet preferences. Instead, they would have to address all issues of concern to Washington. "It would be no use going into a Summit meeting pretending that these other problems did not exist," Reagan had earlier told Thatcher. The administration would not insist on equal movement on all fronts at once, Shultz explained thereafter, but neither would it necessarily refrain from making "progress in one dimension contingent on progress in others." In essence, the goal of diplomatic engagement would be to turn geopolitical leverage into wide-ranging changes in Soviet behavior.[163]

Doing so meant ensuring that the United States retained—and increased—the strength it had built during the early 1980s. "The strategic reality of leverage comes from creating facts in support of our overall design," Shultz said. "We must structure the bargaining environment to our advantage" to show the Soviets that it was "in their own interest" to seek "better relations across the board."[164] Along these lines, Reagan Doctrine aid expanded during the second term, as the CIA opened a new front in Angola and intensified its Afghan program. The U.S. military budget also continued to increase—albeit at lower rates—and Reagan remained committed to moving forward with SDI.[165] That program, administration officials noted, "confers powerful U.S. negotiating leverage."[166] And in the diplomatic realm, Reagan and Shultz informed Soviet officials that expanded East–West trade must await progress on other issues, while insisting that such progress must take the form of verifiable, meaningful changes in Kremlin behavior in the arms race, in the Third World, and on human rights and political issues at home. The U.S. approach, Reagan wrote in 1985, should be that of "just hanging back until we get some of the things we want." "We can afford to set high conditions for agreements," agreed National Security Adviser Frank Carlucci in 1987. "We want accommodation on our terms."[167]

Yet it was equally imperative to maintain balance in U.S. policy—to ensure that sticks were complemented by carrots, that pressure was matched by reassurance. If nothing else, the experience of the early 1980s had shown that Soviet leaders who felt ostracized and existentially endangered were unlikely to be forthcoming diplomatic partners. "We all as politicians understood that progress becomes very difficult if we push the other person into a corner," Reagan said in 1985.[168] Tact was therefore essential. Threats, public demands, and inflammatory rhetoric would probably backfire; Reagan must demonstrate that improved Soviet conduct would elicit less hostility and greater respect from the West. "I think I can work with this guy," he said in 1985. "I can't just keep poking him in the eye!"[169] If the United States were to have productive relations with Moscow, a hard line and a soft touch were both essential.

Admittedly, striking this balance was not always easy in the second term. Within the administration, hardliners such as Weinberger and Casey were never fully reconciled to thoroughgoing engagement with Gorbachev, whom they suspected of being a wolf in sheep's clothing. Outside the administration, key figures from Reagan's GOP base openly derided the administration's diplomacy on these same grounds. Representative Jack Kemp (R–New

York) would label Reagan's arms control efforts vis-à-vis Gorbachev "a nuclear Munich." Columnist George Will charged that the president had "accelerated the moral disarmament of the West—actual disarmament will follow" through the more measured approach he was now taking in superpower relations.[170] Reagan could never entirely ignore such criticism, which occasionally caused him to take a more strident public line toward the Kremlin.

Yet even in the face of these charges, Reagan and Shultz kept their diplomatic goals firmly in mind. And so even amid the continuing disputes and polemics, they worked diligently through the late 1980s to build a productive and mutually respectful relationship with Gorbachev. In summit meetings and private correspondence, Reagan looked to establish personal rapport and trust with the general secretary, while also affirming his commitment to reducing the threat of war. "We harbored no hostile intentions toward the Soviets," he said in 1986. "We recognized the differences in our two systems. But the President felt that we could live as friendly competitors."[171] And even as Reagan and Shultz pressed Gorbachev and Shevardnadze on a wide range of issues, they usually did so politely and privately, they indicated that progress would lead to better relations, and they pledged that they had no intention of humiliating Moscow if concessions were made. "If the Soviets loosened up, we would not exploit it," Reagan promised Gorbachev in one discussion on human rights. "We would simply express our appreciation."[172] On the whole, then, the administration was now pursuing a more carefully calibrated and nuanced strategy for shaping Soviet behavior. That strategy combined positive and negative incentives; it was meant to make moderation at home and abroad seem necessary but also acceptable to Gorbachev. Over time, it would prove very effective in doing just that.

The first milestone came in November 1985 at the Geneva summit. The eventual result of Reagan's early invitation to Gorbachev, the summit was important not for substantive breakthroughs on arms control or Afghanistan— there were none—but, rather, in the basic tone it set. Even as the two leaders sparred over subjects such as SDI and Central America, they began to feel more comfortable with one another. Reagan confirmed for himself that Gorbachev was a dramatic departure from his stolid predecessors: "You could almost get to like the guy."[173] Gorbachev's reservations about Reagan were less easily overcome, but the general secretary did gain greater confidence that the president was not as reckless or unthinkingly anti-Soviet as sometimes portrayed. Observers on both sides noted a degree of personal warmth between the statesmen, and the summit concluded with pledges to sustain the dialogue. The primary accomplishment of Geneva, Gorbachev wrote to Reagan shortly thereafter, was to "overcome the serious psychological barrier which for a long time has hindered a dialogue worthy of the leaders of the USSR and the USA."[174]

The dialogue soon intensified. At Geneva, the two leaders had invoked Reagan's earlier language in declaring that "a nuclear war cannot be won and must never be fought."[175] In January 1986, Gorbachev outdid this statement with a more dramatic one: a public proposal to abolish nuclear weapons by the year 2000. The dominant belief in Washington was that the proposal was a propaganda ploy. But it appealed to Reagan's antinuclearism, and he perceived an opportunity to advance the arms-control agenda. Reagan wrote to Gorbachev, endorsing nuclear abolition as an eventual goal, and in July he made his own proposal: to work toward a near-term agreement to eliminate offensive ballistic missiles. This overture, he wrote, "should open the door to some real arms negotiations if [Gorbachev] is really interested."[176] In the interval, the antinuclear sentiments of both leaders had been stimulated by the reactor explosion at Chernobyl in April, which served, per Gorbachev, "as a serious reminder of the terrible forces contained in the energy of the atom," and of the need for cooperation to subdue that threat.[177]

These events were prelude to the Reykjavik summit in October. Envisioned as a preparatory meeting prior to a 1987 summit in Washington, Reykjavik turned into one of the most surprising and dramatic moments of the Cold War. Gorbachev was now feeling acute pressure to ease the strains on his economy. "We are already at the end of our tether," he had told advisers; "an arms race that we cannot manage" loomed.[178] At Reykjavik, the general secretary thus announced that he was ready to destroy all intermediate-range missiles in Europe, and to cut superpower strategic arsenals by half. That offer, in turn, alerted Reagan to the possibility of a major arms-control breakthrough and led to a series of rapidly escalating proposals: a U.S. bid to eliminate offensive ballistic missiles over ten years, then a Soviet counteroffer to eliminate strategic weapons, and then, tantalizingly, a moment when it seemed the two sides had agreed to abolish their nuclear arsenals entirely. The deal unraveled, however, because Gorbachev demanded potentially fatal restrictions on SDI as the price of any agreement. Reagan saw SDI as essential to maintaining deterrence as the United States reduced or eliminated its nuclear arsenal, and the summit ended amid mutual recriminations.[179]

Reagan later termed this encounter "one of the longest, most disappointing—and ultimately angriest—days of my presidency."[180] In hindsight, however, more was gained than lost in Iceland. It would have been extraordinarily difficult to negotiate the modalities of nuclear abolition, let alone sell that program to the Politburo, Congress, U.S. allies, and other potential veto players. And as tempers cooled after the summit, both leaders grew philosophical about its meaning. "The significance of that meeting at Reykjavik is not that we didn't sign agreements in the end, the significance is that we got as close as we did," Reagan told U.S. officials. Similarly, Gorbachev characterized the summit as "a breakthrough, which allowed us for the first time to look over the horizon," and as evidence that Reagan was committed to improving U.S.–Soviet relations and taming the nuclear beast.[181] Indeed, the fact that the two sides were contemplating such revolutionary measures showed how dramatically the relationship had changed, and how much the mutual distrust and tension were fading.

Reykjavik was equally significant for what it revealed about U.S.–Soviet power dynamics. Reagan's policy rested on the belief that Washington could take a hard line in the negotiations because of the leverage that the U.S. buildup—and Soviet economic decline—afforded. "We *want* peace," he had said in 1985. "They *need* peace."[182] After Reykjavik, it was hard to argue with that analysis, because Gorbachev's desire to head off further competition had led him to alter the Soviet posture in several ways. The general secretary had not only endorsed eliminating intermediate-range missiles in Europe (a proposal that Soviet officials, including Gorbachev, had heretofore ridiculed), but he had also accepted the need for on-site verification, agreed to include Soviet IRBMs in Asia within the INF package, and made important steps toward the U.S. position on START. Gorbachev, Shultz noted, was "laying gifts at our feet . . . concession after concession." Reagan, meanwhile, had given up very little; Gorbachev asked "when the U.S. would start making concessions of its own."[183]

At Reykjavik, of course, the Soviets had made all movement in their position contingent on restricting SDI, but that demand soon proved untenable as well. "As difficult as it is to conduct business with the United States, we are doomed to it," Gorbachev told the Politburo in early 1987. "We have no choice. Our main problem is to remove the confrontation."[184] A final effort to derail missile defense failed after Shultz warned Gorbachev "to weigh carefully the advisability of tying the entire relationship with the United States to SDI." By the end of the year, Gorbachev had set aside the issue and assented to a landmark INF treaty that eliminated U.S. and Soviet intermediate-range missiles worldwide. The treaty mandated the destruction of roughly 1,500 Soviet deployed missiles, as compared to 350 on the U.S. side; it left the British and French nuclear arsenals untouched (another reversal of long-standing Soviet policy); and it effectively represented Moscow's acceptance of Reagan's core position from 1981.[185] From Gorbachev's perspective, there was simply no longer any alternative to accepting this formula. The treaty was necessary to remove "a pistol held to our head" in the form of the Pershing-II, he believed, and to reduce the "funds swallowed up by the insatiable Moloch of the military-industrial complex."[186]

Unsurprisingly, the asymmetrical reductions of the INF treaty, and the firmness of Reagan's arms-control posture, elicited some Soviet resentment. "Two great powers should not treat each other like this," Gorbachev told Shultz in 1987.[187] Frustration aside, however, the INF treaty improved Soviet security by eliminating the Pershing-II, and it provided a friendlier diplomatic climate in which Gorbachev could pursue defense cuts. Reagan and Shultz managed any residual friction quite nicely, through well-timed gestures and conciliatory public relations. When Gorbachev requested the scrapping of seventy-two older, largely symbolic Pershing-1a missiles in West Germany as part of the INF pact, Reagan persuaded Bonn to agree. The president and Shultz also took care to frame the treaty not as a Soviet cave-in but as a mutual triumph. That approach shone through at the Washington summit in December, when Gorbachev received a state dinner, twenty-one-gun salute, and other honors. This treatment gave Gorbachev's image a diplomatic fillip as the Soviet political scene become more fraught, and it underscored the idea that more forthcoming behavior would win legitimacy and respect abroad. Gorbachev clearly appreciated the experience: he testified that the summit showed "how much the human factor means in international politics," and that it marked "a new level of trust in our relations with the United States."[188]

As Reagan maneuvered Gorbachev toward a more positive stance on arms control, he was doing something similar vis-à-vis Soviet policy in the Third World. From 1985 onward, Gorbachev grasped that Moscow had lost momentum in the developing regions, and that the expansion of the 1970s had come at a high price. As scholars have documented, however, he initially refused to give up the struggle. "We cannot afford to lose," he explained. "Even if we cannot move decisively ahead, we still can and should keep what we already have."[189] In letters to Reagan, Gorbachev accused Washington of supporting groups "which are, in essence, terrorists," and he increased Soviet aid to the FMLN and the Sandinistas. Even in Afghanistan, the Soviet military intensified its operations—including cross-border strikes into Pakistan—in hopes of weakening the insurgency and strengthening the Kabul government, and Gorbachev demanded that any Soviet withdrawal be linked to the termination of foreign aid to the rebels. "They should find a balance of concessions," he told Reagan in 1987.[190]

The trouble with this policy was that it was unsustainable. The price of supporting Moscow's Third World allies was becoming harder to bear as the Soviet economy deteriorated; U.S. officials joked that the "colonial regions are exploiting the Soviet Union!"[191] And if it was true, as Gorbachev acknowledged, that the Kremlin had suffered a "total defeat" in Afghanistan, then dragging out that misadventure would only compound its military, diplomatic, and economic onus. "It is obvious," noted a Soviet report in May 1987, "that the absence of a solution to the Afghan problem is being used to harm the interests of all socialist countries."[192]

The effect of U.S. policy during the late 1980s was to accentuate Gorbachev's incentives to accept this reality and begin a broad retrenchment from the Third World. Admittedly, U.S. aid to guerrillas in countries such as Angola and Nicaragua never resulted in the military overthrow of communist regimes during Reagan's presidency, but it did drive home the price of maintaining Soviet positions along the global periphery. This was especially true in Afghanistan, where in 1985–1986 the administration ramped up covert support in hopes of forcing "the removal of Soviet forces from Afghanistan and the restoration of its independent status."[193] That increased support—especially provision of Stinger missiles—took a heavy toll on Soviet forces during 1986–1987 and ensured that the quagmire only worsened for Moscow. Intelligence reports confirmed that the Stingers were undermining Soviet air superiority, allowing the guerrillas to consolidate safe havens, and generally empowering the resistance. "The Stinger missile has changed the course of the war," noted one assessment.[194]

The counterpart to this military pressure was a strong diplomatic offensive. Reagan and Shultz continually reminded Gorbachev that no overarching détente would be possible unless his policies toward Afghanistan and other regional conflicts changed. "The absence of any progress on regional issues is a fundamental impediment to a general improvement of our relations," Reagan wrote before one summit.[195] Yet they also hinted that Soviet retrenchment would allay tensions and be conducive to a better relationship with the West. The occupation of Afghanistan was "a dreadful quagmire," Reagan declared in 1987, but the Soviets could "win accolades from people of good will everywhere . . . by grounding their helicopter gunships, promptly withdrawing their troops, and permitting the Afghan people to choose their own destiny. Such actions would be viewed not as a retreat but as a courageous and positive step."[196]

This two-pronged approach was well suited to maximizing the strain on Soviet positions, while also playing on Gorbachev's need for diplomatic progress and greater access to Western trade and technology.[197] In late 1987–1988, the general secretary began taking steps to cut Soviet losses and decrease East-West frictions. Soviet officials sought U.S. assistance in ending conflicts in Namibia and Angola, and advised their Third World clients that Kremlin aid had limits. In Central America, Gorbachev would soon suspend arms shipments to Nicaragua and begin reducing assistance to the FMLN, as he urged both parties to make peace with their U.S.-backed rivals. "The concerns of our strategic allies in the Soviet Union are concentrated around the geopolitical problems the worldwide struggle against imperialism poses," Nicaraguan leaders lamented, "and not in acting sympathetically with the Revolution."[198]

This retreat from the Third World was most dramatic in Afghanistan, from which Soviet troops began pulling out in May 1988. Gorbachev saw the withdrawal as essential to bettering the Soviet image abroad and facilitating rapprochement with Washington. It would "confirm our new approach to solving international problems," he said, and "deprive our enemies and opponents of their most powerful argument."[199] To further mollify Reagan, Gorbachev set a firm timeline for the withdrawal, and "front-loaded" the removal of Soviet troops into the opening months of that period. These concessions did not convince Reagan to halt aid to the rebels, which U.S. and Pakistani officials saw as critical to toppling the communist regime left behind in Kabul. "Nothing . . . prevented us from continuing to support those we had supported, and . . . we intended to do so," Shultz told Shevardnadze.[200] But the administration did lessen the embarrassment for Moscow, by praising Gorbachev for his statesmanship, and by endorsing diplomatic accords that let him claim that the Soviets were withdrawing as part of an international settlement rather than a unilateral surrender. Matlock, then U.S. ambassador to the Soviet Union, later wrote that the accords "gave Gorbachev the political cover he needed to extract his troops." Similarly, Chernyaev agreed that the withdrawal "would be easier and more graceful to do . . . within the framework of an agreement."[201] In Afghanistan as in arms control, Reagan accomplished key geopolitical objectives without humiliating a weakened Kremlin in the effort.

Nowhere was this balancing act more important than in promoting human rights and political liberalization within the Soviet Union. Reagan had long argued that these domestic matters were in fact crucial geopolitical issues, because a less authoritarian Soviet Union would be a less secretive and dangerous Soviet Union. Human rights, he told Shevardnadze, were "literally at the heart of the U.S.–Soviet relationship."[202] As superpower diplomacy accelerated, Reagan and Shultz continually pushed Gorbachev to release political prisoners, liberalize laws on dissent and political activity, expand emigration for Soviet Jews and other dissidents, and provide greater liberties for religious groups. The president pursued these issues at every summit and in numerous other forums, reminding Gorbachev that little else would be possible without moderation of Soviet rule at home. "If the Soviet Union intended to improve its relations with the United States," he said at Geneva, "it would do well to change its reputation with respect to individual freedom."[203]

This pressure was applied with a relatively light touch, however, because Reagan understood that Gorbachev was unlikely to budge on this most sensitive subject if he felt harangued or disrespected. Washington must not "force Gorbachev to eat crow and embarrass him publicly," Reagan had written in 1985. "We must always remember our main goal and his need to show his strength to the Soviet gang back in the Kremlin."[204] The administration generally pursued the human rights dialogue through quiet diplomacy rather than public challenges, and Reagan and Shultz framed the issue not as one of the United States issuing demands, but as an area in which Moscow could repair its tarnished image. Likewise, they held out the prospect that meaningful progress would bring tangible benefits, from expanded trade to an agreement to hold the next Helsinki follow-on meeting in Moscow. Gorbachev badly wanted the latter reward as a symbol of Soviet international legitimacy; U.S. diplomats and the Western allies dangled the carrot of a positive answer to encourage liberalization. "We must propose a challenge as well as offer an inducement," State Department officials wrote.[205]

Gorbachev did not always take kindly to these exhortations—"he would not sit as the accused before a prosecutor," he once told Reagan.[206] Nor did he require U.S. prodding to understand that some kind of liberalization was imperative to political and economic rejuvenation at home. Yet even taking these issues into account, there is considerable evidence that Reagan's carrot-and-stick approach did advance the cause of Soviet reform. It strengthened the hand of liberalizers such as Shevardnadze, while helping convince even KGB officials that greater respect for individual rights was vital to progress on key priorities like trade and arms control.[207] Eventually, liberal Foreign Ministry officials began asking U.S. diplomats to push the rights question *more* vigorously, for precisely this reason. "Can the Department provide me a list of prisoners that I could pass on to Kashlev?" inquired one State Department official. "I take it that he would like to use it to put some additional pressure on Moscow."[208] Similarly, by putting the issue of reform squarely athwart the path to improved relations, Reagan reinforced Gorbachev's inclination to leaven Soviet repression, and provided an incentive for him to move further and faster than he might otherwise have done. As Chernyaev later said, "Our policy did not change until Gorbachev understood that there would be no improvement and no serious arms control until we admitted and accepted human rights, free emigration, until glasnost became freedom of speech, until our society and the process of perestroika changed deeply."[209]

These advances were most marked from early 1987 onward, as Gorbachev sought to remove human rights as a stumbling block in East-West affairs. In April, he told Shultz that Moscow would consider "any proposal that emerges in the humanitarian area," and the two countries soon formed working groups to address the subject more systematically.[210] Before long, the Soviets were moving forward on numerous fronts: ending the jamming of VOA and other Western broadcasting, releasing 650 political prisoners between early 1987 and early 1989, and allowing the emigration of Jews, Armenians, and ethnic Germans to skyrocket from 1,900 departures in 1986 to 77,800 two years later. As part of the CSCE process, the Kremlin also accepted firmer criteria for judging human rights performance in the Eastern bloc, stronger protections for Helsinki monitoring groups, and provisions to ease the flow of information among citizens. "Under Gorbachev human rights performance has made significant—by Soviet standards, remarkable—progress," CIA analysts noted.[211]

Throughout the late 1980s, Reagan's role in facilitating this progress was based not simply on his ability to apply leverage, but also on his willingness to support and reward advances where they occurred. Just how important this latter aspect of policy was became clear at the Moscow summit in late May and early June 1988. In the year prior, Soviet reform had accelerated. Gorbachev was now working to outflank his opponents and empower greater economic restructuring through a program of unprecedented political liberalization: strengthening the judiciary, introducing democratic elections, improving individual rights and protections, and making other changes that would significantly weaken the institutional bases of Soviet authoritarianism. Those reforms divided the Communist Party, however, with both liberals and hardliners questioning the pace and scope of the proposed changes. Facing growing opposition at home, Gorbachev looked to his chief diplomatic interlocutor for reassurance that political reform would be rewarded abroad. Through private channels, he had Anatoly Dobrynin pass an oral message in March 1988 expressing Soviet concern that "the President still thinks of the USSR as an evil empire whose social and political positions have placed it on the ash heap of history. The Soviets request that, if this in fact is not the President's perception . . . then it would be important for the President to state this prior to the Moscow Summit. The Soviets ask what concrete steps they could take over the next few months to prompt such a statement by the

President."[212] Gorbachev, one U.S. assessment noted, was seeking "Western endorsement of *glasnost.*"[213]

Reagan responded with a careful blend of pressure and encouragement. In April, he gave a tough speech on U.S.-Soviet affairs, and at the summit he pushed energetically for greater reforms "across the board." He asked Gorbachev to decree "that religious freedom was part of the people's rights, that people of any religion—whether Islam with its mosque, the Jewish faith, Protestants or the Ukrainian church—could go to the church of their choice."[214] He and Shultz also pushed for the institutionalization of existing reforms and the repeal of antidissent laws used to limit political discourse. Finally, speaking publicly at Moscow State University, Reagan extolled the virtues of political and economic liberty and the need for change in the Soviet system. "Democracy is the standard by which governments are measured," he declared; an authoritarian Soviet Union would be neither economically competitive nor internationally respected in the modern world.[215]

As Reagan issued this challenge, however, he also expressed his admiration for what Gorbachev had done so far. Appreciating that Gorbachev was now seeking to change the Soviet system in remarkable ways, the president provided a strong endorsement.[216] He publicly praised *perestroika* and *glasnost,* credited Gorbachev with making immense changes in Soviet policies, and stressed the general secretary's personal contributions to the improved East-West relationship. And as the Soviet leadership had requested, he consigned the "evil empire" label itself to the ash heap of history, calling it an artifact of "another time, another era."[217] As historian James Mann has noted, Reagan's rhetoric hit its mark, bolstering Gorbachev prior to a crucial party congress in June, at which he continued with the reform agenda. The general secretary certainly grasped the significance of Reagan's gestures; he and aides such as Chernyaev and Shevardnadze all looked back on the summit as a watershed in cooperation and trust.[218] The two sides had "come a long way," Reagan himself said.[219]

By the close of Reagan's presidency, in fact, it was becoming hard to deny that U.S.-Soviet relations had changed fundamentally. At their last summit in New York in December 1988, the president and Gorbachev reminisced warmly about their previous meetings, and treated each other more as old friends than as leaders of rival superpowers. Reagan reaffirmed that "we were all on Gorbachev's side concerning the reforms he was trying to make in the Soviet Union"; Gorbachev replied that his country "would never go back to what it had been."[220] The general secretary had made that much evident in a speech at the United Nations the same day. In that address, he announced a *unilateral* 500,000 troop reduction in the Soviet military, the removal of 50,000 soldiers and 5000 tanks from Eastern Europe, the endorsement of "freedom of choice" in "the social development of nations," and the renunciation of class struggle and ideological conflict as the basis of Moscow's relations with the world. It was necessary to avoid being "hemmed in by our values," he said; the Kremlin had no claim "to be in possession of the ultimate truth."[221] One longtime observer of U.S.-Soviet affairs later called the speech "the most astounding statement of surrender in the history of ideological struggle."[222]

Gorbachev would not have put it that way, but he did mean his address to show that the Cold War was ending and that the Soviet Union was distancing itself from zero-sum competition with the United States. "This speech should be an anti-Fulton—Fulton in reverse," he told advisers.[223] This retreat from Cold War was rooted in necessity, in that the Soviets could no longer sustain an intense global struggle, and it also reflected the humanistic principles of Gorbachev's new thinking. Yet it was no less a product of Reagan's success in establishing a more stable, productive relationship. It was now possible to demilitarize Soviet policy, Gorbachev said in 1988, "because politically we have entered a new situation in our relations with the United States." Or as he told Reagan in New York, "It had all begun in Geneva."[224]

As we will see in chapter 6, it would fall to George Bush to preside over the final endgame of the Cold War, and to fully reap the harvest of Soviet decline. Through the 1980s, however, the Reagan administration played an indispensable role in seizing the opportunities before it and moving the superpower struggle toward that resolution. From the start, Reagan moved to retake the geopolitical high ground through a determined Cold War offensive. After late 1983 and early 1984, he then blended the hard line and the soft touch necessary to encourage a dramatic reduction of tensions on eminently favorable grounds. The president's second-term diplomacy maintained enough firmness and leverage so that Gorbachev had to make real concessions as the price of an improved relationship, but it also fostered the mutual respect and confidence needed to convince the general secretary that accommodation was a path worth taking. Reagan was, no doubt, very lucky to come along when the Soviet Union was falling into deep systemic crisis, and to find in Gorbachev the exceptionally congenial partner who was so critical to making American diplomacy effective. But even so, Reagan's policies showed that the United States was now putting the structural possibilities at hand to excellent use.

They also demonstrated that vision and adaptation were both central to successful statecraft during the 1980s. From the beginning of his presidency,

Reagan knew where he wanted to go in U.S.-Soviet relations, and he devised a deliberate, multifaceted strategy meant to take him there. Yet through 1983–1984, that strategy was only partially effective. It took time, experience, and the ability to learn and recalibrate accordingly for the administration to find the right mix of policies to achieve its long-range aims. Indeed, had Reagan not moderated his stance toward Moscow, he would have been hard pressed to profit from Gorbachev's ascension or win the diplomatic gains of his second term. Turning bold ideas into good policy is almost always something that requires flexibility as well as perseverance. Reagan's dealings with the Soviets were no exception to this rule.

Blowback

Nor were they an exception to the rule that even good policy has liabilities. As noted previously, Reagan's statecraft was a high-risk endeavor, in that it contributed to a sharp increase in East-West tensions during the first term. Throughout the 1980s, his policies incurred significant costs as well. Several of these costs pertained most directly to issues covered in later chapters, and will be explored more fully there. Yet they still deserve to be discussed briefly here, because they demonstrate the weaknesses of a very productive Cold War strategy, and because they show that U.S. resurgence entailed its own dilemmas.

Many of those dilemmas clustered around the Reagan Doctrine, which was among the administration's most effective—and troubling—endeavors. The upside of the Reagan Doctrine was that it served as a highly economical method of punishing Soviet overextension and creating pressures for Kremlin retrenchment. The downside was that it occasioned a range of negative by-products. Some—not all—of the "freedom fighters" whom the CIA supported were unsavory or downright repugnant characters, from Angola's Jonas Savimbi to anti-Sandinista rebels who engaged in torture, assassination, and devastating economic sabotage. More broadly, the fact that U.S. policy toward countries such as Angola and Nicaragua essentially aimed at fueling ongoing civil wars meant that the Reagan administration bore some responsibility for perpetuating the horrific violence that afflicted these nations.[225] At the time, U.S. officials justified these interventions on grounds of geopolitical necessity, and on the rationale that the likely alternative—Soviet-backed communist regimes—would be worse. "There are degrees of evil," Ambassador to the United Nations Jeane Kirkpatrick said.[226] All the same, there is little question that Reagan's Third World initiatives muddled the moral clarity of U.S. policy, or that they contributed to the carnage and instability that often constituted the Cold War's primary legacies in the global south.

The Reagan Doctrine also fed into dubious behavior within the executive branch. The excesses and ambiguities of the Contra war eroded congressional support for that war as time went on; the resulting restrictions led the administration into the series of improvisations and illegalities that produced the Iran-Contra scandal. The crux of the scandal was that Reagan's aides had sold arms to Iran and diverted some proceeds to the Contras, despite legal prohibitions on such activity. When the story broke in late 1986, it caused a major political blowup that threatened to cripple Reagan's foreign policy—and perhaps even cause his impeachment—just as U.S.-Soviet diplomacy was taking off. The president eventually escaped such punishment, and the controversy subsided, when investigators found no "smoking gun" linking Reagan directly to the illegal activity. Nonetheless, the officials who executed the operation certainly believed that they were carrying out the essence of the Reagan Doctrine. "Do whatever you have to do to help these people keep body and soul together," the president had instructed at one point.[227] Indeed, a major lesson of the scandal was that Reagan's enthusiasm for covert action, and the deficiencies of his management style, could lead the administration onto treacherous ground.

The drawbacks of the Reagan Doctrine were ultimately most pronounced and most lasting in Afghanistan, where, Gates later wrote, "our operations . . . had lingering and dangerous aftereffects."[228] Those aftereffects flowed largely from the fact that, although America's Afghan allies were courageous fighters, many of them possessed a worldview scarcely less hostile to Washington than to Moscow. "You could see at the time that some of them hated us," John McCarthy, the U.S. deputy chief of mission in Pakistan, recalled. "These were very anti-Western kinds of types, very fundamentalist in terms of their approach to modern life."[229] Accordingly, U.S. support to the resistance constituted "the crown jewel" of the Reagan Doctrine and an exemplary form of rollback, but it simultaneously empowered a new generation of enemies. Likewise, the Afghan conflict served as a nexus and finishing school for radical Muslim fighters not just from Afghanistan but from around the world, some of whom would form the core of an international jihad during the 1990s and after. "This networking was facilitated considerably by the Afghan war," U.S. counterterrorism official (and later ambassador to Pakistan) Robert Oakley noted.[230]

Although no one could have fully foreseen the consequences of these developments at the time, Reagan did perhaps miss a chance to limit the ills that grew out of the Afghan war. By the late 1980s, Kremlin officials were seeking U.S. support for a coalition government that could survive the Soviet withdrawal and provide order in postwar Afghanistan. Many resistance leaders "wished to establish a fundamentalist regime," Shevardnadze warned Shultz; the superpowers should "agree to discourage extremism."[231] Yet even though U.S. officials understood the prospects for instability in Afghanistan, they declined to pursue a solution that would have brought communists into the Kabul government. To cut this deal, top officials feared, would enrage congressional conservatives and offer an unneeded concession to a Soviet government whose bargaining position was eroding by the day. "Why take this risk when the Soviet hand is so weak?" wrote one official. "Why face the political heat on the Hill?"[232] Instead, the United States focused on providing the *mujahedin* with enough weapons to defeat the communist government that remained after the Soviet withdrawal. This choice helped ensure the eventual fall of that regime, but it also contributed to the chaos in which the Taliban and its terrorist allies would later flourish.

Nor were these the only pernicious outcomes of the war. As I discuss in chapter 5, cooperation between Washington and Islamabad was essential to supporting the Afghan resistance, but it tied Reagan to a military dictatorship whose authoritarian tendencies and efforts to Islamize Pakistani society were fomenting long-range polarization. "In time," the CIA predicted in 1981, the policies of Muhammad Zia-ul-Haq's government might have "profound and unsettling" effects.[233] In addition, U.S. dependence on Zia was ensuring that Reagan could do little to dissuade that government from developing a nuclear weapons capability.

From the mid-1960s onward, U.S. officials had made concerted efforts to retard the spread of nuclear weapons, in the belief that proliferation—especially in conflict-prone regions such as South Asia—could present a major threat to international security. From the late 1970s onward, U.S. officials also knew that the covert Pakistani nuclear weapons program was reaching critical mass.[234] Yet in 1979–1980, the Carter administration had opted to downgrade its emphasis on the matter in order to facilitate geopolitical cooperation on supporting the anti-Soviet jihad. "Our big problem with Pakistan was their attempts to get a nuclear program," Harold Brown explained, and "although we still object to their doing so, we will now set that aside for the time being."[235] Despite misgivings, the Reagan administration followed the same path. There was "overwhelming evidence that Zia has been breaking his assurances to us" on nuclear matters, Shultz wrote in 1982, but it was necessary to be "mindful of the essential role that Pakistan plays in support of the Afghan resistance."[236] Conscious that Washington could not exert real pressure on Zia without jeopardizing the anti-Soviet resistance, Reagan's diplomats generally soft-pedaled the nuclear issue just as Pakistan was making key strides toward the bomb. All told, Reagan succeeded in bleeding the Soviets in Afghanistan, but in doing so, he courted longer-term dangers in a volatile region.

Finally, and not least of all, there were the financial costs of Reagan's policies. The military buildup of the 1980s was the centerpiece of Reagan's offensive, and it played a key role in restoring U.S. advantage. Yet that buildup was also hugely expensive, and it entailed unavoidable trade-offs between military strength and fiscal discipline. "It is very difficult for me to believe that one can cut the budget as they would like to cut it, that one can cut taxes as they want to cut taxes, increase defense as one wants to increase defense," predicted Chief of Naval Operations Thomas Hayward in 1981.[237] Reagan had campaigned on the notion these priorities were in fact reconcilable, but he soon had to admit that the skeptics were correct. "If it comes down to balancing the budget or defense," he said, "the balanced budget will have to give way."[238]

Give way it did, in spectacular fashion. The price of Reagan's military programs—when combined with the impact of his tax cuts—was an explosion of deficit spending and national debt. Annual deficits reached nearly $250 billion during his presidency, and publicly held national debt tripled from $711 billion to $2.1 trillion. The cost of debt service reached one-sixth of federal outlays when Reagan left office, and the ratio of debt to GDP rose from 26 percent in 1980 to 42 percent in 1989. By historical comparison, Reagan incurred more debt than all previous presidents combined, and on his watch the United States became a debtor nation for the first time in seventy years.[239] As long as Washington could attract large amounts of foreign capital, it could finance this debt without excessive near-term dislocations. Even so, Reagan's fiscal record raised questions about when the country's inability to live within its means might itself become a source of insecurity. By the late 1980s, Reagan himself was acknowledging that "his biggest concern was the budget deficit," and allies like Thatcher warned that this problem might ultimately undermine America's "great strength" in global affairs.[240] As U.S. debts grew in later decades, these concerns would only become more pronounced.

Taken together, these issues showed that while Reagan's approach to the Cold War achieved truly striking results, those results came at a price. The president effectively used U.S. power to exploit Soviet decline, reshape superpower affairs, and make possible a dramatic improvement in America's global position. At the same time, however, his policies were sowing more troublesome legacies, from Afghanistan to Nicaragua to Washington, DC. These legacies did not negate Reagan's historic achievements in the Cold War, nor did they make his statecraft particularly unusual: trade-offs and unintended consequences are the norm in world affairs. They did indicate, however, that America's international renaissance contained the seeds of problems to come.

Conclusion

The Reagan years were a time of profound change in the Cold War. At the dawn of the 1980s, the United States appeared to be reeling from a string of geopolitical reverses, and struggling to handle an emboldened Soviet Union. By mid-decade, however, the tide of the superpower contest had turned unmistakably; by the time Reagan left office, bipolar tensions were easing dramatically and in ways that earlier generations of U.S. statesmen would have found nearly inconceivable. There were still crises to come and issues to be resolved, certainly, and those tasks would fall not to Reagan but to his successor. Yet the U.S.-Soviet relationship the president left behind in early 1989 was virtually unrecognizable from what he had inherited eight years earlier.

That transformation illustrated three key themes regarding America's geopolitical trajectory during the 1980s. The first was that U.S. officials were now aggressively exploiting the emerging chances to reassert American primacy and profit from the tectonic shifts at work. Here as elsewhere, of course, Reagan did not cause those shifts to begin, and he was fortunate to hold power at a time when the global context was becoming far more permissive than before. What can be said, though, is that Reagan and his advisers generally understood the possibilities that were presenting themselves in the Cold War, and that they fashioned policies that ultimately made the most of them. From the outset, the administration deliberately and concertedly used all aspects of national power to exacerbate Kremlin weaknesses and build a position of U.S. strength; from 1983–1984 onward, it adroitly combined positive and negative inducements to facilitate striking improvement in the bilateral relationship. The Reagan team indeed turned structural opportunity into successful strategy, and in doing so, it began to shape global changes to America's decided advantage.

The course of U.S.-Soviet relations also illustrated a second theme, however, which was that this process of turning structural opportunity into successful strategy was precisely that—a process. For all of Reagan's prescience and vision, there was a substantial measure of trial-and-error adaptation in his policies. The geopolitical offensive of the first term may have restored U.S. leverage, but it also led to an alarming spike in Cold War tensions. It would thus take the searing experience of Able Archer, and the resulting Reagan recalibration, to bring about an approach that fused strength with reassurance and permitted the turn in U.S.-Soviet relations after Gorbachev took power. The development of effective U.S. policies during the 1980s was not a seamless or uncomplicated affair, and Reagan's dealings with the Kremlin provided ample demonstration of that fact.

They also showed that the foreign policy breakthroughs of that decade had their downsides. Regarding the Cold War, the primary outcome of Reagan's statecraft was a marked reduction in the Soviet threat and a fundamental improvement in the U.S. global position. Yet that statecraft required trade-offs, and it produced negative second-order effects in the moral, financial, and geopolitical reams. Some of these effects proved fairly transient in their impact; others fed into the threats that would characterize the post–Cold War era. This, then, constituted a third essential theme of Reagan's Soviet policies: that the renewal of U.S. primacy brought about problems—and blowback—of its own.

CHAPTER 3

American Statecraft and the Democratic Revolution

If the United States was geopolitically ascendant during the 1980s, it was ideologically ascendant as well. The democratic revolution that had begun in the 1970s gathered strength, racing across Latin America, pushing into Asia, and creating promising stirrings in Africa. At least twenty countries made or initiated democratic transitions between 1980 and 1990, the vast majority coming even apart from the collapse of communism and subsequent transformation of Eastern Europe at the close of the decade.[1] There were also tragic setbacks for democracy during this period, such as the brutal suppression of China's pro-reform movement in 1989, and the future of many emerging democracies remained uncertain both at the time and for years thereafter. On the whole, however, the 1980s witnessed a major shift in global politics, one in which the democratic values and institutions the United States favored spread far and wide.

The origins of that shift were deep and multifaceted, as discussed in chapter 1. Yet in sustaining, strengthening, and propelling the democratic revolution during the 1980s, U.S. statecraft had an essential role. The Carter administration, for all its difficulties, had laid the groundwork for this achievement by grasping the geopolitical import of democratic change and helping liberalization take hold in several countries. And as in U.S.-Soviet relations, the Reagan administration built upon this foundation with great success. After some pronounced initial skepticism about promoting liberal reform overseas, Reagan and his advisers resolved to seize the moment of democratic opportunity, even as they also sought to avoid repeating Carter's mistakes by marrying their enthusiasm to a healthy dose of strategic prudence. The result, overall, was a strong and strikingly effective approach to democracy promotion: in case after case, U.S. policy increased pressures for liberalization, bolstered reformers at crucial points, and helped democratization succeed where it might otherwise have failed.[2] To be sure, U.S. policy was rarely the *principal* cause of democratization, which usually flowed mainly from internal forces. But in countries from Latin America to East Asia and beyond, U.S. initiatives provided an important—even indispensable— assist. All told, the 1980s thus constituted a veritable golden age of U.S. democracy-promotion endeavors; the Reagan administration compiled a record of democratic internationalism that was arguably unmatched in the postwar era. Here as in the superpower competition, that administration ably deployed American influence to amplify favorable trends and reassert U.S. momentum in the global arena.

This does not mean, of course, that U.S. policies were flawless, or that the process of developing those policies was an uncomplicated one—here too, there were similarities to Reagan's Cold War. At first, Reagan and his key aides were ambivalent about encouraging political change in noncommunist states, and it took a key shift in perspective starting in late 1981–1982 for them to fully recognize and commence exploiting the possibilities of the democratic revolution. Even after the administration made this shift, its efforts in places such as the Philippines or El Salvador were often evolving, arduous, messy, and driven by crises or other pressures as well as by geopolitical design. On aggregate, the record of these efforts turned out to be quite impressive. Yet there were nonetheless cases, such as South Africa, where Reagan's diplomacy brought as much frustration as fruition, and instances, notably in Central America, where the moral and human price of U.S. policy was dismayingly high. Every successful policy has its ambiguities and weaknesses, and Reagan's approach to democracy promotion was no different.

In the end, however, it bears restating that the principal legacy of the Reagan administration in this realm was to contribute signally to the empowerment of democratic reform, and to help fashion a world in which U.S. ideological and political values seemed ever more influential. This result testified to the symbiotic relationship between structural change and assertive statecraft during the 1980s; it also helped enshrine democracy promotion as a core tenet of U.S. policy in the unipolar era that followed.

Reagan's Democratic Evolution

It is no small irony that the Reagan administration became such a strong supporter of the democratic revolution, for this is not at all what one would have expected when the administration began. During the late 1970s, Carter's travails had exposed the risks in a forward-leaning stance on human rights and democracy, and Reagan and several future advisers had been strident critics of that approach. They argued that Carter's policies had alienated allies and fueled disastrous destabilization in Managua and Tehran. "Moderation and democracy" were Carter's goals, Jeane Kirkpatrick alleged; "Khomeini and the Ortega brothers" were the results.[3] More broadly, Reagan associates such as Caspar Weinberger charged that spreading liberalism throughout the world was a quixotic quest, and that trying to do so would only undercut the realism needed to defeat the Soviet threat. "There are clear perils in a foreign policy which attempts to impose or export our morality to all other countries in the world," Weinberger wrote.[4]

During 1981–1982, there was thus great ambivalence in U.S. policy. Reagan undertook a "war of ideas" against Moscow, and championed human rights and political reform in the Soviet bloc. Yet he also distanced himself from Carter's emphasis on encouraging liberalization in noncommunist societies, resolving that efforts to shore up Western security must come first. "We don't throw out our friends just because they can't pass the 'saliva test' on human rights," Reagan told the NSC. "I want to see that stopped."[5] Similarly, Alexander Haig used early speeches and press conferences to downgrade the importance of human rights, and high-level emissaries such as General Vernon Walters carried the same message to estranged authoritarian partners. "There will be no more Irans," Walters said; the United States would "stay by the side of our allies."[6]

This was not just a change in rhetoric; Reagan took action to underscore the break with Carter's legacy. He hosted the leaders of Argentina and South Korea in his first weeks in office, and dispatched envoys like Walters, Vice President George H. W. Bush, and Kirkpatrick to mend relations with authoritarian regimes from the Philippines to Chile during 1981. "Ambassador Kirkpatrick's thinking with respect to world problems," Chilean diplomats noted, "broadly agrees with our government's approaches."[7] U.S. officials also downplayed shocking abuses by the Salvadoran military amid the civil war in that country, while signaling that liberalization would not be a precondition for security assistance to countries fighting Marxist insurgencies. "We no longer have the luxury of using Latin America as a test bed for social experiments," Pentagon official Nestor Sanchez explained. "The stakes are simply too high."[8] Likewise, the administration ceased the practice of voting against multilateral loans to countries such as Argentina and Brazil, and sought to reinstitute economic aid to Chile, Uruguay, and other dictatorships. Finally, as his nominee to head the State Department human rights bureau, Reagan chose Ernest Lefever, a prominent conservative who opined that America had no right "to promote human rights in other sovereign states."[9] Having called the Carter era a "sorry chapter" in U.S. diplomacy, Reagan seemed to be turning the page on that chapter decisively.[10]

The period in which this attitude characterized U.S. policy was fairly brief, but the consequences were significant. When Reagan won the presidency, authoritarian regimes and their supporters took heart. "We celebrated . . . just like New Year's Eve, with mariachis, marimbas, and firecrackers," one Guatemalan politician said.[11] In late 1980 and 1981, there was a corresponding surge in abuses by governments that now felt free from the threat of U.S. interference. South Korean authorities arrested 1,200 dissidents and closed 67 newspapers; Salvadoran death squads ran rampant, leaving bodies adorned with signs reading, "With Ronald Reagan, the miscreants and guerrillas of Central America and El Salvador will be finished."[12] In the Southern Cone, Kirkpatrick's visits presaged renewed crackdowns on human rights and opposition activists. "Military Governments in many countries," a group of U.S. religious leaders admonished Reagan, "are viewing your election as a green light."[13] If the Reagan administration would eventually make a major contribution to advancing democracy and human rights abroad, its early policies often had a far more adverse effect.

This dynamic was particularly salient in Guatemala. Between 1981 and 1983, two successive military governments responded to a raging civil war with a brutal counterinsurgency that deliberately targeted not just guerrillas but vast numbers of noncombatants. "There can be no rules in guerrilla and counter-guerrilla warfare," one Guatemalan officer later explained. "It is the dirtiest war there can be."[14] This campaign would claim tens of thousands of lives, and U.S. officials knew that the army was perpetrating a "reign of terror."[15] Yet the administration still ran interference for that army, because it was locked in a death struggle with Marxist guerrillas that had proclaimed their intent to "carry out socialist revolutions in the style of Cuba, Algeria, Libya, and Nicaragua."[16] Seeking to avert further Cold War setbacks in Central America, U.S. officials cast aspersions on reports by groups such as Amnesty International, and declared that there was "no evidence" of systematic repression. "To blame the . . . government for all the murders of leftists and civilians is like blaming the U.S. government for the Hatfield-McCoy Feud and organized crime killings," State Department officials wrote. And when

Reagan visited Guatemala in 1982, he publicly announced that the regime was "getting a bum rap."[17] These comments could only have signaled U.S. acceptance of the ongoing atrocities, and they showed just how amoral Reagan's early statecraft could be.

Had the story ended here, it might have been appropriate to conclude, as one scholar recently has, that Reagan's policies constituted a "disaster for human rights" and political reform in noncommunist countries.[18] Yet the administration was already undergoing a major evolution in its approach to these subjects, one that reflected several interlocking factors. Prominent among these was congressional and public pressure. The Iranian and Nicaraguan revolutions may have discredited Carter's policy, but they hardly erased the urge for morally sensitive statecraft. There remained a strong contingent of lawmakers—including Democrats such as Kennedy, Tom Harkin, and Stephen Solarz, and Republicans like Charles Percy—who were determined to keep human rights in play, and who were supported by an array of NGOs and advocacy organizations. Reagan's opening moves were deeply offensive to this constituency, which soon made its influence felt. Amnesty International and Americas Watch publicized horrific abuses by U.S-backed regimes, and congressional critics made aid requests and military sales to countries such as El Salvador dependent on progress toward human rights and political reform. Similarly, the Senate Foreign Relations Committee voted decisively against Lefever's nomination, urged on by sixty advocacy groups that decried his indifference to human rights and "blind support of authoritarian allies." Rights proponents exulted when the nomination was then withdrawn, noting that the episode had "elevated human rights to a prominence that even Jimmy Carter was unable to give it.[19]

Within the administration, it was rapidly becoming apparent that a policy that so explicitly devalued human rights and democracy would be politically untenable. The reality, State Department officials wrote, was that "we will never maintain wide public support for our foreign policy unless we can relate it to American ideals and to the defense of freedom."[20] If U.S. policy *did* effectively incorporate democracy and human rights, however, it might harness this idealism and reinvigorate support for American involvement overseas. A wide range of actors—from the AFL-CIO, to Freedom House, to representatives and senators on both the left and right—were already working for greater individual rights and democratic change in countries across several continents. Greater executive-branch engagement on these issues, Haig wrote to Reagan in 1982, would "provide a new focus for *our* idealism . . . gain bipartisan support, and give your Administration a positive,

freedom-oriented face."[21] In case after case during the 1980s, these imperatives encouraged major policy shifts toward countries such as El Salvador and
the Philippines, and incentivized the administration to go further in seeking
liberal reform than it might otherwise have done.

Political pressures interacted with key bureaucratic shifts. The defeat of
Lefever's nomination was an embarrassing setback for the administration, but
it cleared the way for the rise of Elliott Abrams, who became assistant secretary of state for human rights and humanitarian affairs in late 1981, and later
assistant secretary for inter-American affairs. Abrams was a card-carrying
Cold War hawk, but he also had a keen appreciation of human rights and
democracy from both a political and a geopolitical perspective. "Human
rights is at the core of American foreign policy," he wrote; the "very purpose" of U.S. diplomacy must be "the defense and promotion of freedom in
the world." Through the 1980s, Abrams would use his hawkish credentials
to promote policies that sought to win congressional backing and advance
U.S. interests by furthering the cause of political liberalization abroad. He
would also use his bureaucratic savvy to forge alliances with like-minded
State Department officials such as Paul Wolfowitz and L. Paul Bremer, and to
turn the offices he ran into bastions of support for these policies.[22]

Abrams's ascendancy was all the more significant because it intertwined
with a broader strategic reappraisal. By late 1981–1982, Reagan and key
advisers such as Haig were coming to grasp the fundamental insight that had
guided Carter's policy: that the world was indeed undergoing an epochal
political awakening in which demands for democracy and individual rights
were ever-harder to ignore. This trend was apparent within the Soviet bloc,
where the Polish crisis dramatized just how powerful the desires for greater
freedom had become. It was also increasingly prominent in noncommunist
countries, where authoritarian regimes were facing rising popular protests, or
where democratic reformers were struggling against extremists on both the
left and right. "There are growing pressures for political change in communist and authoritarian countries alike," Haig wrote in March 1982.[23] George
Shultz had been making the same argument since the late 1970s, and he
became a forceful proponent of this view after succeeding Haig. "Democracy can be the wave of the future," he said. "A new age of democratic
reform and revolution lies ahead of us."[24] Speaking to British Parliament in
June 1982, Reagan sounded the same theme. "Around the world today," he
said, "the democratic revolution is gathering new strength."

In India a critical test has been passed with the peaceful change of governing political parties. In Africa, Nigeria is moving into remarkable

and unmistakable ways to build and strengthen its democratic institutions. In the Caribbean and Central America, 16 of 24 countries
have freely elected governments. And in the United Nations, 8 of the
10 developing nations which have joined that body in the past 5 years
are democracies.[25]

By mid-decade, it had become an administration mantra that "the tide of
the future is a freedom time, and our struggle for democracy cannot and will
not be denied."[26]

As this comment indicates, the sense that the world was approaching a
democratic tipping point awakened a new enthusiasm for promoting liberal
reform. It certainly tapped into a rich vein of ideological fervor within
Reagan. For all his emphasis on Cold War realism, the president had long
harbored deeply Wilsonian inclinations. He believed that democracy was the
highest form of political organization, and that people everywhere deserved
to shape their own destiny. "We believe in the dignity of each man, woman,
and child . . . the special genius of each individual, and . . . his special right
to make his own decisions and lead his own life," he said.[27] As his presidency
unfolded, Reagan would embrace the implications of this belief, insisting
that the United States had a moral obligation to promote a more democratic
global order. "This is not cultural imperialism," he declared at Westminster:

> It is providing the means for genuine self-determination and protec-
> tion for diversity. . . . It would be cultural condescension, or worse,
> to say that any people prefer dictatorship to democracy. Who would
> voluntarily choose not to have the right to vote, decide to purchase
> government propaganda handouts instead of independent newspa-
> pers, prefer government to worker-controlled unions, opt for land to
> be owned by the state instead of those who till it, want government
> repression of religious liberty, a single political party instead of a free
> choice, a rigid cultural orthodoxy instead of democratic tolerance and
> diversity?[28]

Or, as Shultz put it, "Support for democracy is not simply a policy of the
American Government. It is basic to our history and our world view."[29]

Crucially, however, that policy was also increasingly seen as a way of
advancing concrete national interests. A core insight of Carter's policy had
been that promoting rights and reform could serve strategic ends. As the
Reagan administration grew more attuned to the ongoing democratic revolution in 1981–1982, it grew more aware of this insight, too. Within the
Cold War context, it was becoming apparent that democratization should not

be seen as a hindrance to U.S. policy, but as a prerequisite to stability in countries where repression and popular marginalization were increasing pressures
for radical change. "In non-communist countries," Haig wrote, "we need
to help moderate democratic forces as the best long-term protection against
communism."[30] Moreover, a greater focus on democracy and human rights
would increase the strain on authoritarian Soviet clients such as Nicaragua,
and intensify the onslaught against Moscow by affirming the ascendancy of
Western values. As one high-level strategy document stated, America "must
make clear to the world that democracy, not Communism, is mankind's
future."[31] The United States would therefore "go on the offensive with a
forward strategy of freedom," Reagan declared in 1983; it would promote
democracy and human rights as a means of waging Cold War.[32]

More broadly still, by 1982–1983 the administration had endorsed another
Carter-era concept: that the spread of democracy was the best guarantee of
a secure and congenial international order. "Ultimately a truly stable, cooperative and open international system requires societies based on freedom
of choice and legitimacy rather than force and oppression," Haig wrote.[33]
Shultz's subsequent appointment strongly reinforced this view; so did the
invasion of the Falkland Islands by Argentina that same year, which underscored that even friendly dictators were prone to erratic, violent behavior.[34]
From this point onward, U.S. officials averred that a more liberal world
was overwhelmingly in Washington's interest. They argued that democracies were more peaceful, stable, and productive than authoritarian regimes,
more likely to respect human rights, and more likely to side with the United
States on crucial issues of international order. There was a "truly profound
connection" between democracy and security, Shultz said; "It is no accident . . . that America's closest and most lasting relationships are its alliances with its fellow democracies."[35] Reagan put it similarly. "America must
remain freedom's staunchest friend," he said, "for freedom is our best ally
and it is the world's only hope to conquer poverty and preserve peace."[36]
Spreading liberal values was enlightened self-interest; it was a way of promoting global well-being, and of strengthening U.S. security and influence
in the process.

The result of these convergent factors was a major shift in U.S. policy, and
a determined effort to aid democratic governance and liberal reform abroad.
The opening shot in that campaign was Reagan's Westminster speech, in
which he committed his administration to cultivating the democratic revolution. Over the next several years, this theme would gain greater prominence, as advisers such as Kirkpatrick lost influence or resigned, as Abrams
and like-minded officials seized the bureaucratic initiative, as U.S. diplomats

energetically implemented pro-democracy and human rights policies, and as initial successes provided proof that these aspirations could be achieved. By Reagan's second term, these efforts were widely recognized as a defining theme of U.S. statecraft. "There can be no doubt where America stands," Reagan declared. "The American people believe in human rights and oppose tyranny in whatever form, whether of the left or the right."[37] It was a striking turnabout by the man who had once said that a quasi-genocidal junta was getting "a bum rap."

Of course, this rhetoric did not mean that the administration was making an *absolute* commitment to democracy and human rights. For as Reagan embraced the democratic revolution, he was mindful of the need for a prudent and strategic approach to doing so. The administration never thought twice about cooperating with geopolitically crucial but authoritarian regimes in Pakistan or China, nor did it flinch from partnerships with groups—such as the Afghan guerrillas—whose strategic value clearly outweighed their illiberalism. "The human rights element in making decisions affecting bilateral relations," State Department officials wrote, "must be balanced against U.S. economic, security, and other interests."[38] Similarly, Reagan and Shultz were generally unwilling to use military force in the name of democracy, and they stressed that, because Washington could not foster liberal reform *everywhere,* it must be opportunistic and discerning in deciding where and how to intervene. "We do not have the power to remake the planet," Shultz said; "an awareness of our limits" was essential.[39]

This awareness of limits was particularly crucial to avoiding the type of mistakes that Carter had made in Iran and Nicaragua. Reagan remained aware of how badly an ill-timed, overeager approach to liberalization could backfire, and he was determined not to push this agenda to the point of folly. The administration made clear that it would not destabilize friendly authoritarians or push them to cede power before a democratic alternative could fill the void. "Human rights is not advanced by replacing a bad regime with a worse one, or a corrupt dictator with a zealous Communist politburo," Abrams argued.[40] Nor could policy simply entail shunning governments that fell short of U.S. standards. Rather, it might require working with flawed regimes to promote gradual liberalization; it might also mean pursuing reforms while supporting the repressive institutions—the military, the intelligence services—that were holding the radicals at bay. When facing "the Communist dictatorship seeking to expand," Reagan explained, Washington could not forsake "the imperfect democracy seeking to improve."[41] Abrams was equally direct in discussing Central America in 1983: "In the real world the choice is frequently not between good and bad but between bad and worse or, perhaps more accurately, bad but improvable, or worse and permanent."

> What this means is that the United States is at times reluctantly compelled to support regimes which abuse human rights, because we think that their replacements would be much worse for the cause of human rights, and because we think that American (and other) pressure can greatly improve these regimes over time. . . . Our goal is not purity; we do not live in Utopia. Our goal is effectiveness in a violent and bitterly divided area of the world.[42]

There remained, then, strong elements of caution, realism, and anticommunism in Reagan's policy, and these issues would do much to shape key relationships during his presidency. Yet they were not to be mistaken for cynicism or indifference, because Reagan and his closest aides also understood that the United States had to be assertive—that it had to take risks, that it had to apply its power at key times and places—if it wished to strengthen the democratic momentum. Reagan and Shultz certainly believed that "history is on freedom's side," but they recognized that freedom needed powerful friends if it were to triumph. "History will not do our work for us," Shultz said. "Passive measures are unlikely to suffice."[43] Reagan's view was the same. "While we must be cautious about forcing the pace of change," he said, "we must not hesitate to declare our ultimate objectives and take concrete actions to move toward them."[44]

This desire for concrete action underlay one of Reagan's signature initiatives, the creation of the National Endowment for Democracy (NED). The idea of creating a governmental or quasi-governmental organization to promote democracy dated back to the late 1960s, but it came to fruition only under Reagan. The goal of the NED, he explained at Westminster, was to "foster the infrastructure of democracy."[45] It would do so by building the political and social institutions on which successful democracies depended, and by providing reformers with the skills, resources, and contacts needed to transform their societies from within. "If we want democratic forces to win, they need practical training and financial assistance to become as effective as the communists in the struggle to take and maintain power," Haig wrote in March 1982.[46] In communist countries, NED activities would help sustain and gradually empower those elements seeking reform; in noncommunist autocracies, they would foster robust civil societies and pluralistic alternatives to dictatorial regimes. "If the Endowment is successful," NED officials wrote, "it could help resolve one of the most difficult dilemmas facing the United States in the world—the absence of democratic alternatives to authoritarianism."[47]

The NED initially faced skepticism from congressional observers who worried that it would become a front for CIA destabilization programs, and from administration insiders who considered it too ambitious. "The idea," NSC staffer Norman Bailey wrote, "should be classified with perpetual motion and anti-gravity devices."[48] By 1983, however, the NED had been established as a "quasi-autonomous non-governmental organization"—a nominally private, nonpartisan institution that was nonetheless designed to advance U.S. interests and received taxpayer funding. The "quasi-autonomous" part of that designation was important legally, so that the recipients of NED support would not be tainted by receiving aid directly from the U.S. government. And to ensure its nonpartisan character, the NED carried out its activities through four separate groups that each represented a different aspect of U.S. society or politics: the National Democratic Institute for International Affairs (which represented the Democratic Party), the National Republican Institute for International Affairs (the Republican Party), the Free Trade Union Institute (the AFL-CIO), and the Center for International Private Enterprise (the U.S. Chamber of Commerce). Building democracies would take time, NED officials wrote: "The Endowment will be effective in carrying out its mission only if it stands apart from immediate policy disputes and represents a consistent, bipartisan, long-term approach to strengthening democracy that will be supported though successive administrations."[49]

During the mid- and late 1980s, these organizations implemented a wide array of programs under the NED aegis. They supported democratic trade unions from South Africa to Poland, and opposition political parties from Taiwan to South Korea. They funded independent newspapers and radio stations in authoritarian countries, and sponsored election-monitoring missions and human rights watchdog organizations. They helped opposition groups gain access to expert advice on polling and campaign strategy, and brought together cadres of reformers from different countries to discuss common challenges and best-practices. They funded efforts to organize women's groups and other civic associations, and held seminars and training programs for community leaders. Through its activities, Reagan wrote, the NED represented "the cornerstone of our efforts to promote the growth of democratic institutions throughout the world."[50]

Admittedly, the NED was never lavishly funded—its initial budget was $18.5 million, which grew to $25–35 million in later years. But because NED programs were generally labor- rather than capital-intensive, this was sufficient to support initiatives across dozens of countries.[51] In other ways, too, the NED punched above its budgetary weight. Programs that helped keep an independent newspaper alive, enabled opposition parties to more effectively contest elections, or detected voting fraud could be low-cost but high-impact activities. "Funding for this program is very small," Reagan wrote in 1987; "the potential return on our investment, very high."[52] And even though NED resources were limited, the symbolism was significant. As endowment officials wrote, the NED's existence "sends a message to friend and foe alike that the United States not only cares deeply about the success of democracy in the world, but is prepared to assist those who are struggling on its behalf."[53] Not least of all, creation of the NED helped catalyze a broader reorientation of U.S. foreign aid programs, with organizations such as the U.S. Agency for International Development (USAID) and U.S. Information Agency (USIA) increasingly emphasizing democracy promotion in their own activities.[54]

The NED did not, then, represent the sum total of the administration's pro-democracy agenda, and other aspects of policy—from public rhetoric to covert action—would often prove more important. What the NED did demonstrate was a genuine commitment to promoting reform, and a willingness to put prestige and resources at stake to accomplish that goal. As Tony Smith has written, "No administration since Wilson's [was] as vigorous or as consistent in its dedication to the promotion of democracy abroad as that of Ronald Reagan."[55] Indeed, despite his early ambivalence, from 1982–1983 onward Reagan fully perceived the significance of the democratic revolution, and would use U.S. power to strengthen and propagate that trend. The administration would be enormously successful in doing so, although not without ironies, trade-offs, and frustrations along the way.

Anticommunism and Democracy in Central America

Nowhere were the legacies of Reagan's democratic campaign more contested than in Central America. The focus of U.S. policy in that region was on El Salvador and Nicaragua. In the former country, a Marxist insurgency that reached perhaps 12,000 full-time combatants and received support from Nicaragua, Cuba, and the Soviet bloc seemed dangerously close to overthrowing a narrowly based, deeply repressive political system.[56] In the latter, a Marxist-Leninist regime was consolidating itself at the expense of democratic actors following the 1979 revolution, while establishing close ties to Havana and Moscow and acting—as Sandinista leaders put it—as the "logistical center for the Salvadoran revolution."[57] Given the Cold War climate and the traditional salience of Central America to U.S. security, the Reagan administration viewed these developments with utmost concern. "For us," Kirkpatrick said, the region was "quite simply the most important place in the world."[58]

Reagan's approach to Central America mirrored the trajectory of his democracy-promotion efforts as a whole. In neither Nicaragua nor El Salvador was democracy initially a central aim of U.S. policy. The overriding goal in El Salvador was always to prevent another communist takeover in Central America, and at first the administration downplayed the need for political reforms and placed primary importance on helping the government defeat the FMLN militarily. "Revolutions . . . are caused not by social injustice," Kirkpatrick said; "revolutions are caused by revolutionaries."[59] In Nicaragua, the main objective was to alter that country's external behavior—its Eastern-bloc ties and support for the FMLN—rather than its internal arrangements, and Reagan was willing to pursue a diplomatic modus vivendi if these conditions were met. "The key consideration is that we want Nicaraguan support for the insurgents in El Salvador and the ability of Cuba to use Nicaraguan territory to stop and stay stopped," Haig wrote; the Sandinistas' domestic practices were secondary.[60]

In both cases, however, democracy soon became inextricably interwoven with U.S. geopolitical goals. Kirkpatrick's insights aside, by mid-1981 it was clear that the Salvadoran government desperately needed greater democratic legitimacy to avoid a total collapse of public support, and to win continued assistance from a rights-conscious U.S. Congress that was already imposing restrictions on American aid. "We need a carefully balanced and integrated strategy in which anti-insurgency and anti-Cuban efforts will be accompanied by prompt and decisive actions in the political and economic realms," U.S. officials wrote. The Salvadoran junta had to attack "the Breeding Ground of the Insurgency Virus" to preserve its standing at home and abroad.[61] In Nicaragua, meanwhile, the breakdown of a bilateral dialogue in late 1981, and the Sandinistas' refusal to halt arms shipments to the FMLN, encouraged the conclusion that *only* regime change could secure U.S. interests. "Nicaragua's anti-social regional behavior is after all a mere symptom of a deeper political disease," State Department official (and ambassador to neighboring Honduras) John Negroponte wrote; regional stability would be elusive if that disease went untreated.[62] By 1982, Reagan's policy was unmistakably—if not always publicly—oriented toward "restor[ing] freedom and democracy to Nicaragua," and administration officials would subsequently make the holding of competitive elections a key U.S. demand of the regime.[63] Throughout Central America, Reagan said, the United States was now seeking "to stop the advance of communism . . . by doing what Americans instinctively do best—supporting democracy."[64]

In El Salvador, the administration pursued a two-pronged strategy toward this end. First, Reagan poured economic and military aid into that country to strengthen its government and check the insurgency. El Salvador received over $4.5 billion in U.S. assistance during the 1980s, $1 billion of which went to bolstering the armed forces by giving them the training, equipment, and support needed to stem the FMLN onslaught. By mid-1984, U.S. aid had financed the training of 29,000 military personnel, creation of a modern intelligence system, and acquisition of trucks, helicopters, and other crucial supplies, and American advisers continually pushed Salvadoran officers to prosecute the war more vigorously. The short-term goal was to keep a fragile government from collapsing. Over the longer term, these measures would produce "strategic victory by destroying the insurgents' will and capability to fight."[65]

U.S. assistance would also provide "breathing space" for the second prong of Reagan's strategy—building lasting stability through political and socio-economic reform. U.S. officials urged the Salvadoran government to restrain the rampaging "death squads" that targeted anyone opposed to the status quo, to curb appalling rights violations by an abusive military, to proceed with agrarian reforms to benefit landless peasants, and to hold elections and liberalize the political system. The government "must make every effort to continue disciplining and controlling its troops and to reduce human rights abuses and also show continued progress on reforms," Haig told Salvadoran officials.[66] Over time, these measures would foster a viable democracy that could accommodate dissent and marginalize the FMLN politically, while U.S. economic and security assistance prevented the guerrillas from winning militarily. "Democracy is what we want," Reagan reiterated; the goal was to "enable Salvadorans to stop the killing and sabotage so that economic and political reforms can take root."[67]

From the outset, U.S. officials understood that achieving this goal would entail unavoidable moral compromises. Reagan's policy required interven-ing deeply in Salvadoran politics, to an extent that would have outraged Americans had the roles been reversed. More important, it impelled the United States to work hand-in-glove with the often-murderous Salvadoran military, in order to provide the climate of basic security in which liberalization could occur. This cooperation was deeply distasteful to many observers, but Reagan's aides insisted that there was no good alternative. For if Washington terminated aid or disengaged from El Salvador, the likely outcome would *not* be bloodless reform, but either an FMLN victory or a wave of right-wing repression by elites who now had no incentive to hold back. Shultz put it precisely: "In El Salvador, the United States is supporting moderates who believe in democracy and who are resisting the enemies of democracy on both the extreme right and the extreme left. If we withdrew our support, the moderates, caught in the crossfire would be the first victims—as would be the cause of human rights. . . . Anyone who believes that military support for our friends isn't crucial to a just outcome is living in a dream world."[68] Or, as Abrams said, "We must deal with countries as they are," not as they might ideally be.[69] The United States could promote democracy in El Salvador, but it had to be pragmatic about what this program necessitated.

During the early 1980s, this policy did produce real progress. U.S. aid prevented the disintegration of an already-battered economy, and American military assistance reinforced the Salvadoran military just enough to avert defeat. On the political side, persistent U.S. pressure bolstered an agrarian reform that, despite its many flaws, ultimately benefitted some 570,000 individuals and redistributed 22 percent of Salvadoran farmland.[70] Just as important, firm U.S. warnings helped dissuade right-wing extremists like Roberto D'Aubuisson from staging a coup and imposing what they ominously called an "Argentine solution."[71] A right-wing military takeover was unacceptable, U.S. ambassador Dean Hinton told D'Aubuisson; "the Civilian stamp should be firmly imprinted."[72] In consequence, El Salvador held elections—with strong U.S. support—in 1982 and 1984, in which the vast majority of eligible voters participated despite guerrilla death threats. The 1982 elections, one human rights group noted, constituted "a decisive defeat for those who rejected the electoral process," as they showed that democratization was taking root.[73]

The roots were shallow, however, and CIA officials admitted that "progress in El Salvador is a relative thing."[74] The administration had hoped that the 1982 polls would elect Christian Democratic Party (PDC) leader José Napoleón Duarte, a genuine reformer who, Shultz wrote, "exuded a sense of decency and human concern." Yet despite $2 million in U.S. funding, Duarte's PDC was beaten out by a coalition of conservative groups led by the Nationalist Republican Alliance (ARENA), a far-right party that represented the economic elite and that U.S. officials called "a terrorist network led by D'Aubuisson henchmen."[75] Frantic and crudely interventionist diplomatic maneuvering prevented D'Aubuisson from becoming provisional president, and forced ARENA into a unity government. Even so, that new government deemphasized and obstructed the agrarian reform (yielding only partially and under great U.S. pressure), military atrocities persisted at alarming levels, and the death squads continued to torture and murder political moderates—including PDC members—as well as thousands of actual and suspected guerrilla sympathizers. Hinton gave a blunt appraisal of the situation in a speech in San Salvador. "The 'Mafia' must be stopped," he said in reference to death-squad killings. "Your survival depends on it. The gorillas of the Mafia, every bit as much as the guerrillas of Morazán and Chalatenango, are destroying El Salvador."[76] The United States had helped initiate a democratic *process* in that country, but securing truly reformist and stabilizing *outcomes* was another thing entirely.

This setback, in turn, illustrated two deeper challenges for U.S. policy. The first was that although the dual prongs of Reagan's strategy were meant to be complementary, there was an inherent tension between them. There is no question that supporting the Salvadoran military was vital to preventing a regime collapse and thereby holding open the possibility of democratic reform. But because the military and its death-squad allies were the main *perpetrators* of human rights abuses, U.S. assistance also complicated prospects for liberalization by strengthening some of the most reactionary actors in Salvadoran society. Some American support probably found its way to brutal paramilitary groups, and even U.S.-trained army units committed unspeakable atrocities. More broadly, the majority of the 70,000–75,000 deaths in the civil war occurred in the early 1980s, with the preponderance caused by the U.S.-backed military and the death squads. The Marxist guerrillas "could be cruel terrorists," Shultz later wrote, but "so could the military forces of El Salvador." Moreover, because U.S. officials feared that widespread awareness of these atrocities might cause a congressional aid cut-off, they sometimes sought to obscure or downplay the horror. American aid was supposed to create breathing space for positive change, but in the hands of a repressive military and political leadership, it could have the opposite result.[77]

The most disturbing example of this dynamic was the "massacre at El Mozoté" in late 1981. The Atlacatl battalion, a U.S.-trained, rapid-response infantry unit, conducted a major operation in Morazán Department, near the village of El Mozoté. In the course of that operation, the battalion systematically massacred several hundred civilians who had taken refuge in the village and were suspected of being guerrilla sympathizers. Women old and young were raped; children and adults alike were shot, beheaded, bayoneted, and burned. It was the worst atrocity of the entire war, and one that Reagan's representatives were slippery at best in addressing. With an eye to a crucial upcoming report to Congress on human rights issues in El Salvador, State Department officials presented a vague and evasive account of what had happened, exaggerating the guerrilla presence in El Mozoté and denying that "government forces systematically massacred civilians in the operation zone." In the name of democracy and anticommunism, the U.S. government was, in essence, providing both training and political cover for the perpetrators of heinous crimes.[78]

This first problem of U.S. policy was closely related to a second, which was that the Reagan administration struggled mightily to find the leverage necessary to halt these practices. In theory, this should not have been so hard. The Salvadoran military and government were highly dependent on U.S. assistance; their very survival depended on it. But because Reagan continually stressed that an FMLN victory was intolerable, ARENA and the high command doubted that he would *ever* really terminate aid short of something so blatant as a coup. "Reagan will never let the Communists win here," said one conservative. "It's just a complete bluff."[79] This impression was reinforced by internal infighting among Reagan's advisers, and by unhelpful comments from hardliners such as Kirkpatrick. "Guerrillas win wars by violence," she told D'Aubuisson. "If the government loses militarily none of the other programs matter."[80] Such messages undoubtedly weakened the impetus to reform, and by late 1982 and early 1983, right-wing repression was combining with economic crisis and a renewed guerrilla onslaught to drive El Salvador ever closer to the abyss.

It would ultimately require intense U.S. pressure—executive and legislative alike—to turn the tide. By early and mid-1983, it was obvious that the lack of further progress on political issues might well lose the war, and that it would certainly lose any chance of securing the increased U.S. assistance needed to tip the balance decisively. Proposals to reduce or restrict aid were gaining strength in the House and Senate; criticism of continued repression and death-squad violence was reaching fever pitch. One Democratic representative called on Congress to use "every possible occasion to try to block funds for the Government of El Salvador." Even on the Republican side, key Senate staffers warned that "support for aid was likely to collapse" absent progress on key human rights issues.[81] "Reforms have a great impact on U.S. public opinion and our ability to obtain resources from the Congress," Shultz told Reagan, but the insufficiency of reform had placed those resource flows in grave jeopardy.[82]

The administration therefore made an all-out effort to persuade—or compel—the Salvadorans to change course. A new ambassador, Thomas Pickering, arrived in San Salvador with instructions to "raise hell" about human rights, which he did so vigorously that he was targeted for assassination by D'Aubuisson. U.S. officials issued a stream of urgent warnings about the need for rapid movement on political and social issues.[83] And in late 1983, Bush traveled to El Salvador with the starkest message yet. Without major reforms, he told the high command, "there is no prospect of victory." To keep U.S. support, the authorities must extend and preserve the agrarian reform, make judicial reforms, and punish rights violators. Above all, the military must "do all possible to support and protect the coming elections" in 1984, and the "entire government and particularly the security forces must take all steps required to end death squad activity." "We are at a critical crossroads," Bush said—the relationship, and war, hung in the balance.[84]

This message was reinforced, ironically, by congressional criticism of U.S. policy. Reagan and his aides deplored what they viewed as congressional meddling in El Salvador, which had indeed constrained U.S. support to date. Yet at this critical juncture, the threat of a congressional revolt—or simply a refusal to provide more aid—had salutary effects. It compelled the administration to give added force to its diplomacy; it also lent that diplomacy credibility in San Salvador. "This is no smoke screen. This is a reality," Bush said. "I know the views of the Senate and of the House of Representatives. All who support us know we cannot get done what must be done . . . if you are not able to help yourselves in this way."[85] This symbiotic executive and congressional pressure finally had the necessary impact. In January 1984, the CIA reported that "rightwing violence has been greatly reduced," albeit grudgingly, since December. Death-squad killings dropped, and some key human rights violators were arrested or fired. Crucially, the paramilitaries also largely stopped targeting the PDC, reducing the danger that blanket repression would drive moderates into an alliance with the guerrillas and thereby destroy El Salvador's fledgling democracy. Finally, although the agrarian reform was not extended to the degree U.S. officials desired, neither was it rolled back wholesale as some observers had feared. "A very constructive and excellent start has been made," Pickering observed.[86]

The decisive turning point came in early 1984, when Duarte triumphed in the aforementioned presidential election, again with intensive U.S support. Duarte's campaign received over $2 million in CIA funding, and U.S. officials made plain that an ARENA victory could wreck the relationship.[87] This was unembarrassed meddling, but it shifted the domestic balance. "The CIA . . . won the election here," the ARENA vice-presidential candidate remarked.[88] More important, the fact that Duarte's reform program had strong support from congressional Democrats finally convinced the military to permit liberalization as the surest guarantee of U.S. aid. Political killings fell dramatically, to twenty-two per month in 1986 (a sliver of the rate from 1981–1982), and military conduct improved significantly. "The human rights situation has improved dramatically and meaningfully," U.S.

diplomats reported.[89] Duarte was also able to conduct a controlled democratic opening, with political restrictions relaxed and generally fair elections
held. These measures, in turn, ensured that U.S. aid flowed more freely from
1984 onward, strengthening the Salvadoran armed forces. Admittedly, abuses
persisted, representative institutions remained weak, and the civil war dragged
on until 1992. But Duarte's ascension was vital to minimizing prospects of
a guerrilla victory and consolidating a system that, for all its flaws, was far
more pluralistic than before. "Viewed from the optic of 1979," wrote one
U.S. official, "the progress is nearly unbelievable."[90]

U.S. involvement was thus integral to the emergence of a more democratic El Salvador, as even some critics of that policy recognized.[91] Over
the course of the early and mid-1980s, U.S. efforts played a central role
in reducing rights violations and dissuading coups, strengthening moderates
and promoting reforms, and providing economic and military support that
kept the war from being lost in the interim. These accomplishments showed
the possibility of fruitful executive-legislative branch cooperation on issues
of human rights and democracy, and they demonstrated that it was indeed
possible to use liberalization as a salve for instability in conflict-torn societies. "El Salvador . . . is a model for the type of democratic change the U.S.
would like to see in Central America," Abrams said.[92] The lingering question,
of course, was whether this achievement was worth the costs and compromises it entailed: billions of dollars in aid, intrusive meddling in Salvadoran
affairs, and cooperation—even complicity—with a government and military
that were often savagely repressive toward their own citizens. As Shultz and
Abrams had asserted, these costs were probably the price of effectiveness in
an imperfect world. But they nonetheless showed that democracy promotion
could be a messy and morally ambiguous affair.

That went doubly for the intervention in Nicaragua. The primary tools
of U.S. policy toward Managua were the Contras, a motley crew of anti-
Sandinista insurgents that Reagan supported in hopes of undermining the
government and forcing it—either by overthrow or sustained pressure—to
permit pluralism and democratization.[93] Beginning in late 1981, the CIA
provided arms, supplies, and training to the guerrillas, and occasionally it
used its own assets to attack Nicaraguan targets. With U.S. support totaling
$322 million from 1981 to 1990, the Contras grew rapidly as a fighting force,
reaching 7,000 guerrillas in 1983 and 16,000 in 1985.[94] With U.S. encouragement and direction, the Contras also became more aggressive, attacking
sensitive infrastructure, ambushing Sandinista patrols and convoys, and striking deep into Nicaragua. Due to congressional restrictions, this activity was

not explicitly aimed at toppling the Sandinistas. But Reagan himself said that the Contras were meant to force Managua to "restore a democratic rule and have elections," and he believed that only "sharp pressure" would prevent "the consolidation of a totalitarian state allied with Cuba and the Soviet bloc."[95]

The Contras were only one means of generating that pressure. Large-scale U.S. military exercises and overflights increased the psychological strain on the Sandinistas. Reagan also waged economic warfare by blocking multi-lateral and private loans, slashing Nicaragua's sugar quota, and eventually imposing a trade embargo. This measure would "severely disrupt the economy . . . and cause generalized economic shortages, hardship and dislocations," U.S. analysts wrote.[96] Finally, from 1984 onward, there was a parallel campaign of political warfare via support to domestic critics of the regime. The NED provided funding for what remained of the independent press, assistance to nongovernmental trade unions, and backing for efforts to unite and strengthen the political opposition. "The NED is committed to this promotion of democratic institutions," Ambassador Anthony Quainton noted. "Nowhere are such institutions needed more than in Marxist Nicaragua." Although these activities cost only $5.6 million from 1984 to 1989, they helped fortify political resistance to Sandinista policies, and they assumed greater scope and importance as the 1980s progressed.[97]

If the United States pursued democracy via reform and stabilization in El Salvador, it thus sought democratization through coercion and *de*stabilization in Nicaragua. "Just as there is a classic formula for communist subversion and takeover, there is also a proven method of overthrowing repressive government that can be applied successfully in Nicaragua," Casey said.[98] In this struggle, there was no doubt where Reagan's heart was. The anti-Sandinista campaign fused Reagan's pro-democracy sentiments to his anticommunism, and the president described the conflict in Manichean terms. "The Sandinista rule is a Communist reign of terror," he alleged. "The Nicaraguan people are trapped in a totalitarian dungeon." The Contras, by contrast, were "freedom fighters," "the moral equal of our Founding Fathers." For Reagan, the Contra war was the epitome of a morally and strategically sound program of democracy promotion. "The struggle here is not right versus left; it is right versus wrong."[99]

The reality, unfortunately, was less straightforward. To be clear, the Sandinista government *was* a flawed and authoritarian regime. That regime was fueling the Salvadoran insurgency and forging strong links to the Soviet bloc; it was seeking to steer Nicaragua toward a one-party state through measures ranging from severe political restrictions to the use of imprisonment, torture, and "revolutionary terror"; and despite its initial popularity, it had a decidedly authoritarian allergy to seriously risking its power in fair elections. "The power of the people will never be gambled," military chief Humberto Ortega declared.[100] (The Sandinistas did hold elections in 1984, but even formerly sympathetic observers criticized the conditions.[101]) By mid-decade, the Sandinista regime was holding several thousand political prisoners, and had shown itself capable of many of the same abuses perpetrated by Somoza. The Contras, meanwhile, did start out as a group of former Somoza-era National Guardsmen, but the overwhelming majority of their later recruits were highland peasants, Miskito Indians, and other ordinary people resisting government repression. "All we are," said one guerrilla, "is a whole bunch of *really* pissed-off peasants." With strong U.S. urging, the insurgent leadership also became more democratic over time.[102] By the late 1980s, it was not wildly implausible to say, as Reagan did, that the Contras were "the real democratic alternative to the Sandinistas."[103]

The trouble, however, was that the pursuit of generally worthy ends could involve very dubious means. Particularly at the outset, the Contras engaged in thuggish or even terroristic practices, from raping and murdering Sandinista literacy teachers, to assassinating government officials, to extorting food and supplies from civilians, to torturing and killing prisoners captured in battle. There was "no time to carry on due process," one Contra spokesman explained. "You want to have answers very soon because otherwise you would be risking your own troops."[104] On balance, the Reagan administration discouraged these practices, which dropped off significantly over time. Yet there were nonetheless cases in which overzealous U.S. officials were part of the problem. In 1983, CIA operatives distributed a tactical manual that advocated murdering government officials. "The only way to defeat Communism is by using the same means, the same tactics," CIA officials advised.[105] Needless to say, such episodes undercut the moral clarity that Reagan invoked.

So did other aspects of U.S. policy. By supporting the Contras, Washington was not simply applying "sharp pressure" on the regime; it was fueling a civil war that inflicted hellish punishment on Nicaraguans. That war ultimately caused 30,000–35,000 deaths, and massive economic damage, in a country that had never recovered from the trauma of the anti-Somoza revolt. And within the United States, the imperatives of funding the war amid growing congressional opposition eventually led to downright felonious behavior that challenged the system of checks and balances underpinning *American* democracy. Supporters of Reagan's policy insisted that these measures were vital to maintaining pressure and keeping the Contras active, both of which were essential to democratization in Nicaragua. Even so, they showed—as in El Salvador—that the costs of democracy promotion could be quite high.

For much of Reagan's presidency, in fact, the payoff was only a bloody stalemate. U.S. assistance made the Contras a larger and more capable fighting force, one that could not be eliminated by the Sandinista army. Yet neither could the Contras defeat the Sandinistas, and as U.S. officials reported in 1983, the insurgency did not "yet pose a serious threat" to regime survival.[106] With the level of U.S. support constrained by congressional opposition, and with Moscow and Havana readily resupplying Managua with military and economic aid, the war appeared likely to drag on indefinitely. James Baker, a top Reagan aide, termed the Contra war "our country's Vietnam of the 1980s," and State Department adviser Cresencio Arcos predicted that the administration's approach "will give you nothing but attrition in the end."[107]

Attrition worked both ways, however, and although the Contras could not defeat the government, they did put it under mounting duress. War and sanctions wrecked the economy, costing perhaps $12 billion in damage in a nation whose GNP was only $2 billion annually. "The contras are doing about as well as can be expected," wrote NSC staffer Robert Pastorino, "not great; but it apparently doesn't take much to disrupt the feeble economy and infrastructure of Nicaragua."[108] The insurgency (and NED support) also energized the political opposition, while fomenting a state of perpetual insecurity that was bound to take its toll. Sure enough, the war induced the Sandinistas to take politically costly measures, from forcibly relocating peasants, to severely restricting political freedoms, to enforcing a highly unpopular draft. By the mid- and late 1980s, U.S. and Contra pressure—when combined with the authoritarianism and mistakes of the regime itself—was putting the Sandinistas in a precarious spot. "The social basis of the revolution" was fraying, Comandante Bayardo Arce admitted; "the destabilization of the country" threatened.[109]

This intensifying strain was crucial to the political opening that occurred in the late 1980s. By late 1986–1987, the Contras had seized the military initiative, keeping up to 6,000 fighters on Nicaraguan soil, contesting control of perhaps 60 percent of the country, and mounting a crescendo of attacks that ravaged infrastructure and overextended Sandinista forces. The guerrillas were waging "an increasingly successful and widespread campaign of attacks, ambushes, and sabotage," CIA analysts wrote, and the impact was combining with Sandinista mismanagement to keep the economy "on a bare survival footing."[110] "The economy was on zero," one Sandinista leader recalled, as inflation hit 33,600 percent in 1988, and growth plummeted by 15 percent.[111] Sandinista officials increasingly believed that "their very survival depended on ending the *contra* war," and thereby easing the insecurity, privation, and political agitation it had fostered. As leading analysts concur, this desperation was the "main reason" the regime eventually accepted what it had long resisted—liberalizing the political system, easing curbs on the opposition, and holding genuinely competitive elections—as the cost of ending the conflict.[112]

Reagan could not take full credit for this outcome, though, because U.S. pressure alone would not have forced the Sandinistas to risk the revolution at the polls. Their decision to do so was also due to the collapse of Soviet power, which eroded Eastern-bloc support for Nicaragua and made it imperative to seek greater international legitimacy. More important, it reflected the fact that by 1987–1988 two important influences made an electoral opening look more attractive. There was the Central American peace process, which had taken root despite Reagan's opposition to negotiating with Managua, and which created a path to peace for the Sandinistas if they restored pluralism and moderated their foreign policy. And, paradoxically, there were also key political changes in Washington—ebbing congressional support for the war after Iran-Contra, and Reagan's approaching departure from office—that convinced Nicaraguan leaders that a clean electoral victory might let them escape U.S. pressure once and for all. "We will win this war in Washington," the Sandinista directorate predicted; they would "leave the counterrevolution without resources."[113] Reagan's policy lent the stick that was essential to forcing the regime toward liberalization, but other factors provided the carrot that was also crucial.

When the elections occurred in February 1990, U.S. policy *did* help ensure that the Sandinistas suffered a surprising and resounding defeat. This was most true in the sense that the economic and other deprivations caused by the war had badly undermined Sandinista popularity, and convinced many voters that evicting the incumbent regime was the best guarantee of a better life.[114] It was also true in that the Bush administration coordinated with other international observers to exert pressure for a genuinely fair election, while USAID and the NED committed $9 million to bolstering the opposition coalition. "The whole thrust of this program is to help the opposition coalesce and overcome their historical differences and develop a national political structure with a view to getting their message into all corners of Nicaragua," NED officials explained. This money funded get-out-the-vote projects, training for legions of poll-watchers to deter fraud, programs to improve coordination among the diverse elements of the anti-Sandinista coalition, and support for opinion surveys and the development of electoral and media strategies—all of which strengthened the opposition cause, and contributed to the government's defeat.[115]

As in El Salvador, then, the use of U.S. power was indispensable to democratization in Nicaragua. And as in El Salvador, there was no shortage of ambiguity in an achievement that had to be weighed against undeniably heavy costs: the catastrophic damage inflicted on Nicaragua and its citizens, for instance, or the transgressions against democratic procedures in the United States. For critics, those costs and ambiguities loomed larger than the accomplishments. For most American officials, by contrast, the conflicts in Nicaragua and El Salvador were seen as crucial battles, and ultimately key victories, in the advancing democratic revolution. During the 1980s, in fact, U.S. policy was doing a great deal to strengthen that revolution, not just in El Salvador and Nicaragua, but across much of Latin America as a whole.

A Historic Opening in Latin America

Latin America was frequently a bellwether for the international shifts of the 1970s and 1980s. As I discuss in chapter 4, it was at the forefront of the neoliberal revolution taking the Third World by storm. It was also at the vanguard of the global democratic trend. From 1977 to 1990, sixteen Latin American or Caribbean nations, including nearly all of Central and South America, made or began transitions from dictatorship to democracy.[116] These changes constituted a remarkably broad and rapid transformation, which was particularly striking given how dictatorial the regional political makeup had been just a short time prior. The 1980s would be "recorded in history as a great democratic awakening in the Americas," Reagan said in 1987. "The dominance of democracy in Latin America has fundamentally altered the hemisphere."[117]

In Latin America as elsewhere, the impetus to democratization was usually primarily internal rather than external,[118] and the level of U.S. support for the process varied considerably. As noted previously, the early indifference of the Reagan administration to democracy and human rights may initially have set back prospects for liberalization in some instances, and U.S. policy played virtually no role in consummating ongoing transitions in countries such as Uruguay and Brazil during the early 1980s. In Argentina, too, Reagan had first sought reconciliation with a repressive regime, and he contributed to the democratic opening of 1982–1983 only in unintended ways. In particular, the nascent rapprochement with Buenos Aires—which included a covert partnership to support the Contras—encouraged an increasingly unpopular junta to launch its disastrous invasion of the Falkland Islands, by raising hopes for U.S. support in the crisis that would inevitably follow. In the event, however, Reagan sided with the British, causing the Argentine generals to claim that they had "been stabbed in the back," and ensuring that the junta was so humiliated that a return to the barracks was unavoidable.[119] At best, this was a case of democracy promotion by misperception.

In most cases, however, U.S. involvement was more deliberate and proactive, and Latin America was where U.S. democracy-promotion efforts were ultimately strongest and most effective. Reagan's intensifying commitment to liberalization in Latin America reflected all the same factors that motivated his broader shift on democracy and human rights, as well as some that were more focused on the region itself. There was, for instance, a strong conviction that greater political freedom would reinforce the economic liberalization in train in many Latin American countries.[120] There was also a spillover effect from U.S. involvement in Central America. On the diplomatic front, Reagan's demands for democracy in Nicaragua made it harder to ignore that issue vis-à-vis authoritarian allies on the right. "To get more help" from Latin American countries on Nicaragua, one NSC aide wrote, "We had to be more visible about Chile."[121] At the same time, progress in El Salvador bolstered the idea that liberalization represented the path to lasting stability, and defeated a venerable argument against breaking with authoritarian allies. "Our problem is to do all we can so that democracy takes root and stays," Shultz said. "Democracy is the best insurance we can have against efforts there from the USSR."[122]

More broadly still, Reagan's activism flowed from recognition that Latin America was where the democratic advance had greatest momentum, and that Washington's strong influence in the region provided a golden opportunity to support the trend. "Because the democratic aspirations of the citizens of this region have resulted in a wealth of new democracies," one interagency review concluded, "it is the most obvious place to begin this work."[123] Reagan was even more ambitious. "I have a vision of a democratic Western Hemisphere," he told the NSC, "from the Tierra del Fuego to the North Pole."[124] And near the close of Reagan's presidency, Abrams explained, with only slight exaggeration, that the essence of U.S. policy had been to align U.S. power with the regional transformation at work: "An extraordinary development has unfolded during the Reagan years. A democratic revolution is underway. One country after another has joined the ranks of democratic states. . . . Here was a rare opportunity for American statecraft to respond to a historic opening as it was happening. We in the Reagan Administration gave it our full support."[125]

One way the administration did so was by emulating the Carter-era tactic of interceding at key moments to safeguard fragile transitions. If the Reagan Doctrine entailed promoting "pro-democracy/anti-communist revolution,"

U.S. officials wrote, the corollary was "an activist policy . . . on behalf of democratic consolidation once democracy is won."[126] Following the return of Argentina to democracy in 1983, for instance, the administration sided firmly with the elected government of Raúl Alfonsín during attempted military rebellions in 1987–1988.[127] This intervention had very marginal concrete effects, but it did illustrate good-faith efforts to implement what Frank Carlucci called "the mirror image of the Brezhnev Doctrine": a policy that "insures the irreversibility of democracy gains" by preventing nascent democracies from being waylaid.[128] Abrams underscored U.S. determination on this score in his dealings with Latin American militaries and other regional audiences. "The Reagan administration . . . is 100 percent in favor of electoral democracy in Latin America," he said, "and wants nothing to do with the overthrow of democratic governments by the military."[129]

This was more than rhetoric: several times U.S. policy served as a firewall against authoritarian backsliding. In Peru, strained relations with President Alan García did not prevent American diplomats from forcefully discouraging coups by disgruntled military officers who were counting on U.S. support. In April 1987, embassy officials reported that "we got several feelers about U.S. reaction to a coup . . . in the last ten days of March. We made our opposition clear in each case."[130] In January 1989, another coup was seemingly in the making, and the plotters again sought U.S. endorsement. As before, the response was unequivocal. "From the Ambassador down, American diplomats put out the message that . . . a coup would bring isolation, even from the international financial community," one Western diplomat noted, and face-to-face meetings with military leaders hammered the theme home. These warnings apparently quashed hopes that the coup would be welcomed abroad, and undermined military enthusiasm for the idea.[131]

U.S. policy had similar impact in Bolivia. Due to concerns about the role of the military in drug trafficking, Reagan had never sought rapprochement with that junta. Instead, Ambassador Edwin Corr labored to facilitate a democratic transition by mediating between political groups and reminding the generals that improved relations with Washington required a political opening. Once that opening began, with the choosing of a civilian president (Hernán Siles Zuazo), Corr worked tenaciously to protect it. He and the U.S. military liaison office used their contacts to quietly but firmly restrain incipient coup plotting. When renegade officers did nevertheless kidnap Siles Zuazo in 1984, Corr "telephoned military commands and political leaders around the country telling them that the embassy, and Washington, would oppose any attempt to overthrow the civilian government." Given Bolivia's need for economic assistance and the fact that the plotters had earlier claimed to have U.S. backing, these efforts helped in securing the president's release, and in allowing Bolivia make a peaceful democratic transition for the first time in decades.[132]

Shaky transitions in Central America also benefitted from U.S. support. In Guatemala, the Reagan administration had little direct impact on the controlled liberalization undertaken at mid-decade. But it did later fortify that process through aid that helped keep the economy afloat, and through efforts—including quiet mediation, public statements of support, and threats of an aid cut-off should democratic rule be interrupted—to head off coup threats. In Honduras, U.S. policy promoted the same ends. The massive expansion of American military aid during the Contra war did strengthen the often-repressive armed forces, as critics pointed out. Yet U.S. diplomats also used the leverage that aid conferred to encourage democratic elections in 1981, discourage human rights abuses, and thwart efforts by the newly chosen president to postpone subsequent elections. USAID technical assistance was equally crucial to national elections in 1985, and the embassy preempted concerns that the military might dispute the outcome of that vote by quickly embracing the rightful victor. Along the way, infusions of up to $230 million in annual economic aid helped sustain the struggling Honduran economy and strengthen its fledgling civilian government.[133] In several cases, then, the United States gave impetus to the democratic movement by playing "catcher in the rye, preventing young democracies from falling off the cliff."[134]

Washington was simultaneously helping *initiate* democratic transitions by supporting reformers and undermining long-tenured authoritarian regimes. In Haiti, for example, Reagan hastened the end of the Duvalier dynasty by withdrawing long-standing U.S. backing at a critical time. Amid widespread protests and upheaval in early 1986, the administration declared Haiti out of compliance with human rights conditions attached to its aid allotment, and Shultz announced that Washington wanted a government "that is put there by the democratic process." This statement came just as Jean-Claude Duvalier was wavering between repression and resignation, and the realization that "the United States no longer wanted him in power" helped tip the balance.[135] The United States arranged Duvalier's exit, and sought via economic aid and other measures to encourage elections and "set Haiti on a path toward a true democracy."[136] That path would be incredibly tortuous over the next three decades, but Haiti still stood as an instance in which U.S. power helped rupture a creaking authoritarian system and create an opening for liberalization.

Alfredo Stroessner of Paraguay also had good cause to rue American meddling. Stroessner, an aging strongman with impeccable anticommunist credentials, had long benefitted from the prestige that U.S. support provided. But by the mid-1980s, Reagan was turning on the dictator. In 1985, he publicly called Paraguay "one of Latin America's remaining dictatorships." The NED began supporting independent political groups and the sole antigovernment radio station, and Ambassador Claude Taylor energetically engaged civil society groups and critiqued Stroessner's rule. "We believe that democracy is the best defense against instability," Taylor remarked. "We believe that essential to this policy is respect for human rights." Reagan subsequently increased the pressure by suspending Paraguay's access to the Generalized System of Preferences (GSP), and U.S. envoys were soon meeting conspicuously with opposition leaders and reform-minded generals. The implication was not lost on Stroessner. Paraguayan police at one point tear-gassed a meeting of women's groups hosted by Taylor, and the ambassador was regularly threatened with expulsion or violence.[137]

These U.S. initiatives might not have mattered had there not already been growing dissatisfaction with Stroessner's rule. But as the dissatisfaction mounted, U.S. policy had a compounding effect. It emboldened opposition leaders and forced Stroessner to lift a state of siege long used to muzzle dissent. Revoking Paraguay's access to GSP also resonated, showing business and political elites the economic costs of authoritarianism. Perhaps most important, U.S. pressure undercut one of Stroessner's long-standing political advantages—his ability to point to American support for his regime. The U.S. connection was traditionally "a pillar of his regime's legitimacy," two scholars write, but that pillar had now crumbled. Finally, when Frederick Woerner, the head of U.S. Southern Command, met with suspected military reformers in late 1988, he unmistakably implied that a change of government would ease Paraguay's isolation. When those military reformers did unseat Stroessner in early 1989, the State Department openly supported the new regime as it moved toward democratic elections. U.S. policy, one assessment concludes, was thus "an important factor, not only in the deteriorating image and growing isolation of the regime, but also in its ultimate collapse."[138]

The concurrent struggle for democracy in Chile represented a more difficult case. Carter's human rights efforts during the late 1970s had only a slight impact on prospects for political liberalization, and Reagan initially seemed unlikely to do better. The president had long applauded Augusto Pinochet's anticommunism and criticized those who acted "as if Fascism has been imposed on the Chileans."[139] Reagan also admired Chile's free-market reforms, and well into the mid-1980s, he hesitated to break with the dictator. "He saved his country," Reagan told the NSC.[140] As a result, the administration first sought to reconcile with Santiago, and even as democracy promotion became more important to Reagan's policies, U.S. officials in Chile pursued that objective very tepidly. James Theberge, Reagan's ambassador during the early 1980s, was so close to Pinochet that Chileans dubbed him the junta's "fifth man."[141]

As in so many cases, however, Reagan's policy evolved so much that it became almost unrecognizable. This was partially due to congressional agitation. Congressional democrats such as Harkin and Kennedy contested Reagan's early overtures to Pinochet, blocking attempts to resume unconditional military aid and decrying the "cynicism and hypocrisy" of U.S. policy. Throughout the 1980s, congressional activists would hold hearings that shined light on Pinochet's abuses, and they sought to enact more punitive measures—particularly economic sanctions—absent liberalization. "Chile is going to become a major issue in the Congress, unless there are significant changes," State Department officials warned. Within the administration, this threat served as a consistent impetus to stronger human rights and democracy-promotion measures, so as to preserve some cooperation with congressional critics, and prevent them from seizing control of Chile policy altogether.[142]

Beyond congressional pressure, however, there were also geopolitical matters driving Reagan's shift. There was an obvious diplomatic connection between Chile and Central America, in that Reagan could hardly rally regional opposition to authoritarianism in Nicaragua while ignoring it in Chile.[143] More fundamentally, Reagan's shift reflected growing concerns that if Pinochet clung to power indefinitely—and the authoritarian Chilean constitution of 1980 allowed him potentially to stay until 1997—he would polarize the country and drive the moderate opposition into an alliance with the Communist Party and leftist guerrillas armed by Havana and Moscow. This fear was exacerbated by events in 1983. Amid a disastrous economic contraction and public unrest, Pinochet ordered 18,000 troops into the streets, resulting in mass arrests, hundreds of injuries, and dozens of deaths.[144] The CIA reported that "only agreement on hastening the democratic opening will avoid radicalization and polarization." Shultz agreed: "There is a growing tension between our national interest in an orderly and peaceful process and Pinochet's apparent desire to hang on indefinitely."[145]

Beginning in 1983–84, the administration gradually began taking steps to induce liberalization. Shultz fired a shot across the bow by declaring that amid the "fever of democracy," Chile was "sticking out like a sore thumb."[146] The administration backed up this criticism with economic pressure, as in 1985, when U.S. diplomats won the lifting of Chile's draconian state of siege as the price of a crucial World Bank loan.[147] Simultaneously, U.S. officials and NED representatives broadened their contacts with the opposition, urging moderates to break with the radical left, abandon polarizing tactics, and present a united front in favor of an orderly transition to democracy.[148] The goal of all this was not to force an open break with Pinochet, but to push him to accept real negotiation and reform. The idea, State Department officials had written, was to "support and help ensure the legitimacy of the dialogue process and to encourage and strengthen moderates on both sides."[149]

These measures did force tactical concessions from Pinochet, and they eventually helped unify the opposition and discourage it from ties with the communists.[150] Yet Pinochet remained entrenched in power, and by 1986 U.S. officials were forecasting a grim and violent future if he stayed. "We need to be willing to rock him a little," Shultz told the NSC. "We have to use some muscle, or he won't change."[151] From 1986 onward, U.S. pressure steadily grew. In Congress, Kennedy and his allies introduced harsh sanctions legislation that, among other things, would have barred imports of Chilean copper. While opposing this particular measure, the administration took steps of its own. A new ambassador, Harry Barnes, forcefully criticized the regime and infuriated Pinochet by attending the funeral of a teenager who had been murdered by security personnel. (Chilean hardliners thereafter spread a rumor "that when Barnes left Chile, it would be in a six-foot box."[152]) U.S. representatives abstained from voting on international loans to Santiago; Reagan suspended Chile from GSP and canceled insurance for American private investment. NED activities in Chile increased, and U.S. diplomats visibly courted opposition figures and military reformers. "We are intensifying efforts to identify the USG [U.S. government] with a peaceful, orderly return to full democracy, and where useful to back up our rhetoric with effective action," Abrams and other officials wrote.[153]

The focal point of this campaign was the 1988 plebiscite, held in accordance with Pinochet's own constitution, on whether he should remain in power. Seeing the vote as the best change for peaceful change, U.S. officials worked to empower the opposition's "No" campaign, and to make the playing field as level as possible. "Without outside pressure," wrote State Department officials, "this plebiscite will likely be carried out under undemocratic circumstances geared to obtain a Pinochet victory."[154] The administration used the threat of blocking crucial loans to ensure that the opposition had access to Chilean media, and that Pinochet lifted key restrictions on political activity. NED money funded the training of thousands of election observers, and supported an independent "quick count" meant to prevent fraud. The endowment also sponsored programs to assist the "No" with polling, electoral, and media strategies, and funded a hugely successful voter-registration campaign aimed at anti-Pinochet voters. "We literally organized Chile as we organize elections in precincts anywhere in the United States," one NED consultant said.[155] And prior to the vote, the State Department firmly warned the Chilean government that violence, intimidation, or fraud would cause "the greatest possible disaster" for its relations with the democratic world.[156]

These efforts demonstrated the extent to which Washington had broken with Pinochet and sided with the democratic opposition. They also showed how administration and congressional initiatives were increasingly working in tandem. Through Reagan's second term, there had been sharp disagreements between presidential aides and congressional officials on how hard and fast to push for change in Chile. But as the plebiscite neared, Shultz's State Department seized on congressional opposition to Pinochet as an additional lever in dealing with the regime. U.S. diplomats coordinated visits of representatives and senators who met with the opposition and who, in one case, bluntly told Pinochet that "without a rapid transition to democracy . . . efforts in Congress to impose punitive economic sanctions could not be resisted." In his own meetings with Chilean elites, Barnes warned that Congress might impose such sanctions even if Pinochet won under fair conditions.[157] As had been the case in El Salvador, executive- and legislative-branch efforts were coming into greater alignment, thereby augmenting pressures for change.

This coordinated, multifaceted U.S. campaign was not *primarily* responsible for Pinochet's defeat in the plebiscite in October 1988, or for Chile's return to democracy more broadly. But insofar as Washington *could* influence Chilean affairs, U.S. policy had real impact. U.S. intervention was important in strengthening and unifying the opposition, forcing the regime to hold the plebiscite in a relatively fair climate, and apparently in deterring at least one scheme to disrupt the voting with violence.[158] And, in general, U.S. diplomacy from the mid-1980s onward significantly increased the strains on Pinochet. It helped delegitimize the dictator internationally, bolstered the forces struggling against him, and brought home to observers both inside and outside the regime that continued authoritarianism would cause only ostracism for Chile. Pinochet himself grasped the impact of U.S. policy: he blasted the "'great country to the north' for attacking Chile, for providing the opposition with 'millions of dollars,' and for sending a 'messenger [Barnes] who did nothing but propagandize against the government.'"[159] As Pinochet understood, the Reagan administration had joined the forces of change and contributed to the demise of the regime.

What was ultimately the most dramatic case of U.S. democracy promotion in Latin America came at the very close of the decade, and occurred not under Reagan but under his successor. The invasion of Panama in December 1989 was not principally about democracy; it was about strongman Manuel

Noriega's drug trafficking, and his proclivity to foment violence against U.S. forces and civilians in the Canal Zone. Yet Noriega's authoritarian proclivities, especially his suppression of elections in May 1989, added to the bill of particulars. "The real question is this," Secretary of State James Baker said: "Will the political destiny of Panama be determined by the will of the Panamanian people or by the force of a rifle butt?"[160] When U.S. troops invaded, they not only arrested Noriega but also installed the democratic leaders who had been robbed of victory in the May elections. "We have to get Noriega out," Bush said, "and we hope to promote the institutions of a democratic government."[161] Indeed, although many Latin American leaders deplored this military intervention, it was presumably the restoration of democracy that appealed to the 92 percent of Panamanians who supported it. The operation was "more a liberation than an invasion," Panama's new president said. "Without U.S. help, we couldn't have done it ourselves."[162]

"A legacy of democratic consolidation in this hemisphere," one interagency study from the late 1980s noted, "could be one of this Administration's most enduring accomplishments."[163] Self-congratulation aside, this assessment was not half-wrong. Over the course of the decade, the application of U.S. influence was a key ingredient—if usually a supporting one—in strengthening reformers, undermining dictators, and keeping transitions on track. The result was to add force to a democratic trend that was already quite vibrant, and to help foster a regional environment in which democracy was increasingly the norm. There remained valid concerns about the *depth* of Latin American democracy, and as we will see, political reforms were frequently not accompanied by equally progressive socioeconomic changes. Yet the progress of the 1980s was still remarkable, and U.S. statecraft was a crucial reason why. As Abrams might have phrased it, American engagement helped ensure that a "historic opening" did not go to waste.

From Authoritarian to Democratic Stability in East Asia

There was also a historic opening occurring in East Asia. The liberalizing currents in that region were not as powerful as in Latin America, and in many cases, Reagan was content to coexist with cooperative authoritarians. But contrary to stereotypes about the incompatibility of liberalism and Asian political cultures, strong democratic movements did take hold in a few countries, most notably the Philippines and South Korea. In neither case were U.S. officials initially eager to challenge dictatorships that were also longtime allies, and in the Philippines particularly, Reagan himself remained ambivalent nearly to the end. In both cases, however, the administration eventually identified itself strongly with pro-democratic forces. By doing so, it confirmed that the United States was now embracing democratization—rather than repression—as the route to lasting stability, and it helped ensure that promising windows were not slammed shut.

Making that shift was most difficult in the Philippines, a key strategic outpost that had hosted U.S. air and naval bases for decades. Precisely for this reason, U.S. officials had protested only meekly from the early 1970s onward as Ferdinand Marcos steered that country into a corrupt, repressive dictatorship. The Carter administration downgraded its human rights campaign to secure continued basing rights, and Reagan originally saw no reason to change course.[164] The president had great respect for Marcos's anticommunism, and amid an intensifying Cold War, he had no inclination to weaken America's Pacific flank. When Bush visited Manila on Reagan's behalf in 1981, he thus toasted Marcos in words that clearly downplayed the need for reform. "We will not leave you in isolation to the degree we have any vibrant strength," he promised—"it would be turning our backs on history if we did." Similarly, Reagan hosted Marcos and his wife in Washington in 1982—"I think they will go home reassured and confident of our friendship," he wrote—and aid to the Philippines nearly doubled, to $900 million over five years, during his first term.[165]

Reagan's sympathy for Marcos would persist, but this policy proved difficult to sustain. The political pressures were building in the Philippines, as stagnation, corruption, and repression fueled upheaval. Rural Filipinos were gravitating toward the communist New People's Army (NPA), which by the early 1980s boasted over 6,000 members and was operating in two-thirds of the country's seventy-three provinces. The insurgency, U.S. officials wrote, had "systematically exploited various grievances ranging from corruption, to ineffectiveness of local officials, to military abuse to government neglect of economic needs."[166] Likewise, moderates and the middle class were growing frustrated with weak economic prospects and the strangulation of democratic politics. This simmering discontent exploded into mass outrage in 1983, when military leaders had opposition leader Benigno Aquino murdered upon his return from exile in the United States. "Marcos may remain firmly in control for some time," Ambassador Michael Armacost wrote. "But I doubt that he will ever regain the public confidence and respect he formerly enjoyed."[167]

The potential for destabilization in the Philippines intersected with changing attitudes in Washington. Reagan was facing rising congressional criticism over his partnership with Marcos, particularly from liberals such as Solarz. The New York Democrat had urged political reforms in the Philippines even before the assassination, and warned that U.S. policy was undercutting American ideals and interests alike. After Aquino's murder, Solarz used his position on the House Foreign Affairs Committee to begin restricting military (but not economic) aid, to investigate the dictator's corruption, and to pressure Reagan and Marcos alike. "If calling for the restoration of democracy and free elections in the Philippines constitutes interference in his internal affairs, then I plead guilty," Solarz said.[168]

This advocacy provided an incentive for a more forward-leaning stance on liberalization, as did key geopolitical factors. Officials such as Armacost, Stephen Bosworth (Armacost's replacement), and Assistant Secretary of State Paul Wolfowitz were now worried that U.S. policy was fomenting anti-Americanism among Filipinos. These and other advisers also warned that continued repression would foster radicalization and perhaps revolution. There were "indications of serious instability," Robert Gates noted in 1984. "Politically, the breach between the Marcos regime and the majority of Filipinos is deep and probably irreversible."[169] Planning documents were soon stating that it was not change per se but rather persistent authoritarianism that threatened U.S. "vital interests in the Philippines," and that this country "must be a stable, democratically-oriented ally as a radicalized Philippines could destabilize the entire region."[170]

There thus began a cautious shift in U.S. policy. Reagan publicly stated that there would be no abandoning the Marcoses, no "throwing them to the wolves and then facing a Communist power in the Pacific."[171] But the administration, led by State, did begin seeking to use U.S. influence as Marcos's patron to induce a process of reform from above. In April 1983, Wolfowitz had urged Marcos to prove "that the Philippines is sensitive to the human rights concerns expressed in the democracies of the West."[172] U.S. diplomats subsequently pressed for competitive parliamentary elections, freer rein for the media and opposition, and economic reforms to complement a political opening. The administration hinted that it would be hard to sustain U.S. aid without such reforms, but promised "significantly enhanced bilateral and multilateral economic assistance" if changes occurred. Meanwhile, Bosworth publicly endorsed the goal of creating "functioning pluralistic democracies" in countries such as the Philippines. He also broadened U.S. contacts with opposition forces, as NED funds paid for programs to strengthen trade unions, civic groups, and independent parties.[173] The goal, a key directive reiterated in 1985, was "*not* promoting the dismantling of institutions that support stability—as occurred in Nicaragua during the collapse of the Somoza regime. Our goal is orderly succession that leads to a stable transition."[174]

This carrot-and-stick policy helped temper congressional pressure for a sharper break with Marcos, and convinced him to hold fairer-than-usual parliamentary elections in 1984. (After the opposition scored major gains, Marcos said, "Our instructions to our people to allow the opposition to win some seats might have been taken too literally."[175]) Yet it did not alter his essential authoritarianism, or his desire to remain in power indefinitely. In fact, Marcos interpreted Reagan's often-sympathetic statements as evidence that the president would back him in the end, which significantly decreased the pressure for reform. In late 1985, Marcos outraged domestic and foreign observers by indicating that he would reinstate the general who had allegedly planned Aquino's murder, and the continuing corruption, intransigence, and incompetence of his regime drove the internal situation steadily downward. "A communist takeover is a distinct possibility," Reagan feared.[176]

This threat, combined with renewed congressional pressure, compelled a more active approach. In October, Reagan sent a close friend, Senator Paul Laxalt, to deliver a firm message to Marcos. Laxalt urged major reforms of the military and electoral system, and said that rapid changes were imperative. "The very obvious bottom line of the Senator's mission," Bosworth recorded, "was that we want to be able to continue to work with Marcos, but he must produce early and fairly dramatic accomplishments if we are to avoid crippling political developments in the U.S."[177] Marcos dodged some of Laxalt's prescriptions, but the visit did cause him to call snap presidential elections for February 1986 in a bid to catch the opposition flat-footed and win a victory that would provide democratic legitimacy. "Unless the leopard has changed his spots," Wolfowitz wrote, "Marcos plans to use the vehicle of the democratic electoral process, which his supporters will manipulate to the extent necessary to ensure victory, in order to fend off critics at home and in the U.S."[178]

For U.S. officials, the election presented both threat and opportunity. "If Marcos goes ahead with election fraud, we will be facing a disaster in the Philippines," Wolfowitz wrote, for violence and tumult would follow. If the election was fair, however, whatever government emerged might have the legitimacy to "halt the political and economic downturn, re-energize the military, and turn around the escalating communist insurgency."[179] The State Department therefore worked to improve the ability of the opposition (now led by Corazon Aquino, Benigno's widow) to compete, and to prevent Marcos from stealing the vote. U.S. diplomats turned Marcos's electoral strategy against him by stressing that only a truly clean election would restore his international standing, and they prodded him to relax controls on to the opposition. Reagan also sent observers led by Senator Richard Lugar to monitor the voting, and U.S. money funded Filipino election-monitoring groups as well.[180] In January, Bosworth publicly created distance from Marcos by stating that Washington would work with any democratically elected government. And just before the voting, Reagan stated that fair elections were vital to the increased aid that Manila needed, and to thwarting the deepening polarization. "The Communist strategy can be defeated," he said, "but defeating it will require listening to and respecting the sovereign voice of the people."[181]

Unfortunately, the leopard had not changed his spots, and Marcos attempted, via fraud, violence, and intimidation, to steal a victory during and after the voting on February 7. His machinations, however, were detected immediately by the robust monitoring presence that U.S. policy had enabled.[182] The result was first a tense standoff, with both sides claiming victory, and then the launching of mass popular protests. Amid growing fears that Marcos would order a bloody crackdown, the military splintered. Units and key commanders defected to the opposition, taking several key government installations and engaging in sporadic combat with loyalist troops. The Philippines stood at the brink—of either an inspiring democratic breakthrough, or a brutal and radicalizing relapse.

This was a defining moment for U.S. policy, and Reagan initially failed to rise to the occasion. Although the president sincerely wanted democracy in the Philippines, he had apparently hoped that Marcos would win a relatively fair election, thereby sparing Washington the pain of choosing between an old ally and true reform. When this scenario did not come to pass, Reagan wavered. Influenced by reports of Aquino's inexperience, and still hesitant to abandon Marcos, the president gave a press conference in which he retreated from his new policy to his old one. He speculated that fraud had occurred "on both sides," and characterized the overriding U.S. interest as maintaining basing access.[183] The comments were widely interpreted as being pro-Marcos, and earned rebuttals from an impressive array of critics: liberals and conservatives in Congress; Shultz and other State Department officials; the president's own electoral observers; and not least Aquino herself, who acidly wondered "at the motives of a friend of democracy who chose to conspire with Mr. Marcos to cheat the Filipino people of their liberation."[184] With Reagan hesitating, the House Foreign Affairs Committee took initial steps toward terminating military aid, and Solarz opined that the president's comments were "proof positive that they are smoking marijuana in the White House."[185]

As the crisis intensified, however, U.S. policy became firmer and more decisive. Shultz reminded Reagan that Marcos could no longer ensure stability, and that if he clung to power he would only "destroy the democratic alternative to the Communists."[186] This reasoning, combined with mounting evidence of Marcos's electoral misdeeds, overcame the objections of figures such as Casey and Chief of Staff Donald Regan, and led Reagan to approve a series of actions that progressively put U.S. influence behind the democratic forces. On February 15, the White House condemned the fraud as "so extreme that the election's credibility has been called into question."[187] Thereafter, the administration cautioned Marcos that Washington would not accept a tainted election, and that violence against protestors or rebel military units would "cause untold damage to the relationship."[188] (Shultz's special envoy in Manila, Phillip Habib, used congressional pressure to the administration's advantage in this respect, warning regime loyalists that a fraudulent result would doom the military aid relationship.[189]) Reagan himself even weighed in, telling Marcos that violence would "split your country irrevocably, benefitting only the forces of the left."[190] These admonitions apparently helped dissuade Marcos from using force when he might still have crushed the incipient military rebellion. American units at Clark Air Force Base further fortified the rebels by providing them with intelligence and allowing them to rearm and refuel from U.S. stocks, while CIA operatives lent communications and propaganda support.[191]

Belated as they were, these measures lent key outside sustenance to the anti-Marcos forces, and added to the pressures preventing the regime from settling the crisis on its own repressive terms. By February 23, Reagan was ready for the final push. A presidential directive stated that the goal was to "facilitate a peaceful transition," and the next day, the White House effectively called for Marcos to resign. "Attempts to prolong the life of the present regime by violence are futile," it stated; the only solution was "a peaceful transition to a new government."[192] Laxalt followed with a phone call on Reagan's behalf, telling Marcos to "cut and cut cleanly" and offering him exile in the United States. These signals, complemented by Bosworth's efforts in Manila, left no doubt that Marcos had lost U.S. support, and finally convinced him to surrender power. "We had removed the sign of heaven from him, the mandate of heaven," Bosworth recalled.[193] Following Marcos' departure, the Reagan and Bush administrations worked to sustain the fragile transition to democracy, both through increased economic aid and strong measures—including a minor military intervention in 1989—to thwart attempted coups.

As one assessment of U.S. policy in the Philippines correctly notes, Reagan's support for democracy was often "hesitant, messy, crisis-driven and skewed by the desire to . . . protect the American military installations."[194] Moreover, the U.S. contribution was distinctly secondary to the risks run, efforts made, and resistance generated by Aquino and her "people power" supporters. That said, it is still hard to imagine that Philippine democratization would have occurred when it did without U.S. involvement. It was U.S. pressure that induced Marcos to call the 1986 elections, and that made those elections (as one State Department official noted) "so-well supervised that flaws could not be concealed."[195] And despite Reagan's initial ambivalence, U.S. intervention eventually made it far more difficult for Marcos to overturn the results, and then helped force him from power. This was not a seamless effort, by any means, but U.S. policy had a constructive overall effect. It helped ensure that the democratic tide was not turned back at a key juncture, and it confirmed what that Washington could and would break with long-time authoritarian allies that stood athwart that trend.

This legacy was salient as Reagan confronted another fraught transition the following year, in South Korea. Like the Philippines, South Korea was a deeply authoritarian but strategically important ally, and the latter trait had consistently trumped the former in U.S. policy. During the late 1970s, the Carter administration had desisted from efforts to promote liberalization amid the upheaval that followed the assassination of the dictator Park Chung-hee, and it raised no serious objections to the establishment of another authoritarian regime under Chun Doo-hwan, or to the massacre of hundreds of protestors in Kwangju in May 1980.[196] For Reagan, too, the imperative of anticommunist stability initially overrode all else. The administration quietly persuaded Chun not to execute leading dissident Kim Dae-jung, but otherwise made clear that human rights and democratization were secondary. The "greatest violators of human rights" were "behind the bamboo and iron curtains," Reagan told Chun in 1981; the United States would not harp on allies' imperfections.[197]

Beneath the apparent stability provided by Chun, however, Korean politics were in flux. Rapid growth was creating a middle and upper class that demanded political power to match their economic status. There also remained a diverse and increasingly restive opposition movement, and raucous protests and other dissent persisted during the 1980s. "Many Koreans think that progress toward civilian rule is too slow," the INR reported in 1983. "Even some of Chun's military colleagues seem to feel that he needs to extend more power to the opposition to bring Korea into the modern world."[198] Adding to the flux were the actions of Chun himself. The Korean leader was often a deeply authoritarian figure, but he did at least nod to democratic forms by holding parliamentary elections in 1981 and 1985, and by promising to leave power and hold free elections after a single term. "The people believe that a change of presidents is possible only through violence," he told Reagan. "This is a very dangerous way of thinking."[199] Although the sincerity of this commitment was widely questioned, it nonetheless created a plausible pathway to democratization, and offered points of leverage for those who favored such a process.[200]

By 1982–1983, the Reagan administration was gradually joining this group. As so often, this was partially due to congressional pressure, as Solarz and his allies were maintaining a drumbeat of criticism of U.S. policy. "By doing nothing" to support reform, Solarz argued, "we abdicate our leadership and imperil our interests."[201] Reagan's shift also reflected a growing recognition that U.S. policy was engendering resentment among the Korean opposition (particularly students), a dangerous long-term trend. "Anti-government sentiment has increasingly taken on anti-American overtones," administration officials reported.[202] Most important, with internal dissent mounting, State Department and White House officials worried that stability by repression now might create explosive instability later. In 1984, Shultz explicitly mentioned Korea in saying that "there are countries whose long-term security will probably be enhanced if they have a more solid base of popular support and domestic unity." Although it would be foolish simply to break with an important ally, it would be equally foolish to ignore the need for political evolution, and for intensified U.S. engagement to encourage such reform.[203]

That engagement took two principal forms, the first of which was an effort to strengthen reformist tendencies within the government. U.S. officials urged Chun (with some success) to release political prisoners, restore rights to banned politicians, and decrease overall repression. "The soul of democracy," Reagan told Chun, "is freedom under law."[204] Similarly, Reagan and Shultz subtly invoked U.S. leverage by stressing that reform was imperative to long-term support for South Korean security. "Chun sought continuing reassurance from the United States on the security front," Shultz wrote of one meeting. "The president and I again emphasized the critical importance of Chun's commitment to a democratic succession."[205] In particular, the administration seized on Chun's single-term pledge, repeatedly praising him for that "farsighted" promise—and thereby raising the political and diplomatic costs should the South Korean leader renege.[206] Throughout all this, Reagan reaffirmed the U.S.–South Korean alliance, but he also became a strong advocate of peaceful democratic transition. "The development of democratic political institutions," Reagan told the Korean National Assembly, "is the surest means to build the national consensus that is the foundation of true security."[207]

The second and parallel aspect of U.S. policy was engagement with the opposition, meant to strengthen democratic reformers and discourage radical impulses. The NED supported the development of the relatively centrist New Korea Democratic Party (NDP, which was formed in 1985 and promptly won 29 percent of the vote in parliamentary elections), and State Department officials kept close contact with Kim and other opposition figures. Shultz and other U.S. representatives simultaneously urged (not always with success) caution and moderation on those figures, arguing that confrontation would invite repression, and that working within the electoral system offered the best path to change.[208]

The critical test came in the first half of 1987. The transition in the Philippines the year prior had heightened demands for change in Seoul, creating a mood that was at once optimistic and confrontational. This Korean powder keg nearly ignited between April and June, when Chun backtracked on his pledges to liberalize. He suspended negotiations on a constitutional reform meant to clear the way for open elections later that year, and indicated that a hand-picked successor, Roh Tae-woo, would take his place. These decisions incited large and often violent demonstrations; those protests raised the specter that Chun might declare martial law and forcibly stifle the opposition. Like the Philippines in 1986, South Korea was perched on the precipice: "The choice for the Chun government . . . was narrowed to one of mobilizing troops to quell the demonstrations and risking large-scale violence and possibly a civil war, or making wholesale concessions to the forces of democracy and risking the loss of power."[209]

The Reagan administration was deeply worried that North Korea might profit from turmoil in Seoul, and it was careful to stay officially neutral in the political struggle. Yet with the Philippine episode in the background, there was a strong internal consensus that repression would be far more destabilizing than even a messy democratic opening. As early as February, Assistant Secretary of State Gaston Sigur had publicly called for Seoul to pursue constitutional reforms that would "create a more open and legitimate political system" and thereby "break the tragic cycle of unexpected and violent changes of government."[210] Shultz subsequently declared that he supported "every comma . . . every dot of the 'i,'" of Sigur's address, and as the crisis unfolded, the administration came down strongly against efforts to derail the transition. "We need to keep pressure on democratization," Ambassador James Lilley argued. U.S. officials publicly declared that "fair elections are necessary," and they called on the government to revive the constitutional dialogue while also urging the opposition to eschew violence and participate constructively.[211] Shultz and Sigur maintained close personal contact with NDP leaders and other dissidents, and they warned that any resort to force by the government would be disastrous. "The transition of power must be peaceful," Sigur said, "and the [government] must get a broader base of support."[212]

The most important U.S. intervention came at the peak of the crisis in June, when Chun was on the verge of imposing martial law. Fearing a bloodbath that would stain Korean politics and U.S.-Korean relations for decades, the administration made a concerted push to head off the crackdown. Reagan sent a personal letter to Chun, calling for a democratic transition and warning of irreparable damage to the alliance if force were used. "I believe that political stability based on sound democratic institutions is critical to insuring the long-term security of your country," he wrote. In Seoul, Sigur and Lilley reinforced this message directly, with tacit support from the U.S. military command. Meanwhile, Shultz and other State Department officials pledged U.S. backing for a democratic South Korea, while making clear that repression would not be supported.[213] Confronted with massive opposition from South Korean society, and now from Seoul's essential foreign ally, Chun backed down. Plans to use force were rescinded, opposition demands for constitutional revision were accepted, and South Korea moved toward free elections and the establishment of a vibrant democracy.[214]

As numerous analysts have noted, there were multiple factors that caused democratization in South Korea, the most important of which was the large-scale mobilization by Koreans themselves. Yet it is also widely recognized that U.S. involvement amplified these pressures for change from the mid-1980s onward, and provided a strong—although probably secondary—disincentive for repression when the fate of Korean politics hung in the balance.[215] Leading South Korean dissidents later expressed thanks for the U.S. role, writing to State Department officials that "your support for the cause of democracy and human rights has helped our people sustain their struggle against tyranny."[216]

Within the Reagan administration, the experience in East Asia during the 1980s vindicated the key ideas behind the growing emphasis on democracy promotion in U.S. foreign policy. In a major speech in 1987, Sigur argued that the outcomes in South Korea and the Philippines showed that "democratic government and greater individual freedom now represent the wave of the future," not just in the Western Hemisphere but in Asia as well. These episodes also showed an increasing confidence that promoting democracy was not a distraction from geopolitical interests such as anticommunism and regional stability, but rather a powerful way of securing those ends. Finally, as halting and ambivalent as U.S. policy had sometimes been, these successes confirmed that foreign help was indeed crucial if pro-democracy movements were to win. "An evolving democracy must have *support from abroad,* especially from other democracies," Sigur argued. "Whether principally political, economic, or moral in nature, this collegial support must be evident and reliable."[217] As Sigur recognized, such support was unlikely to be the principal cause of democratization, in Asia or elsewhere. But as U.S. involvement in the Philippines and South Korea showed, it could strengthen the forces of liberalization and improve their chances of success.

Constructive Engagement and South Africa

For all of the challenges that U.S. policymakers faced in Latin America and East Asia, nowhere were the trials of promoting democracy greater than in South Africa. The apartheid government in Pretoria represented one of the world's most odious autocracies. An entrenched white minority of roughly 5 million monopolized political and economic power, and ruled a population of 20–25 million blacks (and smaller numbers of Asians and "coloreds") through institutionalized discrimination. Opposition to this system was becoming steadily more explosive, with black resistance and resentment surging, and the African National Congress (ANC) waging a campaign of revolutionary violence against the regime. The growing polarization, in turn, was fused to Cold War and regional tensions. The existence of Marxist governments that aided the ANC in Mozambique and Angola, the presence of tens of thousands of Cuban troops in the latter country, and the ongoing insurgency against South African rule in Namibia not only fed into a regionalized war; they also exacerbated Pretoria's insecurities and strengthened hardliners who warned that political change would be tantamount to suicide.

This situation ensured that U.S. policy was constantly buffeted by cross-pressures. Top administration officials understood that seeking internal reform was imperative if the White House was not to lose control of South Africa policy to the anti-apartheid movement in the United States. That movement was part of a broader international campaign against the South African regime, and by the early 1980s, it was steadily gaining strength on the campuses, in churches, and in Congress as well. U.S. officials also needed no convincing that apartheid was a moral abomination. "We are opposed to it. We are appalled by it. Let there be no question about that," Haig said. Finally, the Reagan administration feared that attempts to prolong apartheid indefinitely would only heighten the chances for a cataclysmic race war that would turn South Africa red and destabilize the whole region. An "enormous price will be exacted if the pressures in and around South Africa degenerate into destructive revolutionary violence," State Department officials warned. "If we do not bring about understanding," Reagan agreed, "South Africa faces one of the biggest bloodbaths in history."[218]

From the early 1980s onward, U.S. policy statements therefore affirmed that the administration sought "the peaceful dismantling of apartheid for South African society."[219] As dangerous and repulsive as apartheid was, however, Reagan was equally determined not simply to repudiate the South African regime. Amid a reinvigorated Cold War, he argued, doing so would be geopolitical folly: "Can we abandon a country that has stood beside us in every war we've ever fought, a country that strategically is essential to the free world in its production of minerals we all must have and so forth?"[220] Moreover, the experience of the Carter years had convinced many officials that ostracizing or openly chastising Pretoria would backfire by exacerbating the intransigence of a perpetually defensive regime. "We cannot have influence with people if we treat them as moral lepers," Shultz would say; changing the political situation in South Africa required more subtlety.[221]

The strategy that emerged to reconcile these conflicting imperatives was "constructive engagement," a concept devised and largely overseen by Assistant Secretary of State for African Affairs Chester Crocker. Constructive engagement rested on the idea that it was possible to encourage "purposeful, evolutionary change toward a nonracial system" by strengthening liberalizing tendencies within the government of Prime Minister P. W. Botha—a "modernizing autocracy," as Crocker assessed it, which understood that apartheid must change to survive in the modern world. Yet constructive engagement was equally premised on the notion that these tendencies would emerge only in a calm and stable environment, and that fostering this environment would require sustained engagement using both positive and negative incentives. "Pressure for change should be a central ingredient in American policy," Crocker had written in 1980, "but pressure is not enough. Also required is a clear Western readiness to recognize and support positive movement, and to engage credibly in addressing a complex agenda of change."[222]

Constructive engagement therefore required striking a delicate balance. U.S. officials made clear that reform was imperative and that apartheid must end. As Crocker announced in 1981, the United States would not "align ourselves with apartheid policies that are abhorrent to our own multi-racial democracy." Yet the administration simultaneously announced that it had "no intention of destabilizing South Africa in order to curry favor elsewhere," and U.S. officials worked to restore the bilateral ties and mutual confidence that had eroded in recent years.[223] To that end, Reagan and his diplomats stressed that Washington and Pretoria shared an interest in combating communism and radicalism in the region. Reagan also supported IMF lending to Pretoria, and opposed calls for disinvestment or the use of economic sanctions against the government (although he largely maintained the preexisting arms embargo). Above all, the administration sought to handle disagreements privately rather than in high-profile public showdowns— "tests of manhood," Haig called them—that would only empower South African hardliners. "Indignation and strong convictions do not constitute a foreign policy," Crocker argued. "The issue is how to translate those convictions into results."[224]

Indeed, the goal of this engagement was not to perpetuate an unjust status quo, but to build the influence and credibility needed to push for change. The administration (and NED) sought that change in part by promoting moderate black empowerment through a variety of measures: assistance to independent trade unions and civic groups, provision of university scholarships and legal aid, support for black-owned businesses and fair-employment practices, and others.[225] More important, it aimed to use the improved relationship to encourage incremental reforms: ending forced evictions and resettlements of black populations, releasing political prisoners such as Nelson Mandela and ceasing the practice of detention without trial, increasing black rights to urban residency and freer travel, and reducing or eliminating aspects of economic discrimination. Over time, these piecemeal steps would foster cooperation between black and white moderates, marginalizing advocates of violence and making it easier to tackle the thornier questions about power-sharing and a transition away from apartheid. As Crocker had written in 1980, "The innovative feature of constructive engagement is its insistence on serious thinking about the sequencing and interrelatedness of change. Priority ought to be given to those arenas of change that logically lead to, and make possible, future steps. We must avoid the trap of an indiscriminate attack on all aspects of the system—as though each were equally odious and none should be addressed first."[226]

As designed by Crocker, constructive engagement also had a crucial regional dimension. Democratic change, he believed, was highly unlikely so long as Pretoria was caught up in a "climate of constant fighting with adversaries along its borders."[227] Accordingly, the administration sought to broker a process of regional decompression, whereby the Cubans would withdraw from Angola, South Africa would grant independence to Namibia, and Pretoria and its neighbors would cease destabilizing each other. If successful, this process would ease the polarizing regional security competition and thereby lower obstacles to accommodation in South Africa itself.

"We needed to understand the intimate link between regional security and internal change, and get the sequence right," Crocker argued. "As long as cross-border war continued, regional leaders would blame foreign enemies and seek foreign allies rather than reach out to their own people and create legitimate systems at home."[228] Throughout the 1980s, U.S. officials would continually underscore that the crux of constructive engagement was this recognition of the interconnection between regional peace and domestic reform. "A white government that no longer sees itself as besieged from outside its borders will be better able to take the steps it must to reform its own society," Shultz said.[229]

To attain its ends, the administration plunged deeply into the currents of regional diplomacy. It used its unique ability to communicate, either directly or through intermediaries, with all the relevant parties. Meanwhile, Crocker worked creatively to create linkages between core issues such as Cuban withdrawal and Namibian independence, so that one side's goals could come only through recognition of the other side's legitimate interests. "We are not asking any party to commit suicide," one U.S. official said.[230] In dealing with South Africa itself, the administration deployed a mixture of mild pressure and reassurance, pushing Pretoria to engage its neighbors and refrain from too aggressively employing its military power, while also averring that Washington would not allow radical forces to dominate the region. Keeping the issue of Cuban withdrawal at the center of the diplomatic agenda was one way of substantiating these promises; another was pressing Congress to repeal its ban on covert aid to Angolan insurgents led by Jonas Savimbi so as to increase U.S. leverage vis-à-vis the Marxist People's Movement for the Liberation of Angola (MPLA) government in that country.[231]

Taken as a whole, constructive engagement was thus a sophisticated and nuanced strategy. It recognized the linkages between internal and external conflicts; it offered an incremental approach to dealing with the morass of problems posed by apartheid; it held the possibility of gradually facilitating democratic reform and regional decompression without forsaking a U.S. ally. And during Reagan's first term, the strategy appeared to be working. Internal reforms occurred, with the easing of institutionalized discrimination in the workplace and the educational system, greater government acceptance of black trade unions and other moderate civic groups, and the creation of a tricameral parliament with one house each for whites, Asians, and coloreds. Blacks were still excluded from real political participation, of course, and these measures were limited at best. But they did seem to show that Pretoria was moving in the right direction. "In part because of U.S. encouragement, change in South Africa has begun—barely, but it *has begun*," Deputy

Secretary of State Kenneth Dam reported. Reagan agreed: "We've made considerable progress with quiet diplomacy."[232]

There was equivalent progress on the regional front. In early 1984, South Africa signed parallel agreements with Mozambique and Angola. The Nkomati accords pledged Maputo and Pretoria to halt destabilization activities against each other; the Lusaka accords called for a cease-fire between Luanda and Pretoria, the withdrawal of South African forces from Angolan territory, and steps to halt infiltration to support the Namibian insurgency. As U.S. officials understood, these agreements reflected the weariness of both Pretoria and its antagonists, and their corresponding willingness to consider diplomacy. But they also reflected Crocker's efforts to drive the process forward by advancing creative formulas and identifying common interests, enlisting the good offices of third parties, and dangling the reward of better relations with Washington—for South Africa as well as economically struggling rivals such as Angola and Mozambique—if the key parties behaved constructively. By mid-1984, the spiral of regional violence had been disrupted, and the Angolans were discussing the envisioned endgame: Cuban withdrawal for Namibian independence. This forward movement confirmed the value of U.S. engagement, and raised hopes for a virtuous cycle in which regional progress would enable and draw strength from South African liberalization. "We have had undeniable achievements in southern Africa the past four years," State Department officials assessed: "Regional violence is down, there has been movement toward reform inside South Africa, and U.S. strategic interests have been protected."[233]

The momentum, unfortunately, could not be sustained. In retrospect, constructive engagement hinged on two key assumptions: that the Botha government was ultimately willing to make a major transformation of apartheid, and that small reforms would satisfy the black community in the interim. "The relationship which I have sought to build with South Africa," Reagan explained in one letter to Botha, "is based on my belief that positive change is occurring in your country and that you wish this peaceful evolution to continue."[234] Neither of these assumptions, however, could long withstand the harsh realities of polarized South Africa. Anger at the slow pace and modest scope of change produced a surge of antigovernment protest and violence in late 1984, escalating into what the CIA termed "the worst outbreak of black unrest in South Africa's modern history."[235] In response, the Botha government offered only minimal or belated concessions. Worse still, that government imposed a state of emergency, detained up to 30,000 individuals, and unleashed the security forces to the tune of hundreds or perhaps thousands of deaths.[236] And as South Africa descended into radicalism and repression, the regional panorama deteriorated, too. South African hardliners reescalated the conflicts with Mozambique and Angola through cross-border raids and renewed destabilization. The virtuous cycle had become a vicious cycle, raising troubling questions about Pretoria's intentions—and whether constructive engagement could deliver lasting results. "Our efforts and our initiatives . . . have been swamped, even overwhelmed by a circle of setbacks and violence and repression," Crocker acknowledged.[237]

As events in southern Africa veered off course, the political foundation of constructive engagement also collapsed. That policy had always been a tough sell domestically, because as Crocker recognized, calls for engagement often "came across as support for white South Africa."[238] When the progress of the early 1980s dissipated, a broad coalition of anti-apartheid activists alleged that U.S. policy was merely enabling a reprehensible regime. There were demonstrations on college campuses across the country; in Congress, Kennedy led a bipartisan group calling for more punitive measures. Reagan, who continued to believe that "we must . . . seek the end of apartheid . . . through gradualism in the political process," momentarily delayed the congressional push for sanctions in mid-1985, by emplacing more modest executive-branch sanctions on Pretoria, and by securing some South African reforms in the months thereafter.[239] By mid-1986, however, resurgent regional and domestic violence had made Reagan's calls for congressional restraint seem morally obtuse. "The sanctions we have are not strong enough," Kennedy declared. After Reagan gave a tone-deaf speech that made him appear insensitive to the ongoing repression, a veto-proof bipartisan majority passed harsh economic sanctions that could only be lifted upon major steps toward democratization.[240] The president had lost control of the agenda and, with it, the ability to calibrate incentives and disincentives in dealing with South Africa. Botha charged that Reagan's policy was now "worse than Carter's," and his initial response was more defiance.[241] Progress toward democracy seemed as distant as ever, and U.S. policy looked to have failed entirely.

Contrary to what most analysts expected, however, this impression proved misleading, and by the late 1980s, the trajectory of events was improving dramatically. In 1988, painstaking negotiations produced a series of interlocking agreements centered on Cuban withdrawal from Angola, the granting of Namibian independence, and cessation of hostilities between Pretoria and Luanda. South African destabilization of Mozambique also came to a close, facilitating an end to the devastating civil war in that country. And following Botha's succession by F. W. de Klerk in 1989, South Africa itself began a fraught but ultimately successful transition to multiracial democracy. In 1987, the CIA had warned that "conditions conducive to a major racial conflagration" were coalescing in that country; by the early 1990s South Africa was seen as an inspiring—if still deeply troubled—exemplar of the democratic revolution.[242] To be sure, this transformation owed to a complex array of factors, from the visionary leadership of Mandela and de Klerk to the global shifts engendered by the end of the Cold War.[243] Yet even though many of these factors had little to do with the United States, American policy did make two key contributions.

First, even amid the apparent demise of constructive engagement in 1985–1986, Crocker and Shultz had refused to let the regional aspects of the policy die. The State Department remained alert for opportunities to prod South Africa to reengage diplomatically, and Crocker eventually threatened that Washington might wash its hands of the region—thereby leaving Pretoria isolated—if it did not.[244] From 1985 onward, Crocker gained an even stronger card to play against Luanda and Havana, as the repeal of the 1970s-era Clark amendment allowed the CIA to provide military assistance—including Stinger missiles and TOW (tube-launched, optically tracked, wire-guided) antitank weapons—to Savimbi's rebels. Combined with moderate economic sanctions on Luanda, this measure made it possible, U.S. officials wrote, to "pursue a two-track strategy of a) continuing to negotiate with the MPLA and South Africa on Cuban troop withdrawal in the context of Namibian independence while b) applying pressure on the MPLA to negotiate seriously and to accept a negotiated settlement." Indeed, although military aid to Savimbi's forces was no silver bullet, it did raise the costs of continuing the war for Angola and Cuba, and helped drive home the need for an eventual accommodation. Covert assistance, Gates later wrote, "provided . . . the leverage" necessary for diplomacy to work.[245]

By 1987–1988, the conditions for a settlement were falling into place. A series of clashes between the South African military and Savimbi's National Union for the Total Independence of Angola (UNITA) rebels, on one side, and massively reinforced Cuban units and the Angolan armed forces, on the other, showed that there was a rough stalemate on the battlefield and that decisive victory was beyond the reach of all the exhausted combatants. Meanwhile, the relaxation of Cold War tensions provided further impetus for Moscow's African allies to look for a way out of the conflict, and eased South African fears of a Soviet-backed onslaught. Throughout 1988, intensive U.S. efforts helped facilitate dialogue between the parties and translate these propitious conditions into accords that greatly reduced regional tensions and insecurity. For all the travails of constructive engagement, the policy eventually delivered results. Writes one observer, "Even his critics had to describe Crocker's diplomacy as 'triumphant.'"[246]

The regional settlement soon made possible democratic elections in Namibia, and as Crocker had expected, it also had ramifications within South Africa. By reducing the foreign military threat, the accords eased the siege mentality that had gripped Pretoria, and deprived reactionaries of a venerable argument against political change. "By signing the agreements on Angola and Namibia," one ANC official noted, "they are focusing attention on the last remaining problem in the region: South Africa."[247] Equally important, the accords set an essential precedent in demonstrating that negotiation offered a peaceful and positive-sum solution to long-running conflicts. "Peace could not be achieved through the barrel of a gun, which is the central theme running through the network of agreements," Pik Botha, the South African foreign minister, observed. "It is a sobering lesson. . . . There is no reason that can't apply to the political parties in South Africa."[248] However tortuous the process, U.S. diplomacy proved central to fostering a regional environment that was far more conducive to democratization.

The second key contribution of U.S. policy was more paradoxical, for it stemmed from the defeat of constructive engagement, not its triumph. When Congress imposed sanctions in 1986, Reagan had warned that this would simply drive Pretoria into a defensive crouch. This prediction was accurate enough in the short term, but over time U.S. sanctions did add to the pressures for liberalization.[249] Although the cumulative economic impact of the sanctions was marginal (and had less influence than the decision of commercial banks to stop rolling over South African debt), it affected the thinking of a powerful business community that valued its links to the outside world. "In this day and age there is no such thing as economic self-sufficiency and we delude ourselves if we think we are different," said one financier. "South Africa needs the world."[250] More broadly, sanctions drove home the fact that South Africa had become a total pariah state, ostracized even by Cold War allies such as Washington. "The majority of whites continued to desire acceptance in the Western world," writes one scholar; U.S. and other international sanctions made clear that this required ending apartheid. All told, then, sanctions made an important contribution to de Klerk's decision to liberalize, a fact later stressed by both government and ANC officials.[251]

U.S. efforts to promote democracy in South Africa thus left mixed and somewhat messy legacies. Constructive engagement was never as effective as promised when it came to encouraging internal reform, and its shortcomings led Congress to adopt a more coercive approach from 1986 onward. Yet U.S.

sanctions did eventually strengthen the cause of internal liberalization, despite what Crocker and his colleagues had predicted. Moreover, the peacemaking aspects of constructive engagement made critical contributions to the more favorable regional climate in which liberalization occurred. What can probably best be said, then, is that the Reagan administration did genuinely work for democratic change in South Africa, and that for all the disappointments and problems that ensued, American influence had a positive—and in some ways, quite important—overall impact on that process. As in other cases during Reagan's presidency, the record of U.S. involvement was hardly spotless or seamless. But in the end, it was hardly negligible, either.

Conclusion

In certain ways, the South African case therefore demonstrates the limits of U.S. democracy-promotion efforts during the 1980s. In other respects, however, it confirms a basic theme running through numerous episodes during the decade: that U.S. policy had become a significant, even critical element in democracy's advance. From the Southern Cone to South Korea, U.S. officials had worked energetically and effectively to fortify the forces of liberal reform. They had done so through various measures and approaches: by pressuring authoritarian regimes and protecting fragile transitions, by supporting reformers and promoting the development of democratic institutions, by helping moderates defeat radical challenges from both left and right, and by seeking diplomatic settlements conducive to democratization. It merits repeating, certainly, that the onset of electoral democracy was hardly a cure-all for troubled societies, and that the main burdens of democratization were born by the internal actors who risked their lives and livelihoods to stimulate change. But it also merits repeating that these reformers benefitted considerably—in some cases, tremendously—from U.S. support. As Samuel Huntington has noted, "The absence of the United States from the process would have meant fewer and later transitions to democracy."[252]

When it came to democracy promotion, the events of the 1980s thus confirmed what the course of the late Cold War had demonstrated: that there was an increasingly synergistic interaction between U.S. strategy and global change. Beginning in the 1970s, there had been an international groundswell of pro-rights and democratic activism. First under Carter and then more so under Reagan, U.S. officials recognized that trend and progressively put the force of national policy behind it. Over a period of years, these efforts helped produce a world that was far more democratic and politically free than before, and one in which U.S. political and ideological values seemed ever more preponderant. "Nothing can stand in the way of freedom's march," Bush would declare in 1989. "Today is freedom's moment."[253] Here as elsewhere, American policies capitalized on profound international transformations and helped foster a renewed U.S. ascendancy.

As in the case of U.S.-Soviet relations, however, there were important caveats to this success story. Effective democracy-promotion policies did not take shape in a flash of inspiration, nor was the path forward usually a frictionless one. Rather, it took time and adaptation, even stumbles and failures, to set U.S. efforts on the proper trajectory. It is worth remembering that Carter's highest-profile efforts to promote liberal reform were disasters, that Reagan was initially very ambivalent about emphasizing human rights and democratization, and that it was pressure from critics in Congress that repeatedly helped push the administration in more constructive directions. It is also worth remembering that there were numerous cases in which U.S. policies had to evolve considerably to achieve positive results. In the Philippines, for instance, Reagan's stance was shifting and sometimes hesitant until very late in the game. In other cases, such as Nicaragua and El Salvador, democracy promotion was a long, bloody slog that reached fruition only after many years and no little good fortune. Moreover, even though American efforts to foster democracy were ultimately broadly successful, there were cases—South Africa, for instance—in which Reagan's diplomacy was thoroughly imperfect, and the results of policy were mixed and ironic. Overall effectiveness aside, there was ambiguity and messiness aplenty in America's approach to the democratic revolution.

There were also some undeniable costs. Democracy promotion in the 1980s was an inherently interventionist endeavor, one that required deeply pervasive meddling in the affairs of notionally sovereign states so as to produce the victory of one faction over another. In many cases, admittedly, the results of that meddling were largely and probably correctly seen to have been more beneficial than not for the citizens of the country in question. Yet there were also episodes such as El Salvador and Nicaragua, in which the legal and moral compromises in U.S. policy were considerable, and in which the human toll was appallingly severe. "If Ronald Reagan wanted credit for having saved Nicaragua," one scholar writes, "he also had to take responsibility for having destroyed much of it in the process."[254] It may well have been, as supporters of U.S. policy argued, that unsavory means were the only way of accomplishing democratic ends in these countries. But even so, these episodes revealed that the price of promoting democracy could be high indeed.

On the whole, of course, the primary outcome of U.S. policy was to empower a broad international movement away from authoritarianism and toward representative government. And in fact, the gains of the 1980s ensured that democracy promotion would be a central pillar of U.S. statecraft long after Reagan left office. The institutional infrastructure was now in place; the NED and USAID were involved in democracy-promotion initiatives in several dozen countries around the world when Reagan's presidency concluded, and these initiatives only expanded thereafter. Democracy-related activities became better incorporated into the core missions of USAID, USIA, and the State Department during the late 1980s and early 1990s, and overall funding for democracy assistance increased from around $100 million at the end of the 1980s to more than $2.5 billion in 2011. "The rise of democracy assistance in the 1980s," writes ones expert, "helped set the stage" for the growth of such assistance in the 1990s and after.[255]

The record of the 1980s also made democracy promotion an objective that enjoyed widespread political support. As we have seen, the need to secure congressional—particularly Democratic—backing was an important reason why a Republican administration decided to embrace an emphasis on liberal reform. And as time went on, successes in places such as El Salvador, Chile, and the Philippines demonstrated, to observers in the White House and Congress alike, that it was possible to pursue a policy that promoted American values without shortchanging U.S. geopolitical interests. There remained plenty of disagreement on particular episodes or manifestations of U.S. policy, as the cases surveyed in this chapter show. But broadly speaking, there was also emerging what NED analysts called a "new pro-democratic consensus," one that "brings together diverse political elements that can agree on certain crucial propositions":

> That democratic governments tend to be friendly to the United States and peaceful in their foreign relations; that they tend more toward political stability and economic prosperity than non-democratic systems; that the growth of democracy serves our national interests; and that to further those interests we should support those who are struggling to establish democratic systems and defend democratic values.

This basic goal of spreading democracy would subsequently be adopted by both Democratic and Republican administrations, constituting a strong element of continuity in U.S. foreign policy from the 1980s onward.[256]

Finally, the experience of democracy promotion during the Reagan years fed into a powerful sense that the world was once again moving Washington's way ideologically as well as geopolitically, and that the vigorous use of U.S. influence was central to keeping the tides flowing in the right direction. "Democracy, once viewed as an historical relic, now seems like the wave of the future," NED officials wrote in 1987. "Countries across the globe" were "turning away from the ideologies of the past," Reagan agreed in his farewell address, and toward American values and institutions instead. Bush put it even more strongly in his inaugural address: "We know what works: freedom works. We know what's right: freedom is right. We know how to secure a more just and prosperous life for man on earth, through free markets, free speech, free elections, and the exercise of free will unhampered by the state."[257] This sense that freedom and democracy were on the march, and that U.S. involvement was vital to sustaining and accelerating their advance, ensured that such initiatives would remain central to the post–Cold War strategy that took form during the early 1990s. In this sense, the success of American democracy-promotion endeavors during the 1980s helped shape not only the emerging unipolar era; they helped shape U.S. foreign policy for that era, too.

CHAPTER 4

Toward the Neoliberal Order

"In watching the flow of events over the past decade," State Department Policy Planning Staff Francis Fukuyama wrote in 1989, "it is hard to avoid the feeling that something very fundamental has happened in world history." The turning tide of the Cold War and the crisis of the Soviet system showed that Marxism-Leninism was suffering "its death as a living ideology of world historical significance." Conversely, Western concepts of liberalism—political and economic—were ever more dominant. The epic ideological struggles of the twentieth century had ended neither in the triumph of fascism or communism, nor in the "convergence between capitalism and socialism" that was sometimes predicted in the 1960s and 1970s. Rather, those struggles had led "to an unabashed victory of economic and political liberalism" and to the "universalization of Western liberal democracy as the final form of human government." If history was driven by the clash between competing models of societal organization, Fukuyama wrote, the world was seeing not just the end of the Cold War but the "end of history" itself.[1]

Fukuyama's thesis was testament to the impending Western victory in the superpower rivalry, and to the remarkable proliferation of democracy. Yet it also affirmed a third core aspect of U.S. revival—the continuing transformation of the international political economy. During the 1970s, fundamental shifts had begun to foster a new neoliberal order—an increasingly globalized, interconnected economy in which market concepts were supreme and the United States was well situated to prosper. In the decade thereafter, the formation of that system took essential paces forward. The major developed countries successfully managed international economic conflicts that might otherwise have derailed the ongoing processes of integration, and they embarked on an ambitious agenda of global trade liberalization. The progress was even more historic in the developing nations. Only a decade after dependency theory and the NIEO had dominated the discourse, countries from Latin America to China were casting off state-centric approaches and embracing the market ethos. "There's a new and dynamic international order in the economy," George H. W. Bush could affirm by the end of the decade. Globalization was advancing apace, and a U.S.-backed neoliberal order was firmly taking hold.[2] In economics as in politics, America's preferred institutions and ideals were becoming progressively more hegemonic.

The contours of the world economy are often shaped by great impersonal forces, on the one hand, and great-power policies, on the other. This was true of the neoliberal ascent under consideration here. That phenomenon was rooted in the systemic and intellectual currents that had been unleashed previously, and that operated with tremendous force in the 1980s and after. Yet it was also a product of actions taken in Washington. If Nixon, Ford, and Carter had begun to align statecraft with the possibilities that were springing up in the international economy, subsequent leaders did so with even greater energy and effectiveness. From the start, the Reagan administration was committed to forging a more open, market-oriented order that would honor America's ideological proclivities, and augment its influence and wealth. Over time, that administration and its successor deployed a range of initiatives—in dealing with developed and developing countries alike—that applied U.S. leverage to secure this end. "We should boldly seize the new opportunities offered by the world," Treasury Secretary James Baker said in 1987, and broadly speaking, this is what U.S. policymakers did.[3]

As one would expect, of course, the process of achieving those results was no more perfect here than in any other area. Handling Western economic relations, dealing with U.S.-Japan commercial frictions, catalyzing a new round of global trade negotiations, and managing the Third World debt crisis—these were all difficult and sometimes perplexing issues. They taxed the abilities of American officials, inflicted various setbacks and disappointments, and compelled shifting tactics and approaches over time. And even though the eventual success of U.S. policy could be extraordinary, here too that success was rife with contradictions and costs. This fact was apparent in the angry backlash against neoliberal reforms in many Third World countries, for instance, and in the more problematic legacies of U.S. support for China's economic opening. Strategic breakthroughs in one period fed into strategic challenges in the next; that dynamic proved inescapable during the 1980s.

These issues notwithstanding, the most salient outcome of U.S. policy was still to pair national power with structural possibility, and thereby to bring the vision of a neoliberal world much closer to realization. That historic accomplishment paralleled and complemented U.S. breakthroughs in the superpower contest and the campaign to push the democratic revolution. It also presaged efforts to advance the neoliberal order still further in the post–Cold War era.

Reaganomics at Home and Abroad

In the economic realm as in so many areas, the early 1980s marked a key juncture in the trajectory of U.S. power and influence, and in the evolution of the international system. As the decade began, the outlook for the U.S. and the world economies remained gloomy, and sources of peril seemed ubiquitous. The traumas of the 1970s persisted throughout much of the Western world, from high unemployment and soaring inflation, to low growth and plunging self-confidence. Economic stagnation, in turn, threatened to spur resurgent protectionism, as industries rocked by rising energy costs and fiercer competition demanded measures to shield them from their foreign rivals. Across the industrialized world, these appeals would be a fixture of political discourse in the 1980s, and particularly during the first half of that decade, they led many observers to fear for the future of the global trading system. "The world faces extremely difficult economic and financial problems," said Donald Regan (Reagan's first-term treasury secretary) in 1982, "essentially without precedent in the postwar period."[4]

If the immediate challenges were severe, however, more promising trends were working their way to the surface. As discussed in chapter 1, the shifts of the 1970s actually helped preserve and even accentuate America's key economic strengths, from its position of advantage in the emerging post-industrial model, to its ability to attract a seemingly inexhaustible gusher of capital from abroad. "The US clearly has the potential dynamism, the resources and the institutional flexibility" to adapt in this new era, one CIA assessment concluded; "many other countries are not so fortunate."[5] At the same time, even as onrushing globalization was exacerbating protectionist insecurities in vulnerable sectors, it was promoting the greater intertwining of national economies and the rejuvenation of global capitalism. The technological and other trends underlying this phenomenon would only intensify in the 1980s and after, continuing to remake the international system in the process. As World Bank President A. W. Clausen noted in 1983, there was an "unprecedented integration of the global economy" occurring.[6] "The nature of scientific and technological change was such that societies were converging," George Shultz subsequently said.[7] Amid the dangers that menaced the global economy, there were profound opportunities as well.

The Reagan administration had no step-by-step plan for exploiting these opportunities when it took power, and as we will see, it would often take time for U.S. officials to fashion effective approaches. From the early 1980s onward, however, the administration did see that opportunities were indeed emerging, as demonstrated by the speeches and comments of key officials such as Shultz and Reagan, and as reflected in a growing body of intelligence assessments.[8] Perhaps more important, the administration also had, in Reagan himself, a leader with an intuitive feel for—and unwavering belief in—the promise of liberal capitalism at home and abroad. In Reagan's eyes, the U.S. economy was "one of the great wonders of the world," and it would certainly prosper if the right policies were pursued. The president was equally committed to the advance of free markets overseas, viewing this as the route to sustained prosperity "everywhere in the world." The market was "the one true path," Reagan would say, "where I believe we can find the map to the world's future."[9]

When it came to economics, then, the administration's overriding goal was to unleash what Reagan termed "the magic of the marketplace," both in the United States and abroad.[10] As Donald Regan explained, "a deep and abiding faith in the power of the marketplace" represented the "heart and soul of Reaganomics" and the key to the administration's economic program.[11] Similarly, the president and advisers such as Shultz and Regan (and later Baker, Regan's second-term successor) touted the potential of neoliberal policies to transform the global economy, and U.S. officials averred that Washington had a "historic opportunity" to promote these practices and ignite a new era of worldwide growth. Information-age technologies, NSC staffer Norman Bailey wrote, "will totally transform the world and lead to the greatest economic boom in history (unless the world destroys itself first)."[12] Reagan himself referenced the "profound transformation" underway in the world economy, and he outlined his foreign economic policy in unapologetic terms. "We apply the principles of economic freedom at home," he said. "We should not export central planning and statist economics abroad." "Free markets, low tax rates, free trade" were "the most valuable foreign aid we can give"; they were the "weapons of peace we must deploy in the struggle to win a future of liberty for mankind."[13]

Although the international dimensions of this campaign are of primary interest here, it was the domestic aspects that first took precedence for the administration. Reagan saw reinvigorating the U.S. economy as the precursor to any effective foreign policy, and his top priority was to break the grip of inflation. "Inflation is no longer an economic catchword," Reagan had said in 1978. "To all Americans it is something as violent as a mugger, as frightening as an armed robber and as deadly as a hit-man."[14] Following Carter's example, Reagan lent the Federal Reserve (Fed) strong tacit support as it sought to kill the inflationary cycle by raising the prime rate above 21 percent and restricting the money supply. He persisted in this stance even as Paul Volcker's measures sent the country into deep recession in 1981–1982, eliciting angry protests from farmers and other aggrieved constituencies, and causing plummeting Republican popularity prior to the midterm elections. "If not us, who?" Reagan asked critics. "If not now, when?" The short-term pain was intense, but by 1982–1983, inflation was plummeting, falling to 3.2 percent in 1983 and staying at healthy levels for the rest of the decade and after.[15]

The assault on inflation was the vanguard for a larger effort to tap the potential of the U.S. economy through neoliberal reform. From Reagan's perspective, the economy had suffered of late precisely because it was "overgoverned, overregulated, and overtaxed."[16] Like other neoliberal leaders, he seized on the fraying of the Keynesian consensus to push through a raft of measures meant to limit government intervention and restore the supremacy of the market. A bruising legislative battle in 1981 led to a tax reform that cut personal income rates by 23 percent over three years, dropped the top marginal personal rate from 70 to 50 percent, and slashed capital gains taxes while increasing corporate write-offs and investment credits—all told, a cumulative tax reduction of $750 billion over five years, or the largest tax cut in U.S. history to that date. Spiraling budget deficits subsequently forced a tactical retrenchment via "revenue enhancements," but another major tax reform in 1986 further lowered the top individual rate from 50 to 28 percent, while also simplifying the code. The objective, Reagan declared, was to "send one simple, straightforward message to an entire nation: America, go for it!"[17]

The tax cuts were accompanied by other important steps. Again following his predecessors, Reagan launched a deregulatory campaign featuring an early freeze on pending regulatory orders, the appointment of regulatory reformers or deregulators to key positions, curbs on the power of the Federal Trade Commission, and the termination of a major and long-standing anti-trust lawsuit against IBM. Reagan also ordered that all new regulations be subjected to economic cost-benefit analysis, and he pushed for further dereg-ulation of finance and other sectors. "Our economic program is designed to free up the marketplace from government intrusion," Donald Regan said—"to unleash the productive capacity of our economy." The administra-tion simultaneously rolled back the influence of organized labor, to enhance corporate profitability and remove a goad to rising wages and inflationary pressures. Reagan jolted the labor movement by firing over 11,000 air traf-fic controllers who illegally went on strike in 1981, and his appointment of anti-union officials to the National Labor Relations Board ensured that his presidency would be seen as a time when the balance of power shifted deci-sively toward management rather than labor.[18]

As critics alleged, this economic program had some very problematic results. High interest rates pounded "old economy" industries (particularly manufacturing) that were already reeling, and made credit harder to obtain for low- and middle-income Americans. Likewise, the rollback of union power accentuated downward pressure on wages for many workers, just as the Reagan tax cuts increased the inequalities that were being driven by structural economic transformations. The combined effect of these influ-ences was significant: whereas in 1975 the top 1 percent of families possessed 22 percent of U.S. wealth, by 1995 the number was 42 percent and climb-ing.[19] Beyond all this, Reagan's tax cuts—when combined with sky-high defense spending—led to spiraling budget deficits. Over time, these deficits would squeeze social programs, exert a moderate drag on growth, and fuel among many observers a pronounced sense of national vulnerability. Federal finances, embittered Reaganite and former budget czar David Stockman wrote, had become "an utter, mind-numbing catastrophe."[20]

Yet if *Reaganomics* remains a term of opprobrium in some circles, its broadest macro effects were quite positive. Even dramatic budget deficits were not nearly as damaging for America as for other countries, because the inflow of foreign capital made those deficits comparatively easy to finance. And in general, the Reagan years marked the start of one of the most impressive, sustained expansions in U.S. history. By late 1982, the United States was leading the developed countries out of recession, and over the next two years, its economy expanded at a rate three times that of Western Europe.[21] U.S. growth reached over 7 percent in 1984, remained around 3–4 percent through the end of the 1980s, and continued, follow-ing a brief recession in the early 1990s, through end of the millennium.

Consumption boomed, the financial sector sizzled, and corporate profits and investment skyrocketed. The Dow more than tripled between 1982 and 1987, and the crash of October 1987 was a mere speed bump en route to a fourteenfold increase between 1982 and 1999.[22] "The American economy is like a race horse that's begun to gallop out in front of the field," Reagan boasted.[23] At the very least, the economy was demolishing expectations from when Reagan's presidency began. As Herbert Meyer noted in 1983, "Fear that our economy would falter has given way to mounting excitement over the budding recovery. Inflation has dropped from double-digit levels to an annual rate of less than 4 percent, interest rates are easing, and the stock market is at a record level and rising. Today the debate among economists and business executives swirls around the question of whether the coming boom will be the most powerful in recent history or merely one of the most powerful."[24]

Admittedly, Reagan could not claim all credit for this performance. The economy benefitted greatly from falling oil prices as the 1980s proceeded, and from the advantageous structural changes and policy innovations that predated his presidency (and followed it, as well). But even so, there is little question that Reagan's policies were fundamental to the emerging renewal of U.S. economic prowess. "By bringing down the rate of inflation in the mid-1980s," historian Louis Galambos concludes, "the government opened the way for the private sector to fund the transformations essential to U.S. competitiveness."[25] In the same vein, slashing tax rates encouraged investment and increased profitability, and continued deregulation facilitated a wave of mergers and acquisitions that further strengthened American competitiveness. As historian Robert Collins writes, one of Reagan's signal achievements, "now clear in retrospect, was to set in motion . . . what economists label 'the Great Expansion,' an unparalleled twenty-year burst of prosperity at century's end."[26]

If Reagan's initiatives helped fortify U.S. economic power, they also left an indelible imprint on the development of economic policy. *Time* magazine had observed that the administration's proposed tax cuts would "put Ronald Reagan's mark on the U.S. economy and on American society for a generation or more."[27] The prediction was prescient. Reagan's policies were central to reorienting the economy along more market-oriented, neoliberal lines, and to bringing the ideas that had begun to gain sway during the 1970s firmly into the mainstream of U.S. political discourse. The success of those policies in stimulating robust growth, in turn, ensured that tax reduction, deregulation, and an emphasis on strengthening the private over the public sector remained at the forefront of the national agenda for years thereafter.

"What contemporaries somewhat derisively called 'Reaganomics,'" Collins notes, "cast a long shadow."[28]

From the beginning, Reagan hoped to have an equally profound impact abroad. A great enthusiasm for fostering free-market practices overseas characterized Reagan's rhetoric and policy during the 1980s, and constituted the logical counterpart to his administration's domestic program. "The validity of old-fashioned market economics" was universal, Undersecretary of State for Economic Affairs W. Allen Wallis explained; "good economic policy is good economic policy, whether the application is domestic or international."[29] Administration officials believed that neoliberal success at home would have a powerful demonstration effect abroad, and Reagan underscored that support for the "principles of economic freedom" was the connective tissue between domestic and international policy.[30] Free trade and open capital markets, reduced government intervention, the promotion of private enterprise and a pro-market approach to growth—these were the practices that Washington would encourage other nations to adopt.

As was true of Reagan's democratic proselytism, this stress on spreading the market gospel drew on a range of considerations. The deepest taproot was ideological, for Reagan viewed economic liberty as a God-given right and a chief marker of difference between the United States and its totalitarian enemies. "Only when the human spirit is allowed to invent and create, only when individuals are given a personal stake in deciding economic policies and benefiting from their success—only then can societies remain economically alive, dynamic, prosperous, progressive, and free," he argued.[31] Similarly, Reagan averred that the fate of economic liberty was intertwined with that of democracy, because these twin virtues were mutually dependent and mutually reinforcing. "The democratic and free-market revolutions are really the same revolution," he said; there was a "vital nexus between economic and political freedom."[32] For Reagan, then, promoting the market ethos was an indisputable moral good and an essential part of America's national heritage. "We believe in freedom," he said in 1981; America could act on no other basis.[33]

There was no doubting Reagan's conviction here, nor was there any doubting his sincerity about the efficacy of the policies he touted. As strongly as any U.S. official before him, Reagan believed that the principles of free trade and capitalist development were "undeniable and universally true," and that these practices represented the surest—the only—route to lasting prosperity.[34] The president consistently argued that free trade was the ultimate positive-sum game, one that would enrich all participants, just as protectionism would impoverish them.[35] And both before and during his presidency, he contended that market-based reform—particularly in the Third World—was the key to unlocking the potential of countries everywhere. "Poverty *is* not imposed on poor nations by those called rich," he argued in 1980. "They are poor precisely to the extent they have ignored or turned away from free market capitalism and yes to the extent they have placed their faith in Marxist-controlled economies."[36] Or, as he said in 1981,

> History demonstrates that time and again, in place after place, economic growth and human progress make their greatest strides in countries that encourage economic freedom. . . . The critical test is whether government is genuinely working to liberate individuals by creating incentives to work, invest, and succeed. Individual farmers, laborers, owners, and managers—they are the heart and soul of development. Trust them.[37]

By empowering the hidden hand of capitalism, Reagan believed, countries would serve their own best interests, as well.

Promoting market policies was no matter of charity, however, because such reforms would also serve U.S. interests. During the 1970s, Anthony Solomon had explained that "no nation has benefitted more than the United States" from an open system, and the Reagan administration firmly endorsed this conclusion.[38] Because America had the world's largest and most advanced economy, it was well placed to reap the benefits of a more liberal order. Opening financial and capital markets overseas would further enable Washington to tap the world's savings; promoting liberalized trade would create new outlets for U.S. goods and services. Likewise, encouraging countries to welcome foreign investment would foster possibilities for American corporations operating abroad, adding to the growing flow of investment income back to the United States. Expanding the realm of market economics, a Treasury report concluded, meant "expanding opportunities for U.S. exports, investments, and finance."[39] A U.S. Trade Representative (USTR) report reached the same conclusion: "One of the principal requirements of a strong U.S. economy is the maintenance of open markets both at home and abroad."[40]

Such statements had long been staples of U.S. foreign policy, but this objective was especially salient in the Reagan years. As administration officials noted, the explosion of world commerce during the 1970s had left the country "more dependent on international trade than at any time in recent history."[41] U.S. capital markets were more open and globally oriented than at any time in the postwar era, and the share of GDP provided by trade had doubled in the decade before 1981.[42] Export-related jobs had risen by more than 75 percent during the 1970s, and roughly 80 percent of U.S. manufacturing jobs created between 1977 and 1980 were tied to exports.[43] Accordingly, Washington now had an even greater stake in beating back protectionism and driving forward globalization. There was pressing need, a presidential briefing paper noted, to "provide external environment that can liberate creative energies of our people and provide the markets we need to build the world-class high technology industries on which our futures depend."[44] "Shaping the international economic environment," Baker would say during Reagan's second term, was a policy imperative.[45]

Ultimately, this "shaping" would pay more than economic dividends. It would also further U.S. geopolitical aims and affirm the American resurgence. Just as Reagan saw capitalism as the best guarantee of prosperity, he saw prosperity as the best guarantee of global stability. "Those which put freedom as the first priority find that they have also provided security and economic progress," he said.[46] More broadly, insofar as the United States could spread its preferred economic policies, it would further demonstrate the bankruptcy of the Soviet model and underscore America's revitalized global influence. This was a consistent theme of Reagan's speeches, which contrasted the success of the market model with the failures of statist approaches, and the same ideas filled Shultz's statements as well.[47] A core U.S. goal, he argued in 1983, must be "the demonstration of the strength and viability of market-oriented economies and the democratic form of government with which they are associated." The American model had the momentum, he wrote subsequently, and Washington must press the advantage:

A worldwide revolution in economic thought and economic policy is underway. . . . After more than a century of fashionable Marxist mythology about economic determinism and the "crisis of capitalism," the key to human progress turns out to be those very Western concepts of political and economic freedom that Marxists claimed were obsolete. . . . Today—in a supreme irony—it is the communist system that looks bankrupt, morally as well as economically. The West is resilient and resurgent.

American values, he concluded, "turn out to be more central to the world's future than many may have realized."[48]

Indeed, for all the ideas that drove Reagan's policies, what lent those endeavors such confidence was the familiar sense that history was again working in America's favor, and that any challenges were therefore accompanied by wonderful possibilities. "We have no mission of mediocrity," Reagan said in 1983. "We were born to carry liberty's banner and build the very meaning of progress, and our opportunities have never been greater."[49] As the decade went on, U.S. officials would reference "the worldwide trend towards political and economic freedom" as "the most significant development of this decade," and Shultz would declare that "we are winning" the battle between freedom and statism.[50] "America is again in a position to have a major influence over the direction of events," he wrote. "We have a duty to help shape the trends, as they evolve, in accordance with our ideals and interests, to help construct a new pattern of international stability that will ensure peace, prosperity, and freedom for coming generations."[51] In economics as elsewhere, the United States would thus retake the offensive. This was the core ambition behind the administration's foreign economic policy, and the ethos that would guide it amid the crises and challenges ahead.

Trade, Finance, and Policy Coordination in the Western World

Reagan's approach would certainly be tested by his dealings with the major developed countries. With hindsight, we can now see that the 1980s were a time of convergence among the Western powers: an era in which globalization was interlinking the leading economies more tightly, in which international trade and economic coordination took major strides forward, and in which the neoliberal ascendancy that had originated in the 1970s gained force and breadth across the developed world. The success of the policies implemented by Thatcher and Reagan, and the emulation that success inspired; the rise of leaders such as Helmut Kohl in West Germany and Nakasone Yasuhiro in Japan; and the generalized trend toward deregulation and liberalization—all these phenomena ensured that the 1980s would eventually be seen as a "neo-liberal golden era," a time when market-oriented approaches achieved dominance. "Nations already bound together by common political ideals and economic interests," Shultz and Baker wrote in 1986, "have come even closer together in their thinking on how best to pursue those interests."[52]

For much of the 1980s, however, it was not the concord but the conflicts that ruled the headlines in U.S. relations with the major Western economies. Intense trade competition, confrontations over commercial imbalances and currency valuations, the threat of resurgent protectionism at home and abroad, and the dislocations caused by the very openness of the post–Bretton Woods order all posed formidable obstacles to Reagan's agenda, and often made it seem that the developed world was not coming together but coming apart. The future may have been promising, in other words, but just getting there would be no easy task.

The challenges that U.S. officials faced were particularly pronounced in the realm of trade. The completion of the Tokyo Round in 1979 had signaled that the Western powers were determined to preserve the postwar trading system even amid severe economic trauma, but by the early 1980s, that system was again under strain. Amid widespread recession, world trade contracted in 1981–1982, as slow growth and high unemployment fueled a protectionist clamor throughout the West. "Protectionist pressures in the major trading countries today are the most severe that they have been since the Second World War," Wallis noted; a "vicious whirlpool" was forming as one restrictive measure gave impetus to the next.[53]

That whirlpool, ironically, drew strength from precisely the globalizing forces that had been unleashed in the 1970s. The explosion of commercial and financial interchange touched off during that decade had begun the long-term rejuvenation of global capitalism. Yet globalization could have paradoxical effects, and that same explosion had intensified international competitive pressures just as industries across the developed world were already being battered. "Basically, international competition is a healthy reflection of the economic development process and the growing integration of the world economy," the NIC reported in 1982. "But competitive pressures are far more severe than ever before because they are appearing on so many fronts at the same time, and the industrial economies are far more open to foreign trade."[54] In these circumstances, prospects for further trade liberalization to capitalize on the promise of globalization seemed dismal. The possibility of a protectionist backlash that might strangle that phenomenon, conversely, looked all too likely.

No trade relationship was more fraught during the early 1980s than that between the United States and Japan. Since the 1970s, Japan's rapid postwar growth had fueled fears of U.S. decline and stimulated speculation that Tokyo might one day rule the world economy. The fact that Japan had achieved its success via an aggressive form of export-led growth, which exploited open Western markets while simultaneously sheltering domestic industry behind dense protectionist barriers, only heightened the tensions. The U.S. annual merchandise trade deficit with Japan ballooned from $5 billion in 1976, to $16 billion in 1981, to $46 billion in 1985, and industries from autos to semiconductors faced existential threats from Japanese competition.[55] Tokyo, one U.S. expert noted, was "eating our lunch."[56] Although Japanese formal tariffs fell significantly following the Tokyo Round, the persistence of ubiquitous nontariff barriers (NTBs), subsidies, and other discriminatory tactics elicited charges of predatory trade, injecting tension into the bilateral relationship and raising fears of a catastrophic trade war between the world's two largest economies. "Something has to change—soon," wrote Reagan's first U.S. trade representative, William Brock. Japanese practices, a paper prepared by Brock's staff argued, were "threatening to poison not only our bilateral relationship, but indeed the whole world trading system."[57]

Compounding international trade frictions were issues of exchange-rate volatility and macroeconomic coordination. As noted previously, the shift away from fixed rates had dramatically heightened the fluidity of international commerce and finance, but it had fostered significant instability, too. "The great interdependence of nations that resulted from the expansion of an open system of trade and payments has, almost by definition, increased each country's vulnerability to developments in other nations," Baker said.[58] During the 1970s, this reality had spurred U.S. policymakers to pursue the type of policy cooperation achieved at the Bonn Summit, and to take measures to steady the dollar—and thereby the exchange rates structuring global trade—following its long post–Bretton Woods slide. By the early 1980s, however, major problems of coordination and volatility were again becoming evident. The spike in U.S. interest rates under Volcker attracted a surge of foreign investment, draining capital from other Western economies and driving the value of the dollar upward by 59 percent from 1980 to early 1985. That trend, in turn, destabilized international trade flows. Prices of American exports soared and those of imports plummeted, fueling massive trade imbalances and stimulating inflationary pressures in countries that consumed U.S. goods. "Currency relationships oscillated wildly," notes one scholar, "straining the world trading system."[59]

This was an undeniably challenging set of conditions, even for a leader with as much purpose as Reagan. There was never any doubt about what the president wanted in U.S. relations with the developed West. He called for further liberalization of world trade through a new GATT round and other negotiations if necessary, and he strongly advocated for market solutions and against protectionism. As U.S. officials wrote before a Western economic meeting in 1984, "The challenge for Summit leaders is to consolidate improvement towards worldwide economic recovery, reconfirm our commitment to resist protectionism, promote early progress in liberalizing trade and improving the trade system, and agree on the need for new multilateral trade negotiations to achieve comprehensive liberalization."[60] During the early 1980s, however, turning aspiration into achievement was no easy matter.

With Western Europe slow to emerge from recession, politicians in that region saw little hope of public support for deepening trade—and thus increasing competition—through a new GATT round, and NTBs crept upward across the developed world. The proportion of developed-country manufactures subject to NTBs rose from 20 percent in 1980 to 30 percent in 1983, U.S. officials reported: "The world is moving away from, rather than toward, comprehensive free trade."[61] Nor could Reagan claim dramatic early progress with Japan. Although U.S. officials continually lobbied Tokyo to liberalize its economy and commercial practices, the entrenched nature of Japanese protectionism meant that the resulting gains seemed quite modest compared to a spiraling trade deficit.[62] Bilateral tensions seemed close to a boiling point, with even administration insiders accusing Japan of pursuing a systematic campaign to destroy U.S. industry. "They clearly intend to dominate by 1990/2000," Commerce Secretary Malcolm Baldrige warned. "Can we afford to be 'Adam Smith' if they do not want to play?"[63] Most officials offered more measured assessments, but there was nonetheless widespread frustration hanging over U.S. dealings with Tokyo.

In some ways, in fact, Reagan's policies initially exacerbated the problems he faced. During the early 1980s, the administration dismissed the need for coordinated intervention on exchange rates and brushed aside allies' complaints about the Volcker shock. U.S. officials insisted, not unreasonably, that Washington could best spur global recovery by getting its own house in order. Similarly, Treasury officials argued that exchange-rate intervention would only distort the free market, allowing countries to delay the broader policy changes that would promote stronger growth and thereby ease the uneven economic performance that caused unstable rates. "We remain convinced," a Treasury Department memo stated, "that the lasting way to achieve greater stability in exchange rates is to move toward better convergence of economic conditions among the major economies."[64] Insofar as the administration stressed international coordination, it emphasized "policy convergence"—the idea that other countries should follow the U.S. lead in curbing inflation, cutting taxes, and slashing regulation as the best path to stability and growth. "'Convergence,'" Regan said, "is simply a rather fancy word for what is really common sense."[65]

As even some critics admitted, this approach gave Washington the flexibility it needed to defeat inflation, and to set off a recovery that would pull in huge quantities of imports and ultimately stimulate foreign economies as well.[66] In addition, over time the success of the U.S. economy would provide a strong argument for the "policy convergence" that Reagan championed. Amid the difficult circumstances of the early 1980s, however, the immediate effects were more negative. Reagan's apparent indifference to the allies' discomfort exacerbated trans-Atlantic tensions, adding to the pressures on international trade. German officials memorably charged U.S. policy with causing the "highest rates of interest . . . since the birth of Christ." Not to be outdone, the French complained that Western summits had become "nearly worthless," and they threatened to block movement on multilateral trade talks until the dollar was brought under control.[67] "The United States," Reagan's aides conceded, "has not yet developed an effective and convincing international dimension for its economic program."[68]

There was blowback at home, too. By ensuring the continued rise of the dollar, Reagan's hands-off approach to exchange rates also ensured a flood of comparatively cheap imports and a crunch for U.S. exporters—both of which outcomes hit domestic industry hard and fed a soaring overall trade deficit that reached a record-setting $123 billion in 1984.[69] Political support for free trade dwindled, with business groups, organized labor, and other constituencies arguing that U.S. policies were leading to ruin. "This administration," Regan said in 1984, "is going to be under a great deal of political pressure this year to raise the barriers of Fortress America."[70] From the White House, Reagan steadfastly defended the principles of free trade, but his willingness to accept domestic dislocation as its price infuriated the critics all the more. When the president denied protective relief to a U.S. shoe industry that was being eviscerated by foreign competition, his admonition that Americans must "live according to our principles" was cold comfort to those who suffered.[71] With other key industries—from automobiles to steel and beyond—undergoing their own agonizing restructurings, it seemed that Reagan's stance might soon become politically untenable. In 1985, the New York Times offered an obituary for the era of postwar trade liberalization. "Industry by industry," it noted, "the battle to maintain open markets is being lost."[72]

This was a damning provisional assessment of Reagan's foreign economic policy. Even as that judgment was rendered, however, the outlook was beginning to brighten. The economic recovery that had started in the United States in 1982–1983 was taking hold across the Western world, easing recession-induced strains and improving the climate for international cooperation.[73] Simultaneously, the neoliberal trend was accelerating, as the cohort of reformist leaders grew, and the attraction of emulating the steps that were enabling the vigorous U.S. expansion increased. There had been a "remarkable transformation of attitudes on economic policies," Wallis observed in Reagan's second term. "Market-oriented policies that were once dismissed as old-fashioned, naïve, and impractical are now seen to work in practice, and there is a major trend toward such policies throughout the world."[74]

The conversion of François Mitterrand was noteworthy in this regard. The first socialist president of the French Fifth Republic had come to power pledging to "break with capitalism," and his initial policies evinced determination to favor the state over the market. The government nationalized banks and other large corporations, boosted public spending and social benefits, and raised taxes on high-income individuals. But rather than jump-starting growth, these measures provoked a severe crisis featuring inflation, rising unemployment, and capital flight. Faced with economic disaster and political humiliation, Mitterrand switched course dramatically. Guided by Finance Minister Jacques Delors, and encouraged by Washington and Bonn, the Élysée embraced austerity and market-based reforms, including the de facto privatization of state-owned enterprises and modernization of the financial sector. "The state must know how to efface itself," said Mitterrand. As one of Reagan's economic advisers noted, this striking French U-turn was among several indicators of "the spreading conviction . . . that growth based on non-market interventions and increasing prices was not viable in the 1980s."[75]

The French experience was certainly crucial in what it portended for Europe. Mitterrand's experiment had initially threatened to reverse recent moves toward greater European integration, as the falling franc put great strain on the EC coordinated exchange-rate system. His subsequent reversal, however, combined with other factors—namely the resolution of a long-standing dispute over the British financial contribution to the EC—to enable great leaps in both liberalization and integration. In 1986, EC members concluded the Single European Act. That agreement put Europe on the path to a true common market in which goods, money, and people could flow far more freely than before. It also presaged the final removal of national capital controls and a wave of neoliberal financial reforms, and it foreshadowed the even more significant steps that would soon follow: the creation of the European Union and of a common European currency.

The process of achieving these advances was both convoluted and contested, and the reforms themselves reflected a wide range of motives among EC members. For many Europeans, in fact, the drive for integration was impelled by a sense that only a more cohesive unit could compete economically with America, and through the late 1980s and after, U.S.-European trade disputes were as much the norm as the exception. In an important sense, though, the revival and deepening of the European project from the mid-1980s onward was a reflection of the moment of ideological consensus that Mitterrand's reversal had made possible. From London to Paris to Bonn, the leading EC players now agreed that freer trade, greater integration, and liberalized capital flows were vital to escaping the doldrums of the 1970s and early 1980s, and to competing effectively in the new global system. Trade disputes notwithstanding, this consensus marked a significant evolution in world political economy, one that generally made Europe a more attractive destination for U.S. trade and capital, and one that thus comported well with the basic goals and assertions of global Reaganomics.[76]

Meanwhile, the Reagan administration had become better positioned to capitalize on this neoliberal trend, because it was adopting policies that would allow it more effectively to navigate pressing challenges and opportunities. By 1985, for instance, the administration was reversing itself on exchange-rate and policy coordination, catalyzed by Shultz's increasingly outspoken advocacy on the issue from State, and particularly by the rise of the more politically astute James Baker at Treasury. As Baker understood, the hands-off policy toward the dollar and issues of coordination more broadly was killing support for free trade at home, while also introducing dangerous instability into global trade. The benefits of floating rates were undeniable, he acknowledged, but so were the "substantial volatility and unpredictability" that system courted.[77] Greater international cooperation was therefore essential to restoring exchange-rate equilibrium, stemming the rise of the dollar, and easing pressures on the world trading system. As Reagan himself now affirmed, "An unpredictable world exchange rate system serves to destroy the very foundation of international trade." Or, as he said in another instance, "We must never again permit wild currency swings to cripple our farmers and other exporters."[78]

This shift set the stage for a renewal of the collective international economic management that the administration had earlier spurned. The most important milestone in this process was the Plaza Accord, an agreement reached among the finance ministers of the United States, United Kingdom, West Germany, France, and Japan at a meeting in New York in September 1985. (This Group of 5, or G-5, would soon become the G-7 with the addition of Italy and Canada.[79]) The Plaza Accord had been hammered out in intense secrecy over three months of behind-the-scenes negotiations leading up to the September meeting in New York. As implemented, the accord entailed a coordinated, $10 billion central-bank intervention in the exchange markets, in order to achieve, in Baker's words, "some orderly appreciation of the main non-dollar currencies against the dollar."[80] As the *New York Times* noted, this intervention marked the first attempt at coordinated, multilateral currency stabilization since the final collapse of Bretton Woods in 1973, and it had the desired effect and then some.[81] By March 1986, the dollar had declined 24 percent against the mark and 26 percent against the yen. By early 1987, it had fallen by 40–50 percent against these currencies from its peak in early 1985, essentially reversing the appreciation of the half-decade prior.[82]

In some ways, the Plaza Accord and resulting dollar devaluation were simply a testament to U.S. power in the global economy. This episode demonstrated that meaningful coordination was possible only with U.S. participation. It also showed that Washington could leverage its security presence abroad, as well as the threat of a protectionist backlash at home, to secure a major competitive devaluation that slashed the value of the U.S. foreign debt by perhaps one-third, and that significantly advantaged American exports. (In fact, U.S. exports boomed in the decade after 1985, growing by an average of over 10 percent annually.)[83] At the same time, however, the accord had a broader multilateral significance, for it confirmed that Reagan's shift toward coordination was enabling a concerted counterattack to thwart protectionism and reinvigorate global liberalization. "What's new here is that we're all here together," Baker commented.[84] Indeed, Plaza reflected the fact that *all* the Western economies had an immense stake in averting the trade-restrictive measures that threatened in the United States, and in giving Reagan the political and economic leeway to ward off the threat. In this respect, the pact succeeded brilliantly; it immediately gave Reagan the domestic credibility he needed to veto a protectionist textile bill "without fear of challenge." As one aide said, Plaza was "the most successful public relations operation of the decade."[85]

If anything, Plaza worked *too* well. By 1986–1987, the dollar had sunk to a level that was inflicting considerable pain on exporters in Europe and Japan, and threatening renewed destabilization of trade. In response, at a meeting in Paris in February 1987, the summit countries resolved that currency values had reached a level "consistent with underlying economic fundamentals."[86] With Baker again at the forefront, the parties reached a private understanding that their central banks would preserve equilibrium and keep exchange rates within a fairly steady range. Tokyo invested heavily in dollar securities to arrest the drop of that currency; other central banks took similar actions. As Baker confided to Bush in April, "We have, in fact, been intervening in large amounts with other countries to stabilize the dollar—something of course I wouldn't acknowledge or make public."[87] In essence, the Louvre accords built on foundations laid by Plaza, signaling a firmer G-7 and U.S. commitment to pursuing the exchange-rate stability needed to protect and advance world trade.

Significantly, the coordination that evolved during 1985–1987 did not pertain solely to exchange rates; it also touched macroeconomic policy more broadly. These twin forms of cooperation, U.S. officials now appreciated, had to be seen as mutually reinforcing. There was no longer a doubt, Baker noted, "that closer coordination of economic policies will be required to achieve the stronger, more balanced growth and compatible policies necessary to reduce the large trade imbalances that remain and foster greater exchange rate stability."[88] Beginning with Plaza in 1985, intensive negotiations led to progressive advances toward this goal. At the Tokyo Summit in 1986, Baker and Reagan secured agreement to strengthen the ability of the IMF to monitor the policy fundamentals of the G-7 countries, and to suggest remedial action when necessary.[89] The summit also led to joint interest-rate reductions, meant to provide coordinated stimulus to Western economies.[90] Another breakthrough came the next year at the Louvre, where deals on macroeconomic policy accompanied exchange-market coordination. Bonn agreed to augment and accelerate a tax-reduction package; Japan committed to cut interest rates and stimulate domestic demand; the United States, building on recent congressional legislation, pledged to restrain spending and reduce deficits. Holding to these promises, particularly in the U.S. case, was sometimes easier said than done. But a coordination process had been established, and it would continue at future summits. "The major countries," Baker said in 1988, "have . . . agreed on the basic directions that their policies should follow and . . . have made specific commitments to achieve these ends."[91]

Although the shortcomings of these dual coordination processes were not negligible, neither were the benefits. In the seven years after Louvre, exchange rates were significantly less volatile than in the fourteen years between the end of Bretton Woods and the Plaza Accord. That stability helped U.S. exports surge by perhaps 20–30 percent in 1987–1988 and contributed to a broader easing of protectionist sentiments.[92] "We have been successful in beating back the protectionists," Reagan declared, and pressures for broad, congressionally mandated trade restrictions were largely contained or diffused.[93] Increased coordination, IMF officials added, had also helped "maintain growth at relatively high rates, dampen inflationary pressures, stabilize exchange rates at more realistic levels, and reduce external imbalances."[94] These processes of cooperation proved their worth in late 1987 when, following the October stock market crash in New York, G-7 banks made a coordinated intervention to increase liquidity and prevent the onset of recession or worse. "After that crash, all the major economic countries could have turned inward, but they chose not to do so," Baker said.[95] By the end of the decade, the achievement of imperfect but improved multilateral coordination was easing the conflicts that had roiled intra-Western relations—and facilitating the stability and confidence that were prerequisites to further liberalization of the world economy.

During the mid- and late 1980s, the administration was also making progress toward these goals in the difficult context of U.S.-Japan relations.

Contrary to some of the more alarmist assessments during Reagan's presidency, that relationship was never as adversarial or one-sided as sometimes thought. The security alliance provided a strong degree of underlying cohesion between Washington and Tokyo, and Reagan enjoyed warm ties with Japanese leaders such as Nakasone. ("He would be the 'catcher' and the President the 'pitcher,'" Nakasone told Reagan in 1983.[96]) Moreover, despite concerns that Washington was impotent to combat Japanese protectionism, the United States possessed real leverage. Because Japan depended on America for security, it could not risk an outright break; because the U.S. market absorbed a whopping 37 percent of Japanese exports, Tokyo had huge incentives to avert an outbreak of retaliatory protectionism. "Japan has little choice but to negotiate the best terms it can for access to U.S. and West European markets," the CIA reported in 1982. "It has nowhere else to go."[97] Other U.S. officials noted that "Japan has more to lose from U.S. retaliation or use of leverage" than vice versa.[98]

Even in these circumstances, the existence of entrenched interests within the Japanese economy, along with the consensual, deliberate style of the political system, ensured that moves toward liberalization were slow and unsatisfying at best. "Strong resistance from vested interests" was inevitable, INR analysts correctly assessed.[99] By the early and mid-1980s, however, there was an emerging group within Japan that favored a less protectionist approach. Politicians such as Nakasone, who wished to maintain strong ties with Washington; exporters who feared losing access to the U.S. market; banks and financial firms that stood to profit from more open currency and financial markets; and observers who understood that Japan was nearing the limits of its postwar economic model—these groups constituted a potentially receptive audience for American overtures and a possible force for change. "Those Japanese who share our views about structural change in Japan will want to 'use' us to strengthen their position and attain our shared objectives," U.S. officials noted; American influence should be applied in ways that amplified these voices.[100]

By late in Reagan's first term, the administration had begun to find ways of doing so. In late 1983 and early 1984, U.S. negotiators secured the yen/dollar agreement, which paved the way for a significant opening of Japanese capital markets. The accord included a variety of specific measures—internationalizing the yen and lowering barriers to capital flows, allowing foreign institutions greater access to Japanese financial markets, and others—along with detailed timetables for implementation. Many of these reforms had previously been desired by the Japanese financial sector. Nevertheless, the use of U.S. leverage, including the implicit threat of a protectionist backlash if Japan did not move forward, provided a critical boost to internal calls for change. "Action, action, action, that's what I want now," Regan declared late in the negotiations. "I'm through with patience."[101] "By playing hardball," CEA official Jeffrey Frankel wrote, "the U.S. side in the end won most of what it had sought."[102]

The gains were considerable. Most broadly, the yen/dollar reforms—which were largely implemented on or ahead of schedule, and which were complemented with additional steps in later years—marked a key step toward freeing Japanese capital flows and drawing that country into a more open financial order.[103] More specifically, they stimulated American financial service exports to Japan, and dramatically expanded Japanese capital flows to the United States. By making Japanese capital more mobile, the accords effectively accentuated the power of a strong U.S. economy, with deep and sophisticated financial markets, to pull in Japanese savings and investment. "The net effect," two analysts note, "was to liberate large sums of Japanese savings for American use."[104] During the negotiations, Regan had urged Japanese officials to "open up your capital markets and learn to share," and this was exactly what happened. Japanese net long-term capital outflow exploded from $17.7 billion in 1983 to $137.1 billion in 1987, with the proportion destined for the United States expanding rapidly.[105] This influx of foreign capital boosted U.S. growth, while also facilitating U.S. deficit spending and offsetting the impact of American trade imbalances. "An enormous tide of money" was now rolling eastward across the Pacific, one financial reporter wrote; skyrocketing Japanese capital exports were "helping finance the budget deficits of the United States Government."[106] Or, as Robert Gilpin notes, Japan was becoming the chief "financial backer of the continued economic and political hegemony of the United States."[107]

The yen/dollar agreement was no panacea for the broader economic relationship, of course. Trade frictions remained omnipresent throughout Reagan's presidency and after, manifesting in alarmist warnings about Tokyo's impending economic mastery, and sometimes in ugly Japan-bashing in the United States. Charged atmospherics aside, however, here too the administration eventually forged a strategy that at least managed the tensions and began making progress. To maintain executive leadership in trade policy and prevent Congress from enacting severe protectionism, the administration made several moves to signal that it was taking the Japanese challenge seriously. These measures included pushing Tokyo to accept "voluntary" restraints on auto exports to the United States beginning in the early 1980s, a step that contradicted Reagan's free-trade philosophy but was useful, aides wrote, in avoiding charges of "'selling-out' to the Japanese."[108] An agreement reached in 1986 to protect the semiconductor industry against Japanese discrimination and dumping served a similar purpose, as did the decision to impose up to $300 million in sanctions when Tokyo failed to heed that accord.[109] By the time he left office, Reagan had threatened additional sanctions on several other issues, not out of desire to use them, but to maintain his domestic credibility. "It is necessary," he had earlier written, "that we stem the strong and growing protectionist sentiment in the Congress which, if not contained, risks overtaking our concerted efforts to achieve significant and measurable progress in resolving our serious bilateral disputes."[110]

Yet the administration struck a delicate balance in doing so, because the second prong of its strategy entailed strong, sustained pressure to secure Japanese concessions on trade reform. Throughout the 1980s, the administration used a variety of media—formal negotiations, public statements, and private communications—to urge movement on key issues. It equally used these media to threaten, tacitly and sometimes explicitly, that Tokyo was courting trouble absent "some significant and meaningful steps."[111] "We must maintain sufficient pressure on the Japanese," a key NSDD averred.[112] Officials such as Baldrige, Regan, and Baker took this counsel to heart, often bluntly criticizing Japanese trade practices. And while Reagan generally played "good cop," he also punctuated U.S. policy by threatening to use the retaliatory authority conveyed by Section 301 trade legislation to punish Japan for unfair commercial practices—a maneuver, like the semiconductor sanctions, that allowed him to intensify pressure on Tokyo while ensuring that pressure from Congress did not explode.[113]

Not surprisingly, this approach engendered some hard feelings. One set of negotiations, Shultz wrote, "produced positive results in a painful, tooth-pulling effort that left everyone involved a little ragged and frustrated."[114] Despite the frustration, gradual and sometimes significant movement did occur in several areas: from decreased tariffs on cigarettes and chocolate ("two very sensitive items," U.S. officials wrote), to liberalized treatment of certain high-tech goods and medical equipment, to concessions on oranges and beef, to decisions to allow greater foreign participation in infrastructure projects.[115] Similarly, the fact that Japanese imports in sectors that were emphasized in one particular process—the market-oriented sector-selective (MOSS) talks—grew nearly twice as fast as those in other sectors (6.7 vs. 3.4 percent in 1985) indicated that U.S. policy was having an effect.[116] Admittedly, the bilateral trade deficit remained an enormous $60 billion in 1987, and Japanese barriers were still formidable in many sectors. Yet what liberalization did occur—along with Tokyo's acceptance of dramatic currency revaluation via the Plaza Accord—caused U.S. exports to Japan to increase substantially in the late 1980s, soaring between 34 and 46 percent in 1987–1988 alone.[117]

By this point, Reagan's diplomacy had obtained another significant result, which was simply enmeshing Japan in a continuing process of dialogue and negotiation on trade issues and broader structural changes in the Japanese economy. This represented a deliberate shift by the administration. After initially focusing on increasing U.S. market share, Reagan's negotiators pivoted to addressing the causes of that problem, first by attacking trade barriers themselves, and then by launching a campaign "to help foster structural adjustment in the Japanese economy to move it away from its export-led growth orientation toward greater growth through internal investment and demand."[118] The resulting initiatives—first MOSS and then the structural adjustment dialogue—were important in several ways. They provided a forum for sustained engagement and pressure, and a mechanism through which U.S. officials could consistently support Japanese counterparts who were seeking to reorient that economy. Politically, they also eased bilateral strains somewhat, by giving the Japanese an institutionalized opportunity to address U.S. structural problems such as budget deficits, and by ensuring that American officials could point to ongoing negotiations as reason to reject more precipitous retaliation.[119] Not coincidentally, the Bush administration would later adopt this same approach, launching its Structural Impediments Initiative (SII) to address difficult problems and keep control of the trade policy agenda at home.

In key respects, then, the trajectory of U.S.-Japan economic relations during the 1980s was more favorable than met the eye. Most basically, the Reagan administration had managed that relationship in a way that prevented commercial tensions from boiling over and undermining the world trading system. And if many U.S. commentators remained frustrated that Washington had not gotten more, Japanese observers were more impressed by how *much* change had occurred. Notes one author:

> From a Japanese perspective, the country had moved far and fast under Western prodding to liberalize trade. Under heavy pressure, Japan had opened up a variety of protected markets, such as telecommunications, cigarettes, beef, citrus, and airport construction. It had liberalized its financial markets, opening the securities and trust banking business to foreigners. . . . In the mid-1980s, under pressure from the West and from a revalued yen, Japan had stimulated domestic demand and had moved toward reducing its dependence on export-led growth.[120]

Reagan's goal was a more fluid global economy; his policy toward Japan furthered that aspiration through what it achieved and what it prevented.

By containing U.S.-Japan trade frictions, the administration also facilitated a broader international move toward trade liberalization. This shift was due partially to good fortune, in that plunging oil prices strengthened the Western recovery from mid-decade onward and created tailwinds for difficult negotiations. Yet it was also due to U.S. policy. Throughout the mid- and late 1980s, Reagan remained unbendingly opposed to any major departure from the free-trade agenda. "If the ghost of Smoot-Hawley rears its ugly head in Congress, if Congress crafts a depression-making bill, I'll fight it," he pledged.[121] Similarly, the administration recommitted itself to multilateral trade liberalization, arguing that the best way to defeat protectionism was to demonstrate the benefits of free trade by opening new markets abroad. "The only effective way to head off the forces of protectionism," U.S. officials explained, "is to be engaged in a negotiating process designed to increase—not just maintain—the openness of world markets."[122] By this logic, starting a new GATT round remained the gold standard, because it would enable the broadest opening of world commerce, and allow proponents of liberalization across numerous countries to join forces to offset the influence of protectionist elements at home. "Multinational trade negotiations permit us to counterbalance powerful groups that benefit from protection with groups that would benefit from a reduction in trade barriers and a more stable and comprehensive set of trading rules," Baker argued.[123]

By the mid-1980s, Reagan was pairing this steadiness of purpose with a more nuanced and effective strategy for realizing that aim. To dampen protectionist forces at home, the president made a series of rhetorical and tactical concessions. He mixed advocacy of free trade with calls for "fair trade," promising that Washington would not tolerate predatory practices.[124] The administration gave substance to this policy by sharply critiquing discriminatory trade practices abroad, and by using targeted sanctions and duties to defend U.S. industries that were being gutted by such practices. The threat and employment of sanctions against Japan was only one manifestation of this approach; Reagan used similar tactics against the EC, Brazil, South Korea, Taiwan, and others. "We are pursuing an aggressive program against unfair trade practices," Baker reassured U.S. senators.[125] The goal, he said privately, was to "slowdown [sic] protectionism and give our Republican allies on the Hill something to fight back with."[126]

Borrowing another tactic employed in U.S.-Japan relations, Reagan simultaneously used this campaign to remind key trade partners that the alternatives to negotiation and liberalization were not attractive. The threat of Section 301 sanctions had pushed Tokyo to make concessions and agree to launch the MOSS talks (and later, SII); given how dependent so many countries were on access to the gigantic U.S. import market, this approach was also effective against other actors. In early 1986, for instance, Reagan used this technique to halt new EC restrictions affecting U.S. farm exports and to channel that dispute into broader negotiations.[127] The threat of U.S. retaliation, Baker commented, had proven "a powerful weapon for opening markets" and a persuasive reason for countries to recommit to the GATT process.[128] Washington, he said at another point, was now pursuing "free trade with a bite."[129]

The administration heightened the pressure to revitalize global trade talks by adopting what was termed the "minilateral" strategy. To circumvent lingering roadblocks—principally in Europe—to a new GATT round, U.S. negotiators pursued an indirect route to the destination. They focused on reaching free-trade agreements (FTAs) with willing individual participants, on the theory that doing so would create momentum toward broader trade liberalization, and foster fears among other countries that they might be left behind. This was a key rationale behind projects such as the Caribbean Basin Initiative in the early 1980s, and then FTAs with Israel and, more important, Canada. The minilateral approach, Baker candidly explained, was a "lever to achieve more open trade. Other nations are forced to recognize that we will devise ways to expand trade—with or without them."[130]

The U.S.-Canada FTA, negotiated during Reagan's second term and signed in 1988, was the foremost example of this approach. A bilateral trade agreement made sense given the immense commerce between the two countries: in 1985, Canada sold 76 percent of its exports to the United States, while the corresponding American figure was 26 percent. Yet it also reflected the way that congressional protectionism could actually be used to strengthen the attraction of free-trade talks. By the mid-1980s, Reagan's fair-trade rhetoric, and the threat that Congress might enact harsh punitive measures against Canadian industries, provided powerful motivation for Ottawa to lock in access to the U.S. market via a formalized FTA.[131] The resulting deal ultimately eliminated all tariffs on U.S.-Canadian trade, and created the largest free-trade area in the world. It also catalyzed the process that would lead to the broader North American Free Trade Agreement (NAFTA), and provided just the type of breakthrough that minilateralism emphasized. The agreement, Baker said, would strengthen GATT and "the entire world trading system."[132] For his part, Reagan argued that the FTA would set "an example of cooperation" on trade. "To those who would hunker down behind barriers . . . Canada and the United States will show the positive way."[133]

This multipronged approach to reenergizing global trade took time to develop, but in the end it worked quite well. As in U.S.-Japan relations, Reagan maintained control of the trade agenda at home, a prerequisite to effectiveness abroad. His emphasis on fair trade, and his use of retaliatory threats and sanctions, helped contain protectionist pressures and head off crippling legislation. "Last Fall you will recall that there were predictions of Congressional action in any number of protectionist areas," Regan (now chief of staff) wrote in 1986. "Partially due to administration action on 301 cases and international negotiations, none materialized."[134] Congress did produce an omnibus trade bill in 1988 with protectionist language and themes, but this outcome was actually a victory for the administration because the bill did not "impose statutory protections [on trade], and it did not impose direct congressional control over trade."[135] Even foreign leaders appreciated Reagan's success in this regard. "We have always seen in President Reagan a partisan fighter against protectionism," Hans-Dietrich Genscher, the West German foreign minister, said.[136]

In the international realm, too, Reagan's tactics provided an essential impetus. The renewed multilateral coordination of the late 1980s was now easing the currency fluctuations that had earlier impeded broad trade liberalization. The president's continual advocacy of GATT negotiations, the threat of sanctions that would constrict access to the U.S. market, and the incentives—positive and negative—underscored by the minilateral approach also played a central part in eliciting agreement by the G-7 to begin the immensely ambitious Uruguay Round of trade talks in 1986, and in prodding those talks along over time. "The series of FTA negotiations" begun in the 1980s, one scholar writes, "energized the next installment in America's multilateral trade liberalization strategy."[137] (Or as Baker immodestly put it, that round was underway "largely as a result of our initiative and persistence."[138]) To be sure, it would take nearly eight years to complete the Uruguay Round, which proved every bit as contentious as trade negotiations usually are. Yet it was notable that the Bush and Clinton administrations eventually employed many of the tactics developed during the 1980s—such as the use of bilateral or regional trade pacts such as NAFTA to "galvanize the rest of the world"—to consummate the process.[139] When that conclusion came, it resulted in the most comprehensive liberalization of the postwar era, slashing developed-country tariffs by an average of 40 percent, creating the World Trade Organization (WTO), and bringing key areas like financial services and intellectual property into the realm of global trade rules. "The Uruguay Round," Andrew Brown writes, "initiated a new phase in the trend toward more open markets."[140]

By the close of Reagan's presidency, the movement toward economic openness was thus gathering critical policy momentum in the developed world, thereby encouraging the structural changes unleashed in the previous decade to continue reshaping the global system. "At each economic summit," Reagan wrote, "I could feel the mood shift more strongly in favor of free trade."[141] Over the course of the 1980s, the administration had facilitated that shift by diverting protectionist pressures, and by promoting renewed coordination to calm the vicissitudes of a more fluid world economy. It had deepened Tokyo's immersion in a more globalized financial system, and made important progress on bilateral trade issues while avoiding a disastrous commercial conflict. Finally, in multilateral trade issues, Washington had helped catalyze a new GATT round and recommit the West to a far-reaching agenda of liberalization. Despite all the struggles and frustrations, U.S. officials had made integral contributions to preserving and deepening global integration at a time when the world economy was, as Reagan said in 1987, "in the midst of a profound transformation."[142] As we will see, that transformation, and the U.S. role in promoting it, was even more pronounced in the developing world.

Debt, Leverage, and Neoliberal Ascendancy in the Third World

In economics as in politics, the 1980s saw sweeping change in the Third World. When the decade started, most LDC economies were still characterized by state-centric approaches such as import-substitution industrialization (ISI), and North-South relations bore the scars of confrontation over the NIEO and other redistributive battles of the 1970s. Ten years later, by contrast, the Third World was moving headlong toward economic liberalization and an embrace of policies championed by Washington. At least thirty-four developing countries either opened or started opening their economies in the decade after 1984, a total that may have understated the changes at work.[143] Whatever the precise number, the LDCs were reforming their economies and opening themselves to the world in unprecedented ways. Globalization and neoliberalism were zipping ahead; U.S. economic and ideological influence had been reaffirmed in striking fashion. "History has decided," Bush declared in 1989; free-market principles reigned supreme.[144]

The proximate catalyst for this shift was the Third World debt crisis. As noted, that crisis was an ironic result of the 1970s. At the time, the oil shocks and NIEO had made it seem, one World Bank official recalled, "that the Third World was trying to beat the developed world into submission."[145] In reality, the lasting consequence of the decade was exploding Third World debt. With financial markets awash in liquidity and banks aggressively expanding overseas lending, the LDCs borrowed furiously. Oil importers did so to pay soaring energy bills and fund otherwise unsustainable domestic programs. Oil exporters did likewise, calculating that debt incurred now to promote industrialization and increase social spending could be repaid with petro-proceeds later. In Latin America, overall debt soared from $59 billion in 1975 to $331 billion in 1982, with most loans featuring short maturities and variable interest rates.[146] In the Third World writ large, non-oil LDC debt quadrupled from 1973 to 1980.[147]

This debt-led approach temporarily helped LDC governments avoid hard choices and preserve decent growth. By the end of the decade, however, swelling debt burdens were causing economic turmoil in places such as Peru and Turkey, and leading to slower growth and rising inflation in numerous countries. The collapse came in 1981–1982, when a perfect storm of factors— spiking interest rates, a brutal drop in commodity prices, and lender skittishness brought on by the Polish crisis and the Falklands War—devastated LDC balance sheets and spooked commercial banks just as major borrowers needed fresh loans to roll over their debt. With oil prices descending from their 1979–1980 high, not even exporters such as Mexico were immune from the crunch that followed. That country ushered in the debt crisis proper by announcing that it could no longer make interest payments in August 1982; that announcement sparked a domino effect that caused private lending to LDCs to dry up almost entirely. "The day of reckoning has arrived," Peru's finance minister announced.[148] For the next decade, LDC debtors would be staring down the barrel of national bankruptcy, and living in excruciating economic upheaval.

The debt crisis was undoubtedly wrenching for those who experienced it. In Latin America—the epicenter of both this episode and the reforms it ultimately induced—per capita GDP fell by an average of 1.8 percent annually from 1982 to 1986, while unemployment hit 20–30 percent and inflation surpassed 20,000 percent in some countries.[149] National economies threatened to implode entirely; rising poverty and declining food consumption brought the pain home on an individual basis. Yet crises also can be transformative moments, and this was true of Third World political economy. Even in the heyday of dependency theory and the NIEO, the LDCs felt the neoliberal gusts that had begun to blow in the 1970s, and the debt crisis broke as inherited economic models were already coming under fire. In Latin America, a new generation of economists critiqued an ISI model that fostered domestic industry at the cost of inefficiency, instability, and a failure to develop the robust export sectors needed to profit from greater global trade. In Africa, the persistent inability to achieve sufficient growth after independence was also challenging the statist, anti-Western precepts that prevailed in many capitals. And throughout the developing world, observers were beginning to take note of China's astonishing turn toward the market, and of the gains made by East Asian countries that had embraced an outward orientation. The LDCs were showing "increased dissatisfaction with centralized economic planning, controls, and intervention," the CIA reported. "LDC governments are increasingly willing to contemplate and experiment with market-oriented approaches."[150]

Through the late 1970s, the resulting policy changes were most pronounced in Pinochet's Chile, which had conducted virtually wholesale economic liberalization after the 1973 coup. The junta slashed import duties and public spending, lifted price controls and privatized industry, and courted foreign investment. This shift could be immensely painful for the poor and working-class Chileans who bore the brunt of the shocks, but it nonetheless suppressed inflation, restored growth, and won the esteem of free-marketers everywhere. "They stand on Adam Smith," Shultz would remark.[151] And while the entrenched nature of ISI and other state-centric models initially made Chile an outlier, there was growing ferment elsewhere. LDC bureaucracies were increasingly staffed by more technocratic, better-educated elites that had often trained at Western universities and were more receptive to fundamental policy shifts.[152] In Latin America especially, free-market policies were being touted by conservative intellectuals, business groups, and political parties as a way of reducing distortions and unleashing untapped potential. By the early 1980s, this "New Right" was coalescing in countries from Mexico to Bolivia, raising the profile of neoliberal concepts and exerting sustained pressure for change.[153]

In Latin America and elsewhere, the debt crisis would strengthen these groups by rupturing the prevailing order, and by affirming—ever-more convincingly over time—the need for far-reaching reform. "Things that seemed impossible to do became possible," one planning minister said; the pressures of crisis impelled and empowered governments to strike out in new directions.[154] Just as important, the debt crisis opened the door to an alliance with external actors seeking the same end. During the late 1970s, the Ford and Carter administrations had begun to use Third World economic distress to encourage pro-market adjustment. The Reagan administration intensified and expanded this policy. Deeply troubled by the recent upsurge of LDC economic nationalism in recent years, Reagan resolved to retake the initiative in the battle to shape Third World development. Washington would not support large-scale redistributive schemes that propped up inefficient economies, he declared, nor would it speak "with a sense of guilt about the gap between the rich & poor nations." Rather, it would denounce the false promise of statism and promote "free market capitalism" as the way forward.[155] The LDCs, Donald Regan explained, were promising and essential terrain for this endeavor: "Developing country economies are among the most dynamic and diverse in the world. They are on the frontier of economic progress. Opportunities in those economies for creative, worthwhile, and rewarding efforts abound. These are the economies that hold a major key to future economic expansion." The Third World, in other words, was to be a central theater in America's international economic offensive.[156]

Even before the debt crisis, Reagan was energetically pursuing this offensive. In 1981, the administration indicated that it would not use foreign assistance to support "unsound" economic programs, and underscored the point by cutting development aid from $7.1 billion to $5.8 billion.[157] The same year, Reagan killed any lingering prospects of large-scale global redistribution. At a summit between developed and developing countries in Cancun in October, his negotiators undermined calls for meaningful "global negotiations" on North-South issues. In his address to the conference, Reagan sang the praises of capitalism and argued that North-South cooperation must begin with Third World reform. "With sound understanding of our domestic freedom and responsibilities," he said, "we can construct effective international cooperation. Without it, no amount of international good will and action can produce prosperity."[158]

During 1981–1982, the administration also waged a campaign to make the international financial institutions (IFIs) more responsive to this agenda. Both the IMF and the World Bank had expanded their LDC lending considerably after the oil shocks, and despite the fears of some U.S. officials, both institutions were moving in neoliberal directions by 1981. The advent of the World Bank's Structural Adjustment Lending (SAL) program was critical in this regard; these loans, President Robert McNamara wrote, required borrowers to make major reforms seeking "increased efficiency of resource use and improved responsiveness of the economy to changes in economic conditions."[159] McNamara's replacement by A. W. Clausen, a prominent U.S. banker, in 1981 accentuated this trend, as did the rise of Managing Director Jacques de Larosière at the IMF. De Larosière believed that the accumulation of LDC debt had revealed deep problems that required major liberalizing reforms: "There is no other path to follow."[160] During the late 1970s, the IMF had begun strengthening its "conditionality," the policy changes it demanded from borrowers, to induce such reforms. "Adjustment and financing must go hand in hand," Fund officials wrote.[161]

The Reagan administration moved quickly to confirm these shifts. From the outset, it tied U.S. support for increasing IFI resources to even tighter IMF conditionality, and to an even greater focus by the World Bank and other development banks (e.g., the Inter-American Development Bank, IDB) on rolling back the state. "Our approach in the multilateral financial institutions," noted James Burnham, the U.S. executive director at the World Bank, "has been to stress the need for greater market-oriented conditionality in lending operations."[162] At the same time, the administration encouraged the replacement of IMF and especially World Bank officials deemed hostile to U.S. views with advisers committed to the free-market ethos. Given that the IFIs could not survive without American support, the administration was thereby able to lock in the neoliberal shift and ensure that these institutions acted as generally reliable conduits for U.S. influence. As Reagan's last national security adviser, Colin Powell, would write, "The Bank and the Fund make tough demands on governments needing their assistance because we insist on it."[163]

When the debt crisis erupted, U.S. officials thus recognized it as both threat and opportunity. It was a threat in that persistent economic turmoil could stir sociopolitical upheaval. "We should remember," Assistant Secretary of State Thomas Enders warned, "that few of the governments with which Latin America entered the Great Depression were there at the end."[164] The crisis also severely depressed U.S. exports to the LDCs. In Latin America, sales to Mexico plummeted from $17.789 billion in 1981 to $11.817 billion in 1982, and exports to Argentina and other countries suffered similar drops. Overall, U.S. exports to the LDCs dropped by 46 percent by the end of 1983. As Regan noted, "The export sector of our economy—a leader in creating new jobs—is tremendously vulnerable to any sharp cutbacks in imports by the LDCs."[165] Most troubling of all, the crisis raised the prospect of an outright breakdown of international finance. Petrodollar recycling had not simply made the LDCs dependent on commercial loans; it had fostered inverse dependency by making commercial banks dependent on LDC repayment. Were the major debtors now to default, they might touch off a chain reaction of Western—and U.S.—bank failures that would wreak havoc on a world financial system that had grown dramatically more interconnected. If Washington did not confront the crisis, Volcker wrote in October 1982, "then the consequences are essentially unpredictable, ranging from a 'manageable mess' to real chaos, political and economic, around the world in a way the U.S. could not expect to escape."[166]

The debt crisis thus threatened to turn integration into vulnerability, and it offered an early warning about the dangers of instability and contagion in a more globalized world. More positively, however, the crisis also presented an opening for policymakers to exploit. "The depth of the current economic and financial problems" in the LDCs, U.S. officials wrote, "has produced a search for new approaches" and a chance to push the developing countries down a different path.[167] The administration and the IFIs could make their help in combating the debt problem contingent on greater receptivity to free trade, foreign direct investment (FDI), and other reforms. It could thereby turn back LDC economic nationalism and draw the developing countries into a more open system under U.S. leadership. From the start, U.S. officials referred to the crisis as a "historic opportunity," and a chance to think big.[168] "If the U.S. is ever going to try to form a Western Hemisphere free trade area," Norman Bailey wrote, "now would be the time to do so. The Latin American countries recognize that they must export to the U.S. if they are able to pay their debt and recover, and they realize that in order to do so they must make concessions as well." Likewise, Casey and the CIA argued that the crisis would allow Washington to reinforce the "more pragmatic" turn in Third World political economy, and "strengthen trade, finance, and investment links with LDCs." Still other officials put it even more baldly. "The debt," they wrote, "can and should be used as leverage."[169]

From late 1982 onward, then, the aim of the U.S. debt strategy was to avoid a disaster that might unravel the global economy, while also seeking transformative changes that would integrate that economy all the more. To accomplish the first aim, U.S. officials quickly resolved to provide the debtors—especially the three major debtors (Argentina, Brazil, and Mexico) known as the "ABM threat"—with the resources to make interest payments and avoid snowballing defaults that might cause "a major break down in the structure of international credit."[170] In the near term, this meant working creatively to assemble bridging loans and provide liquidity. Over a single weekend in August 1982, Volcker and Regan spearheaded a multiplayer effort involving the Fed, the Treasury, other U.S. offices and agencies, and Western central banks to compose a package of over $3 billion for Mexico. Buenos Aires, Brasilia, and other debtors received similar treatment when they teetered on the brink of insolvency. "Speed in implementation is absolutely essential," Volcker wrote. "We are behind 'the curve' now, and we have to get at least abreast of it *quick* to maximize chances for success."[171]

The point of moving fast was actually to slow things down: to buy time, avert otherwise-certain defaults, and find breathing room to arrange more substantial financing.[172] To this end, the IMF—which U.S. officials now termed the "centerpiece" of the debt strategy, and for which Reagan supported a major resource bump in 1983—dramatically ramped up its LDC lending. By late 1984, sixteen Latin American countries had negotiated IMF stabilization agreements, and the Fund had made loans totaling $22 billion to seventy debt-distressed countries since August 1982.[173] In many cases, IMF loans were accompanied by new commercial lending, which U.S. and IMF officials worked diligently to secure for countries undertaking adjustment. In late 1982, Mexico concluded a $4 billion IMF loan that was matched by $5 billion in private lending, establishing the model that was replicated in subsequent cases. Even a bulked-up IMF could not manage the crisis by itself, Regan explained. "An orderly resolution" required commercial banks to restructure old debt and make new loans.[174]

Because most banks were not eager to send good money after bad, obtaining this result required measures both innovative and subtly coercive. With strong U.S. support, de Larosière unveiled the concept of "concerted lending," which stipulated that no IMF program would proceed until commercial banks had committed a critical mass (up to 90 percent) of the necessary private loans. Because a failure to provide new lending to the LDCs would likely cause a string of bank-killing defaults, commercial lenders had little choice but to agree.[175] To further facilitate this process, Fed and Treasury officials intervened deeply in negotiations among debtors, commercial banks, and the IMF, urging the banks not to declare delinquent debtors in default, and helping shape the terms of debt restructuring and new lending packages. "Both Mr. Volcker and Mr. Solomon [Anthony Solomon, now head of the New York Fed] played a constructive intermediary role, trying to edge the banks towards the Fund position," IMF officials noted of one negotiation.[176]

The first prong of U.S. strategy thus involved stabilizing LDC finances. The second entailed securing meaningful adjustment. These issues always were explicitly linked. Access to emergency liquidity required a commitment to deal with the IMF; the resulting stand-by arrangements (which were the price of new commercial loans) inevitably entailed dramatic reforms. This meant undertaking austerity and import-compression programs to shore up a country's balance sheet; it also meant slashing government intervention and subsidies, lowering barriers to trade and foreign investment, and liberalizing currency markets and exchange rates. "All Fund-supported adjustment programs," IMF officials noted, "reflect an effort to open an economy up, to liberalize economic activities . . . and to reduce controls."[177] U.S. and IMF officials expected that these reforms would help debtor countries regain their footing; the policy changes would also bring the LDCs into the more open global system taking hold. "The current situation . . . presents both opportunities and risks," de Larosière said. "The task for policy is to ensure that the opportunities are exploited and the risks averted."[178]

IMF officials generally took the lead in negotiating these reforms, because of their technical competence, and because this approach allowed the Fund—rather than the United States—to absorb the lion's share of the criticism that often resulted. "We all hid behind the IMF," one State Department Latin America hand recalled.[179] In numerous ways, however, the administration used its own influence to encourage adjustment. Washington used PL-480 food assistance and Export-Import Bank credits to reward leaders who undertook major reforms, while strongly urging the recalcitrant to cooperate. In 1983–1984, for instance, U.S. diplomats informed Mobutu Sese Seko of Zaire that "the USG could no longer consider helping Zaire unless the country was able to institute massive, sustained economic stabilization measures in conjunction with a new fund program."[180] To reinforce these messages, USAID tied assistance programs such as its Economic Support Fund to the implementation of liberalizing measures. "We will be seeking policy changes and reform more aggressively than before," agency officials wrote.[181] U.S. representatives also reminded borrowers that they risked losing access to IMF resources if they broke their stand-by arrangements, and that defaulters would be locked out of international finance completely.[182] Finally, USAID and NED funds supported pro-reform groups such as business associations and conservative think-tanks, raising their profile and amplifying their voices. "AID's support . . . can help private enterprise flourish in most developing countries," that agency stated.[183]

Through the mid-1980s, this two-pronged strategy produced some good results. By easing liquidity crunches and encouraging new lending streams, U.S. policy played an indispensable role in keeping debtors afloat and avoiding catastrophe. "A global financial panic was averted," CIA analysts wrote, "mainly as a result of the quick action of the United States and other industrial countries to shore up the foreign positions of Mexico and several other key LDC debtors."[184] In conjunction with the IFIs, moreover, the administration had established the principle that stabilization and adjustment must go hand in hand, thereby strengthening LDC reformers and inducing numerous debtors to begin restructuring. Ghana initiated a wrenching but determined transition in 1983 under World Bank and IMF supervision; Zaire acceded to strong pressure by launching an adjustment program that Reagan deemed "courageous and far-sighted."[185] The Philippines made first moves toward an eventual, far-ranging liberalization, and numerous Latin American governments undertook austerity and other reforms. Altogether, IMF officials calculated that nearly forty countries were pursuing major adjustment programs in mid-1983. "Adjustment is now virtually universal," de Larosière declared. "Never before has there been such an extensive yet convergent adjustment effort."[186]

Any satisfaction was premature, however, because progress toward reform was ephemeral. In retrospect, sustaining and consummating the changes that Reagan and the IMF envisioned would have been tough under any circumstances, because economic restructuring required confronting constituencies—from government bureaucrats, to favored trade unions, to poor and middle-class citizens who benefitted from social programs—that had immense stakes in the existing order. Many Third World statesmen understood that structural reforms were needed, CIA analysts judged, but those reforms "are extremely difficult to undertake because they represent attacks on entrenched interest groups whose support is usually essential to LDC leaders' maintenance of political power."[187] Amid the debt crisis, attacking these interests was all the more fraught. With growth stagnant or negative, real wages falling by up to 60 percent in some countries, and unemployment and inflation reaching dangerous levels, doing so could well provoke a furious—even explosive—response.

In theory, the debt strategy was meant to insulate reform programs from this danger, by providing resources that would make adjustment easier to bear. "The choice for debtor countries is not between adjustment today or adjustment tomorrow," Deputy Secretary of State Kenneth Dam said. "It is between orderly adjustment—cushioned by external support—and disorderly adjustment forced by economic decline and attempts to sustain ineffective policies."[188] In practice, however, U.S. strategy fell short in this regard. Liquidity infusions, IMF loans, and concerted lending provided enough money to avoid default, but not to do much else. In net terms, massive debt-service obligations and capital flight actually ensured that capital flowed *out* of debtor countries. In 1985, commercial banks provided $3.7 billion in new lending to seventeen key debtors, but collected $22 billion in interest payments.[189] The LDCs were hemorrhaging cash, prompting Latin American debtors to complain of "forced insolvency," and compounding the economic and political dilemmas that Third World leaders faced.[190]

In many ways, in fact, adjustment programs seemed to intensify the pain. Because these programs emphasized austerity, they increased recessionary pressures on economies that were already being pummeled. Moreover, because adjustment entailed slashing subsidies, freeing prices, and rolling back protections for key industries and their employees, it tended to cause particular distress for vulnerable segments of the population. In Latin America, for instance, the number of people in poverty rose from 130 million in 1981 to 150 million in 1986, at a time when protections for the poor were in retreat.[191] The upshot, frequently, was to ratchet up internal strains so severely as to put the social fabric at risk. In the Dominican Republic, austerity measures introduced in 1984 led to riots, raging street battles, and a brutal police response that left at least dozens (and perhaps over one hundred) dead. "A bomb is being formed here, and an explosion is taking shape," one Dominican communist said.[192] In Brazil, officials warned of a coming "convulsion that threatens the entire social and political structure."[193] Nor were these isolated concerns. At least thirty-nine countries experienced austerity protests or riots during the debt crisis, leading observers to fear for the basic stability of their political systems.[194]

In these conditions, even leaders who grasped the need for reform took a stop-and-go approach to implementing it. "Governments of many financially troubled countries face intense political and social pressure to abandon or weaken austerity measures," the CIA noted.[195] Many governments hesitated to take sensitive steps such as privatizing or closing unproductive, but politically powerful, state-owned enterprises (SOEs). And even though while some LDCs, such as Mexico, showed striking perseverance, others could not or would not carry these programs to completion. Major debtors such as Argentina and Brazil, and smaller ones from Nigeria to Peru, came out of compliance (sometimes repeatedly) with IFI packages during the 1980s, breaching spending targets or balking at reforms. "We can't foster policies that lead to hunger and misery," Argentine President Raúl Alfonsín said.[196]

By mid-decade, the debt strategy was in trouble. Even cooperative figures, like Miguel de la Madrid of Mexico, warned that "debtor countries were running out of options."[197] Brazil, Argentina, and other countries occasionally threatened to halt or reduce payments (and sometimes temporarily did so), calculating that the specter of default would compel the IMF and the banks to give easier terms. Across Latin American, debtors were considering banding together to forge a stronger position, and U.S. officials feared formation of a "debtor cartel" that might undercut pressure for adjustment.[198] "Embassy . . . reportings reveal support for a tougher posture against creditors—such as a payments moratorium—gaining political popularity in Argentina, Brazil, Ecuador, and Peru," the CIA assessed.[199] In mid-1985, Alan García of Peru actually took this step, declaring that Lima would pay only what it could afford. The Reagan administration remained committed to using the debt as leverage, but whether it could effectively do so was in doubt.

As it became clear that Washington faced what Volcker called "a continuing hard-slogging effort . . . extending certainly for several more years ahead," U.S. policy began its own process of adjustment. The key, U.S. officials realized, was to "find a 'carrot' that can be used to reward debt-troubled LDCs that undertake substantial structural reforms."[200] To this end, Volcker's Fed encouraged the IMF to promote multiyear rescheduling deals that spaced out repayment over longer periods. U.S. officials also worked closely with IMF and bank representatives to help key debtors, starting with Mexico, secure significant new financing on more generous terms. These packages would reduce the odds that a major debtor would break with the IFIs altogether, the thinking went, while demonstrating to other LDCs that good behavior would be rewarded. "The time had come," Volcker said, to make Mexico "an example to other Latin American countries."[201]

The goal of recommitting debtor governments to adjustment also drove a broader U.S. initiative, the Baker Plan. Announced in October 1985 and quickly endorsed by the IFIs, the plan had three components. The first was a renewed pledge by debtors to undertake structural reforms. The second was a commercial-bank commitment to lend an additional $20 billion to the fifteen main LDC debtors (ten of them in Latin America) over the next three years. The third was a promise that the IFIs—led by the World Bank and IDB— would raise their annual lending to principal debtors by some 50 percent, from $6 billion to $9 billion, to be accompanied by new IMF money as well.[202]

The Baker Plan did not envision any weakening in conditionality, and it stressed the need for all LDC debtors to make fundamental economic changes. "The same basic policy prescriptions," World Bank officials wrote, "apply to every country."[203] What made the initiative a departure, rather, was that it promised new money that would allow debtors to reform while also generating the economic expansion necessary to avoid crushing hardship and ultimately "grow out of debt."[204] At the same time, the plan was designed to induce the new lending that would make such growth possible by assuring the commercial banks (and the IFI capital subscribers) that their money would facilitate lasting structural changes that would eventually make borrowers more creditworthy. In essence, then, the plan would revitalize the debt strategy by forging a strengthened bargain between lenders and borrowers, empowering LDC reformers, and allowing Washington to reassert leadership of the process. "Far better for us to take the initiative rather than be taken on the defensive," Assistant Secretary of the Treasury David Mulford said.[205]

Although the Baker Plan drew criticism from the outset, it made important—if incremental—contributions to the eventual achievement of U.S. aims. The plan helped prod private banks to make new loans, most notably a massive $7.7 billion package for Mexico, and to reschedule $70 billion in LDC debt between late 1985 and early 1987.[206] The provision of new resources, in turn, diverted pressure for more radical steps by key debtors by showing that cooperation with the financial community, for all its drawbacks, was still more profitable than confrontation. "There was some left-wing pressure . . . to repudiate the debts," de la Madrid told Bush, but "Mexico was not going to do that."[207] The plan thereby purchased time for banks to strengthen their capital reserves and loan-loss provisions so that an LDC default would no longer be so fatal, and it led to a wave of new World Bank, IDB, and IMF agreements. By 1987, Mulford was touting these agreements as proof that U.S. policy had fostered a "most important change . . . in debtor attitudes," strengthening liberalizers and helping LDC countries recommit to reform.[208]

There was some real truth in this assessment. Mexico's liberalization began in earnest in the mid-1980s, as the government cut tariffs and import barriers, joined the GATT, and moved—first gingerly and then more forcefully—to shutter or sell SOEs. In 1982, there had been 1,200 SOEs in Mexico; by 1988, there were 500. "The Baker Plan and the IMF have pushed them in the right direction," Poindexter said.[209] Brazil made meaningful (if still halting) steps toward reducing its wide-ranging import prohibitions, and Chile resumed its neoliberal project with renewed vigor after some crisis-induced backsliding. In Bolivia, the government undertook radical austerity to defeat the hyperinflation that was threatening to destroy the country, and moved boldly to restructure the economy through trade reform, privatization, and deregulation. There had been "more progress in Latin America toward fundamental economic reform than at any time in the last 50 years," Volcker said.[210] There was progress elsewhere, too. The Philippines, for instance, continued the adjustment begun under Marcos with key trade and other measures under Aquino. "The debtor nations themselves," Baker said, "are increasingly adopting market and growth-oriented reforms."[211]

As before, however, the momentum was uneven and hard to sustain. And as before, the root of the problem was that the debt burden was just too large. Although the banks collectively fulfilled most of their Baker Plan obligations, they did so very reluctantly, and they remained wary of going any further with countries that were swimming in a sea of red ink. Commercial lending, an IMF official admitted, was "the 'wobbly leg' of the Baker plan."[212] As a result, despite the new lending that did occur, continued capital flight and debt service meant that net capital flows to Latin America were negative $22 billion in 1986, with the outflow persisting through the end of the decade.[213] With capital still scarce, and with debt service devouring national income, economic performance was far too weak to "grow out of debt." GDP per capita did rise slightly for the "Baker 15" in 1987, and the average debt-service ratio declined modestly. But, the World Bank acknowledged, "most of the indebted countries are still no better off than in 1982."[214] The total debt for the fifteen most indebted countries grew from $422.7 billion in 1985 to $482.7 billion in 1987, inhibiting growth and leading some officials to say that repayment was impossible.[215]

With the debt growing and depression-like conditions persisting in many LDCs, a reaction was inevitable. Alfonsín turned sharply against the IMF in 1987, declaring that "the debt cannot be paid," and that he would no longer heed "ridiculous prescriptions that have nothing to do with the people." The Reagan administration took note. "We're going to be hearing more and more of this from the debtor countries," one official said.[216] Sure enough, in 1987 the specter of default or other noncooperation returned, with Brazil declaring a unilateral moratorium on repayment of $67 billion in foreign debt. Costa Rica, Honduras, and other countries enacted similar measures. Latin American debtors demanded limitations on interest payments at a regional summit in November, and Argentina briefly suspended debt service in early 1988 because it was had nearly exhausted its foreign reserves.[217]

As LDC frustration peaked, progress toward liberalization remained precarious and incomplete. Essential reforms were delayed or canceled, and even leaders who accepted the rationale for change came out of compliance with lending agreements. Zaire, a former poster child for adjustment, broke with the IFIs after it found itself paying 50 percent of its annual budget to the IMF. "Zaire was a model student of the IMF," one Mobutu associate lamented, "but was not compensated for being such a good student."[218] In Mexico, officials feared a popular backlash that might make reform untenable. "The longer the debt overhang lingers with no tangible solution in sight," World Bank officials wrote, "the more uncontrollable the handling of the economic and political situation will become."[219]

When Reagan left office, the debt strategy again looked to be losing steam. The United States and the IFIs had promoted unprecedented liberalization in the LDCs, but the gains remained fragile and reversible amid a crisis that showed few signs of easing. De Larosière's successor, Michel Camdessus, noted that the debt strategy "is clearly not living up to all of the expectations for it." Elliott Abrams agreed that while "much progress has been made," new measures were essential to fortify and reenergize LDC reform. "It would be a genuine tragedy if the extraordinary democratic leaders who have borne the brunt of painful adjustment measures were to pay for their courage rather than being rewarded for it."[220] With this specter still very much lingering, there was no denying that U.S. ambitions remained unfulfilled as Bush took power in 1989.

By the time this transition occurred, however, the conditions were gradually emerging for a resolution to the crisis, and for the consummation of the Third World's neoliberal turn. Within the LDCs, this evolution simply reflected the fact that the alternatives to deep reform were disappearing. By the late 1980s, the halfway, "heterodox" programs undertaken by countries such as Brazil and Argentina had failed disastrously, causing hyperinflation over 10,000 percent in some cases. In Brazil, the payments moratorium had exacerbated the chaos by alienating lenders and intensifying capital flight. "The fact is that we can't destroy the international financial system," President José Sarney conceded. "We can scratch it, but it can destroy us." Peru's revolt was similarly catastrophic: the economy contracted by 23 percent from 1988 to 1990, and inflation skyrocketed.[221] Meanwhile, it was impossible to ignore that countries that had truly pursued neoliberal or export-oriented projects earlier—such as Chile and South Korea—were recovering more vigorously, and that China was booming due to its reforms. The result was to intensify the economic soul-searching underway in many LDCs, and to cause greater receptivity to the approaches of the New Right.[222]

The growing resonance of neoliberal ideas was captured in the popularity of *The Other Path,* the 1987 book by Peruvian economist Hernando de Soto. De Soto described a Peruvian economy that was smothered by a parasitic state, forcing citizens to seek salvation in an informal system where market rules prevailed. This informal economy constituted "the most important rebellion against the status quo ever waged in this history of independent Peru," and for the country to survive it must embrace the rebellion. "We must draw on what actually works," de Soto wrote; "economic freedom" must triumph. Coming at the tail of a decade in which existing models had been so disastrously discredited, de Soto's book hit like a lightning bolt, becoming a best-seller across Latin America.[223]

As borrower attitudes were changing, so were lender perspectives. By this point, most objective observers acknowledged that LDC debts were so massive that they could not be repaid in full without wrecking prospects for meaningful growth and recovery. And because commercial banks had used the time afforded by the debt strategy to strengthen themselves against default, there was gradually developing greater scope for alternative solutions.

In 1987, Citicorp became the first big bank to essentially write down a major chunk of its Latin American exposure.[224] Other banks were starting to sell LDC debt at a discount or trade it for equity, and in 1988 Mexico—with U.S. support—conducted an auction in which it bought back some debt at reduced prices. The level of debt retired was modest, but as NSC aide Stephen Danzansky wrote, "the plan represents a significant turning point in the debt strategy by tacitly acknowledging that some LDC debt will not be repaid."[225]

This set of circumstances cleared the way for a further, decisive revision of U.S. policy. "The principles which have guided us in the past . . . remain valid," Assistant Treasury Secretary Charles Dallara explained, but "new directions for our strategy are needed."[226] This insight informed the Brady Plan (named for Baker's successor, Nicholas Brady), announced in March 1989. In a bid to "reinvigorate a process that has become debt weary," Brady proposed actual debt reduction—not just new loans—for countries undertaking reform. LDCs could exchange their debt either for par bonds at below-market interest rates, or for discount bonds with market rates. These bonds, in turn, would be guaranteed by $30 billion in U.S. government securities provided as collateral by the IFIs and Japan. The plan would "provide debtor countries with greater hope for the future," Brady said; it would conclusively incentivize adjustment by offering concrete rewards for resolute actions.[227]

The Brady Plan was well-matched to changing attitudes among lenders and borrowers alike. The negotiations that the initiative entailed were unavoidably tortuous and difficult, but even in 1989, the first Brady Plan deals were taking shape. Mexico signed an accord that cut its debt by $42 billion and reduced interest payments by one-third. The Philippines, Costa Rica, Morocco, and Venezuela soon followed, and by late 1990, "virtually every eligible debtor country was requesting Brady Plan treatment."[228] By 1994, eighteen deals had been made, culminating with a settlement between Brazil and its creditors. Combined with a fortuitous fall in interest rates, these pacts cut the debt burden to more manageable levels. For the seventeen leading debtors, the ratio of net debt to GNP fell from 67 percent in 1986 to 42 percent in 1993. "The Brady Plan," World Bank president Barber Conable noted, "has added a potent weapon for debt reduction in countries committed to economic reform."[229]

As Brady deals proliferated, so did the reforms U.S. policy had long aimed to promote. In the Philippines, Morocco, and elsewhere, Brady deals and the promise of debt reduction facilitated the consummation of major trade and structural reforms. In Argentina and Peru, new leaders who had campaigned against the IMF switched course dramatically once elected, carrying out aggressive reform programs. "The economic system has been revolutionized," U.S. officials in Peru noted.[230] Across Latin America, SOEs were sold off at an unprecedented clip, financial and currency flows were liberalized, regulations were reduced, and the average tariff fell from 49.98 percent in the mid-1980s to 12.35 percent in the mid-1990s.[231] "From the Rio Grande to Tierra del Fuego, countries have been undertaking economic policy reforms that in many cases are as deep-seated and far-reaching as the dismantling of communism in Eastern Europe," one observer wrote.[232] Even Brazil, which U.S. officials had labeled the "most protectionist country in the world," began its own paradigm shift, abolishing state monopolies, liberalizing treatment of FDI, restoring fiscal discipline, and implementing what the IMF called a "dramatic change in the economic setting."[233]

In few places were those changes more striking than Mexico, the country that had always been central to the debt crisis and U.S. policy. There the administration of Carlos Salinas accelerated the economic transition by slashing import barriers, opening the financial sector, vastly improving treatment of FDI, and privatizing hundreds of remaining SOEs. This economic revolution culminated in an FTA with the United States (which eventually became the broader NAFTA), a step intended to signal that Mexican reforms were irreversible. "I want to consolidate the new policies for a market-oriented economy," Salinas said. Mexico had certainly done "fundamental economic reform," Brady agreed.[234]

In Washington, this dramatic change in Third World political economy produced a powerful sense of triumph. Just over a decade after the oil shocks and Third World nationalism had menaced the global economy, so many LDCs were adopting the neoliberal ethos and integrating into that economy more fully than ever before. "I used to call this a silent revolution," Camdessus said, "but it is no longer so silent; it is now being embraced by countries in all regions of the world."[235] Focusing on Latin America, Brady commented that the region was undergoing an "exhilarating revolution, as a whole new generation of leaders spells out their hopes for economic reform." The "lessons" of that revolution were unambiguous, he argued: "Freedom works. Free markets work. These simple principles have moved nations; they have altered the course of history; they have turned the tide of our economic future."[236]

With respect to American policy, there was cause for satisfaction. Over the course of a decade, U.S. officials had recognized the transformative potential of the debt crisis, established a framework that stressed the imperative of structural reform, and used various forms of influence and leverage to stave off a global financial meltdown and encourage the remaking of Third World political economy. This process was as messy and halting as any aspect of U.S. statecraft during the 1980s, but the results were impressive in the end. American strategy may have left things to be desired, Enders observed, it "kept us engaged, moved us to respond at critical junctures, and contributed to, rather than thwarted, the historic transformation now under way."[237]

From Washington's perspective, the benefits of this transformation were vast. LDC trade liberalization led to a surge in U.S. exports as Third World economies began to recover. In March 1992, Baker reported that U.S. exports to Latin America had increased by 29 percent over the previous two years; trade with Mexico rose from $35 billion in 1987, to $75 billion in 1992, to over $247 billion by 2000.[238] U.S. investment in LDC economies also boomed, as American individuals and firms (encouraged by the signing of twenty-seven bilateral investment treaties between Washington and foreign capitals from 1990 to 1995) took advantage of the new climate. "Latin America, once a pariah, is now an area of great interest to investors," Citicorp executive William Rhodes wrote.[239] More generally, the economic reforms undertaken in the 1980s and afterward made it possible to broaden the GATT regime and address North-South trade and investment issues more fully in the Uruguay Round than in any previous negotiation.[240] As the Third World went neoliberal, the goal of a world where market capitalism was progressively more accepted—and U.S. opportunities were correspondingly greater—seemed ever closer to realization.

For many LDCs, too, there were important gains. Privatization generally made industry more efficient; economic reforms helped LDCs attract investment, repatriate flight capital, and reenter private lending markets on a voluntary basis. Trade often rose substantially; inflation fell. In Latin America, where the prevalence of neoliberal reform was greatest, growth averaged 3.4 percent between 1990 and 1998 (nearly 1.5 times faster than the world average of 2.3 percent), and exports rose at nearly 10 percent annually. Average (unweighted) cross-country inflation fell to 10 percent by the end of the 1990s, down from 1,200 percent a decade earlier. Average real wages grew by 17.8 percent between 1991 and 1998 after falling sharply during the 1980s, and poverty returned to its 1980 level. As careful analysts have noted, the overall effects of reform were broadly positive.[241]

Yet even so, the neoliberal triumph left a bitter taste in many mouths. Most of sub-Saharan Africa saw little profit from the repeated bouts of adjustment during the 1980s, and remained mired in crisis and deprivation for years thereafter. Even in Latin America, the gains of the 1990s sometimes seemed paltry compared to the misery—the poverty and infant mortality, the declining incomes and caloric intake—that the debt crisis had inflicted. "Our debt, by the hunger it provokes in our people, kills more people than wars," Luiz Inácio da Silva, Brazilian Workers' Party candidate (and future president), declared in 1989.[242] And if the balance sheet on the reforms themselves was still generally positive, there were nonetheless causes for grievance. Just as the debt crisis had illustrated the instability that could result from greater openness, for instance, the opening of LDC economies left those countries more vulnerable to external shocks in the years thereafter. "Life in a world of free-flowing capital," one analyst writes, "proved to be something of a roller-coaster."[243]

When one moved from the macro- to the micro-level, the consequences could be even more disconcerting. In highly stratified societies, neoliberal policies helped the rich get richer—for example, by allowing them to buy SOEs at bargain prices, and to establish what were sometimes essentially private monopolies in place of the old public ones. Neoliberal reforms, one U.S. diplomat said, were "fixed for the people on top."[244] For the less fortunate, "adjustment" was often a euphemism for a host of evils: the removal of subsidies or price controls on essential goods, budget cutbacks that decimated social programs, the loss of jobs or wages due to privatization and greater competition. "The social costs have been high," U.S. diplomats wrote of one Latin American country—"unemployment continues to rise, hunger is not uncommon."[245] These traumas of adjustment were tragically illustrated in early 1990s Peru, when a cholera outbreak, caused in part by the fact that many families could no longer afford cooking oil to boil water or prepare food, killed around 2,000 people. As a World Bank symposium had earlier concluded, "For those already poor—or for those now newly poor—structural adjustment can mean hunger, infant mortality, and great deprivation."[246]

One should not take this critique too far. Pro-market policies eventually fostered stability and growth that enabled modest reductions in poverty. More important, for all the ills of neoliberal reform, *not* reforming could be even worse. To return to the Peruvian example, the economic chaos unleashed by García's policies during the mid- and late-1980s inflicted far more damage than even a draconian austerity program would have caused. Real wages fell by 75 percent between 1987 and 1990, inflation hit 3,400 percent in 1989, and food consumption declined alarmingly.[247] Countless Peruvians were impoverished, or worse. In Bolivia, by contrast, where adjustment was pursued doggedly from 1985 onward, the pain was intense, but continuing hyperinflation likely would have been even more devastating. "The stabilization probably helped the relative position of the poor compared to what would have happened in the absence of stabilization,"

World Bank analysts concluded.[248] In this sense, the undeniable downsides of neoliberal reform may, to some degree, have been necessary evils. "Not all problems can be solved painlessly," World Bank Vice President and Treasurer Eugene Rotberg said.[249]

Whatever the case may have been, there was nonetheless substantial resentment, and sometimes resistance, generated by the policies that Washington backed. In Africa, the IMF was tarred as the "Infanticide Memorial Foundation."[250] In Venezuela, massive riots broke out after the government undertook an austerity and reform program in 1989, leading to a brutal crackdown and hundreds of deaths. The reforms continued, but the anger they provoked figured in a 1992 coup attempt led by an obscure paratrooper named Hugo Chávez, who soon became a leading critic of the neoliberal model. "The coup attempt unleashed widespread dissatisfaction with corruption and the pain of economic reform," U.S. officials reported.[251] There was similar blowback in Mexico, where the implementation of NAFTA precipitated a revolt by Zapatista rebels who deemed that pact a "death sentence" for poor indigenous peoples.[252] As the post–Cold War era unfolded, challenges to the neoliberal order would remain a fixture of global politics. Here, as elsewhere, U.S. successes left lasting contradictions.

The Market and the Middle Kingdom

The contradictions of success also marked U.S.-China economic relations. Any analysis of U.S. efforts to foster a more integrated global economy during the 1980s requires a discussion of that relationship, because Beijing's pivot to capitalism constituted the most dramatic manifestation of the neoliberal turn, and because China's size made that pivot so consequential. "By any measure," Undersecretary of State Michael Armacost said in 1985, "Beijing's economic reforms of the past 6 years represent one of the boldest and most far-reaching attempts to restructure a major economy anywhere in the world."[253] It was a restructuring that U.S. administrations did much to support, and one whose ramifications would eventually prove both beneficial and problematic.

For China as for so many developing nations, the 1980s marked an economic watershed. Although some policy changes had begun in the twilight of Mao Zedong's rule, it was in 1978 that Deng Xiaoping launched reforms that truly propelled China toward the market. First cautiously, and then with building speed, Deng's government introduced measures to make policy more responsive to economic incentives, and to foster rapid modernization through greater ties to the world. This turn toward "neoliberalism with Chinese characteristics" emphasized measures such as de-collectivizing agriculture and allowing farmers to earn a profit, introducing rewards for more efficient performance in industry, incrementally but unmistakably liberalizing controls on foreign investment and trade, and promoting private businesses and joining institutions such as the World Bank.[254] "China was striving to reach marked results by the end of the century," Deng said, and the old model would not suffice.[255] The results of Deng's measures were nothing short of breathtaking. Chinese GDP more than doubled over the next decade, with per capita GDP close behind, and imports and exports multiplied several-fold. The world's largest country was undergoing an economic revolution, and entering the global economy in ever-greater ways.[256]

From the start, the United States was a key player in that revolution. In one sense, it was Deng's desire to emulate Western prosperity that drove his reforms. "What he saw in the United States," one scholar writes of Deng's early 1979 trip, "was what he wanted for China in the future."[257] More tangibly, U.S. officials labored to ensure that reform succeeded. Determined to draw closer to Beijing as détente with Moscow crumbled, the Carter administration laid the groundwork with several initiatives. Carter granted MFN status to China, a crucial precondition for expanded bilateral trade, and helped it join the IMF and World Bank. U.S. envoys negotiated agreements to expand bilateral scientific and technological cooperation, and the administration took initial steps to ease the transfer of both civilian and military technology. American representatives promoted greater investment in China, and established forums for developing economic cooperation. Partially in response to these measures, two-way trade quadrupled between 1978 and 1980, and U.S. investment in China began to surge. The U.S.-China economic relationship, Carter announced, "is a new and vital force for peace and stability in the international scene. In addition it holds a promise of ever-increasing benefits in trade and other exchanges."[258]

Reagan took up the same policy with even greater vigor. Broadly speaking, promoting the liberalization and integration of the thriving Pacific Rim economies was a high priority for Reagan and top advisers such as Shultz and Baker, who believed that the dynamism of that area was making it an ever-more vital hub of world commerce. "If you want to understand the future," Shultz said, "you must . . . understand the Pacific region."[259] The administration persistently pursued this agenda vis-à-vis Japan and other countries, in some cases with considerable success. U.S. engagement helped induce the South Korean financial and industrial reforms of the 1980s, for instance.[260]

Despite some initial misgivings, the administration became an even stronger supporter of Deng's reforms. During the 1980 campaign, Reagan had alarmed Chinese authorities by calling for a restoration of U.S. ties with Taiwan, and by labeling the communist regime in Beijing a "government that believes in destroying governments like ours."[261] Once in office, however, he committed to helping that very government modernize the Chinese economy. From a strategic perspective, doing so would make China a firmer bulwark against Soviet power. "Only the interests of our adversaries would be served by a weak China that had failed to modernize," State Department officials argued.[262]

From an economic perspective, the prospect of a more open and prosperous China was even more enticing. Bringing China into the international economy would powerfully attest to the ascent of the market model. It would also promote a potentially massive enlargement of regional and global commerce, while creating great opportunities for the expansion of U.S. trade and investment. "I need hardly elaborate for those in this room the economic benefits a modernizing China could bring to U.S. business," Paul Wolfowitz told a group of entrepreneurs.[263] By 1983–1984, presidential directives pledged Washington to "lend support to China's ambitious modernization effort," and Reagan carried this message to Beijing. As papers prepared for his 1984 visit stated, "My country stands ready to contribute in whatever way possible to China's ambitious goals for the 21st century."[264]

This approach was well matched to Deng's understanding of what rapid development required. "The Chinese seem to recognize," INR analysts wrote, "that Western economic and technological help is essential for their modernization."[265] In this context, Reagan was able to deploy numerous measures to fortify reformist tendencies in Beijing. The administration used the Commodity Credit Corporation and Export-Import Bank to facilitate Chinese purchases of U.S. goods, and worked, through the Overseas Private Investment Corporation, to encourage U.S. investment. Recognizing that the private sector would be the leading edge of foreign involvement in China, American officials also offered to play matchmaker between U.S. firms and their Chinese counterparts by gathering and relaying information on potential partnerships. At the same time, the administration consistently pushed Beijing to continue liberalizing its trade, investment, and financial policies, and to clarify the legal and regulatory framework in which foreign firms would operate. And through the Joint Economic Committee and other bodies, U.S. and Chinese officials conducted regular dialogues on ways of expanding economic ties.[266] All the while, Reagan heartily lauded Deng's reforms, indicating that a more open China would enjoy greater international stature and respect. Beijing was pursuing the course of "vision" and "vitality," Reagan declared in 1984. "We welcome the opportunity to walk at China's side in this endeavor."[267]

By far the most important step the administration took, however, was to dramatically increase the flow of technology and know-how that Beijing so desperately needed. Again building on Carter-era initiatives, Reagan quickly began to loosen export controls on the transfer of advanced industrial and economic technologies. Export-license approvals involving technology transfer increased threefold from 1979 to the end of 1982, and administration officials noted that U.S. firms "now sell exceptionally broad range of both equipment and technology, much state-of-the-art."[268] In 1983, Reagan liberalized export controls further, to permit sale of all technologies save a few categories with "direct and significant military applications," and to streamline approval procedures.[269]

With U.S. companies eager to sell technology, trade in this area immediately soared. Export licenses doubled from 1982 to 1984, and sales of high-tech goods—including mainframe computers and semiconductors, hydroturbines and petrochemical equipment—increased sevenfold, from $144 million in 1982 to over $1 billion in 1986. "Technology transfer," Armacost said, "has become a touchstone of Sino-U.S. relations."[270] This more relaxed policy also encouraged other initiatives that brought Western technology to bear on Chinese modernization: co-production ventures between U.S. and Chinese firms, participation of U.S. companies in energy exploration and development of the Chinese transportation network and electronics industry, and others. Here as elsewhere, the thrust of policy was not to use huge quantities of public resources to spur Chinese modernization, but to exploit the role of the U.S. government as facilitator and gatekeeper to help the private sector fulfill this task.[271]

It is hard to overstate the contribution that this U.S. involvement made to the success of Deng's reforms during the crucial early period. America was a leading source of foreign investment in China during the 1980s, when this investment was so critical to catalyzing prosperity. (The centrality of U.S. and other foreign capital, in turn, nudged Beijing to take additional steps to improve the investment climate.)[272] Sales of advanced technology, and the provision of expertise through corporate partnerships and other arrangements, also allowed modernization to progress far more rapidly than it otherwise would have, a fact that Chinese officials tacitly acknowledged by continually seeking more cooperation along these lines.[273] "Importing foreign technology," the Defense Intelligence Agency concluded, "plays a central role in China's modernization strategy."[274] Not least of all, the granting of MFN status and the opening of the U.S. market to Chinese goods helped Beijing achieve the export sales that so propelled its growth. As Odd Arne Westad assesses, "The relationship with the United States stood left, right, and center in Communist China's initial market revolution."[275]

That relationship was certainly near the forefront of China's insertion into the global economy. Beijing's formerly autarkic system was being internationalized during this period. The Chinese share of world trade quadrupled between 1978 and the early 1990s, and trade as a share of GNP multiplied from 7 to roughly 40 percent.[276] Amid this boom, U.S.-China commerce soared. Bilateral merchandise trade grew fourteenfold, from $374 million to $5.2 billion, between 1977 and 1982, and would reach roughly $8 billion in 1985 and $25 billion in 1991.[277] Beijing and Washington were rapidly becoming mutually indispensable trade partners, and China was being pulled inexorably into an increasingly interconnected world economy. "China's 1 billion people are entering the mainstream of the international economic system," John Holdridge, a State Department Asia hand, could say as early as 1982. "The volume and value of bilateral trade between our two countries has grown tremendously."[278]

As the 1980s progressed, U.S. officials therefore viewed China's transformation as a signal triumph. Shultz hailed China's "long march to the market" as "a truly historic event," and as confirmation that the neoliberal tide was rolling in.[279] Speaking at Moscow State University in May 1988, Reagan himself cited the Chinese experiment as proof that "the power of economic freedom" was "spreading around the world."[280] Indeed, there was little question that China's economic revolution was a major step forward for market capitalism worldwide, or that Washington had enabled that revolution in important ways. In the decades that followed, the rewards of the bilateral economic relationship ensured that preserving and deepening that engagement remained a core aspect of U.S. policy.

For all of the satisfaction that accompanied China's opening, however, even in the 1980s there were aspects of that phenomenon that were more problematic. One issue concerned the relationship between economic and political reform. Reagan's expectation was that the latter would follow the former: once the Chinese people had their "first taste of freedom," political liberalization would come close behind.[281] Unfortunately, the progression was not so straightforward. Deng's economic reforms did destabilize existing political arrangements, and figured in the flowering of popular dissent leading up to 1989.[282] Yet the Chinese government responded not by initiating a process of democratization, but via a bloody massacre that reasserted the dominance of the Communist Party at a cost of hundreds of civilian lives. "If we had not suppressed them, they would have brought about our

collapse," Deng reportedly said.[283] In later years, the party would use prosperity as a substitute for political reform, not as a prelude thereto. Economic
and political liberalization, it turned out, were not always as indivisible as
U.S. officials believed. From Tiananmen Square onward, American presidents
would therefore face charges that the U.S.-China economic relationship was
merely strengthening an incorrigibly authoritarian regime.

There was also the question of what an economically prosperous China
would ultimately mean for U.S. security interests. During the 1970s and
1980s, the Cold War context meant that the growth of Chinese power
was seen as a check on Moscow and a geopolitical gain for Washington.
Even during Reagan's presidency, however, concerns occasionally surfaced
that successful economic modernization might provide the foundation for a
military buildup that would eventually make China a danger to East Asian
stability. That prospect "now seems remote," Pentagon analysts reported in
1983, but "the possibility of Chinese conflicts with U.S. allies and friends
and the United States itself cannot be excluded" over the longer term.
A China that continued to thrive economically, and that developed military
capabilities commensurate with its wealth, would someday be able to pursue
more aggressive policies toward Taiwan, South Korea, or Japan, and perhaps
even challenge the United States for supremacy in the Western Pacific.[284]
In the 1980s, this concern—that U.S. policy might actually be feeding a
monster—remained muted and generally latent. In subsequent decades, it
would become all too prominent.

Conclusion

American statecraft in the 1980s did not lack for ambition. At a time of profound global transitions, U.S. officials believed, Washington need not content
itself with status-quo policies or simply reacting to events. Rather, it should
use its power proactively, to engage the forces of historical change and drive
them decisively forward. Amid great global fluidity and promise, Reagan-era
officials liked to say, the United States could aspire to "shaping the international environment."[285]

This approach paid dividends in the Cold War and in U.S. efforts to spread
democracy overseas. It had similar results in the international economic arena.
From the beginning, the Reagan administration dedicated itself to expanding and deepening the global market economy. Over time, U.S. officials
gradually pulled together the policies needed to achieve this ambition—to
contain the dangers that afflicted Western economic relations, to bring Japan
more fully into global finance while also avoiding a trade war, to spearhead

a renewed drive toward multilateral trade liberalization, and above all to use American leverage to promote a dramatic turn in LDC political economy. By the close of the 1980s, the more globalized economy that U.S. officials desired was thus coming steadily closer to reality. America's favored liberal model was racing forward economically as well as politically; the neoliberal ascendancy seemed just as incontestable as democracy's advance. As so often during this period, U.S. statecraft had indeed pushed the pace of change and been crucial to "shaping the international environment."

This theme, then, held true across broad swaths of American policy. But so did the key caveats that attended 1980s-era U.S. statecraft. For one thing, the work of assembling effective approaches was no briefer or easier here than elsewhere. It required, in instances ranging from the dollar crisis to the debt crisis, a process of adjustment and adaptation in the ways that American officials sought to turn opportunity and ambition, on the one hand, into concrete outcomes, on the other. And although the end results of that process were generally quite satisfying, the more disconcerting legacies bequeathed by U.S.–Third World and U.S.-China economic relations showed that the rise of the neoliberal order contained resentments and insecurities anew. American officials would soon find themselves confronting the challenges that sprang from their earlier triumphs; this too was a theme that cut across U.S. policy in the Reagan years.

At the close of the 1980s and 1990s, however, many of these rising challenges were but dimly apparent, and it was the recent successes of U.S. policy that shone brightest. Those successes attested to the breadth and multidimensionality of American renewal in the years preceding; they also ensured that Washington would keep pursuing its neoliberal agenda in the future. The partnership with the IFIs having proved its worth, U.S. officials would continue to use those institutions to seek the consolidation and further proliferation of market reforms. More broadly, the confidence that American and IFI officials took away from the 1980s made it highly likely that they would aim to replicate their achievements in new areas when given the chance. This was the heart of the Washington Consensus identified by John Williamson in 1990—the feeling of assurance that free-market reforms were right for countries everywhere, and that they could be put into effect around the world through the right mix of internal determination and external encouragement.[286]

Indeed, as was the case with democracy promotion, a most consequential legacy of U.S. foreign economic policy during the 1980s was to instill a firm belief that the global order was remaking itself to reflect America's core preferences, and that energetic engagement was integral to keeping the process going. "We stand here at this point in history," one U.S. official declared in 1989, "with free market economics in triumph."[287] "Countries across the globe are turning to free markets," Reagan himself had said earlier that year; America could not but lend its full support to this trend.[288] As the post–Cold War era unfolded, this sense of great optimism and vindication would help ensure that U.S. statecraft remained decidedly on the offensive.

CHAPTER 5

Structure versus Strategy in the Greater Middle East

The American ascendancy of the 1980s was fundamentally rooted in propitious global conditions. From the Cold War, to the promotion of democracy, to the shaping of a neoliberal order, U.S. officials were able to harness strong historical forces that were remarkably conducive to national purposes. This does not mean that U.S. policy was simply lucky rather than good, of course, for structure and strategy went together in the impressive breakthroughs of the decade. What it means, rather, is that such breakthroughs were far more likely with the geopolitical winds at Washington's back.

This synergy between good policy and good fortune was the dominant theme of U.S. statecraft in the 1980s. It was not a universal theme, however, because there were areas in which the prevailing winds remained more adverse than advantageous. In these cases, the arc of American policy was far less pleasing, and the outcomes were far less impressive. When structure and strategy aligned, in other words, the United States did very well; when they clashed, transformative achievements went wanting.

This latter dynamic found its clearest expression in U.S. dealings with the greater Middle East.[1] If the world was basically evolving to Washington's liking, the structural trends in the Middle East were heading in the opposite direction. Here the geopolitical bequest of the 1970s was ominous, as the Iranian revolution of 1979 fused together three deeply rooted developments that would bedevil U.S. policymakers for years to come. The growth of insecurity and instability in the Persian Gulf, the empowerment of an often-radical political Islam, and the alarming rise in Middle Eastern terrorism—all these phenomena were both symbolized and catalyzed by Ayatollah Ruhollah Khomeini's revolution, and all were far more menacing than encouraging for the United States. In other areas, American statecraft could reap the dividends of positive change. Here the dominant trends ran primarily *against* U.S. interests, auguring recurrent strife and danger that would last through the end of the Cold War and beyond.

That crucial difference was reflected in the record of U.S. policy in the greater Middle East in the decade after 1979. Throughout these years, American officials wrestled with the complex and interwoven challenges posed by Gulf insecurity, terrorism, and the upsurge of political Islam, and they sought to bring U.S. power to bear as they had done so effectively in addressing other crises and opportunities around the world. Yet despite great efforts and some undeniable accomplishments, the results of these endeavors were ultimately ambiguous at best. The structural issues that the United States confronted in the greater Middle East were simply resistant to decisive breakthroughs or neat solutions, and American policies were often inconclusive, unsatisfying, or even counterproductive in their effects. Overall, the 1980s were an era of great global gains for Washington. But in this more difficult regional setting, lasting victories were harder to come by, and America's problems were only beginning. As the unipolar order was taking form, then, so were the persistent threats that would most disturb and complicate U.S. dominance.

The Iranian Revolution and the Three Challenges

If there was a single event that served as the nexus of the structural challenges that Washington faced in Middle Eastern affairs from the late 1970s onward, it was the Islamic revolution in Iran. As late as 1977, Iran had been a seemingly stable, modernizing, pro-Western bulwark in the Gulf. Two years later, it was rapidly becoming a militant theocracy and a severe threat to U.S. interests. At home, Iranian leaders were erecting a political system based on a fundamentalist version of Shiite Islam; abroad, they were destabilizing their neighbors and espousing one of the bitterest forms of anti-Americanism ever seen in international politics. Khomeini's supporters shocked U.S. observers with chants of "Death to America"; the ayatollah himself labeled Washington "the Great Satan" and "the number one enemy of the oppressed and deprived nations of the world."[2] As we have seen in chapter 1, Khomeini's revolution and the hostage crisis that followed were often taken as indicators of a broader U.S. decline in the geopolitical context of the late 1970s. This view was overstated, but the Iranian revolution still crystallized and drew together three interwoven challenges that would confront, and often confound, U.S. policymakers in the 1980s and after.

The first of these challenges was the collapse of the existing balance of power in the Persian Gulf. By Carter's presidency, the Gulf was fast becoming an increasingly vital, and threatened, region in world affairs. The geopolitical importance of the area dated back decades, of course, but it had grown dramatically during the 1970s. By mid-decade, the Gulf contained 54 percent of world proven oil reserves. The oil shocks had demonstrated just how dependent the West had become on those supplies, and how essential it was to maintain U.S. access and influence in the region. "Without Middle Eastern oil," Energy Secretary James Schlesinger said in 1979, "the Free World as we know it is through."[3] At the same time, however, the rise of internal upheaval in countries from Pakistan to Saudi Arabia to the Horn of Africa, and the growth of Soviet influence in nations such as Iraq, South Yemen, and Ethiopia, were casting greater doubt on the security of the Gulf and the areas surrounding it. "There is no question in my mind that we are confronting the beginning of a major crisis, in some ways similar to the one in Europe in the late 40's," Brzezinski wrote in 1978. "Fragile social and political structures in a region of vital importance to us are threatened with fragmentation."[4]

The Iranian revolution dramatized and intensified this crisis. Since the British withdrawal from "East of Suez" in 1971, Iran had been the linchpin of U.S. strategy in the Gulf. The shah was the world's largest consumer of American weaponry ($16.2 billion in purchases from 1972 to 1977), and had acted as a strategic surrogate amid U.S. retrenchment.[5] His regime served as a crucial bulwark against Kremlin power to the north. It also maintained pressure on the pro-Soviet Baathist regime in Iraq, helped defeat leftist rebels in Oman, and generally allowed the United States to enjoy relative stability in the Gulf while making only a token U.S. military commitment—three ships stationed at Bahrain—to the region. "The Shah is a tough, mean guy," Kissinger said in 1974. "But he is our real friend."[6]

The Iranian revolution, therefore, was a strategic shock of the first order. It shattered the keystone of the existing security architecture in the Gulf. It threw the largest and most powerful country in the area into chaos. It opened a power vacuum that hostile forces from within or outside the region might be tempted to exploit. In short, the revolution unraveled America's position in the Gulf and left U.S. interests in that region terribly exposed. "The Iranian crisis has led to the collapse of the balance of power in Southwest Asia,"

Brzezinski wrote, "and it could produce Soviet presence right down to the edge of the Arabian and Oman Gulfs."[7]

At first, the Carter administration believed it could mitigate the strategic consequences of the shah's fall by forging cordial relations with the fairly moderate leaders that initially succeeded him. During 1979, the administration even shared sensitive intelligence on regional security issues with the provisional government.[8] Yet these overtures came to naught as Khomeini and his more radical followers seized control of the revolution, and it soon became clear that the new Iran would be an exporter of *in*security. "We must endeavor to export our Revolution to the world," Khomeini declared, and his regime used tools from propaganda to armed subversion in hopes of undermining nearby governments and reshaping the region in its image.[9] Support for radical opposition groups in Iraq and Kuwait, efforts to incite unrest among marginalized Shiite populations in Saudi Arabia and elsewhere, the promotion of violence and extremism in countries from Bahrain to Lebanon—these tactics made Iran the scourge of its neighbors, and they fed the upheaval in the area. "Iran," U.S. officials wrote, "became the major source of instability rather than the main buttress of regional security."[10]

Even before the Soviet invasion of Afghanistan, then, policymakers feared that a critical region was, as Brzezinski wrote, on the verge of veering "dangerously out of control."[11] The invasion made this prospect loom larger still. As JCS Chairman General David Jones reported, Soviet forces were now within striking distance of Gulf oilfields, and Soviet fighter aircraft could range the Strait of Hormuz—the chokepoint for Gulf oil shipments—from Afghan airfields. "One Soviet airborne division, about 8,000 troops, with organic armored vehicles, could land anywhere in the vicinity of the Persian Gulf in two to three days if all Soviet airlift is employed," Jones added.[12] Even if Moscow refrained from such dramatic steps, it might use its presence in Afghanistan to coerce, intimidate, or merely stoke ongoing turmoil in neighboring countries such as Iran or Pakistan, or even in Iraq and Saudi Arabia farther afield. "They have in effect changed a proper nation into a puppet nation," Carter said, "and I think it will have profound strategic consequences on the stability of that entire region."[13]

By 1979–1980, the effect of all this was to convince U.S. officials that Gulf security was endangered in unprecedented ways, just when the strategic value of the region had never been greater. It followed that redressing this insecurity must become a top-tier priority. This theme was evident in Carter's declaration, in January 1980, that further Soviet aggression in the region would be grounds for a military response.[14] It was equally underscored by Brzezinski, who argued in a series of memos that the geopolitical salience of the Gulf was now equal to that of Western Europe and Japan. The Gulf had become the "third central strategic zone" of U.S. policy, he wrote. Securing that region would constitute the "third phase of the great architectural task undertaken by the United States after World War II," and an abiding preoccupation going forward.[15]

From the late 1970s onward, the difficulties of addressing that issue would be compounded by a second challenge connected to the Iranian revolution—the resurgence of often-radical political Islam across much of the Middle East and beyond. This turn toward political doctrines that focused on reordering government and society according to Islamic precepts, and which in some cases were quite literalist and fundamentalist in nature, reflected a confluence of factors. For many Muslims, the Six-Day War of 1967 was key. The Arabs' humiliating defeat by Israel led to widespread soul-searching in the Muslim world, centering on why a community that had once been so powerful was now rendered so impotent. The answer that many Muslim intellectuals and clerics offered up was that insufficient piety was to blame. It was because Muslim peoples and polities had strayed from God that they were mired in weakness and malaise; the community would regain its earthly glories only when it returned to a more righteous path. In this sense, the rise of Islamism was a product of military defeat, and of astonishment at the power disparity between the Muslim world and its most immediate enemy.

The impact of the 1967 war dovetailed with other causes. By the 1970s, the failures of Arab nationalism and corrupt secular dictatorships had gone far in discrediting rival ideological paradigms. At the same time, the dislocations wrought by ambitious modernization programs, and by the influx of oil money, were spurring conservative resistance and a retreat to traditional values amid disorienting change. Not least of all, the Islamist resurgence was rooted in a backlash against foreign and particularly Western influence. Amid the intellectual ferment of the period, that influence was increasingly associated with the persistence of unresponsive dictatorships across the region, and viewed as a reason for Muslim weakness vis-à-vis Israel and in international politics. As a result of these factors, by the late 1970s Islamist movements were gaining strength from Pakistan to Saudi Arabia to the Maghreb, challenging existing political orders and exerting what would ultimately be pervasive impact. "There is no mistaking the awakening of Islam," the CIA assessed. "Islamic feeling is on the upswing and this must be factored into our relationships with Muslim states."[16]

This awakening burst into U.S. and Western consciousness with the Iranian revolution. The revolt against the shah exemplified many key factors that

informed the broader Islamist resurgence. It was the shah's rapid modernization of Iranian society—and the concurrent expansion of the U.S. presence
in the country—that alienated conservative clergy such as Khomeini from
the mid-1960s onward. The socioeconomic disjunctures that flowed from
modernization and the oil boom simultaneously caused growing numbers
of citizens to seek refuge in Islamist ideas. When the climactic crisis broke
in 1978–1979, the growing popular salience of those ideas helped fortify
many revolutionaries in their showdown with the regime, and then allowed
Khomeini to steer the revolution in a theocratic direction.

Khomeini's ascendancy, in turn, invigorated the Islamist revival all the
more. The revolution energized Islamist groups everywhere by showing that
this movement could defeat faithless regimes and their foreign backers, and
that it was possible to construct a polity where religious concepts reigned
supreme. The demonstration effect was an extremely powerful one not just
for Khomeini's co-sectarian Shiites in the Gulf and Levant, but for religiously inspired dissidents across the Muslim world. "Khomeini has shown
the power of Islam as a force for mobilizing the masses," the CIA noted.
"Other antiregime protest movements will no doubt use Islam as a rallying
cry."[17] This was precisely what the ayatollah desired. From Tehran, Khomeini
declared that the revolution was a model for all who sought to restore Islamic
influence and power:

> Our problems will not disappear until we return to Islam, the prophet's
> Islam. Until such a time we will not be able to solve the problem of
> Palestine, the problem of Afghanistan or any other problems. Nations
> must return to genuine Islam. Should governments also do accordingly,
> so much the better; otherwise nations must separate their accounts from
> those of their governments and deal with them as the Iranian nation
> dealt with its government. It is then that problems will be solved.[18]

So what did the Islamic revival mean for Washington? Few U.S. officials had forecast that revival before Khomeini's triumph, and most were
unsure what to make of it. Islamism, Brzezinski wrote, was something that
"America doesn't have much experience of dealing with."[19] Dealing with
the phenomenon was unavoidable, however, for its geopolitical implications were immense. In Tehran, for instance, Islamist ideology was a fount of
Khomeini's hostility to the United States and many of Iran's neighbors. The
ayatollah believed that an Islamic revolution was inherently an anti-Western
revolution—that Islamic civilization could recover neither its purity nor its
glory without expunging the foreign influences that had strengthened Israel,
propped up secular regimes, and corrupted Muslim societies. This emphasis

on breaking with the West informed Khomeini's support for the taking of hostages in November 1979, and his broader determination to drive the United States out of the Middle East. "The Khomeini regime views itself at war with the U.S., which is viewed not only as a foe of Iran but the chief enemy of all Islam," the CIA assessed.[20] Likewise, the idea that Iran was divinely commanded to spread the Islamic revolution guided its subversive and confrontational approach to other Gulf states. "We have no choice but to destroy those systems that are corrupt and to overthrow all oppressive and criminal regimes," Khomeini announced; such behavior was a matter of religious duty.[21]

The Islamist resurgence had broader geopolitical ramifications, as well. As we will see, it catalyzed the Afghan jihad against an atheistic communist regime and occupying Soviet forces, a development that U.S. officials would seek to exploit. By and large, however, the consequences were far more troubling for Washington. Across the region, Islamist movements challenged moderate or pro-Western regimes that they deemed insufficiently pious and excessively accommodating of foreign prerogatives. In late 1979, for instance, religious radicals launched a bloody takeover of the Grand Mosque in Mecca, raising questions about the stability of the Saudi regime. Two years later, Islamist militants assassinated Anwar Sadat of Egypt, the visionary leader who had made peace with Israel and aligned his country with the West. The killing appalled American leaders—Reagan confessed "a great sense of loss"—while also exposing the vulnerability of pro-U.S. governments.[22] By this point, in fact, the frequently anti-Western cast of Islamist ideas was giving voice to strident critiques of U.S. policy throughout the Middle East, and was generally promising to complicate American relations with the region. "The Islamic people . . . are now awake from their slumber," one group of students wrote. "They will never [again] surrender to domination and submissiveness."[23] CIA analysts summed up the situation in 1981. The Islamic revival, they wrote, had often been "destabilizing for the societies concerned and detrimental to the strategic and economic interests of the United States."[24]

The revival would prove particularly problematic for U.S. policymakers because it also intertwined with a third emerging challenge: an upsurge of international terrorism, especially in or emanating from the Middle East. Terrorism, of course, was hardly original to this period. If we define *terrorism* as the threat or use of violence by substate actors in order to create fear and thereby achieve political ends, then the phenomenon already had a distinguished pedigree.[25] But the profile of the problem did rise significantly in the 1970s. Palestinian and other groups mounted high-profile international attacks to publicize their causes, and the same advances that facilitated globalization—improved travel and communications—made such operations easier to conduct and harder to ignore. The number of terrorist attacks worldwide each year increased roughly fivefold, from 142 to 709, between 1968 and 1981. "The trend is unmistakably upward," Brian Michael Jenkins of the RAND Corporation wrote in 1980; attacks were becoming more common and deadlier.[26]

The "global offensive" prosecuted by the Palestine Liberation Organization (PLO) during this period offered a prime example of the trend. Led by Yasser Arafat, the PLO turned to terrorism as a way of pursuing Palestinian national aspirations in the face of overwhelming Israeli military superiority. To strike at Israel and its supporters, and garner attention for the Palestinian cause, the PLO and its subgroups launched deliberate attacks against noncombatants, not just within Israel and the Middle East, but in Western Europe and other areas as well. The campaign began with the hijacking of an El Al flight in 1968; its most notorious moment was the massacre of Israeli athletes at the 1972 summer Olympics in Munich. During the 1970s, as in later years, Palestinian attacks failed to achieve the stated goal of national liberation. Yet they did generate enormous publicity and prestige for the PLO, and provided a means of bloodying a far stronger opponent. Through the example it set, and the ties it forged to other radical groups in the Middle East and beyond, the PLO helped usher in the age of modern international terrorism.[27]

As of the late 1970s, that age was one for which the United States was ill-prepared. Even as increasing terrorist attacks had occasioned growing concern in certain government circles, the problem had only sporadically received top-level attention. The Nixon administration engaged in a flurry of activity to address airline hijackings, and near the end of the decade, the Pentagon created what would become Delta Force as a specialized hostage-rescue unit. These measures aside, however, terrorism still elicited comparatively little sustained urgency in the highest echelons of the executive branch. "For the U.S. government," one author writes, "terrorism remained the annoying little gnat that buzzed around the superpower while it was trying to handle truly dangerous matters." As late as 1977, NSC officials were looking for ways of "making it easier for us to ignore the alarmists who want to make combatting terrorism the biggest business of government." And with the PLO now decreasing its own reliance on terrorism in the late 1970s, some U.S. officials concluded that the threat was waning.[28]

This was a spectacularly erroneous forecast, unfortunately, and the epicenter of international terrorism from the late 1970s onward was the Middle

East. Here, rising Islamic fervor was adding a deadly new element to the equation by fostering the advent of more groups that were willing to use violence to defend the faith and attack its purported enemies. "Most such groups are identified with religious fundamentalism or 'fanaticism,'" CIA analysts noted, "and assert their religious purity as justification for their actions against an 'impure' government or some other group or institutions."[29] This religious zealotry combined with familiar drivers such as the Arab-Israeli and Israeli-Palestinian conflicts, and growing resentment against established regimes and foreign powers. Crucially, it also fed on the increasing willingness of numerous Middle Eastern states to sponsor terrorists as a tool of asymmetric warfare—a low-cost, semicovert means of advancing their aims and gaining leverage on stronger actors. "Terrorism is warfare 'on the cheap' and entails few risks," Pentagon analysts wrote. "It permits small countries to attack U.S. interests in a manner, which if done openly, would constitute acts of war and justify a direct U.S. military response." Cumulatively, these factors drove a sustained growth in terrorism, one that would prove highly threatening to U.S. interests. By 1984, U.S. officials were calling the Middle East "the crucible of terrorism," and nearly half of recorded attacks occurred or originated in the region.[30]

As with the Islamic revival and the rise of Persian Gulf insecurity, the explosion of Middle Eastern terrorism was deeply entangled with the Iranian revolution. That revolution marked "America's first encounter with radical Islam," and the hostage crisis brought home the rising danger that terrorism posed.[31] The seizing of the U.S. embassy and holding of over 50 hostages for 444 days was, CIA analysts wrote, "a model for terrorist operations."[32] It showed that religious extremists could exploit the vulnerability of American civilians abroad to capture global attention and utterly humiliate a superpower. It demonstrated the political utility that governments such as Khomeini's—which ruthlessly perpetuated the confrontation as a way of marginalizing its moderate opponents—could derive from sponsoring terrorist groups. It illustrated how long-standing U.S. policies in the region—in this case, support for the shah—could make Washington the focus of the boiling anger underlying many terrorist acts. Above all, it revealed how difficult it could be address the problem. Carter struggled mightily to gain the diplomatic leverage needed to free the hostages peacefully, and the disastrous rescue effort underscored how unprepared the U.S. military was for counterterrorism missions. "They have us by the balls," Carter lamented; the United States seemed paralyzed by this startling act of terror.[33] "To fundamentalist groups elsewhere," the CIA subsequently warned, "the 'lesson' of the hostage crisis might not be that it was highly costly to the state, but that it was a heroic example of defiance of the West by a group of believers unwilling to compromise and accept Western values."[34]

The warning was prescient, because the hostage crisis presaged things to come. Acts of terrorism—often religiously inspired—proliferated across the Middle East during the 1980s and after, frequently abetted by radical states in the region. Tehran made promoting terrorism a central pillar of its foreign policy, using it to attack U.S. and Israeli influence, and to subvert governments that resisted the export of the Islamic revolution. "The regime makes no distinction between military or civilian targets or tactics," U.S. intelligence noted, "and it increasingly appears willing to strike at its enemies' interests anywhere in the world." Iranian financial, logistical, and even operational support flowed to Shiite extremists throughout the region. During the early 1980s, for example, the Iranian Revolutionary Guard Corps (IRGC) organized Shiite factions in Lebanon into Hezbollah, which would soon become the world's most feared terrorist group.[35] Other governments were pursuing similar policies. Syria's Hafez al-Assad supported Hezbollah and Palestinian organizations as proxies in the struggle against Israel and its supporters; Libya's Muammar Qaddafi was patron to Islamist radicals and "almost every major international terrorist group."[36] In Washington, William Casey was soon remarking on a "contagious" epidemic of international terrorism. "The last several years," CIA analysts reported, "have seen a sharp rise in the numbers and activities of religiously inspired terrorists in the Middle East."[37]

At the time and after, the majority of these attacks targeted Middle Eastern citizens and governments. Yet as the hostage crisis indicated, the United States could hardly stand immune from the threat. Terrorist attacks on pro-Western regimes in the Middle East might further destabilize the region, or force those governments to distance themselves from Washington. And as American officials would note during Reagan's presidency, the international role of the United States virtually ensured that it, too, would come under fire. "We are a prime target," one analyst wrote, "because we have an extensive official and commercial presence overseas which is high in numbers of people and profile; our citizens and facilities are accessible and open to the public; our policies are opposed to the interests of many terrorist groups; and we often support governments which terrorists are attempting to bring down."[38] Backing for Israel and moderate Arabs, opposition to Iran and other radical actors—these initiatives were central to protecting U.S. interests in the Middle East, but they were also sure to incur the enmity of terrorist groups and state sponsors with drastically different visions for the region. If terrorism was the weapon of the weak, in other words, it was the bane of a strong and assertive American superpower. As the level and lethality of international terrorism increased, the United States would frequently find itself at the center of the storm.

In sum, if U.S. policymakers generally enjoyed a very favorable global climate during the 1980s, they had no such luxury in the Middle East. Here America faced a nasty tangle of emerging issues, from rising insecurity in the Gulf, to the resurgence of political Islam, to the spreading cancer of Middle Eastern terrorism. Over the course of the decade, these convergent crises would lend themselves not to the type of striking advances scored in other areas of U.S. foreign policy, but to a less satisfying and more problematic set of outcomes.

Persian Gulf Security and the Iran-Iraq War

This dynamic was evident as the United States set about constructing a new Persian Gulf security architecture. Doing so was a matter of urgency beginning in 1979–1980. With the Iran-centric order having collapsed, and threats from inside and outside the region looming, building what Brzezinski termed a "Persian Gulf security framework" was imperative. "We are facing as acute a dilemma as when the British came to us to say that Greece and Turkey were our problem," he said; a historic crisis demanded decisive measures.[39]

As initially developed by Carter, and later adopted by Reagan, the Gulf security framework featured two interlocking elements. The first consisted of fortifying friendly governments by providing them with security assistance and stressing the U.S. commitment to their independence and stability. "Sound regional security," one NSC document asserted, "rests primarily on the internal strength of the nations of the area and their ability, separately and collectively, to defend their independence and territorial integrity."[40] During 1979–1980, the Carter administration significantly increased military sales, aid, and training to countries such as North Yemen, Saudi Arabia, and Egypt; it initiated or expanded intelligence-sharing programs on key security threats; and it dispatched U.S. officials to help Gulf countries coordinate their defense activities. Just as important, Carter gave explicit assurances that there would be no more Irans or Afghanistans—America would support its friends against internal upheaval and foreign aggression.[41]

Making these promises credible required strengthening U.S. military capabilities in the region, and this was the second key element of the framework. "We need to do something to reassure the Egyptians, the Saudis, and others on the Arabian Peninsula that the U.S. is prepared to assert its power," Brzezinski wrote, "and that requires a visible military presence in the area now."[42] The United States should not seek to replicate NATO or station large numbers of troops in Gulf countries, because the appearance of dependency on Washington could prove politically fatal to fragile regimes. Yet the United States must augment its skeletal presence in the region, by building the capacity to insert sizable forces on short notice, and by developing the infrastructure—basing agreements, prepositioning of supplies, and enhanced lift and logistics—that would enable this surge capacity. Once developed, this military shield would act as the ultimate guarantor of regional security; it would also deter conflict and empower the Gulf kingdoms to resist the threats they faced.[43]

As early as 1977, these calculations had led to planning for a Rapid Deployment Force (RDF) capable of moving quickly into the region to deal with internal or external crises.[44] Subsequent development of the RDF lagged due to bureaucratic inertia, but the shocks of 1979 galvanized the process. The RDF began to take shape in earnest. It was now slated to consist of 1.33 armored divisions, 2 Army light infantry divisions, 6 Air Force wings, 3 carrier battle groups, and 1 division of Marines with accompanying airpower.[45] The U.S. naval presence in the Persian Gulf and Indian Ocean was also more than doubled. Meanwhile, State and Defense representatives were negotiating basing and access agreements with countries such as Kenya, Somalia, Egypt, and Oman, and a major expansion of the base at Diego Garcia was underway.[46] In mid-1980, the RDF (now the Rapid Deployment Joint Task Force, RDJTF) conducted its first overseas exercise with Egyptian forces, providing proof of concept and sensitizing U.S. officials to the challenges of desert operations. The building of strength and stability in the Gulf would be a long-term endeavor, Brzezinski wrote, but "considerable progress" had been made.[47]

Progress was a tenuous thing in the Gulf, however, and any gains threatened to evaporate with the outbreak of the Iran-Iraq War in September 1980. Saddam Hussein's decision to invade Iran started a conflict that would claim 200,000 lives and dominate Gulf affairs for nearly a decade, and it stemmed from a lethal mix of insecurity and opportunism.[48] Like many Gulf rulers, Saddam felt profoundly threatened by the hostile rhetoric, subversion, and ideological foment emanating from Islamic Iran. But he was simultaneously tempted by the post-revolutionary chaos that had decimated the Iranian armed forces. "Iran has no power to launch wide offensive operations against Iraq, or to defend on a large scale," Iraqi intelligence reported.[49] With Baghdad having conducted a major military buildup during the 1970s, Saddam felt both impelled and empowered to launch a blitzkrieg against a weakened Iran, in hopes of toppling Khomeini, seizing oil-rich Khuzestan, and realizing his dream of making Iraq—and Saddam—hegemonic in the Gulf and Arab politics. "The result of our calculations," he predicted, "is that we can reach into the heartland of Iran."[50]

The aims were grand, and the results catastrophic. The Iraqi invasion did not destroy Khomeini's revolution; it strengthened it by allowing the clerics to fuse Islamic fervor to Persian nationalism. "You are fighting to protect Islam and he [Saddam] is fighting to destroy it," Khomeini declared.[51] Within weeks, the Iraqi advance had stalled amid logistical problems, poor planning and performance, and determined enemy resistance, leaving Baghdad to fight a protracted war against a country with a 3:1 population advantage and a burning desire for vengeance. By 1982, Iran had turned the tables entirely, recouping earlier losses and invading Iraq with the purpose of toppling Saddam, "liberating" the Shiite south, and bringing the Islamic revolution to Basra if not Baghdad. Besieged with little prospect of relief, Saddam responded by escalating in dangerous and destabilizing ways. Iraqi forces used chemical weapons to blunt Iranian offensives, and carried the war into the Gulf with aerial attacks on enemy shipping and infrastructure. These tactics produced a rough stalemate, but one that left Iraq and the region under severe duress. A "Middle Eastern Armageddon" portended, Assistant Secretary of State Richard Murphy recalled.[52]

From the start, the war posed serious difficulties for Washington. In 1979–1980, Carter had unsuccessfully courted Saddam, hoping to bring him into the Gulf security framework despite his ties to Moscow and adversarial relationship with the West. Contrary to numerous allegations, however, the administration neither expected nor welcomed Saddam's attack on Iran.[53] "The war came as a shock," INR analyst Wayne White recalled.[54] U.S. officials worried that the war might disrupt delicate negotiations to free the hostages, give Moscow an excuse to indulge its own territorial ambitions vis-à-vis Iran, and destabilize a region—and a world oil market—that were already on the brink. "A widening conflict . . . runs a number of grave risks," the State Department assessed.[55] Accordingly, U.S. diplomats passed word to Saddam that "we will not support your dismemberment of Iran," and they intervened to prevent Iraq from enlarging the war by using the territory of Oman and the United Arab Emirates (UAE) to stage attacks on Iranian targets. U.S. policy, Haig reaffirmed in 1981, was to "prevent widening the conflict, bring an end to the fighting and restore stability to the area."[56]

Yet if the outbreak of the war was troubling for U.S. officials, the prospect that Saddam might *lose* from 1981–1982 onward was even worse. If Iran decisively defeated Iraq—and the size imbalance made that prospect seem more likely over time—the consequences would be devastating.[57] An Iranian victory would allow Tehran to establish a radical Shiite regime in at least part of Iraq, and would give fresh momentum to Islamic fundamentalism. It would put Tehran in position to coerce or undermine the exposed Gulf monarchies and, potentially, to dominate that region and its resources. The Gulf contained so much of the world's proven oil reserves, NIC Chairman Henry Rowen wrote in 1982: "The power to interrupt the supply of this flow entails the power to wreak havoc on the economies of the West."[58] "An Iranian victory," CIA analysts agreed, "could lead fairly rapidly to Iranian hegemony over the entire Gulf."[59]

This scenario gave rise to the U.S. "tilt" toward Iraq. The tilt was not based on any sympathy for Saddam, a leader who supported Palestinian terrorist groups, who had evinced a fierce hostility toward Israel and the United States, and who had distinguished himself, even among Middle Eastern dictators, as a ruthless tyrant. "Saddam Hussein is a 'no good nut,'" Reagan wrote.[60] The tilt, rather, was based on the time-honored strategic principle that desperate times called for desperate measures. U.S. policy, McFarlane wrote, "is not out of political affection for Saddam Hussein, but rather because of the instability and chaos his regime's collapse would trigger throughout the Gulf. Should the war end, Iraq's interest would no doubt once again be hostile to our own."[61] The key, then, was not to enable Baghdad to win the war, but to provide the bare level of assistance necessary to stymie Iran and prevent Khomeini from attaining regional hegemony. Elsewhere, U.S. policy might aspire to transformative victories; in the Gulf, it was simply about balancing evils and escaping calamity.

The first phase of the tilt unfolded from 1982 to 1986. The State Department removed Iraq from its list of state sponsors of terrorism in February 1982, and full diplomatic relations were restored in late 1984. Economic assistance began to flow, as Baghdad received $1.65 billion in Commodity Credit Corporation (CCC) guarantees from fiscal years 1983 to 1986, and Iraq was approved for nearly $700 million in Export-Import credits. Saddam's regime was never permitted to purchase U.S.-made weapons, but there were sales of $201 million in "nonmilitary" equipment such as helicopters and trucks, as well sales of industrial components such as high-speed computers, machine tools, and other goods with both civilian and military uses. Meanwhile, American representatives encouraged France, Italy, and other countries to sell Baghdad the arms it needed, while mounting a diplomatic offensive, known as Operation Staunch, to prevent U.S. allies in Europe and elsewhere from exporting materiel to Iran. The United States, presidential envoy Donald Rumsfeld told Saddam in 1983, would "regard any major reversal of Iraq's fortunes as a strategic defeat for the West."[62]

As Shultz later recalled, U.S. support for Iraq "increased in rough proportion to Iran's military successes."[63] This applied particularly to a final aspect of
U.S. assistance—sharing sensitive military intelligence. This program began
in 1982, when U.S. satellites detected a major Iranian buildup opposite a
gap in Iraqi lines.[64] The relationship expanded as Iraqi fortunes deteriorated,
with U.S. officials providing reports (derived largely from satellite imagery;
Airborne Warning and Control System, or AWACS, reconnaissance aircraft;
and signals intelligence) on Iranian troop dispositions and the results of Iraqi
bombing. Intelligence sharing increased further in 1986, with establishment
of a direct CIA-Baghdad link that relayed U.S. information just hours after
its collection.[65] By October, the CIA was providing Baghdad with "specific
targeting data" on economic and logistical facilities deep in Iran. "Iraqi air
has significantly reduced Iran's oil exports," one official wrote. "Iraq should
be encouraged to sustain these economic attacks because they do degrade
Iran's offensive capabilities."[66] In principle, the United States remained neutral in the war; in practice, it was intervening to steady Baghdad and keep the
conflict stalemated.

The tilt went hand in hand with other initiatives to build stability and
bolster U.S. influence in the Gulf. Picking up on Carter's security framework,
Reagan continued efforts to strengthen the Gulf monarchies—virtually all
of which were now supporting the Iraqi war effort—and shield them from
threats. "We are ready to help support the security of Saudi Arabia and its
Gulf state neighbors during the conflict," Reagan wrote to King Fahd.[67] The
administration expanded security assistance to the Gulf and surrounding
areas, reaching $1.7 billion in fiscal year (FY) 1986. It encouraged Gulf lead-
ers to band together, supporting the development of the Gulf Cooperation
Council (GCC) and urging the creation of an integrated regional air-defense
network.[68] Viewing Saudi Arabia as the crucial "regional power" and anchor
of these arrangements, the administration also sold that country AWACS,
KC-135 tankers, advanced equipment for its fleet of F-15 fighters, Stinger
ground-to-air missiles, and Sidewinder air-to-air missiles. And again following Carter's lead, Reagan affirmed that Washington would protect the Gulf
regimes from aggression, and prevent Iran from attacking Iraq's supporters or
closing the Strait of Hormuz. Vital U.S. interests were at stake, Reagan said.
"We cannot be found wanting now."[69]

The president was simultaneously pursuing the second element of the
security framework, by further developing the infrastructure and capabilities
necessary to project U.S. power. "Measures must be taken now to improve our
immediate ability to deter any expansion of the conflict in the Persian Gulf
and, if necessary, defend U.S. interests," Reagan directed.[70] By mid-decade,

the RDJTF had become U.S. Central Command (CENTCOM), a unified regional command with increased bureaucratic stature and autonomy, and control of nearly 292,000 individuals across the four services.[71] Moreover, it was increasingly able to deploy significant forces into the Gulf in a matter of weeks, thanks to a dramatic expansion of air- and sealift capabilities, prepositioning of key supplies, and major investments in developing ports, airfields, and other facilities. The Pentagon spent nearly $900 million on military construction in Oman, Somalia, Kenya, Bahrain, and Diego Garcia from FY 1980 to 1985. American representatives also secured Saudi agreement to "over-build" the kingdom's military facilities to enable their use by U.S. forces in times of crisis. As a result of all this, the aspiration of being able to surge significant military power into the Gulf was becoming a reality.[72]

By mid-decade, in fact, U.S. officials could reasonably claim to be making the best of a bad situation. The United States was making real gains toward the military capabilities necessary to act as stabilizer of last resort in the region—an achievement, ironically, that would be highlighted after Saddam invaded Kuwait in 1990. More immediately, the combination of U.S. military initiatives and support for the Gulf monarchies was helping maintain a thin but vital layer of security in a turbulent environment. Had the United States not asserted and substantiated its commitment to the area, for instance, it seems unlikely that the Gulf states could have resisted Iranian intimidation and continued their critical support—at least $30–40 billion in loans and grants, as well as other aid—for the Iraqi war effort.[73]

The development of a more robust security framework thus had positive spillover effects on the Iran-Iraq War. During the early and mid-1980s, U.S. policy influenced that conflict in other ways, too. Operation Staunch helped Iraq maintain a qualitative edge over numerically superior Iranian forces by severely constraining Tehran's ability to buy top-quality weapons and spare parts. Staunch reduced the number of West European countries selling arms to Tehran from fifteen to six, and slashed the value of that trade from $1 billion in 1984 to $200 million in 1987. "We believe that this has had a significant effect on Iranian military capabilities," Murphy said.[74] U.S. intelligence was equally valuable. It increased the impact of Iraqi airpower via better targeting and damage assessment; it also saved Iraqi troops from being surprised and overrun in at least one (and perhaps several) key battles. "We are providing the Iraqis with very good intelligence on [Iranian] troop dispositions and movements which in itself is a great asset in this type of war," wrote NSC staffer Geoffrey Kemp.[75] More broadly, U.S. backing gave Saddam newfound international legitimacy and facilitated Iraqi ties to other supporters. As Iraqi military intelligence reported, the United States had "helped Iraq on many occasions" in its desperate struggle for survival.[76]

The Reagan administration was thus managing the crisis of Gulf security. The crisis itself, however, was hardly nearing an end. The situation in the region remained perpetually precarious, as shown when Iranian forces overran al-Faw Peninsula in early 1986. That operation endangered Basra and essentially severed Iraqi access to the Gulf; it also resurrected the prospect that unremitting pressure might cause Saddam's outnumbered military to collapse. "The essential point is incontrovertible," Murphy wrote. "The longer the war continues, the greater the risk of an Iraqi defeat."[77] And while Washington was actively working to forestall this outcome, its policies were simultaneously exposing new dangers and challenges.

The growth of U.S. military influence in the Gulf, for example, was a source of security in the area, but it was a source of potential vulnerability as well. The Gulf kingdoms had long been wary of appearing to rely on a foreign—particularly non-Muslim—power such as the United States, and the Islamic resurgence made this concern more acute. "The moderate regimes may . . . suffer a loss of legitimacy in the eyes of their own people if they appear to become tools of the U.S.," one analyst warned, "a factor which could lead to greater unrest and internal instability."[78] The "over-the-horizon" approach of the RDF and then CENTCOM was specifically designed to accommodate this sensitivity, but the obvious expansion of the U.S. role in the region still risked embarrassing friendly governments and stimulating Islamist resentment. "Xenophobia is an exploitable vulnerability," one assessment noted.[79] And should American facilities actually be used for combat purposes, one NSC group predicted, they might become magnets for "a wave of terrorist attacks" by Iranian proxies or other groups that resented this foreign military intrusion into the heart of the Muslim world. The inescapable paradox of U.S. policy, then, was that "increasing our military presence in the Gulf region" was necessary, but that it also "increases the likelihood of such attacks."[80]

The U.S. partnership with Saddam was equally a double-edged sword. That partnership was indispensable in checking Iranian expansion and preventing a complete unraveling in the Gulf. As Barbara Bodine, a State Department official who served in Baghdad, put it, the hard reality was that "if you don't like Saddam, we have Khomeini."[81] The downside, however, was that the tilt also involved strengthening a ruler whose messianic ambitions and proclivity for violence might make him just as dangerous as Khomeini in the long run. A senior White House official put the problem precisely: "I don't think it's in anybody's interest, any country in the world, to have either side win."[82]

As the tilt developed, U.S. officials hoped that they could somehow escape this predicament—that consistent support and engagement would eventually mellow Saddam and make him a better partner. The thinking, Bodine recalls, was that "if I have to get in bed with the devil, maybe I can redeem him—a little bit." Saddam's regime was at least a secular alternative to Islamic radicalism; over time, perhaps, it might develop into a more moderate and stabilizing presence in the region. At a minimum, U.S. assistance should provide leverage that could be used to modify the worst aspects of Iraqi behavior. "Our strengthened relations enable us to encourage Iraq's trend toward more moderate positions on a range of issues important to us," Shultz's aide, Charles Hill, wrote in 1984.[83]

Yet even as Saddam availed himself of U.S. support, he often seemed determined to disprove this theory. Despite minor adjustments, Iraq maintained extensive ties to Palestinian terrorists, including some who killed U.S. citizens.[84] Baghdad also continued to develop large-scale chemical and biological weapons programs, using dual-use Western industrial imports to do so. Iraq must "make every possible effort to achieve manufacture of toxic agents in large quantities as quickly as possible," Saddam ordered.[85] As Iraqi forces struggled to stem the Iranian onslaught, they soon began using these weapons, as U.S. officials reported in 1983, "almost daily."[86] The Baathist regime would eventually use around 100,000 chemical munitions against Iranian forces and rebellious Iraqi Kurds, the greatest employment of such weapons since World War I. Aside from their terrible human toll, these attacks threatened to erode the long-standing international norm against chemical weapons use. "If the use of chemicals continues or increases," a U.S. intelligence report noted, "it would be an indication to Third World states that chemical weapons have military utility, and a worldwide chemical protocol or treaty could become more difficult to obtain."[87]

The chemical issue demonstrated the inherent liabilities of supporting Saddam, and the limits of U.S. leverage in the relationship. Iraqi officials made clear that a regime fighting for its survival—and defending U.S. interests in the process—would brook no questioning of its methods. "You have to understand we're fighting these benighted medieval Khomeini types," Foreign Minister Tariq Aziz told foreign officials. "They want to destroy our country, conquer us, of course we'll use every means at our disposal. Why if we had nuclear weapons we'd use those too."[88] And so, despite expectations that aid would buy influence, the administration quickly concluded that it could not confront Saddam over this issue without compromising the relationship and undercutting an effective tool of the Iraqi defense. U.S. and Iraqi diplomats cooperated to dilute UN criticism of Baghdad's sins, and the administration reassured Saddam of its support. "Our desires and our actions to prevent an Iranian victory and to continue the progress of our bilateral relations remain undiminished," Shultz told Iraqi officials in 1984. Washington, the State Department reiterated, did "not want this issue to dominate our bilateral relations."[89] Facing the possibility of an Iranian-dominated Gulf, the Reagan administration could not be picky in its friends.

Midway through the 1980s, then, the dilemmas of Gulf geopolitics showed few signs of easing. U.S. policymakers had made important contributions to shoring up Iraq, containing Iran, and building a regional security framework backstopped by real military muscle. Yet the progress toward greater stability remained extremely fragile so long as the Iran-Iraq War persisted, and the measures that had produced that progress had disconcerting implications of their own. In these circumstances, it was virtually guaranteed that U.S. policies would leave a conflicted legacy, and that Gulf security would pose daunting problems for the remainder of the war and after.

The Travails of Counterterrorism

The issues posed by Middle Eastern terrorism proved no less troublesome. Taking office in the wake of the Iran hostage crisis, Reagan had staked out a forward position on that threat from day one. With the dangers from extremists and their state sponsors metastasizing, he argued, it was imperative to stand firm and act assertively—to refuse to be coerced or extorted, to hinder terrorists' operations whenever possible, and to strike back powerfully when attacks did occur. "Let terrorists be aware," Reagan warned in January 1981, "that when the rules of international behavior are violated, our policy will be one of swift and effective retribution." "We are determined," he added two weeks later, "to wage an effective fight against terrorism."[90] As the decade unfolded, however, U.S. officials would continually struggle to gain the initiative in this fight, and mastery of the terrorist challenge remained frustratingly elusive.

Those frustrations began to manifest quite early, via the confrontation with Qaddafi's Libya. If Iran was viewed as the very epitome of a terrorist state by U.S. policymakers, Qaddafi's regime was a strong challenger for the title. Driven by eclectic influences including Islamist ideology, pan-Arabism, and anti-imperialism, the Libyan leader had established himself as a leading Middle Eastern radical and bitter opponent of U.S. influence. His regime made major purchases of Soviet arms, sought to deny the U.S. Navy and other maritime traffic access to international waters in the Gulf of Sidra, and destabilized moderate or pro-Western governments across the region. These initiatives, in turn, were underwritten by support for myriad terrorist groups, which offered a low-cost, plausibly deniable means of punishing Qaddafi's enemies and waging his militant agenda abroad. By 1981, Libyans or Libyan-supported extremists had murdered anti-Qaddafi dissidents in Europe and America, targeted Saudi royals and other U.S. allies for assassination, and pursued violent subversion in countries such as Chad, Egypt, and Sudan. "Libya under Qadhafi is a significant threat to U.S. interests throughout the Middle East/African region and, in the broader sense, to our concept of an international order," Haig wrote.[91]

Within months of taking power, the administration was developing a multi-pronged campaign to contain the threat. Reagan ordered the closing of the Libyan People's Bureau (embassy) in Washington, allegedly a hub for terrorists seeking to operate on U.S. soil. The administration also gave covert and overt military support to anti-Qaddafi leaders in neighboring countries, to bolster them while increasing the strains on Tripoli.[92] Most dramatically, the Navy conducted aggressive Freedom of Navigation exercises in the Gulf of Sidra, to show that the United States would not be intimidated by Qaddafi's threats, and that it possessed its own powerful tools of deterrence and coercion. This approach, Haig said, "will be helpful . . . to show that we are 'putting screws' on Qadhafi."[93] When Libya interfered with the exercises, naval aviators downed two of Qaddafi's Soviet-made jets. The United States, Reagan reiterated, would use its power energetically, to throw Qaddafi off balance and show that terrorist activities carried a price. He did "not want Colonel Qadhafi dead but just confined," the president remarked. Libya, in this sense, was an early test case of the administration's forward stance on terrorism.[94]

U.S. policy did influence Qaddafi's calculus, but not as Reagan intended. Prior to the Gulf of Sidra clash in August 1981, intelligence analysts had warned that a show of force might cause "a Libyan desire to punish the United States through the use of anti-American terrorism, particularly if Tripoli believed the Libyan hand could be plausibly denied."[95] Qaddafi's first instinct was rarely to retreat from a challenge—as one U.S. assessment noted, he interpreted confrontation "as a dare, not a deterrent."[96] Moreover, although Qaddafi understood that he could not match U.S. military capabilities, he also grasped that his extremist contacts provided a tool of asymmetric warfare against an otherwise-dominant adversary. In fall 1981, he responded to Reagan's measures by approving the targeting of U.S. embassy compounds and personnel in Europe. The CIA received information that Libyan hit squads even planned to assassinate high-ranking officials, including Reagan. "The Libyan campaign against U.S. officials is without precedent," CIA officials assessed, "and the potential effectiveness of security, and other deterrant [sic] measures is hard to gauge."[97] Doubts later arose regarding whether these plans had become operational, but the episode was sobering nonetheless. Far from being confined, Qaddafi was using the threat of terrorism to escalate the conflict. As Casey aptly summarized the situation, "Qadhafi has attempted—by act or just leaks of an act—to strike at senior American officials at home and abroad. In doing so he has caused disruption of our normal way of life on the official level, the expenditure of millions, and some degree of skepticism among our allies about our intelligence and subsequent actions. All this at very little cost and a great deal of 'revolutionary' publicity for him."[98]

The administration responded to Qaddafi's threats with a sharp warning of its own, that "we would consider any Libyan terrorist attack against a U.S. target to be tantamount to an armed attack upon the U.S. and that we would respond accordingly."[99] Yet in considering how to constrain the Libyan leader, it became evident that Reagan himself faced perhaps the more cumbersome constraints. Actually attacking a Muslim country might inflame Islamist sentiment and embarrass Middle Eastern allies; it could also cause Qaddafi to retaliate against the roughly 2,000 U.S. oil workers in Libya. Measures such as economic sanctions carried fewer risks of blowback, but unless Libya's major European trading partners participated—not likely, given their fear of Qaddafi's wrath—sanctions would be "essentially devoid of serious impact."[100] Finding it difficult to exert American power in meaningful ways, Reagan settled on a response that administration officials termed "symbolic": a ban on U.S. purchases of Libyan oil and other minor economic sanctions, and a request that U.S. firms evacuate their employees. The measures were modest, as were the expectations. Qaddafi would not "abandon his goals," NSC officials wrote, but he might "be willing to modify temporarily some of his more extreme methods."[101] Meanwhile, Reagan reinforced the regional containment of Tripoli by augmenting military support to neighboring countries.[102]

These measures, along with economic and political difficulties at home, did apparently give Qaddafi some pause. There was a lull in his terrorist activities in 1982–1983, leading Shultz to say that "Qaddafi is back in his box where he belongs."[103] Yet the effect was temporary, and U.S. officials acknowledged that the enemy retained the initiative. "Even if the terrorists had been called off," Casey warned, "they could resume at any time." Sure enough, as Qaddafi reconsolidated his domestic position and U.S. attention shifted elsewhere, Libyan-sponsored terrorism resurged. Qaddafi was "on a binge," INR analysts wrote.[104] U.S. intelligence linked Qaddafi to as many as forty-two terrorist plots in 1984–1985, from the murder of dissidents abroad to the mining of Red Sea shipping lanes, to the attempted killing of U.S. diplomats and foreign leaders. The Libyan leader supported groups such as the vicious and indiscriminate Abu Nidal organization, and avowed his intention of "exporting terrorism to the heart of America."[105] U.S. policy "has not been without merit or effect," NSC aide Donald Fortier, wrote, "but it has obviously not eliminated the problem."[106] Reagan had sought a catalytic early victory against state-sponsored terrorism; he had received a rude lesson in just how persistent and hard to counter that threat could be.

In this respect, the confrontation with Libya was prelude to a far more shattering episode—the bombings of the U.S. embassy and Marine barracks in Beirut in 1983. Those attacks resulted from the U.S. intervention in Lebanon from 1982–1984, a textbook case of good intentions gone catastrophically awry. The goals of that mission had been multiple: to mitigate the carnage that followed the Israeli invasion of Lebanon in mid-1982, to enable the Lebanese government to reassert control of its own territory, and to provide a buffer that would separate the various combatants in Lebanon's ongoing civil war and induce the withdrawal of Israeli and Syrian forces from the country.[107] The outcome, however, proved tragic. The 1,200-troop U.S. presence (part of a larger multinational force) was envisioned as an honest broker between the myriad domestic and foreign factions vying for supremacy. Yet that force quickly, and not unreasonably, came to be perceived as supporting a Christian, Israeli-backed government against Muslim groups aligned with Syria and Iran. The upshot was to suck the Marines into a conflict they were meant to mediate. U.S. forces began to take casualties from hostile fire; they responded with defensive measures that made them seem less impartial still.[108]

This process brought America squarely into the cross-hairs of Hezbollah and its sponsors. In many ways, Hezbollah represented the apex of the Islamic radicalism coursing through the Middle East. Composed of militant Shiite factions that united amid the Israeli occupation, Hezbollah's armed wing boasted a core of highly disciplined, intensely devoted fighters who aimed to drive Israel and its Western backers out of Lebanon and establish an Islamic state. Aided by IRGC operatives and based in the Syrian-controlled Bekaa Valley, Hezbollah quickly became a lethally effective force that pioneered tactics such as suicide truck-bombings. And by 1983, Hezbollah was on a collision course with Washington. Its leadership viewed the Marines as a hostile presence that was colluding with Israel and standing athwart a Shiite Islamist ascendancy in Lebanon; its patrons in Tehran were equally eager to contest U.S. intervention and punish Washington for supporting Iraq. What followed, CIA analysts wrote, was the onset of a "war of terrorism . . . against U.S. interests in Lebanon."[109] In April 1983, Hezbollah bombed the U.S. embassy, killing sixty-three people, including seventeen Americans. In October, the group struck even more viciously, using a powerful truck bomb to destroy the Marine barracks in Beirut at a cost of 241 American lives. The Reagan administration had sought to stabilize Lebanon; it ran into a buzz-saw of religiously inspired, state-backed terrorism instead.

The Beirut barracks bombing caused the worst loss of American life due to terrorism prior to September 11, 2001, and the highest number of U.S. military casualties between Vietnam and Desert Storm. Beyond their terrible human toll, the Lebanon attacks were an excruciating reminder of how exposed the United States was to the actions of committed, well-organized terrorists. The bombings confirmed, for instance, that Washington's role in the Middle East made it a target for those whose goals were obstructed by American influence in the region, and that the extensive U.S. presence offered inviting opportunities for attack. They demonstrated that even the American military remained immensely vulnerable to ruthless and innovative terrorist tactics. As U.S. officials admitted, the use of a "flying truck bomb" had caught the Marines utterly flat-footed.[110] Perhaps most worrisome, the fact that these attacks caused such awesome damage raised the terrifying possibility of repetition—that terrorist groups would continue using similar methods to exploit U.S. weaknesses and achieve their goals. Marine Corps Commandant P. X. Kelley put it starkly in testimony after the barracks bombing: "Let me say, with all of the emphasis I can, that there are skilled and professional terrorists out there right now who are examining our vulnerabilities and making devices which are designed to kill Americans, lots of Americans around the world, in further acts of mass murder by terrorism. Let there be no doubt about it!"[111]

If the attacks themselves were alarming enough, their aftermath cast serious doubt on whether the administration could actually deliver "swift and effective retribution." Reagan's own initial instinct was to strike back hard. "Those who directed this atrocity must be dealt justice, and they will be," he said.[112] Within days, U.S. intelligence had evidence of Hezbollah's responsibility and Iran's complicity, and military planners were readying airstrikes on Hezbollah targets in the Bekaa Valley. Inside the White House, there was little doubt that these attacks were necessary to disrupt Hezbollah operational capabilities, and that the credibility of U.S. policy was on the line. "State-sponsorship of terrorism . . . can only be expected to grow unless we act forcefully now," NSC aide Howard Teicher wrote. "At a minimum, United States forces cooperating with our European and Middle East allies, should wipe out terrorist infrastructure wherever it may exist within Lebanon."[113] Other officials went further, advocating counterterrorist operations by U.S. ground forces in Lebanon, and even striking Syrian or Iranian targets.[114] The gauntlet had been thrown down, it seemed, and national security demanded a punishing riposte.

As preparations to attack proceeded, however, doubts arose as to whether the case for military retaliation was so clear-cut. The intelligence community was confident in assigning blame for the barracks bombing, but some officials remained skeptical of how hard the proof was. Even more pressing was the concern raised by Weinberger and other officials: that a military strike might actually make matters worse, by causing civilian casualties that would stoke Muslim anger, or by inciting Hezbollah or other Iranian-sponsored groups to retaliate with new attacks. The remaining Marines in Lebanon, one U.S. assessment noted, were "an exceptionally vulnerable presence and a natural target," while Shiite radicals could easily attack embassies or other facilities in the Gulf.[115] Military reprisals, then, might draw Washington deeper into a conflict against enemies who recognized no rules of warfare, and who had already demonstrated their lethal proficiency. "The question," Weinberger would repeatedly ask during the 1980s, "is whether an attack from us will deter the next attacks" or encourage them.[116] Believing the latter more likely than the former, Weinberger and Kelley lobbied against airstrikes, and argued that the best way to prevent future attacks was to remove the Marines from Lebanon.[117]

With his advisers divided, Reagan decided that the risks of action out-weighed the likely benefits, and he canceled the airstrikes at the last minute.[118] As the situation in Lebanon then deteriorated, he also reluctantly heeded Weinberger's counsel by "redeploying" the Marines back onto their ships. The defense secretary argued that the administration was prudently cutting its losses and removing the troops from an impossible situation. Other offi-cials warned that this combination of inaction and retreat was simply show-ing that terrorism worked. Washington had been hit hard, Shultz lamented, and "we really haven't faced up to it."[119] "Radical leaders," the CIA agreed, "almost certainly viewed the withdrawal of the Marine contingent from Beirut . . . as proof of the effectiveness of terrorist tactics."[120] U.S. credibil-ity had definitely suffered. When in early 1984 State Department officials obliquely warned Syria to stop facilitating Iranian support for Hezbollah or face retaliation, President Hafez al-Assad flatly refused on grounds that Washington would not carry out its threats.[121]

This was a portent of things to come, because from October 1983 to December 1985, anti-American terrorism intensified dramatically. Iranian-backed Shiite radicals bombed the U.S. embassy in Kuwait in December 1983, and tortured and killed American citizens after hijacking a Kuwaiti airliner in 1984. Hezbollah continued its onslaught, murdering Americans in Beirut, bombing the rebuilt U.S. embassy in that city, and seizing several U.S. hostages (including CIA station chief William Buckley), most of whom were eventually killed or held in captivity for years. In April 1985, Hezbollah operatives also bombed a restaurant frequented by U.S. service-men in Spain, killing eighteen people and wounding fifteen Americans; in June, the group staged yet another dramatic attack by hijacking a TWA flight from Athens to Rome.[122] The hijackers killed a U.S. Navy diver on board, and then held thirty-nine Americans hostage for seventeen days before releasing them in a thinly veiled swap for hundreds of prisoners held by Israel. Meanwhile, Palestinian terrorists hijacked the cruise ship *Achille Lauro* in October 1985, killing a wheelchair-bound U.S. citizen in the process. Not to be outdone, Qaddafi sanctioned numerous operations, notably an Abu Nidal attack on airline ticket counters in Rome and Vienna in December 1985 that killed twenty people, including five Americans. Overall, the U.S. government recorded more than eight hundred interna-tional terrorist incidents in 1985, "a 60 percent increase over the rate of the previous two years."[123] Terrorism, Casey remarked, was "a cancer that is spreading," "a scourge that increasingly is beginning to dominate our lives and times."[124]

This spike in attacks ensured that terrorism remained front and center in administration debates during 1984–1985. One relatively hawkish faction of advisers coalesced around George Shultz. To Shultz, terrorism was not just a criminal activity or something that could be combated solely through intelligence, law enforcement, and diplomacy. It was "an unbridled form of warfare" waged by ruthless groups seeking political ends, and Washington would be continually pummeled until it took the fight to the enemy. "The way to get after these people," he said, "is to get after them with both bar-rels."[125] The U.S. government had to disrupt terrorist groups by destroying their training grounds, logistics, and leadership; it even had to strike these organizations before they actually attacked. To do otherwise, Shultz con-tended, was to lock the United States into an untenably passive posture and ensure that terrorism could be perpetrated without serious cost. "We cannot allow ourselves to become the Hamlet of nations," he argued; bold measures featuring "active prevention, preemption, and retaliation" were essential. The fight against terrorism would not "be a clean or pleasant contest," but it was one that America could win by bringing its formidable power to bear.[126] "If we remain firm, we can look ahead to a time when terrorism will cease to be a major factor in world affairs."[127]

As during the Lebanon episode, however, these arguments were contested by a second group of advisers, who cautioned that excessive activism could be more problematic than restraint. Bush, for instance, worried that Washington would have "great difficulty in fine-tuning retaliation"—in hitting terrorist targets hard enough to be effective, but not so hard as to provoke international outrage over a disproportionate response.[128] Weinberger, for his part, argued that the promiscuous use of force would drain public support for U.S. foreign policy by embroiling the country in a series of indecisive conflicts. "We must never reflexively resort to a military option," he said.[129] Likewise, Weinberger contended that a policy of preemption would force the military to conduct difficult operations based upon insufficient intelligence, potentially causing major collateral damage and inflaming Muslim sentiment. "Preemptive . . . retaliation would be analogous to firing a gun in a crowded theater in the slim hope of hitting the guilty party," he scoffed.[130] Even more hawkish officials conceded that Weinberger had a point. "If we respond against Hezbollah," McFarlane said in 1984, "our actions could very well drive the Shias into more of a frenzy." Direct attacks on state sponsors such as Iran or Libya, the CIA agreed, might well cause retaliation against U.S. targets or even within the United States.[131]

These debates raged through the mid-1980s, spilling over into dueling speeches between Shultz and Weinberger, and eliciting charges that Reagan's indecisiveness was paralyzing U.S. policy. There was some truth to this assessment, but the fundamental issue was simply that there was no obvious solution to the problem at hand. As recent history had shown, terrorism was, by its very essence, a devilishly difficult threat to tackle. It was a form of violence that ignored the conventions and constraints to which democracies generally held themselves, and one that turned the vastness of America's international presence into a source of vulnerability. It was an arena in which superior U.S. military power could be counteracted by an attacker's fanatical commitment, and by the use of unconventional tactics cloaked in secrecy and surprise. For actors "unable to mount a conventional military challenge against a militarily superior foe," one RAND Corporation analyst wrote, "terrorism provides an 'equalizer.'"[132] Above all, terrorism was a threat that arose in part from the very global activism that made the United States a superpower, and one that would probably persist as long as it sought to shape the destiny of societies in the Muslim world. "Terrorism," a State Department panel concluded in 1985, "will be with us for a long time."[133]

In these circumstances, it was hardly self-evident what course Reagan should follow. Shultz was undoubtedly right that only an outright U.S. flight from the Middle East would halt the attacks altogether, and that violent extremists would wreak havoc so long as it was relatively cost-free to do so. As even Weinberger acknowledged at one point, "We need to stand up to this or it will just continue."[134] The trouble, however, was that Shultz's opponents were also right in arguing that a more assertive policy was full of risk. Retaliatory and especially anticipatory attacks would place severe demands on U.S. intelligence and military capabilities, and there was no guarantee that the adverse results would be less than the positive ones. This was the cruel dilemma of the U.S. struggle with terrorism: it was a conflict that seemed to demand a vigorous response, but one that made such a response difficult and dangerous to execute. One congressional report put the issue squarely: "There can be no easy policy recommendation that would guarantee immunity from future terrorism. . . . The world cannot be ordered as to satisfy all aspirations and assure every destiny, and there is simply no solution to the sufficiently dedicated fanatic with a moment of luck."[135]

It is thus not surprising that U.S. policy had a distinctly halting character during the mid-1980s. At times, Reagan leaned toward Shultz's position. Following the kidnapping of Buckley in March 1984, he signed NSDD-138, which approved a range of aggressive measures including the use of military and paramilitary assets to conduct sabotage, retaliation, and preemptive attacks. U.S. strategy, the document stated, must support "an active, preventive program to combat state-sponsored terrorism before the terrorists can initiate hostile acts"; "pre-emptive neutralization of anti-American terrorist groups" would be energetically pursued.[136] This plan soon unraveled, however, amid internal opposition and fears that such operations could spiral out of control. The United States must not "combat terrorism with more of what others would see as terrorism," argued Robert Oakley, the top State Department counterterrorism official. "It would be morally, ethically, politically unacceptable to the American public for its government to engage in such distasteful activities." These arguments were dramatized when an anti-Hezbollah group that the CIA had considered supporting staged a car bombing that killed eighty civilians.[137]

Reagan subsequently remained adamant that the administration must do *something* to stem the tide of terror. "Wouldn't an attack slow things down?" he asked in one discussion on Hezbollah.[138] But the Pentagon continued to

oppose military options, and even more hawkish advisers struggled to identify opportunities to use force effectively and without intolerable risk. The
result was indeed something like paralysis. Every incident seemed to elicit
a long, inconclusive debate about how to respond; in the vast majority of
cases, the upshot was no retaliation whatsoever. On the rare occasion when
Reagan did order the military into action, the results were discouraging. U.S.
fighter jets forced an airliner carrying the *Achille Lauro* hijackers to land in
Sicily in October 1985, but Italian authorities refused to allow the extradi-
tion of the suspects and eventually allowed the mastermind of the plot to
go free. The United States, it appeared, was stuck in a worst-of-both-worlds
policy that involved tough talk and very little action. "There is an impression
in the Middle East that the West is on the defensive with regard to terrorism,"
CIA officials reported. "Despite U.S. talk of retaliation, we have not done
so, which makes our statements seem like bluster."[139] If U.S. foreign policy
was generally confident and effective during the 1980s, here it was weak,
uncertain, and persistently back-footed.

What finally galvanized more forceful action in 1985–1986 was the fact
that the problem was getting badly out of hand. The lethality and frequency
of attacks was increasing, CIA officials reported, and terrorism was becoming "institutionalized" in the policies of radical states.[140] Washington, meanwhile, seemed a paper tiger—as two of Bush's advisers put it, "powerless,
easily manipulated, and at the mercy of those who attack us because we cannot fight back."[141] Throughout the government, there was a growing sense
that current trends threatened unacceptable consequences. "Left unchallenged," Oakley warned, "the rise of terrorism will undermine the system of
political, economic, and military relationships which the United States and its
allies have come to rely upon to preserve, protect and promote their national
and mutual interest in an orderly and peaceful fashion."[142] It remained true,
hawks such as Casey conceded, that there were "very difficult and sensitive
problems" in choosing how to respond. "Yet we cannot allow this to freeze
us into paralysis" any longer.[143]

These sentiments were shaping public debate, as well. Since the Iran hostage crisis, terrorism had been a sore spot for Americans. As the wave of
terror crested in the mid-1980s, so did frustration with the government's
inability to respond. By September 1985, 78 percent of Americans favored a
"major effort" to "take steps to combat terrorism," up from 54 percent a year
prior. "Concern about controlling terrorism now matches the level of concern reached only by a few domestic issues during this last decade; nuclear
weapons, crime, inflation, and unemployment," officials reported.[144] One of

Bush's aides put it more vividly: "The American people seem to be waiting for Dirty Harry, Rambo and John Wayne to 'stick it to 'em.'"[145]

The resulting urgency informed numerous concrete programs. The Pentagon continued to develop capabilities in counterterrorism missions such as hostage rescue, while also—under pressure from Congress—placing greater emphasis on special-operations forces and low-intensity conflict. For its part, the State Department ramped up its Anti-Terrorism Assistance (ATA) program, designed to strengthen the counterterrorism capabilities of friendly countries and promote greater multilateral cooperation. Seventeen new countries joined the initiative in 1985; by 1989, more than 60 countries and 9,000 personnel had participated.[146] The CIA, meanwhile, increased intelligence sharing with foreign counterparts in the Middle East and elsewhere. Charged with establishing "a clandestine service capability for preventing, pre-empting, and/or disrupting international terrorist activity," it also created a dedicated Counterterrorism Center (CTC) within its Directorate of Operations.[147] Most significant, military planners developed more up-to-date attack portfolios on key targets, and Reagan resolved to lean forward in future crises. "States that practice terrorism or actively support it, will not be allowed to do so without consequence," affirmed NSDD-207, signed in January 1986. "Whenever we have evidence that a state is mounting or intends to conduct an act of terrorism against us, we have a responsibility to take measures to protect our citizens, property, and interests."[148]

This determination to take the offensive brought the administration back around to Qaddafi. The bilateral confrontation had escalated since 1982–1983, with Qaddafi becoming bolder in his threats and attacks, and Reagan exploring and sometimes approving covert operations to undermine the Libyan regime.[149] Following the Abu Nidal attacks in Rome and Vienna, Reagan resolved to make an example of "Libya's top clown." "Our earlier actions clearly have not been enough to deter Qadhafi and other governments from supporting terrorism," he wrote. "More dramatic steps are now needed that make clear to Qadhafi, and leaders like him, that they will pay a price for such support and encouragement."[150] In March 1986, the U.S. Navy conducted more aggressive exercises in the Gulf of Sidra, precipitating a clash that led to the sinking of four Libyan vessels and the destruction of radar and missile installations along the Libyan coast. Reagan had hoped that this provocation might also tempt Qaddafi to launch another terrorist attack that would offer pretext for a harsher military response: "a h—l of a punch," the president termed it.[151] When Qaddafi obliged by ordering the bombing of a West Berlin nightclub frequented by U.S. soldiers, the administration had its chance.

The U.S. air raid on Libya in April 1986 was the most extensive counterterrorism operation performed by the American military between 1979 and 2001. It involved airstrikes by F-111 fighter-bombers staging out of the United Kingdom, and by carrier-borne jets operating from the Mediterranean. The targets including training camps, airports and airbases, terrorist command-and-control centers, and Qaddafi's residential compound and headquarters. The goal was to demonstrate, with unmistakable clarity, that America was no longer holding back.[152] "If we are to offer our peoples a respite from fear on our streets, on the seas, and in the air," Reagan wrote to NATO leaders, "Qadhafi and others like him must know that terrorism has severe and adverse consequences."[153] In fact, although U.S. officials did not explicitly aim to kill Qaddafi, it was no secret that this would be a welcome by-product. As it happened, the Libyan leader escaped unharmed, but some family members were reportedly injured or killed, and most of the targets suffered moderate to extensive damage. "We did what we had to," Reagan wrote.[154]

The administration kept tightening the screws following the attack. Responding to reports that Qaddafi had been badly frightened by the raid, and that internal discontent was rising, Reagan approved operations to further unsettle the regime. "We believe that the situation inside Libya is still unstable and could well be exploited by further pressure," one NSC document asserted.[155] Navy SEALs conducted sabotage and disinformation activities within Libya, as U.S. warships and planes maintained a threatening posture nearby. The CIA continued to support anti-Qaddafi exiles and dissidents, and the Sixth Fleet used balloons to spread messages calling for his overthrow. "Qadhafi is an enemy and a terrorist," Shultz said, and the United States had to keep the pressure applied.[156]

U.S. officials hoped that the campaign against Libya would be a tide-turning event in the struggle against terrorism. In the aftermath, there was cause for optimism. Although most NATO allies had opposed the April raid—even denying the F-111s overflight rights—the attack spurred them to take stronger counterterrorism measures so as to reduce the need for additional U.S. military action in the future. Some five hundred Libyan diplomats were expelled from Europe, and NATO countries began to cut purchases of Qaddafi's oil.[157] Qaddafi himself assumed a lower profile, and the number of attacks attributed to Libya fell from nineteen in 1986 to six in 1987. "Our actions last spring had a clear effect on his terrorist activities," Weinberger argued.[158] Other state patrons, such as Syria, became more cautious as well, with the CIA reporting that "most regimes that sponsor or otherwise support terrorism have become less active or more discreet."[159]

Additionally, in the late 1980s, the nonmilitary measures developed in recent years began to bear fruit. Initiatives such as the CTC, ATA, and expanded intelligence sharing and diplomatic cooperation allowed for significant gains against Abu Nidal and other groups, and helped disrupt perhaps one hundred plots.[160] By decisively employing U.S. power, it seemed, Washington had finally gained the upper hand. "History is likely to record that 1986 was the year when the world, at long last, came to grips with the plague of terrorism," Reagan said.[161]

There had been progress, yes, but the reality remained far more ambiguous. Military coercion of Qaddafi did nothing to solve the problem of the U.S. hostages in Beirut—from early 1985 to late 1987, the number of captives had risen from five to nine. "Hostages and the threat of Americans being taken hostage will be with us for a considerable period," Frank Carlucci, the national security adviser (and later secretary of defense) said. "Taking hostages and conducting terrorist activities is the only way these small groups have to make war on the U.S."[162] Initial impressions to the contrary, Qaddafi himself was also still using terrorism to wage war against America. In revenge for the airstrikes, his operatives quietly purchased and murdered a U.S. hostage being held in Lebanon, and killed an embassy employee in Sudan. By late 1986, the Libyan regime was again abetting major terrorist attacks, while also taking greater care to cover its tracks. By 1988, Oakley was reporting that "Libya's support for terrorism . . . has again increased to dangerous levels." That much became evident in December 1988, when Libyan operatives bombed a Pan Am flight over Scotland, killing 270 people, including 189 Americans. It was Qaddafi's deadliest blow yet, but Libyan involvement was concealed sufficiently to make near-term retaliation impossible.[163]

Reagan's campaign against terrorism had not had such decisive impact after all. The president had taken office determined to defeat that growing menace, but his aspiration proved maddeningly difficult to realize. The very nature of Middle Eastern terrorism made it a tenacious foe, and one that often confounded the expectation that unrivaled U.S. power could be used to satisfying and definitive ends. "Experience has taught us," Reagan himself acknowledged in 1987, "that there is no clear, easy solution to this problem."[164] True enough—despite whatever short-term progress the administration had made, the threat from Middle Eastern and Islamic terrorism would be an enduring security challenge well into the unipolar era. And that challenge, it so happened, was actually drawing fuel from other U.S. policies of the Reagan years.

Radical Islam and the Afghan Jihad

The policy in question was U.S. support for the anti-Soviet jihad in Afghanistan. As discussed in chapter 2, U.S. involvement in that insurgency was an integral component of Reagan's Cold War offensive. Given the religious and ideological basis of the conflict, however, it also intertwined with the emerging security issues that the United States faced in the Greater Middle East during the 1980s. Whereas Washington was generally on the defensive vis-à-vis the Islamic resurgence during this period, here U.S. policymakers channeled the anti-Soviet nature of that phenomenon for strategic profit. As with backing for Saddam, though, this initiative ultimately proved to be a Faustian bargain. For just as Reagan was seeking to counter Islamist radicalism and terrorism across much of the Middle East, his support for the Afghan jihad was helping invigorate those very influences.

The fact that this odd symbiosis was even possible owed to what U.S. policymakers often saw as the one redeeming feature of Islamist movements during the late 1970s and after—that they were usually just as anti-Soviet as anti-American. In Tehran, for instance, Khomeini argued that there was "no difference" between two domineering and anti-Islamic superpowers, and his regime conducted a bloody purge of the Iranian left to excise Soviet influence from the country.[165] More broadly, the same blend of religious pride, piety, and anti-imperialism that made many Islamists so hostile to U.S. influence in Muslim countries also made them intensely suspicious of Soviet inroads. Islamic fundamentalism posed a problem for all outsiders, one State Department report concluded, "because . . . anything foreign or non-Muslim becomes the perceived enemy."[166] If anything, the rigidly secular Kremlin faced greater ideological hurdles in relating to movements that put religion at the core of governance. Political Islam might be compatible with aspects of socialism, one analyst assessed in 1979, "but it is inimical to atheistic Communism."[167]

The rise of the Afghan insurgency powerfully demonstrated, and intensified, the anti-Soviet aspects of the Islamic awakening. Even before the Soviet invasion in December 1979, the Afghan rebellion had begun as a backlash against a communist regime that was perceived to be attacking the tribal and religious basis of that society. The subsequent Soviet occupation was meant to blunt this backlash and prevent ideological contagion into Muslim areas in Soviet Central Asia, but instead it inflamed the religious dimension of the conflict all the more. Precisely when Afghanistan—and much of the Islamic world—was experiencing a profound religious revival, an ideologically alien, foreign power had brutally subjugated a Muslim land. It was akin to trying to douse a fire—with gasoline. Muslim scholars issued edicts deeming the conflict a holy war. Afghan recruits flocked to fundamentalist resistance groups that had begun to operate out of Pakistan, and volunteers poured in from across the Muslim world.[168] "The guerrilla war has acquired the character of a *jihad*," noted an analysis prepared for the Pentagon, "in which there can be no compromises and no concessions."[169] Afghanistan was now a focal point of Islamic militancy, and Moscow was reaping the whirlwind.

From Carter onward, U.S. policymakers saw the Afghan conflict principally in cold geopolitical terms, as way of blunting a feared Soviet drive toward the Gulf, and of halting and eventually reversing Moscow's expansion. "The U.S. objective," NSDD-75 stated, "is to keep maximum pressure on Moscow for withdrawal and to ensure that the Soviets' political, military, and other costs remain high while the occupation continues."[170] In pursuing this objective, however, U.S. officials were not blind to the religious overtones of the insurgency. As CIA analyst Arnold Horelick noted, America could now "encourage a polarization of Muslim and Arab sentiment against the USSR."[171] Within days of the invasion, the Carter administration was therefore determined to play up the religious nature of the war. "We should portray regime as Soviet puppet and Soviet action as *anti-Afghan* and *anti-Moslem*," NSC staffer Stephen Larrabee wrote. "Aim should be to isolate Soviets within Moslem world."[172] From Brzezinski's perspective, stoking that conflict was vital to focusing Islamic anger on Moscow: "A low-level and enduring insurgency is essential to keep the Islamic states mobilized against the Soviets."[173] Even as the United States was struggling with the Islamic revival, it was seeking to redirect the fury of that movement against its greatest enemy.

This ethos persisted under Reagan. The entire Reagan Doctrine was premised on coopting geopolitically useful but otherwise distasteful allies. Despite the fact that the Islamic tide was causing such preoccupation, the administration thus made strengthening that tide a key aspect of its semicovert war in Afghanistan. Expanding on an initiative first devised by Brzezinski, William Casey partnered with the deeply Islamist government of Saudi Arabia, which played an indispensable part in bankrolling the insurgents and bringing non-Afghan Muslims to the fight. By one estimate, perhaps 50,000 foreign fighters would eventually participate in the jihad, the plurality from Saudi Arabia. The CIA also directed money to Islamic charities that recruited Muslim volunteers, and it cooperated with Pakistani intelligence to foster religious upheaval not just in Afghanistan but in Soviet Central Asia. Korans printed in Uzbek, and pamphlets with titles such as "The Life of the Great Muhammad," were clandestinely distributed. The Muslims of this region, Casey believed, "could do a lot of damage to the Soviet Union." As Soviet officials clearly grasped, Moscow's enemies were now using the "Islamic factor" against it.[174] "Washington's policy," Kremlin leaders had written as early as 1980, was one of "reorienting Islamic fanaticism on an anti-Soviet course."[175]

More than anything else, however, it was the contours of the U.S. partnership with Pakistan and Muhammad Zia-ul-Haq that accentuated the Islamist character of the insurgency. From 1980 onward, Pakistan was the linchpin of U.S. support for the *mujahideen*. The key resistance groups were based in Peshawar, and Pakistan was the only feasible corridor for delivering supplies and money to the guerrillas. "We must remember that without Zia's support, the Afghan resistance, key to making the Soviets pay a heavy price for their Afghan adventure, is effectively dead," Shultz wrote.[176] To cinch that support, the administration concluded a multiyear, $3.2 billion aid package for Pakistan in 1981, and provided that country with advanced weapons such as F-16s. It also gave Zia remarkable leeway in governing the day-to-day workings of the jihad. Even as the CIA played an integral role in supporting and equipping the rebels, it left direct management of these groups to Pakistan's Inter-Services Intelligence. Training, weapons, and other support were delivered through Pakistani intermediaries, giving Islamabad the final say in how such resources were allocated.[177] This arrangement was necessary because Zia insisted that Pakistan be the chief foreign influence in the insurgency. It was also desirable because a more visible U.S. presence might antagonize the Soviets, or even hardline Islamists who had little love for Washington. "A low U.S. profile is essential to . . . success," CIA analysts wrote. "U.S. leverage can best be exerted through third parties."[178]

As U.S. officials understood, one consequence of the "low profile" was to ensure that Zia could use American resources to sharpen the Islamist features of the insurgency. Even before the Soviet invasion, a mix of piety and politics had already led Zia to begin a wide-ranging domestic Islamization, which was reshaping the Pakistani economy, educational system, and military and intelligence services. "Zia probably sees himself as a man with a mission imposed by God to make Pakistan into a stable, Islamic nation," the CIA assessed.[179] As the war unfolded, he pursued a parallel approach to managing the Afghan insurgency.

To ensure that Pakistani influence and ideological preferences were well protected, the Inter-Services Intelligence channeled weapons, money, and other support primarily to the most religiously oriented, fundamentalist groups based in Peshawar—those organizations, U.S. diplomats wrote, that "see the jihad . . . as not just a freedom fight, but also a means to establish a 'revolutionary' Islamic state" in Kabul.[180] Zia's primary proxy was a group called Hezb-i-Islami, which advocated the establishment of a political order rooted in archaic Islamic precepts, and which was led by a man—Gulbuddin Hekmatyar—who was already legendary for his viciousness toward those who flouted his puritanical vision. Meanwhile, Pakistani intelligence officials were effectively starving the more liberal or secular resistance groups of support—"penalizing the democrats and the royalists," one U.S. diplomat recalled.[181] In Islamabad, Zia made little secret of the sort of regime he desired for post-occupation Afghanistan: "The new power will be really Islamic, a part of the Islamic renaissance which, you will see, will someday extend itself to the Soviet Muslims." This basic approach was shared by other U.S. partners as well. Saudi Arabia directed large amounts of funding to the most radically Islamist organizations in the resistance, and promoted fundamentalist Wahhabi concepts among the insurgents and Pakistani society.[182]

If the Afghan war was the bane of Soviet power, then, it was a boon for militant Islam. On the former count, the religious character of the insurgency helped sustain the *mujahideen* in their fight against superior forces, and provided a gaping asymmetry of motivation as time went on. As INR analyst Eliza van Hollen wrote, "The Soviet soldier whose father fought heroically at Stalingrad does not have a cause in Afghanistan, but his opponent is fighting a holy war."[183] On the latter score, the conflict injected energy and dynamism into the ongoing Islamist resurgence. Zia's strategy ensured that fundamentalist groups were ascendant within the fragmented Afghan insurgency, and later in the post-conflict struggle for power in Kabul. The resistance, one U.S. analyst noted in 1988, was now led by "the most ideologically militant, fundamentalist leader, Gulbuddin Hekmatyar."[184] Outside Afghanistan, the war catalyzed Islamist sentiment throughout the Muslim world, and forged a vast cohort of individuals who came to fight, assist in other ways, or simply absorb the intoxicating ideological climate. "Something akin to a radical Islamic foreign legion was taking shape," one scholar writes. Indeed, Abdullah Azzam, the Palestinian organizer who worked with Saudi officials to bring thousands of fighters to Afghanistan, saw the war as the advent of an armed Islamic vanguard that would defend the faith on future battlefields as well.[185]

In Reagan's eyes, the Afghan *mujahideen* were "freedom fighters" and invaluable strategic partners for the United States.[186] Given the difficulties that Washington was having elsewhere with radical Islam, however, there were nagging doubts about the long-term ramifications of empowering the jihad. State and Defense Department observers worried about whether supporting Zia might align America with authoritarian and Islamist tendencies that it would later rue.[187] Contemporary analysts also understood just how retrograde fundamentalists such as Hekmatyar were—he "personi-fies a thirteenth-century vision of Islam," one noted—and they doubted that the marriage of convenience would do more than obscure a deep underlying hostility to the United States. "I would put my arms around Gulbuddin and we'd hug, you know, like brothers in combat and stuff, and his coal black eyes would look back at you, and you just knew that there was only one thing holding this team together and that was the Soviet Union," the CIA station chief in Islamabad recalled.[188] Looking beyond Afghanistan, it was hard not to wonder whether the Islamist international taking shape might eventually turn against U.S. interests. "Sure, we're taking American help to fight the Russians," said Ayman al-Zawahiri, an Egyptian revolutionary who traveled to Afghanistan, "but they're equally evil."[189]

At the time, of course, there were sound reasons not to let these concerns derail U.S. policy. Given Pakistan's centrality to the jihad, there was no good alternative to backing Zia and giving him discretion in managing the insur-gency.[190] There was also a grudging recognition that the most ideologically noxious figures in the resistance were among the best fighters. "The ones you and I would feel most comfortable having a cup of tea with, had the fewest fighters on the ground," John McCarthy, the deputy chief of mission in Pakistan, said. "The ones that you and I would like to see go away as a bad dream, were the ones who were laying booby traps, ambushing Soviet convoys, blowing up the occasional tanks."[191] Finally, in view of the immense near-term stakes in play—the security of the Gulf and the trajectory of the Cold War—there was an understandable calculation that longer-term, far-hazier risks were worth running. Years later, Brzezinski would defend U.S. policy on these grounds: "Which is more important in world history: The Taliban or the fall of the Soviet Empire? A few over-excited Islamists or the liberation of Central Europe and the end of the Cold War?"[192]

Support for the jihad was certainly valuable in the Cold War context. But viewed in the context of the security challenges now emanating from the greater Middle East, American policy did in fact exacerbate some key emerg-ing threats. In Afghanistan, the war (and the subsequent U.S. withdrawal) did contribute to an Islamist ascendancy that ultimately produced a regime even more retrograde than Khomeini's, and just as hostile. In Pakistan, U.S. assistance to Zia did underwrite the rule of a leader who was both repressing and radicalizing the political culture. "Zia has declared Islamic law is law of Pakistan," Reagan wrote in 1988. "That puts them into the Fundamental-ist Revolution with the Ayatollah and Quadaffi [sic]."[193] More broadly still, the war caused ideological spillover from Central Asia to Saudi Arabia and beyond, fanning Islamist sentiment and radicalizing individuals who fought in the jihad and then took their beliefs and experiences home with them. Washington was not wholly or uniquely responsible for these outcomes, but its role was not inconsequential, either. Through its intervention in Afghanistan, the United States had helped shift the political atmosphere of the Muslim world in ways that were bound to complicate longer-term diplomacy.

It had also provided a fillip to a form of violent extremism that would prove even more lethal than the Iranian- and Libyan-sponsored variant of Reagan's day. Contrary to popular mythology, the CIA never directly aided Osama bin Laden or his closest colleagues. But a conflict sponsored and encouraged by Washington did foster the conditions for a flourishing global jihad. The war in Afghanistan was an incubator for networks of Muslim extremists who were proficient in deadly violence and willing to kill for religious ends. In this sense, Oakley said, the conflict was a sort of "Spanish Civil War" for international terrorism.[194] The eventual success of the Afghan insurgency left these groups filled with confidence and a sense of divine purpose; it also led them to seek new enemies and new battlefields, from Kashmir to Egypt to the United States. And tragically, American policy aided this phenomenon in more direct ways, too. After all, the CIA had provided or funded the provision of weapons (such as Stinger missiles) and training (in paramilitary and insurgent tactics) that were easily ripped from their original context and turned to nefarious ends. "The paramilitary training and weapons we provided, after the conflicts ended, were put to unwelcome purposes and even used in actions hostile to U.S. interests," Gates later wrote.[195] As Washington was desperately combating Islamist terrorism during the 1980s, it was also helping generate a newer strain of the same disease.

There was thus a conflicted and even self-defeating quality to U.S. policy during this period. In the Persian Gulf and the broader Middle East, the Carter and Reagan administrations generally strove to confront and contain the rising threats that were now shaping the regional agenda. U.S. involvement in Afghanistan, however, had the reverse effect. Supporting the jihad made sense in a Cold War framework, and it allowed Washington to temporarily turn the Islamist resurgence to geopolitical advantage. The longer-term price, unfortunately, was to compound some of the key Middle Eastern adversities that were already causing such grief.

Iran-Contra and After

If there was a single incident that encapsulated just how *much* grief those adversities were causing, it was the Iran-Contra fiasco that marred Reagan's second term. In the context of U.S. politics, the most controversial part of that episode was its *Contra* aspect, the illegal provision of funds to the Nicaraguan resistance. Within the framework of Middle East policy, however, it was the *Iran* element that was so damaging and so revealing. The Iranian revolution of 1979 had originally fused together the three challenges that so perplexed U.S. officials in the years that followed; the Iran arms sales of 1985–1986 again brought those issues to an intersection, and demonstrated just how vexing they remained.

At first glance, the opening to Tehran was one of the more bizarre chapters in U.S. diplomacy under Reagan. For precisely when Washington was escalating its tilt toward Iraq, it was undertaking a convoluted covert operation that placed it in the awkward position of supporting Iran as well. First in partnership with Israel, and then operating independently, CIA and NSC officials provided Iran with over 2,000 TOW antitank missiles, 18 HAWK anti-aircraft missiles, and several shipments of HAWK spare parts between mid-1985 and late 1986, all despite Operation Staunch and the U.S. arms embargo on Tehran. The CIA also gave Iran a small amount of military intelligence prior to the battle for al-Faw in early 1986, disregarding Gates's objections that this was "a very dangerous thing to do." In a series of clandestine meetings, moreover, the administration pursued a broader dialogue with the Iranians and stressed its desire for a bilateral partnership. "We are interested in a long-term political and strategic relationship," McFarlane (recently resigned from his NSC post) said in 1986.[196] As Washington and Tehran clashed—sometimes lethally—across the Middle East, Reagan's representatives were supporting and wooing that very regime.[197]

They were doing so for reasons that went to the very heart of America's Middle Eastern quandaries. From Reagan's perspective, the Iran opening was mainly a last-gasp ploy to deal with the menace of state-sponsored terrorism. By 1985, the administration felt helpless to prevent the taking of U.S. captives in Beirut or—despite the development of improved special-forces capabilities—to get them back.[198] Moreover, and despite his official "no concessions" stance on terrorism, Reagan had already tacitly violated that policy by encouraging Israel to release hundreds of prisoners during the TWA Flight 847 saga. Deeply pained by the hostages' plight, and angered by U.S. impotence vis-à-vis Hezbollah, Reagan was therefore driven to pay the very ransoms he had publicly deplored. "He could answer charges of illegality," Reagan said, "but he couldn't answer charge that 'big strong President Reagan passed up a chance to free hostages.'" Washington would send Iran "a modest amount" of badly needed arms for its struggle against Saddam; Tehran would reciprocate by inducing Hezbollah to release the hostages.[199] "In that we have been unable to exercise any suasion over Hizballah during the course of nearly two years of kidnappings," John Poindexter wrote, "this approach through the government of Iran may well be our only way to achieve the release of the Americans held in Beirut."[200]

For the NSC and CIA officials who masterminded it, the Iran operation was also an audacious strategic gambit to remake the political climate of that country. By the mid-1980s, Iran appeared to many U.S. observers to be reaching a critical crossroads. A costly war and an overtaxed economy were unsettling the political scene, and rumors of Khomeini's failing health raised the possibility of an epic power struggle once he died. CIA and NSC officials warned that such turmoil could redound to Soviet advantage, while also predicting that political change in Iran might, if handled deftly, create opportunities to rebuild some U.S. influence.[201] What was needed, wrote Graham Fuller, the national intelligence officer for the Near East and South Asia, was a "bolder and perhaps slightly riskier policy which will at least ensure greater U.S. voice in the unfolding situation. Right now—unless we are very lucky indeed—we stand to gain nothing, and lose more, in the outcome of developments in Iran, which are all outside our control." It was essential, Howard Teicher agreed, to proceed "in a manner that reinforces the prospects for restoring U.S. influence in Iran to the maximum extent possible."[202]

To its proponents, the Iran initiative thus became a vehicle for shaping the Iranian succession and cracking the broader regional issues unleashed by the revolution. Advisers such as McFarlane, Poindexter, Casey, and Oliver North argued that arms sales could provide access to Iranian moderates who reportedly desired improved relations and opposed the more radical of Tehran's policies. "We have seen evidence of a growing cleavage between those loyal to the regime and those opposed to it," Casey wrote. "U.S. actions . . . can exploit this cleavage and activate the uncommitted."[203] Because the diplomatically isolated Iranians had such dire need of advanced weapons and spare parts, the thinking went, the establishment of even a modest military supply relationship could have profound impact in Tehran. Specifically, it could allow the United States to strengthen and gain leverage with the moderates, helping them succeed in the post-Khomeini struggle—and thereby begin rolling back the tide of Islamic radicalism at its source. The goal, U.S. officials averred, was a "more moderate," "Western-oriented" government.[204] By building influence with the right groups, Teicher argued, Washington could seek "Iran's emergence, as steadily and as soon as possible, from the extremism of its fundamentalist revolution and from its attachment to state-sponsored terrorism as a tool of policy."[205]

Such an approach might also redress the otherwise-intractable dilemmas of Gulf security. The fact that Iran remained the major strategic prize in the region, and that U.S. ties to Saddam were uncomfortable at best, had never been lost on American officials. The reason for backing Iraq in the first place, Fuller noted, was "because we lack our preferred access to Iran."[206] In this context, the arms sales were about more than freeing hostages. By engaging and empowering a group of supposedly receptive moderates, the administration might also begin reconstructing a vital strategic relationship that would fortify the U.S. position in the Gulf and reduce its dependence on Iraq. The ultimate objective, wrote one participant, was "establishing gradually a rapprochement between the United States and Iran," and reforging an "alliance" with Tehran.[207] "Iran is not going to go away," Casey later commented; it would "remain a geopolitical force" that Washington must bring back into the fold.[208] To this end, U.S. officials stressed (and exaggerated) the common Soviet danger in their meetings with Iranian officials, while reiterating their desire for a new beginning in bilateral ties. "We have a great opportunity to establish a relationship between our countries," North said in May 1986. "Men of good will have a chance to build a bridge of confidence."[209]

In theory, then, the Iran gambit was meant to be a sort of silver bullet—a single shot that would permit the United States to escape the interrelated problems posed by state-sponsored terrorism, Islamic radicalism emanating from Tehran, and continuing Gulf insecurity. Even as the operation unfolded, however, skeptics raised questions about whether any of this was really achievable. Given the recent record of hostility and the entrenched nature of Iranian anti-Americanism, Weinberger deemed the whole scheme "almost too absurd to comment on." It was "like asking Qadhafi to Washington for a cozy chat," he scoffed.[210] Shultz too pronounced himself "very unenthusiastic." Trading arms for hostages would incentivize more hostage-taking: "If we start paying now, it will never stop." Additionally, selling weapons to a radically anti-American regime was unlikely to produce a strategic reorientation in Tehran, but it might well prolong the Iran-Iraq War, strengthen Khomeini versus Saddam, and horrify U.S. allies in the Gulf when the secret inevitably leaked. "The whole story will come out someday and we will pay the price," the secretary warned.[211] For Shultz and Weinberger, then, the Iran opening was not a clever cure-all. It was a reckless endeavor driven by that intoxicating brew of wishful thinking and desperation.

The fact that Reagan nonetheless overruled his two most influential advisers, and proceeded with such a risky operation, just confirmed how desperate he had become for a game-changing breakthrough in the Middle East.

As Shultz and Weinberger had predicted, however, the initiative was a disaster. The execution was comically inept. It was beset by a reliance on dishonest and self-interested intermediaries, and characterized by a range of embarrassing mishaps, from protocol blunders caused by religious and cultural incomprehension, to delivery of the wrong type of HAWK missiles, to the Iranians' discovery that the CIA was overcharging them for the weapons (to generate funds for the Contras). "It's amateur hour over there," said one State Department critic. High-ranking U.S. envoys were foisted off on low- and mid-level Iranian counterparts, and McFarlane's entreaties about a "strategic relationship" were met only by demands for more arms. Most damaging of all, in November 1986 leaks—from Iranian hardliners or perhaps Hezbollah—revealed the entire operation, forcing its termination and enveloping Washington in scandal.[212]

As the Iran initiative unraveled, it became apparent just how badly Reagan had erred. The arms sales had no positive impact on Iranian sponsorship of terrorism. The CIA discovered in 1987 that Tehran's relationship with Hezbollah was even closer than it had earlier believed, and Iranian involvement in terrorism actually increased during that year.[213] By demonstrating that the United States would pay handsomely for hostages, moreover, the arms sales had a predictably counterproductive effect. "The willingness of the U.S. to provide weapons to the Iranians, who then . . . would pay the Hezbollah, just increased Hezbollah's appetite for hostages," John Kelly, the American ambassador to Lebanon, acknowledged. Sure enough, Hezbollah seized additional hostages even as it released three captives as part of the Iran operation, and by January 1988, there were *more* Americans being held in Lebanon than before.[214] More broadly, revelations that Reagan was making the very concessions he officially scorned had a devastating impact on international perceptions of U.S. counterterrorism policy, just as the administration had finally given substance to its rhetoric by hitting Qaddafi. U.S. policy, one adviser noted, "has . . . crumbled around our feet."[215]

Nor did the operation have the desired effects within Iran. In retrospect, the notion that Washington could manipulate Iranian politics so profoundly, with such minimal investment of resources, was fanciful, and the officials who pushed this line were grasping at straws on the basis of low-quality intelligence. To be sure, there was a comparatively moderate faction that was willing to entertain improved relations with Washington, but that group was never powerful enough to displace the more extreme element led by Khomeini himself. (Nor, for that matter, was it as "moderate" as sometimes believed.) The supreme leader, meanwhile, was willing to sanction covert dealings with Washington to secure weapons for the fight against Saddam, but he remained adamantly opposed to any real rapprochement with the "Great Satan."[216] As a result, North's overtures fell on deaf ears. Even worse, when news of the arms sales eventually broke, Iranian hardliners used the revelations to discredit the moderates and reconsolidate their control in Khomeini's waning years. "The disclosure of the Iran initiative has exacerbated the leadership struggle in Tehran and damaged our influence in the Middle East and Persian Gulf," Poindexter acknowledged.[217]

Rather than having positive spillover effects throughout the region, in fact, the arms sales caused negative consequences to flow far and wide. The scandal jeopardized everything America had worked for in the Gulf since 1979, by damaging the credibility and relationships that Carter and Reagan had built. Gulf governments had taken great risks in opposing Iran and facilitating the buildup of U.S. military infrastructure; they now discovered that Reagan was secretly arming the country that most threatened them. Shultz had warned that "our moderate Arab friends" would "be badly shaken if they ever find out that we are breaking our commitment to them and helping the radicals in Tehran fight their fellow Arab Iraq," and the Iran revelations did cause a cooling of U.S. relationships from Jordan to the UAE.[218] "The distancing by Gulf states from the U.S. over the past several months has been in large part due to the combination of Iranian pressure and our apparent unwillingness to respond, as well as the embarrassment caused by revelations of arms for hostages," Oakley reported.[219]

Nowhere was the impact more corrosive than in U.S.-Iraqi relations. Throughout the early 1980s, Saddam had never truly trusted Washington. U.S. policy, he said, was to "let this group of lunatics bash each other."[220] Even so, the arms sales came as a shock to a regime that had grown accustomed to U.S. support. The fact that Reagan had been aiding Saddam's mortal enemy, at a time when the Iraqi military position was so precarious, elicited a mix of fear and visceral outrage in Baghdad. Saddam termed the incident "this stab in the back," and worried that it might tip the delicate military balance against Iraq. "The Americans are creating an imbalance of power in the region," he told advisers, "as Iran is known as an aggressive country and four times bigger than Iraq."[221]

This fear that U.S. weaponry might give Iran a decisive edge proved unfounded, given the relatively small quantity of arms delivered. But the impact on U.S.-Iraqi relations was substantial. In the short term, moderate members of the regime were badly discredited. "Those who favor the American connection feel too compromised to defend it against hardliners," one Iraqi official said.[222] Over the longer term, the incident cast a dark shadow over Saddam's views of the United States. For the remainder of the war, he would harbor suspicions that Reagan was continuing to aid Iran. And according to one detailed report, the "Irangate" scandal (as Saddam called it) convinced him "that Washington could not be trusted and that it was out to get him personally."[223] If the Reagan administration had hoped to build a productive, lasting relationship with Baghdad, it had done grave damage to its own aspiration.

This was the cumulative upshot of the arms sales: an enraged Saddam, a still-hostile and now modestly strengthened Iran, a discredited counterterrorism policy, and a plethora of alienated allies. In search of a panacea for the problems confronting it, the Reagan administration had gambled on an ill-conceived venture that accomplished little and undercut many of the interests it was meant to advance. The effects were concisely summarized during the preparation of Reagan's speech in response to the leaking of the operation in November 1986. After an early draft claimed that "this initiative has been particularly successful, and, if we can recognize its full potential, holds enormous promise for stabilizing the dangerous situation in the Middle East," an unidentified speechwriter offered a perfect one-word rebuttal: "Bullshit."[224]

The blowback from this episode put the administration squarely in recovery mode from early 1987 onward. The White House restated its no-concessions policy on terrorism, and reviewed the range of the actions being taken to deal with this threat.[225] More urgent still, amid a major Iranian offensive against Basra in January, the administration faced the twin tasks of rebuilding a damaged Gulf security framework and preventing an empowered Tehran from consummating its onslaught. "There is a general interagency consensus on the need to do something to deter or forestall an Iranian victory and to shore up our position with our Arab friends in the Gulf," NSC staffer Dennis Ross wrote. Weinberger agreed, framing a stronger tilt toward Saddam as a strategic necessity. "We should not only be supportive of Iraq, but should be seen to be supportive," he told the NSC. "This is an opportunity to recoup some of our standing in the region and regain credibility with the Arab states."[226]

These imperatives set the tone for U.S. policy in the closing stages of the war. Reagan made a determined effort to repair relations with Saddam and to further bolster that regime. Economic assistance grew significantly, with Iraq receiving $653 million in CCC guarantees in FY 1987 and over $1.1 billion in FY 1988, along with Export-Import financing.[227] Restrictions on dual-use exports were further loosened, to the point that Baghdad, in the latter part of the war, procured numerous shipments of industrial and high-tech goods with applications for Saddam's weapons programs.[228]

More direct support for the Iraqi war effort was also forthcoming. Intelligence sharing intensified, with the Defense Intelligence Agency (DIA) dispatching over sixty analysts to Iraq. Using data gathered primarily from satellite and aerial reconnaissance, the DIA team provided targeting information on Iranian command-and-control, logistical, and economic assets. The analysts focused particularly on bridges, railroads, brigade and divisional headquarters, and other targets that, if degraded or destroyed, would make it harder for the Iranians to mass troops for effective offensive operations. The purpose, DIA analyst Rick Francona recalled, was to give the Iraqis "something that their Air Force could hit that would make a difference." U.S. intelligence agencies also continued to provide information on Iranian troop dispositions, helping the Iraqis plug "some real gaping holes in their line" around Basra. In addition, as Saddam's forces gradually transitioned from defense to offense in late 1987–1988, DIA targeting packages helped them strike key Iranian assets, particularly in the battle to retake al-Faw peninsula. The ethos of this intensified intelligence sharing was imparted by Reagan himself: "An Iranian victory is unacceptable."[229]

All this was accompanied by efforts to exert greater pressure on Iran itself. Reagan reemphasized Operation Staunch, and imposed a ban on oil imports as well as strict limitations on other trade with Tehran.[230] In the UN Security Council, American diplomats were simultaneously using the improvement of U.S.-Soviet ties to increase Iranian isolation. State Department officials worked with Moscow to push a Security Council resolution calling on both parties to cease fire and accept the status quo ante. The Iranians—who controlled large chunks of Iraqi territory and were committed to overthrowing Saddam—would presumably refuse, inviting international condemnation and potentially opening the way to UN sanctions against Tehran. It was "imperative to make it as difficult as possible for the Iranians to prosecute the war," said Ambassador Joseph Petrone.[231]

The drive for UN sanctions ultimately proved unavailing, but by mid-1987 the administration was taking the far more dramatic step of inserting U.S. forces directly into the fighting. Back in early 1984, Saddam had precipitated the "tanker war" by attacking Iranian (and sometimes neutral) shipping, in an attempt to strain Tehran's economy and perhaps goad the mullahs into an overreaction that would imperil Gulf oil flows and thereby elicit superpower intervention. As the attacks continued, the Iranians took the bait. Iranian mines and torpedoes damaged sixty-seven oil tankers from 1984 to 1986, with attacks increasing over time. By late 1986, Tehran was focusing primarily on Kuwaiti shipping (and ships visiting Kuwaiti ports), in a bid to force that small and essentially defenseless country to cease its massive economic support for Iraq.[232] With Iran also importing Silkworm antiship missiles from China, the tanker war appeared to be nearing a dangerous escalation. "The danger in the Persian Gulf to maritime trade . . . and to oil facilities is growing," the CIA reported.[233]

By late 1986 and early 1987, this threat that Iran might succeed in intimidating Kuwait or other Gulf countries, or in disrupting oil flows, was already pushing Reagan to consider more decisive action. When Kuwait forced the issue by asking both Washington and Moscow for protection, the president acted to preempt a larger Soviet role in the region.[234] American naval forces soon began escorting Kuwaiti tankers, which were reflagged to emphasize that an attack on them was an attack on U.S. interests. "We are doing this to support a friendly state—Kuwait—against Iranian intimidation," Murphy said. To underscore U.S. resolve, the Pentagon deployed additional naval assets and planned attacks against Iranian targets should Tehran interfere.[235] In effect, the United States was now using its own forces to preserve access to Gulf oil, and to protect the diplomatic alliances that were keeping Saddam afloat. During this same period, Reagan made only tepid efforts to restrain Iraqi attacks, even after an accidental strike on the frigate USS *Stark* killed thirty-seven sailors. U.S. policy in the Gulf, one Iraqi official acknowledged, "prevents Iran from imposing its control on the region."[236]

Given the less-than-neutral role that the U.S. Navy was now playing in the war, it was unsurprising that reflagging brought Washington and Tehran into head-to-head conflict. Fall 1987 saw periodic naval clashes, with the Iranians laying additional mines, shelling convoys, and attacking tankers, and the Americans responding with strikes against enemy ships as well as against oil platforms used as bases for gunboats and mining operations. The hostilities spiked in 1988. After the USS *Samuel B. Roberts* struck an Iranian mine in mid-April, U.S. forces retaliated with Operation Praying Mantis, the largest American surface engagement since 1945. U.S. vessels and aircraft sank or incapacitated two enemy frigates, a fast attack craft, and several smaller attack boats—roughly half of the Iranian navy. American forces destroyed two oil platforms as well. The United States, as Carlucci later acknowledged, had gone from neutrality in 1980 to an "undeclared war" against Iran. Two months later, this undeclared war escalated, both tragically and unintentionally, still further. The guided-missile cruiser USS *Vincennes* mistook an Iranian passenger jet for an attacking F-14, and used surface-to-air missiles to destroy the plane, killing 290 passengers and crew.[237]

Although the destruction of Iran Air 655 was hardly premeditated, the administration did certainly mean U.S. military pressure to coerce Tehran into abandoning its hopes of dominating the Gulf and defeating Iraq. U.S.

operations, Weinberger had written, were a "signal of our determination to stand up to intimidation, to support our friends, and to help contain, and eventually end, the Iran-Iraq war."[238] In conjunction with other factors, U.S. policy did gradually have this effect. In hindsight, 1987 marked a turning point in the war. The major Iranian offensives of that year failed to have decisive impact, and in 1988, a retrained Iraqi army retook the offensive. Using vastly superior firepower, foreign (including U.S.) intelligence, and devastating chemical weapons attacks, Saddam's forces began routing an enemy that was now exhausted by enormous casualties and suffering from severe shortages of weapons and spare parts. Khomeini's regime was also confronting grave challenges at home, with the economy in free-fall, and Scud missile attacks on Tehran and other cities depressing domestic morale. Iran no longer seemed ascendant; it was struggling just to hold the line.[239]

In these circumstances, U.S. military action sent a strong signal. Iranian leaders interpreted the clashes in the Gulf as evidence that America was preparing to intervene decisively in the conflict. Although Tehran retained the option of retaliating with terrorism—and had in fact sponsored recent attacks in Kuwait, Bahrain, and Saudi Arabia—the regime reluctantly concluded that it could not sustain a continuing war with Baghdad *and* an intensifying conflict with Washington. As Akbar Hashemi Rafsanjani, chairman of the Iranian parliament, lamented, "It is obvious the Global Arrogance has decided to prevent our victory."[240] In July 1988, Iran accepted a cease-fire, largely restoring the status quo ante. Saddam's regime and the existing order in the Gulf had survived, with a substantial assist from the United States.

U.S. military intervention in 1987–1988 showed how deeply and directly Washington had now implicated itself in Gulf security affairs. And for most officials, the cease-fire that followed was evidence that the United States had finally turned the corner in its quest for renewed stability in the region. The perceived Kremlin threat to the Gulf was receding with the Soviet withdrawal from Afghanistan; Tehran's drive for hegemony had also been turned back. "The Iranian challenge to stability in the Middle East and Southwest Asia has been blunted," Murphy said. "The Iranians overreached themselves and learned a lesson, at least for the time being."[241] The fact that the war had so drained the Islamic Republic seemed to portend a period of respite for the crisis-weary region, and—in conjunction with Khomeini's death in 1989— perhaps even a longer-term moderation of Iranian policies. A few U.S. officials thought the danger to the Gulf so reduced that they advocated disbanding CENTCOM.[242] This argument never got very far, but U.S. naval deployments in the Gulf did shrink after the cease-fire. In 1989, a NIC assessment concluded that "a new regional order has emerged in the Persian Gulf that will reduce the likelihood of regional hostilities over at least the next two years."[243]

The basic problem of Gulf security, however, would prove more resilient than American officials expected. If anything, the close of the war had exacerbated Iranian animosity toward the United States, by convincing so many Iranians that Washington had deliberately shot down Iran Air 655, and that it had deliberately enabled Iraqi chemical attacks. In addition, Khomeini successfully reintensified the revolution in his final months in power, ensuring the dominance, the NIC wrote, of "radicals who favor continued revolutionary ferment at home and confrontation abroad."[244] After a brief period of relative quiescence, Iran would reemerge during the early 1990s as what the State Department called "the world's most active and dangerous state sponsor of terrorism," and what the Pentagon deemed "both a serious immediate and an important long-term threat to the security of the Gulf."[245]

Even more dangerous was the rising challenge from Iraq. In many ways, the length and course of the Iran-Iraq War had obscured the fact that Saddam had been first to make a destabilizing bid for regional hegemony. As the war ended, it was hard not to wonder whether he might someday try again. For on the one hand, the war had confirmed Saddam's messianic belief that he was destined to lead the Arab world against its enemies, and it had left him with a massive military machine composed of up to 1 million soldiers, 5,500 main battle tanks, and copious high-tech weaponry. "Iraq has the largest and best equipped armed forces in the Arab world, and its victory effectively removes Iran as a regional counterbalance for the next few years," the CIA assessed.[246] On the other hand, the conflict left Iraq with crippling foreign debts—$58 billion by one count—and economic problems that were fueling internal discontent. Saddam was further angered that the Gulf states were refusing to write off their wartime loans to Baghdad or endorse his claim to regional leadership. The Iraqi strongman emerged from the war as a well-armed but increasingly desperate actor, in other words, confident in his martial prowess but also feeling aggrieved and cornered. "Pakistan and Turkey could 'handle' Iran," one Pakistani official warned, "but . . . who would handle Iraq? For Saddam Hussein to survive . . . he needed a state of confrontation, if not with Iran then with somebody else."[247]

Saddam also came out of the war with an extremely fraught relationship with the United States. In Washington, U.S. officials recognized the troubling aspects of Saddam's behavior and capabilities, but they believed that the familiar recipe of support and engagement might yet turn the wartime partnership into more lasting cooperation. During the conflict, the Iraqi dictator had somewhat modified his position on issues such as Arab-Israeli peace, and the calculation of the incoming Bush administration was that "the lessons of war may have changed Iraq from a radical state challenging the system to a more responsible, status-quo state working within the system, and promoting stability in the region."[248] Given that Iraq would need foreign help with postwar reconstruction, and that it seemed unwise to isolate the Gulf's strongest military power, Bush resolved to treat Saddam as a friend in hopes of making it so. An early directive affirmed the goal of pursuing "normal relations" in order to "promote stability in both the Gulf and the Middle East," and in 1989 the administration approved another $1 billion CCC program for Iraq.[249] "They had shown an ability to work with us during the Iran-Iraq war," State Department official Joseph McGhee later said: it seemed reasonable to expect that this would continue.[250]

Even during 1988–1989, however, there were indications that Saddam might be growing more rather than less dangerous. In the period surrounding the end of the war, the regime had launched a brutal counterinsurgency against rebellious Kurds, complete with forced relocations, free-fire zones, and chemical weapons attacks on civilian targets. One particular chemical strike, against Halabja, killed perhaps 5,000 victims. "The regime of Saddam Hussein has long been known as one of the most brutal and repressive in the world," Murphy and other State Department officials reported. "But its actions in 1988 outdid its previous performance."[251] After the cease-fire, the regime continued to expand its chemical- and biological-weapons programs apace. It also worked determinedly toward a nuclear weapons capability and sought to extend the range of its Scud missiles. These developments (all monitored by U.S. intelligence) raised concerns that Iraq might be a source of regional turmoil rather than stability, a possibility that loomed larger as Saddam's rhetoric toward Israel and other foes turned more confrontational.[252]

As we can now see, in fact, Saddam had come to view the United States as one of these foes. Baathist ideology, a conspiracy-minded personality, and Washington history of meddling in the region had long made Saddam suspicious of American intentions. Reagan's double-dealing during "Irangate" had now convinced him that the United States was a dangerous enemy that was implacably opposed to his regime. "Did they not conspire against us during the war?" Saddam asked advisers. "Their conspiracy was obvious." Even as Saddam accepted American assistance in 1988–1989, he therefore attributed all manner of intrigues to Washington—alleging that it was seeking to topple the Iraqi government, ruin the economy, and perhaps even assassinate him. "I have a strong feeling that they were behind it," he said after one apparent assassination attempt.[253] Likewise, the regime condemned U.S. ties to the Gulf countries as an effort to encircle Iraq and thwart its rightful claim to regional primacy. "The real danger is the United States and its follower Israel," Saddam's half-brother, Barzan Ibrahim al-Tikriti, wrote to him in 1989. "The Americans want to control the region and we are the only obstacle in front of them."[254] In the first half of 1990, these suspicions would deepen, and Saddam's behavior would grow more erratic. Far from serving as a U.S. asset, Iraq was becoming the primary source of regional insecurity.

As the 1980s came to an end, then, the Gulf was on the verge of a new era of violent conflict. One severe threat to regional order and U.S. interests had been beaten back, but another was taking its place. A decade after the Iranian revolution, Washington had found no real respite from the problems of Gulf security. That area, and the United States, were simply moving from one crisis to another.

Conclusion

The decade after 1979 was undoubtedly a taxing time for U.S. officials charged with addressing the changing regional landscape in the greater Middle East. The Iranian revolution had crystallized the rising challenges posed by Persian Gulf insecurity, Islamic radicalism, and Middle Eastern terrorism, leaving Washington to grapple with these phenomena thereafter. And as one might expect, U.S. policymakers frequently struggled to master the problems they confronted. From the persistent dilemmas and contradictions of Gulf security, to the frustrations of counterterrorism, to the blowback from the Afghan jihad, to the fiasco of the Iran arms sales and their aftermath, the events of the 1980s made clear that U.S. policies had left only a mixed and conflicted legacy, and that there was no easily escaping the issues that were increasingly dominating the regional panorama. Dramatic advances and decisive victories were conspicuously absent; the same themes that preoccupied Carter- and Reagan-era policymakers would endure into the 1990s and beyond.

The story of Washington's engagement with these issues thus provides a crucial counterpoint to the general trend of U.S. foreign policy in the 1980s. In so many other areas, America had once again become the self-confident superpower, one that was purposefully exerting its influence to make major strategic advances. But in this region, the situation was very different. Here the key tectonic shifts cut largely against American interests, and here the record of U.S. policy was less inspiring. The great achievements of the 1980s had come when structural change and American strategy acted symbiotically; when that relationship was more conflicted, the outcomes were more pedestrian and problematic.

The record of U.S. policy in the greater Middle East therefore reminds us that there were important exceptions to the broadly favorable flow of global events, and to the generally impressive performance of American statecraft. No less significant, it underscores that the 1980s were a transitional decade in more ways than one. As we have seen in the previous chapters, this was the period when the United States truly began to shift from the apparent malaise of the 1970s to the reinvigorated dominance of the 1990s. Yet as this chapter indicates, it was also the period when America began to face many of the most troubling threats that would ensure continued insecurity and travail even in that unipolar era. For the perils posed by terrorism, Islamic radicalism, and instability in the Gulf were not going away as the 1980s ended. If anything, they were poised to play an even larger role in a world that would no longer be principally defined by U.S.-Soviet rivalry. In fact, it would not take long at all to see just how large that role would be, because events in the Persian Gulf would soon unleash one of the first, and most defining, crises of the unipolar era.

CHAPTER 6

The Dawn of the Unipolar Moment

By the late 1980s, the international system, and America's position therein, were nearing a historic watershed. Only a decade before, it had often seemed self-evident that the United States was a beleaguered, declining colossus. Since then, however, America's diplomatic stock had soared. The arc of the Cold War had shifted fundamentally, with superpower tensions receding rapidly, and Washington and its allies now on the brink of winning that contest altogether. Democracy and free markets were making their torrid advance, fostering a veritable sea change in global politics and economics, and recasting the international environment according to U.S. interests and values. Through a combination of profound trends and proactive policies, the United States had moved from the apparent gloom of the 1970s to the verge of a decisive breakthrough into a new era of supremacy.

The culmination of that paradigm shift came in the 1989–1992 period. During these years, the more and more tenuously bipolar system that had prevailed into the late 1980s unraveled completely, and a new, unipolar order took its place. That unipolar order featured the United States as the world's sole superpower: a country that enjoyed an extraordinarily favorable configuration of power and influence in the international arena, and whose values, preferences, and overall global leadership seemed as privileged as ever before. This new system was one in which America's longtime strategic and

ideological competitor had fallen by the wayside, with no comparable challenger to take its place. Not least, the unipolar environment that emerged
in this period was one in which the leading global power was determined
to maintain and profit from its dominance—to lock in the gains from the
collapse of the old order, and to continue reshaping world affairs to its own
advantage. This was the dawn of the post–Cold War "unipolar moment":
an era in which the United States possessed, and was determined to keep,
unrivaled international primacy.

This transition from one geopolitical era to another was crystallized by
three major strategic shocks of the 1989–1992 period. The fall of the Berlin
Wall and the collapse of Eastern European communism, the Persian Gulf
crisis and war, and the disintegration of the Soviet Union and its aftermath—
each of these events represented a vital turning point. Each episode shattered
old certainties and arrangements, and each created new opportunities and
dangers. Each event revealed the fluidity of global politics at a time of transition and upheaval, and each put the very terms of the international order in
play. In sum, each of these strategic shocks demonstrated the extent to which
fundamental change was now sweeping the international system, and each
one created a moment of flux in which determined actors could remold that
system further still.

This was the context for U.S. policy in the George H. W. Bush years.
Bush is often considered an adroit tactician who lacked longer-range vision
or a sense of guiding purpose.[1] The record of his foreign policy gives the lie
to such critiques. Granted, Bush's administration did not foresee with any
clarity the shocks that would mark its time in power, and a degree of improvisation necessarily characterized its response to earth-shaking events. Yet
that improvisation was always rooted in a coherent and perceptive strategic
outlook. From the start, the administration appreciated that the world was
entering a period of tremendous fluidity, one in which it might be possible
to assert U.S. interests even more ambitiously than before. As crises arose and
events became malleable, the Bush team therefore acted—and reacted—in
ways that established U.S. primacy as the bedrock of the new global order.
After the fall of the Berlin Wall, Bush used U.S. leverage to help secure
German reunification within NATO and fundamentally remake the postwar
European order to American advantage. After Iraq invaded Kuwait in August
1990, the administration catalyzed a multilateral response that showcased just
how crucial America's unmatched diplomatic and military power was to
the well-being of the post–Cold War world. And before, amid, and after
the terminal crisis of the Soviet Union, the administration laid the basis for

a post–Cold War strategy that envisioned the indefinite retention and exploitation of U.S. preeminence. At the climax of the American resurgence, U.S. policy remained generally purposeful, if imperfect, indeed.

The Bush Administration on the Eve of Unipolarity

Profound historical changes may occur over an extended span of time, but they often culminate in moments of intense and unpredicted upheaval. Such was true of the global paradigm shift that climaxed between 1989 and 1992. The events of this period were frequently stunning not just for their impact, but also for the astonishing rapidity with which they unfolded, and for the fact that virtually no one had accurately forecasted them in advance. The improbable had now become commonplace; the pace of history had accelerated dramatically. "I admit that we were shocked by the swiftness of the changes that unfolded," Bush said in late 1989. "Dynamic, and at the same time fundamental changes" were happening at breakneck speed.[2] "A tidal wave of history was about to break upon us," Gates later recalled; not even expert observers fully anticipated what was coming.[3]

It was only natural, then, that there would be a certain improvisational nature to policy in the Bush years. As Secretary of State James Baker later wrote, this was a time when defining characteristics of the postwar system were being upended, "when long-held beliefs about grand strategy were being turned upside down." No policymaker could possess a step-by-step plan for navigating such transformations; rather, a capacity to "roll with the changes" was imperative.[4] Dennis Ross, the incoming PPS director, took the same perspective in a memo drafted in late 1988. "We're entering a period that is really unlike any we've seen through the whole postwar era," Ross wrote, "and this is not the time to put our thinking in a straightjacket." Amid fundamental global upheaval, Ross argued, officials that failed to "stretch our minds and accept the importance of thinking unconventionally" would surely be left behind by events.[5]

Yet if no one could have predicted or been entirely prepared for the revolutionary shifts of this period, the Bush administration was marvelously equipped to handle them in intelligent ways. For one thing, the administration possessed an embarrassment of riches in foreign policy expertise. That expertise began with Bush himself, who had earlier been vice president, director of central intelligence, head of the U.S. mission in China, and ambassador to the United Nations. Bush's top advisers were similarly seasoned. Baker had been Reagan's chief of staff and then treasury secretary; National Security Adviser Brent Scowcroft had run the NSC for Gerald

Ford. Secretary of Defense Richard Cheney was a respected former congressman and White House chief of staff with long experience in foreign policy; Colin Powell, who became JCS chairman in late 1989, had previously been national security adviser in addition to his decades of military service. Cumulatively, Bush and his inner circle had unparalleled credentials, and they were supported by an exceptionally talented group of second- and third-tier officials: Gates (now deputy national security adviser), Robert Blackwill, and Richard Haass at the NSC; Ross, Robert Zoellick, and Lawrence Eagleburger at State; Paul Wolfowitz at the Pentagon; and many others.

The Bush team also benefitted from having an efficient and generally effective decision-making process, managed by Scowcroft and Gates. The efficacy of that system rested in part on the striking collegiality of the inner circle, a situation that was partly fortuitous and partly a reflection of Bush's emphasis on these qualities. Yet it rested equally on the efforts of Scowcroft, whom Bush termed the "ult[imate] honest broker," to devise a system that was more structured than Reagan's and less conspiratorial than Kissinger's.[6] This "Scowcroft system" featured regular and transparent consultation among principals, emphatic discouragement of leaking and other intrigues, and a strong coordinating and advisory role for Scowcroft himself. It also stressed efforts, as Gates recalled, "to cut away all the extraneous bull shit"—to protect Bush's time by fleshing out and sharpening policy differences before taking an issue to him for decision.[7] This system certainly had its share of strains and failures from 1989 to 1993, and it hardly precluded the disputes that are inevitable among strong-willed individuals. On the whole, however, it proved far more successful than not in leveraging the abilities of its participants, reducing gamesmanship without smothering disagreements, and imparting coherence to policy in a hectic time.[8]

Administration decision making was even more firmly anchored by the core strategic ideas that top U.S. officials, and especially Bush himself, brought to the job. Although Bush was never seen as a strategic visionary in the mold of his predecessor, in reality his statecraft was always guided by a set of basic convictions and aims. The president believed that American leadership was integral to a stable and congenial world order, and that renewed U.S. strength and vigor had been crucial to the positive developments underway. "America has set in motion the major changes in the world today," he said in 1988—"the growth of democracy, the spread of free enterprise, the creation of a world market in goods and ideas."[9] And in contrast to a spate of pessimistic literature that had appeared in the 1980s, Bush argued that the United States was, in fact, at the brink of a new era of geopolitical ascendancy. "America is not in decline," he declared. "America is a rising nation. . . . We're on the verge of a new century, and what country's name will it bear? I say it will be another American century."[10]

Indeed, if Bush and his advisers did not foresee precisely what would happen during their time in power, they certainly did understand that they were entering a moment of great promise, a period when it might be possible to seek major changes in the global order. "There are times when the future seems thick as a fog; you sit and wait, hoping the mists will lift and reveal the right path," Bush stated in his inaugural address. "But this is a time when the future seems a door you can walk right through into a room called tomorrow."[11] The president and Baker touted the recent expansion of democracy and markets, and predicted that these institutions were making a decisive global breakthrough. "Freedom's advance is evident everywhere," Bush declared. "Democracy . . . really is on the offensive," Baker added.[12] Likewise, the secretary of state noted that the "correlation of forces" in the Cold War had shifted remarkably in America's favor, and in February 1989, Bush signed a National Security Review stating that U.S. policies toward Moscow had been "extraordinarily successful." "Containment is being vindicated," it noted, "as the peoples of the world reject the outmoded dogma of Marxism-Leninism in a search for prosperity and freedom."[13] Almost everywhere, it seemed, history was headed in the right direction. "This was a time of great optimism," Bush said. "The West's success was so great, and the future was so exciting."[14]

From his earliest days in office, then, Bush believed that the United States had an opportunity to lean forward in its statecraft, to "dream big dreams" about what it might achieve.[15] Democracy and markets were surging ahead, he said in January 1989, and America must "keep those trends going with the United States at the forefront."[16] The United States was in a position to think boldly about its global aspirations, Bush reiterated in a major address in May. "We and our allies are strong, stronger really than at any point in the postwar period, and more capable than ever of supporting the cause of freedom," he declared. "There's an opportunity before us to shape a new world." "What is it we want to see?" he asked in the same speech. "It is a growing community of democracies anchoring international peace and stability, and a dynamic free-market system generating prosperity and progress on a global scale."[17] Such themes were ubiquitous in Bush's statements. As Jeffrey Engel has noted, far from being aimless, Bush was part of a tradition of policymakers "determined to place America at the head of a world system considered in Washington's best interest, and . . . in the world's best interest as well."[18]

This did not mean, of course, that the president saw positive transformations as inevitable. "Happy endings," his first *National Security Strategy* (*NSS*) stated, "are never guaranteed."[19] There remained plenty of threats to U.S. interests, from a still heavily armed Soviet Union, to newer and emerging dangers such as the proliferation of weapons of mass destruction (WMD), terrorism and Islamic extremism, and even the possibility that reduced super-power tensions might lead to a resumption of historical frictions within the Western world. Accordingly, officials such as Bush, Cheney, and Scowcroft warned that change might bring instability as well as opportunity. They also feared that premature euphoria might cause the abandonment of policies that had proven so useful in containing Moscow and advancing U.S. goals, or that it might induce overzealous actions that would invite blowback and disrupt progress where it remained fragile.[20] A president determined to "dream big dreams" was therefore equally determined to employ "prudence and com-mon sense" in pursuing them. "The magnitude of change we sense around the world compels us to look within ourselves and to God to forge a rare alloy of courage and restraint," Bush said in mid-1989. "We all wish to take advantage of opportunities," he later told British officials, "but not do any-thing foolish" in the process.[21]

Prudence would be a recurring feature of Bush's statecraft, and it would suffuse his rhetoric to the point that the very word came to serve as a com-mon caricature of the administration as plodding, unimaginative, and slow to respond to epochal change.[22] Yet prudence and vision are not mutually exclu-sive, and the administration was far better poised to respond to such change than its critics understood. Even in the opening innings of Bush's presidency, there was a recognition that the global order was approaching a moment of potentially profound flux, as old and new dangers were mixed with great pos-sibilities. As a paper prepared by Zoellick noted in October 1989, the United States was entering a "dynamic period in foreign policy," and it faced a chal-lenge "analogous to [the] task after 1945—devising a new world order for changed circumstances." "Our task," Zoellick wrote, "is to manage change effectively to serve U.S. interests."[23] It was just this mind-set that would guide the administration as it addressed the cascading strategic shocks that marked the end of the Cold War and the dawn of the unipolar era.

German Reunification and the Shaping of Post–Cold War Europe

The first shock was the collapse of East European communism in 1989. At the beginning of the year, the Warsaw Pact regimes had been under grow-ing strain but were very much intact. By the end of the year, nearly all these regimes were dead or headed to the grave. Poland and Hungary were making negotiated transitions from one-party rule; communist regimes in Bulgaria and Czechoslovakia had fallen under popular pressure. In Romania, the Ceausescu dictatorship had been violently swept away following a last-ditch attempt to prevent revolution via repression. Most dramatically of all, the Berlin Wall had fallen, physically rending the Iron Curtain and commencing the death spiral of the East German regime. Through all of this, Moscow remained passive, declining to intervene to save the governments that formed the core of its Cold War empire. "We stand against any interference in the domestic affairs of other states and we intend to pursue this line firmly and without deviations," Soviet diplomats told U.S. officials. "Thus, the American side may consider that 'the Brezhnev Doctrine' is now theirs as our gift."[24]

This astounding turn of events traced back to the profound structural problems that had increasingly plagued the bloc regimes since the 1970s, and to the rising popular resentment and mobilization those problems had triggered. Persistent and worsening economic crises, declining ideological legitimacy, and growing political dissent—by the mid- and late 1980s, these strains were reaching a breaking point. Many regimes were in dire financial straits that left them in thrall to their Western creditors, and with few options for appeasing their disaffected populations. Throughout the bloc, there were inescapable signs that the communist model was simply exhausted. Some countries, such as Hungary, had begun experimenting with economic and political liberalization in hopes of regaining legitimacy and momentum. Others, such as East Germany and Romania, stood pat and lost what little vitality they had left. "The entire socialist community is experiencing the most difficult period in its development in the entire postwar period," Soviet officials reported in February 1989. At risk was "the fate of socialism in a number of countries of this region, the future of the Warsaw Pact, [and] the fundamental interest of the Soviet Union."[25]

Ironically, it was Gorbachev himself who turned this tenuous situation into the reverse domino effect of 1989. The Kremlin leader had not intended to liquidate socialist rule in the bloc. "We clearly have to draw boundaries," he told Hungarian officials in March 1989. "The limit . . . is the safekeeping of socialism and assurance of stability." But Gorbachev also appreciated that Moscow could no longer afford the costs of rescuing the Pact governments economically or crushing their internal opposition militarily. "Today we have to preclude the possibility of repeated foreign intervention in the internal affairs of socialist states," he said. His preference, then, was to reinvigorate East European communism—and safeguard the Soviet sphere of influence—through determined but controlled reform, a course he urged upon bloc leaders both publicly and privately.[26]

As was often the case with Gorbachev, however, this policy had unin-tended results. By pushing the bloc regimes to pursue managed liberaliza-tion, the general secretary implicitly condemned the old system and thereby encouraged ferment that could *not* so easily be managed. When Gorbachev visited East Germany in October 1989, for instance, his calls for reform served mainly to energize a population that was now turning on its own govern-ment. And because Gorbachev was unwilling to undertake the massive eco-nomic or military interventions necessary to restore socialist stability, he also pulled the traditional Soviet props from beneath the wobbling Pact regimes.[27] "We are excluding the possibility of bloody methods," Gorbachev told Soviet officials in early 1989; as his *public* statements conveyed this message in the succeeding months, there was no holding back the deluge.[28] The fear that sustained communist rule was gone, and the pressures for change became uncontrollable. "The total dismantling of socialism as a world phenomenon has been proceeding," Chernyaev wrote in October. "And a common fellow from Stavropol set this process in motion."[29]

The result was the liberation of Eastern Europe, and a tremendous rip in the fabric of the postwar order. The division of Europe had been the defin-ing mark of Cold War bipolarity; the collapse of communism in the East showed that this system had been ruptured decisively. A great "shift in the world balance of forces" was occurring, Chernyaev wrote. "This is the end of Yalta . . . of the Stalinist legacy."[30] With the Iron Curtain breached, there were now unprecedented opportunities for reordering European geopolitics and the international system. The looming question was what forms those changes would take. "Historians are likely to view 1989 as a year, like 1848, which transformed a continent," Scowcroft wrote. "The past is irretrievably gone, but the future remains cloudy."[31]

The Bush administration's first ten months in power had gradually put it in position to answer that question. Granted, Bush had not left the gate quickly in U.S.-Soviet relations. The president and his aides all agreed that Washington had a very strong hand vis-à-vis Moscow, but there were differ-ences about how to play it. Baker and Ross called for intensive diplomatic engagement, to test Gorbachev's sincerity and encourage greater reforms at home and abroad. A group led by Scowcroft, conversely, worried that those reforms might actually be intended to revitalize Soviet power and "disband the Western coalition by smothering us with kindness," and that declaring an end to the Cold War might surrender the sources of leverage that had brought Washington to the point of victory.[32] The upshot was a roughly three-month "pause" in superpower diplomacy, as Bush ordered a set of policy reviews to fix the U.S. course. Speaking on behalf of the administration, Gates claimed that the president was "resisting the siren song of the quick fix and the big headline"; critics jeered that Bush was dissipating the diplomatic momentum of the Reagan years.[33]

By mid-spring, however, Bush was adopting a more active policy. That shift derived partly from concern that Gorbachev, through the peace offensive he had launched at the United Nations in December 1988, was now threatening to fracture NATO through conciliation rather than confrontation. "Gorbachev has, like a kind of surfer, caught a wave of public support," Bush said. "It would be nice to get agreement on a broad vision of our own."[34] More important, there was a growing sense that the opportunities at hand were too attractive to pass up. Whatever Gorbachev's long-term intentions, he was certainly a new type of Kremlin leader, one who seemed open to major departures, and one who clearly needed good relations with the West to address the intensifying crises of Soviet power. The Soviets were increasingly desperate for a calm external environment and expanded foreign trade and investment, U.S. officials noted, and Gorbachev's new thinking "makes it difficult for him to appear unresponsive to bold, new ideas." The administration thus had a chance to pursue deep changes in Soviet behavior as the price of normalized relations—and perhaps, thereby, to begin constructing a post–Cold War order on U.S. terms. The goal, as Bush's guiding directive on superpower relations affirmed, was to seek "fundamental alterations in Soviet military force structure, institutions, and practices which can only be reversed at great cost, economically and politically, to the Soviet Union."[35]

The president unveiled this vision in May 1989, in a major speech that outlined a program for moving "beyond containment" and integrating the Soviets "into the community of nations." "We are approaching the conclusion of an historic postwar struggle between two visions: one of tyranny and conflict and one of democracy and freedom," Bush stated. To end this conflict, the Kremlin should take concrete steps. It should dramatically reduce its military power and make its force structure less threatening. It should promote human rights and genuine democratization at home. It should help resolve Third World conflicts on Western terms. It should also permit true political change and self-determination in Eastern Europe. "Tear down the Iron Curtain," Bush exhorted. As these steps were taken, the door would open to a new and more normalized East-West relationship. In essence, Bush was publicly outlining the conditions on which the Cold War could fully end.[36] As aides explained, "These conditions are the foundation on which the Soviet Union's relationship to us and to the international system would rest."[37]

Eastern Europe was the centerpiece of this program. "The potential for real and sustained change in Eastern Europe is greater now than at any time in the post-war world," one of Bush's earliest policy reviews had noted. "The time may have come when creative American policies can make a more significant difference."[38] To this end, the administration emphasized that it would prioritize relations with bloc countries that pursued internal reform. It also laid down markers that Soviet willingness to allow continued liberalization and independence in the region was a prerequisite to moving beyond containment. "The Cold War began with the division of Europe," Bush declared in Germany in May. "It can only end when Europe is whole." From spring 1989 onward, this aspiration of making Europe "whole and free," of ending its division "on the basis of Western values," would be a guiding principle of U.S. policy.[39]

It would also motivate tangible initiatives. In May, the administration advanced an aggressive proposal for cutting conventional forces in Europe (CFE). The proposal was intended to test Gorbachev's willingness to accept disproportionate cuts that would vitiate the long-standing Kremlin edge on the continent; it was equally meant to leaven the military domination that had long thwarted Eastern European reform. An ambitious CFE agreement, Baker argued, would help liberate "the political process in Eastern Europe from the heavy weight of an excessive Soviet military presence."[40] In July, Bush then traveled to Poland and Hungary, praising ongoing reforms and promising U.S. financial and trade assistance if they continued. Admittedly, Bush did not offer nearly as much aid as some observers had hoped, and with the example of Hungary in 1956—and China in 1989—in mind, he refrained from doing anything that might appear as incitement to rebellion and provoke a harsh reaction. ("Americans . . . do not want to see people crushed under tanks, as in 1956," he had said.)[41] But even as Bush struck this delicate balance, he left little doubt that Washington was encouraging deep change in the Soviet bloc. "America stands with you," he declared in Poland. "It is in your power to help end the division of Europe."[42]

By this point, the administration was even grappling with the issue of German reunification. The "German question" had long been among the most sensitive in world politics, and Bush had no intention of forcing the issue prematurely. Yet the president and his inner circle did grasp that it was impossible to confront the division of Europe without also confronting the division of its most powerful country. "Even if we make strides in overcoming the division of Europe through greater openness and pluralism," Scowcroft wrote in March, "we cannot have a vision for Europe's future that does not include an approach to the 'German question.'" As policy toward Eastern Europe developed, the administration staked out a position meant to provide "some promise of change, of movement" by advocating democratization and self-determination in the German Democratic Republic (GDR), and the eventual reunification of the German states.[43] Change was afoot in the bloc, Bush said in May; "Let Berlin be next!"[44]

American policy during spring and summer 1989 may have had a marginal impact on the unfolding process of political change in Eastern Europe, by encouraging the forces of liberalization and underscoring disincentives for Soviet intervention.[45] Where U.S. policy was more important, however, was in preparing the administration to react to what was about to occur. By mid-1989, Bush and his closest aides saw that the postwar congealment of power and ideology on the continent was loosening, and they had advanced a vision of a post–Cold War Europe freed from authoritarianism and Soviet domination—a Europe reunified "on our terms," Zoellick had written to Baker in May.[46] "New and extraordinary possibilities exist," Baker agreed in notes written the next month. And by October, Bush himself was speculating that the Warsaw Pact might disintegrate. "That may seem naïve," he said, "but who predicted the changes we are seeing today?"[47] On the eve of the Berlin Wall's collapse, the administration was dreaming big dreams about the shape of things to come.

Admittedly, those ambitions only partially mitigated the surprise when the wall was breached on November 9. "We've imagined it," Bush admitted that evening, "but I can't say that I foresaw this development at this stage."[48] The pace and extent of change in Eastern Europe was exceeding everyone's expectations, he subsequently said: "It seems like the world is changing overnight."[49] Indeed, the opening of the wall had greatly accelerated the economic and political collapse of the GDR, and unleashed an exodus of emigrants to the West. "This is a catastrophe for the GDR," Helmut Kohl, the chancellor of the Federal Republic of Germany (FRG), observed. "This is a dramatic thing; an historic hour." Sensing opportunity in crisis, Kohl seized the initiative. In late November, he unveiled a ten-point plan meant to lead to free elections in the GDR, the progressive strengthening of ties between Bonn and Berlin, and the eventual reunification of the two states. Kohl's program, British diplomats wrote, was "a major event." Reunification, long viewed as an essentially dormant issue, had now rushed insistently to the fore.[50]

Given Germany's history, that prospect sent shivers through countries East and West. Within NATO, the French were wary and the British downright hostile, fearing that reunification might create a new German juggernaut and destabilize Europe. Mitterrand privately expressed doubts that "the issue of changing borders can realistically be raised now," and into early 1990 he was saying that the Germans "did not have the right to upset the political realities of Europe."[51] Thatcher was even less amenable. "We do not want the unification of Germany," she had said even before the wall came down. "Such a development could undermine the stability of the entire international situation and could lead to threats to our security."[52] In Eastern Europe, too, old memories were vivid. "The widespread fear of German aggression, German tanks, continues to have an effect," said Lech Walesa.[53]

Then there was the response from Moscow. Gorbachev had wanted reform in Eastern Europe, and he had tolerated epoch-making political change there. But he had not expected that socialism would collapse so entirely and so precipitously, nor had he reckoned that the Soviets might soon be facing a near-total loss of influence.[54] For all Gorbachev's advocacy of "freedom of choice," the idea that Moscow's key European outpost might disappear, and that the country that had savaged the Soviet Union during World War II would be reconstituted, produced a visceral reaction. Moves toward reunification would cause "not only the destabilization of the situation in Central Europe, but also in other parts of the world," he warned Western leaders on November 10. The world had "paid a high price for past mistakes," Shevardnadze added days later. "The Soviet people have not forgotten and never will forget history's lessons."[55]

For many leaders, then, the initial impulse was to oppose the dramatic changes that were now possible. What was striking about the U.S. response was how quickly and unambiguously the administration supported those changes. To be sure, administration officials understood that the situation in Europe was rife with risk. Escalating instability in the GDR, a State-Defense planning group wrote in early November, "is among the World War III scenarios for which U.S. and NATO planners have been preparing for decades."[56] Conscious of these perils, Bush carefully measured his public statements to avoid provoking Gorbachev or stoking further chaos in East Germany. It made no sense to "stand on the Berlin Wall and 'beat my chest,'" he said.[57] To Bush, this restrained posture made good diplomatic sense; to many outside observers, it played into the caricature of a president so "prudent" that the world was passing him by.

What this criticism misunderstood, however, was that Bush was actually moving rapidly to put the United States behind the goal of reunification. Within days of the wall's breaching, the administration affirmed that it supported self-determination for the GDR, a step that would likely lead to eventual reunification.[58] The president subsequently responded to Kohl's ten-point program by telling the chancellor that "I'm with you completely," and at a U.S.-Soviet summit in Malta in early December, he gently informed Gorbachev that "you cannot expect us not to approve of German reunification."[59] At a NATO meeting in Brussels the next day, Bush openly endorsed that objective and urged the allies to do likewise. "The task before us," he said, "is to consolidate the fruits of this peaceful revolution . . . to end the division of Europe and Germany."[60] As numerous observers later testified, this early support for reunification was vital—it ensured that European and Soviet anxieties did not foreclose the process before it could gather critical momentum.[61]

This was a very forward-leaning stance by the Bush administration, and it derived from two powerful sources. First, Bush simply did not share the reflexive apprehension about Germany that remained so potent in Europe. Precisely because he was not European, Bush had greater emotional and psychological remove from Germany's past. He also had far greater faith in a reunified Germany's future. Bush appreciated that German nationalism was a powerful force, and one that might now make reunification inevitable. Yet he believed that four decades of democracy had buried any authoritarian impulses, and that a Germany that remained within the Western community and alliance system would hardly be a threat to peace. "I know your position and think I know the heartbeat of Germany," he had told Kohl in October; the Germany of 1989 was not the Germany of 1939.[62] These convictions guided U.S. policy thereafter. As Scowcroft wrote prior to the Brussels summit, "We are not afraid of a new Germany that is part of the commonwealth of free nations, firmly tied to Western values."[63]

Indeed, the administration welcomed this prospect, because reunification offered a transcendent, once-in-a-lifetime chance to close out one era and begin another. "The opportunities are manifest," Scowcroft wrote. "We are on the verge of realizing an end to the artificial division of Europe, with the East-West military confrontation of forty years transfigured beyond recognition."[64] The struggle over German power had been a fundamental issue of the Cold War, and the GDR had been the centerpiece of the Soviet alliance bloc in Europe. As Scowcroft noted, reunification under Western auspices would thus "rip the heart out of the Soviet security system," confirming a decisive strategic shift and ending the Cold War unquestionably on U.S. and Western terms.[65] It would also facilitate the spread of democracy and capitalism into the former Soviet bloc, and testify powerfully to those institutions' ascent. In short, a reunified Germany would reshape the basic architecture of Europe, and create a post–Cold War order in which Washington, its allies, and their values were dominant. "We were witnessing the sorts of changes usually only imposed by victors at the end of a major war," Scowcroft later noted; reunification was central to locking in those changes. Or, as Bush wrote, "Our deepest hopes for a transformation of the continent are coming closer to being realized."[66]

Crucial to reaping those gains was keeping a reunified Germany in NATO. In theory, the fall of the wall had made possible a variety of geopolitical statuses for a post–Cold War Germany, ranging from full NATO membership, to association with both NATO and the Warsaw Pact, to neutralization and demilitarization, to greater reliance on pan-European institutions such as CSCE. For U.S. officials, however, only the first option was acceptable. In one sense, NATO membership was a hedge against instability, as it would bind a more powerful Germany to the security system that had allowed the FRG to thrive without upsetting the postwar European order. "We want to tie the Germans to the West," Scowcroft wrote. U.S. officials doubted that alternative institutions, such as CSCE, could fulfill this role, because those institutions were not anchored by a stabilizing and pacifying American presence. "Twentieth century gives no encouragement to those who believe the Europeans can achieve and sustain this balance of power and keep the peace without the United States," Scowcroft wrote.[67]

The administration also had a second goal in seeking to hold Germany within NATO, which was to keep U.S. power and influence at the center of post–Cold War Europe. As U.S. officials acknowledged, NATO was "the raison d'etre for keeping U.S. forces in Europe."[68] The alliance made Washington the dominant player in European security and gave it leverage on a vast range of issues. If NATO were enervated because the most powerful state on the continent remained outside of it, NSC aide Robert Blackwill wrote, "such an outcome would forfeit the prime assets that have made the United States a postwar European power and thus have a devastating effect on the U.S. ability to influence Europe in ways that protect our political, commercial, and strategic interest."[69] America would have won the Cold War, only to lose its relevance in the peace that followed. German membership in a strong and healthy NATO, anchored by a U.S. troop presence, was therefore the central pillar of the new European order Bush aimed to construct. The president left no room for doubt on this key question: "This is vitally important for European security and stability and for the U.S."[70]

Virtually from the start, then, U.S. policy was one of backing reunification as a way of shaping the terms on which it would occur. "Our strong support for the process," Zoellick explained, "would make it more likely that the German people would voluntarily stay within Western structures."[71] The question that followed was how assertively to push that process. In Washington and Bonn alike, the original preference was for a measured approach that would take several years to unfold, that would integrate the two Germanys in stages, and that would mollify the volatility and fears that accompanied great change.[72] This was the approach Bush pursued in November and December 1989. His position, as developed by the State Department and then announced at Brussels, was that reunification should occur within the context of NATO and the European Community, respect Helsinki principles, and be "peaceful, gradual, and part of a step-by-step process."[73] Bush and Baker began building allied support for this policy, while also gently probing Gorbachev for any give in his stance. This had been a key U.S. objective at Malta, and the fact that Gorbachev did not explicitly draw a red line—instead complaining that Kohl was "in too much of a hurry"—gave hope that the gradualist approach might bring a weakened Kremlin around in the end without causing a panicky backlash along the way. "We need a formulation which doesn't scare him, but moves forward," Bush told Kohl.[74]

This commitment to gradualism even led Baker to travel to East Berlin in December, to encourage reforms that would allow the GDR government to survive long enough for a step-by-step process to work.[75] But by early 1990, the patient approach was being overtaken by events. Baker's efforts notwithstanding, the GDR government was hemorrhaging legitimacy and power. The progressive collapse of that regime, in turn, caused Kohl to conclude that it was necessary and desirable to forge ahead more quickly. "The situation is dramatic in the GDR," he told Bush; the government "has hardly any authority at all."[76] In early February, Kohl again grabbed the initiative, mooting plans for a near-term economic union between Bonn and Berlin. With pressure for unity building among the GDR population, and with that country's first democratic elections scheduled for March, there was a growing likelihood that reunification might come in months rather than years.[77]

As reunification loomed larger, so did its uncertainties and dangers. There was the question of what diplomatic arrangements would be required, given that Washington, Paris, London, and Moscow still had four-power rights in Berlin. There was the danger that a dash toward reunification might split NATO by provoking open resistance from Britain and France. Then there was the possibility that the Soviets might dig in their heels. The Kremlin understood that reunification within NATO would overturn the strategic balance and cripple Soviet power in Europe. And after taking a moderate tone at Malta, Gorbachev had veered the other way as the momentum increased. He complained that Kohl's behavior "resembles that of an elephant in a China shop," and Shevardnadze warned that "the specter of revanchism is haunting Europe in the embrace of unity and unification."[78] Soviet concerns could not be ignored, for Moscow still had roughly 400,000 troops in the GDR. Gorbachev could also cause problems via diplomacy: by allying himself with Western skeptics of German unity, demanding a full European conference to settle the German question, or insisting that reunification occur only after *both* Cold War blocs had dissolved and new pan-European structures emerged. Most disconcerting of all, Gorbachev might offer Kohl a grand bargain—reunification on the condition of German neutrality—that would severely undermine NATO and U.S. influence in Europe if accepted. Scowcroft "doubted whether Kohl wanted to leave NATO," he told British officials, "but if Gorbachev made the offer of unification in return for neutrality, he would be very tempted."[79]

For Washington, these scenarios all pointed to the need for a more active U.S. role in managing reunification, and navigating its pitfalls. It was important to get ahead of events, Scowcroft wrote. "The most dangerous course of all . . . may be to allow others to set the shape and character of a united Germany and of the future structure of European security." The United States was in strong position to mold the process if it acted decisively, Scowcroft's staff agreed, because it alone had substantial leverage with all the key players. "This constellation gives us great potential influence and opportunities to shape an outcome that meets our goals."[80]

During January and February 1990, the administration therefore began to develop a strategy to assure that the remaking of the European order proceeded according to U.S. interests. That strategy was premised, somewhat paradoxically, on the idea that speed should be treated as ally rather than adversary. As Bush and Scowcroft now realized, an accelerated process would harness, rather than fight, the energy of the East and West Germans who were driving toward unity. It would reduce the possibility that the GDR might cease to function as a state, with all the ensuing chaos and potential for violence, before that process was consummated. Just as important, an accelerated timetable would create facts on the ground building steadily toward the outcome desired by Washington, while depriving opponents of the chance to gather themselves and mount effective resistance. Scowcroft put it directly: "As absorption of the GDR into the FRG becomes a fait accompli, Soviet leverage to reshape the new FRG will decline."[81] Kohl's desire to go quickly should be affirmed; Bush should encourage the German chancellor to grasp the opportunities presented by rapid change.

Because speed carried risks, however, an accelerated process would also demand skilled diplomacy to keep events moving along the proper path. "We are about to enter the most crucial period for American diplomacy toward Europe since the formation of NATO in 1949," Scowcroft wrote to Bush. The administration must ensure that Germany was not pressured or enticed to renounce NATO membership as the price of reunification. It must forge a broad diplomatic coalition in support of U.S. and German goals. It must find a formula that would obtain Soviet acquiescence without provoking a perilous East-West confrontation. The stakes were sky high. "We are entering the end-game of the Cold War," Scowcroft wrote. "We must be impeccably prepared so that when the end-game is over, the North Atlantic Alliance and the U.S. position in Europe remain the vital instruments of peace and stability that we inherited from our predecessors."[82]

During early and mid-1990, the administration pursued three intertwined lines of diplomacy to attain this end. The first consisted of securing tight cooperation with Kohl. U.S.-German consultation was frequent and intensive throughout this period, and Bush provided diplomatic cover for the chancellor as he pushed ahead. Prior to a key summit between Kohl and Gorbachev in February, for instance, Bush sent the chancellor a letter declaring his "complete readiness . . . to see the fulfillment of the deepest national aspirations of the German people," and pledging that Washington would not let Moscow have a veto on German self-determination. "If the events are moving faster than we expected," he added, "it just means that our common goal . . . will be realized even sooner than we had hoped."[83] This letter, Kohl commented after reading it, "will one day be considered one of the great documents in German-American history."[84] Indeed, Bush's support shielded Bonn from opposition and criticism—from whatever quarter—by demonstrating that there was no daylight between Kohl and his superpower ally. It also reinforced the accelerated pace of the process by encouraging the chancellor to drive forward the internal (inter-German) aspects of reunification.

U.S. support for Kohl had a further logic as well, which was to beat back any neutralist or anti-NATO tendencies in Germany. In late January, Foreign Minister Hans-Dietrich Genscher had made worrying comments indicating that the FRG might forgo or deemphasize NATO membership to secure reunification, and that the alliance might cede pride of place to pan-European structures such as CSCE in post–Cold War Europe.[85] The Bush administration responded, over the next several weeks, by unmistakably conveying that the flip side of U.S. commitment to Kohl must be Kohl's commitment to NATO. The goal, Scowcroft and Blackwill wrote to Bush before his meeting with Kohl in February, was to "cement a historic bargain" that would alleviate concerns about Germany's future and deprive the Soviets of any chance to split Washington and Bonn on this subject. "The concept of Germany being in NATO is absolutely crucial," Bush told Kohl at the summit.[86] This approach underscored that U.S. support was essential but conditional, and thereby confirmed Kohl's own Atlanticist tendencies. The summit produced a joint statement affirming the German commitment to NATO, its military structures, and the forward deployment of U.S. troops.[87] From this point onward, Bush and Kohl projected a united front on virtually all key issues surrounding reunification.

That unity, in turn, served a second line of diplomacy, which focused on building consensus within NATO. Gorbachev would have difficulty opposing an initiative that enjoyed broad NATO support, U.S. officials believed, whereas Western dissension would abet Soviet obstruction. Accordingly, Bush and Baker undertook a series of initiatives to ensure Western cohesion. They eased allies' fears about future instability by underscoring that U.S. troops would remain in Europe. They also pledged that Washington would insist on firm German solidarity with NATO—a crucial point for Thatcher in particular—before proceeding. He would "get it from the horse's mouth and in the clearest and most specific terms," Bush told Thatcher before meeting with Kohl in February.[88] Notwithstanding Thatcher's avowed skepticism of reunification, the administration had reason to hope that these assurances might bring her along. The prime minister was "not against [reunification], but reluctant," Foreign Secretary Douglas Hurd had told Bush in January. "She sees things that need to be sorted out."[89]

In cooperation with Bonn, the administration was also sorting out the issues surrounding Mitterrand's position on reunification. In early 1990, the United States and FRG launched parallel campaigns to overcome French ambivalence. Kohl struck a key bargain with Paris, agreeing to support decisive advances in European integration in order to reassure Mitterrand that a reunified Germany would remain committed to cooperation with its neighbors. For their part, U.S. officials affirmed that Washington, too, would back further European integration and the development of CSCE, two key French priorities, as long as Paris and other countries supported a strong NATO as the bedrock of continental security.[90] What the administration wanted via its intra-alliance diplomacy, NSC aides wrote, was "a 'cocoon' of Western ties . . . to support the FRG as it faces Soviet demands."[91] Nor were sticks entirely absent from this campaign: Bush's strong advocacy of reunification conveyed the message that Washington would not look kindly upon noncooperation by the countries it protected.

As U.S. officials pursued agreement within NATO, they broadened the coalition further by addressing Eastern European concerns. Bush and Baker pointed out to Vaclav Havel that countries such as Czechoslovakia would almost certainly be safer with Germany firmly bound to a strong NATO, and that there was no other institution that could provide the same level of post–Cold War security. "We think that our presence in Europe—military and economic—has been a stabilizing presence, not a threatening presence," Bush told Havel in February. "We're convinced of that in our heart of hearts." The administration also worked to neutralize emerging friction between Bonn and Warsaw by helping obtain guarantees that a reunited Germany would respect the Oder-Neisse boundary.[92] Altogether, these measures never entirely succeeded in removing anxieties about reunification in either Eastern or Western Europe. But by mid-spring, they were at least reducing those anxieties, and narrowing the possibilities for successful opposition, sufficiently to foster consensus. "All of our allies and several Eastern European countries" were united, Bush could announce.[93]

That left the third, and most challenging, line of U.S. diplomacy: the effort to win Soviet assent. By early 1990, the U.S. approach to this task was coalescing around a bet that Soviet resistance would prove less absolute than it often appeared. Reunification within NATO would be a "bitter pill for Gorbachev to swallow," Scowcroft wrote, and Moscow had many ways to frustrate or delay that initiative.[94] Yet the calculation in Washington was that Gorbachev would ultimately decline a showdown. For if the Kremlin used force to prevent reunification, it would destroy the entire basis of Gorbachev's foreign policy and return a fading Soviet Union to the worst depths of the Cold War. Even prolonged diplomatic obstruction would be costly, because it would jeopardize East-West ties when Moscow could least afford it. By early 1990, Gorbachev's economic reforms were floundering and the treasury was bare. His political reforms—meant to create space for economic restructuring—were unleashing domestic polarization. Gorbachev's need for diplomatic achievements and foreign support to offset these other weaknesses was thus paramount. "They have little leverage," Baker would assess, "so ultimately they will have to come along."[95] The trick, then, was to structure U.S.-Soviet dealings in ways that reinforced the costs of resistance while highlighting the benefits of cooperation.

Doing so meant employing a mix of persuasion, reassurance, and pressure. The administration would have to persuade Moscow that its security was better assured with Germany inside rather than outside NATO. It would have to reassure the Soviets, by treating them with dignity, involving them in the process, and working with Bonn to devise ways of reconciling German membership in NATO with Moscow's understandable anxieties. Gorbachev "will want to see that legitimate Soviet security interests are being taken into account," Baker noted.[96] Finally, the administration must tactfully pressure the Soviets, by reinforcing that events were racing ahead, that the allies were increasingly united, and that Moscow's ties to the West hinged upon its cooperation. Washington would have to combine diplomatic soft soap with a willingness to play hardball. "The Soviets are not in a position to dictate Germany's relationship with NATO," Bush said. "To hell with that! We prevailed, they didn't. We can't let the Soviets clutch victory from the jaws of defeat."[97]

Emblematic of this approach was the Two-plus-Four mechanism devised by Baker's staff in early February. The Two-plus-Four was to serve as the diplomatic forum through which the four World War II victors settled international aspects of reunification, while the two Germanys negotiated domestic aspects. The Soviets had proposed some sort of six-power forum in January, so Two-plus-Four would meet Gorbachev's desire for an official voice and role. The group, Bush said, offered "a chance to satisfy the Soviet wish to be fully involved."[98]

The Two-plus-Four was also designed, however, to maximize Western leverage in the negotiations. Its terms of reference made reunification the explicit goal of the talks, and specified that a reunified Germany should not face restrictions on its choice of alliance. Moreover, because the Two-plus-Four brought the internal and external aspects of reunification into a single forum, U.S. officials correctly calculated that the speed of events on the ground would drive the negotiations forward, decreasing Soviet bargaining power over time. Finally, the creation of Two-plus-Four was accompanied by creation of One-plus-Three, a parallel, informal group in which the Western powers met to coordinate their positions in advance of formal negotiations with Moscow. "I prefer to call two plus four the 'two by four,'" PPS official Harvey Sicherman wrote, "because it represents in fact a lever to insert a united Germany in NATO whether the Soviets like it or not, but which gives them a role that ought to keep them out of a desperate corner." Bush himself put it more obliquely: "We are going to win the game, but we must be clever while we are doing it."[99]

The U.S. strategy began to bear fruit in February. By then, the quickening demise of the GDR had resigned Gorbachev to the inevitability of union at some future time, and left him grasping for ways to delay the process and prevent it from happening within NATO.[100] When Baker visited Moscow in early February, he subtly reminded the Soviets that their position on that issue was becoming weaker every day. "Soon Germany's internal integration will become a fact," he said. Yet Baker also emphasized persuasion and reassurance. He told Gorbachev and Shevardnadze that a neutral Germany would have to develop the military strength to defend itself—"it could very well decide to create its own nuclear potential"—whereas a Germany within NATO would be subject to U.S. constraint. At the same time, he offered a face-saving solution to the NATO question. Drawing on an idea earlier floated by Genscher, Baker proposed that a reunified Germany would be in NATO, but that the alliance would not expand its jurisdiction or military deployments into the territory of the former GDR. (This formulation was soon modified to specify that NATO jurisdiction would extend to GDR territory, but not non-German troops.) "Not an inch of NATO's present military jurisdiction will spread in an eastern direction," he said. In essence, Baker was proposing a means of bringing the new Germany into NATO, while also alleviating Kremlin concerns that the alliance would be creeping closer to Soviet borders.[101]

This proposal would later become a fount of controversy when NATO expanded beyond Germany under Clinton.[102] In early 1990, however, the idea of "special military status" for the GDR seemed a reasonable way of squaring U.S. interests with Soviet fears. Without making commitments, Gorbachev told Baker that "much in what you have said appears to be realistic." The Soviet leader accepted the Two-plus-Four mechanism, and said that "there is nothing terrifying in the prospect of a unified Germany."[103] When Kohl—buoyed by Bush's letter of support and bearing promises of economic aid—visited Moscow the next day, Gorbachev agreed in principle that the Germans themselves could decide whether to reunify.[104]

Baker came away encouraged, thinking that Gorbachev—having acceded to the concept of reunification—would eventually yield on NATO membership. As had happened after Malta, however, the Soviet position on that issue again began to harden. Gorbachev and Shevardnadze were badly conflicted, wanting cooperation with the West, but still blanching at the thought of a reunified Germany within NATO, and resenting the haste of the process. During February and March, these concerns were reinforced as other East European countries began to demand the removal of Soviet troops, and as hardliner opposition mounted in Moscow. "There could be no future for a reunified Germany in NATO," Marshal Sergey Akhromeyev said. These officials, particularly in the armed forces, demanded the neutralization and demilitarization of a reunified Germany, and argued that anything else would be an unforgivable betrayal of Soviet security.[105] Feeling this pressure, Gorbachev pivoted, declaring in March 1990 that NATO membership was "absolutely out of the question."[106]

Yet as so often since the mid-1980s, Gorbachev's position was crumbling beneath his feet. In March, pro-Kohl forces scored a huge victory in GDR elections, accelerating plans for economic union and catalyzing negotiations on other aspects of reunification. Meanwhile, the growing unity among the Western allies, and even East European countries, was leaving Moscow ever-more isolated. Having first opposed reunification, State Department officials later noted, "The Soviets became resigned to its inevitability only to find themselves outpaced by the consensus building for German membership in NATO." Finally, as Gorbachev's economic and political problems intensified, and issues such as ethnic tensions and nationalities disputes exacerbated the situation, the value of calm and productive foreign relations loomed ever larger.[107] On multiple dimensions, Gorbachev's leverage was waning and his options were narrowing.

As Moscow's position weakened, the Bush administration continued to chip away at Soviet resistance. In mid-May, Baker met Gorbachev and Shevardnadze in Moscow, carrying the message that "events in Europe will not stand still, and you risk leaving yourselves out with your current position." As a positive inducement, however, he also presented a package of nine assurances—coordinated with Kohl beforehand—to allay Soviet anxieties and neutralize the hardliner critique. He promised, among other things, that reunification would be accompanied by further East-West arms reductions, that a united Germany would reaffirm its renunciation of WMD, that non-German forces would not deploy into the former GDR, and that reunification would produce "enhanced German-Soviet economic ties." The Soviet Union could face an embittered and unconstrained Germany if it did not relent, Baker implied, or it could deal with a grateful and generous Germany if it did. Gorbachev was unlikely to accept this set of assurances on the spot, U.S. officials predicted, but "we want to foster a spirit of cooperation with the Soviets and try to gain their acquiescence over time."[108]

The administration was simultaneously taking care not to overplay its hand by seeking additional rows with Moscow. When Gorbachev imposed economic sanctions against Lithuania after it declared its independence in March, Bush resisted congressional calls for a showdown. "We do not want to complicate, for the Soviet leadership, problems that you view as internal problems," he told Shevardnadze.[109] Bush quietly urged Gorbachev to negotiate with Lithuania, as he pushed the Lithuanians to go slowly and seek dialogue. When the confrontation persisted, he firmly but nonprovocatively informed Gorbachev that he could not get Congress to approve MFN status for Moscow—a trade-boosting measure that the Soviets badly needed—without progress in resolving the crisis. Bush absorbed considerable domestic criticism for not responding more sharply, and what steps he took still annoyed Gorbachev. But the Soviet leader nonetheless acknowledged Bush's "amazing restraint," which eventually secured a pledge to deescalate the confrontation, while also avoiding a nasty rupture that might have spilled over into delicate discussions about Germany's future.[110]

None of this had been enough to win agreement when Baker visited Moscow in May. But Gorbachev's policy was evolving. The West had the upper hand and would not wait forever, Chernyaev had recently warned: "Germany will be in NATO and you will again miss the train."[111] Gorbachev and Shevardnadze were also beginning to accept the idea that a neutral Germany might well be more dangerous than a Germany anchored to NATO. "The presence of American troops can play a containing role," Gorbachev had allowed as early as February. A neutral Germany "would be a big problem," Shevardnadze agreed.[112] And finally, with multiplying domestic difficulties in the background—and with U.S. officials starting more explicitly to warn that a failure to cooperate could poison East-West relations—the conditions were aligning for a breakthrough at Gorbachev's summit with Bush in Washington in late May and early June.[113]

That summit demonstrated Bush's persistence in applying all the key elements of U.S. diplomacy. He reminded Gorbachev that the processes of reunification would soon reach fruition: "There is no force that can put a brake on them." He pointed out that the West was united, and that NATO would be "the anchor of stability" in post–Cold War Europe. He stressed the need to continue improving U.S.-Soviet relations, and told Gorbachev that "we do not have any intention to hurt the dignity of your country." Facing this full-court press, Gorbachev made a last effort to deflect the alliance issue by suggesting that Germany be tied to both NATO and the dying Warsaw Pact (a "screwy idea," Bush thought). But when Bush responded by arguing that the Helsinki accords gave Germany the right to choose its own alliance, Gorbachev unexpectedly agreed, handing a major concession to the United States.[114]

That concession did not entirely resolve the issue, because Gorbachev—having surprised and angered his own delegation—immediately began backtracking, and Shevardnadze demanded harsh restrictions on German sovereignty in the next Two-plus-Four meeting.[115] It had become clear, though, that Gorbachev himself had largely accepted that Germany would be in NATO. What remained was to find a formula that would help him swallow that outcome and sell it at home. "Although the Soviets appear to be gradually resigning themselves to the emerging realities," U.S. analysts wrote, "Moscow will require evidence that we are acting in good faith to protect its interests."[116]

Proof of good faith soon arrived in two initiatives—one U.S. and one German—meant, in Gates's words, to "bribe the Soviets out of Germany."[117] The German initiative was support for the Soviet economy. It had long been evident that economic aid would be a key bargaining chip with Moscow, and that the FRG was the obvious candidate to provide it. "You've got deep pockets," Bush had told Kohl.[118] After Gorbachev had acceded to the principle of reunification in February, Kohl had arranged for German banks to lend Moscow up to DM 5 billion. The FRG subsequently pledged another DM 1.25 billion to support Soviet troops stationed in the GDR, and in July, Kohl provided a major package of DM 12 billion, along with an interest-free loan of DM 3 billion. For Gorbachev, who had compared cash to the "oxygen" his gasping reforms needed to survive, these infusions of capital provided tangible, near-term proof of the benefits of diplomatic cooperation.[119]

The U.S. initiative was a package of NATO reforms, pushed through by Bush and Baker at an alliance summit in July. The rationale for these measures, Zoellick noted, was to "give Gorb. some things to make him more comfortable with the process"—to make a post–Cold War NATO look less menacing.[120] Adopted after difficult negotiations with leaders such as Thatcher, the July reforms included several key features: an offer to conclude nonaggression treaties with individual Warsaw Pact countries, a pledge that NATO would field smaller active forces and deploy them in less assertive ways, and a declaration that the alliance would use nuclear weapons "only as a last resort." The alliance also invited Gorbachev to address the North Atlantic Council and established military liaison programs for the bloc countries. The reforms had "begun a major transformation of the North Atlantic alliance," Bush declared. "What we tried to do," he told Gorbachev, "was to take account of your concerns."[121]

The reforms had the desired impact in Moscow; Shevardnadze said they were crucial "in making it possible for the Soviet Union to accept a united Germany as a member of NATO."[122] By this point, in fact, Gorbachev had concluded that Moscow had received what assurances and concessions it could reasonably expect, and that the Soviets now risked being left behind altogether. (Baker had continued to underscore that prospect, hinting that the Western countries might terminate their four-power rights in Berlin unilaterally, leaving Moscow isolated as reunification occurred.) Kohl's pledge to limit the size of the post-reunification *Bundeswehr* provided a final inducement for Gorbachev, who acceded to reunification within NATO at a Soviet-FRG summit in mid-July.[123] The Two-plus-Four soon concluded its work, and in early October, the FRG and the GDR were formally reunified. "Forty-five years of conflict and confrontation between East and West are now behind us," Bush reflected. "In this past year, we've witnessed a world of change."[124]

The transformations were truly profound. German reunification clearly signified the end of the Cold War, in that it accomplished the peaceful resolution of that conflict's most intractable issue. By the same token, the process of reunification demonstrated just how fundamentally the balance of power and influence between Moscow and Washington had shifted. Gorbachev ultimately acquiesced in the overturning of arrangements that his predecessors had been willing to threaten nuclear war to preserve, and as a result, the Soviet alliance structure was now broken beyond repair with the loss of its East German keystone. The Warsaw Pact would soon collapse altogether; Soviet military power was banished from Europe. The U.S. security system, by contrast, had been expanded, strengthened, and confirmed in its continuing relevance. Washington retained its preeminent role in European security—even former adversaries now agreed that the continent needed an American presence—and NATO had become a vehicle for integrating Moscow's erstwhile allies into the U.S.-led democratic community in the West.[125] If this was not "a system on our terms," as Zoellick had put it, then it was hard to imagine what would be.[126] The Cold War, bipolar era in Europe was over, and the emerging post–Cold War order on that continent bore unmistakable signs of U.S. primacy.

That emerging order also reflected the influence of deliberate U.S. policy. The Bush administration could not claim sole or even primary credit for German reunification, of course, because that event had flowed from the long-term breakdown of East European communism, because it had subsequently been propelled primarily by Kohl and the Germans themselves, and because it had involved essential contributions from Gorbachev and other actors. Yet as observers from virtually all of the principal countries involved have testified, U.S. policy was still indispensable.[127] "Without NATO's stance, and the American stance, none of this would have been possible," Kohl said.[128] Indeed, the administration had identified the goal of a united Germany and a transformed Europe even before the wall had fallen. Once the wall did come down, the administration grasped the implications, and aligned itself beside Kohl and reunification when virtually all others were reluctant or opposed. As the pace of the process then quickened, U.S. diplomacy proved vital to managing lurking dangers, to coordinating the crucial coalitions, to firmly but tactfully exploiting Western strength and Soviet weakness, and to finding opportunity and advantage in the fluidity of events. At a time when rapid change had shattered the European status quo, the Bush administration helped guide that change peacefully, purposefully, and in a distinctly unipolar direction.

The Persian Gulf War and the Unveiling of Unipolarity

The reunification of Germany on Western terms was therefore an accomplishment in which U.S. policymakers could take pride. It was not one they could savor at length, however, because the strategic shocks followed hard upon each other in the Bush years. German reunification was not yet complete when Saddam Hussein stunned the world by dispatching 1,800 tanks and 140,000 troops to invade Kuwait on August 2, 1990. The conquest and annexation of that oil-rich kingdom triggered a great international crisis over the future of the Persian Gulf and the shape of the global order, and it eventually led to by far the largest use of American force since Vietnam. When the Persian Gulf War ended in February 1991, it left Saddam humiliated and defeated but still in power, an outcome that was rather more ambiguous than the Bush administration would have liked. Where the Gulf crisis was far less ambiguous, however, was in demonstrating how unipolar the emerging post–Cold War system truly was.[129]

As discussed in chapter 5, Saddam's aggression against Kuwait grew out of an explosive cocktail of strength and weakness. Baghdad had exited the Iran-Iraq war as a regional military superpower, but one with crippling debts and incipient domestic instability. As these problems deepened in 1989–1990, Saddam became more bellicose and desperate. He issued chilling threats to "make the fire eat up half of Israel" with chemical weapons, and he increasingly focused on Kuwait as both the cause of and solution to Baghdad's economic crisis. Saddam accused the Kuwaitis of trying to destroy Iraq economically by flooding the market with cheap oil, and by slant-drilling from the Iraqi side of the contested border. "It is an aggression that is not less effective than military aggression," Saddam's foreign minister, Tariq Aziz, declared; the survival of the Iraqi regime was at stake.[130] When intimidation failed to elicit the concessions that Saddam demanded, he overpowered his wealthy but militarily defenseless neighbor instead.

Saddam's relationship with America figured centrally in this decision, but not in the way that is often supposed. By the close of the Iran-Iraq war, Saddam viewed the United States as a deeply malevolent power that was determined to thwart Iraqi ambitions and break the Baathist government. Despite Bush's efforts at engagement, these suspicions only deepened. Saddam worried that Soviet decline had left Washington hegemonic in world politics, freeing it to pursue domination of the Middle East. "If the Gulf people, along with all Arabs, are not careful," he warned, "the Arab Gulf region will be governed by the U.S. will."[131] And as Iraq's predicament worsened, Saddam frequently identified an American hand in those travails. Baathist officials alleged that Washington was inciting Israeli military action against Iraq, conspiring with dissidents to overthrow the regime, and masterminding the Kuwaiti economic strangulation campaign. "Imperialist and Zionist circles" were out to ruin Iraq, Saddam charged in July 1990. "They have used every arrow in their quiver except direct military aggression."[132] In this context, a lightning attack against Kuwait held appeal as a way of solving Iraqi economic problems *and* disrupting a U.S.-led conspiracy against the revolution. "The Americans didn't give us any rest," Saddam explained. "Our only choice was to go after the . . . circle of conspirators tasked with this mission."[133]

As these comments indicate, Saddam almost surely did not see a U.S. "green light" preceding the invasion. What he probably believed, rather, was that Iraq could overrun Kuwait and then use the threat of a prolonged, costly war to deter the United States from intervening to reverse the conquest. "Yours is a society which cannot accept 10,000 dead in a single battle," he told U.S. Ambassador April Glaspie in late July.[134] Accordingly, Saddam's diplomacy during this period was geared not toward securing American approval, but rather toward lulling Washington sufficiently to prevent it from intervening *before* the attack. If Iraq broadcast its intentions too clearly, he and his advisers worried, then outside forces would interfere. Saddam therefore ended his meeting with Glaspie on a note of reassurance, promising not to strike as long as negotiations continued. "When we meet and when we see that there is hope, then nothing will happen," he said. "Saddam has blinked," the U.S. embassy duly reported.[135]

If Saddam aimed to gain a measure of surprise, then, he clearly succeeded. U.S. officials were not blind to the more aggressive tone of Iraqi statecraft in 1989–1990, and CENTCOM had begun planning for the possibility that the next threat to Gulf security might be Baghdad rather than Tehran. Yet up until the eve of the invasion, U.S. policy remained torn between a desire to engage Iraq and the growing need to contain it. As Iraqi intimidation of Kuwait became more pronounced, for instance, the administration restated its commitment to Gulf security, and it approved token U.S. participation in military exercises with the UAE to signal that commitment. But there remained persistent hopes that Saddam would accept a diplomatic settlement, and a belief that if military action came it would be limited rather than total. When the full-on invasion occurred, Washington was thrust into a crisis for which it had hardly prepared. "Improvisation was the order of the day," recalled Haass, Scowcroft's key adviser on Gulf affairs. "There was no playbook and no contingency plan for dealing with this scenario or anything like it."[136]

What the administration did have, from the invasion onward, was a realization that Saddam's gambit represented a defining moment in American statecraft and the evolution of international politics. Most immediately, the invasion had put Saddam in a position to command the Gulf and its resources, and thereby to destroy everything that the United States had worked for in that region since 1979. By taking Kuwait, Iraq had gained control of 22 percent of the world's proven oil reserves. If Iraqi forces continued into Saudi Arabia, a scenario that initially seemed all too real, that figure would approach 50 percent.[137] Either way, Saddam would possess an outsized ability to affect global energy flows and prices, and he would have set a precedent, and attained the resources, necessary to bully his way to regional hegemony. Hussein "has clearly done what he has to do to dominate OPEC, the Gulf and the Arab world," Cheney said at an NSC meeting on August 3. "The problem will get worse, not better." "There is too much at stake," Scowcroft agreed. "We have to seriously look at the possibility that we can't tolerate him succeeding."[138]

Saddam's power grab was especially threatening because it came as Western dependence on Gulf oil was increasing. Despite conservation efforts since the 1970s, America still received 24 percent of imports from the Gulf as of the late 1980s, and its overall import dependence had grown since the shocks of 1973–1974. U.S. allies in Europe and Asia received an even greater proportion of their oil from the Gulf, with that reliance slated to increase further in coming years. Overall, the Gulf's share of world proven oil reserves had grown to nearly 70 percent by the late 1980s, with that number also expected to rise.[139] If anything, the Gulf was becoming even more critical to U.S. strategy. "It would be inimical to U.S. interest to permit any power—including Iraq—to gain dominance over Gulf oil supplies," Wolfowitz had written in July 1990. "Such dominance by a single country would enable it to dictate oil prices and production, placing the economies of the U.S. and its allies in an extremely vulnerable position that would become more precarious as Western dependence on Gulf oil continued to grow."[140]

Crucial as the oil issue was, however, the Gulf crisis transcended any specific concern about that region or its energy supplies. For as U.S. officials immediately grasped, Saddam's attack had put the very contours of global politics at risk. Following the invasion, Bush and his advisers frequently argued that the world had reached a critical juncture between the Cold War and the still-unfolding era to come, and that how the United States responded would have a defining impact on the character of that era. If Washington acquiesced, Scowcroft warned (in a memo drafted by Haass), "we would be setting a terrible precedent—one that would only accelerate violent centrifugal tendencies—in this emerging 'post-Cold War' era." The increasing fluidity of global politics might devolve into anarchy; aggressive despots like Saddam would be emboldened. Deputy Secretary of State Lawrence Eagleburger voiced this concern clearly at an early NSC meeting. "This is the first test of the post [Cold] war system," he said. "If [Hussein] succeeds, others may try the same thing. It would be a bad lesson." Bush himself soon took up the same theme. "At stake," he commented, "is the shape of the world to come."[141]

The goal of shaping that world was central to U.S. thinking throughout the crisis. If administration officials feared that passivity would lead to a dark era of chaos, they believed that decisive action could foster a very different global order. Washington could take the Gulf crisis as an opportunity to catalyze international cooperation in dealing with emerging threats, to assert American leadership in the post–Cold War environment, and to lay the foundations of a system more stable and congenial to U.S. interests. "We stand today at a unique and extraordinary moment," Bush would declare in September. "Out of these troubled times . . . a new world order can emerge: a new era—freer from the threat of terror, stronger in pursuit of justice, and more secure in the quest for peace." "There is no substitute for American leadership" in shaping that order, he argued; the United States must meet this "first test of our mettle" with firmness and resolve.[142] Bush would put it even more plainly thereafter. "The rules of the post-Cold War world are being written," he said, and America intended to lead the way in writing them.[143]

This expansive conception of U.S. interests in the Gulf predisposed the administration to take strong, and virtually immediate, action to oppose Saddam's gambit. By August 3, Bush was telling foreign leaders that "Saddam Hussein simply cannot get away with this." By the next day, Bush was lobbying Saudi officials to permit the deployment of U.S. ground troops to prevent further Iraqi advances. "We must be viewing this with more urgency," he told King Fahd. "We need to get those forces there soon or Saddam, flushed with victory, might grab the oil fields and the eastern province."[144] And by August 5, Bush was publicly declaring that "this will not stand"—a statement implying that he would do whatever necessary not simply to defend Saudi Arabia, but to reverse the aggression that had already occurred.[145] As in the case of German reunification, there was little hesitation or ambiguity in Bush's decision making. At another critical moment, he leaned forward to assert U.S. interests and shape the emerging environment.

This ethos informed a response that was extraordinarily expansive in both military and diplomatic terms. For its part, the Pentagon began a massive deployment of forces to shield Saudi Arabia and, perhaps, eventually to liberate Kuwait. "We need to get the Americans in—we need to show the flag," Powell said. The Saudis had initially balked at this idea, fearing—with the U.S. pullout from Lebanon in mind—that Washington might do enough to antagonize Saddam but not enough to defeat him. "The Saudis are concerned about our seriousness," Scowcroft said, and there were indications that the kingdom might cut its own deal with Saddam.[146] After intensive persuasion by Cheney and Bush himself, however, Fahd accepted that the Iraqi threat was sufficiently imminent, and U.S. resolve sufficiently real, to take the dramatic step of permitting non-Muslim troops on Saudi soil. Within two weeks, there were 30,000 U.S. troops with accompanying airpower in Saudi Arabia; by November, there were 250,000 troops, including heavy mechanized forces. By the time the war began in January 1991, the United States had nearly 550,000 personnel, 2,000 tanks, 1,990 aircraft, and 100 warships in the Gulf—all told, about half of U.S. combat forces worldwide.[147]

This enormous buildup was enabled by the major improvements in lift, logistics, and infrastructure that Washington and its regional partners had undertaken since 1979, without which Operation Desert Shield would have been impossible. It was equally facilitated by the global shifts underway. In mid-1990, the United States still had a Cold War–size military, but the disappearance of Cold War tensions made it feasible to redeploy assets such as the Army VII Corps from Europe to Saudi Arabia. "We could now afford to pull divisions out of Germany that had been there for the past forty years to stop a Soviet offensive that was no longer coming," Powell recalled.[148] The end of the superpower struggle freed Washington to act more boldly in post–Cold War hotspots such as the Gulf.

It also empowered the diplomatic aspect of U.S. strategy, which focused on assembling a large and diverse international coalition, operating under the aegis of the UN Security Council, to confront Saddam. From the outset, the administration had emphasized multilateralism in responding to the crisis. In part, it did so from the genuine belief that the easing of Cold War polarities allowed for greater collective security against common threats, a theme that Bush continually stressed in his public speeches.[149] In equal part, however, the administration saw multilateralism as a way of securing broadened global support and legitimacy for what was essentially hard-headed action to advance U.S. interests. The goal, Bush and Scowcroft later wrote, was to give "a cloak of acceptability to our efforts and mobilize world opinion behind the principles we wished to project." Intensive multilateral diplomacy could serve as a force multiplier and cost-defrayer for U.S. efforts, and establish a model for assertive yet consensual American leadership in the post–Cold War era. "The United States henceforth would be obligated to lead the world community to an unprecedented degree," Scowcroft believed. It should therefore "pursue our national interests, wherever possible, within a framework of concert with our friends and the international community."[150]

This diplomatic campaign began just hours after the invasion, when Baker pressed Moscow to substantiate its desire for friendship with the West by abandoning its erstwhile Iraqi client and unequivocally opposing Saddam's actions. From that point onward, tireless and often very personal diplomacy was a hallmark of Bush's policy. The president and Baker worked to rally a range of countries, from traditional U.S. allies such as Australia and the United Kingdom, to long-standing Soviet clients such as Syria and Poland, to Saddam's fellow Arabs such as Egypt and Morocco. The administration coordinated economic support and diplomatic cover to induce weaker or more vulnerable states like Turkey to support the coalition, and it prodded more affluent nations to underwrite that coalition financially. "We are protecting their interests as well as ours," one memo explained, "and it is only fair that they share the burden."[151] Moreover, Bush used subtle pressure to remind leaders such as Gorbachev how important their cooperation was to the broader relationship with America, while also remaining flexible enough to make key tactical concessions when necessary. In September 1990, for instance, Bush agreed that Moscow and Washington would cosponsor a postwar conference on Arab-Israeli issues as a way of giving Gorbachev a tangible diplomatic reward he could use to justify his policy at home.[152]

The result was a remarkable level of international solidarity. In the days after the invasion, the Security Council condemned Saddam's actions and enacted harsh economic sanctions on Iraq. In the weeks that followed, the administration mobilized a political-military coalition that cut across traditional geopolitical lines. Twenty-seven nations provided military forces, adding a total of 270,000 troops, 66 warships, 750 combat aircraft, and 1,100 tanks to the coalition effort. Likewise, Bush and Baker secured pledges of $53.8 billion in cash and in-kind assistance from countries such as Saudi Arabia, Kuwait, Japan, and Germany, covering the overall U.S. bill of $61.1 billion for operations in the Gulf almost entirely.[153] "We are seeing international cooperation that is truly historic," Bush said. "The Soviets, the Chinese, our traditional allies, our friends in the Arab world—the cooperation is unprecedented."[154]

That cooperation was a testament to the permissive diplomatic context of the early 1990s, and to the fact that Saddam's invasion had threatened and horrified so many countries around the world. What it also demonstrated, though, was just how central U.S. power and activism were to the functioning of the dawning post–Cold War order. There was simply no other country with the diplomatic leverage and connections to orchestrate a coalition of such breadth. Nor did anyone else have the power-projection capabilities to anchor that coalition militarily. "We remain the one nation that has the necessary political, military, and economic instruments at our disposal to catalyze a successful collective response," Baker said.[155] Indeed, the fact that so many countries were willing to support or subsidize U.S. action in the Gulf reflected not simply the virtues of Bush's multilateralism; it also showed a broad recognition that American leadership and power were vital to ensuring global stability after the Cold War. "The Japanese people, in the last 45 years, have been used to peace provided by you," Prime Minster Kaifu Toshiki told Bush. The Gulf crisis had underscored that reliance.[156]

The U.S.-led coalition was initially mobilized for explicitly defensive purposes: to protect Saudi Arabia while giving sanctions time to compel Saddam's withdrawal from Kuwait.[157] Bush, however, had always assumed that offensive action might be necessary, and by mid- and late October this looked ever more likely. The sanctions were battering the Iraqi economy, but Saddam remained unrepentant and his troops continued to dig in. "The basic premise" of present policy, "that sanctions will eventually present Iraq with a choice between capitulating or escalating, may prove wrong," Haass wrote.[158] If this was true, then indefinite delay would only give Saddam time to fortify his defenses, improve his WMD programs, and fracture a coalition that included Arab countries and centered on the politically awkward presence of U.S. forces on sacred Muslim ground. "Frankly, I am far from sanguine that time works in our favor," Bush said. In early November, the administration therefore secured Saudi consent to deploy the extra troops needed for an "offensive option." That option would strengthen coercive diplomacy, Scowcroft wrote, and provide a "real alternative should diplomacy fail."[159]

For Bush, the shift from defense to offense required no great agonizing, because a willingness to fight over Kuwait flowed naturally from his perception of what was at stake in the crisis. In many ways, in fact, war was actually the most attractive way of resolving the dispute. Saddam's invasion had shown that the regional balance of power that Washington had sought to construct during the 1980s was really no balance at all, and that Gulf stability would be tenuous so long as Iraq was armed to the teeth and ruled by aggressive leadership. "It is not clear that an outcome that leaves Saddam in power and Iraq's industrial and war-making capability intact constitutes a viable much less optimal outcome from our perspective," Haass had written in August. At best, a peaceful Iraqi withdrawal would leave the United States faced with an expensive and diplomatically awkward commitment, probably involving large numbers of American troops stationed permanently in the Gulf, to contain a still-dangerous Saddam. At worst, Washington might soon face an even deadlier foe. "Simply pushing Iraq back with its industrial, military and leadership intact all but ensures that in a few years we will have a much more aggressive and capable Iraq (with biological and nuclear weapons) on our hands," Haass noted.[160]

That prospect powerfully underscored the appeal of military solutions. Bloody as a war with Saddam might be, it would offer an opportunity to smash his armed forces, degrade or destroy his WMD programs, and perhaps so humiliate him that he fell from power. To be sure, the administration did not want to so weaken Iraq that the country fractured or Iran was able to dominate the Gulf. But from August onward, Bush and many top aides had seen the wrecking of Iraq's offensive capabilities—and ideally, the toppling of Saddam—as the optimal outcome. "All will not be tranquil until Saddam Hussein is history," Bush said.[161] In this context, there was no substitute for decisive military action. For as the DIA predicted in a key estimate circulated before the war, a major conflict would have numerous positive effects flowing from the reduction of the Iraqi military: "The probable end to Saddam Husayn's rule . . . the preservation of friendly moderate regimes in the region . . . the containment of Iraq, and at least the temporary slowdown of the arms race." Washington could then help craft a more durable and organic regional equilibrium; major peacetime deployments of U.S. troops would probably be unnecessary. War, in other words, offered the best path to stability and peace in the Gulf.[162]

Setting the conditions for that war entailed new military, diplomatic, and political tasks. On the military front, the Pentagon had to craft a war plan to achieve U.S. aims at tolerable cost. While CENTCOM had cobbled together a serviceable defensive plan after August 2, its initial offensive plan was so unimaginative—it featured an up-the-gut assault into the Iraqi defenses—that civilian leaders wondered whether it was designed to be unworkable. Under heavy pressure from Cheney and other civilian officials, the uniformed military changed tack, with CENTCOM head Norman Schwarzkopf overseeing preparation of a more creative plan that better exploited U.S. advantages. That plan envisioned a strategic air campaign to pound Iraqi infrastructure, military-industrial, and command-and-control targets; a theater air campaign to isolate and attrite enemy units in the forward Kuwaiti Theater of Operations (KTO); and a land campaign that would use dominant fires and mobility to paralyze, envelop, and destroy Saddam's best forces. In essence, CENTCOM aimed to liberate Kuwait and shatter Saddam's military in the process. "We have the capability to obliterate his military structure," Bush told Israeli prime minister Yitzhak Shamir. "We have a beautifully planned operation, calculated to demoralize him forever."[163]

Putting that plan into effect, in turn, required a renewed diplomatic campaign to win international approval of military action should Saddam refuse to withdraw. During November, Bush and Baker lobbied relentlessly among UN Security Council members, Arab states, and other constituencies. They argued that the credible threat of war was essential to any hopes for a peaceful outcome, and that reversing Iraqi aggression was vital to establishing a secure post–Cold War order. They made clear that Washington earnestly sought multilateral endorsement, while also subtly warning countries such as China that opposition to the relevant Security Council resolution would come at a price. "We would not understand if they stood in the way," Baker told Chinese officials.[164] Similarly, the administration traded on the need of the Soviets and other countries for good relations with Washington to ensure their support or acquiescence. "People wanted to stay close to us," Baker later said, and U.S. diplomacy made the most of that fact.[165] Saddam's refusal to make any move toward withdrawal, and his continued holding of U.S. and other hostages, further bolstered the American case. In late November, the Security Council passed a resolution authorizing military action if Iraq did not withdraw by January 15.

That left the political preparations for war, which were perhaps most daunting. The administration had built strong domestic support for the initial, defensive deployment by using a mix of arguments it would draw on throughout the crisis. Baker stressed the economic case for intervention, saying that the Gulf crisis was "about a dictator who, acting alone and challenged, could strangle the global economic order."[166] Bush cast the issue in strategic and moral terms. He frequently compared Saddam to Hitler, and warned that the consequences of appeasement now would be as devastating as in the 1930s. He also argued that the country had a chance—and responsibility—to set post–Cold War affairs on a steadier and more humane footing. What the United States sought, he declared, was "a world where the rule of law supplants the rule of the jungle. A world in which nations recognize the shared responsibility for freedom and justice. A world where the strong respect the rights of the weak."[167] Vital issues of principle and pragmatism were at issue, Bush contended, and America must not falter.

Powerful as these arguments were, however, the prospect of moving from deterrence to combat proved controversial. The U.S. ascendancy of the 1980s had not erased post-Vietnam qualms about military intervention, and misadventures such as Lebanon had only accentuated those fears. In late 1990, polling revealed that two-fifths of Americans thought it "somewhat" or "very likely" that war against Iraq would become "another prolonged situation like the Vietnam conflict."[168] Antiwar observers—including most congressional

Democrats, as well as numerous former military officials—called for giving sanctions more time, and accused Bush of a rush to war that might cause 15,000 U.S. casualties. "We must recall the lessons of the Vietnam war," warned one senator. Likewise, Edward Kennedy would ask the Senate to "save thousands of American soldiers . . . from dying in the desert in a war whose cruelty will be exceeded only by the lack of any rational necessary for waging it."[169] Bush believed that shaping the post–Cold War era required unleashing U.S. power; whether he could secure domestic backing for that mission remained open to question.

Bush eventually overcame this resistance, but only narrowly and with great effort. Despite some initial reservations about asking Congress to vote on the prospective use of force against Saddam, the administration did ultimately invest its full prestige in such a campaign. In public and in private, Bush argued that the Vietnam analogy was a red herring—that the United States *had* learned the lessons of the past and would bring overwhelming power to bear. "If we must use force it will be decisive," he told congressional leaders. "The parallels to Vietnam do not and will not bear scrutiny." Bush also rebutted arguments that time was on America's side, warning that hesitation now would lead to less attractive options later. "We . . . pay a high economic price for every day that passes," he said. "And Saddam is using time to upgrade his military forces and to develop unconventional weapons. Should war come, waiting could result in higher U.S. and allied casualties."[170]

These arguments began to shift the debate in Bush's favor preceding the January 15 deadline. Meanwhile, the administration deflected charges of a rush to war by demonstrating that it was exhausting avenues for a peaceful settlement. To this end, Bush sent Baker to meet Aziz in Geneva on January 9. The secretary brought no concessions: he restated the demand for immediate and unconditional withdrawal, and informed Aziz that the coalition was prepared to inflict catastrophic damage. "If conflict comes, your forces will face devastating superior fire-power and forces," Baker said. "Should war begin—God forbid—it will be fought to a swift decisive conclusion." Baker also sharply warned Aziz against using chemical weapons, promising that "the American people will demand vengeance."[171] As Bush had expected, this approach did not produce a diplomatic breakthrough. But the meeting did highlight Iraqi determination to hold onto Kuwait, and thereby clinched the case for action. On January 12, Congress passed a use-of-force resolution, 250-183 in the House and 52-47 in the Senate. Three days later, the UN deadline passed, and on January 17, coalition airstrikes began.

As the war commenced, Bush reaffirmed his desire for a resounding victory. On January 15, he had signed NSD-54, which explicitly committed the United States not simply to liberating Kuwait but to eviscerating Iraqi military might. U.S. forces were to destroy Saddam's WMD facilities and his command, control, and communications capabilities; to eliminate the elite Republican Guards "as an effective fighting force"; and to inflict such damage as to "weaken Iraqi popular support for the current government." The United States had once aligned with Saddam's regime to shore up Gulf stability. It now aimed to emasculate, and perhaps destroy, that regime in the name of post–Cold War security in the Gulf and beyond.[172]

The coalition military campaign that began on January 17 was thus focused on breaking Iraqi power. Yet what was most remarkable about that campaign was what it revealed about American military muscle. During the 1970s and 1980s, the United States had invested in advanced concepts and weapons systems that were meant to offset Soviet numerical superiority and give Washington a competitive edge over a dangerous rival. In early 1991, American forces were now applying those capabilities in a world where the Soviet threat was disappearing, and where the enemy was a Third World military that looked impressive on paper but was far less capable than the global superpower U.S. troops had trained to fight. The result was a historic mismatch. The Gulf War demonstrated how yawning the gap between the United States and its potential post–Cold War adversaries was, and it showed how information-age technology was ushering in a "revolution in military affairs" with America at the forefront.

These dynamics were amply demonstrated by the air war. Iraq possessed a fairly sophisticated air defense system, featuring 700 fighter aircraft, 7,000 antiaircraft guns, and 16,000 surface-to-air missiles. Yet despite fears that this system might inflict heavy losses, the United States and its allies seized command of the skies almost immediately. Terrain-hugging Tomahawk cruise missiles, F-117A stealth fighter-bombers, EF-111 electronic warfare aircraft, Navy F/A-18s and A-6s armed with high-speed antiradiation missiles, and other weapons and platforms that had been developed for use against the Soviets now laid waste to Iraqi air defenses on the first night of the war. Likewise, U.S. interceptors began to wreak havoc on Iraq's fighter force, in many cases using the over-the-horizon perspective provided by AWACS to destroy enemy jets before they were even within visual range. What remained of the Iraqi air force soon fled to Iran, giving the coalition nearly uncontested aerial supremacy, and allowing it to mount 116,000 sorties during the war while incurring astonishingly low losses of just 52 fixed-wing aircraft.[173]

Many of those sorties were part of a punishing six-week bombing campaign against targets in Kuwait and Iraq. That campaign was an exercise in relentlessness, involving daytime and nighttime strikes, carried out from different altitudes and directions, by a range of aircraft, from B-52s to F-111Fs to F-15Es to F-117As. U.S. airpower pummeled strategic targets such as Iraqi government facilities, WMD programs, command-and-control nodes, and critical infrastructure, making effective use of precision-guided munitions to inflict significant—in some cases, catastrophic—damage at historically efficient rates of expenditure. U.S. and coalition aircraft were also hammering Iraqi forces in the KTO, destroying hundreds of tanks and artillery pieces, badly disrupting command and logistics, and putting Saddam's army in a severely weakened position before the ground war even began. By mid-February, Air Force officials were reporting the "destruction of 30 per cent of tanks, 31 per cent of armored vehicles, [and] 44 per cent of artillery pieces with Iraqi front-line units estimated at 50 per cent of troop strength." "Iraqi army starting to crack," Powell reported.[174] After the war, analysts debated just how effective U.S. airpower had been; what was indisputable was that the conflict revealed a level of aerial dominance that took even experts by surprise.[175]

That aerial dominance was particularly manifest when Saddam surprised the coalition by ordering a multidivision attack toward the Saudi port of al-Khafji in late January. The operation was intended to disrupt the coalition war plan, by provoking a premature ground campaign that would allow Iraqi defenders to inflict unacceptable casualties on U.S. forces. In the event, however, the attacking Iraqi units soon found themselves taking terrible punishment from above. American A-10s and other ground-attack craft mauled some units so badly as to prevent them from even joining the battle. One brigade, an Iraqi after-action report noted, was so damaged that the "only thing that they had [left] was their name." Those units that did reach al-Khafji were forced to withdraw lest they, too, be decimated. One Iraqi prisoner later said that his unit had absorbed more damage from thirty minutes of bombing around al-Khafji than from eight years of combat against Iran. The battle even had a chastening effect on Saddam himself; he claimed victory but refrained from further offensive operations.[176]

As the air campaign progressively neutralized Iraqi capabilities, the chief diplomatic priority was to neutralize threats to coalition solidarity. Bush had expected that Saddam would try to short-circuit Operation Desert Storm by rupturing the anti-Iraq forces, and once the airstrikes started, the Baathist leader had moved to do just that. His forces fired dozens of Scud missiles at Israel, in hopes of inciting a disproportionate response that would polarize regional sentiment and split the coalition along Arab-Israeli lines. The human toll of these attacks was minimal, but the psychological impact on Israelis was not. "There's feeling in Israel that we are at war," Defense Minister Moshe Arens said. "Israelis are on edge living with fear." On more than one occasion, the Israeli military stood poised to strike back with air and potentially also commando operations into western Iraq—just the sort of reaction that Bush worried might cleave Washington from its Arab partners.[177]

Preventing that reaction required all of the administration's leverage and acumen. The Pentagon sent Patriot air defense missiles to Israel, and CENTCOM devoted a sizable proportion of airstrikes to hunting Scud launchers. Neither the Patriots nor the Scud hunt were nearly as effective in *destroying* enemy missiles as was initially thought, two blots on the U.S. military's wartime performance. Nevertheless, the Patriots did provide psychological reassurance to Israelis, and the Scud hunt drastically *reduced* the number of launches.[178] Meanwhile, Bush and Cheney exerted strong pressure on the Israelis not to retaliate—even denying them the IFF (identification, friend or foe) codes necessary to safely transit coalition airspace—while also reminding Arens and Shamir that a successful reprisal could still have counterproductive effects. It was imperative to "keep in mind our mutual goal of dealing a decisive blow to Iraq—something that can only be accomplished by the continued effectiveness of the U.S.-led coalition," Bush wrote to Shamir.[179] In the end, these tactics produced the intended restraint. Israel refrained from intervention, removing the gravest diplomatic danger to the war effort.

Bush dispatched another diplomatic challenge as coalition forces prepared to initiate the ground offensive. Throughout the Gulf crisis, Gorbachev had sought to balance his need for U.S. support with his desire to win domestic and international plaudits by brokering a diplomatic settlement. Once the air war began, he had asked Bush to halt the bombing and negotiate. Iraq "has been taught a lesson," he argued. "What is the purpose of continuing military action?"[180] As a subsequent ground war loomed, Gorbachev redoubled his efforts. He proffered a series of Soviet-brokered agreements whereby Saddam would pledge to remove some or all of his troops from Kuwait by a specified date, in exchange for a cease-fire, a rapid lifting of economic sanctions, and perhaps other concessions. "What do we prefer," Gorbachev asked Bush, "a political method or a military action, i.e. a ground offensive?"[181]

None of Gorbachev's proposals were remotely acceptable in Washington, precisely because the administration did prefer a "military action" to a "political method." "If [Iraqis] crack under force, better than [withdrawal]," Bush said.[182] Accordingly, the president responded with the mix of politeness and firmness that increasingly characterized U.S.-Soviet relations. To avoid alienating Gorbachev, Bush listened carefully to each proposal and assured him that "I do appreciate your efforts."[183] But he also affirmed that there would be no cease-fire "until a massive withdrawal is underway," and he rejected each of Gorbachev's ideas in turn. "We just can't let this guy off the hook," Bush believed.[184] With Soviet influence continually eroding, Gorbachev had little choice but to accept the decision. "We're doomed to be friends with America, no matter what it does," Chernyaev wrote. "Otherwise we'd again face isolation and everything will go haywire."[185] The entire episode indicated how much the power dynamics between Moscow and Washington had shifted in recent years, and how determined Bush was to see the war to a successful conclusion.

That determination was amply evident in the ground campaign that began on February 24. The final CENTCOM plan for that campaign featured synchronized operations across hundreds of miles of battlefield. U.S. and coalition troops would assault the main defensive belts in Kuwait, to fix enemy forces and lure reinforcing Republican Guard units forward. Simultaneously, 18,000 Marines would feign an amphibious landing on the Kuwaiti coast to distract Iraqi forces and pull them deeper into the KTO. As all this happened, the decisive action would unfold far from the principal Iraqi defenses. Airborne units would execute coordinated drops in the Iraqi rear, to seize staging areas and help seal the forward theater. Finally, some 270,000 U.S., British, and French troops that had covertly crossed 200 miles of Saudi desert prior to the fighting would execute a giant "left hook," driving north before slicing across southern Iraq from west to east. This left hook would pin Iraqi units—especially armor and Republican Guard—in the KTO, where they would be destroyed by coalition tanks and airpower. All the while, intensive airstrikes would hamper and immobilize Iraqi forces, preventing them from maneuvering effectively to blunt the coalition attack.

It was a bold plan, and the initial execution exceeded all reasonable expectations. U.S. forces breached the key belts in Kuwait almost immediately, and within two days the coalition had reached Kuwait City. Airborne assaults were simultaneously creating chaos in the enemy's rear, while the left hook—although moving more slowly than other parts of the attack—was progressively flanking the KTO and demolishing Iraqi armor in its path. Overall, what Saddam had touted as the "mother of all battles" had become an unmitigated rout. Iraqi forces were being cut to pieces, surrendering en masse, or fleeing northward to escape the onslaught. As they did so, coalition airpower took a horrific toll, turning the main road from Kuwait to Iraq into the aptly named "Highway of Death." By February 26–27, Kuwait was largely liberated and the coalition was on the verge of trapping huge swaths of Saddam's forces. As one postwar survey concluded, Desert Storm was "one of the most operationally successful wars in history."[186]

The effectiveness of U.S. arms in the Gulf was partially a function of Iraqi military weaknesses, which were glaringly exposed by combat against a first-world adversary.[187] As with the air war, however, what allowed U.S. forces to so ruthlessly exploit those weaknesses were the leaps in training, doctrine, and technology made over the prior fifteen years. The Gulf war demonstrated the potency of concepts such as AirLand Battle, which coalition forces implemented (in adapted fashion) by combining bold maneuver and penetration with immobilizing strikes deep in the enemy's rear. It likewise validated the importance of recent technological breakthroughs. Joint Surveillance Target Attack Radar System (JSTARS) battle management aircraft provided real-time situational awareness, while satellite navigation enabled coordinated movement across unmarked desert. Thermal imaging and infrared technology allowed U.S. forces to "own the night," and digital fire-control computers and advanced sensors dramatically improved the accuracy and lethality of American fires. As William Perry, an original author of the offset strategy, assessed after the war, Desert Storm revealed that the United States had achieved "a revolutionary advance in military capability." In the Gulf, the net result was devastating damage to Iraqi forces, achieved at historically low loss rates (around 350 dead) for the coalition. Iraqi losses "were so lopsided—roughly a thousand to one—that there is virtually no historical precedent," Perry wrote.[188]

The coalition advance was so rapid, in fact, that it became a catastrophic success. CENTCOM had not planned for such a precipitous Iraqi collapse, and by February 27, the one-sided nature of the conflict was causing problems. With Kuwait essentially freed, and the coalition killing large numbers of fleeing Iraqis, there were growing pressures—from Schwarzkopf and Powell, and also from U.S. allies—to declare victory and end the war. Bush and his top aides unanimously agreed, believing (mistakenly) that nearly all of Saddam's armor had been trapped by the left hook. "Their armor was so decimated that they no longer constitute a military threat to their neighbors," Bush said. Noting that he liked "the symbolism of this war having been over in just 100 hours," Bush decided to end the fighting almost immediately, via unilateral cease-fire early on February 28.[189] Any desire to press on to Baghdad, or simply continue the onslaught for another day, was tempered by diplomatic concerns, a belief that Saddam was unlikely to survive the drubbing he had already absorbed, and fear of stumbling into an occupation for which U.S. forces had not prepared. "We do not want to screw this up with a sloppy, muddled ending," Bush said.[190]

That, however, was precisely what Bush got. It soon emerged that improved situational awareness had not fully dispelled the fog of war, and that Bush had halted the fighting one day too early. For contrary to Schwarzkopf's assurances, his forces had not fully "closed the gate" on Iraqi units in the KTO. The speed of the U.S. advance into Kuwait had actually pushed those units farther north than CENTCOM had expected, and amid poor communication between Schwarzkopf and his subordinates, he and Powell had recommended—and Bush approved—halting the left hook just short of severing the remaining escape routes. A generally effective decision-making system had misfired amid imperfect information and the exhaustion produced by months of incessant crisis management. Following the cease-fire, over 800 Iraqi tanks and 100,000 soldiers exploited this unintended generosity to elude the trap. Furthermore, because Schwarzkopf lacked detailed instructions for handling the abrupt termination of hostilities, he made the additional error of allowing Iraqi forces to continue using their helicopters when the terms of the cease-fire were officially settled at a hastily arranged conference on March 3.[191]

Both of these mistakes soon took on enormous significance. As the fighting ended, Gates recalled, "We genuinely believed . . . that the magnitude of the defeat was so overwhelming that the army would take out Saddam when the war was over."[192] Yet what transpired was not a military coup but mass uprisings by southern Shiites and northern Kurds. Saddam's regime momentarily teetered on the brink, but the Iraqi leader soon steadied himself and used his remaining forces to brutally suppress the revolts. The Bush administration sat passively to the side. Having hoped to catalyze Saddam's removal *without* destroying the Iraqi state, the administration now declined to intervene in a bloody, sectarian civil war that might indeed fracture Iraq or bring Iranian-backed Shiites to dominance. The paralyzing fear in Washington, Ross recalled, was that "this was going to create a new Lebanon" in the Gulf.[193] Given a free hand, Saddam reconstituted his domestic authority at a cost of tens of thousands of lives. "I'm not sure how to get him out of power," Bush soon confessed.[194]

Ironically, then, a war that was halted to avoid a sloppy ending left an aftermath that was undeniably messy. Saddam remained in power, his military might dramatically reduced from pre-1991 levels but still potent enough to cause concern. "Even in its presently weakened state," Assistant Secretary of Defense Henry Rowen reported, "Iraq is still much stronger than any of its neighbors to the south."[195] In this setting, the administration affirmed that

Iraq would remain a pariah state as long as Saddam ruled, and the Security Council enforced a harsh sanctions-and-inspections regime to ensure that Iraqi WMD stockpiles were destroyed and the terms of the cease-fire honored. "Saddam Hussein is sanctioned forever," Bush said.[196] That endeavor, however, quickly turned into a prolonged cat-and-mouse game with the still-cagey Saddam. It also necessitated a persistent U.S. military presence throughout the 1990s—punctuated with periodic strikes on Iraq—to ensure compliance and hold containment in place. It was becoming undeniable, as one Pentagon study noted as early as 1992, that "decisive military victory in regional conflict does not necessarily bring permanent peace."[197] The war against Saddam had not resolved the long crisis of Gulf security; it had simply given that crisis different form.

As the 1990s progressed, this state of semiwar in the Gulf would also give crucial momentum to the problems of terrorism and Islamic radicalism. Even as Operation Desert Storm was ongoing, one NSC paper had predicted that "a permanent U.S. presence will provide a rationale for, and could become a target for, the terrorist threat which will outlive the war."[198] Sure enough, the long-term stationing of American troops in Saudi Arabia would become increasingly destabilizing for the Saudi regime over time, while also motivating lethal jihadist attacks against a perceived U.S. occupation of Muslim holy ground. By 1995–1996, Islamist radicals were bombing U.S. military facilities and personnel in Saudi Arabia. More broadly, the U.S. presence was becoming what Wolfowitz would later call a "principal recruiting device" for an al-Qaeda organization that was now setting its sights on American targets in the region and beyond.[199] Well into the post–Cold War era, the aftermath of the conflict with Saddam would remain a source of frustration and blowback for Washington. By the late 1990s, some analysts were claiming that America's stunning operational triumph had turned into a strategic defeat.

This was not the legacy Bush had hoped the war would leave. But amid the regret about Saddam's political survival and its consequences, it was easy to forget what had been accomplished. From the earliest days of the crisis, Bush had recognized that the Iraqi invasion was a critical moment in both regional and global affairs, and that decisive action was imperative. From a more or less standing start, the administration had then directed a prodigious shift of personnel and materiel halfway around the world, it had coordinated an international coalition of striking size and diversity, and it had mobilized domestic support for America's largest war since Vietnam. When that conflict eventually came, the administration oversaw a campaign that liberated Kuwait far more quickly and cheaply than virtually anyone had thought possible, that ensured continued access to the Gulf oil on which the global market economy depended, and that significantly diminished Iraqi military power and left Saddam much weaker and more isolated than before. In doing all of this, Bush had sent a strong signal that Washington would not allow the post–Cold War world to devolve into anarchy. Rather, it would use its power to maintain a certain level of order and stability. Messy ending aside, this was a record of enviable achievement.

At the level of global politics, in fact, the Persian Gulf War represented a key inflection point in the opening of the unipolar era. The conflict underscored that military power was still the *ultima ratio* of world affairs, and that U.S. military power was the indispensable guarantor of post–Cold War security. Indeed, it showed that the United States had a truly commanding military lead over any likely adversary, and the will to use that advantage decisively when vital interests were at stake. Just as significantly, the conflict demonstrated that America possessed a unique ability to rally international support in dealing with common threats, and that it could win widespread legitimacy for the assertive use of its power—all at a time when the Soviet capacity to influence major global crises had become minimal. In each of these respects, the Gulf crisis signaled the rise of America's post–Cold War primacy. "The U.S. clearly emerges from all of this as the one real superpower in the world," Cheney observed. "The capacity of the United States for leadership . . . has been demonstrated once again."[200]

From early 1991 onward, this impression was widely shared, both in Washington and abroad. "Today, no one questions the reality of only one superpower and its leadership," Gates declared in May.[201] He was not exaggerating by much. U.S. officials in Europe reported that the war had caused "a renewed sense of reliance on America for security and global leadership," by demonstrating that international security required powerful defenders. "If before the war we were convinced of the need for a U.S. presence, after the effectiveness and efficiency shown by the U.S., we are all the more convinced now," Italian Prime Minister Giulio Andreotti said.[202] The conflict had an equivalent effect in Japan. "The leadership, determination, diplomatic skill, and military efficiency displayed by the U.S. stunned many Japanese," the American embassy reported. "There is a renewed recognition here that for the foreseeable future Japan cannot match our ability in any of these areas nor should it try to do so."[203]

For many observers, then, the Persian Gulf War revealed the reality of U.S. primacy far more starkly than before. For American leaders, the conflict also underscored the necessity of that primacy. From the perspective of the Bush administration, events in the Gulf confirmed quite sharply that the post–Cold War world would be a promising but also a potentially very nasty place. Saddam's gambit had raised the possibility that a world characterized by an overriding Soviet threat might give way to a world in which newer dangers—such as aggressive authoritarian powers seeking to dominate critical regions—menaced the global order. It followed that decisive U.S. leadership, rooted in unchallenged U.S. power, was vital to ensuring that the era of bipolar rivalry was replaced by something better and not something worse. "It's only the United States that can lead," Bush wrote during the crisis. "All countries in the West clearly have to turn to us."[204] This idea would remain centrally important as the administration articulated a U.S. global strategy for the unipolar era.

Primacy and Post–Cold War Strategy

The need to articulate that strategy was highlighted by the third strategic shock of the Bush years, the fall of the Soviet Union. That event represented the culmination of the far-reaching global changes that had been remaking the world environment since the 1970s, and it turned what years earlier had been a powerful strategic rival into a collection of independent states consumed by their own weakness and instability. By doing so, the Soviet collapse did more than just dramatize how commanding America's post–Cold War position really was. It also helped crystallize a primacist U.S. strategy meant to perpetuate and exploit that position.

As discussed in earlier chapters, the breakdown of the Soviet state was rooted in deep-seated trends that had been enervating Moscow's power since the 1970s and even before, and that had continued to worsen during the 1980s. Yet in crucial respects, the primary author of that breakdown was the man who set out to reverse those trends.[205] By 1989–1990, reforms that Gorbachev had meant to revitalize the Soviet system were destroying its pillars instead. Perestroika had become radical enough to destroy the old command economy, but not radical enough to force a decisive shift to a functioning market system. Stagnation thus turned into unmitigated free fall. GNP growth went from an anemic 1.5 percent in 1989 to a cataclysmic negative 12 percent in 1990, and shortages of basic goods were alarmingly frequent and severe. Economic collapse, in turn, undercut Gorbachev's popularity and raised fundamental questions about the future of the Soviet state. "The people do not want to pay for 70 years of criminal policies," Chernyaev noted. "They will never understand why, in order to become a civilized country . . . you have to go through hunger, collapse, depravity, crime."[206]

Political liberalization was just as destabilizing. Gorbachev had launched his "democratization" program to outflank hardliners and create room for economic reform. He never fully succeeded in that respect, but the increasingly aggressive political opening had momentous consequences nonetheless. It undermined the unity and authority of the Communist Party, whose iron discipline was so central to the Soviet system. It mobilized new political actors that Gorbachev could not control, and created competing loci of power and legitimacy. In effect, political reform fractured the existing order without achieving consensus around what should take its place. "Gorbachev has yet to fashion a coherent system of legitimate power around new state institutions to replace the old party-dominated, Stalinist one he has extensively dismantled," Jack Matlock, now the U.S. ambassador to the Soviet Union, reported.[207] Nor was this the extent of it—still other reforms were compounding the basic effect. Gorbachev's repudiation of key Marxist-Leninist concepts was vital to his foreign-policy and domestic innovations, but it undermined the socialist ideal that had long united Soviet elites, and weakened the ideological glue that held the multinational state together. Finally, the loss of Eastern Europe led to recriminations that further splintered the Soviet elite and emboldened proponents of radical change at home. The very integrity of the system was now fraying; the drive for reform had unleashed the forces of disintegration.

As the strength of the Soviet state withered, those centrifugal forces began to pull the union apart. The Baltic states agitated for independence, and nationalism ran rampant. Politicians such as Russia's Boris Yeltsin worked assiduously to strengthen the republics at the expense of the center, using Gorbachev's own democratic reforms to strengthen their leverage in an escalating political war against the Soviet state. Political polarization surged, while ethnic tensions and violence threatened. Amid the mounting chaos, Gorbachev—who had been lionized in the West for his reforms—now found himself isolated and even reviled at home. The Soviet leader was forced to execute a series of political zigzags meant to sustain his reforms while also conciliating hardliners, but the effect was to alienate him from reactionaries and liberals alike. "He is no longer regarded with respect or interest; at best, he is pitied," Chernyaev wrote. "He has outlived his achievements, while disasters and chaos exacerbate the people's irritation with him."[208] Gorbachev had fundamentally changed the Soviet Union, but hardly as he intended. "The USSR is in the midst of a historical transformation that threatens to tear the country apart," the CIA had reported in November 1990. "The old Communist order is in its death throes."[209]

Those death throes climaxed in 1991, as last-ditch efforts at resuscitation failed. Gorbachev had said that he wanted to have "a renewal take place in Russia without blood, without civil war," and his refusal to endorse massive repression left him only the option of preserving a looser union through a new voluntary association among the republics.[210] That initiative looked promising for a time, but it was consistently complicated by the growing assertiveness of Gorbachev's rivals, and by the disintegrative processes that he himself had catalyzed. By threatening to dilute the power of the Soviet state, moreover, the new union treaty provoked the hardliners into attempting their own final gambit, which backfired far more spectacularly. That gambit took the form of an ill-executed coup attempt in August 1991, which quickly collapsed amid popular resistance, international opprobrium, and divisions within the military. The upshot was not to save the Soviet system, but to fatally discredit the institutions—the party, the KGB, the military—that might conceivably have rallied to hold it together. In the aftermath, what remained of Gorbachev's authority evaporated, power flowed irreversibly away from the center, and the republics declared independence and gutted the union from within. By the end of the year, the Soviet state had ceased to exist. "The debate in our union on what kind of state to create took a different track from what I thought right," Gorbachev lamented.[211]

As the Soviet Union endured its terminal crisis in 1990–1991, U.S. views on that process were actually quite ambivalent. More hawkish advisers, such as Cheney, favored using U.S. influence to encourage the devolution of power from the center to the republics, from Gorbachev to Yeltsin, and generally to accentuate the disintegrative forces that might kill off America's adversary once and for all. "I wanted to be more aggressive," Cheney later said.[212] Bush, Baker, and Scowcroft were more restrained, however, because there was as much reason to fear as welcome what might follow. The collapse of the Soviet state was hardly guaranteed to birth stable democracies. It might instead cause chaos, violence, and resurgent authoritarianism across a huge landmass; it might also throw the status of the mammoth Soviet nuclear arsenal into question. Similarly, American support for declension might spook Soviet hardliners and incite just the right-wing coup that U.S. officials had long feared. Perhaps most important, a president who would take calculated risks but disliked unnecessary ones hesitated to abandon a leader—Gorbachev—who had been so incredibly forthcoming in favor of politicians—such as Yeltsin—who were unknown quantities at best. "I hope Gorbachev survives," Bush said. "He's been good to work with so far."[213]

Seeking a Soviet breakup was thus an alluring but potentially a very dangerous idea. These competing impulses produced a policy that was itself hedged and cautious in several respects. Diplomatically, the administration began reaching out to figures such as Yeltsin, but it also affirmed its support for Gorbachev and warned him of impending coup threats. "You are our man," Bush said.[214] Economically, Bush and Baker arranged an emergency infusion of Saudi funds to bolster Gorbachev, but turned aside pleas for more sizable Western aid. "We should get away from schemes that simply pour money down a rathole," Scowcroft commented.[215] With respect to the fate of the union itself, Bush's policy was equally ambiguous. The president urged Moscow not to use force or coercion against the republics, thereby effectively encouraging the nationalism at work. Yet he also supported Gorbachev's union treaty, and warned the leaders of republics such as Ukraine against making a destabilizing rush to the exit. "Americans will not support those who seek independence in order to replace a far-off tyranny with a local despotism," Bush declared in Kiev. "They will not aid those who promote a suicidal nationalism based on ethnic hatred."[216] Confronting a fraught and uncertain situation, Bush hewed to the middle ground.

At the time and after, this policy was maligned for its apparent indecisiveness.[217] Yet while it is true that the administration did not do as much as it might have to encourage a Soviet collapse, it is easy to take this criticism too far. A policy of sidelining Gorbachev—and openly supporting the forces that were subverting the Soviet state—almost certainly would have added to the polarization underway, raising rather than lowering the likelihood of violence. It also would have made it impossible to transact the remaining diplomatic business with the Kremlin. As it was, Bush's continued solicitude for Gorbachev helped seal the still-pending CFE and START treaties in late 1990 and 1991, both of which brought substantial and asymmetric Soviet force reductions and thereby accentuated the decline of Moscow's military power. Bush's middle ground was not such a bad place to be.

To a significant degree, the president sought to remain in that position until the very end. After brief hesitation, Bush strongly condemned the August 1991 coup attempt, and lent support to Yeltsin and other leaders who resisted it. Thereafter, the president recognized Baltic independence, and privately affirmed that a Soviet breakup was increasingly likely and desirable. "The best arrangement," he thought, "would be diffusion, with many different states, none of which would have the awesome power of the Soviet Union." But even so, Bush still believed that Gorbachev could play a constructive role in the move to a less centralized system. He also feared that dissolution might be violent and anarchical rather than peaceful, and so he remained torn between Cheney's calls for boldness and Baker's preference for restraint.[218] Even as Bush welcomed Russian and Ukrainian independence in late 1991, Baker thus continued to consult with Gorbachev on "how best to deter disintegration to lowest common denominator?"[219] Only when the final breakdown came did Bush act unambiguously, establishing diplomatic and economic ties with the successor states to "institutionalize the collapse of the Soviet Union."[220] On the whole, then, U.S. policy did not play as clear or decisive a role as one might have expected in accelerating the final Soviet demise.

That demise, however, played a key role in further clarifying the post–Cold War environment that the United States was entering. For what the Soviet disintegration confirmed—in almost cinematically dramatic fashion—was that America was not simply ascendant in global affairs, but that in many ways it was fundamentally unrivaled. "We were suddenly in a unique position," Scowcroft believed, "without experience, without precedent, and standing alone at the height of power."[221] America's long-standing global competitor had fallen into chaos and then collapse; the rival ideology the Kremlin espoused had been thoroughly discredited. With the decline and fragmentation of the Soviet military, the United States alone now possessed armed forces with global reach and impact, and American defense expenditures would soon equal those of the next six countries (including Russia) combined. Other nations, such as Japan and Germany, were sometimes touted as rising contenders for global power. But they still lagged far behind America in economic power (the U.S. economy was more than twice the size of the Japanese economy in the early 1990s), to say nothing of military might. In sum, America's major international rival had fallen, and there was no one to take its place. "In all the usual measures of national power—economic, military, cultural, political even philosophical—we have no challengers," Gates assessed.[222]

If anything, America's overall position was even stronger than such comparisons indicated. For not only was the United States by far the world's most powerful country, but many of the most vibrant and influential nations behind it were U.S. allies, linked to Washington by organic relationships that provided stability and entrenched American influence in crucial regions. The U.S. ideological model also had all the momentum, with democracy and markets having expanded impressively since the mid-1970s, and perhaps poised to advance further still with the collapse of communism in Eastern Europe and the Soviet Union. In addition, U.S. leadership had just been strongly affirmed by German reunification and the Gulf crisis, which demonstrated how essential that leadership remained to guiding change and preserving order in tumultuous times. All told, it was a truly astounding configuration of power and influence that the United States enjoyed in the early 1990s: the country stood atop an increasingly open and democratic system that seemed more receptive to American guidance than ever before. The question, for those who looked closely, was not *whether* the emerging order was unipolar; it was what the United States would *do* with the primacy it wielded.

Even prior to the final Soviet collapse, the debate on this issue had begun. Some commentators, notably Charles Krauthammer, called for Washington to double-down on its postwar global activism. "If America wants stability, it will have to create it," he wrote amid the Gulf crisis. "The alternative to unipolarity is chaos."[223] Other observers argued for retrenchment. Following the intellectual example of historian Paul Kennedy, whose 1987 best-seller had warned that the United States might soon succumb to "imperial overstretch," they contended that the end of the Cold War offered a much-needed escape from taxing global burdens that had too long distracted the country from pressing domestic problems. Paul Tsongas, a Democratic senator running for president in 1992, would soon take up this cry on the left. "The Cold War is over," he quipped; "Japan won." Yet it was not only liberals who believed that the United States should tend its own garden as the Soviet peril faded. Conservatives such as Patrick Buchanan offered similar prescriptions, as did even recent hawks such as Jeane Kirkpatrick. "It is time to give up the dubious benefits of superpower status," she wrote in 1990. America should again become "a normal country in a normal time."[224]

Well before the hammer-and-sickle was lowered for the last time, the Bush administration had staked out its own position in the debate. From 1989 onward, Bush and his aides repeatedly stated that the United States would not retire into a posture of geopolitical repose as the superpower struggle ended. "Far from becoming less of a force in the world," Cheney stated in 1990, "America is going to be taking on greater global responsibilities in the years ahead."[225] The United States would consolidate and deepen the gains of recent years; it would embrace its role as leader of the international system. In essence, even as the Cold War was ending, the Bush administration began laying the foundations of a post–Cold War strategy meant to extend U.S. primacy and render the global order still more conducive to American interests.

From the outset, this approach to post–Cold War policy flowed from a mixture of confidence and anxiety. On the one hand, the Bush administration could not but feel affirmed and empowered by the recent trends in America's international position and the broader global environment. The resolution of the Cold War on Western terms, the successes of democracy and markets, the decline of America's chief rival and the ascendance of U.S. influence—these phenomena fostered a sense that the opportunities were practically limitless. "It is a reconstruction of international relations the likes of which we haven't seen since the late 1940s," Baker said in 1990; the basic contours of world order were apt for reshaping.[226] The United States must therefore press its advantages and sustain the forward momentum. Washington had "a once-in-a-century opportunity to advance American interests *and* values throughout the world," Baker would subsequently say; the task was to "help shape this new era and to define it for generations to come."[227]

On the other hand, this commitment to primacy was equally forged from perceptions of danger and instability. Saddam Hussein had already given U.S. officials reason to fear that the post–Cold War world might be a volatile place, with over-armed tyrants exploiting a period of transition to make bold plays for regional hegemony. The postwar discovery that Iraq had been as little as one year away from manufacturing a crude nuclear device, moreover, surfaced troubling implications about the threat of post–Cold War proliferation by hostile and aggressive regimes. Nor were these the only signs of emergent upheaval as the early 1990s unfolded. The prospect of post-Soviet chaos and nuclear instability, the possibility of resurgent tensions in Central and Eastern Europe following the collapse of communism, the continuing dangers posed by terrorism and Islamic fundamentalism, and the devastating civil war that ripped Yugoslavia apart beginning in mid-1991—all these issues made U.S. officials apprehensive that Bush's "new world order" might turn disorderly indeed. "A monolithic, powerful Soviet Union is no longer the enemy," Bush said in 1991. "The enemy is uncertainty. The enemy is unpredictability." Powell conveyed same message to foreign officials: "He did not know exactly where the next crisis would be, but that it was out there waiting to happen."[228]

In pondering this incipient disorder, Bush was always careful to reiterate that the United States had neither the intention nor the capability to intervene in every conflict or address every problem. "We don't want to put a dog in this fight," he wrote as Yugoslavia descended into its fratricidal nightmare; there was no immediate, compelling strategic argument for U.S. military involvement in that war.[229] What there was a compelling case for, Bush believed, was the overall engagement and activism needed to keep the most pressing dangers at bay. Because of its unmatched power and influence, the United States was uniquely equipped to offer reassurance and security amid rapid change, and to catalyze collective action to address problems that did merit a decisive response. This was the role that Washington had played in the West during the Cold War; it must continue to shoulder the burden thereafter. "The pivotal responsibility for ensuring the stability of the international balance remains ours, even as its requirements change in a new era," Bush's first *NSS* stated.[230]

As early as 1990–1991, the administration had therefore begun to develop several essential principles of a post–Cold War strategy geared to shaping that new era. First and foremost, the administration planned to maintain unequaled, globe-spanning U.S. military power. "The rebuilding of America's strength during the past decade was an essential underpinning of the positive change we now see in the international environment," the 1990 *NSS* stated. "Our challenge now is to adapt this strength to a grand strategy that looks beyond containment."[231] Reductions from the peak of the Reagan buildup were inevitable given decreased superpower tensions and congressional pressure for a "peace dividend." What was imperative was to preserve a defense posture sufficient to ensure continued U.S. superiority, and to anchor the international order that Washington envisioned. "It is absolutely vital that we retain sufficient military force to sustain our worldwide commitments," Cheney argued, and to foster "an environment in which freedom and democracy and market economies can flourish."[232]

This was the rationale behind the "Base Force" concept developed by the Pentagon in 1989–1990. The Base Force constituted a meaningful decrease in U.S. military power from its previous heights, envisioning eventual cuts of 25 percent in overall personnel levels, reductions in carrier battle groups and other tools, and the withdrawal of a significant portion of American troops from Europe. Yet the Base Force was designed to accommodate these cuts without undermining U.S. influence or jeopardizing a congenial global environment. The concept entailed the retention of still-robust overseas deployments in Europe and East Asia; maintenance of the unmatched air, naval, and expeditionary capabilities necessary to surge into regional hot spots around the world; and preservation of the ability to command the global commons. It also emphasized intensive R&D designed to maintain and even increase U.S. technological superiority, and a "reconstitution" capacity to hedge against the revival or emergence of a peer military competitor.[233] "America must possess forces able to respond to threats in whatever corner of the globe they may occur," Bush explained; it must "protect the gains that 40 years of peace through strength have earned us."[234] By fortuitous coincidence, the presidential rollout of the Base Force occurred on August 2, 1990. The subsequent Gulf crisis eased pressures for more draconian reductions, tempered what cuts did occur, and allowed the administration to begin gradually gathering consensus around the idea of a post–Cold War preponderance of military power.[235]

That preponderance, in turn, would contribute to a second strategic goal— locking in the more favorable configuration of power that America's Cold War victory was making possible. In countless documents, speeches, and meetings with foreign officials, the administration stressed that the United States would not retreat from its forward force deployments and alliance commitments after the Cold War; it would maintain those arrangements well into the future. It would do so to reinforce stability in key regions such as Europe and East Asia, to prevent power vacuums and deter the emergence of new threats, and to maintain what Cheney called the "enormous influence" that alliances and troop commitments afforded Washington. "As a new global order takes shape," Pentagon officials wrote, America would act as the "irreplaceable balancing wheel" in vital theaters.[236] Through both words and actions—particularly in the Gulf crisis—the administration also made clear that it would prevent adversaries from gaining the regional dominance that might allow them to threaten the broader global order. "We did not stand united for forty years to bring the Cold War to a peaceful end in order to make the world safe for the likes of Saddam Hussein," Baker said; the United States intended to protect the position of security and advantage it had won.[237]

If anything, it intended to improve that position, for a third strategic principle entailed the continued promotion of markets and democracy overseas. From the beginning of his presidency, Bush had stressed the expansion of these liberal institutions. As the administration contemplated the post–Cold War era, that emphasis become more pronounced. The spread of democracy and markets would reinforce post–Cold War peace by promoting greater prosperity and removing sources of conflict, U.S. officials argued; it would also make the global order steadily more reflective of American values and American interests. "America stands at the center of a widening circle of freedom," Bush declared in 1990—"today, tomorrow, and into the next century."[238] It was "common sense," Baker agreed, "for the United States to lead alliances of free-market democracies in Asia, Europe, and the Americas in support of democracy and economic liberty."[239]

Throughout the Bush years, this logic drove concrete action. In the realm of democracy promotion, the administration twice intervened militarily—in Panama and the Philippines—to protect or help establish democratic rule, and it used diplomatic and economic tools to support democracy in places as varied as Latin America, South Africa, and the former Soviet bloc. "Our idea is to replace the dangerous period of the Cold War with a democratic peace," Baker stated, covering not just "half a world" but "the whole world" instead.[240] The administration was more energetic still in pushing free trade and market economics. It consummated the NAFTA negotiations with Mexico and Canada, guided the Third World debt crisis to its resolution, and made significant progress toward the agreement that eventually sealed the Uruguay Round. It also promoted endeavors such as the Enterprise for the Americas Initiative and the Asia-Pacific Economic Cooperation forum, which were meant to institutionalize—and ensure U.S. influence in—the ongoing liberalization of regional economies in Latin America and East Asia.[241] "By furthering the development and integration of market economies within the international system," Baker explained, "we strengthen the collective force of those that share our principles."[242] Washington would not just hold what it had in the post–Cold War era; it would build on the liberal advances of the 1970s and 1980s, and continue to press the global offensive.

Finally, the administration began formulating a fourth principle of post–Cold War statecraft, which was that the United States should meet emerging threats early—before they became full-on systemic crises or existential dangers such as the Cold War–era Soviet Union, and perhaps before they emerged in the first place. This idea was central to the administration's emphasis on retaining alliances and forward deployments in key regions—a primary point of which was to keep new threats from arising—and even more so in its refusal to let Saddam become hegemonic in the Gulf. More broadly, U.S. officials repeatedly stated that although Washington could not solve every problem, it must engage proactively to address those issues that might jeopardize global stability and key American interests if allowed to fester. "We want to help avoid or settle regional conflicts," Baker said. "We want to stem the proliferation of weapons of mass destruction, weapons that can explode local conflicts into large disasters."[243] U.S. resources were not limitless, Bush agreed, but the employment of diplomatic, political, and even military power would be crucial to ensuring that the Soviet danger was not replaced by new first-order threats. "Terrorism, hostage-taking, renegade regimes and unpredictable rulers, new sources of instability—all require a strong and an engaged America," he said.[244] Eternal vigilance was the price of a better post–Cold War peace.

By mid-1991, these themes were gradually coalescing into a more integrated view of the new international order and the U.S. role therein. This being the case, the final Soviet collapse did not upend the emerging strategic paradigm but rather sharpened and reinforced it. The disappearance of America's rival added enormously to the sense of power and possibility that was already driving U.S. thinking about the post–Cold War world. "We have reached a turning point," Bush declared. "We have defeated imperial communism."[245] At the same time, the fragmentation of the Soviet state into its unstable and, in some cases, nuclear-armed successors underscored perceptions of potential danger and volatility.[246] Above all, then, the Soviet collapse provided both the opportunity and the necessity to spell out a more fully defined, comprehensive approach to the new era. A world that was now unipolar demanded a strategy to match. As Baker said, "Either we take hold of history or history will take hold of us."[247]

It was Cheney's Pentagon that most eagerly embraced this challenge, and that most cohesively drew together the tenets of U.S. thinking. Since 1989, that department had been planning intensively for the post–Cold War era. Amid the Soviet collapse in late 1991, the key Pentagon policy office—Wolfowitz's Office of the Undersecretary of Defense for Policy—began assembling a document known as the "Defense Planning Guidance" (DPG). In normal times, the DPG served mainly to fix budgetary and acquisitions priorities for the coming five-year period. In this extraordinary time, it was something bigger. Wolfowitz's office took the drafting of the DPG as a chance to assess the "fundamentally new situation" that had arisen, and to "set the nation's direction for the next century."[248] The result was a sort of grand unified theory of U.S. strategy in the unipolar era. That theory would incite much controversy, but its core elements would prove quite enduring.

The draft DPG was completed in February 1992, and its analysis proceeded from an unvarnished assessment of power realities. The document argued that "the collapse of the Soviet Union," "the discrediting of Communism as an ideology with global pretensions and influence," and the dramatic U.S. victory in the Gulf had given America a level of political-military predominance that was historically very rare, and beyond near- or medium-term challenge. The United States enjoyed a clear and growing military superiority, and unrivaled economic and diplomatic influence. It headed a "system of collective security and . . . democratic 'zone of peace'" that already encompassed most of the industrial world and might now grow further. In essence, the United States possessed what Cheney termed great "strategic depth"—a generous margin of power, an absence of existential threats, and a corresponding ability to exercise great influence over world events.[249]

It followed that the fundamental goal of U.S. strategy should be to extend, and improve, this position for as long as possible. "Our first objective is to prevent the re-emergence of a new rival . . . that poses a threat on the order of that formerly posed by the Soviet Union," the DPG stated. "This is a dominant consideration . . . and requires that we endeavor to prevent any hostile power from dominating a region whose resources would, under consolidated control, be sufficient to generate global power." The United States should maintain favorable balances in Europe, East Asia, and the Persian Gulf; it should also seek to prevent the revival of a new enemy superpower in the former Soviet space. The goal of unipolar strategy, in other words, must be to make unipolarity permanent. "Our strategy," the authors reiterated, "must now refocus on precluding the emergence of any potential future global competitor."[250]

American strategy should simultaneously deepen and reinforce the unipolar order, by checking sources of instability that might disrupt it, and by continuing to recast the international system in the U.S. image. Washington should "limit international violence" by combating scourges ranging from regional conflict to WMD proliferation to terrorism; it should also "encourage the spread of democratic forms of government and open economic systems," particularly in Eastern Europe and the former Soviet Union. After all, the Kremlin had "achieved global reach and power" by dominating the territory and resources of the former USSR; the way to avert a recurrence of that threat was to help countries such as Russia and Ukraine "become peaceful democracies with market-based economies." By promoting economic and political liberalization—by extending the "democratic zone of peace"—the United States would extend its geopolitical mastery as well.[251]

This goal of locking in a unipolar and progressively more liberal order was nothing if not ambitious. And as the DPG clearly stated, achieving that goal would require wide-ranging efforts across various realms. Economic and diplomatic engagement would certainly be necessary to address crises, pursue initiatives such as nonproliferation and counterterrorism, and sustain the advance of democracy and markets. Moreover, attaining the overarching aim of preventing a new peer competitor would require the United States to wield carrots as well as sticks. Washington must foster an international order that would allow other countries to prosper, and it must continue to provide the public goods that would convince key nations such as Japan and Germany to embrace unipolarity rather than contest it. "We must account sufficiently for the interests of the advanced industrial nations to discourage them from challenging our leadership or seeking to overturn the established political and economic order," the document stated. The durability of U.S. primacy would hinge significantly on how other countries perceived that primacy, and American policy must be sensitive to that fact.[252]

The DPG, in this sense, was more nuanced than some subsequent caricatures allowed.[253] Yet it was also very blunt in arguing that a unipolar order would ultimately rest on unchallenged military power and the benefits it bestowed. The DPG emphasized the stability and influence that flowed from force deployments in East Asia and Europe, and raised the prospect of greater U.S. presence in the Gulf. It endorsed the existing system of U.S. alliances and the dominant configuration of power that system had fostered, and suggested offering security guarantees to Eastern Europe to extend that configuration further. It spoke of the importance of U.S. military power in fostering a climate of peace in which democracy and markets could flourish. Most important, the DPG laid great stress on the need to make the military costs of challenging America so prohibitively high that no country would even dare to try: "We must maintain the mechanisms for deterring potential competitors from even aspiring to a larger regional or global role." And finally, the document argued that in an uncertain world, military supremacy was the indispensable safeguard against rising threats to the global order the United States wished to project. Washington would not be "righting every wrong," but "we will retain the preeminent responsibility for addressing selectively those wrongs which threaten not only our interests, but those of our allies or friends, or which could seriously unsettle international relations." In the final analysis, the DPG stated, "the world order is ultimately backed by the U.S."[254]

As with NSC-68 some forty years earlier, the February 1992 DPG was somewhat oblique in discussing just how much military power was enough to sustain this order. But there was little doubt that the document envisioned a vast rather than a marginal superiority, particularly at the crucial higher ends of the conventional spectrum. Earlier drafts had emphasized that "U.S. forces must continue to be at least a generation ahead in weapons technology."[255] For its part, the February draft stressed the deterrent power afforded by overall technological superiority, and the need to be able to win decisively in Desert Storm–like conflicts—potentially against WMD-armed opponents—in the future. It also asserted that while the United States preferred to act through multilateral organizations such as NATO and the United Nations, it should "be postured to act independently when collective action cannot be orchestrated or when an immediate response is . . . necessary." This was a recipe for a military that was not just the best, but the best by far.[256]

The February 1992 DPG was only a draft document. It had been prepared by mid-level officials (particularly Zalmay Khalilzad), and had not been approved or, in some cases, even read by key decision makers such as Wolfowitz and Cheney. As a milestone in the evolution of post–Cold War strategy, however, the DPG was enormously important. It forcefully articulated the overall goal of sustaining and deepening U.S. primacy, and outlined the policies and approaches needed to achieve that goal. It sharpened, and made a coherent whole of the ideas that were already shaping the administration's strategic outlook: the need for unrivaled military dominance, the desire to lock in a profoundly positive balance of power, the imperative of advancing markets and democracy, and the concept of meeting threats before they metastasized or even manifested. The DPG thus crystallized U.S. strategic thinking in the early 1990s. It represented a strikingly candid and fairly comprehensive attempt to chart the country's path in the unipolar era.

It was precisely that candor that made the DPG so controversial when the document leaked to the *New York Times* in March 1992. Seizing on Khalilzad's more provocative themes and language, critics expressed shock and outrage at what the Pentagon seemed to have in mind. Senator Alan Cranston (D-California) declared that the administration wanted to make the United States "the one, the only main honcho on the world block, the global Big Enchilada." Other observers decried the "muscle-flexing unilateralism" of the document, and pointed out that the DPG seemed as focused on preventing the rise of longtime allies—such as Germany and Japan—as adversaries. Edward Kennedy, who had advocated far greater defense cuts, alleged that the DPG "aimed primarily at finding new ways to justify Cold War levels of military spending."[257]

Stung by this criticism of a still-unfinished product, the administration seemed to retreat. Bush and Cheney pointed out that they had not formally approved or even read the document, and NSC aides prepared talking points that the president could use to play down the DPG in meetings with foreign leaders.[258] The draft was subsequently rewritten by Lewis "Scooter" Libby, a top Wolfowitz aide, who excised some of the more muscular language and more ostentatiously advertised U.S. relationships with key allies and international organizations. The narrative soon took hold that the Pentagon had retreated from a radical bid for global hegemony, and returned to the more multilateral ethos of the Gulf War. "Pentagon Drops Goal of Blocking New Superpowers," the *Times* reported.[259]

This, however, was not really what had happened, and the entire episode was not what the frenzied public commentary made it seem. As we have seen, the DPG was hardly an outlier in official thinking about post–Cold War strategy; in many ways, it represented the culmination of that thinking. Nor was the goal of preventing a hostile peer challenger from dominating a crucial region anything new; it was a World War II– and Cold War–era idea extended to the post–Cold War world. Powell and Cheney had actually conveyed the basic themes of the DPG in public speeches and appearances before Congress in early 1992, without great controversy. "We are . . . the world's sole remaining superpower," Powell had said. "Seldom in our history have we been in a stronger position relative to any challengers we might face. This is a position we should not abandon."[260] Bush himself subtly expressed support for the essential content of the DPG once he was made aware of it, and his statements during this period equally stressed the need for U.S. assertiveness and primacy. "We must remain the active leader of the entire world," he wrote. "We must not only have the convictions about democracy and freedom, but we must have a strong National Defense posture."[261] Other officials, including Baker, made similar points and argued that, although the administration valued multilateralism, "we can hardly entrust the future of democracy or American interests exclusively to multilateral institutions."[262]

In hindsight, the real problem with the DPG was not one of content but of language and politics. As a classified document, the DPG had stripped away the banalities and euphemisms that were often used in public discussions of America's global role. It asserted the reality—and goal—of primacy in starker form than many observers were used to hearing. That alone would have caused controversy; what added to the furor was the political context. The DPG was swept up not simply in ongoing debates about military spending but, more important, in the Democrats' election-year critique of Bush's policy. It was no coincidence that some of the strongest critics of the draft were Democratic presidential candidates who were wooing the liberal base in a heated primary. Bill Clinton's campaign called the DPG an attempt "to find an excuse for big budgets"; Paul Tsongas scored the administration for allegedly downgrading the United Nations. When the political roles were reversed during the Clinton years, many Democratic officials would find that the key themes of the DPG were not so outrageous.[263]

Far from being discarded, in fact, the DPG proved to be foundational in the shaping of post–Cold War strategy. Libby's rewrite was approved with fairly minimal edits from the NSC staff, and was eventually released as the Regional Defense Strategy (RDS) in January 1993. Semantics aside, this new document contained every core theme of Khalilzad's draft. It stressed the fact of U.S. preeminence and the imperative of preserving that advantage. "America's strategic position is stronger than it has been for decades," the RDS stated; the task now was "maintain the strategic depth that we won through forty years of the Cold War." It explained the need to sustain favorable regional balances through alliances and forward deployments, and affirmed that U.S. forces would be postured to "preclude hostile nondemocratic powers from dominating regions critical to our interests." It underscored the importance of strengthening the international order by countering challenges such as terrorism and WMD proliferation, and by promoting liberal institutions to "extend the remarkable democratic 'zone of peace.'" The RDS also politely restated that the United States would not hesitate to use force—unilaterally if necessary—to defeat or head off the most serious emerging threats. Perhaps most important, it endorsed the idea that Washington must "dominate the military-technological revolution" to make challenges to its primacy point-less. The DPG had been changed in name only; its basic strategy had now gained official approval.[264]

As the Bush presidency wound down, the administration took other opportunities to convey its commitment to that strategy. In December 1992, Bush had dispatched U.S. troops to combat famine in Somalia. In two major speeches given thereafter, he sought to reassure his audiences that this decision did not portend frequent military interventions in all the world's crisis spots. The United States "should not seek to be the world's policeman," he said; it must not go "running off on reckless, expensive crusades." But Bush also urged that America use its unmatched influence to shape the world environment, preclude a return to great-power conflict, and "win the democratic peace . . . for people the world over."[265] Similarly, the administration's legacy NSS, released in January 1993, endorsed the tenets of the RDS and reaffirmed the vision of a sole superpower using its great influence to deepen a liberal global system. "The United States remains the nation whose strength and leadership are essential to a stable and democratic world order," the report explained; to forsake this position would be to squander historic opportunities and invite renascent dangers.[266] By the time Bush left office, his administration's thinking had coalesced around a primacist approach to world affairs.[267]

That approach would prove remarkably durable over time. To be sure, at various points during the early 1990s it appeared that counsels of retrenchment might be taking hold. The Soviet collapse temporarily revived downward pressures on defense spending (which Cheney and Powell accommodated through additional, largely nonessential cuts), and congressional trimmers continued to talk of a major peace dividend. In addition, of course, Bush lost the presidency in 1992, in an election that initially seemed to augur a strategic shift. That election was dominated by concerns about a domestic economy in recession, it featured a quasi-isolationist third-party candidate who gained 19 percent of the vote, and its victor—Bill Clinton—had promised significant defense reductions and bashed Bush for spending too much time on foreign policy. (Confusingly, Clinton also bashed Bush for not doing more to spread democracy or end the Balkan conflict.) Clinton's first secretary of defense, Les Aspin, had earlier advocated a "threat-based" force that would have been smaller than the "capabilities-based" force that Powell and Cheney supported, and he promised a "bottom-up review" of U.S. capabilities.[268]

In the end, however, the changes to U.S. defense posture were minimal, and the primacist ethos soon became a bipartisan, near-consensus viewpoint among national security elites. In retrospect, the Gulf War had already largely drawn the venom from calls for truly draconian retrenchment. And as the new Democratic administration found itself facing many of the same opportunities and dangers as its predecessor, it ultimately embraced virtually all the key strategic precepts that had emerged during the Bush years. Aspin, earlier very critical of the Base Force and the RDS, wound up effectively endorsing both concepts, and U.S. defense strategy remained focused on deterring and winning "major regional contingencies" against emerging challengers. By the mid-1990s, the Pentagon was advocating "full spectrum dominance" to shape the international environment and dissuade rivals from seeking to compete.[269] "As we move into the next century," administration officials wrote, "it is imperative that the United States maintain its military superiority in the face of evolving, as well as discontinuous, threats and challenges."[270] Indeed, as U.S. defense spending remained robust and other countries slashed their own budgets, American military dominance increased. Over the course of the 1990s, the United States "consistently accounted for a little more than a third of all the military spending in the world," far more than all potential enemies *combined*. Presidents changed, but the emphasis on perpetuating unipolarity remained.[271]

One hardly had to wait to see the continuity. In September 1993, National Security Adviser Anthony Lake gave a major speech that enunciated the Clinton administration's approach to foreign policy, and that showed how axiomatic the tenets of primacy had become. A defining "feature of this era is that we are its dominant power," Lake said. Washington possessed unmatched economic and military power, and "America's core concepts— democracy and market economics—are more broadly accepted than ever." In these circumstances, "the successor to a doctrine of containment must be a strategy of enlargement—enlargement of the world's free community of market democracies." The United States would strengthen "the core from which enlargement is proceeding" by deepening economic ties and providing continued stability in Europe and East Asia. It would energetically promote markets and democracy in key regions such as Eastern Europe and the former Soviet Union. It would employ military and political influence to isolate aggressive regimes and prevent them from upsetting a liberalizing global order. And finally, America would use its unique capacity for leadership to selectively address civil wars, humanitarian crises, and other sources of instability. "We should act multilaterally where doing so advances our interests," Lake said—"and we should act unilaterally when that will serve our purpose." The world had reached a "historic crossroads," and a dominant United States must act to reap the benefits and repress the dangers of that situation.[272]

By 1992–1993, then, the basic paradigm of post–Cold War strategy had taken form. That paradigm had begun to develop even before the Cold War fully ended and the Soviet Union fell. It was subsequently refined and enunciated through key initiatives like the DPG, the RDS, and the advent of "enlargement." Over time, the specific ways in which that paradigm was operationalized would vary, both across and within presidencies. Yet the core objective and the guiding ideas would remain the same. The United States would not retrench after its Cold War victory; it would consolidate existing gains and seek new ones. The American resurgence that had begun in the 1970s had now brought the country to a place of global primacy. The goal of national strategy, henceforth, would be to make that status enduring.

Conclusion

The years between 1989 and 1992 marked a decisive transition in the evolution of the international system and the rise of unipolarity. During the 1970s and 1980s, global change and strategic choice had begun to reorder the world environment. During the 1989–1992 period, that process climaxed in dramatic upheaval that ushered in America's post–Cold War primacy. The fall of the Berlin Wall shattered the bipolar order in Europe, and let the Bush administration play an indispensable role in reunifying Germany and remaking the geopolitical architecture of the Cold War's central theater. The Persian Gulf crisis then showed the potential for great instability in the post-bipolar world; it also demonstrated how essential America's vast military and diplomatic superiority would be in controlling that instability and shaping the new era. Finally, the demise of the Soviet Union destroyed Washington's longtime adversary definitively, casting the nature of the post–Cold War world into sharpest relief, and evoking the most coherent articulation of a primacist global strategy.

As the Bush years became the Clinton years, the contours of the unipolar order were thus coming into place. From a position of seeming weakness in the late 1970s, the United States had surged to unrivaled international supremacy just over a decade later. American dominance was evident in the military, economic, diplomatic, and ideological realms; a postwar system characterized by the clash of two superpowers had given way to a post–Cold War system in which there was manifestly only one. The American century would not die the premature death that so often had been predicted in previous years. Rather, U.S. policymakers were now looking forward to a prolonged and fruitful period of unipolarity.

What remained to be determined, of course, was just how long, and how fruitful, that period would actually be. At the dawn of the unipolar moment, there were so many reasons for optimism. Yet there were also, perhaps, reasons for greater concern. The Gulf War had already indicated that unipolarity was not synonymous with peace or security, and that unmatched power did not necessarily translate into fully satisfying outcomes. As the post–Cold War era subsequently unfolded, it would become all the more evident that primacy did not free the United States from a host of thorny problems and challenges—and that it might create new ones, as well.

Conclusion
Understanding the Arc of American Power

The term *superpower* was coined during World War II, to denote those countries that wielded and competed for influence on a global scale.[1] The phrase grafted nicely onto the bipolar U.S.-Soviet rivalry that followed, but by the close of the Cold War, some observers were beginning to wonder whether the age of the superpowers had reached its end. Even before the final collapse, Soviet power and authority were becoming steadily and perhaps irretrievably less super. The United States, by contrast, seemed to have found another gear and was now manifesting not just global influence but global superiority along multiple dimensions. From the striking—and increasing—imbalance of military power, to the preponderance of economic might, to the advance of the political and economic institutions that Washington cherished, to the myriad alliances and other relationships that projected U.S. influence into key regions of the world, America had attained a perch that was not simply favorable but, by historical comparison, quite extraordinary. "There are now no longer two superpowers," British journalist Peregrine Worsthorne wrote in 1991. "There is one hyper-power with all the rest far behind."[2]

This assessment reflected the afterglow of the U.S. performance in the Gulf War, and in some ways, it obscured the fact that America's international superiority was actually less pronounced in the early 1990s than it had been at the dawn of the superpower era a half-century earlier. The United States possessed but half of the share of global output it had commanded when the world lay in ruins in 1945, for instance, and its economic lead over the next most productive country was much reduced, too. Yet in other ways, observers such as Worsthorne and Krauthammer were right to sense that the dawning unipolar moment was not simply a restoration—or pale imitation—of the early postwar era. Unlike in 1945, the United States did not now confront a hostile superpower that dominated large parts of the world's geopolitical core and was poised to compete for supremacy across Eurasia and eventually beyond. Nor did it face a rival ideology with the prestige that socialism had enjoyed at the outset of the postwar period; rather, the American-backed liberal model now had such unmatched momentum.[3] Finally, whereas in the late 1940s the rise of the Cold War had effectively confined U.S. influence to the areas of the noncommunist world, in the early 1990s the easing of long-standing global cleavages meant that there were still fewer geographical constraints on the exertion of American power. In these and other regards, the unipolar moment was something new and exceptional indeed.

The situation that the United States inhabited in the early 1990s was all the more remarkable given what the arc of American power had looked like not so long before. Throughout much of the 1970s, the postwar order had been eroding, and U.S. policy was in disarray. The oil shocks and the economic traumas, the adversity in the Cold War and the divisions within the West, the setbacks in the Third World and the repeated crises of U.S. influence—these issues so often made it seem that America was a superpower in trouble. "America's power, its will and its sense of purpose all seem to be in a state of advanced decline," Reagan had lamented. "Respect for, and confidence in the United States are at an all-time low."[4] To be clear, Reagan contested this view, as did other sharp-eyed observers. But the recent record of U.S. policy was not inspiring, and the trials of the 1970s had created a pervasive sense of decline that would last through the close of that decade and, in some quarters, deep into the 1980s as well. Concerns about "malaise" were the predecessors to "Japanophobia" and fears of "imperial overstretch": all these phenomena testified to a belief that the American age was crashing to a close.[5]

The U.S. position did change markedly from the 1970s onward, but not in the way that the "declinists" had predicted.[6] In retrospect, we can see that those predictions often attributed too much importance to American difficulties that ultimately proved transitory, and too little to the crippling long-term problems faced by rivals such as the Soviet Union. They underestimated the terrific resilience of U.S. economic power, and the attractiveness of core American ideals and principles abroad. Above all, they misjudged the extent to which key international trends were actually making the international climate more receptive to the reassertion of American influence and authority, and the degree to which U.S. policy would harvest the rewards in years to come. By the early 1990s, these factors had produced not a steady slide away from global leadership, but a new and, in many ways, improved American primacy. As the post–Cold War era then progressed, even former skeptics were impressed. "Nothing has ever existed like this disparity of power; nothing," Paul Kennedy wrote in 2002; earlier empires would have marveled at the reach and extent of American might.[7]

The specifics of Kennedy's claim were perhaps debatable, but there was no denying the basic global power dynamics that inspired the assertion. The foregoing chapters have related how this unipolar moment took form, tracing the story from the rejuvenating global departures of the 1970s, to the forward-leaning and generally effective statecraft of the 1980s, to the astonishing ruptures and opportunistic policies of the George H. W. Bush years. This concluding chapter now distills several core themes that have run throughout the analysis; it also reflects, briefly, on the trajectory of U.S. power and statecraft in the post–Cold War period.

Key Themes and Conclusions

A first theme to arise from this story is that the primacy that the United States achieved during this period was about more than an imbalance of material capabilities and the absence of a global competitor. Leading political scientists have often relied on this fairly narrow definition of *unipolarity*, treating it as a situation in which the distribution of hard-power resources— namely military and economic resources—is slanted dramatically in favor of the leading state. "I define a unipolar system as one in which a single power is geopolitically preponderant because its capabilities are formidable enough to preclude the formation of an overwhelming balancing coalition against it," writes Christopher Layne. "Unipolar systems," another scholar agrees, "possess only one great power which enjoys a preponderance of power and faces no competition" for leading-power status.[8] By these standards, the post–Cold War order was assuredly unipolar. As noted in the previous chapter, the United States accounted for between one-fifth and one-fourth of the world economy during the 1990s, at least twice the share of the next-most productive country. By mid-decade, its military spending and capabilities were equal to those of at least the next several states combined. "If today's American primacy does not constitute unipolarity," two leading authorities were soon writing, "then nothing ever will."[9]

What the history of the period under consideration demonstrates, however, is that this narrow frame of reference actually understates the dominance that the United States had come to wield as its unipolar moment began. For starters, looking solely at the *distribution* of power does not adequately capture the full *configuration* of power that America enjoyed. As the Bush administration had recognized in contemplating post–Cold War strategy, the alliances, forward military deployments, and diplomatic relationships that Washington had originally developed during the superpower conflict now continued to serve as force multipliers for American power, securing positive ties with second-tier states and thrusting U.S. influence deep into crucial regions. Moreover, the fact that so many of those second-tier states were U.S. friends and allies further added to the overall level of capacity that America could assemble in dealing with important global issues. As the Persian Gulf War demonstrated, in fact, the emerging unipolar order was really more like a "unipolar concert"—a system in which many second-level states not only declined to balance strongly against the leader, but actively assisted in the exercise of its power.[10] Strange as it sounds, then, the world's most powerful country was actually in position to punch *above* its own geopolitical weight.

Perhaps even more central to America's post–Cold War primacy—and to the U.S. renewal that had enabled it—were the ideological dimensions. As we have seen, the period between the late 1970s and early 1990s was not simply one in which the United States was renascent geopolitically. It was equally a period in which its favored ideas and institutions flourished so impressively as to become increasingly hegemonic. By the outset of the post–Cold War era, globalization and the Washington Consensus were sweeping forward in the Third World, as well as in many of America's former Second-World adversaries. Political liberalization was continuing the awesome advance that would increase the number of electoral democracies worldwide from less than 40 in the early 1970s to roughly 120 by the turn of the millennium.[11] Nearly around the globe, it seemed, the liberal practices of free trade, free markets, and free political institutions were on the rise, and alternative models—whether economic or political—were embattled or in some cases essentially defeated. The significance of this phenomenon for the overall global balance was not to be underestimated. For insofar as power and influence are measured by the prevalence of one's core values and concepts, the United States had attained a growing ideological superiority to go along with its emerging geopolitical and strategic preponderance.

To be sure, this ideological superiority was never as complete or conclusive as Fukuyama's "end of history" thesis made it out to be. Nor did this—or any other—form of U.S. dominance ever equate to omnipotence or invulnerability. But Washington's ideological preeminence was nevertheless a striking manifestation of how broadly ascendant the United States had become by the 1990s, and how extensive and multidimensional its post–Cold War primacy truly was. "The realist who focuses only on the balance of hard power will miss the power of transnational ideas," Harvard scholar Joseph Nye wrote in 1990; this "soft power" element was also fundamental to America's overall position.[12] Understanding this point is central to grasping the compound nature of the U.S. resurgence from the 1970s onward, and of the unipolar order that resurgence created.

This first theme relates to a second, which has to do with the manner in which that unipolar order took shape. Just as many analysts define *unipolarity* primarily in quantifiable hard-power terms, it is common to argue that the unipolar moment was something that arose suddenly—virtually overnight by historical standards—with the end of the Cold War and the collapse of the Soviet Union. The United States "emerged suddenly as a unipole as a result of the Soviet decision to stop competing with it in 1989 and the subsequent dismemberment of the Soviet state two years later," Nuno Monteiro writes. Similarly, leading historians have framed the rise of the post–Cold War order as a development that happened rapidly—even accidentally—in the period surrounding the opening of the Berlin Wall, or have argued that the rise of the unipolar moment was something that came almost as a *deus ex machina* for a "disoriented giant" in a more difficult world.[13] It is true, certainly, that the events of 1989–1991 marked the dramatic culmination of the unipolar turn, by conclusively killing off a fading bipolar system and throwing the contours of the new order into sharp relief. At the same time, however, focusing too intently on the events surrounding the final Soviet collapse can obscure the fact that unipolarity was actually a longer-term and more complex process, one that drew on wide-ranging historical transformations as well as conscious policy choices.

As we have seen, that process originated in the 1970s, with the unchaining of an entire set of profound global trends: trends that touched on issues ranging from the Cold War, to the spread of democracy and human rights, to the onset of globalization and the rise of a post-industrial economy; and trends that would gradually reorder the international landscape in the years that followed. Those trends were then considerably amplified and channeled by well-aimed U.S. policy interventions in the 1980s, and they eventually converged and climaxed in the remarkable breakthroughs—which were also often influenced by American statecraft—during the George H. W. Bush years. In this sense, it is simplistic and ahistorical to think of the rise of the unipolar order as something that abruptly "happened" with the Soviet collapse and the undeniably astonishing conclusion of the Cold War in 1989–1991. It was, rather, something that played out across a longer span of time and a broader span of issues, and something that involved a mix of inputs, actions, and influences that all inter-reacted with one another to result in momentous historical change.

Seeing the advent of unipolarity as a multifaceted and multistage process, as opposed to a more singular or discrete event, is important for a variety of reasons. It gives us a better sense of how historical change accumulated and acquired momentum over time, and across several diverse issues and realms. It reminds us that tracing the renewal of American primacy requires looking beyond the Cold War competition with Moscow, to the wider range of global shifts that unfolded to U.S. advantage from the 1970s onward. Finally—and this leads to a third essential theme of this book—it underscores the centrality of volition and circumstance alike in reviving American fortunes, and in making the unipolar moment.

The relationship between structure and strategy is a perennial theme in debates about historical causality and the sources of great change in the international order. The making of the unipolar moment occurred squarely at the nexus of these powerful factors. From a structural perspective, the deep global currents that began to flow so strongly in the 1970s constituted the essential precondition to everything that followed. The onset and progression of terminal Soviet decline, the onrush of democratization and a more prominent human rights consciousness, and the rise of globalization and the associated changes in the world economy—all these trends originated from influences that were beyond the control of any U.S. policymaker, and all were foundational to the renewed American ascendancy. These trends created a broadly and in some cases enormously favorable context for the advancement of U.S. interests, and they generally allowed American officials to align their efforts with, not against, the most vibrant forces in the global arena. Good results were thus a product of good fortune. If the United States did so well during the 1980s and after, it was because it had the impetus of history at its back.

Good results were also a product of good strategy, however, because those structural forces interacted synergistically with American statecraft as time went on. From the Cold War to democracy promotion to the contours of the global economy, U.S. officials progressively came to understand the profound changes that were coursing through the international system, and to make the most of them via the calculated employment of national power.

The result was first to accentuate and direct the favorable shifts so as to markedly improve America's international position, and then to capitalize on a moment of great fluidity to lock in decisive change in the global order. The unipolar turn was therefore a function of choice and circumstance together—it was the interplay of those elements that shaped the history of this period.

Understanding this interplay is central to grasping, in a broad sense, the role that U.S. agency and initiative had in forging the post–Cold War order. It also sheds light on the parts played by specific leaders and administrations. We can now see, for example, that the process of fitting strategy to structural opportunity actually began in the 1970s, under the Ford and especially the Carter administrations. This was not, by any stretch, a golden age of American strategy. U.S. officials were so frequently battered by the crises of the period, and they often struggled to overcome difficult global conditions and the shortcomings of their own statecraft. Even amid the travails and occasional self-inflicted wounds, however, these administrations were starting to grapple with the international changes underway, and to develop some of the core insights and innovations that would enable more effective strategy in years ahead. From economic deregulation to the Volcker shock, from the institutionalization of Western economic summitry to the Tokyo Round, from Carter's human rights policies to his late-stage military buildup, the initiatives of the 1970s sowed the seeds of later successes. As structure was turning in America's direction, strategy was slowly and sometimes haltingly positioning the United States to benefit.

The Reagan administration had the luck, and the skill, to build on these foundations. There is a continuing debate among scholars as to the quality of Reagan's statesmanship and the impact of his administration's policies.[14] What the evidence presented in this book shows is that Reagan and his advisers facilitated a veritable strategic renaissance. From the beginning, Reagan combined a generally astute strategic sensibility with an unwavering belief in the greatness and long-term prospects of the United States. Over the course of Reagan's presidency, he and his aides—from Shultz and Baker at the top, down to the array of mid- and lower-tier officials who supported them—developed ambitious strategic frameworks that put the force of American power behind the vital tectonic shifts at work. In the Cold War, in dealing with the international economy, in addressing processes of political change in the Third World, the administration was thereby able to harness and guide positive trends, and to achieve historic gains across a range of essential issues. This was the Reagan administration's indispensable contribution to the American resurgence: to help translate the structural possibilities that had opened up beginning in the 1970s into the strategic breakthroughs of the decade that followed. This growing symbiosis between structure and strategy was a critical factor in turning global affairs sharply to U.S. advantage during the 1980s, and in bringing the international system to the verge of an epochal transition.

This was the context in which George H. W. Bush took power. Bush was often derided, at the time and after, as a leader who lacked boldness or foresight. Yet even though Bush's statecraft was far from perfect, these caricatures badly miss the mark. The president and his key advisers—particularly individuals such as Baker and Brent Scowcroft—generally understood that the world was entering a time of great flux and contingency, a period when dangers lurked but alluring possibilities beckoned. And so, amid the successive strategic shocks that marked his tenure, Bush and his team usually responded quite purposefully, via initiatives that helped solidify a decisive U.S. primacy in the emerging post–Cold War era. From German reunification, to the Persian Gulf War, to the crafting of a new global strategy in the period surrounding the Soviet collapse, the common threads that ran through Bush's policies were an awareness that the international system had reached a fundamental transition point, and a willingness to use U.S. power to shepherd that transition toward its unipolar outcome. At the dawn of a new era in global politics, American strategy remained deeply intertwined with transformative structural change.

Otto von Bismarck once remarked that the essence of statecraft resides not in remaking the world from scratch, but rather in sensing the flow of history and positioning one's country accordingly. "The best a statesman can do," he explained, "is listen to the footsteps of God, get hold of the hem of His cloak, and walk with Him a few steps of the way."[15] U.S. strategy accomplished something like this in the run-up to the unipolar moment. U.S. officials were not in any deliberate sense the authors of the tectonic trends that would so benefit the country from the 1970s onward, and it is hard to imagine such a dramatic renewal occurring absent the vital assistance those trends provided. Yet when opportunities presented themselves and the international system became ripe for the reshaping, American statecraft was generally able to perceive and make the most of the conjuncture. U.S. strategy allowed the country to get hold of the hem of a structural revolution. Bismarck, one imagines, would have approved.

The history of this period is thus testament to what ambitious, forward-looking strategy can accomplish at a pivotal moment in global affairs. A fourth theme of this book, however, is that the history of this period is also testament to how messy and iterative the task of making such strategy can be. For it was simply not the case that good strategy took root in a flash of insight and then allowed U.S. policymakers to march smartly from triumph to triumph. No, the formulation and execution of American strategy was itself a process, one that required foresight and flexibility alike, and one that could be complex and imperfect indeed.

Consider, as the essential example, the Reagan years. By and large, these years were a time of highly productive strategy—a time when U.S. officials not only perceived the key international trends that had begun to leave their mark during the 1970s, but also effectively mobilized U.S. power and resources to reap the benefits. Looking back on this period, it is hard not to be struck by the degree of strategic vision and intentionality shown by officials like Reagan and Shultz, and by the extent that they were able to actualize those ideas via concrete policy initiatives that brought aspiration into closer alignment with reality.

It is also hard not to be struck, however, by the fact that this process was rarely a smooth or straightforward one. Strategic vision did not translate immediately or seamlessly into effective policy. Across every important dimension of resurgence, U.S. statecraft had to evolve and adapt in order to succeed. In the case of U.S.-Soviet relations, this meant shifting the blend of confrontation and conciliation that characterized Washington's policy from 1983–1984 onward, so as to tamp down escalating superpower tensions and best employ the strategic leverage the administration had begun to generate. In the case of international economic relations, it meant adapting policy—sometimes repeatedly—on individual issues from Third World debt to exchange-rate management, in order to achieve the consistently held goal of a more open and market-oriented global system. (Regarding the Third World debt crisis specifically, it took nearly a decade of such alterations, lasting into Bush's presidency, to elicit a conclusive outcome.) In the case of democracy promotion, it required a significant change in overall perspective from late 1981–1982 onward, followed by another period of evolution—sometimes disorderly and crisis-driven in nature—in U.S. policies toward a number of specific countries. Real breakthroughs and significant gains would eventually come in all of these areas, but the pathway from conception to achievement was invariably a tortuous one.

It was one that entailed plenty of bumps and stumbles, as well. There was Reagan's initial backtracking on human rights and democracy, which came at a real cost in places such as Guatemala, and the hesitation and contradictions that sometimes marred his later policy toward countries like the Philippines and El Salvador. In the Cold War, there was the fact that Reagan's early approach actually raised East-West hostility to potentially dangerous levels, even as it helped restore U.S. advantage. In the realm of international monetary and economic policy, the administration's opening stance on issues such as exchange rates and policy coordination significantly increased the frictions caused by globalization, and jeopardized political support for freer trade. The list of examples could go on, but the point is that the record of U.S. policy during the 1980s was far from unblemished. Indeed, it was precisely those blemishes that often occasioned the adaptation that would eventually conduce to greater success.

To note these issues is not to dispute the overall efficacy of Reagan-era strategy, much less to argue—as some have—that there were no coherent strategies to speak of.[16] It is simply to recognize that strategy is *inherently* a tortuous and imprecise affair. It is a discipline that places a premium on long-term purpose and vision, but it is equally a discipline that requires frequent reassessment and recalibration at the level of tactics and methods. It is something in which missteps and course corrections are virtually inevitable, and in which learning and iteration are thus imperative. This much has always been true of U.S. strategy, and the period assessed here was no exception.[17] Nor—and this leads to a fifth and final theme—was it an exception to the rule that even great achievements can leave troubling legacies.

The story of U.S. foreign policy from the late 1970s through the early 1990s was primarily one of revival and accomplishment. This was a period when the country roared back from malaise and widespread pessimism, and surged forward to a perch of unrivaled and in some ways unprecedented international primacy. It was a time when American statecraft made essential contributions to ending the Cold War resoundingly on U.S. and Western terms, to enabling electoral democracy and free markets to race ahead at breakneck pace, and ultimately to forging a unipolar order amid the wreckage of bipolarity's collapse. Not least of all, it was an era in which American policymakers could be positively Bismarckian in their ability to gauge the flow of history, and thereby to guide it as well. These were all truly impressive outcomes—outcomes that together thrust the United States into a spot of tremendous power and authority in world affairs, and outcomes that must surely rank this period as one of the more constructive chapters in the history of American foreign policy. When measured against the dreary expectations that were so prevalent in the mid- and late 1970s, in fact, the subsequent achievements of U.S. policy seem all the more staggering by comparison.

Yet still there remains reason to resist the triumphalism that can infuse interpretations of such periods, because this era of resurgence left more problematic residues as well.[18] For one thing, the global forces that arose and developed during those years were not entirely fortuitous. In the Middle East especially, the rise of Islamic radicalism, Persian Gulf instability, and international terrorism created a web of interwoven challenges that were far more disruptive to U.S. interests. The travails of American officials in redressing those dangers gave the lie to any illusion that U.S. policy was *uniformly* successful during the 1980s, while also ensuring that those phenomena would continue to afflict the country's security posture long thereafter. Not even the U.S. victory in the Gulf War in 1991 offered an escape from this predicament— that conflict left the embers of regional instability to smolder, while providing fuel for the fires of terroristic jihad. The United States might have been ascendant, in other words, but so were the threats that would often render its post–Cold War primacy so fraught indeed.

In few areas, of course, were America's difficulties as pronounced as they had been in the Middle East. But even where the sweep of events was far more encouraging, ambiguities were ineluctable. Globalization may have acted as a powerful stimulant to U.S. renewal beginning in the 1970s, for instance, but it stimulated new insecurities and inequalities as well. At home, increased global integration gave impetus to the growing socioeconomic disparities that characterized the American experience from that decade onward. When combined with the impact of Reaganomics, this integration also exacerbated the effects of an economic paradigm shift that was rejuvenating for U.S. power but excruciating for many Americans. On the international front, a more fluid world economy brought with it the potential for greater turmoil and instability, as demonstrated by the dramatic currency swings of the 1970s and 1980s, and the threat that the Third World debt crisis had posed to the entire global financial system. Life in a more open world carried liabilities as well as benefits, a fact that would become all the more salient as the post–Cold War era progressed.

If the global forces that transformed America's position could be bivalent in their effects, so could the particular policies U.S. leaders pursued to profit from those trends. For the very initiatives that did so much to facilitate resurgence often entailed real costs and compromises along the way. Those costs were perhaps most literal in the Cold War, where Reagan's military buildup helped turn the tide in that struggle, while also helping to produce an explosion of red ink that raised questions about the long-term fiscal footing of the United States. Other U.S. policies involved serious moral compromises, whether via the undemocratic law-breaking of Iran-Contra, or the sponsorship of disreputable and sometimes downright murderous clients such as the Salvadoran armed forces and the Nicaraguan rebels. In cases such as these, Washington ultimately obtained the ends it sought in the realms of superpower competition and democracy promotion. But it became a party to devastating Third World conflicts, and even horrifying atrocities, in doing so. Productive as it may have been, the reassertion of U.S. power had its darker side.

It also had its contradictions, in the sense that American strategy helped lay the groundwork for crises and conflicts to come. To be sure, U.S. policy was far from solely or even primarily responsible for problems such as nuclear proliferation in South Asia or the rise of an international jihad, and it takes a special American narcissism to believe otherwise.[19] Yet the Cold War initiatives that the United States pursued from the late 1970s onward did nonetheless *assist* in the emergence of these dangers, and helped set the geopolitical context in which they flourished. In the same vein, the great progress that Washington made in promoting globalization and neoliberalism during the 1980s occasioned dilemmas of its own. The resentment and dislocations that pro-market reforms fostered in the global south, and the security challenges that explosive Chinese growth would soon uncover—both issues would be persistent challenges for U.S. officials in the post–Cold War era, and both flowed, at least partially, from the achievements of earlier years. As the United States moved into the unipolar moment, a fair amount of blowback would come with it.[20]

One must be careful not to take this line of argument too far, by portraying U.S. strategy as distinctly counterproductive or even Pyrrhic in its results. Successful strategies *always* have negative by-products, because it is simply impossible to optimize on every dimension simultaneously. American strategy in this particular era generally optimized on the most important dimensions—those that enabled the country to attain such a formidable primacy as the 1990s started—and the costs and blowback that resulted were in many cases the price of effectiveness. What remains undeniable, however, is that there was indeed a price to be paid. "Almost every achievement," James Baker later wrote, "contains within its success the seeds of a future problem."[21] The story of America's rise to unipolarity affirms this essential truth. The history of the succeeding years, in turn, demonstrates a second and similar truth: that unmatched power can be a double-edged sword.

American Power and Policy in the Post–Cold War Era

"We have within our grasp an extraordinary possibility that few generations have enjoyed," Bush's 1991 *NSS* proclaimed—"to build a new international system in accordance with our own values and ideals, as old patterns and certainties crumble around us."[22] This claim, issued as the Bush administration was first defining the nation's strategy for the post–Cold War era, captured the spirit of U.S. statecraft as that era progressed. Contradictions and ambiguities aside, the American resurgence had given the country unique leverage in the global arena, at a time when that arena itself seemed uniquely malleable. Under both Republican and Democratic leaders, and across the most crucial aspects of U.S. international engagement, the conduct of American policy thereafter showed that Washington intended to hold and exploit the initiative.

Consider the arc of U.S. alliance relations. The case of German reunification had already established that the United States was more inclined to expand than contract its alliance system as the superpower struggle ended and old geopolitical boundaries disappeared. That tendency would only grow more pronounced. During the 1990s, the Clinton administration undertook initiatives to fortify the U.S. position in East Asia by consolidating and deepening American alliances with Japan and South Korea. It also launched what would become a multiphase, bipartisan project to push NATO deep into the former Soviet bloc and even the former Soviet Union itself. Poland, Hungary, and the Czech Republic joined NATO in 1999; within another decade, nine more countries, including Romania, Bulgaria, and the Baltic states, had followed. The rationales for enlargement were numerous, ranging from preempting potential instability and nationalism in Eastern Europe, to creating the climate of security that would allow transitioning post-communist states to consolidate economic and political reforms. But at a very basic level, enlargement reflected a drive to capitalize on the collapse of Russian influence, extend the U.S.-led "democratic zone of peace," and seize an even more favorable configuration of power in post–Cold War Europe. "Countries that were once our adversaries now can become our allies," the Clinton administration asserted. Contrary to predictions that its alliances might wither absent the Soviet threat, Washington was now pushing past its Cold War sphere of influence to extend U.S. geopolitical reach even farther than before.[23]

Post–Cold War administrations followed the same approach in the economic and political sphere, through the further promotion of free markets, free trade, and democracy. The most ambitious prong of this offensive came in Russia itself, where the Clinton administration strongly supported Boris Yeltsin's fairly democratic and reformist government, while also encouraging neoliberal "shock therapy" under IMF and World Bank auspices. Yet the offensive itself lasted beyond Clinton's presidency, and was much broader (and often more effective) than this single campaign. It entailed promoting political and economic liberalization in Eastern Europe through NATO expansion and other means, and supporting democratic breakthroughs—or discouraging authoritarian revivals—in countries from Haiti and Guatemala in the 1990s, to Georgia and Ukraine a decade later. It likewise involved measures to promote global trade liberalization through the conclusion of NAFTA and the Uruguay Round, support for the creation of the WTO, and the signing of additional free-trade and investment pacts with countries from Colombia to Chile to South Korea. Not least, it featured a consistent advocacy of globalization and democratization as pathways to a more secure, prosperous, and peaceful world, one in which the United States would be ever more advantaged and influential. America's "cherished goal," Clinton declared in 1995, was a "more secure world where democracy and free markets know no borders." It was a statement that just as easily could have come from George H. W. Bush before him, or George W. Bush after.[24]

All these endeavors were backstopped by a military posture that remained very forward-leaning and, if anything, became more interventionist with the Cold War over. Through the 1990s and after, U.S. forces would remain deployed in significant numbers in Europe, East Asia, and the Middle East, so as to reassure allies, deter potential threats, and suppress the instability and security competitions that might halt the march of free institutions or otherwise unsettle the unipolar order. In support of these goals, American forces were now structured to fight two major wars against regional challengers such as Iraq, Iran, or North Korea virtually simultaneously. "Such a capability is the *sine qua non* of a superpower," Pentagon officials wrote, "and is essential to the credibility of our overall national security strategy."[25] Washington also used military power, economic pressure, and other tools to contain and undermine such "rogue states," and to inhibit them from developing nuclear arsenals that might counteract American conventional dominance or underwrite aggressive behavior. The United States had stymied and eventually defeated an "outlaw empire" during the postwar era, Anthony Lake wrote in 1994; it would now use its unparalleled capabilities to prevent this new "band of outlaws" from spoiling a more promising post–Cold War moment.[26]

The counterpart to these measures was a growing willingness to use force to vindicate the American concept of how that post–Cold War system should work. In hindsight, an enduring result of the Persian Gulf War in 1991 was to propagate the notion that the "revolution in military affairs" was making it possible to achieve low-casualty, virtually immaculate victories over the weaker opponents that the United States now confronted. Despite the rude ending to the humanitarian mission in Somalia, where eighteen servicemen were killed in bloody urban combat in late 1993, the effect was gradually to loosen the constraints on sending U.S. forces into battle even when less-than-vital interests were at stake. "What's the point of having this superb military that you're always talking about if we can't use it?" Madeleine Albright famously asked Colin Powell in 1993. Per Albright's query, the tendency was indeed to "use it" as the 1990s progressed.[27]

In 1994, for example, the Clinton administration employed military coercion—even mobilizing and dispatching an invasion force—to overthrow a repressive junta that had seized power in Haiti three years prior. Between 1995 and 1999, U.S. and NATO forces would then fight two separate wars in the Balkans, so as to extinguish volatility on Europe's southern flank, and end the "ethnic cleansing" of vulnerable civilian populations. The lesson of the 1999 conflict over Kosovo, Clinton announced, should be understood by all: "If somebody comes after innocent civilians and tries to kill them en masse because of their race, their ethnic background, or their religion, and it's within our power to stop it, we will stop it."[28] Enjoying a surfeit of military power and a death of existential threats, Washington could increasingly intervene to support democracy and human rights, and to enforce its desired norms of the unipolar order.

At the time and after, analysts vigorously debated the wisdom of these interventions, and questioned whether U.S. policies added up to a coherent program for utilizing American primacy.[29] But if the overall goal of U.S. statecraft was to extend and deepen that primacy, then the outcome of the first post–Cold War decade was generally quite positive. America's soft-power ideological preeminence certainly increased, with global economic integration and market institutions sustaining their forward momentum, and the number of electoral democracies growing from 89 in 1991 to 121 in 2001.[30] And in hard-power terms, America's pursuit of an assertive post–Cold War strategy led to a near-term accentuation of U.S. dominance. Because Washington maintained relatively robust military spending as most other countries slashed theirs, U.S. defense outlays went from equaling those of the next six nations combined in 1996–1997 to equaling those of roughly the next fifteen countries five years later.[31] Meanwhile, the United States had been extending its alliance system and the geopolitical influence that came with it, and pressing its interests and ideals in areas that had formerly been locked away by Cold War divisions. Finally, the fact that America rode a globalization-aided economic boom for most of the decade meant that the U.S. share of global GDP slightly increased from 1991 to 2001.[32] In sum, the world did not revert to a multipolar mean during the 1990s—it grew *more* unipolar with time.

Unipolarity, for its part, provided a relatively high degree of international stability, at least compared to what many academic experts had expected. During the early 1990s, a common fear was that the post–Cold War world would see a return to febrile geopolitical volatility. Prominent international relations realists such as John Mearsheimer argued that it was Cold War bipolarity that had largely maintained the peace and suppressed sources of turmoil for the past forty-five years. The breakdown of bipolarity, then, would have lamentable systemic consequences. It would lead to the fracturing of long-standing alliance blocs as Soviet power faded, and to the rampant spread of nuclear weapons as countries rushed to provide for their own security. It would precipitate the return of more independent and nationalistic behavior by Germany and Japan, and the eruption of intense, multisided security rivalries in areas such as Central Europe and the Far East. "We will soon miss the Cold War," Mearsheimer famously warned; "the prospect of major crises, even wars . . . is likely to increase dramatically now that the Cold War is receding into history."[33]

But whatever problems the post–Cold War system produced, this was one dog that mostly did not bark. Bipolarity did not give way to a viciously competitive and tumultuous multipolarity; it gave way to a unipolar system in which U.S. policymakers were set on preventing precisely the sort of dangerous instability that Mearsheimer envisioned. By and large, the results of that project were not half-bad. German and Japanese revanchism did not materialize, contrary to the fears of so many observers. As U.S. officials had intended, rather, American force deployments and alliance commitments kept Tokyo and Berlin anchored firmly within the Western community, and reduced whatever need they might otherwise have felt to strike out fully on their own in military and geopolitical terms. NATO expansion enveloped Germany in a group of democratic, Western-oriented states while also ensuring continued U.S. presence in Europe; the persistence and deepening of American security ties in the Pacific likewise helped keep historical frictions between Japan and its neighbors comparatively muted. In fact, both Germany and Japan actually decreased their military spending markedly during the 1990s—a sure sign that both countries remained nested quite comfortably within a U.S.-led order.[34]

America's unipolar strategy was mitigating the prospects for instability in other ways, as well. In the former Soviet Union, the determined application of U.S. influence was integral to achieving the denuclearization of Ukraine, Kazakhstan, and Belarus in the early 1990s, easing fears that the Soviet collapse might birth a plethora of poor, precarious, and nuclear-armed states. In Eastern Europe, U.S. commitments helped smother potential flare-ups and security dilemmas following the breakdown of Soviet hegemony. The extension of NATO security guarantees, for example, reduced incentives for nuclear proliferation or major military buildups in traditionally vulnerable states such as Poland, as U.S.-led military interventions ended—albeit belatedly—the ethnic conflicts that had erupted in the Balkans before they could destabilize southeastern Europe more broadly. "Let a fire burn here in this area," Clinton had said in announcing the beginning of U.S. operations in Kosovo, "and the flames will spread."[35] Even in the Persian Gulf, the much-maligned—and deeply problematic—U.S. presence continued to play an important prophylactic role, checking the ambitions of a tyrannical Iraqi regime that had twice before made bids for regional dominance, and that once again menaced Kuwait in 1994. In these and other respects, what one scholar terms "the American pacifier" suppressed renascent geopolitical competition and upheaval in key areas, and provided the reassurance that permitted global economic integration and other positive trends to continue their good work.[36] The unipolar system was far from perfect, as we will see, but its benefits—for the United States and for broader international security—were nonetheless quite substantial.

Both the stability and deepening of the unipolar system, of course, testified to the impact of forces that U.S. officials did not control, as well as those they did. But the flow of events in the 1990s nonetheless offered evidence to suggest that the basic premise of a primacist strategy—that unipolarity was sustainable and desirable—was not wildly unrealistic. In consequence, by the turn of the millennium, there was a growing tendency to see unipolarity in the same way that the authors of the 1992 DPG had seen it—as something that might well become a semipermanent feature of the international landscape. Just a decade earlier, leading international relations scholars such as Kenneth Waltz had argued that unipolarity was a systemic aberration that would soon give way to a renewed balance of power.[37] In the late 1990s and early 2000s, by contrast, the debate was more and more shaped by analysts such as William Wohlforth, who contended that the unipolar *im*balance was so pronounced and stable that it could endure as long as bipolarity before it. Similarly, Krauthammer himself now declared that the "unipolar moment" had become a "unipolar era," and that this essentially benign form of U.S. empire could, and should, last for generations. As long as a primacist strategy was properly resourced, these analysts believed, American preeminence and its blessings need not fade anytime soon.[38]

These assessments spoke to the heady condition of U.S. power a decade into unipolarity. The horizon was far from cloudless, however, because America's post–Cold War statecraft also had its liabilities. In the broadest sense, the primacist ethos that drove U.S. policy ensured that there was little rest for the Cold War weary—that America would not, as Jeane Kirkpatrick had recommended, again become "a normal country in a normal time." The hundreds of billions of dollars spent annually on defense and foreign affairs, the troops dispatched to patrol faraway frontiers, the lives risked and sometimes lost in unfamiliar lands, the disproportionate responsibility borne for world order—these costs of superpowerdom lived on even after the Soviet Union perished. To be sure, the direct financial costs of the primacist strategy were not especially high by historical standards: Washington spent 3–4 percent of GDP on defense in the late 1990s, as opposed to well over 10 percent at the peak of the Cold War. But those costs remained significantly higher than they would have been under a more circumspect foreign policy, and in some respects—such as frequency of significant military interventions—the United States was actually more active than it had been during the superpower struggle. The Clinton administration liked to call America "the indispensable nation"; indispensability, it turned out, could be a taxing role to play.[39]

Relative geopolitical stability notwithstanding, that role was also rife with tensions and dangers. As discussed previously, the surge of globalization and neoliberalism during the 1970s and 1980s had been broadly but not unambiguously beneficial for the United States. Those ambiguities became more prominent with time. Even as the freer international flow of goods and capital invigorated post–Cold War capitalism, it ever more baldly revealed what one leading economist called the "deep fault line between groups who have the skills and mobility to flourish in global markets" and those without.[40] The risks and instability associated with interconnectedness were also becoming more tangible, as crises that began in one area regularly raised the specter of broader, systemic contagion. In 1994–1995, a Mexican currency crisis—itself exacerbated by the greater mobility of capital—threatened to spread to other Latin American countries and the United States, necessitating a $50 billion emergency package provided by Washington and others to staunch the bleeding. In 1997–1998, another financial crisis smashed through East Asia and then spread to Russia and parts of Latin America, leaving economic havoc in its path. In both cases, the epidemics were contained, just as the Third World debt crisis earlier had been, before the results turned truly catastrophic for the global economy. But the very need for such containment was becoming a more commonplace occurrence, confirming that the age of globalization was a tumultuous time indeed.[41]

Tumults aside, the mantra in Washington remained that globalization was overwhelmingly a net positive for America and that—as Undersecretary of State Joan Spero put it in 1996—"efforts to resist the powerful technological and economic forces behind globalization . . . are misguided and, in the long run, futile."[42] If resistance was truly futile, however, that didn't stop plenty of people in the United States and other countries from trying. The protests and riots that marred the WTO Summit in Seattle in 1999, the rise of neopopulist leaders in Latin America who inveighed against neoliberalism and the Washington consensus, the resentment of Russians who blamed post-communist shock therapy and financial crises for destroying their livelihoods and savings, the community leaders in India and elsewhere who led boycotts against foreign goods, and even the rising domestic resistance within the United States to the further proliferation of FTAs—all these issues were part of a growing global discomfort with growing global integration. By the late 1990s, they constituted what a writer for the *Financial Times* called a "powerful backlash against globalization," and thus against a core element of America's unipolar agenda.[43]

Nor was globalization the only area in which the habits of hegemony had begun to elicit an adverse response. America's primacist strategy was generally reassuring to states that benefitted from U.S. protection, and in line with the tenets of the 1992 DPG, Washington also sought to render unipolarity palatable to countries such as Russia and China by drawing them more deeply into the international economic order. Clinton shepherded Yeltsin's Russia into APEC and the G-7 (rechristened the G-8) in 1998. The administration likewise waged a successful campaign, in the face of considerable domestic criticism regarding human rights and other issues, that paved the way for China's accession to the WTO in 2001. The approach, as Clinton wrote in his final *NSS*, was one of "seizing on the desire of both countries to participate in the global economy and global institutions, insisting that both accept the obligations as well as the benefits of integration."[44]

The effect was not all that U.S. officials had desired, however, in part because other aspects of American policy appeared far more sinister to these key regional players. Despite Clinton's close personal relationship with Yeltsin, many Russians officials not unreasonably saw NATO expansion as an effort to exploit Moscow's debility and extend the U.S. sphere of influence ever deeper into the former Soviet empire. The enlargement of the alliance, the director of the Russian foreign intelligence service had warned as early as 1993, "would bring the biggest military grouping in the world, with its colossal offensive potential, directly to the borders of Russia." Russian observers equally resented America's repeated use of force in the Balkans, another area where Moscow had traditionally held much sway. Accordingly, these initiatives created an undercurrent of tension in the relationship—one that the Clinton administration managed fairly well during the 1990s, but one that would nonetheless grow stronger and more explosive as the Kremlin gradually recovered from its extreme post-collapse weakness.[45]

In East Asia, meanwhile, Washington's determination to uphold regional stability and protect a favorable status quo was starting to run smack into the ambitions of a China that was rapidly becoming stronger and more assertive in its own right. In 1995–1996, China sought to intimidate Taiwan on the eve of its first direct presidential election by conducting provocative missile tests in the waters surrounding the island. Clinton responded by dispatching two carrier battle groups—the foremost symbols of U.S. military power—to the area. The show of force achieved its immediate purpose, and it hammered home the fact that Washington set the geopolitical rules of the road even in China's backyard. "Beijing should know, and this will remind them," Defense Secretary William Perry said, "that while they are a great military power, the premier—the strongest—military power in the western Pacific is the United States." Perhaps not surprisingly, however, the crisis also underscored the incentives for Beijing to invest the fruits of its ongoing economic boom in a long-term military buildup meant to counteract that U.S. dominance and give China greater authority in regional affairs. From the mid-1990s onward, a flourishing bilateral economic relationship could only partially obscure the emerging geopolitical tensions between Washington and a fast-rising power that was simultaneously profiting from, and chafing at, the contours of the unipolar order.[46]

The revival of open great-power rivalry was still an incipient danger to that order in the late 1990s. The threat of Islamist terrorism, by comparison, represented the most severe near-term form of resistance to U.S. hegemony. Osama bin Laden's al-Qaeda network had been born amid the Afghan jihad, and turned its venom on Washington following the deployment of U.S. troops in Saudi Arabia during the Gulf War and after. Bin Laden viewed this manifestation of the globe-spanning, post–Cold War U.S. military presence as a grave insult to Islam. He also argued that the strategic goal of al-Qaeda—the destruction of faithless, pro-Western regimes and the establishment of a religious caliphate stretching across the Muslim world—could be accomplished only by driving the domineering superpower out of the Middle East. Righteous holy warriors must kill Americans, civilians and soldiers alike, "in order for their armies to move out of all the lands of Islam, defeated and unable to threaten any Muslim," he declared. Beginning in the mid-1990s, this ambition gave rise to a series of escalating strikes against American citizens and targets, including the bombing of U.S. embassies in

Kenya and Tanzania in 1998, and the attack on the USS *Cole* off Yemen in 2000. The culmination came with the stunning mass-casualty attacks on the United States itself in September 2001, which left nearly 3,000 people dead, and shattered the atmosphere of post–Cold War security that America had enjoyed.[47]

The 9/11 attacks offered Americans a tragic reminder that, as one expert put it, "the overweening power that they had taken for granted over the past dozen years is not the same as omnipotence."[48] What's more, they were the starkest example of how U.S. dominance and the world order it upheld could themselves be founts of danger and defiance. The attacks demonstrated that Washington's post–Cold War agenda could inspire homicidal resistance from actors who saw U.S. policies as a check on their own ambitions. They showed how enemies could exploit some of the most prominent features of globalization—the ease of international travel and communications, for instance, and the ability to move money across borders—to strike at the American homeland itself. Beyond that, 9/11 illustrated how the very depth of America's military supremacy encouraged its foes to adopt innovative, asymmetric tactics—like using knives and box-cutters to turn commercial airliners into lethal missiles—as their means of waging war against the hyper-power. In so many ways, 9/11 encapsulated the insecurities and pernicious consequences of U.S. primacy. At the apex of its post–Cold War power, the nation also seemed to have reached the apex of its vulnerability.

It was perhaps paradoxical, then, that the immediate upshot of the attacks was to *heighten* the hegemonic impulse in U.S. statecraft. As historians such as John Lewis Gaddis have noted, America has often responded to looming dangers by seeking security in expansion rather than retrenchment.[49] After 9/11, too, the combination of enormous fear and enormous power led the country to push forward rather than pull back. Military spending leapt dramatically, increasing by a real-dollar average of 7.4 percent annually between 2001 and 2009, and the George W. Bush administration unabashedly embraced the cause of perpetuating U.S. primacy. "America has and intends to keep military strengths beyond challenge," the president announced in 2002, "thereby making the destabilizing arms races of other eras pointless and limiting rivalries to trade and other pursuits of peace."[50]

Bush also pushed forward in the employment of those strengths. Following 9/11, the administration mobilized U.S. power, not only to strike al-Qaeda leadership, bases, and infrastructure in Afghanistan, but also to destroy the Taliban regime that had sheltered bin Laden and to supplant it with a representative democracy. Then, in 2002–2003, the administration pivoted to destroy Saddam Hussein's regime in Iraq as the second phase of a broader "global war on terror." Toppling Saddam, Bush and his top aides calculated, would offer an unmistakable warning to other regimes or actors that might be tempted to target the United States, and would depose a government whose suspected WMD programs and extensive terror ties now seemed to pose an intolerable threat. Moreover, it would remove a long-standing source of regional instability in a crucial area, and enable the replacement of Saddam's stifling tyranny with a free-market democracy whose success would reverberate throughout the Middle East. "The great struggles of the twentieth century" had left only a "single sustainable model for national success: freedom, democracy, and free enterprise," Bush wrote in his 2002 NSS. In a new era of danger, the United States would now spread that liberal model still further—and via the decisive application of military force—as a way of attacking the root causes of violent extremism and transforming a persistently troubled region.[51]

America's post-9/11 wars, aimed at destroying enemies and remaking governments half a world away, were campaigns that only a superpower could undertake. The early outcomes of those interventions, in turn, seemed to indicate that the nation had reached a whole new level of supremacy. The United States routed al-Qaeda and the Taliban from Afghanistan in less than one hundred days in late 2001, through a creative mix of precision airstrikes, special-forces and paramilitary operations, and targeted support to local proxy militias.[52] If anything, the initial campaign in Iraq was even more impressive. The Pentagon and CENTCOM had crafted a war plan that would use "surprise, speed, shock, and risk" to decimate the Iraqi military and achieve "decapitation of government" with a relatively small attacking force.[53] When the fighting began, roughly 150,000 U.S. ground troops (augmented by air and naval power, as well as 20,000 British soldiers) made short work of Saddam's regime. Mechanized units charged northward from Kuwait, as special-forces operatives secured oil fields and destroyed Scud missiles. U.S. airpower rained destruction on enemy formations and command-and-control assets, and dramatic armored thrusts into the capital precipitated the collapse of the regime after just three weeks of combat. In all, the war showcased an overwhelming conventional military superiority that was now being used in audacious ways and for transformational ends. "By a combination of creative strategies and advanced technologies," Bush declared, "we are redefining war on our terms."[54]

The boast was premature, however, and in retrospect America's post-9/11 wars may have represented the point at which the tide of U.S. power crested and began to recede. For as soon became clear, it was one thing to use

U.S. military supremacy to defeat weaker opponents and break authoritarian regimes. But even for a hyperpower, it was another thing entirely to occupy and stabilize shattered foreign societies, and to implant liberal democracy in countries that had rarely or never really known it before. In Afghanistan and Iraq alike, then, what had initially looked like sweeping victories soon devolved into bloody and protracted insurgencies, in which U.S. troops ran head-on into powerful forces ranging from nationalism to tribalism to Islamic radicalism. The technological superiority of which Bush had bragged meant comparatively little in these conflicts, as determined foes used innovative tactics such as suicide bombings and improved explosive devices to offset U.S. advantages and inflict appalling damage. The Iraq and Afghanistan wars would eventually claim roughly 7,000 American lives through 2015. They would also consume trillions of dollars in either direct or indirect costs, while leaving U.S. forces deprived of anything approximating decisive triumphs. The wars thus became symbols not of American preeminence, but of American hubris and overreach.[55]

Particularly so the Iraq War, which like Vietnam four decades earlier had traumatic and wide-ranging effects. The decision to wage that war had produced a wide rift with key European allies, who worried that amid the fevered post-9/11 climate, U.S. power was now being wielded in destabilizing and even destructive ways. "Our most important partner," lamented German foreign minister Joschka Fischer, "is making decisions that we consider extremely dangerous."[56] The war itself then had a host of unintended consequences. It undermined U.S. credibility when Saddam's vaunted WMD stockpiles turned out to be largely nonexistent, and it cast doubt on the entire democracy-promotion agenda when Iraqi liberation ushered in an orgy of chaos and sectarian blood-letting that claimed well over 100,000 civilian lives. The war simultaneously handed an invaluable recruiting tool and training ground to an international jihadist movement that had been badly weakened in Afghanistan, while empowering a longtime U.S. nemesis—Iran—to assert its influence in the regional power vacuum that the war created. Perhaps most broadly, the conflict consumed U.S. foreign policy for years, detracting attention and resources from other priorities, and sapping the confidence and energy of American statecraft. In multiple respects, excessive ambition had rendered U.S. leadership weaker and less impressive than before.[57]

As Bush's presidency came to a close, there were other signs that America's post–Cold War expansion might have gone too far. By 2008, NATO had already incorporated three former Soviet republics, and it was considering taking on two more, Georgia and Ukraine. Unfortunately, there had been too little serious consideration of whether the alliance could actually *defend* these new members in a crisis, or whether the continued expansion of NATO might eventually stretch Moscow's tolerance to the breaking point. Both questions were answered in August 2008, when Russia—following a period of rapidly escalating tensions and mutual provocations—prosecuted a short, sharp war against Georgia and its pro-U.S. government. That conflict quickly led to the dismemberment of Georgia as Washington and NATO stood passively by, and it signaled that the Kremlin was now willing to fight to prevent the further encroachment of U.S. influence.[58] When Vladimir Putin repeated the performance six years later—carving apart Ukraine after it began to move toward the Western orbit—the result was to return U.S.-Russian relations to something near a Cold War climate, to cast a pall of insecurity over Eastern Europe and the Baltic states, and to raise serious questions about whether NATO could honor even its existing commitments in those areas. In geopolitics as in war, driving forward creates new possibilities and new dangers alike. This latter aspect of NATO expansion was now coming more clearly into view.

At the same time, and more seriously still, the economic strength that underpinned U.S. global leadership had also come under doubt. The economic model that had arisen from the crises of the 1970s was driven by globalization, neoliberal reform, and an ability to borrow cheaply from abroad. That model fueled the long expansion of the 1980s and 1990s, and another period of respectable growth after a recession in 2000–2001. Yet the downsides to this performance were a dramatic accumulation of debt, both public and private, and the dangers inherent in a financial sector in which deregulation had now gone to an extreme. The reckoning occurred in 2007–2008, with the eruption of a financial crisis that sent the United States and other countries plunging into recession, destroyed perhaps $34 *trillion* in global wealth, and very nearly led to an outright breakdown of international finance and another worldwide depression. As in the 1980s and 1990s, constructive improvisation by Washington and other parties prevented the worse-case scenarios from materializing. The experience, though, was chastening nonetheless. The crisis badly undermined the attractiveness of the American economic model, and it thrust the United States into a period of sluggish growth and government austerity that accentuated post-Iraq counsels of retrenchment.[59] Along the way, the crisis underscored the extent to which real economic dynamism now seemed to have shifted decisively eastward, and especially to China.

"In 20 years, if they keep developing the way they have, they could be a pretty scary outfit," Kissinger had said during the 1970s.[60] By the second decade of the twenty-first century, what Kissinger envisioned was manifestly coming to pass. China had averaged perhaps 10 percent annual growth since 1979, allowing it double the size of its economy every eight years and to climb the ranks of the global economic powers at unprecedented pace.[61] By the mid-point of Barack Obama's presidency, China had already surged past Japan as the world's second-largest economy, and it had a GDP that was more than half as large as that of the United States. With growth rates still in the neighborhood of 7–8 percent per year, most observers disagreed only on *when* Beijing would eventually surpass Washington. Economic power, in turn, was rapidly being translated into military might. Chinese defense outlays grew roughly sevenfold between 1996 and 2013, and the country amassed precisely the air and sea capabilities needed to project its own power while also contesting U.S. preeminence in the Western Pacific. "China is reshaping the military order in Asia," a Pentagon official noted in late 2008, "and it is doing so at our expense."[62] As Beijing more aggressively pressed its interests in that region, as it competed for influence in places as far afield as Africa and Latin America, and as it rejected U.S. concepts of democracy and touted the benefits of its own political-economic model, it was hard not to wonder whether the world's next leading power was making its ascent and bringing the unipolar moment to an end.

The cumulative result of these factors was to bring the domestic debate on U.S. prospects almost full circle to where it had been in the 1970s. During the late Bush and early Obama years, scholars and pundits heralded "the end of the American era" and the advent of a "post-American world." International relations experts who had earlier predicted the swift rise of multipolarity following the Cold War now revived those forecasts, and argued that Washington could best adapt to its diminished circumstances by dramatically rolling back overseas commitments and accepting a far more modest foreign policy.[63] Among the public at large, a poll taken in 2011 showed that 69 percent of respondents believed that the United States was now in decline.[64] Other observers pushed back against this gloomy outlook, touting the extensive benefits that assertive U.S. global engagement afforded, and writing that the principal danger to American primacy was one of "committing preemptive superpower suicide out of a misplaced fear of declining power."[65] But it was still becoming less and less common to talk of a unipolar era lasting generations, and even as U.S. leaders continued to evoke the imperative of American leadership, they occasionally spoke simply of making a virtue of necessity by turning the approaching multipolar world into a "multi-partner world."[66]

Was this merely another wave of premature pessimism, or was the wolf finally here when it came to American decline? The evidence was more mixed than it first appeared. In one sense, by Obama's second term there was no disputing that U.S. primacy was more contested than at any time since the Cold War. Virtually around the world, Washington confronted serious threats to the global system it anchored—from a revisionist Russia that was using force to coerce its neighbors and redraw the boundaries of the post-Soviet space, to rampant instability and Islamic extremism in the Middle East, to the stalling of democracy's advance in the face of smarter and more resilient authoritarian regimes.[67] Post–financial crisis defense cuts were simultaneously impairing U.S. capabilities, and forcing hard choices about priorities and presence in a seemingly more volatile world. And in the midst of all this trouble, the rise of China loomed ever larger. That rise had already cut into America's post–Cold War economic lead, and the two-decade Chinese military buildup was markedly altering the strategic equation—and perceptions of relative power and influence—in East Asia.[68] If Beijing continued to advance at anything approximating recent rates, and if Washington remained on its current trajectory, then it was indeed just a matter of time until unipolarity had run its course, and the United States faced a rival that could challenge it not simply regionally but perhaps globally as well.

Yet there was also good reason to question the narrative of U.S. decline, just as there had been in the days of stagflation and malaise. For one thing, all the talk about America's travails and China's rise often obscured the fact that the United States still had a very formidable overall lead. As of 2014, the United States had a $17.4 trillion economy that remained roughly $7 trillion larger than that of China.[69] U.S. per capita GDP—a crucial measure of how much wealth the country could extract from its citizenry to pursue geopolitical goals—was over four times that of China.[70] In military terms, the overall U.S. defense budget represented a meaty one-third of global outlays—a figure that remained enormously impressive compared to other historical eras—and it outstripped Chinese spending by more than three to one.[71] Finally, in the crucial realms of global power-projection capabilities and alliance partnerships, there was still simply no comparison—the United States had advantages that would probably not be surmounted by any competitor for many decades, if even then. The international system was no longer as unipolar as it had been a decade and a half before, but it remained markedly slanted in America's direction.

The question was how long things would stay this way, but here too there was cause to wonder if the future was really so foreboding. For all its momentum, China still had to overcome imposing difficulties that stood athwart its continued rise. A corrupt and often-unresponsive government, a rapidly aging population, a dangerous-looking asset bubble, and the slowdown in growth rates that was all but certain to occur as China reached middle-income status were but some of the domestic issues that made straight-line projections of Beijing's ascent seem rather shaky.[72] In geopolitical terms, China faced the challenge of asserting its power in a neighborhood where so many states seemed likely to fear and resist those efforts. For all its difficulties, by contrast, the United States still possessed real long-term advantages. It had a relatively young and growing population, a peerless higher education system, and an unmatched capacity for high-tech innovation. More broadly, the United States boasted an economy that possessed terrific underlying strengths, and a political system that, for all of its plentiful flaws and dysfunction, nonetheless enjoyed organic legitimacy at home and widespread esteem overseas.[73] If the history of the run-up to the unipolar moment had demonstrated anything, it was that American power had outperformed the skeptics before. Once all of these various factors were taken into account, it seemed plausible—if far from assured—that it might do so again. As always, the ultimate outcome would hinge on those deep structural factors that shaped the context of U.S. policy, as well as the specific strategies that American officials pursued in response.

The future of U.S. primacy thus remained murky a decade and a half into the new millennium, and a quarter-century into the unipolar period. What had become crystal clear was that that primacy had proven to be both blessing and burden. From the start of the post–Cold War era, the United States had enjoyed a historically exceptional power position and a unique capacity to steer the course of world events. It had often deployed those assets constructively, to advance its own interests and continue shaping the global environment in ways that other actors could only envy. And yet just as America's rise to unipolarity had not been without its drawbacks, neither were these subsequent efforts to make the most of that status. For all its virtues, the primacist ethos left the United States bearing heavy global responsibilities, and promoting forces that were both beneficial and problematic in their effects. It invited the hostility of those that American power threatened, and exposed alarming vulnerabilities as well as showcasing impressive strengths. Finally, and as the Iraq War particularly had demonstrated, it courted the hubristic ambitions that could ultimately lead to overstretch. Regardless of whether it endured, then, America's unipolar moment had illustrated something fundamental about international politics—that even as great power brought great opportunity, it could also bring great insecurity and great cost.

Notes

Introduction

1. Robert Tucker, "America in Decline: The Foreign Policy of 'Maturity,'" *America and the World 1979,* special issue of *Foreign Affairs* 58, no. 3 (1979/1980): esp. 449, 456–57.

2. MemCon between Kissinger, Rusk, Vance, et al., 3/31/1975, Digital National Security Archive (DNSA); Kissinger-Yigal Allon MemCon, 12/9/1974, DNSA. Throughout this book, dates for archival, speech, newspaper, and most magazine citations are given in MM/DD/YYYY format.

3. James Schlesinger, "Is America in Retreat?" *Newsweek,* 11/19/1979.

4. The word *unipolarity* was not invented in the 1990s, but it was popularized then. See Charles Krauthammer, "The Unipolar Moment," *America and the World 1990,* special issue of *Foreign Affairs* 70, no. 1 (1990/1991): 23–33.

5. George Bush and Brent Scowcroft, *A World Transformed* (New York: Vintage, 1999), 564.

6. Francis Fukuyama, "The End of History?" *National Interest* 16 (summer 1989): 3–18.

7. Krauthammer, "Unipolar Moment," 23–24.

8. The outlines of the issue-specific literature on U.S. policy can be traced in the chapters that follow, although space constraints preclude—lamentably—citation of all the relevant books and articles.

9. There are books that take similarly broad-gauge or integral approaches to other key periods. On the 1970s, see Daniel Sargent, *A Superpower Transformed: The Remaking of American Foreign Relations in the 1970s* (New York: Oxford University Press, 2015); and on the 1990s, Andrew Bacevich, *American Empire: The Realities and Consequences of American Diplomacy* (Cambridge, MA: Harvard University Press, 2002). The work with a focus closest to my own is James Cronin, *Global Rules: America, Britain, and a Disordered World* (New Haven: Yale University Press, 2014), which uses the U.S.-UK relationship as a lens through which to view global changes from the mid-postwar era to the present.

10. One note on declassification may be useful at the outset. At some repositories I consulted in the research for this study (particularly the Reagan and George H. W. Bush presidential libraries), the ongoing process of declassification has introduced more fluidity into archival locations and citations than would ideally be the case. At the Reagan Library, for instance, I found that box numbers for certain documents (although not the broader collections) had shifted over the course of my various trips to that archive since 2007. The same is true at the Bush Library. Documents found in Box 42 of FOIA 1998–0099-F (files pertaining to the Persian Gulf War) during my first trips to that archive in 2004–2005, for instance, might have moved to

Box 43 or 44 by the time of my later trips in 2012 and 2013. The number of documents affected seems to be fairly small, and the movement seems to have occurred most frequently in cases in which declassification has been driven primarily by Freedom of Information Act (FOIA) requests rather than more systematic processes. When I found that box numbers did change over the years, I have cited the location in which I found the relevant document most recently.

11. Even within this framework, space constraints dictate leaving some important issues to the side. This book does not address issues of popular culture at any length, for instance, even though such issues were indeed part of the broader soft-power/ideological resurgence of the period. My belief, however, is that these issues—although significant—were ultimately less crucial to the U.S. resurgence than the shifts emphasized here: changes in global power relations, and in the political and economic climate of world politics.

12. As I make clear in the chapters that follow, the divisions between these three periods were rough rather than precise, and there was, obviously, some overlap.

13. Shultz, Statement to Senate Foreign Relations Committee (SFRC), 1/31/1985, *American Foreign Policy: Current Documents* (Washington, DC, 1986), 8 [this collection is hereafter cited as *AFP: CD,* followed by year and page number].

14. For a representative portrait of George H. W. Bush (and his team) as highly skilled tacticians who lacked longer-range vision, see Zbigniew Brzezinski, *Second Chance: Three Presidents and the Crisis of American Superpower* (New York: Basic Books, 2007), 45–82.

15. For an example of this narrower definition of *unipolarity,* see William Wohlforth, "The Stability of a Unipolar World," *International Security* 24, no. 1 (summer 1999): esp. 9–22. Wohlforth defines *unipolarity* as a system "in which one state's capabilities are too great to be counterbalanced" (9).

16. For the idea that the United States "emerged suddenly as a unipole as a result of the Soviet decision to stop competing with it in 1989 and the subsequent dismemberment of the Soviet state two years later," see Nuno Monteiro, *Theory of Unipolar Politics* (New York: Cambridge University Press, 2014), 58. For similar interpretations, see Michael Hunt, *The American Ascendancy: How the United States Gained and Wielded Global Dominance* (Chapel Hill: University of North Carolina Press, 2007), esp. 257–64; Wohlforth, "Stability of a Unipolar World," esp. 10. The role of accident in the end of the Cold War is stressed in Mary Sarotte's insightful account, *The Collapse: The Accidental Opening of the Berlin Wall* (New York: Basic Books, 2014).

17. The "great man" or "individual agency" approach is exemplified in Peter Schweizer, *Victory: The Reagan Administration's Secret Strategy That Hastened the Collapse of the Soviet Union* (New York: Atlantic Monthly Press, 1994); Peter Schweizer, *Reagan's War: The Epic Story of His Forty-Year Struggle and Final Triumph over Communism* (New York: Doubleday, 2002); Paul Kengor, *The Crusader: Ronald Reagan and the Fall of Communism* (New York: HarperCollins, 2006). The "structural forces" approach is perhaps best argued by Stephen Brooks and William Wohlforth, "Power, Globalization, and the End of the Cold War: Reevaluating a Landmark Case for Ideas," *International Security* 25, no. 3 (2000/2001): 5–53. There is a parallel "great man versus structural forces" debate on the Soviet side of the end of the Cold War, revolving around Mikhail Gorbachev's role. For one insightful take, see Vladislav Zubok,

A Failed Empire: The Soviet Union in the Cold War from Stalin to Gorbachev (Chapel Hill: University of North Carolina Press, 2007), esp. 303–35.

18. The idea that strategy entails assessing "the propensity of things" and moving accordingly is discussed in Aaron Friedberg, *A Contest for Supremacy: China, America, and the Struggle for Mastery in Asia* (New York: W. W. Norton, 2011), 123–24.

19. On strategy and its limitations, see Hal Brands, *What Good Is Grand Strategy?: Power and Purpose in American Statecraft from Harry S. Truman to George W. Bush* (Ithaca: Cornell University Press, 2014); Richard Betts, "Is Strategy an Illusion?" *International Security* 25, no. 2 (2000): 5–50; Lawrence Freedman, *Strategy: A History* (New York: Oxford University Press, 2013).

20. The triumphalist tendency is most pronounced in the Reagan hagiography. See, for instance, Schweizer, *Reagan's War*; Kengor, *Crusader*. A deeply insightful account that contains traces of the same tendency is John Lewis Gaddis, *The Cold War: A New History* (New York: Penguin, 2005).

1. Roots of Resurgence

1. See Samuel Huntington, "Why International Primacy Matters," *International Security* 17, no. 4 (1993): 68–83. See also Nuno Monteiro, *Theory of Unipolar Politics* (New York: Cambridge University Press, 2014). In this book, I treat *primacy* and *unipolarity* as functional synonyms, although I am aware that other analysts differentiate them.

2. Melvyn Leffler, *A Preponderance of Power: National Security, the Truman Administration, and the Cold War* (Stanford: Stanford University Press, 1992), 2–4; G. John Ikenberry, *After Victory: Institutions, Strategic Restraint, and the Rebuilding of Order after Major Wars* (Princeton: Princeton University Press, 2002), 168. See also Michael Hunt, *The American Ascendancy: How the United States Gained and Wielded Global Dominance* (Chapel Hill: University of North Carolina Press, 2007).

3. Kissinger Background Briefing, 12/18/1969, *Foreign Relations of the United States 1969–1976,* Vol. I (Washington, D.C., 2003), Doc. #47 [hereafter, documents from this series are cited as *FRUS,* followed by year, volume, and document number].

4. Daniel Sargent, *A Superpower Transformed: The Remaking of American Foreign Relations in the 1970s* (New York: Oxford University Press, 2015), chap. 1.

5. Jonathan Kirshner, *American Power after the Financial Crisis* (Ithaca: Cornell University Press, 2014), 38.

6. Richard Nixon, *First Annual Report to the Congress on United States Foreign Policy for the 1970's,* 2/18/1970, American Presidency Project (APP), http://www.presidency.ucsb.edu/ws/?pid=2835.

7. "Telephone Interview with the Honorable Paul O'Neill," 8/17/1994, 12, Box 1, Yanek Mieczkowski Research Interviews, Gerald Ford Library (GFL).

8. See Richard Rosecrance, ed., *America as an Ordinary Country: U.S. Foreign Policy and the Future* (Ithaca: Cornell University Press, 1976); Robert Keohane, *After Hegemony: Cooperation and Discord in the World Political Economy* (Princeton: Princeton University Press, 1984); Paul Kennedy, *The Rise and Fall of the Great Powers: Economic Change and Military Conflict from 1500 to 2000* (New York: Random House, 1987).

9. Davis to Clift, 4/2/1975, Box 16, Presidential Subject File (PSF), National Security Adviser (NSA) File, GFL; Interagency Intelligence Memorandum, "Latin

American Perceptions of the United States," 4/26/1976, Box 2, President's Country File for Latin America (PCFLA), NSA, GFL.

10. Kissinger-Shah MemCon, 7/27/1973, Box 1027, Presidential-Henry A. Kissinger (HAK) MemCons, National Security Council (NSC) Files, Richard Nixon Presidential Library (RNPL); Ejército Guerrillero de los Pobres, *Guerra Popular,* No. 8, Aug. 1979, Colección Documentos, Centro de Investigaciones Regionales de Mesoamérica (CIRMA).

11. Kissinger-Yigal Allon MemCon, 12/9/1974, DNSA; Nixon Remarks to Media Executives in Kansas City, 7/6/1971, APP.

12. "Interview of Secretary Simon," 6/4/1976, 7, Box 58, William Simon Papers, GFL; Thomas Borstelmann, *The 1970s: A New Global History from Civil Rights to Economic Inequality* (Princeton: Princeton University Press, 2011), 57.

13. Kevin Mattson, *"What the Heck Are You Up to, Mr. President?": Jimmy Carter, America's "Malaise," and the Speech That Should Have Changed the Country* (New York: Bloombury USA, 2009), 14.

14. Harry Truman, Remarks at Baylor University, 3/6/1947, APP; G. John Ikenberry, *After Victory: Institutions, Strategic Restraint, and the Rebuilding of Order after Major Wars* (Princeton: Stanford University Press, 2002), 167–68; Judith Stein, *Pivotal Decade: How the United States Traded Factories for Finance in the Seventies* (New Haven: Yale University Press, 2011), 155.

15. See data in Angus Maddison, "Statistics on World Population, GDP, and Per Capita GDP, 1–2008 AD," http://www.ggdc.net/MADDISON/oriindex.htm (accessed 11/1/2013).

16. Peter Peterson, "The United States in the Changing World Economy: Statistical Background Material," 12/27/1971, Box 31, James Schlesinger Papers, Library of Congress (LC); I. M. Destler, *American Trade Politics,* 4th ed. (Washington, DC: Institute for International Economics, 2005), 51.

17. Peter Peterson, "A Foreign Economic Perspective," 12/27/1971, Box 31, Schlesinger Papers, LC; Robert Collins, *More: The Politics of Economic Growth in Postwar America* (New York: Oxford University Press, 2000), 105.

18. On the nature, costs, and ultimate decline of Bretton Woods, see Francis J. Gavin, *Gold, Dollars, and Power: The Politics of International Monetary Relations, 1958–1971* (Chapel Hill: University of North Carolina Press, 2004). See also Michael Mastanduno, "System Maker and Privilege Taker: U.S. Power and the International Political Economy," *World Politics* 61, no. 1 (2009): esp. 128–34.

19. International Monetary Fund (IMF) Research Department, "(A) Reform of the International Monetary System: A Sketch of Its Scope and Content," 3/7/1972, in *The International Monetary Fund, 1972–1978: Cooperation on Trial, Vol. 3: Documents,* edited by Margaret de Vries (Washington, DC: IMF, 1985), 3.

20. MemCon between Nixon and Advisers, 9/11/1972, *FRUS 1969–1976,* Vol. III, Doc. #100; Rogers to Nixon, 12/2/1971, *FRUS 1969–1976,* Vol. III, Doc. #83.

21. Harold James, *International Monetary Cooperation since Bretton Woods* (New York: Oxford University Press, 1996), 217–51, esp. 227.

22. Leonard Silk, "The Dollar's Tribulations," *New York Times,* 7/4/1973; James Boughton, *Silent Revolution: The International Monetary Fund, 1979–1989* (Washington, DC: IMF, 2001), 14.

23. James Akins, "The Oil Crisis: This Time the Wolf Is Here," *Foreign Affairs* 51, no. 3 (1973): 462–90. The price information in this paragraph and the next is from F. Gregory Gause, *The International Relations of the Persian Gulf* (New York: Cambridge University Press, 2010), 27–30.

24. On the background and effects of the oil shock, see Gause, *International Relations*, 25–34; Daniel Yergin, *The Prize: The Epic Quest for Oil, Money, and Power* (New York: Simon & Schuster, 1991), 563–632.

25. Ford-Prince Saud bin Faisal Al-Saud MemCon, 9/17/1976, Box 21, Mem-Cons, NSA, GFL; Ford to Shah of Iran, 10/29/1976, Box 2, Presidential Correspondence with Foreign Leaders, GFL. On consumer cooperation, see Ethan Kapstein, *The Insecure Alliance: Energy Crises and Western Politics since 1944* (New York: Oxford University Press, 1990), 178–88, esp. 185–86.

26. Henry Kissinger, Secretary's Staff Meeting, 1/7/1974, DNSA.

27. MemCon between Kissinger, Fraser, et al., 12/17/1974, DNSA. See also MemCon between Ford, Schmidt, et al., 5/29/1975, DNSA; Andrew Scott Cooper, *The Oil Kings: How the U.S., Iran, and Saudi Arabia Changed the Balance of Power in the Middle East* (New York: Simon & Schuster, 2011), esp. 180, 194–96.

28. Statistics in Yergin, *Prize,* 635; Borstelmann, *The 1970s,* 60–61, 134, 308. See also Jeffrey Frieden, *Global Capitalism: Its Fall and Rise in the Twentieth Century* (New York: W. W. Norton, 2006), 372–73.

29. Jimmy Carter, *White House Diary* (New York: Farrar, Straus and Giroux, 2010), 321.

30. Jimmy Carter, Address to the Nation, 7/15/1979, APP.

31. Danny Leipziger, "The Cost of a Credible Foreign Economic Policy," 5/5/1980, Box 6, Anthony Lake Records, Record Group (RG) 59, National Archives and Records Administration (NARA).

32. Kissinger-Schumann MemCon, 8/4/1969, DNSA.

33. Report by Nixon to Congress, 2/18/1970, *FRUS 1969–1976,* Vol. I, Doc. #60.

34. NSC Minutes, 4/9/1975, GFL; Robert McMahon, *The Limits of Empire: The United States and Southeast Asia since World War II* (New York: Columbia University Press, 1999), 170–73, 180–81, 189; Interagency Intelligence Memorandum, "Latin American Perceptions of the United States," 4/26/1976, Box 2, PCFLA, NSA, GFL.

35. NSC Minutes, 7/23/1975, GFL.

36. John Kifner, "Putting the Hostages' Lives First," *New York Times,* 5/17/1981.

37. Richard Nixon, Remarks to Inter-American Press Association, 10/31/1969, APP.

38. Ford-Scowcroft-Moynihan MemCon, 8/27/1975, Box 14, MemCons, NSA, GFL. See also CIA, "Political Perspectives on Key Global Issues," Mar. 1977, NLC-132-64-1-1-2, Jimmy Carter Library (JCL).

39. Vernie Oliveiro, "The United States, Multinational Enterprises, and the Politics of Globalization," in *The Shock of the Global: The 1970s in Perspective,* edited by Niall Ferguson, Charles S. Maier, Erez Manela, and Daniel Sargent (Cambridge, MA: Belknap Press, 2010), 144; Hal Brands, "Richard Nixon and Economic Nationalism in Latin America: The Problem of Expropriations," *Diplomacy & Statecraft* 18, no. 1 (2007): 215–35, esp. 216.

40. On NIEO and its context, see Stephen Krasner, *A Structural Conflict: The Third World against Global Liberalism* (Berkeley: University of California Press, 1985), esp. 3–94.

41. Carlos Andrés Pérez to Ford, 9/21/1974, Box 6, PCFLA, GFL; General Assembly Resolution A/RES/S-6/3201, "Declaration on the Establishment of a New International Economic Order," 5/1/1974, http://www.un-documents.net/s6r3201. htm (accessed 11/3/2013).

42. Robinson to Kissinger, 6/22/1976, Box 6, Lot 77D117, Charles Robinson Records, RG 59, NARA.

43. Carter, *White House Diary*, 335.

44. National Foreign Assessment Center (NFAC), "Changing Power Relations among OECD [Organization for Economic Cooperation and Development] States," 10/22/1979, NLC-7-16-10-14-1, JCL.

45. X (George F. Kennan), "The Sources of Soviet Conduct," *Foreign Affairs* 25, no. 4 (1947): 581.

46. Untitled draft by Odom, Box 3, General Odom File, National Security Affairs File (NSAF), JCL. See also "Power Equilibrium," 11/12/1979, Box 30, Odom Papers, LC; Robert S. Norris and William M. Arkin, "Estimated U.S. and Soviet/ Russian Nuclear Stockpiles, 1945–94," *Bulletin of the Atomic Scientists,* Nov.–Dec. 1994, 59.

47. Alan Smith, *Russia and the World Economy: Problems of Integration* (New York: Routledge, 1993), 81.

48. "Extracts from General Secretary Brezhnev's Speeches to the 25th Soviet Party Congress," 2/24/1976, Box 51, Schlesinger Papers, LC; "Can Capitalism Survive?" *Time*, 7/14/1975, 52–63.

49. Kissinger Background Briefing, 8/14/1970, *FRUS 1969–1976*, Vol. I, Doc. #69; Hal Brands, *What Good Is Grand Strategy?: Power and Purpose in American Statecraft from Harry S. Truman to George W. Bush* (Ithaca: Cornell University Press, 2014), 59–101.

50. NSC Minutes, 9/14/1974, GFL; Vladislav Zubok, *A Failed Empire: The Soviet Union in the Cold War from Stalin to Gorbachev* (Chapel Hill: University of North Carolina Press, 2007), 242.

51. Odom, "Whither the Soviet Union," 3/4/1981, Box 11, Odom Papers, LC. See also CIA, "Soviet Defense Spending: Trends in Ruble Expenditures," Mar. 1975, Box 46, William Seidman Files, Office of Economic Affairs Files, GFL; "Statement of the Honorable Donald H. Rumsfeld, Secretary of Defense," 1/27/1976, Box 8, PSF, NSA, GFL; NFAC, "Estimated Soviet Defense Spending: Trends and Prospects," Aug. 1978, Box 12, Odom File, Brzezinski Material (BM), NSAF, JCL.

52. Odd Arne Westad, "Moscow and the Angolan Crisis, 1974–1976: A New Pattern of Intervention," *Cold War International History Project Bulletin*, no. 8–9 (winter 1996): 21.

53. Ermarth to Aaron and Brzezinski, 1/8/1980, NLC-6-1-3-12-8, JCL.

54. Christopher Andrew and Vasili Mitrokhin, *The World Was Going Our Way: The KGB and the Battle for the Third World* (New York: Basic Books, 2005), esp. 471. This paragraph also draws on Odd Arne Westad, *The Global Cold War: Third World Interventions and the Making of Our Times* (Cambridge, UK: Cambridge University Press, 2006), 202–87; National Intelligence Estimate (NIE), "Soviet Military Policy

in the Third World," 10/21/1976, DNSA; Bureau of Intelligence and Research (INR), "Soviet Military Policy and Communist Military Activities in Sub-Saharan Africa," 10/18/1978, NLC-6-3-3-1-8, JCL.

55. George Herring, *America's Longest War: The United States and Vietnam, 1950–1975,* 2nd ed. (New York: McGraw-Hill, 1985), 274.

56. Robinson to Kissinger, 4/17/1975, Box 7, Robinson Records, RG 59, NARA.

57. MemCon between Ford, Rumsfeld, et al., 3/24/1976, Box 18, MemCons, NSA, GFL; also Richard Boverie to William Hyland, 9/23/1976, Box 9, PSF, NSA, GFL; U.S. Census Bureau, *Statistical Abstract of the United States, 1998* (Washington, DC: Bernan Associates, 1998), 358; Allan R. Millett, Peter Maslowski, and William Feis, *For the Common Defense: A Military History of the United States from 1607 to 2012,* 3rd ed. (New York: Free Press, 2012), 568. In constant (1992) dollars, spending fell from $352.2 billion in 1968 to $216.8 in 1976.

58. Kissinger-Scowcroft-Ford MemCon, 12/18/1975, Box 17, MemCons, NSA, GFL; Henry Kissinger, *Years of Renewal* (New York: Simon & Schuster, 1999), chaps. 15–17.

59. NFAC, "The Invasion of Afghanistan: Implications for Soviet Policy," Jan. 1980, Electronic Briefing Book (EBB) 396, National Security Archive (NSArch).

60. Brzezinski to Carter, 1/3/1980, Box 17, Geographic File (GF), Zbigniew Brzezinski Donated Material (ZBDM), JCL.

61. Carter-Lee Kwan Yew MemCon, 10/7/1977, Box 35, Subject File (SF), BM, NSAF, JCL; MemCon between U.S. and Chinese Officials, 12/2/1975, Box 2, Kissinger Reports on USSR, China, and Middle East Discussions, NSA, GFL.

62. NFAC, "Soviet-American Relations: The Outlook of Brezhnev's Successors," Nov. 1979, Box 59, Odom File, BM, NSAF, JCL. See also Zbigniew Brzezinski, *Power and Principle: Memoirs of the National Security Adviser, 1977–1981* (New York: Farrar Straus & Giroux, 1983), 517.

63. Walter LaFeber, Richard Polenberg, and Nancy Woloch, *The American Century: A History of the United States since the 1890s,* 7th ed. (New York: Routledge, 2013), 367.

64. Meeting of the Political Consultative Committee (PCC) of the Warsaw Pact, 11/22–11/23/1978, Cold War International History Project (CWIHP) Digital Archive.

65. Yuri Andropov, Speech at PCC Meeting, 1/4–1/5/1983, in Vojtech Mastny and Malcolm Byrne, eds., *A Cardboard Castle?: An Inside History of the Warsaw Pact, 1955–1991* (Budapest: CEU Press, 2005), 472.

66. A good contemporary analysis was Presidential Review Memorandum (PRM)/ NSC-10, "Comprehensive Net Assessment: The Current Balance and Trends," undated (1977), NLC-15-105-4-14-0, JCL.

67. During the late 1970s and early 1980s, the CIA believed that the Soviet economy had reached perhaps 57 percent of the size of the U.S. economy. This estimate is now believed to have been high; other observers have put the figure as low as one-sixth or as high as 40–50 percent. It should be noted, however, that the CIA was keenly attuned to overall Soviet weakness during the 1970s. The assertion that Moscow's relative position peaked around 1970 is referenced in Stephen Brooks and William Wohlforth, "Power, Globalization, and the End of the Cold War: Reevaluating a Landmark Case for Ideas," *International Security* 25, no. 3 (2000/2001): 21.

Roughly similar conclusions can be drawn from Maddison, "Statistics on World Population"; CIA, "A Comparison of Soviet and U.S. Gross National Products, 1960–83," Aug. 1984, CIA Records Search Tool (CREST) Archival Database, NARA.

68. NFAC, "The Soviet Economy in 1978–79 and Prospects for 1980," June 1980, NLC-29-12-2-1-4, JCL; CIA, "The Slowdown in Soviet Industry, 1976–82," June 1983, CREST; David Reynolds, *One World Divisible: A Global History since 1945* (New York: W. W. Norton, 2000), 540; Stephen Kotkin, *Armageddon Averted: The Soviet Collapse, 1970–2000* (Oxford: Oxford University Press, 2008), 24–28.

69. Intelligence Memorandum, "The Next Two Years: Brezhnev, or a Succession? Implications for U.S. Policy," Sept. 1977, NLC-6-79-1-23-3, JCL; CIA, "Soviet Economic Problems and Prospects," July 1977, NLC-29-10-6-2-1, JCL.

70. Brzezinski, *Power and Principle*, 343; Archie Brown, *The Rise and Fall of Communism* (London: Bodley Head, 2009), 401–2; Robert Gates, *From the Shadows: The Ultimate Insider's Story of Five Presidents and How They Won the Cold War* (New York: Simon & Schuster, 1996), 116–17.

71. NFAC, "The Soviet Economy in 1978–79 and Prospects for 1980," June 1980, NLC-29-12-2-1-4, JCL; Evgeny Andreev, "Life Expectancy and Causes of Death in the USSR," in *Demographic Trends and Patterns in the Soviet Union before 1991*, edited by Wolfgang Lutz, Sergei Scherbov, and Andrei Volkov (London: Routledge, 1994), 288–89.

72. Anatoly Chernyaev Diary, 5/1/1972 and 4/3/1972, EBB 379, NSArch.

73. Politburo Minutes, 1/7/1974, in Michael Scammell, ed., *The Solzhenitsyn Files* (Chicago: Edition Q, 1995), 284; CIA, "The Spectrum of Soviet Dissent," May 1977, NLC-6-78-8-25-5, JCL; Andropov Memo, 1/5/1977, EBB 387, NSArch.

74. Stephen Kotkin, "The Kiss of Debt: The East Bloc Goes Borrowing," in *The Shock of the Global: The 1970s in Perspective*, edited by Niall Ferguson, Charles S. Maier, Erez Manela, and Daniel Sargent (Cambridge, MA: Belknap Press, 2010), esp. 86–89; Matthew Ouimet, *The Rise and Fall of the Brezhnev Doctrine in Soviet Foreign Policy* (Chapel Hill: University of North Carolina Press, 2003), 39–98; EN N 77-10525, "The Value to the USSR of Economic Relations with the U.S. and the West," Aug. 1977, Box 2, Odom File, BM, NSAF, JCL.

75. Reagan, "Two Worlds," Sept. 1978, Box 8, Ronald Reagan Subject Collection (RRSC), Hoover Institution.

76. Vladislav Zubok, "The Soviet Union and Détente of the 1970s," *Cold War History* 8, no. 4 (2008): 438–42; Kotkin, *Armageddon Averted*, 41–42.

77. Report in Odom to Brzezinski, 2/25/1977, Declassified Documents Reference System (DDRS); CIA, "Eastern Europe: The Growing Hard-Currency Debt," July 1977, NLC-31-24-2-2-7, JCL.

78. Anatoly Dobrynin, *In Confidence: Moscow's Ambassador to Six Cold War Presidents* (New York: Random House, 1995), 346; Sarah Snyder, *Human Rights Activism and the End of the Cold War: A Transnational History of the Helsinki Network* (Cambridge, UK: Cambridge University Press, 2011), 53–80.

79. Special National Intelligence Estimate (SNIE), "Poland's Prospects over the Next Six Months," Jan. 1981, DNSA; Daniel C. Thomas, "The Helsinki Accords and Political Change in Eastern Europe," in *The Power of Human Rights: International Norms and Domestic Change*, edited by Thomas Risse, Stephen C. Ropp, and Kathryn Sikkink (New York, 1999), 219.

80. In Ouimet, *Rise and Fall,* 113–15.

81. Conversation between Kulikov and East German Officials, 6/13/1981, in Mastny and Byrne, *Cardboard Castle,* 447.

82. Ouimet, *Rise and Fall,* 131–235, esp. 234–35; but see also Mark Kramer, "Poland, 1980–81, Soviet Policy during the Polish Crisis," *Cold War International History Project Bulletin,* no. 5 (spring 1995), 116–23.

83. Dobrynin to Foreign Ministry, 3/8/1972, in David C. Geyer and Douglas E. Selvage, eds. *Soviet-American Relations: The Detente Years, 1969–1972* (Washington, DC: U.S. Department of State, 2007), Doc. #267.

84. Mao-Kissinger-Zhou MemCon, 2/17/1973, Box 6, President's Personal File, Nixon Presidential Materials (NPM); Kuisong Yang and Yafeng Xia, "Vacillating between Revolution and Détente: Mao's Changing Psyche and Policy toward the United States, 1969–1976," *Diplomatic History* 34, no. 2 (2010): 408.

85. See "Extracts from General Secretary Brezhnev's Speeches," 2/24/1976; Westad, *Global Cold War,* 169–70.

86. Xiaoming Zhang, "Deng Xiaoping and China's Decision to Go to War with Vietnam," *Journal of Cold War Studies* 12, no. 3 (2010): 3–29.

87. Gribkov, in Svetlana Savranskaya and David Welch, eds., *Global Competition and the Deterioration of U.S.-Soviet Relations, 1977–1980: Transcript of the Proceedings of a Conference of Russian and U.S. Policymakers and Scholars held at Harbor Beach Resort, Fort Lauderdale, Florida, 23–26 March 1995,* p. 59, Carter-Brezhnev Docs, Global Competition Collection, NSArch.

88. Georgy Shakhnazarov, in ibid., 38–39.

89. Dobrynin, *In Confidence,* 475.

90. Savranskaya and Welch, *Global Competition,* 24.

91. Kosygin-Taraki Conversation, 3/17 or 3/18/1979, in *Cold War International History Project Bulletin,* no. 8–9 (winter 1996/1997), 145; Amin Saikal, "Islamism, the Iranian Revolution, and the Soviet Invasion of Afghanistan," in *Cambridge History of the Cold War, Vol. 3: Endings,* edited by Odd Arne Westad and Melvyn Leffler (New York: Cambridge University Press, 2010), 127–30.

92. O. Bogomolov, "Some Ideas about Foreign Policy Results of the 1970s (Points)," 1/20/1980, CWIHP.

93. On Soviet views of the arms race, see BDM Corporation, *Soviet Intentions 1965–1985,* EBB 285, NSArch.

94. In Thomas Nichols, "Carter and the Soviets: The Origins of the U.S. Return to a Strategy of Confrontation," *Diplomacy & Statecraft* 13, no. 2 (June 2002): 28, 37. See also David Walsh, *The Military Balance in the Cold War: U.S. Perceptions and Policy, 1976–1985* (New York: Routledge, 2008), 178–79.

95. Nichols, "Carter and the Soviets," 30; Kristina Spohr Redman, "Conflict and Cooperation in Intra-Alliance Nuclear Politics: Western Europe, the United States, and the Genesis of NATO's Dual-Track Decision, 1977–1979," *Journal of Cold War Studies* 13, no. 2 (2011): 39–89.

96. Brown-Deng Xiaoping MemCon, 1/8/1980, DDRS; Jesus Velasco, *Neoconservatives in U.S. Foreign Policy under Ronald Reagan and George W. Bush: Voices behind the Throne* (Baltimore: Johns Hopkins University Press, 2010), 111.

97. A good recent study is Barbara Zanchetta, *The Transformation of American International Power in the 1970s* (New York: Cambridge University Press, 2013), chaps. 8–12.

98. PRM/NSC-10, "Comprehensive Net Assessment: The Current Balance and Trends," 1977, NLC-15-105-4-14-0, JCL; also PD/NSC-18, "U.S. National Strategy," 8/24/1977, DNSA; "Agenda Paper for SCC Meeting," 7/7/1977, NLC-17-4-9-11-8, JCL.

99. Jimmy Carter, *Keeping Faith: Memoirs of a President* (Fayetteville: University of Arkansas Press, 1995), 597; NSC Meeting, 3/18/1980, NLC-17-2-19-4-7, JCL.

100. Cyrus Vance, *Hard Choices: Critical Years in America's Foreign Policy* (New York: Simon & Schuster, 1983), 395. See also Jordan to Carter, 5/31/1978, NLC-47-4-13-2-0, JCL; "Memo on NSC Accomplishments," Dec. 1980, Box 34, SF, ZBDM, JCL; Raymond Garthoff, *Détente and Confrontation: Soviet-American Relations from Nixon to Reagan* (Washington, DC: Brookings Institution Press, 1994), esp. 633–35, 1076–82.

101. Oksenberg to Brzezinski, 2/16/1979, Box 9, Country File (CF), BM, NSAF, JCL.

102. "North-South Affairs: Evaluative Comments—Retrospective and Prospective," undated [late 1980], Box 34, SF, ZBDM, JCL.

103. NSC Meeting, 12/17/1980, Box 36, William Odom Papers, LC. See also Oral History Interview with Brzezinski, Albright, Denend, and Odom, 49, 2/18/1982, Presidential Oral History Project (POHP), Miller Center, University of Virginia; Gates, *From the Shadows*, 90–95; Christian Philip Peterson, "The Carter Administration and the Promotion of Human Rights in the Soviet Union, 1977–1981," *Diplomatic History* 38, no. 3 (2014): 628–56.

104. Carter-Gromyko MemCon, 9/23/1977, Box 35, SF, BM, NSAF, JCL.

105. U.S. Census Bureau, *Statistical Abstract,* 358.

106. PD/NSC-59, 7/25/1980, EBB 390, NSArch; Brown, "Remarks at Naval War College," 8/20/1980, Box 9, Odom Papers, LC; State to All NATO Capitals, 6/11/1980, EBB 390, NSArch.

107. Andrew Krepinevich, Simon Chin, and Todd Harrison, *Strategy in Austerity* (Washington, DC: Center for Strategic and Budgetary Assessments, 2012), 31–33; Benjamin S. Lambeth, *The Transformation of American Airpower* (Ithaca: Cornell University Press, 2000), 54–55, 72–75; Robert Komer, "What Decade of Neglect?" *International Security* 10, no. 2 (1985): 70–83.

108. Brown-Deng MemCon, 1/8/1980, DDRS; Brown-Zhang Ziping MemCon, 1/8/1980, DDRS; Brown-Geng Biao MemCon, 5/29/1980, DDRS.

109. Brzezinski to Carter, 3/18/1980, Box 12, GF, ZBDM, JCL. See also Brzezinski to Carter, 1/9/1980, NLC-33-6-2-8-9; Odom to Brzezinski, 1/9/1980, NLC-17-45-1-15-7, JCL; Gates, *From the Shadows*, 150–52.

110. "Summary of the President's Telephone Conversation," 12/28/1979, EBB 396, NSArch.

111. Brzezinski Remarks, 12/20/1978, Box 139, Hedrick Smith Papers, LC.

112. A concise history of human rights can be found in Peter Sterns, *Human Rights in World History* (New York: Routledge, 2012).

113. Zbigniew Brzezinski, *Between Two Ages: America's Role in the Technetronic Era* (New York: Viking Press, 1970), 19–22. See also Michael Morgan, "The Seventies and the Rebirth of Human Rights," in *The Shock of the Global: The 1970s in Perspective,* edited by Niall Ferguson, Charles S. Maier, Erez Manela, and Daniel Sargent (Cambridge, MA: Belknap Press, 2010), 237–50; Samuel Moyn, *The Last Utopia: Human*

Rights in History (Cambridge, MA: Harvard University Press, 2010), 121–76; Kenneth Cmiel, "The Emergence of Human Rights Politics in the United States," *Journal of American History* 86, no. 3 (1999): 1231–50.

114. John Stremlau, *The International Politics of the Nigerian Civil War, 1967–1970* (Princeton: Princeton University Press, 1977); Lasse Heerten, "The Dystopia of Postcolonial Catastrophe: Self-Determination, the Biafran War of Secession, and the 1970s Human Rights Moment," in *The Breakthrough: Human Rights in the 1970s,* edited by Jan Eckel and Samuel Moyn, 15–32 (Philadelphia: University of Pennsylvania Press, 2013); Sargent, *Superpower Transformed,* 70–80.

115. Moyn, *Last Utopia,* esp. 121, 133; Morgan, "Seventies," esp. 237–38; Aryeh Heier, *The International Human Rights Movement: A History* (Princeton: Princeton University Press, 2012), esp. 138–204.

116. Barbara Keys, *Reclaiming American Virtue: The Human Rights Revolution of the 1970s* (Cambridge, MA: Harvard University Press, 2013), 103–26, esp. 121–22.

117. MemCon between Kissinger, Fraser, et al., 12/17/1974, DNSA.

118. Scowcroft to Adams and Rodman, for Kissinger, 6/11/1975, Box 16, Trip Briefing Books and Cables, NSA, GFL. See also House Committee on Foreign Affairs, Subcommittee on International Organizations and Movements, *Human Rights in the World Community: A Call for U.S. Leadership* (Washington, DC: U.S. Government Printing Office, 1974).

119. "Human Rights Today," undated (1975), Box 1, Human Rights Subject File, Bureau of Human Rights and Humanitarian Affairs, RG 59, NARA. See also Barbara Keys, "Congress, Kissinger, and the Origins of Human Rights Diplomacy," *Diplomatic History* 34, no. 5 (2010): 823–51.

120. Samuel Huntington, *The Third Wave: Democratization in the Late Twentieth Century* (Norman: University of Oklahoma Press, 1993), 7. See also Robert Alan Dahl, *Polyarchy: Participation and Opposition* (New Haven: Yale University Press, 1971), 1–9. In this book, I treat *democracy* and *electoral democracy* as functional synonyms.

121. Larry Diamond, *The Spirit of Democracy: The Struggle to Build Free Societies throughout the World* (New York: Times Books, 2008), 6–7. See also Michel Crozier, Samuel Huntington, and Joji Watanuki, *The Crisis of Democracy: Report on the Governability of Democracies to the Trilateral Commission* (New York: New York University Press, 1975).

122. The variations are noted in Huntington, *Third Wave*; Jarle Simensen, "Democracy and Globalization: Nineteen Eighty-Nine and the 'Third Wave,'" *Journal of World History* 10, no. 2 (1999): esp. 392–93.

123. The sources of democratization are laid out in Samuel Huntington, "Democracy's Third Wave," *Journal of Democracy* 2, no. 2 (1991): 12–34; Huntington, *Third Wave,* esp. 38–106. See also Daniel Brinks and Micha Coppedge, "Diffusion Is No Illusion: Neighbor Emulation in the Third Wave of Democracy," *Comparative Political Studies* 39, no. 4 (May 2006): 463–89; Barbara Geddes, "What Do We Know about Democratization after Twenty Years," *Annual Review of Political Science* 2 (1999): 115–44; Peter Smith, *Democracy in Latin America: Political Change in Comparative Perspective* (New York: Oxford University Press, 2011).

124. On hybrid regimes and other limitations, see Steven Levitsky and Lucan Way, *Competitive Authoritarianism: Hybrid Regimes after the Cold War* (New York: Cambridge

University Press, 2010); Fareed Zakaria, *The Future of Freedom: Illiberal Democracy at Home and Abroad* (New York: W. W. Norton, 2003).

125. Larry Diamond, *Developing Democracy: Toward Consolidation* (Baltimore: Johns Hopkins University Press, 1999), 25.

126. Freedom House, *Freedom in the World 2013: Democratic Breakthroughs in the Balance*, 2013, 29, https://www.freedomhouse.org/sites/default/files/FIW%20 2013%20Booklet.pdf (accessed 3/9/2015).

127. Larry Diamond, "Facing Up to the Democratic Recession," *Journal of Democracy* 26, no. 1 (2015): 141.

128. Jimmy Carter, Inaugural Address, 1/20/1977, APP.

129. Kissinger Staff Meeting, 10/6/1975, DNSA; John Gaddis, "Rescuing Choice from Circumstance: The Statecraft of Henry Kissinger," in *The Diplomats: 1939–1979*, edited by Gordon Craig and Francis Loewenhiem (Princeton: Princeton University Press, 1994), 567–68, 585–87.

130. "Meeting with Foreign Minister Gromyko," 9/20/1974, Box A1, Kissinger-Scowcroft West Wing Office File, NSA Temporary Parallel File, GFL.

131. Médici-Kissinger MemCon, 12/8/1971, Box 911, VIP Visits, NSC, NPM. See also Nixon-Suharto MemCon, 5/28/1970, DNSA.

132. Kissinger Staff Meeting, 10/1/1973, DNSA; Tanya Harmer, *Allende's Chile and the Inter-American Cold War* (Chapel Hill: University of North Carolina Press, 2011).

133. Kissinger–Pinochet MemCon, 6/8/1976, DNSA.

134. Kissinger-Guzzetti MemCon, 10/7/1976, DNSA; Keys, "Congress, Kissinger," 824, 833–34, 838–50.

135. Keys, *Restoring American Virtue*, 153–77; Kathryn Sikkink, *Mixed Signals: U.S. Human Rights Policy and Latin America* (Ithaca: Cornell University Press, 2004), 106.

136. Schaufele, Lewis, Armitage, and Luers to Kissinger, 4/30/1976, Box 1, HAK, RG 59, NARA.

137. Jimmy Carter, Address at University of Notre Dame, 5/22/1977, APP.

138. See Department of State Draft Study, "A Human Rights Strategy for the United States," 3/2/1977, Box 33, Warren Christopher Records, RG 59, NARA.

139. Draft of Carter address to the Chicago Council on Foreign Relations, 3/15/1976, Box 17, 1976 Presidential Campaign Files, JCL. See also "Congressional Foreign Policy Briefing," 6/8/1977, Box 15, SF, BM, NSAF, JCL.

140. Jimmy Carter, Address at University of Notre Dame, 5/22/1977, APP.

141. PRM/NSC-28, "Human Rights," 7/7/1977, Box 19, White House Counsel Files (WHCF), JCL. The drafting process of PRM/NSC-28 went through several stages, but the main ideas were in place with this draft.

142. Carter, Inaugural Address.

143. Lipshutz to Carter, 12/7/1977, Box 18, WHCF, JCL; PRM/NSC 28, "Human Rights," 8/15/1977, NLC-132-44-6-1-9, JCL.

144. Lake to Vance, 1/16/1978, Box HU-1, White House Central Files, JCL; David Schmitz and Vanessa Walker, "Jimmy Carter and the Foreign Policy of Human Rights: The Development of a Post-Cold War Foreign Policy," *Diplomatic History* 28, no. 1 (2004): 113–43.

145. PRM/NSC-28, "Human Rights," 7/7/1977, Box 19, WHCF, JCL.

146. Ibid.

147. Pastor to Brzezinski, "Accomplishments of the Carter Administration in Latin America and the Caribbean," 11/20/1980, Box 34, SF, ZBDM, JCL.

148. An early directive noted, "There will clearly be situations in which efforts to achieve our human rights goals will have to be modified, delayed or curtailed in deference to other important objectives." PRM/NSC-28, "Human Rights," 7/7/1977.

149. Cauas to Ministry of Foreign Relations (MRE), 6/27/1977, Telex Recibidos, EmbaChile Estados Unidos (EEUU), Chilean Foreign Ministry Archive (MRE Chile).

150. Sikkink, *Mixed Signals,* 138–142; Alex Thomson, "The Diplomacy of Impasse: The Carter Administration and Apartheid South Africa," *Diplomacy & Statecraft* 21, no. 1 (2010): 107–24; Lake and Moose to Vance, 2/16/1978, Box 3, Lake Records, RG 59, NARA.

151. Dobrynin, *In Confidence,* 375.

152. Manila to State, 8/29/1978, DNSA; Pinochet to Guzmán, 12/26/1977, in Cauas to MRE, 2/15/1978, Oficios Secretos Recibidos, EmbaChile EEUU, MRE Chile; Carter-Pinochet MemCon, 9/6/1977, Box 9, North-South (N-S) Files, NSAF, JCL.

153. "Remarks Prepared for an Address by General George S. Brown," 2/28/1978, Box 27, N-S Files, NSAF, JCL.

154. Carter, *Keeping Faith,* 147; PRM/NSC 28, "Human Rights," 8/15/1977, NLC-132-44-6-1-9, JCL.

155. Brzezinski, *Power and Principle,* 356. See also Vance, *Hard Choices,* 316–19; Carter, *White House Diary,* 137; "Iran: U.S. Government Objectives," 3/11/1977, DNSA; "Goals and Objectives in Iran," 1/11/1978, DNSA; Department of State, "Human Rights Goals—Iran," 5/31/1978, DNSA; Department of State, "The U.S. and Human Rights in Iran," 1/29/1980, DNSA.

156. Managua to State, 2/8/1978, DNSA.

157. Managua to State, 3/13/1978, Box 42, Christopher Records, RG 59, NARA. On Carter's policy, see Robert Pastor, *Condemned to Repetition: The United States and Nicaragua* (Princeton: Princeton University Press, 1988).

158. National Intelligence Daily Cable, 6/25/1977, CIA FOIA Electronic Reading Room; INR, "Progress on Human Rights in Iran," 11/12/1977, NLC-31-38-3-2-1, JCL.

159. Frederick L. Shiels, *Preventable Disasters: Why Governments Fail* (Savage, MD: Rowman & Littlefield, 1991), 116; MemCon between U.S. officials and Iranian observers, 11/6/1978, DNSA; Gary Sick Journal, 9/7 and 9/10/1978, NLC-25-37-5-2-7, JCL.

160. Stanley Escudero, "What Went Wrong in Iran?" June 1979, DNSA.

161. Brzezinski, *Power and Principle,* 356; Saunders and Lake to Vance, 12/27/1978, Box 4, Lake Records, RG 59, NARA; Gary Sick Journal, 12/27/1978, NLC-25-37-7-1-6, JCL.

162. "Review of U.S. Policy toward Nicaragua," undated, NLC-24-33-6-3-0, JCL. See also CIA, "Significant Developments Related to the U.S. Stand on Human Rights," 9/23–9/29/1977, NLC-31-38-7-6-3, JCL; Kreisberg and Bushnell to Christopher, 2/14/1978, Box 38, Christopher Records, RG 59, NARA; Hal Brands, *Latin America's Cold War* (Cambridge, MA: Harvard University Press, 2010), 178–79.

163. William Michael Schmidli, "The Most Sophisticated Intervention We Have Seen: The Carter Administration and the Nicaraguan Crisis, 1978–1979," *Diplomacy & Statecraft* 23, no. 1 (2012): 66–86; Vaky to Christopher, 9/11/1978, Box 40, Christopher Records, RG 59, NARA.

164. MemCon between U.S. and Nicaraguan Officials, 9/24/1979, NLC-7-37-6-2-6, JCL.

165. Jeane Kirkpatrick, "Dictatorships and Double Standards," *Commentary*, Nov. 1979, 38.

166. Anthony Lake, *Somoza Falling: A Case Study of Washington at Work* (Boston: Houghton Mifflin, 1989), 273; Lake to Vance, 1/19/1980, DDRS.

167. Brzezinski-Fumihoko Togo MemCon, 11/2/1978, Box 33, SF, BM, NSAF, JCL.

168. The failures of the administration in this and other regards loomed large in early scholarly assessments of Carter's presidency, as well. See Gaddis Smith, *Morality, Reason, and Power: American Diplomacy in the Carter Years* (New York: Hill & Wang, 1986).

169. Mondale to Carter, 1/22/1979, DDRS.

170. Brzezinski Exit Interview, 7, 2/20/1981, Oral Histories, JCL.

171. NFAC, "Impact of the U.S. Stand on Human Rights," 4/20/1977, NLC-28-10-3-2-5, JCL.

172. Huntington, *Third Wave*, 96. See also Fiora Lewis, "Their Rights, Our Interest," *New York Times*, 8/1/1980.

173. "Human Rights Policy: Accomplishments," 12/4/1978, Box 29, SF, BM, NSAF, JCL. See also NFAC, "Human Rights Performance: January 1977–July 1978," Sept. 1978, NLC-28-17-15-9-8, JCL; Brzezinski to Carter, 3/25/1977, NLC-SAFE 16 A-41-87-5-1, JCL; Inderfurth to Brzezinski, 12/1/1978, NLC-11-3-7-10-8, JCL.

174. State to Santo Domingo, 5/19/1978, Box 32, Christopher Records, RG 59, NARA; Christopher to Vance, 5/17/1978, Box 28, Christopher Records, RG 59, NARA; Vance to Balaguer, 5/17/1978, Box 28, Christopher Records, RG 59, NARA.

175. Pastor to Brzezinski, 1/18/1981, Box 34, SF, ZBDM, JCL.

176. INR, "Current Reports," 9/26/1978, NLC-SAFE 17 B-13-72-12-8, JCL. See also Pastor to Aaron, 7/27/1978, NLC-24-19-8-1-6, JCL; State to Quito, 9/22/1978, NLC-16-102-7-3-1, JCL; Pastor, "Daily Activities," 8/11/1978, NLC-24-54-1-9-6, JCL.

177. Brzezinski to Carter, 1/12/1978, NLC-128-9-14-2-3, JCL.

178. William Michael Schmidli, "Institutionalizing Human Rights in U.S. Foreign Policy: U.S.-Argentine Relations, 1976–1980," *Diplomatic History* 35, no. 2 (2011): 351–77, esp. 377; Christopher testimony to International Organizations Subcommittee, 5/2/1979, Box 45, Christopher Records, RG 59, NARA.

179. Brzezinski to Carter, 12/13/1979, NLC-15-28-5-3-7, JCL; Brzezinski to Carter, 12/3/1977, NLC-133-109-3-11-8, JCL.

180. "Can Capitalism Survive?" *Time*, 7/14/1975, 52–63.

181. Eizenstat Memo for Carter, 3/26/1980, CF BE4, White House Central Files, JCL.

182. These paragraphs draw on Daniel Sargent, "The Cold War and the International Policy Economy in the 1970s," *Cold War History* 13, no. 3 (2013): 393–425; Charles Maier, "Malaise: The Crisis of Capitalism in the 1970s," in *The Shock of the Global: The 1970s in Perspective,* edited by Niall Ferguson, Charles S. Maier, Erez Manela, and Daniel Sargent (Cambridge, MA: Belknap Press, 2010), 44–48. See also Daniel Bell, *The Coming of Post-Industrial Society: A Venture in Social Forecasting* (New York: Basic Books, 1973).

183. Here, I am defining *globalization* essentially in economic terms, as the process by which national economies have become progressively more interlinked and integrated. This was not, of course, a process that began only in the 1970s; I am referring to the most recent phase of a phenomenon that stretches back centuries, if not longer.

184. Robinson to Kissinger, 6/22/1976, Box 6, Robinson Records, RG 59, NARA.

185. Peter Stearns, *Globalization in World History* (New York: Routledge, 2010), 129–30; Clayton Brown, *Globalization and America since 1945* (Wilmington, DE: Rowman & Littlefield, 2003), 43–51; John Micklethwait and Adrian Wooldridge, *A Future Perfect: The Challenge and Promise of Globalization* (New York: Random House, 2003), 27–45.

186. These two paragraphs draw on Ethan Kapstein, *Governing the Global Economy: International Finance and the State* (Cambridge, MA: Harvard University Press, 1994), esp. 56; Maurice Obstfeld and Alan Taylor, *Global Capital Markets: Integration, Crisis, and Growth* (Cambridge, UK: Cambridge University Press, 2004), 27–28, 160; Michael C. Webb, *The Political Economy of Policy Coordination: International Adjustment since 1945* (Ithaca: Cornell University Press, 1995), 92–186, 195–198. Current-account data are from Joan Spero and Jeffrey A. Hart, *The Politics of International Economic Relations,* 7th ed. (Belmont, CA: Wadsworth, 2010), 25.

187. Frieden, *Global Capitalism,* 397; Alfred Eckes and Thomas Zeiler, *Globalization and the American Century* (Cambridge, UK: Cambridge University Press, 2003), 244.

188. Theodore Levitt, "The Globalization of Markets," *Harvard Business Review* 61, no. 3 (1983): 93.

189. Robert Gilpin, *The Political Economy of International Relations* (Princeton: Princeton University Press, 1987), 237–38. See also William Robinson, *A Theory of Global Capitalism* (Baltimore: Johns Hopkins University Press, 2004).

190. Jefferson Cowie, *Stayin' Alive: The 1970s and the Last Days of the Working Class* (New York: The New Press, 2010), 222.

191. On this shift, see Daniel Yergin and Joseph Stanislaw, *The Commanding Heights: The Battle for the World Economy* (New York: Simon & Schuster, 1998), esp. chaps. 1–2, 4, 6–7, 9, 12. See also Robert Leeson, *Ideology and the International Economy: The Decline and Fall of Bretton Woods* (London: Palgrave Macmillan, 2003); Maier, "Malaise," 33–38.

192. National Intelligence Officer (NIO) at Large to Director of Central Intelligence (DCI) and Deputy Director of Central Intelligence (DDCI), 3/26/1982, CREST.

193. National Intelligence Council (NIC), "The United States in the World Economy: Elements of Strength," May 1982, CREST; Angus Maddison, *The World Economy: Historical Statistics* (Paris: OECD, 2003), 260–61.

194. See Barry Eichengreen, *Exorbitant Privilege: The Rise and Fall of the Dollar* (New York: Oxford University Press, 2011), 62–68; Dale Helleiner, *States and the Reemergence of Global Finance: From Bretton Woods to the 1990s* (Ithaca: Cornell University Press, 1996), 113–14; Kati Suominen, *Peerless and Periled: The Paradox of American Leadership in the World Economic Order* (Stanford: Stanford University Press, 2012), 180–83.

195. Barry Bluestone and Bennett Harrison, *The Deindustrialization of America: Plant Closings, Community Abandonment, and the Dismantling of Basic Industry* (New York: Basic Books, 1992), 4.

196. NIO at Large to DCI and DDCI, 3/26/1982, CREST; W. Carl Biven, *Jimmy Carter's Economy: Policy in an Age of Limits* (Chapel Hill: University of North Carolina Press, 2001), 219–22; Giovanni Arrighi, "The World Economy and the Cold War, 1970–1990," in *Cambridge History of the Cold War, Vol. 3: Endings,* edited by Odd Arne Westad and Melvyn Leffler (New York: Cambridge University Press, 2010), 33.

197. Manuel Castells and Peter Hall, *Technopoles of the World: The Making of Twenty-First Century Industrial Complexes* (New York: Routledge, 1994), 12–28, esp. 12, 14, 19; Christophe Lécuyer, *Making Silicon Valley: Innovation and the Growth of High Tech, 1930–1970* (Cambridge, MA: MIT Press, 2006), esp. 287–94.

198. Trilateral Commission, *The Crisis of International Cooperation,* 10/22–10/23/1973, 9, http://www.trilateral.org (accessed 8/8/2013). See also Sargent, *Superpower Transformed*; Bluestone and Harrison, *Deindustrialization of America.*

199. Charles Maier, *Among Empires: American Ascendancy and Its Predecessors* (Cambridge, MA: Harvard University Press, 2006), 239.

200. Spero and Hart, *Politics of International Economic Relations,* 135.

201. Borstelmann, *1970s,* 141, 307–8. McDonald's had established an initial presence in Canada in 1967.

202. NIC, "United States in the World Economy"; Sam Gindin and Leo Panitch, *The Making of Global Capitalism* (New York: Verso, 2012), 147–48.

203. W. D. Eberle to Various Recipients, 7/29/1974, DDRS.

204. Gindin and Panich, *Making of Global Capitalism,* 150–51. See also Saskia Sassen, *The Mobility of Labor and Capital: A Study in International Investment and Labor Flow* (Cambridge, UK: Cambridge University Press, 1990), esp. 178–79; Helleiner, *States and the Reemergence,* 113–14.

205. Daniel Sargent, "The United States and Globalization in the 1970s," in *The Shock of the Global: The 1970s in Perspective,* edited by Niall Ferguson, Charles S. Maier, Erez Manela, and Daniel Sargent (Cambridge, MA: Belknap Press, 2010), 52–53, 59.

206. Hormats to Kissinger, 10/24/1975, Box 4, International Economic Affairs (IEA) Staff Files, NSA, GFL. See also Arthur Burns to Gerald Ford, 8/12/1974, Box 1, Burns Papers, Duke University Special Collections; Deporte to Lake, 6/15/1978, Box 4, Lake Records, RG 59, NARA.

207. Paul Volcker and Toyoo Gyohten, *Changing Fortunes: The World's Money and the Threat to American Leadership* (New York: Times Books, 1992), 124; Barry Eichengreen, *Globalizing Capital: A History of the International Monetary System* (Princeton: Princeton University Press, 2008), 130–37; Sargent, *Superpower Transformed,* 119–30.

208. Flanigan to Shultz, 3/27/1974, Box 2, Papers of George Shultz, RG 56, NARA; James, *International Monetary Cooperation*, 257–58. See also Kapstein, *Governing the Global Economy*, 59–77; Helleiner, *States and the Reemergence*, 111, 115–18.

209. Thomas Enders to Kissinger, 1/15/1976, Box 19, HAK, RG 59, NARA.

210. Carter to Fukuda, 8/26/1977, DDRS. See also Carter to Helmut Schmidt, 3/27/1978, DDRS; Carter Statement on Multilateral Trade Negotiations, 4/12/1979, APP.

211. Robert Putnam and Nicholas Bayne, *Hanging Together: Cooperation and Conflict in the Seven-Power Summits* (Cambridge, MA: Harvard University Press, 1987). See also Solomon to Blumenthal, 9/22/1977, DDRS.

212. Owen to Carter, 6/23/1978, DDRS; also Owen to Carter, 7/3/1978, DDRS.

213. Carter, *WHD*, 206; Carter to Schmidt, 3/27/1978, DDRS; Schultze to Carter, 6/27/1978, Box 93, Handwriting File, Staff Secretary File, JCL; Putnam and Bayne, *Hanging Together*, 73–92.

214. "Proposed Course of Action on the Dollar," 10/25/1978, Box 59, Charles Schultze SF, JCL.

215. Federal Reserve Press Release, 11/1/1978, Box 59, Schultze SF, JCL; Volcker and Gyohten, *Changing Fortunes*, 149–51.

216. Yergin and Stanislaw, *Commanding Heights*, 347–48; Biven, *Jimmy Carter's Economy*, 242–46. As Biven points out, it is not clear that Carter understood just how aggressive Volcker would be in fighting inflation.

217. NIC, "United States in the World Economy"; Reynolds, *One World Divisible*, 408; Destler, *American Trade Politics*, 56–57; NIO at Large to DCI and DDCI, 3/26/1982, CREST.

218. Stein, *Pivotal Decade*, 267; Robert Schaeffer, *Understanding Globalization: The Social Consequences of Political, Economic, and Environmental Change* (Lanham, MD: Rowman & Littlefield, 2009), 15; Gindin and Panitch, *Making of Global Capitalism*, 168.

219. Maddison, *World Economy*, 260–61.

220. "Declaration on the Establishment."

221. ECLA, *Economic Survey of Latin America, 1973* (Santiago: Economic Commission for Latin America, 1974), 3.

222. Robinson to Kissinger, 4/17/1975, Box 7, Robinson Records, RG 59, NARA.

223. MemCon, 5/26/1975, *FRUS 1969–1976*, Vol. XXXI: Doc. #294; also MemCon, 5/24/1975, *FRUS 1969–1976*, Vol. XXXI: Doc. #293; Kissinger, "Global Consensus and Economic Development," 9/1/1975, Box 38 (Series I), Robert McNamara Papers, LC.

224. CIA, "The International Setting for North-South Relations in 1978," NLC-24-59-3-1-7, JCL.

225. IMF, "A Facility to Assist Members in Meeting the Initial Impact of the Increase in Oil Prices," 2/19/1974, Box B66, Arthur Burns Papers, GFL.

226. External Finance Division, "Global External Debt Indicators for Developing Countries," 3/29/1982, in Bahram Nowzad to Various Recipients, 3/29/1982, Box 30, WHD Division SF, IMF Archives.

227. Margaret De Vries, *The International Monetary Fund, 1972–1978: Cooperation on Trial, Vol. 1: Narrative and Analysis* (Washington, DC: IMF, 1985), 423.

228. Solomon statement to Subcommittee on Foreign Economic Policy, SFRC, 9/21/1977, Box B72, Burns Papers, GFL; Blumenthal to Carter, 9/22/1977, DDRS.

229. Scowcroft to Ford, undated, Box 3, PSF, IEA, NSA, GFL; "Talking Points: Conversation with Callaghan," undated (late 1976), Box 3, PSF, IEA, NSA, GFL; Kathleen Burk and Alec Cairncross, *Goodbye, Great Britain: The 1976 IMF Crisis* (New Haven: Yale University Press, 1992).

230. MemCon between Carter and Peruvian Officials, 9/6/1977, Box 35, SF, BM, NSAF, JCL. See also E. Walter Robichek to Managing Director, 4/7/1977, Box 10, CF, Central Files Collection, IMF; "Briefing for Mission to Peru," 9/5/1980, Box 155, Western Hemisphere Department, WHDAI CF, IMF; "Comments on the Mexican Program in Light of Recent Developments," 10/8/1976, Box B80, Burns Papers, GFL.

231. Ron Chernow, "The Roughest Bank in Town," *Saturday Review*, 2/3/1979, 18.

232. NIC, "United States in the World Economy."

233. Mattson, "What the Heck," 2.

2. The Reagan Offensive and the Transformation of the Cold War

1. See Gorbachev in MemCon, 5/30/1988, Morning Session, Fritz Ermarth Files, Ronald Reagan Presidential Library (RRL); PCC Meeting in Bucharest, 7/7–7/8/1989, in Vojtech Mastny and Malcolm Byrne, eds., *A Cardboard Castle?: An Inside History of the Warsaw Pact, 1955–1991* (Budapest: CEU Press, 2005), 644; Reagan in John Prados, *How the Cold War Ended: Debating and Doing History* (Washington, DC: Potomac Books, 2011), 84.

2. For widely varying perspectives just on Reagan's role, see John Lewis Gaddis, *Strategies of Containment: A Critical Appraisal of American National Security Policy during the Cold War*, 2nd ed. (New York: Oxford University Press, 2005), chap. 11; Steven Hayward, *The Age of Reagan: The Conservative Counterrevolution* (New York: Crown Forum, 2009); Peter Schweizer, *Victory: The Reagan Administration's Secret Strategy That Hastened the Collapse of the Soviet Union* (New York: Atlantic Monthly Press, 1994); John Arquilla, *The Reagan Imprint: Ideas in American Foreign Policy from the Collapse of Communism to the War on Terror* (Chicago: Ivan R. Dee, 2006); Beth Fischer, *The Reagan Reversal: Foreign Policy and the End of the Cold War* (Columbia: University of Missouri Press, 1997); James Mann, *The Rebellion of Ronald Reagan: A History of the End of the Cold War* (New York: Viking, 2009); Paul Lettow, *Ronald Reagan and His Quest to Abolish Nuclear Weapons* (New York: Random House, 2005); James Graham Wilson, *The Triumph of Improvisation: Gorbachev's Adaptability, Reagan's Engagement, and the End of the Cold War* (Ithaca: Cornell University Press, 2014); Raymond Garthoff, *The Great Transition: American-Soviet Relations and the End of the Cold War* (Washington, DC: Brookings Institution Press, 1994); Frances FitzGerald, *Way Out There in the Blue: Reagan, Star Wars, and the End of the Cold War* (New York: Simon & Schuster, 2000). See also the sources cited later in the chapter.

3. As I argue in this chapter, this shift was less than the full-fledged "Reagan reversal" described in Fischer, *Reagan Reversal*.

4. Paul Nitze, "Reagan as Foreign Policy Strategist," in *Foreign Policy in the Reagan Presidency: Nine Intimate Perspectives*, edited by Kenneth W. Thompson (Lanham, MD: University Press of America, 1993), 145; Garthoff, *Great Transition*, 759.

5. George Keyworth Oral History, 9/28/1987, RRL.

6. George Shultz, *Turmoil and Triumph: My Years as Secretary of State* (New York: Scribner, 1993), 263.

7. Governor Reagan's Nation-Wide Television Address, 3/31/1976, Box 1, RRSC, Hoover.

8. "America's Strength," 12/22/1976, in Kiron Skinner, Annelise Anderson, and Martin Anderson, eds., *Reagan, in His Own Hand: The Writings of Ronald Reagan That Reveal His Revolutionary Vision for America* (New York: Free Press, 2001), 12.

9. Ronald Reagan, Inaugural Address, 1/20/1981, APP.

10. Ronald Reagan, Address to Los Angeles World Affairs Council, 12/14/1978, THCR 2/2/1/27, Margaret Thatcher Foundation (MTF) Archive, http://www.margaretthatcher.org/archive/.

11. NSC Minutes, 7/6/1981, Box 91282, NSC Meetings File, Reading Room Files, RRL. See also Governor Reagan's Nation-Wide Television Address, 3/31/1976.

12. "Viewpoint with Ronald Reagan: Communism, the Disease," undated (1975), Box 1, Ronald Reagan Radio Commentary (RRRC), Hoover.

13. "Soviet Workers," undated (1976–1977), Box 8, RRSC, Hoover; Reagan, "The Russian Wheat Deal," Oct. 1975, in Skinner, Anderson, and Anderson, *Reagan, in His Own Hand,* 30; "Soviet Workers," undated (1976–77), Box 8, RRSC, Hoover.

14. Richard Reeves, *President Reagan: The Triumph of Imagination* (New York: Simon & Schuster, 2005), 6.

15. "Reagan's Foreign Policy Views: West Should Bolster Defenses," undated (1975), Box 2, RRSC, Hoover.

16. "Intelligence," 3/23/1977; "Russian Wheat Deal," in Skinner, Anderson, and Anderson, *Reagan, in His Own Hand,* 118, 30.

17. Reagan, "World Challenges, 1979," 1/12/1979, Box 3, RRSC, Hoover.

18. "Reagan's Foreign Policy Views: West Should Bolster Defenses," undated (1975), RRSC, Box 2, Hoover; "Strategy I" and "Strategy II," 5/4/1977, in Skinner, Anderson, and Anderson, *Reagan, in His Own Hand,* 110–13; Reagan to Edward Langley, 1/15/1980, Box 3, RRSC, Hoover.

19. "Bukovsky," 6/29/1979, in Skinner, Anderson, and Anderson, *Reagan, in His Own Hand,* 149–50; "Détente: Viewpoint with Ronald Reagan," undated (1975), Box 1, RRRC, Hoover. See also "Korea," 8/15/1977, in Skinner, Anderson, and Anderson, *Reagan, in His Own Hand,* 42; "Soviet Trade," 7/9/1979, in Skinner, Anderson, and Anderson, *Reagan, in His Own Hand,* 73–74; Douglas Brinkley, ed. *The Reagan Diaries* (New York: HarperCollins, 2007), 2; Reagan, "Soviet Workers," undated, Box 8, RRSC, Hoover.

20. "Rostow VI," 10/10/1978, in Skinner, Anderson, and Anderson, *Reagan, in His Own Hand,* 99.

21. Lettow, *Ronald Reagan,* 47; "Defense IV," Sept.–Oct. 1979, Box 2, RRRC, Hoover.

22. Address to West German Bundestag, 6/9/1982, APP. See also Reagan-Casaroli MemCon, 12/15/1981, Box 49, SF, NSC Executive Secretariat File (ESF), RRL.

23. "Are Liberals Really Liberal?" circa 1963, in Skinner, Anderson, and Anderson, *Reagan, in His Own Hand,* 442.

24. Reagan-Casaroli MemCon, 12/15/1981. See also Lou Cannon, "Arms Boost Seen as Strain on Soviets," *Washington Post,* 6/19/1980.

25. "Opening Presentation: Strategic Overview," June 1981, DNSA.

26. See, for instance, NSC Meeting, 11/10/1981, Box 91283, NSC Meetings, ESF, RRL; Gates, "Meeting the Soviet Challenge in the Third World," 4/8/1983, CREST.

27. In Robert David Johnson, *Congress and the Cold War* (New York: Cambridge University Press, 2005), 251.

28. Caspar Weinberger, *Fighting for Peace: Seven Critical Years in the Pentagon* (New York: Grand Central Publishing, 1990), 39–79, esp. 64–65, 71.

29. It is generally thought that the hardliners resided at the Pentagon, the CIA, and the NSC, and that the moderates were at the State Department. This idea is broadly correct, but it does obscure important exceptions such as Robert McFarlane and Jack Matlock. And in general, even moderates such as Haig generally favored a hard line toward Moscow; they simply thought that a reinvigorated Cold War offensive should be coupled with a willingness to negotiate, and worried that too much assertiveness might alienate U.S. allies.

30. Kenneth Adelman Oral History, 9/30/2003, 9, POHP.

31. Pipes to Richard Allen, 6/3/1981, Box 3, Richard Pipes Files, RRL. See also White House memorandum, undated, Box 77, James Baker Papers, Seeley Mudd Manuscript Library, Princeton University; Lou Cannon, *President Reagan: The Role of a Lifetime* (New York: Simon & Schuster, 1991), 172–205.

32. Alexander Haig, *Caveat: Realism, Reagan, and Foreign Policy* (New York: Scribner, 1984), 85–86.

33. Iran-Contra is the most noteworthy example. Historical judgments on the Reagan NSC include David Rothkopf, *Running the World: The Inside Story of the National Security Council and the Architects of American Power* (New York: Public Affairs, 2005), 210–59; John Prados, *Keepers of the Keys: A History of the National Security Council from Truman to Bush* (New York: William Morrow, 1991), 447–558.

34. Richard Pipes, *Vixi: Memoirs of a Non-Belonger* (New Haven: Yale University Press, 2003), 164.

35. Henry Kissinger, *Diplomacy* (New York: Simon & Schuster, 2011), 766.

36. See data in U.S. Census Bureau, *Statistical Abstract of the United States, 1998* (Washington, DC: Bernan Associates, 1998), 358. See also "Review of Defense Budget Numbers," undated (1983), Box 77, Baker Papers; SecState to NATO Capitals and Other Posts, 10/2/1981, Box 35, Head of State File (HOS), ESF, RRL.

37. National Security Planning Group (NSPG) Meeting, 1/13/1983, Box 91683, ESF, RRL; NSC Meeting, 11/12/1981, Box 91283, NSC Meetings, ESF, RRL.

38. Weinberger, "The Defense Policy of the Reagan Administration," 6/17/1981, Box 491, Council on Foreign Relations (CFR) Records, Mudd.

39. Weinberger, "Defense Policy."

40. Weinberger, "U.S. Defense Strategy," *Foreign Affairs* 64, no. 4 (1986): 694.

41. On these concepts, see Douglas W. Skinner, *Airland Battle Doctrine* (Alexandria, VA: Center for Naval Analyses, 1988); Benjamin S. Lambeth, *The Transformation of American Airpower* (Ithaca: Cornell University Press, 2000), 85–88; David Walsh, *The Military Balance in the Cold War: U.S. Perceptions and Policy, 1976–1985* (New York: Routledge, 2008), 50–52; Thomas Runge, "Firepower and Follow-On Forces Attack: Making Every Round Count," Airpower Research Institute, Maxwell Air Force Base, Montgomery, AL, March 1991.

42. "The Maritime Strategy," 1984, in John B. Hattendorf and Peter Swartz, *U.S. Naval Strategy in the 1980s: Selected Documents* (Newport, RI: Naval War College, 2008), 69–70. See also "The Strategy of Global Flexibility," 4/12/1982, Part III: Box 3, Caspar Weinberger Papers, LC.

43. "Reprint of a Radio Program entitled 'Rostow IV,'" October 1978, Box 168, Committee on the Present Danger (CPD) Papers, Hoover.

44. See NSDD-12, "Strategic Forces Modernization Program," 10/1/1981, and NSDD-13, "Nuclear Weapons Employment Policy," 10/19/1981, http://www.fas.org/irp/offdocs/nsdd/.

45. See Austin Long and Brendan Green, "Stalking the Secure Second Strike: Intelligence, Counterforce, and Nuclear Strategy," *Journal of Strategic Studies* 38, no. 1–2 (2015): esp. 48–56.

46. NSDD-13, "Nuclear Weapons Employment Policy"; George Wilson, "Preparing for Long Nuclear War Is Waste of Funds, Gen. Jones Says," *Washington Post*, 6/19/1982.

47. Andy W. Marshall, *Long-Term Competition with the Soviets: A Framework for Strategic Analysis* (Santa Monica: RAND Corporation, Apr. 1972), 33, 35. Marshall wrote this paper while at the RAND Corporation; he would later become Director of Net Assessment at the Pentagon.

48. "The President's Concluding Remarks at the National Security Council Meeting," 6/18/1982, Box 3, Pipes Files, RRL.

49. Richard Halloran, "Pentagon Draws Up First Strategy for Fighting a Long Nuclear War," *New York Times*, 5/30/1982. See also Arquilla, *Reagan Imprint*, 39–40.

50. Weinberger Memo, "MX Missile Deployment," Fall 1982, Part III: Box 3, Weinberger Papers, LC.

51. NSC Meeting, 11/30/1983, Box 91303, ESF, RRL.

52. "Summary of President's NATO Consultations: Special Session of the North Atlantic Council," 11/21/1985, OA 92178, Robert Linhard Files, Geneva Summit Record, RRL; Reagan, Address to the Nation, 3/23/1983, APP.

53. Reagan-Thatcher MemCon, 12/28/1984, Box 90902, European and Soviet Affairs Directorate (ESAD), ESF, RRL. See also NSC Meeting, 11/30/1983, Box 91303, NSC Meetings, ESF, RRL; Margaret Thatcher, *The Downing Street Years* (New York: HarperCollins, 1993), 467; "Interview of Bud McFarlane," 10/9/1989, esp. 5, Box 2, Don Oberdorfer Papers, Mudd.

54. NSC Meeting, 4/16/1982, Box 91284, NSC Meetings, ESF, RRL.

55. Reagan-Roberto Viola MemCon, 3/17/1981, Box 48, SF, ESF, RRL; Reagan-Chun Doo-hwan MemCon, 2/2/1981, Box 48, SF, ESF, RRL.

56. NSDD-120, "Visit to the United States of Premier Zhao Ziyang," 1/9/1984, Box 1, National Security Decision Directives (NSDDs), RRL; Shultz to Reagan, 4/3/1984, Box CF0375, Edwin Meese Files, RRL; James Mann, *About Face: A History of America's Curious Relationship with China, from Nixon to Clinton* (New York: Vintage, 2000), esp. 134–54.

57. NSC Meeting, 2/11/1981, Box 91282, NSC Meetings, ESF, RRL. See also Comptroller General, "U.S. Military Aid to El Salvador and Honduras," 8/22/1985, Box 2, Oliver North Files, RRL; William LeoGrande, *Our Own Backyard: The United States in Central America, 1977–1992* (Chapel Hill: University of North Carolina Press, 1996).

58. NIC Analytic Group, "The USSR and the Vulnerability of Empire," 11/27/1981, CREST.

59. "Reuters News Dispatch," 3/18/1981, Box 46, Richard Allen Papers, Hoover; NSC Meeting, 11/3/1982, Box 91305, ESF, RRL; Draft National Security Study Directive (NSSD) 11–82, in Bremer to Interagency Group, 9/9/1982, CREST.

60. Casey Remarks at Brown University, 10/15/1981, CREST.

61. "Response to NSSD 11–82: U.S. Relations with the USSR," late 1982, Box 91278, NSDDs, ESF, RRL. See also Steve Coll, *Ghost Wars: The Secret History of the CIA, Afghanistan, and bin Laden, from the Soviet Invasion to September 10, 2001* (New York: Penguin, 2004), esp. 53–106; James Scott, *Deciding to Intervene: The Reagan Doctrine and American Foreign Policy* (Durham: Duke University Press, 1996), 40–81.

62. Interview with Bud McFarlane, 3/20/1986, esp. 6–7, Box 48, Smith Papers, LC; NSC Meeting, 11/10/1981, Box 91283, NSC Meetings, ESF, RRL.

63. Reagan to Thatcher, 10/25/1983, Box 36, HOS, ESF, RRL; State to Kingston, 10/21/1983, DDRS; Cannon, *President Reagan,* 445–51.

64. Herbert Meyer to DCI, 6/28/1984, Box 9, William Clark Files, RRL.

65. Reagan-Casaroli MemCon, 12/15/1981, Box 49, SF, ESF, RRL; Ronald Reagan, *An American Life* (New York: Simon & Schuster, 1990), 237–38.

66. Clark to Reagan, undated, NSC 0070, NSC Meetings, ESF, RRL; "A Reagan Soviet Policy," Oct. 1981, Box 3, Pipes Files, RRL.

67. Remarks to National Association of Evangelicals, 3/8/1983, APP; Address at University of Notre Dame, 5/17/1981, APP.

68. Toasts by Reagan and Thatcher, 2/27/81, APP.

69. "East-West Policy Study," 7/8/1981, CREST; also "Response to NSSD 11–82: U.S. Relations with the USSR," late 1982, Box 91278, NSDDs, ESF, RRL.

70. Wick to Gergen, 8/7/1981, DDRS; Wick to Reagan, 1/4/1982, Box OA86, SF, ESF, RRL.

71. Kampelman to Eugene Rostow, 11/18/1982, Department of State Staff Correspondence, Kampelman Papers, Minnesota Historical Society (MHS); "The Madrid CSCE Review Meeting," Nov. 1983, Box 13, Kampelman Papers; Sarah Snyder, *Human Rights Activism and the End of the Cold War: A Transnational History of the Helsinki Network* (Cambridge, UK: Cambridge University Press, 2011), 140–59.

72. NSC Meeting, 12/22/1981, Box 91283, NSC Meetings, ESF, RRL.

73. Reagan to Brezhnev, 4/3/1981, Box 38, HOS, ESF, RRL.

74. Reagan, *American Life,* 304; NSC Meeting, 12/21/1981, Box 91283, NSC Meetings, ESF, RRL.

75. State to Bonn, Paris, and London, 1/2/1982, DDRS; Reagan to Jaruzelski, 12/23/1981, Box 91283, ESF, RRL.

76. Caspar Weinberger Oral History, 11/19/2002, POHP, 32; Reagan-Casaroli MemCon, 12/15/1981, Box 49, SF, ESF, RRL.

77. George Weigel, *The End and the Beginning: Pope John Paul II—the Victory of Freedom, the Last Years, the Legacy* (New York: Doubleday, 2010), 147–49; Robert Gates, *From the Shadows: The Ultimate Insider's Story of Five Presidents and How They Won the Cold War* (New York: Simon & Schuster, 1996), 236–39, esp. 237; Reagan in Carl Bernstein, "The Holy Alliance," *Time,* 2/24/1992, http://www.carlbernstein.com/

magazine_holy_alliance.php (accessed 6/12/2015). See also Gregory Domber, *Empowering Revolution: America, Poland, and the End of the Cold War* (Chapel Hill: University of North Carolina Press, 2014), 17–18.

78. NSC Meeting, 5/24/1982, Box 91284, ESF, RRL; NSC Meeting, 12/21/1981, Box 91283, ESF, RRL.

79. NIC, "The Soviet Bloc Financial Problem as a Source of Western Influence," Apr. 1982, DNSA; Kenneth Aaron Rodman, *Sanctions beyond Borders: Multinational Corporations and U.S. Economic Statecraft* (Lanham MD: Rowman & Littlefield, 2001), 80–81; State to Bonn, Paris, and London, 1/2/1982, DDRS; Schweizer, *Victory,* 72–74.

80. Douglas Brinkley, ed., *The Reagan Diaries Unabridged: Volume I* (New York: HarperCollins, 2009), 95.

81. "Discussion Paper for 16 SEPTEMBER Meeting of SIG/IEP on Sanctions Paper," Sept. 1982, NSC 00061, NSC Meetings, ESF, RRL. On sanctions, see also NSC Minutes, 7/6/1981, Box 91282, NSC Meetings, ESF, RRL; NSC Meeting, 12/22/1981, Box 91283, NSC Meetings, ESF, RRL; USDEL Secretary Aircraft to SecState, 1/29/1982, Box 35, HOS, ESF, RRL; Meeting in Cabinet Room, 3/25/1982, Box 91283, NSC Meetings, ESF, RRL; "The President's Concluding Remarks at the National Security Council Meeting," 6/18/1982, Box 3, Pipes Files, RRL.

82 "TV Interview for BBC," 9/1/1982, MTF; Thatcher-Weinberger MemCon, 9/8/1982, Box 91130, ESAD, ESF, RRL. See also State to Bonn, 8/11/1982, DDRS.

83. NIC, "Soviet Bloc Financial Problem."

84. On negotiations and compromise, see State to Bonn, 8/11/1982, DDRS; NSC Meeting, 11/9/1982, Box 91284, NSC Meetings, ESF, RRL; McFarlane, "East-West Economic Relations," undated, Box 20, Country File, ESF, RRL; NSDD-66, "East-West Economic Relations and Poland-Related Sanctions," 11/29/1982, NSDD 1–220, Box 1, Records Declassified and Released by the NSC, RRL.

85. Thomas Reed, *At the Abyss: An Insider's History of the Cold War* (New York: Presidio Press, 2005), 267–70, esp. 269; Schweizer, *Victory,* 31–32, 96–100, 141–43, 202–5, 232–34.

86. NSSD 11–82, "U.S. Policy toward the Soviet Union," 8/21/1982, Box 2, NSDD 221–325, Reading Room Files, RRL; "Response to NSSD 11–82: U.S. Relations with the USSR," NSC 00070, NSC Meetings, ESF, RRL; Draft NSSD 11–82, in Bremer to Interagency Group, 9/9/1982, CREST.

87. NSDD-32, "U.S. National Security Strategy," 5/20/1982, Box 91297, NSDD File, ESF, RRL; Clark to Reagan, 1/10/1983, Box 91306, ESF, RRL.

88. "Meeting in the Cabinet Room, Debrief of Under Secretary Buckley's Trip to Europe," 3/25/1982, Box 91283, NSC Meetings, ESF, RRL; Douglas Selvage, "The Politics of the Lesser Evil: The West, the Polish Crisis, and the CSCE Review Conference in Madrid, 1981–1983," in *The Crisis of Détente in Europe: From Helsinki to Gorbachev, 1975–1985,* edited by Leopoldo Nuti (New York: Routledge, 2009), 46; also Brinkley, *Reagan Diaries,* 142.

89. Shultz to Reagan, 1/19/1983, Box 41, Matlock Files, RRL.

90. Remarks to National Press Club, 11/18/1981, APP.

91. Reagan-Schmidt MemCon, 5/21/1981, Box 48, SF, ESF, RRL; NSDD-15, "Theater Nuclear Forces (Intermediate-Range Nuclear Forces)," 11/16/1981, Box 1,

Records Declassified and Released by the NSC, RRL; Address at Eureka College, 5/9/1982, APP.

92. Reagan-Thatcher Meeting, 9/29/1983, MTF.

93. "Congressional Meeting on Nuclear Freeze," 4/12/1983, Box 1, Meeting File, Presidential Handwriting File, RRL.

94. This was the famous "Walk in the Woods" proposal. See MemCon, 7/16/1982, Box 3, Clark Files, RRL; Rostow to Reagan, 7/30/1982, Box 3, Clark Files, RRL; Memorandum for the President, 8/5/1982, Box 3, Clark Files, RRL; Nitze, "Speech to Council on Foreign Relations," 12/22/1983, Box 501, CFR Records, Mudd. It is worth noting that the Soviets also eventually rejected this formula. For Weinberger's views on arms control, see NSC Meeting, 10/13/1981, in "The Euromissiles and the End of the Cold War: 1977–1987," CWIHP Document Reader (Washington, DC, 2009), Part 3.

95. NSC Meeting, 12/16/1982, Box 91285, NSC Meetings, ESF, RRL; Brinkley, *Reagan Diaries,* 142.

96. "Text of President Reagan's Handwritten Message to President Brezhnev," Apr. 1981, Box 38, HOS, ESF, RRL.

97. NSDD-75, "U.S. Relations with the USSR," 1/17/1983, Box 91287, NSDD File, ESF, RRL; Radio Address to the Nation, 11/13/1982, APP; Jack F. Matlock, *Reagan and Gorbachev: How the Cold War Ended* (New York: Random House, 2004), 65–66; Brinkley, *Reagan Diaries,* 220.

98. NSDD-75, "U.S. Relations with the USSR."

99. Meyer to DCI, 4/12/1983, CREST. See also Clark to Reagan, undated, Box 36, Matlock Files, RRL.

100. Andropov's Speech at PCC Meeting, 1/4–1/5/1983, in Mastny and Byrne, *Cardboard Castle,* 472–79, esp. 473. See also Georgi Mirski, "Soviet-American Relations in the Third World," in *Turning Points in Ending the Cold War,* edited by Kiron K. Skinner (Stanford: Hoover Institution Press, 2007), 167; Robert Patman, "Reagan, Gorbachev, and the Emergence of 'New Political Thinking,'" *Review of International Studies* 25, no. 4 (1999): 591–99.

101. See comments in Edward Atkeson to DCI, 12/6/1983, CREST.

102. Meyer to DDCI and DCI, "Can Gorbachev Pull It Off?" 5/17/1985, CREST. See also NIE, "Domestic Stresses on the Soviet System," Nov. 1985, CIA FOIA; Stephen Brooks and William Wohlforth, "Power, Globalization, and the End of the Cold War: Reevaluating a Landmark Case for Ideas," *International Security* 25, no. 3 (2000/2001): esp. 14–27.

103. See "Record of Interview" with Vitalii Leonidovich Kataev, 6/23/1993, EBB 285, NSArch.

104. In reality, the Pershing-II was able to reach targets as far east as Ukraine and the western Soviet Union. The Soviets apparently feared, however, that the publicly announced range had been deliberately understated by several hundred kilometers and that the missiles could therefore reach crucial Soviet command-and-control targets around Moscow as well. See CIA, "Soviet Thinking on the Possibility of Armed Confrontation with the United States," 12/30/1983, CIA FOIA.

105. Ustinov statement to Extraordinary Session of Warsaw Pact Defense Ministers, 10/20/1983, CWIHP. See also "Summary of Narrative" of A.S. Kalashnikov, Apr. 1993, EBB 285, NSArch.

106. Ben Fischer, "The 1983 War Scare in U.S.-Soviet Relations," Center for the Study of Intelligence, 1996, EBB 426, NSArch, esp. 67; Anatoly Chernyaev, *My Six Years with Gorbachev* (University Park: Penn State University Press, 2000), 9.

107. "Dinner with Andrei Grachev," 5/27/1990, Box 1, Oberdofer Papers, Mudd.

108. Fischer, "1983 War Scare," 67. On Soviet views of SDI, see also Pavel Palazchenko, *My Years with Gorbachev and Shevardnadze: The Memoir of a Soviet Interpreter* (University Park: Penn State University Press, 1997), 41; Peter J. Westwick, "'Space-Strike Weapons' and the Soviet Response to SDI," *Diplomatic History* 32, no. 5 (2008): 955–79; Interagency Intelligence Assessment, "Possible Soviet Responses to the U.S. Strategic Defense Initiative," 9/12/1983, CIA FOIA.

109. NIC, "The U.S.-Soviet Competition for Influence in the Third World: How the LDCs Play It," 4/22/1982, CREST.

110. "Statement of George Shultz," Executive Session, House Select Committee on Intelligence, Draft of 4/16/1983, Box 4, Clark Files, RRL. U.S. policy in Central America is also discussed in chap. 3.

111. Coll, *Ghost Wars,* 53–106. See also Craig Karp, INR, "Afghanistan: Six Years of Soviet Occupation," 12/1/1985, DNSA.

112. Ustinov Statement to Warsaw Pact Defense Ministers, 12/5–12/7/1983, in Mastny and Byrne, *Cardboard Castle,* 490; Report on Ogarkov Speech to Warsaw Pact Chiefs of Staff, 9/8–9/10/1982, in Mastny and Byrne, *Cardboard Castle,* 467.

113. Prados, *How the Cold War Ended,* 156–58; Gates, *From the Shadows,* 237–38; Garthoff, *Great Transition,* 31–32; Reed, *At the Abyss,* 267–70. There is still much debate over whether Casey's endeavors were responsible for the Saudi decision to increase production in the mid-1980s. It now appears that the Saudis made this decision independent of U.S. efforts. Dick Combs, *Inside the Soviet Alternate Universe: The Cold War's End and the Soviet Union's Fall Reappraised* (University Park, Penn State University Press, 2008), 230–31. Either way, this decision also severely compounded Soviet economic troubles.

114. Eric Bourne, "Soviet Bloc Digging Deep into Pockets to Help Poland," *Christian Science Monitor,* 4/16/1982; Ned Temko, "Soviets Find It Hard to Keep Supplying Poland," *Christian Science Monitor,* 3/4/1982.

115. Andropov, Speech at PCC Meeting, 1/4–1/5/1983, in Mastny and Byrne, *Cardboard Castle*, 472–73.

116. Meyer to DCI, 4/12/1983, CREST.

117. CPSU CC Politburo Meeting (Excerpt), 6/4/1981, CWIHP; Ustinov's Statement to Warsaw Pact Defense Ministers, 10/20/1983, CWIHP. See also Anatoly Dobrynin, *In Confidence: Moscow's Ambassador to Six Cold War Presidents* (New York: Random House, 1995), 527.

118. Brezhnev to Brandt et al., 2/22/1982, Euromissiles, CWIHP; Garthoff, *Great Transition,* 132–33.

119. "Three Minutes to Midnight," *Bulletin of the Atomic Scientists,* Jan. 1984, 2.

120. NIE, "Domestic Stresses on the Soviet System," Nov. 1985, CIA FOIA; McFarlane to Reagan, 2/28/1984, DDRS.

121. Fischer, "1983 War Scare," 61.

122. SNIE, "Soviet Policy toward the United States in 1984," 8/14/1984, CIA FOIA. See also Gates in Small Group Meeting, 11/19/1983, Box 34, Matlock Files, RRL.

123. Dobrynin, *In Confidence*, 551; Andrei Grachev, *Gorbachev's Gamble: Soviet Foreign Policy and the End of the Cold War* (Cambridge, MA: Polity Press, 2008), 39–41. See also Odom to Secretary of the Army, 2/10/1984, Box 14, Odom Papers, LC.

124. Report on Ogarkov Speech to Warsaw Pact Chiefs of Staff, 466; Garthoff, *Great Transition*, 137; Melvyn Leffler, *For the Soul of Mankind: The United States, the Soviet Union, and the Cold War* (New York: Hill and Wang, 2007), 358.

125. Minutes of the CC Communist Party of the Soviet Union (CPSU) Politburo, 5/31/1983, CWIHP; Andropov-Harriman MemCon, 6/2/1983, Euromissiles, CWIHP.

126. Matlock-Vishnevsky MemCon, 10/11/1983, Box 2, Matlock Files, RRL.

127. "Reuters News Dispatch," 3/18/1981, Box 46, Allen Papers, Hoover; Anthony Lewis, "Nuclear Hawks Aim for All-Out Arms Race," *Atlanta Constitution*, 11/9/1982; Robert Scheer, *With Enough Shovels: Reagan, Bush, and Nuclear War* (New York: Vintage, 1983).

128. Matlock to McFarlane, 12/13/1983, Box 2, Matlock Files, RRL; Bernard Nossiter, "'Murder' and 'Massacre' Charged as U.N. Council Starts its Debate," *New York Times,* 9/3/1983; Gates, *From the Shadows,* 266–70.

129. Vladislav Zubok, *A Failed Empire: The Soviet Union in the Cold War from Stalin to Gorbachev* (Chapel Hill: University of North Carolina Press, 2007), 274.

130. Gates, *From the Shadows,* 270–72. For various perspectives, see also David Hoffman, *The Dead Hand: The Untold Story of the Cold War Arms Race and Its Dangerous Legacy* (New York: Doubleday, 2009), 94–95; Fischer, "1983 War Scare"; Vojtech Mastny, "How Able Was 'Able Archer'? Nuclear Trigger and Intelligence in Perspective," *Journal of Cold War Studies* 11, no. 1 (2009): 108–23.

131. NSDD-137, "U.S. Nuclear Arms Control Strategy for 1984," 3/31/1984, NSDDs, RRL.

132. "Draft Reagan Campaign Action Plan," 10/27/1983, Box 136, Baker Papers. See also "A Public Affairs Campaign to Support and Follow Up President Reagan's Trip to Europe June 2–11," undated, Box 90100, Sven Kraemer Files, RRL; Ronald Powaski, *Return to Armageddon: The United States and the Nuclear Arms Race, 1981–1999* (New York: Oxford University Press, 2000), 18.

133. "Estimate of the Anti-INF Threat for the Fall," Box 73, SF, ESF, RRL.

134. INR, "Western Europe: Neutralism and Anti-INF Sentiment," date obscured, Euromissiles, CWIHP.

135. NSDD-86, "U.S. Approach to INF Negotiations," 3/28/1983, Euromissiles, CWIHP. See also Burt in Foreign and Commonwealth Office (FCO) to Washington, 9/20/1983, MTF.

136. "German Views on INF," Bonn to FCO, 3/15/1983, MTF; Reagan-Kohl MemCon, 3/5/1984, Euromissiles, CWIHP; Reagan-Thatcher Meeting, 9/29/1983, MTF.

137. Reagan, *American Life,* 588. See also Brinkley, *Reagan Diaries,* 199; Don Oberdorfer, *From the Cold War to a New Era: The United States and the Soviet Union, 1983–1991* (Baltimore: Johns Hopkins University Press, 1998), 66–67.

138. Reagan-Mitterrand MemCon, 3/22/1984, DDRS.

139. Matlock, *Reagan and Gorbachev,* 76.

140. See NSDD-137, "U.S. Nuclear Arms Control Strategy for 1984," 3/31/1984, NSDDs, RRL; Remarks at National Leadership Forum of the Center for Strategic and International Studies, 4/6/1984, APP.

141. Reagan, Address to the Nation and Other Countries, 1/16/1984, APP.

142. Reagan, State of the Union Address, 1/25/1984, APP.

143. Reagan to Chernenko, 4/16/1984, Box 39, HOS, ESF, RRL.

144. Reagan-Gromyko MemCon, 9/29/1984, Box 47, Matlock Files, RRL.

145. "Interview of Charles Hill," 7/20/1989, esp. 6–7, Box 2, Oberdorfer Papers, Mudd.

146. Gates, *From the Shadows,* 292; Brinkley, *Reagan Diaries,* 277; Wilson, *Triumph of Improvisation,* 75, 77–80.

147. Dam to Reagan, 7/14/1984, Box 5, Matlock Files, RRL; "U.S.-Soviet Relations: Bilateral Issues," undated, Box 5, Matlock Files, RRL; Reagan-Gromyko MemCon, 9/29/1984, Box 47, Matlock Files.

148. Phrase in Odom to Secretary of the Army, 2/10/1984, Box 14, Odom Papers, LC.

149. Shultz, *Turmoil and Triumph,* 478, 531–32.

150 Reagan to Loeb, 11/25/1985, in Kiron Skinner, Annelise Anderson, and Martin Anderson, eds., *Reagan: A Life in Letters* (New York: Free Press, 2003), 414; Chernyaev, *My Six Years with Gorbachev,* 46.

151. "Conference of the Secretaries of the CPSU," 3/15/1985, EBB 504, NSArch; Mikhail Gorbachev, *Memoirs* (New York: Doubleday, 1995), 401. See also Archie Brown, *The Gorbachev Factor* (New York: Oxford University Press, 1996), 221–27, 249–50; Archie Brown, *Seven Years That Changed the World: Perestroika in Perspective* (New York: Oxford University Press, 2007), 242–43.

152 Peter Rodman, *Presidential Command: Power, Leadership, and the Making of Foreign Policy from Richard Nixon to George W. Bush* (New York: Knopf, 2009), 155.

153. Grachev, *Gorbachev's Gamble,* 84. On fears of Pershing-II, see Gorbachev to Reagan, 12/24/1985, Box 66, Matlock Files, RRL; Gorbachev, *Memoirs,* 444.

154. "Summit Notes—11/20/85—Second Day," Box 215, Donald Regan Papers, LC. See also Gorbachev-Mitterrand Conversation, 7/7/1986, EBB 504, NSArch; William Jackson, "Soviet Reassessment of Ronald Reagan, 1985–1988," *Political Science Quarterly* 113, no. 4 (1998–1999): 618–22.

155. NIE, "Domestic Stresses on the Soviet System," Nov. 1985, CIA FOIA.

156. Shultz to Reagan, 11/12/1985, Box 47, Matlock Files, RRL; Gorbachev to Reagan, 12/24/1985, Box 66, Matlock Files. See also Jackson, "Soviet Reassessment of Ronald Reagan, 1985–1988," 621–22, 629–30; Dobrynin, *In Confidence,* 570.

157. Carolyn Ekedahl and Melvin Goodman, *The Wars of Eduard Shevardnadze* (University Park: Penn State University Press, 1997), 100–101; and Gorbachev in Politburo Meeting, 2/26/1987, EBB 238, NSArch. These two paragraphs also draw on Zubok, *Failed Empire,* 279–80, 316; Jack Matlock, *Autopsy on an Empire: The American Ambassador's Account of the Collapse of the Soviet Union* (New York: Random House, 1996), 57–67, esp. 58.

158. Views of this subject include Zubok, *Failed Empire,* 280–302; William Wohlforth, "Realism and the End of the Cold War," *International Security* 19, no. 3

(1994–1995): 91–129; Anatoly Chernyaev, "Gorbachev's Foreign Policy: The Concept," in *Turning Points in Ending the Cold War*, edited by Kiron K. Skinner (Stanford: Hoover Institution Press, 2007), esp. 111–17.

159. Reagan to Gorbachev, 3/11/1985, EBB 172, NSArch.

160. Reagan to Murphy, 12/19/1985, in Skinner, Anderson, and Anderson, *Reagan: A Life in Letters*, 415–16; "Summary of President's NATO Consultations," 11/21/1985. See also Shultz to Reagan, 3/25/1985, Box 39, HOS, ESF, RRL.

161. Frederic Bozo, *Mitterrand, the End of the Cold War, and German Unification*, translated by Susan Emanuel (New York: Berghahn, 2009), 10; "TV Interview for BBC," 12/17/1984, MTF.

162. Reagan-Thatcher MemCon, 12/28/1984, Box 90902, ESAD, ESF, RRL.

163. "Record of a Meeting Held at the White House on Thursday 26 February (1981)," MTF; Shultz, "Managing the U.S.-Soviet Relationship over the Long Term," 10/18/1984, Box 128, Charles Hill Papers, Hoover; also Shultz to Reagan, 5/21/1983, Box 91278, NSDD File, ESF, RRL; Matlock, *Reagan and Gorbachev*, 83–85.

164. Shultz, "Managing the U.S.-Soviet Relationship."

165. Defense budget figures are in U.S. Census Bureau, *Statistical Abstract*, 358.

166. "Options for Nuclear Arms Control," undated (1986), Box 215, Regan Papers, LC.

167. Reagan's notes, "Gorbachev," Oct. 1985, Box 215, Regan Papers, LC; Carlucci to Reagan, undated, Box 92132, Linhard Files, RRL; Brinkley, *Reagan Diaries*, 457; Reagan to Gorbachev, 5/11/1985, Box 47, Matlock Files, RRL.

168. "Summary of President's NATO Consultations," 11/21/1985.

169. Matlock, *Reagan and Gorbachev*, 164; Reagan's notes, "Gorbachev," Oct. 1985. See also Reagan-Mitterrand MemCon, 3/22/1984, DDRS.

170. David Broder, "Kemp Denounces Arms-Control Plan," *Washington Post*, 5/23/1987; George Will, "How Reagan Changed America," *Newsweek*, 1/9/1989.

171. Reagan-Gorbachev MemCon, 10/12/1986, EBB 203, NSArch. See also Reagan to Gorbachev, 3/11/1985, EBB 172, NSArch; "First Private Meeting," 11/19/1985, EBB 172, NSArch.

172. Reagan-Gorbachev MemCon, 10/12/1986, EBB 203, NSArch; Reagan's notes, "Gorbachev," Oct. 1985.

173. "Debriefing of President," 11/19/1985, Box 215, Regan Papers, LC.

174. Gorbachev to Reagan, 12/24/1985, Box 66, Matlock Files, RRL; Dobrynin, *In Confidence*, 592–93; Joint U.S.-Soviet Statement, 11/21/1985, APP; MemCon, "Second Private Meeting," 11/19/1985, EBB 172, NSArch.

175. Joint U.S.-Soviet Statement, 11/21/1985.

176. Brinkley, *Reagan Diaries*, 425–26; NSPG Meeting, 2/3/1986, NSPG 00127, RRL; Reagan to Gorbachev, 2/22/1986, Box 66, Matlock Files, RRL.

177. Gorbachev to Reagan, 6/1/1986, Box 214, Regan Papers, LC.

178. Chernyaev, *My Six Years with Gorbachev*, 83–84.

179. For the negotiations, see MemCon, "First Meeting," 10/11/1986, EBB 203, NSArch; MemCon between U.S. and Soviet Officials, 10/11/1986, EBB 203, NSArch; various MemCons, 10/12/1986, EBB 203, NSArch; Reagan, *American Life*, 675–79; Shultz, *Turmoil and Triumph*, 757–73.

180. Reagan, *American Life*, 675.

181. Reagan, Remarks to Arms Control and Disarmament Agency (ACDA) and State Department Officials, 10/14/1986, Box 142, CPD Papers, Hoover; Gorbachev, *Memoirs,* 419; "Session of the Politburo of the CC CPSU," 10/14/1986, EBB 203, NSArch; Interview with Alexander Yakovlev, undated, 3, Box 1, Oberdorfer Papers, Mudd.

182. NSC Meeting, 9/20/1985, Box 91303, NSC Meetings, ESF, RRL. Reagan was restating a formulation recently expressed by Richard Nixon.

183. Reagan-Gorbachev MemCon, 10/12/1986, EBB 203, NSArch; Shultz, *Turmoil and Triumph,* 760, also 758–59, 764–68; MemCon, "First Meeting," 10/11/1986, EBB 203, NSArch; MemCon, Meeting between U.S. and Soviet Officials, 10/11/1986, EBB 203, NSArch; Poindexter to Reagan, undated, Box 91639, Alton Keel Files, RRL.

184. Politburo Meeting, 2/26/1987, EBB 238, NSArch.

185. Lettow, *Ronald Reagan,* 234. See also Shultz, *Turmoil and Triumph,* 1006; Reagan to Loeb, 12/18/1987, in Skinner, Anderson, and Anderson, *Reagan: A Life in Letters,* 384; William Odom, *The Collapse of the Soviet Military* (New Haven: Yale University Press, 1998), 134.

186. Gorbachev, *Memoirs,* 444; Jonathan Haslam, *Russia's Cold War: From the October Revolution to the Fall of the Wall* (New Haven: Yale University Press, 2011), 359.

187. Shultz-Gorbachev Meeting, 4/14/1987, Box 5, Oberdorfer Papers, Mudd.

188. Chernyaev, *My Six Years with Gorbachev,* 142; Gorbachev, *Memoirs,* 445; Mann, *Rebellion of Ronald Reagan,* 238–40, 272–78.

189. Svetlana Savranskaya, "Gorbachev and the Third World," in *The End of the Cold War and the Third World: New Perspectives on Regional Conflict,* edited by Artemy Kalinovsky and Sergey Radchenko (New York: Routledge, 2011), 29–30.

190. Gorbachev to Reagan, 12/14/1985, Box 214, Regan Papers, LC; Working Luncheon with Gorbachev, 12/10/1987, EBB 238, NSArch. See also INR, "Afghanistan: Seven Years of Soviet Occupation," Dec. 1986, DNSA; Hal Brands, *Latin America's Cold War* (Cambridge, MA: Harvard University Press, 2010), 216–17; Artemy Kalinovsky, *A Long Goodbye: The Soviet Withdrawal from Afghanistan* (Cambridge, MA: Harvard University Press, 2011), chap. 4.

191. Odom to Secretary of the Army, 5/11/1984, Box 14, Odom Papers, LC.

192. Chernyaev, "Gorbachev's Foreign Policy," 129; "Soviet Memorandum on the Present Situation in Afghanistan," 5/6/1987, CWIHP.

193. NSDD-166, "U.S. Policy, Programs, and Strategy in Afghanistan," 3/27/1985, NSDDs, RRL. See also NSDD-270, "Afghanistan," 5/1/1987, NSDDs, RRL.

194. Joint Chiefs of Staff (JCS) Cable, probably Mar. 1987, DNSA. See also JCS Cable, 2/27/1987, DNSA; Foreign Broadcast Information Service (FBIS) Bangkok to FBIS Reston, 9/27/1987, DDRS; Alexander Alexiev, "The United States and the War in Afghanistan," RAND Corporation, Jan. 1988, esp. 14, DNSA.

195. NSDD-288, "My Objectives at the Summit," 11/10/1987, EBB 238, NSArch. See also Reagan to Gorbachev, undated (1985–1986), Box 41, HOS, ESF, RRL; MemCon, "First Private Meeting in Geneva," 11/19/1985, EBB 172, NSArch.

196. Address on Soviet-United States Relations, 11/4/1987, APP.

197. On impact of U.S. policy, see Grachev, *Gorbachev's Gamble,* 111–12; Savranskaya, "Gorbachev and the Third World," 30; Odd Arne Westad, *The Global Cold War: Third World Interventions and the Making of Our Times* (Cambridge,

UK: Cambridge University Press, 2006), 371–72, 376, 380; Mirski, "Soviet-American Relations in the Third World," 172–73, 179–80.

198. "Protócolo 1740: Sesión Extraordinario No. 47," undated (1987–1988), Box 4, Robert Claxton Collection on Allende's Chile, Latin American Library, Tulane University; Brands, *Latin America's Cold War,* 217; Leffler, *For the Soul of Mankind,* 409–10.

199. Anatoly Chernyaev, "The Afghanistan Problem," *Russian Politics and Law* 42, no. 5 (2004): 41–42.

200. Shultz-Shevardnadze MemCon, 3/23/1988, RAC Box 1, Nelson Ledsky Files, RRL.

201. Matlock, *Reagan and Gorbachev,* 288; Chernyaev Diary, 4/1/1988, EBB 250, NSArch.

202. Reagan-Shevardnadze MemCon, 3/23/1988, Box 5, Dennis Ross Files, RRL.

203. Anatoly Adamishin and Richard Schifter, *Human Rights, Perestroika, and the End of the Cold War* (Washington, DC: United States Institute of Peace, 2009), 103. See also MemCon, Third Private Meeting, 11/20/1985, Box 92151, Rodman Files, RRL; Shultz to Reagan, undated, Box 2, Howard Baker Papers, RRL; Lisa Jameson to various officials, 11/12/1987, DDRS; "President's First One-on-One Meeting with General Secretary Gorbachev," 5/29/1988, NSC System File Folder 8791367, RRL.

204. Reagan's notes, "Gorbachev," Oct. 1985.

205. Department of State Cable to Shultz, 11/14/1987, DDRS. See also NSC Meeting, 9/20/1985, Box 91303, Meeting Files, ESF, RRL; USDEL Sec in Austria to State, 11/6/1986, DDRS; MemCon between U.S. and Soviet Officials, 10/12/1986, EBB 203, NSArch; "Dubinin-Ridgway Meeting 11/02: Moscow Human Rights Conference and Human Rights Issues," 11/9/1987, DDRS.

206. Reagan-Gorbachev MemCon, 12/8/1987, EBB 238, NSArch.

207. Snyder, *Human Rights Activism,* 158–73, 197; Zubok, *Failed Empire,* esp. 298.

208. Vienna to State, 6/20/1988, DDRS.

209. Matlock, *Reagan and Gorbachev,* 251. See also Mirski, "Soviet-American Relations in the Third World," 172–73; Chernyaev, "Gorbachev's Foreign Policy," 125.

210. Shultz, *Turmoil and Triumph,* 894.

211. Office of Soviet Analysis, "Where Is the USSR Headed?" undated (early or mid-1989), CIA FOIA; Sarah Snyder, "Principles Overwhelming Tanks: Human Rights and the End of the Cold War," in *The Human Rights Revolution: An International History,* edited by Akira Iriye, Petra Goedde, and William Hitchcock (New York: Oxford University Press, 2012), 270–73; "Vienna Breakthrough," *Freedom Monitor,* Feb. 1989, 1, Freedom House Papers, Mudd; "Second Plenary Meeting," 5/31/1988, NSC System File Folder 8791367, RRL.

212. MemCon between Reagan, Massie, et al., 3/11/1988, RAC Box 1, Lisa Jameson Files, RRL; "Background Book for the Meetings of President Reagan and General Secretary Gorbachev," 5/29–6/2/1988, RAC Box 5, Tyrus Cobb Files, RRL. See also Rodman to Powell, 6/9/1988, RAC Box 2, Rudolph Perina Files, RRL; Mann, *Rebellion of Ronald Reagan,* 282–85.

213. "CSCE/Moscow Human Rights Meeting," in "Background Book."

214. "President's First One-on-One Meeting," 5/29/1988; NSDD-305, "Objectives at the Moscow Summit," 4/26/1988, NSDD File, RRL; Remarks to World Affairs Council of Western Massachusetts, 4/21/1988, APP.

215. Remarks at Moscow State University, 5/31/1988, APP. See also "Talking Points for Aspen Journalists' Conference, Wye Plantation," 5/18/1988, RAC Box 2, Perina Files, RRL; Matlock, *Autopsy on an Empire*, 123–24.

216. For U.S. assessments of Soviet liberalization, see Carlucci to Reagan, 2/21/1987, Box 214, Regan Papers, LC; Background Briefing by Senior Administration Official on INF and U.S.-Soviet Summit, 10/30/1987, Box 92151, Rodman Files, RRL; Rodman to Powell, 6/9/1988, RAC Box 2, Perina Files, RRL; Reagan, *American Life*, 686, 702–3; Matlock, *Autopsy on an Empire*, 121–23.

217. News Conference following U.S.-Soviet Summit, 6/1/1988, APP; Garthoff, *Great Transition*, 352–53; "President's First One-on-One Meeting," 5/29/1988.

218. Chernyaev Diary, 6/19/1988, EBB 250, NSArch. See also "Interview of Foreign Minister Eduard Shevardnadze," 1/17/1990, 9, Box 1, Oberdorfer Papers, Mudd; Gorbachev, *Memoirs*, 457; Mann, *Rebellion of Ronald Reagan*, 304–6.

219. Reagan-Gorbachev MemCon, 5/29/1988, NSC System File Folder 9791367, ESF, RRL.

220. Reagan-Gorbachev MemCon, 12/7/1988, EBB 261, NSArch.

221. "Excerpts from Speech to U.N. on Major Soviet Military Cuts," *New York Times*, 12/8/1988; Gorbachev, *Memoirs*, 459–60.

222. Daniel Patrick Moynihan, "The CIA's Credibility," *National Interest* 42 (winter 1995): 111.

223. "Conference with Advisers," 10/31/1988, EBB 261, NSArch.

224. Odom, *Collapse of the Soviet Military*, 136; Reagan-Gorbachev MemCon, 12/7/1988, EBB 261, NSArch.

225. These issues are discussed in John Patrick Diggins, *Ronald Reagan: Fate, Freedom, and the Making of History* (New York: W. W. Norton, 2007), 219–62.

226. Kirkpatrick, Speech to Conservative Political Action Conference (CPAC), 3/21/1981, Box 45, Richard Allen Papers, Hoover.

227. Robert McFarlane and Zofia Smardz, *Special Trust* (New York: Cadell & Davies, 1994), 68. See also NSPG Meeting, 6/25/1984, EBB 210, NSArch; Theodore Draper, *A Very Thin Line: The Iran-Contra Affair* (New York: Hill and Wang, 1991).

228. Gates, *From the Shadows*, 561.

229. John T. McCarthy Oral History, 75, Foreign Affairs Oral History Collection (FAOHC), LC.

230. Robert Oakley Oral History, 153, FAOHC; William Webster Oral History Interview, 8/21/2002, 33, POHP. See also John Prados, "Notes on the CIA's Secret War in Afghanistan," *Journal of American History* 89, no. 2 (2002): 466–71.

231. Shultz-Shevardnadze MemCon, 4/21/1988, DDRS.

232. "End Game on Afghanistan in Geneva," 3/10/1988, RAC Box 1, Ledsky Files, RRL. See also Shultz, *Turmoil and Triumph*, 1089–92; Kalinovsky, *Long Goodbye*, 128–32.

233. NFAC, "Pakistan: Prospects for the Zia Government," Feb. 1981, CREST.

234. See, for instance, David Swartz to Hartman, 1/30/1976, EBB 6, NSArch.

235. Extract of Brown-Deng MemCon, 1/8/1980, EBB 377, NSArch.

236. Shultz to Reagan, 11/26/1982, EBB 377, NSArch. See also Department of State, "The Pakistani Nuclear Program," 6/23/1983, EBB 6, NSArch.

237. Thomas Hayward, "National Security and the Navy Today and Tomorrow," 1/29/1981, Box 740, CFR Sound Recordings, Mudd.

238. Robert D. Hormats, *The Price of Liberty: Paying for America's Wars* (New York: Times Books, 2007), 234.

239. Ibid., 245, 247; Diane B. Kunz, *Butter and Guns: America's Cold War Economic Diplomacy* (New York: Free Press, 1997), 286; Fareed Zakaria, "The Reagan Strategy of Containment," *Political Science Quarterly* 105, no. 3 (1990): 380. See also Dennis S. Ippolito, "Defense, Budget Policy, and the Reagan Deficits," in *President Reagan and the World,* edited by Eric Schmertz, Natalie Datlof, and Alexej Ugrinsky (Westport, CT: Praeger, 1997), 217–22.

240. Reagan-Thatcher MemCon, 11/16/1988, DDRS; Thatcher to Reagan, 10/22/1987, MTF.

3. American Statecraft and the Democratic Revolution

1. For an overview of cases, see Samuel Huntington, *The Third Wave: Democratization in the Late Twentieth Century* (Norman: University of Oklahoma Press, 1993), 21–26. From this and other sources, a reasonable count would include Bolivia, El Salvador, Nicaragua, Haiti, Honduras, Guatemala, Panama, Grenada, Argentina, Brazil, Chile, Uruguay, the Philippines, South Korea, Taiwan, Mongolia, Namibia, Pakistan, Hungary, Poland, Czechoslovakia, Romania, Turkey, and possibly South Africa. I discuss U.S. policy toward the collapse of the Soviet bloc in chap. 6.

2. As Robert Kagan notes, "Democratic transitions are not inevitable, even where conditions may be ripe. Nations may enter a transition zone—economically, socially, and politically—where the probability of moving in a democratic direction increases or decreases. But foreign influences, usually by the reigning great powers, are often catalysts that determine which direction change takes." *The World America Made* (New York: Knopf, 2012), 33.

3. Jeane Kirkpatrick, "United States Foreign Policy: Alternative Approaches to Human Rights," 3/10/1981, Box 740, CFR Digital Sound Recordings, Mudd; Jeane Kirkpatrick, "Dictatorships and Double Standards," *Commentary,* Nov. 1979; Reagan, "Foreign Affairs: The Need for Leadership," 3/17/1978, Box 3, RRSC, Hoover.

4. Weinberger to Casey, undated, Part 1: Box 572, Weinberger Papers, LC.

5. NSC Meeting, 2/6/1981, Box 91282, NSC Meetings, ESF, RRL.

6. Christopher Dickey, "Haig's Emissary, in Guatemala, Discounts Charges of Human Rights Abuse," *Washington Post,* 5/14/1981; Haig Remarks to Trilateral Commission, 3/31/1981, RAC Box 6, Carnes Lord Files, RRL; Haig Press Conference, 1/28/1981, *American Foreign Policy: Current Documents* (Washington, DC, 1981), 394–95 [hereafter *AFP: CD,* followed by year and page number].

7. MRE to Washington, 9/7/1981, EmbaChile Washington, Oficios Secretos Enviados, MRE Chile; Manila to State, 6/29/1981, DNSA; Reagan-Viola MemCon, 3/17/1981, Box 48, SF, ESF, RRL.

8. "Remarks of Nestor D. Sanchez," 12/11/1981, Box 5, Latin American Subject Collection, Hoover; "An Interview with Ronald Reagan," *Time,* 1/5/1981.

9. Tamar Jacoby, "The Reagan Turnaround on Human Rights," *Foreign Affairs,* 64, no. 5 (1986): 1069–70; Douglas Martin, "Ernest W. Lefever, Rejected as a Reagan Nominee, Dies at 89," *New York Times,* 8/4/2009.

10. Ronald Reagan, Acceptance Speech at Republican National Convention, 7/17/1980, Box 3, RRSC, Hoover.

11. Gerald F. Seib and Steve Frazier, "Uneasy Neighbors: Central American Strife Grows, Posing Problem for the Reagan Team," *Wall Street Journal*, 12/23/1980.

12. Alan Riding, "Reagan Impact Felt in Central America," *New York Times*, 11/16/1980; Jacoby, "Reagan Turnaround on Human Rights," 1068–69.

13. "Speak Out on Rights, Say Churches," *The Age*, 12/19/1980; Kathryn Sikkink, *Mixed Signals: U.S. Human Rights Policy and Latin America* (Ithaca: Cornell University Press, 2004), 152–54.

14. "Entrevista con el Capitán Rodolfo Muños Piloña," 4/17/1986, Colección Documentos, CIRMA.

15. MemCon, 1/28/1981, DNSA; CIA Cable, Apr. 1981, EBB 11, NSArch.

16. Guatemala City to MRE Mexico, 10/29/1979, Expediente (Exp.) 9, Legajo (Leg.) 127, Archivo Histórico Genaro Estrada, Mexico City.

17. "Guatemala and El Salvador," Department of State Briefing Memorandum, 5/27/1981, DNSA; Question-and-Answer Session with Reporters, 12/4/1982, APP; Sikkink, *Mixed Signals*, 158–69.

18. Brad Simpson, "Bringing the Non-State Back In: Human Rights and Terrorism since 1945," in *America in the World: The Historiography of American Foreign Relations since 1941*, 2nd ed., edited by Frank Costigliola and Michael Hogan (New York, 2014), 270.

19. Charles Mohr, "Coalition Assails Reagan's Choice for State Dept. Human Rights Job," *New York Times*, 2/25/1981; Robert Borosage and William Goodfellow, "Rights 1, Lefever 0," *New York Times*, 6/14/1981. See also Allen to Reagan, 4/16/1981, Box 30, CF, ESF, RRL; Hauke Hartmann, "U.S. Human Rights Policy under Carter and Reagan, 1977–1981," *Human Rights Quarterly* 23, no. 2 (2001): 422–25; Mark Peceny, *Democracy at the Point of Bayonets* (University Park: Penn State University Press, 1999), 115–16, 121–22.

20. "Excerpts from State Department Memo on Human Rights," *New York Times*, 11/5/1981.

21. Haig to Reagan, 3/8/1982, DDRS; Wolfowitz and Eagleburger to Haig, 10/2/1981, Department of State FOIA Electronic Reading Room.

22. "Excerpts from State Department Memo." The memo was signed by higher-ranking officials, but Abrams was a principal drafter. On Abrams, see Jesus Velasco, *Neoconservatives in U.S. Foreign Policy under Ronald Reagan and George W. Bush: Voices behind the Throne* (Baltimore: Johns Hopkins University Press, 2010), 101–2; Barbara Crossette, "Strong U.S. Human Rights Policy Urged in Memo Approved by Haig," *New York Times*, 11/5/1981.

23. Haig to Reagan, 3/8/1982, DDRS.

24. Shultz, Remarks to Conference on Democratization of Communist Countries, 10/18/1982, *AFP: CD*, 1982: 378; George Shultz, *Turmoil and Triumph: My Years as Secretary of State* (New York: Scribner, 1993), 10–11.

25. Address to British Parliament, 6/8/1982, APP.

26. State of the Union Address, 1/25/1984, APP.

27. Reagan, Remarks at Fudan University in Shanghai, 4/30/1984, APP; Henry Nau, "Ronald Reagan," in *U.S. Foreign Policy and Democracy Promotion: From Theodore Roosevelt to Barack Obama*, edited by Michael Cox, Timothy Lynch, and Nicolas Bouchet (New York: Routledge, 2013), 142–48.

28. Reagan, Address to British Parliament, 6/8/1982, APP.

29. Shultz, Remarks to Conference on Democratization of Communist Countries, 10/18/1982, *AFP: CD*, 1982: 378.

30. Haig to Reagan, 3/8/1982, DDRS; Shultz Statement in Executive Session, Draft of 4/16/1983, Box 4, Clark Files, RRL.

31. "Response to NSSD 11–82: U.S. Relations with the USSR," late 1982, NSC 00070, NSC Meetings, ESF, RRL.

32. Reagan, Remarks at Heritage Foundation, 10/8/1983, APP.

33. Haig to Reagan, 3/8/1982, DDRS.

34. Thomas Carothers, *In the Name of Democracy: U.S. Policy toward Latin America in the Reagan Years* (Berkeley: University of California Press, 1991), 130.

35. Shultz, Statement to SFRC, 1/31/1985, *AFP: CD*, 1985: 7; Shultz Address to Organization of American States (OAS), 11/17/1982, *AFP: CD*, 1982: 1283–85.

36. Inaugural Address, 1/21/1985, APP.

37. Message to Congress, 3/14/1986, APP.

38. "Excerpts from State Department Memo."

39. Shultz, Address to Creve Coeur Club of Illinois, 2/22/1984, *AFP: CD*, 1984: 280. See also Shultz, Address to Trilateral Commission, 4/3/1984, *AFP: CD*, 1984: 1.

40. "Excerpts from State Department Memo."

41. Reagan, Radio Address to the Nation, 3/24/1984, APP.

42. Abrams, Address to East-West Round Table of New York, 4/19/1983, *AFP: CD*, 1983: 329.

43. Shultz, Statement to SFRC, 1/31/1985, *AFP: CD*, 1985: 4–5, 8. See also Shultz, Address to Veterans of Foreign Wars, 8/20/1984, *AFP: CD*, 1984: 63.

44. Reagan, Address to British Parliament, 6/8/1982, APP.

45. Ibid.

46. Haig to Reagan, 3/8/1982, DDRS. See also NED, *Annual Report 1984*, DNSA.

47. NED, *Annual Report 1985*, 5, DNSA.

48. Bailey to Blair, 3/14/1982, Box 90304, Kimmitt Files, RRL. See also Blair to Clark, 4/19/1982, Box 90304, Kimmitt Files, RRL; Jeff Gerth, "Problems in Promoting Democracy," *New York Times*, 2/4/1983.

49. NED, *Annual Report 1984*, DNSA.

50. Reagan to Hatfield, 6/12/1984, RAC Box 9, Ronald Sable Files, RRL.

51. NED, *Annual Report 1985*, 3, DNSA; Thomas Carothers, "The NED at 10," *Foreign Policy* 95 (summer 1994), 124; Larry Diamond, "Promoting Democracy," *Foreign Policy* 87 (summer 1992), 39.

52. Message to Congress, 1/27/1987, APP.

53. NED, *Annual Report 1985*, 5, DNSA.

54. On these other agencies, see Diamond, "Promoting Democracy," 35–36; Kimmitt to Hill et al., 12/12/1983, RAC Box 7, Walter Raymond Files, RRL; Joshua Muravchik, *Exporting Democracy: Fulfilling America's Destiny* (Washington, DC: AEI Press, 1992), 183.

55. Tony Smith, *America's Mission: The United States and the Worldwide Struggle for Democracy in the Twentieth Century* (Princeton: Princeton University Press, 1994), 304.

56. Insurgent peak strength in CIA, "El Salvador's Insurgents: Key Capabilities and Vulnerabilities," June 1990, CIA FOIA.

57. Meeting between Erich Honecker and Daniel Ortega, 2/14/1984, DY 30/2473, Stiftung Archiv der Parteien und Massenorgenisationen der DDR im Bundesarchiv (SAPMO).

58. Kirkpatrick, Speech to CPAC, 3/21/1981, Box 45, Allen Papers, Hoover.

59. Ibid.; "U.S. Military Aid to El Salvador and Honduras," Report by Comptroller General, 1–2, 8–12, 8/22/1985, Box 2, Oliver North Files, RRL.

60. Haig to Reagan, 1/26/1981, Box 32, CF, ESF, RRL; Managua to State, 9/3/1981, Box 32, CF, ESF, RRL; Michael Grow, *U.S. Presidents and Latin American Interventions: Pursuing Regime Change in the Cold War* (Lawrence: University Press of Kansas, 2008), 128–31.

61. "Executive Summary of Strategy Paper for the NSC on U.S. Policy in Central America and the Caribbean," undated (1981), Box 91282, NSC Meetings, ESF, RRL; Allen to Reagan, 4/16/1981, Box 30, CF, ESF, RRL.

62. Negroponte to DCI and Chief of Latin America Division, 5/20/1982, CREST; CIA, "Nicaraguan Support for Central American Revolutionaries," 9/30/1981, CREST. There is a continuing debate over why the diplomatic dialogue ended. The most carefully researched study demonstrates that the Sandinistas were committed to supporting the FMLN and creating a Marxist-Leninist state, even if it meant breaking with Washington. Robert Kagan, *A Twilight Struggle: American Power and Nicaragua, 1977–1990* (New York: Free Press, 1996).

63. "Scope of CIA Activities under the Nicaragua Finding," 7/12/1982, DNSA.

64. "Talking Points," late 1982/early 1983, Box 1, Presidential Meetings, Handwriting File, RRL.

65. "U.S. Military Aid to El Salvador and Honduras," esp. 2, 8–25; Benjamin Schwartz, *American Counterinsurgency Doctrine and El Salvador: The Frustrations of Reform and the Illusions of Nation Building* (Santa Monica, CA: RAND Corporation, 1991), 2.

66. San Salvador to State, 3/8/1982, Box 29, CF, ESF, RRL; San Salvador to State, 6/24/1981 and 12/7/1982, Box 29, CF, ESF, RRL.

67. Remarks to National Association of Manufacturers, 3/10/1983, APP.

68. Schultz, Address to Trilateral Commission, 4/3/1984, *AFP: CD*, 1984, 5. See also "Strategy II: Substantially Deminished [*sic*] U.S. Involvement . . . ," 6/10/1983, NSDD-82 Folder, NSDDs, ESF, RRL.

69. Abrams, Remarks to East-West Round Table, 4/19/1983, *AFP: CD*, 1983: 328.

70. CIA, "El Salvador: Guerrilla Capabilities and Prospects over the Next Two Years," Oct. 1984, CIA FOIA. See also INR, "El Salvador: Brighter Prospects for Land Reform," 3/17/1983, RAC Box 2, Jacqueline Tillman Files, RRL; "Talking Points: The Reagan Administration and the Violent Extremes in El Salvador," 12/3/1983, Latin American Affairs Directorate (LAAD), ESF, RRL.

71. State to SOUTHCOM, 2/9/1982, DNSA; "NSPG re Central America," 7/13/82, CREST; Carothers, *In the Name of Democracy*, 41; San Salvador to State, 6/24/1981, Box 30, CF, ESF, RRL; San Salvador to State, 3/29/1982, Box 29, CF, ESF, RRL; Caracas to State, 2/14/1983, DNSA.

72. San Salvador to State, 3/29/1982, Box 29, CF, ESF, RRL.

73. Testimony by James Finn (Freedom House) to SFRC, 8/3/1982, RAC Box 7, Roger Fontaine Files, RRL.

74. CIA, "El Salvador: Performance on Certification Issues," July 1983, Box 102, North Files, RRL.

75. Shultz, *Turmoil and Triumph,* 409; CIA, "El Salvador: Controlling Rightwing Terrorism," Feb. 1985, CREST.

76. Hinton, Speech to American Chamber of Commerce in El Salvador, 10/29/1982, RAC Box 2, Robert Lilac Files, RRL. See also San Salvador to State, 4/13/1982, Box 29, ESF, RRL; San Salvador to State, 6/10/1982, DNSA; Peceny, *Democracy at the Point of Bayonets,* 132–33; William LeoGrande, *Our Own Backyard: The United States in Central America, 1977–1992* (Chapel Hill: University of North Carolina Press, 1996), 161–70.

77. Shultz, *Turmoil and Triumph,* 129. This paragraph and the next draw on Mark Danner, *The Massacre at El Mozoté: A Parable of the Cold War* (New York: Vintage, 1994); San Salvador to State, 1/15/1982, Box 90502, Jacqueline Tillman Files, RRL; Carnes Lord to Clark, 3/2/1982, Box 29, CF, ESF, RRL.

78. San Salvador to State, 1/31/1982, DNSA.

79. Joanne Omang, "As Salvadoran Politics Boil, U.S. Envoy Shifts Attention," *Washington Post,* 4/24/1982.

80. Caracas to State, 2/14/1983, DNSA.

81. David Forsythe, *Human Rights and U.S. Foreign Policy: Congress Reconsidered* (Gainesville: University Presses of Florida, 1988), 87–88; Cynthia Arnson, *Crossroads: Congress, the President, and Central America, 1976–1993* (University Park: Penn State University Press, 1993), 140.

82. Memorandum for the Record, 6/23/1983, Box 30, CF, ESF, RRL.

83. Sikkink, *Mixed Signals,* 172; Hill to McFarlane, 5/17/1984, DNSA; State to San Salvador, 4/7/1983, DNSA; Alfonso Sapia-Bosch to Clark, 1/29/1983, Box 27, CF, ESF, RRL; Shultz to Reagan, 4/5/1983, Box 30, CF, ESF, RRL.

84. "Vice President Bush's Meetings with Salvadoran Officials," 12/14/1983, DNSA; "Talking Points Used by the Vice President in El Salvador," undated, Box 28, CF, ESF, RRL.

85. "Vice President Bush's Meetings with Salvadoran Officials."

86. Robert McCartney, "U.S. Lauds Drive to Halt Death Squads," *Washington Post,* 1/8/1984; CIA, "El Salvador: Dealing with Death Squads," 1/20/1984, DNSA. See also CIA, "El Salvador," Oct. 1984; Department of State, "Report on the Situation in El Salvador," 7/12/1984, Box 102, North Files, RRL.

87. "El Salvador: Elections Strategy," undated, Box 28, CF, ESF, RRL; Robert J. McCartney, "U.S. Seen Assisting Duarte in Sunday's Salvadoran Vote,"*Washington Post,* 5/4/1984; David Schmitz, *The United States and Right-Wing Dictatorships, 1965–1989* (New York: Cambridge University Press, 2006), 216.

88. Edward Cody, "Duarte Declared El Salvador Victor," *Washington Post,* 5/12/1984.

89. San Salvador to State, 7/5/1986, Box 1, North Files, RRL. See also "El Salvador: Where We Are and What's Needed," 12/12/1985, Box 1, North Files, RRL; "El Salvador," in Department of State, 1988 Human Rights Report, Box 92385, ESF, RRL; CIA, "El Salvador: Controlling Rightwing Terrorism," Feb. 1985, CREST.

90. San Salvador to State, 12/9/1985, DNSA; Department of State, "Report on the Situation in El Salvador," 7/12/1984; San Salvador to State, 2/24/1988, DNSA.

91. "Since America's intervention," one critic wrote, "El Salvador has held six free elections and has peacefully transferred power for the first time in its history from one political party to its opposition; the country has also seen a significant

decline in political murders and in the armed forces' human rights abuses." Schwartz, *American Counterinsurgency Doctrine and El Salvador,* 12.

92. San Salvador to State, 3/22/1986, DDRS.

93. There was internal debate over which possibility was most likely or preferable. Hardliners such as Casey favored overthrow; Shultz thought the Contras might force the Sandinistas to adapt policy and hold elections. The original rationale for the Contras had been to interdict weapons shipments to El Salvador, but this objective was quickly superseded.

94. Richard Sobel, "Contra Aid Fundamentals: Exploring the Intricacies and the Issues," *Political Science Quarterly* 110, no. 2 (1995): 303; Army Intelligence Survey, "Nicaragua: Volume III—Armed Forces," May 1984, DNSA; North to McFarlane, 4/11/1985, DNSA.

95. Interview with *New York Times,* 3/28/1984, APP; Reagan to Speaker of the House et al., 11/14/1985, DNSA.

96. "Possible Economic Sanctions against Nicaragua," undated, Box 28, CF, ESF, RRL; Managua to State, 4/5/1983, DDRS; Reagan to Mejía, 6/29/1984, Box 14, HOS, ESF, RRL.

97. Managua to State, 3/6/1984, DDRS; "Issue Preview: U.S. Efforts to Promote Democracy in Nicaragua," 8/3/1989, DNSA; State to Managua, 4/4/1985, DNSA; NED, "Programs of the Endowment and Its Institutes in Nicaragua," Sept. 1988, DNSA.

98. "Remarks of William J. Casey," Washington, DC, 9/18/1986, DDRS.

99. Reagan, Address on Central America, 5/9/1984, APP; Remarks on U.S. Policy in Central America, 7/18/1984, APP; Remarks to CPAC, 3/1/1985, APP.

100. Bonn to State, 10/16/1981, DNSA. See also J. Michael Waller, "Tropical Chekists: The Sandinista Secret Police Legacy in Nicaragua," *Demokratizatsiya* 12, no. 3 (2004): 427–49; Roger Miranda and William Ratliff, *The Civil War in Nicaragua: Inside the Sandinistas* (New Brunswick: Transaction Publishers, 1992).

101. "Nobody Won in Nicaragua," *New York Times,* 11/7/1984; Robert Pastor, *Condemned to Repetition: The United States and Nicaragua* (Princeton: Princeton University Press, 1988), 249–50.

102. Timothy Charles Brown, *The Real Contra War: Highland Peasant Resistance in Nicaragua* (Norman: University of Oklahoma Press, 2001), esp. 3–6, 167, 204; CIA, "Somocista Influence in the Nicaraguan Democratic Force," 5/23/1983, CREST; State to Managua, 2/13/1986, Department of State FOIA.

103. "Meeting with NDR Directorate," undated, Box 1, Presidential Meetings, Handwriting File, RRL.

104. Author's interview with Bosco Matamoros, 6/14/2007, Washington, DC. See also Ministerio de Educación, "Parte de Guerra," 8/23/1980, CNA 0028, IHNCA; Fernando Cardenal to Lenin Cerna, 5/26/1980, CNA 0004, IHNCA; LeoGrande, *Our Own Backyard,* 413–15.

105. Notes of telephone conversation with Edgar Chamorro, undated, Box 148, Smith Papers, LC. See also Affidavit of Edgar Chamorro, 7/14/1990, Box 148, Smith Papers, LC; "Psychological Operations in Guerrilla Warfare," Oct. 1983, DNSA. On efforts to improve human rights, see "Talking Points," 10/25/1984, DNSA; Gregg and Watson to Bush, 5/27/1987, OA/ID 19835–018, Gregg Files, Vice-Presidential Files, George H. W. Bush Presidential Library (GHWBL).

106. Department of State Telegram, 7/20/1983, Box 32, CF, ESF, RRL; NIE, "Nicaragua: Outlook for the Insurgency," 6/30/1983, Box 32, CF, ESF, RRL.

107. James Baker, *The Politics of Diplomacy: Revolution, War, and Peace, 1989–1992* (New York: Putnam, 1995), 48; author's interview with Cresencio Arcos, 6/13/2007, Washington, DC.

108. Robert Pastorino, "Outline of Strategy for Peace and Democracy in Central America," undated, Box 92348, Pastorino Files, RRL; William Robinson, *Promoting Polyarchy: Globalization, U.S. Intervention, and Hegemony* (Cambridge, UK: Cambridge University Press, 1996), 219–20.

109. Meeting of Erich Honecker and Bayardo Arce, 3/4/1988, SAPMO. See also Ortega to Honecker, 4/2/1985, DY 30/2473, SAPMO; "Massive Forced Conscription Effort in Chinandega," undated, Box 148, Smith Papers, LC.

110. CIA, "Nicaragua: Domestic and Foreign Policy Trends," CIA FOIA, Feb. 1988; Lindsey Gruson, "For Contras in One Area, Growing Civilian Support," *New York Times*, 11/5/1987; Kagan, *Twilight Struggle*, 524, 556.

111. Author's interview with Víctor Tirado, 8/31/2007, Managua; statistics in William LeoGrande, "Making the Economy Scream: U.S. Economic Sanctions against Sandinista Nicaragua," *Third World Quarterly* 17, no. 2 (1996): 343.

112. Kagan, *Twilight Struggle*, esp. 577, 556–58, 721–22; LeoGrande, *Our Own Backyard*, esp. 582.

113. "Protócolo 1740: Sesión Extraordinario No. 47," undated, Box 4, Claxton Collection on Allende's Chile, Tulane; Carothers, *In the Name of Democracy*, 104–7; Pastor, *Condemned to Repetition*, 321.

114. David Close, *Nicaragua: The Chamorro Years* (Boulder: Lynne Rienner, 1999), 43–44; Harry Vanden and Gary Prevost, *Democracy and Socialism in Sandinista Nicaragua* (Boulder: Lynne Rienner, 1996), 140.

115. Quoted in Robert Pear, "U.S. Allots $2 Million to Aid Anti-Sandinistas," *New York Times*, 4/25/1989. See also "NED Program Support: Nicaraguan Electoral Process," 2/13/1990, DNSA; General Accounting Office (GAO), "Central America: Assistance to Promote Democracy and National Reconciliation in Nicaragua," Sept. 1990, DNSA; "Issue Preview: U.S. Efforts to Promote Democracy in Nicaragua," 8/3/1989, DNSA.

116. They were Argentina, Bolivia, Brazil, Chile, the Dominican Republic, Ecuador, El Salvador, Grenada, Guatemala, Haiti, Honduras, Nicaragua, Panama, Paraguay, Peru, and Uruguay.

117. Reagan, Remarks to OAS, 11/9/1987, APP.

118. The two most obvious exceptions were Grenada and Panama. The internal causes of democratization are discussed in Peter Smith, *Democracy in Latin America: Political Change in Comparative Perspective* (New York: Oxford University Press, 2011); Frances Hagopian and Scott P. Mainwaring, eds., *The Third Wave of Democratization in Latin America: Advances and Setbacks* (New York: Cambridge University Press, 2005).

119. Transcript of Meeting between Galtieri and U.S. Military Attaché, 6/6/1982, Box 13, Odom Papers, LC; Deborah Norden and Robert Guillermo Russell, *The United States and Argentina: Changing Relations in a Changing World* (New York: Routledge, 2002), 25–26.

120. Baker, Remarks at Pan American Economic Leadership Conference, 6/15/1987, Box 153, Baker Papers.

121. Tillman to Poindexter, 11/17/1986, Box 91304, NSC Meetings, ESF, RRL.

122. NSC Meeting, 3/13/1987, NSC 00142, NSPG MTG Minutes & Presidential MemCons, RRL. See also Motley to Dam, 11/21/1984, Department of State FOIA.

123. "Report of the NSSD Interagency Group: South America: Supporting, Protecting and Preserving Democracy," undated, NSC 00142, NSC Meeting Files, ESF, RRL.

124. Reagan, NSC Meeting, 3/13/1987. See also Radio Address to the Nation, 4/7/1984, APP.

125. "The Reagan Legacy in Latin America: Active Support for Democracy," 1/12/1989, Current Policy No. 1144, Bureau of Public Affairs, Department of State.

126. "Report of the NSSD Interagency Group."

127. "U.S. Supports Alfonsin," *New York Times,* 4/18/1987; Alan Riding, "U.S. Policy on Latin America Is Well Received—in Washington," *New York Times,* 10/30/1988; Ridgway, Holmes, and Abrams to Shultz, undated, Box 91740, LAAD, ESF, RRL.

128. NSC Meeting, 3/13/1987.

129. Abrams Interview, 8/7/1985, *AFP: CD,* 1985: 1077.

130. Lima to State, 4/13/1987, DNSA. See also U.S. Embassy in Lima, "FY 1989 Goals and Work Plans: Peru," 10/19/1988, DNSA.

131. Alan Riding, "Peru's Twin Crises Raise Coup Rumors," *New York Times,* 1/15/1989; Riding, "As Peru's Crisis Grows, Drastic Steps Are Urged," *New York Times,* 11/30/1988.

132. Marlise Simons, "U.S. Envoy Linked to Foiling of Bolivia Coup," *New York Times,* 7/6/1984; Carothers, *In the Name of Democracy,* 127–29; Reagan to UN Secretary General, 2/20/1985, Box 26, CF, ESF, RRL.

133. Donald Schulz and Deborah Schulz, *The United States, Honduras, and the Crisis in Central America* (Boulder: Westview Press, 1994), esp. 321; Carothers, *In the Name of Democracy,* 50–53, 65–68; author's interview with Arcos; CIA, "Guatemala: Prospects for the New Government," Feb. 1986, Box 91173, LAAD, ESF, RRL; Bush-Cerezo MemCon, 1/14/1986, Box 91176, LAAD, ESF, RRL.

134. The phrase is from Kagan, *World America Made,* 30.

135. Edward Cody, "Shultz's Words Heeded," *Washington Post,* 2/10/1986; Keith Richburg, "Our Haiti Meddling Worked: America Helped Topple a Government and Everybody Cheered," *Washington Post,* 2/23/1986; Shultz, *Turmoil and Triumph,* 621–23.

136. NSDD-220, "Haiti," 4/2/1986, NSDD Files, RRL.

137. Alan Riding, "Paraguay Regime Vilifies U.S. Envoy," *New York Times,* 3/24/1987; Frank Mora, "From Dictatorship to Democracy: The U.S. and Regime Change in Paraguay, 1954–1994," *Bulletin of Latin American Research* 17, no. 1 (1998): 68–71, esp. 68. See also Frank Mora and Jerry Wilson Cooney, *Paraguay and the United States: Distant Allies* (Athens: University of Georgia Press, 2007), 213–29; NED *Annual Report 1987,* DNSA; State to Various American Posts, 2/25/1988, DDRS.

138. Mora and Cooney, *Paraguay and the United States,* 213–14, 223, 228–29, 232–36; Mora, "From Dictatorship to Democracy," 68–70, esp. 69; Andrew Nickson, "The Overthrow of the Stroessner Regime: Re-Establishing the Status Quo," *Bulletin of Latin American Research* 8, no. 2 (1989): 203.

139. "Chile," undated (1973–1974), Box 40, Series I, Pre-Presidential File, RRL. As noted, Carter did help reduce the worst human rights abuses in Chile.

140. NSC Minutes, 11/18/1986, Box 91304, Meetings File, ESF, RRL.

141. Santiago to State, 8/10/1981, Department of State FOIA; Pinochet-Walters MemCon, 5/13/1982, Department of State FOIA; Abraham Lowenthal, "Chile and the No Vote—a Bravo for U.S. Role," *Los Angeles Times,* 10/13/1988.

142. "Harkin Cites Hypocrisy," 2/20/1981, DNSA; State to Santiago, 12/6/1984, DNSA; Motley to Dam, 11/21/1984, Department of State FOIA; "Statement of Senator Edward M. Kennedy Introducing Economic Sanctions against Chile," 3/10/1986, DNSA; Kim Flower to Abrams, 12/19/1986, Department of State FOIA.

143. Tillman to Poindexter, 11/17/1986, Box 91304, NSC Meetings, ESF, RRL.

144. Motley to Eagleburger, 9/19/1983, Department of State FOIA; CIA, "The Chilean Communist Party and Its Allies: Intentions, Capabilities, and Prospects," May 1986, Box 91703, Flower Files, RRL.

145. CIA, "Prospects for Chile," 9/2/1983, Box 28, CF, ESF, RRL; Shultz to Reagan, 9/3/1985, Department of State FOIA.

146. Shultz in State to Santiago, 2/22/1984, Department of State FOIA.

147. Platt to Poindexter, 11/13/1986, DNSA; Paul Sigmund, *The United States and Democracy in Chile* (Baltimore: Johns Hopkins University Press, 1993), 151.

148. "Strengthening the Democratic Center in Chile," *International Democrat* 2, no. 2 (1986), 1–2; Raymond to Poindexter, 7/20/1986, Box 91719, LAAD, ESF, RRL; Shultz to Reagan, 9/3/1985, Department of State FOIA. See also Morris Morley and Chris McGillion, "Soldiering On: The Reagan Administration and Redemocratization in Chile, 1983–1986," *Bulletin of Latin American Research* 25, no. 1 (2006): 1–22.

149. Motley to Eagleburger, 9/23/1983, Department of State FOIA.

150. Platt to Poindexter, 11/13/1986, DNSA; "Strengthening the Democratic Center in Chile," 1–2; Morley and McGillion, "Soldiering On," 13–14, 16–17.

151. NSC Minutes, 11/18/1986, Box 91304, Meetings File, ESF, RRL; CIA, *Terrorism Review,* June 1986, CIA FOIA.

152. Charlotte Roe Oral History, 44, FAOHC.

153. Abrams, Keyes, and Schifter to Shultz, undated, Box 91528, Flower Files, RRL. See also Santiago to State, 8/26/1987 and 12/7/1987, Department of State FOIA; Department of State Cable, 11/9/1987, DDRS; various officials to Shultz, 12/10/1987, DDRS; *NDI Reports,* fall 1988, 6; Sigmund, *United States and Democracy,* 156–72.

154. Department of State Cable, 11/9/1987, DDRS.

155. Robinson, *Promoting Polyarchy,* 182–86, esp. 185; Santiago to State, 3/4/1988, Department of State FOIA; "National Endowment for Democracy," 1/27/1988, DNSA; *NDI Reports,* fall 1988, 1, 6; *NDI Reports,* spring 1988, 3; "U.S. Statement on Support for Democracy in Chile," 12/17/1987, Department of State FOIA; Pamela Constable and Arturo Valenzuela, *A Nation of Enemies: Chile under Pinochet* (New York: W. W. Norton, 1991), 304; Carothers, *In the Name of Democracy,* 158–60.

156. State to Rome, 10/26/1988, Department of State FOIA; State to Santiago, 10/1/1988, Department of State FOIA.

157. Santiago to State, 8/25/1987, Box 91528, Flower Files, RRL; "Summary Notes," 5/27/1988, Box 1, Harry Barnes Papers, LC; Santiago to State, 7/10/1987,

Department of State FOIA; Santiago to State, 6/14/1988, Box 1, Harry Barnes Papers, LC.

158. See State to Seoul, 10/4/1988; "Foreign Minister Garcia-Ambassador Barnes Discussion," 10/4/1988; Arcos to Acting Secretary, 10/4/1988, Department of State FOIA.

159. Santiago to State, 11/29/1988, Department of State FOIA.

160. "Baker Remarks before OAS," 5/17/1989, Box 158, Baker Papers; Bush-Menem TelCon, 12/20/1989, Presidential MemCons/TelCons, GHWBL.

161. Bush-Mulroney TelCon, 12/20/1989, Presidential MemCons/TelCons, GHWBL.

162. Russell Crandall, *Gunboat Democracy: U.S. Interventions in the Dominican Republic, Grenada, and Panama* (Lanham, MD: Rowman and Littlefield, 2006), 209.

163. "Report of the NSSD Interagency Group."

164. Robert McMahon, *The Limits of Empire: The United States and Southeast Asia since World War II* (New York: Columbia University Press, 1999), 201–2. For historical background, see H. W. Brands, *Bound to Empire: The United States and the Philippines* (New York: Oxford University. Press, 1992).

165. Department of State *Bulletin* 81, 2053 (Aug. 1981), 30; Douglas Brinkley, ed. *The Reagan Diaries* (New York: HarperCollins, 2007), 101; Sara Steinmetz, *Democratic Transition and Human Rights: Perspectives on U.S. Foreign Policy* (Albany: SUNY Press, 1994), 170.

166. State to Various Posts, 4/22/1982, DNSA.

167. Manila to State, 9/19/1983, DNSA; Manila to State, 8/22/1983, DNSA.

168. "Solarz Denies Interference," *New York Times,* 3/19/1984; "Solarz Presses Marcos to Hold Free Election," *New York Times,* 8/21/1983; "House Panel Approves Philippines Aid Shift," *Washington Post,* 2/29/1984; Stephen Solarz Oral History, FAOHC.

169. Gates to DCI, 3/7/1984, CREST; Manila to State, 3/3/1984, DNSA; Singapore to State, 4/15/1983, DNSA; Steinmetz, *Democratic Transition and Human Rights,* 170–72.

170. NSDD-163, "United States Policy towards the Philippines," 2/20/1985, DNSA.

171. Presidential Debate between Reagan and Walter Mondale, 10/21/1984, APP.

172. Manila to State, 4/15/1983, DNSA.

173. NSDD-163, "United States Policy towards the Philippines"; Bosworth Address in Manila, 10/25/1984, *AFP: CD,* 1984: 759–61. See also Wolfowitz to Shultz, 2/6/1985, DNSA; Statement by Deputy Assistant Secretary Monjo, 9/13/1983, *AFP: CD,* 1983: 1086; NED, *Annual Report 1986,* 3, DNSA.

174. NSDD-163, "United States Policy towards the Philippines."

175. Shultz, *Turmoil and Triumph,* 611; Wolfowitz to Shultz, 2/6/1985, DNSA.

176. Brinkley, *Reagan Diaries,* 351; Senate Select Committee on Intelligence Staff Report, "The Philippines: A Situation Report," 11/1/1985, DNSA.

177. Manila to State, 10/17/1985 and 10/16/1985, RAC Box 5, James Kelly Files, RRL; David Ottaway, "U.S. Criticizes Acquittal of Gen. Ver," *Washington Post,* 12/3/1985.

178. Wolfowitz to Shultz, Nov. 1985, DNSA; "Implications of the Presidential Elections in the Philippines," undated, DNSA; Gaston Sigur Oral History, 32, FAOHC.

179. Wolfowitz to Shultz, Nov. 1985, DNSA.

180. "Background: Criteria for Honest Philippine Elections," 11/8/1985, DNSA; Wolfowitz to Acting Secretary, 12/26/1985, DNSA; State to Manila, 12/27/1985, DNSA; Armacost to Shultz, 12/24/1985, DNSA; Prepared Statement by Wolfowitz, 1/23/1986, *AFP: CD,* 1986: 554–555; Brands, *Bound to Empire,* 332.

181. Statement on Presidential Election in the Philippines, 1/30/1986, APP; Shultz, *Turmoil and Triumph,* 617.

182. Manila to State, 2/10/1986, DNSA; *International Democrat* 2 (Mar. 1986): 1–2.

183. Reagan's News Conference, 2/11/1986, APP. See also John J. Taylor Oral History, 103–4, 107–8, FAOHC; Stanley Karnow, *In Our Image: America's Empire in the Philippines* (New York: Random House, 1989), 411–12; Shultz, *Turmoil and Triumph,* 618.

184. Manila to State, 2/12/1986 and 2/13/1986, DNSA; State to Manila, 2/15/1986, DNSA; Dyer to Armacost, 2/15/1986, DNSA.

185. Stephen Solarz, *Journeys to War and Peace: A Congressional Memoir* (Waltham, MA: Brandeis University Press, 2011), 122.

186. Shultz, *Turmoil and Triumph,* 635.

187. Statement on Presidential Elections in the Philippines, 2/15/1986, APP.

188. Steinmetz, *Democratic Transitions and Human Rights,* 175–77; Brinkley, *Reagan Diaries,* 392–93; NSDD-215, "Philippines," 2/23/1986, DNSA.

189. Manila to State, 2/22/1986, DNSA.

190. State to Manila, 2/23/1986, DNSA.

191. Karnow, *In Our Image,* 417–18.

192. NSDD-215, "Philippines"; Statement by Principal Deputy Press Secretary, 2/24/1986, *AFP: CD,* 1986: 565.

193. Stephen Bosworth Oral History, 86, FAOHC; Gaston Sigur Oral History, 32–34, FAOHC; Karnow, *In Our Image,* 420–22.

194. James Mann, *Rise of the Vulcans: The History of Bush's War Cabinet* (New York: Viking, 2004), 133–34.

195. Finney to Shultz, 2/24/1986, DNSA.

196. James Fowler, "The United States and South Korean Democratization," *Political Science Quarterly* 114, no. 2 (1999): 266–70, 279–84; Seoul to State, 11/8/1979 and 5/10/1980, DNSA.

197. Reagan-Chun MemCon, 2/2/1981, EBB 306, NSArch. See also State to Seoul, 2/5/1981, EBB 306, NSArch. On pressure not to execute Kim (which began under Carter), see Carter to Chun, 12/1/1980, Box 12, President's Correspondence with Foreign Leaders, JCL; Seoul to State, 1/23/1981, Box 9, CF, ESF, RRL; James Lilley Oral History, 113, FAOHC.

198. INR, "South Korea: The Domestic Situation," 12/12/1983, RAC Box 10, Sigur Files, RRL; INR, "South Korea: The Domestic Political Outlook," 4/5/1985, DNSA; Gregg Brazinsky, *Nation Building in South Korea: Koreans, Americans, and the Making of a Democracy* (Chapel Hill: University of North Carolina Press, 2007), 245–46.

199. "November 13 Meeting between Presidents Reagan and Chun," 11/18/1983, DNSA.

200. State to Seoul, 12/28/1983, DNSA.

201. Stephen Solarz, "Crucial Interests in Asia," *New York Times,* 10/6/1983; Solarz Oral History, FAOHC.

202. "U.S.-Korea Relations Overview," undated, RAC Box 10, Sigur Files, RRL.

203. Shultz, Remarks to Creve Couer Club, 2/22/1984, *AFP: CD,* 1984:282. See also "Meeting with Foreign Minister Lee, May 3 at 1100AM," Box 9, CF, ESF, RRL.

204. "November 13 Meeting between Presidents Reagan and Chun"; Hill to Gregg, 4/19/1983, RAC Box 10, Sigur Files, RRL.

205. Shultz, *Turmoil and Triumph,* 978.

206. "Second Meeting with Chun," Nov. 1983, DNSA; "U.S.-Korea Relations Overview," undated, RAC Box 10, Sigur Files, RRL.

207. Address to Korean National Assembly, 11/12/1983, APP.

208. NED, *Annual Report 1986,* 15, DNSA; Shultz, *Turmoil and Triumph,* 978–79. See also Lister to Abrams, 2/20/1985, Lister Papers; Seoul to State, 6/24/1987, DNSA.

209. Han Sung-Joo, "South Korea in 1987: The Politics of Democratization," *Asian Survey* 28, no. 1 (1988): 53–54; James Lilley, *China Hands: Nine Decades of Adventure, Espionage, and Diplomacy in Asia* (New York: PublicAffairs, 2004), 276.

210. Sigur Remarks to U.S.-Korea Society, 2/6/1987, *AFP: CD,* 1987: 565–66.

211. Sigur Oral History, 15, FAOHC; Statement by Sigur, 5/6/1987, *AFP: CD,* 1987: 569–71; Seoul to State, 4/18/1987, DNSA.

212. Seoul to State, 6/24/1987 (2 cables), DNSA; Shultz Press Conference, 6/19/1987, *AFP: CD,* 1987: 571–72.

213. Don Oberdorfer and Robert Carlin, *The Two Koreas: A Contemporary History,* 3rd ed. (New York: Basic Books, 2014), 131–33; Shultz Press Conference, 6/19/1987, *AFP: CD,* 1987: 571–72; Seoul to State, 6/24/1987, DNSA; Lilley, *China Hands,* 274–78.

214. An irony of the transition was that the government candidate, Roh, won the elections because the opposition could not unite behind one candidate.

215. Fowler, "United States and South Korean Democratization," 280; Oberdorfer and Carlin, *Two Koreas,* 131–33; Han, "South Korea in 1987," 60.

216. Kim Dae-jung to Lister, 8/10/1989, Lister Papers.

217. Sigur, "Democratization and Political Reform in the Asian-Pacific Region," 12/9/1987, RAC Box 4, Kelly Files, RRL.

218. Haig, Testimony to House Appropriations Committee, 3/4/1982, DNSA; Meeting with Secretary Shultz and Ambassador Edward Perkins, 6/1/1987, DDRS; Chester Crocker, "Regional Security for Southern Africa," 8/29/1981, DNSA.

219. See, for instance, Scoon to Searby, 4/6/1982, DNSA; NSDD-272, "United States Objectives in Southern Africa," 5/7/1987, DNSA.

220. Reagan, Excerpts from Interview with Walter Cronkite, 3/3/1981, APP.

221. Shultz, "Toward an American Consensus on Southern Africa," 4/16/1985, DNSA; Interagency Intelligence Memorandum, "South Africa: The Politics of Racial Reform," Jan. 1981, CIA FOIA.

222. Chester Crocker, "South Africa: Strategy for Change," *Foreign Affairs* 59, no. 2 (1980): esp. 324, 325, 337.

223. Crocker, "Regional Security for Southern Africa."

224. State to All Posts, 3/31/1981, DNSA; Crocker Testimony to Subcommittee of SFRC, 9/26/1984, DNSA. See also Department of State, "IMF Loan for South Africa," 11/3/1982, DNSA; Crocker to Haig, 5/12/1981, DNSA.

225. State to Cape Town, 3/29/1986, DNSA; "Project South Africa: Final Report to the National Endowment for Democracy," June 1986, DNSA; "Positive

U.S. Programs in South Africa," undated, Box 91028, African Affairs Directorate (AAD), ESF, RRL; "Southern Africa: Constructive Engagement," Feb. 1985, Box 92241, Herman Cohen Files, RRL.

226. Crocker, "South Africa," 346–47; Herman Nickel Oral History, FAOHC; Reagan to Botha, 5/11/1984, Box 91876, AAD, ESF, RRL; Shultz, "Toward an American Consensus on Southern Africa"; Crocker, Testimony to Subcommittee of SFRC, 9/26/1984, DNSA; NSDD-187, "United States Policy toward Southern Africa," 9/7/1985, RAC Box 14, Sable Files, RRL.

227. Crocker, Testimony to Subcommittee of SFRC, 9/26/1984, DNSA.

228. Chester Crocker, *High Noon in Southern Africa: Making Peace in a Rough Neighborhood* (New York: W. W. Norton, 1992), 77.

229. Shultz, "Toward an American Consensus on Southern Africa."

230. Department of State Briefing, "The Status of the Namibia Negotiations," 6/10/1982, DNSA; Chas W. Freeman Jr., "The Angola/Namibia Accords," *Foreign Affairs* 68, no. 3 (1989): 130, 133.

231. Crocker to Haig, 5/12/1981, DNSA; State to All African Posts, 3/19/1981 and 5/4/1981, DNSA; Crocker, *High Noon in Southern Africa,* 85–86, 170–71, 189.

232. Dam, "The Case against Sanctions," 4/16/1985, DNSA; Brinkley, *Reagan Diaries,* 285. See also "U.S. Policy in Southern Africa after Four Years," undated, RAC Box 10, AAD, ESF, RRL; "Southern Africa: Constructive Engagement," Feb. 1985, Box 92241, Cohen Files, RRL.

233. "Opening Talking Points for NSC Meeting on South Africa," 7/26/1985, DDRS. See also "Southern Africa Status Report," undated, Box 92295, Cohen Files, RRL; "U.S. Policy in Southern Africa after Four Years," undated, RAC Box 10, AAD, ESF, RRL; Crocker, *High Noon in Southern Africa,* chaps. 4–10, esp. pp. 143, 162, 203–9, 237.

234. Reagan to Botha, 5/11/1984, Box 91876, AAD, ESF, RRL.

235. SNIE 73.2-85, "Prospects for South Africa: Stability, Reform, and Violence," Aug. 1985, CIA FOIA.

236. Chester Crocker, "Southern Africa: Eight Years Later," *Foreign Affairs* 86, no. 4 (1989): 156–57.

237. International Political Committee Meeting, 11/8/1985, Box 91876, AAD, ESF, RRL.

238. Chester Crocker Oral History, esp. 58–59, FAOHC.

239. NSC Meeting, 7/26/1985, NSC 00119, NSC Meetings, ESF, RRL; Reagan's Remarks on South Africa Sanctions, 9/9/1985, APP; Reagan to Botha, 9/6/1985, DDRS.

240. C. William Waldorf, *Just Politics: Human Rights and the Foreign Policy of Great Powers* (Ithaca: Cornell University Press, 2008), 127; Karl Lamb, *Reasonable Disagreement: Two U.S. Senators and the Choices They Make* (New York: Routledge, 1998), 146–147.

241. Crocker, "Southern Africa," 159–60; Princeton Lyman, *Partner to History: The U.S. Role in South Africa's Transition to Democracy* (Washington, DC: United States Institute of Peace, 2002), 34–35; Carlucci to Reagan, 10/1/1987, Box 91876, AAD, ESF, RRL.

242. SNIE 73.2-85, "Prospects for South Africa: Stability, Reform, and Violence," Feb. 1987, CIA FOIA.

243. For overviews of the transition, see Patti Waldmeir, *Anatomy of a Miracle: The End of Apartheid and the Birth of the New South Africa* (New York: W. W. Norton, 1997); Hermann Giliomee, "Democratization in South Africa," *Political Science Quarterly* 110, no. 1 (1995): 83–104.

244. Crocker, *High Noon in Southern Africa,* esp. 381–82; "Remarks by Assistant Secretary Crocker," 12/1/1986, DNSA.

245. NSDD-212, "United States Policy toward Angola," 2/10/1986, DNSA; Crocker, *High Noon in Southern Africa,* 297, 462; Robert Gates, *From the Shadows: The Ultimate Insider's Story of Five Presidents and How They Won the Cold War* (New York: Simon & Schuster, 1996), 347–48.

246. Lyman, *Partner to History,* 36. See also Freeman, "Angola/Namibia Accords," 132–37; Crocker, *High Noon in Southern Africa,* 353–72. For a different interpretation that stresses the role of Cuba, see Piero Gleijeses, *Visions of Freedom: Havana, Washington, Pretoria, and the Struggle for Southern Africa, 1976–1991* (Chapel Hill: University of North Carolina Press, 2013).

247. Roger Thurow, "Main Anti-Apartheid Group is Certain Namibia Settlement Will Help Its Cause," *Wall Street Journal,* 1/26/1989. See also Chas Freeman Oral History, 192, FAOHC.

248. Roger Thurow, "Pretoria Accedes to Black Rule Next Door," *Wall Street Journal,* 3/21/1990.

249. For administration views on sanctions, see Reagan to Robert Michel, 9/29/1986, RAC Box 3, Alton Keel Files, RRL; Carlucci to Reagan, 10/1/1987, Box 91876, AAD, ESF, RRL.

250. Roger Thurow, "South Africa Facing a No-Growth Future," *Wall Street Journal,* 7/26/1988. On private sanctions, see Kenneth Rodman, "Public and Private Sanctions against South Africa," *Political Science Quarterly* 109, no. 2 (1994): 313–34.

251. Giliomee, "Democratization in South Africa," 90, 88; Philip Levy, "Sanctions on South Africa: What Did They Do?" *American Economic Review* 89, no. 2 (1999): 418–19; Joe Davidson, "Mandela Thanks Congress for Sanctions but Repeats Request for Aid to the ANC," *Wall Street Journal,* 6/27/1990.

252. Huntington, *Third Wave,* 98.

253. Bush, Address to UN General Assembly, 9/25/1989, *AFP: CD,* 1989: 12.

254. LeoGrande, *Our Own Backyard,* 582–83.

255. Thomas Carothers, *Aiding Democracy Abroad: The Learning Curve* (Washington, DC: Carnegie Endowment for International Peace, 1999), 40. See also Nau, "Ronald Reagan," 150; Diamond, "Promoting Democracy," 35–39.

256. NED, *Annual Report 1987,* 5–6, DNSA. See also Paul D. Miller, "American Grand Strategy and the Democratic Peace," *Survival,* 54, no. 2 (2012): 49–76.

257. NED, *Annual Report 1987,* 3, DNSA; Reagan, Farewell Address, 1/11/1989, APP; Bush, Inaugural Address, 1/20/1989, APP.

4. Toward the Neoliberal Order

1. Francis Fukuyama, "The End of History?" *National Interest* 16 (summer 1989): 3–18, esp. 3–4.

2. Bush, Remarks at Swearing-In Ceremony for U.S. Trade Representative, 2/6/1989, APP.

3. Baker, Remarks to Institute for International Economics, 9/14/1987, Box 154, Baker Papers.

4. Regan, Statement to House Banking, Finance, and Urban Affairs, 12/21/1982, *AFP: CD,* 1982: 256; Bonn to State, 12/8/1981, DDRS.

5. "Global Economic Forces," in NIO-E to DCI, 1/22/1982, CREST.

6. Clausen, "Third World Debt and Global Recovery," 2/24/1983, Box 188, Regan Papers, LC.

7. Shultz in Reagan-Kohl MemCon, 2/19/1988, DDRS.

8. See, for instance, NIO at Large to DCI and DDCI, 3/26/1982, CREST; "Global Economic Forces," in NIO-E to DCI, 1/22/1982, CREST; NIC, "The United States in the World Economy: Elements of Strength," May 1982, CREST; George Shultz, "New Realities and New Ways of Thinking," *Foreign Affairs* 63, no. 4 (spring 1985): esp. 714–16, 719; Reagan Remarks at Commonwealth Club of California, 3/4/1983, APP.

9. Ronald Reagan, *An American Life* (New York: Simon & Schuster, 1990), 205; Remarks at World Affairs Council of Philadelphia, 10/15/1981, APP; Address to UN General Assembly, 9/21/1987, APP.

10. The phrase was ubiquitous in Reagan's speeches. See Reagan, Remarks in Sao Paulo, 12/2/1982, APP.

11. Regan, Remarks to U.S. International Finance Seminar, 9/21/1983, Box 94, Regan Papers.

12. "Is U.S. Foreign Economic Policy Bold Enough?" undated (1982), Box 9, Norman Bailey Files, RRL; Bailey to Clark, 1/27/1983, Box OA85, SF, ESF, RRL.

13. Reagan, Address from Venice Economic Summit, 6/5/1987, APP; Address to Canadian Parliament, 4/6/1987, APP; Remarks to World Affairs Council of Philadelphia, 10/15/1981, APP.

14. "Excerpts from Remarks by the Hon. Ronald Reagan," 9/6/1978, Box 168, CPD Papers, Hoover.

15. Robert Collins, *More: The Politics of Economic Growth in Postwar America* (New York: Oxford University Press, 2000), 198; Paul Volcker and Toyoo Gyohten, *Changing Fortunes: The World's Money and the Threat to American Leadership* (New York: Times Books, 1992), 175–77; Michael C. Webb, *The Political Economy of Policy Coordination: International Adjustment since 1945* (Ithaca: Cornell University Press, 1995), 191.

16. Reagan, "State of the Union," 3/13/1980, in Kiron Skinner, Annelise Anderson, and Martin Anderson, eds., *Reagan, In His Own Hand: The Writings of Ronald Reagan that Reveal His Revolutionary Vision for America* (New York: Free Press, 2001), 473.

17. Address to the Nation, 5/28/1985, APP; Collins, *More,* 198; Judith Stein, *Pivotal Decade: How the United States Traded Factories for Finance in the Seventies* (New Haven: Yale University Press, 2011), 264.

18. Regan, Remarks to Council of the Americas, 6/22/1982, Box 91, Regan Papers; Steven Hayward, *The Age of Reagan: The Conservative Counterrevolution* (New York: Crown Forum, 2009), 169–74, 213–16; Richard H. K. Vietor, "Government Regulation of Business," in *The Cambridge Economic History of the United States,* Vol. 3, edited by Stanley Engerman and Robert Gallman (Cambridge, UK: Cambridge University Press, 2008), 1008–11; Robert Brenner, *The Economics of Global Turbulence* (London: Verso, 2006), 195–96.

19. Michael J. Heale, *Contemporary America: Power, Dependency, and Globalization since 1980* (New York: Wiley-Blackwell, 2011), 37. See also Brenner, *Economics of Global Turbulence,* 189, 209–11.

20. David Stockman, *The Triumph of Politics: How the Reagan Revolution Failed* (New York: Harper & Row, 1986), 356; Collins, *More,* 202–13.

21. "Governors' Speech," 8/5/1985, Box 147, Baker Papers.

22. Growth, in Stein, *Pivotal Decade,* 267–68; Dow, in Robert Schaeffer, *Understanding Globalization: The Social Consequences of Political, Economic, and Environmental Change* (Lanham, MD: Rowman & Littlefield, 2009), 15.

23. Reagan, Remarks at New York Stock Exchange, 3/28/1985, APP.

24. Meyer to DCI, 4/12/1983, CREST.

25. Louis Galambos, "The U.S. Corporate Economy in the Twentieth Century," in *The Cambridge Economic History of the United States,* Vol. 3, edited by Stanley Engerman and Robert Gallman (Cambridge, UK: Cambridge University Press, 2008), 960.

26. Robert Collins, *Transforming America: Politics and Culture in the Reagan Years* (New York: Columbia University Press, 2007), 88, 111–12.

27. Donald Regan, *For the Record: From Wall Street to Washington* (New York: Harcourt, 1988), 215.

28. Collins, *Transforming America,* 59.

29. Statement by Undersecretary of State Wallis, 2/7/1984, *AFP: CD,* 1984: 129.

30. Reagan, Address to Canadian Parliament, 4/6/1987, APP. See also Clyde Farnsworth, "The Third World Has New Respect for Reaganomics," *New York Times,* 10/13/1985; Poindexter to Reagan, May 1986, DNSA.

31. Reagan, Remarks at Annual Meeting of World Bank and IMF, 9/29/1981, APP.

32. Reagan, Remarks at University of Virginia, 12/16/1988, APP.

33. Reagan, Statement at First Plenary Session of Cancun Summit, 10/22/1981, APP.

34. Reagan, Remarks at Annual Meeting of World Bank and IMF, 9/25/1984, APP.

35. Reagan, Remarks to Commonwealth Club of California, 3/4/1983, APP.

36. Reagan, "State of the Union," 3/13/1980, 472.

37. Reagan, Statement at First Plenary Session at Cancun Summit, 10/22/1981, APP.

38. Solomon, Statement to Subcommittee on Foreign Economic Policy, 9/21/1977, Box B72, Burns Papers, GFL.

39. U.S. Treasury Department, *United States Participation in the Multilateral Development Banks in the 1980s* (Washington, DC: Department of the Treasury, 1982), 48; Dale Helleiner, *States and the Reemergence of Global Finance: From Bretton Woods to the 1990s* (Ithaca: Cornell University Press, 1996), 148–49; Robert Hormats, Address to International Insurance Advisory Council, 5/19/1981, *AFP: CD,* 1981: 194–95.

40. U.S. Trade Representative (USTR), "Statement on U.S. Trade Policy," May 1981, Box 186, Regan Papers.

41. Ibid.

42. Address by Undersecretary of State Rashish, 12/7/1981, *AFP: CD,* 1981: 200.

43. Regan, Remarks to Pre-Williamsburg International Monetary Conference, 5/17/1983, Box 94, Regan Papers; Paul Taylor, "U.S. Jobs 'Linked to Exports,'" *Financial Times,* 8/13/1982.

44. "Friday, June 8 Morning Meeting," briefing paper attached to McFarlane to Reagan, 5/18/1984, DDRS.

45. Baker, Testimony to House Ways and Means Subcommittee on Trade, 2/10/1987, Box 80, Baker Papers.

46. Reagan, Remarks at Annual Meeting of World Bank and IMF, 9/29/1981, APP; U.S. Treasury Department, *United States Participation,* 48, "Executive Summary," 6.

47. For instance, Reagan, Address to British Parliament, 6/8/1982; Reagan, Remarks to Members of Council of the Americas, 5/12/1987, APP.

48. Shultz, Testimony to SFRC, 2/15/1983, *AFP: CD,* 1983: 172; Shultz, "New Realities," 715, 720.

49. Reagan, Remarks to Commonwealth Club, 3/4/1983, APP.

50. Poindexter to Reagan, May 1986, DNSA; Shultz, "The Rising Tide of Protectionism," 7/30/1986, *AFP: CD,* 1986: 118. See also Shultz and Baker to Reagan, May 1986, DNSA.

51. Shultz, "New Realities," 705.

52. Shultz and Baker to Reagan, May 1986, DNSA; Hugo Dobson, *Japan and the G7/8: 1975 to 2002* (London: Routledge, 2004), 46.

53. Wallis, Address to Business Council, 10/9/1982, *AFP: CD,* 1982: 237–38.

54. "Global Economic Forces," in NIO-E to DCI, 1/22/1982, CREST.

55. Michael Schaller, *Altered States: The United States and Japan since the Occupation* (New York: Oxford University Press, 1997), 252, 254. For background, see Walter LaFeber, *The Clash: A History of U.S.-Japan Relations* (New York: W.W. Norton, 1997), 363–85.

56. Dept. of Commerce, Japan Seminar, 10/1/1984, DNSA.

57. Brock to Trade Policy Committee and Cabinet Council on Commerce and Trade and attachment, 12/7/1984, DNSA; Leland to Regan, 3/18/1981, DNSA.

58. Remarks to International Monetary Conference, 6/3/1986, Box 150, Baker Papers.

59. Yoichi Funabashi, *Managing the Dollar: From the Plaza to the Louvre* (Washington, DC: Institute for International Economics, 1988), 4; statistics from Jeffrey Frankel, "The Making of Exchange Rate Policy in the 1980s," in *American Economic Policy in the 1980s,* edited by Martin Feldstein (Chicago: University of Chicago Press, 1994), 293.

60. "Key Summit Economic Themes," in McFarlane to Reagan, 5/18/1984, DDRS.

61. *Economic Report of the President* (Washington, DC: Council of Economic Advisers, 1985), 114.

62. Brock to Trade Policy Committee and Cabinet Council on Commerce and Trade and attachment, 12/7/1984, DNSA; Maureen Smith for Undersecretary for International Trade (Commerce), 12/4/1984, DNSA.

63. Minutes of Senior Interdepartmental Group on International Economic Policy (SIG-IEP), 12/5/1984, in Hicks Memo, 12/11/1984, DNSA.

64. "The Search for Discipline," in Regan to Reagan, 3/31/1983, DDRS.

65. Regan, Remarks to International Forum of U.S. Chamber of Commerce, 2/22/1984, Box 172, Regan Papers; "Economic Strategy for the Williamsburg Summit: Talking Points," 3/8/1983, DDRS.

66. Henry R. Nau, *The Myth of America's Decline: Leading the World Economy into the 1990s* (New York: Oxford University Press, 1990), 204; Volcker and Gyohten, *Changing Fortunes*, 183; Regan, Remarks to Council of Americas, 5/8/1984, Box 97, Regan Papers.

67. Leonard Silk, "The Interest Rate Issue: Reagan Blames Inherited Inflation for Rise, but Others Cite Tight Money Policy of U.S.," *New York Times*, 7/21/1981; John Vinocur, "Mitterrand Asks Streamlining of Annual Economic Meeting," *New York Times*, 10/12/1982. See also Paul Lewis, "Paris Said to Link Free-Trade Talks to Dollar Parley," *New York Times*, 3/28/1985.

68. "Strategy Paper for Versailles Economic Summit," June 1982, Box 9, Bailey Files, RRL.

69. Statistics in Shultz, Address at Princeton, 4/11/1985, *AFP: CD*, 1985: 127. See also I. M. Destler and C. Randall Henning, *Dollar Politics: Exchange Rate Policy-making in the United States* (Washington, DC, 1989), 33–39.

70. Regan, Remarks to National Association of Manufacturers, 3/8/1984, Box 96, Regan Papers.

71. Reagan, Statement on Nonrubber Footwear Industry, 8/28/1985, APP; Alfred Eckes and Thomas Zeiler, *Globalization and the American Century* (Cambridge, UK: Cambridge University Press, 2003), 209.

72. "Even Out the Free Trade Pain," *New York Times*, 1/14/1985.

73. See "Key Summit Economic Themes," in McFarlane to Reagan, 5/18/1984, DDRS.

74. Wallis, Address to World Affairs Council of Baltimore, 5/10/1988, *AFP: CD*, 1988: 97.

75. Daniel Yergin and Joseph Stanislaw, *The Commanding Heights: The Battle for the World Economy* (New York: Simon & Schuster, 1998), 312–19; Henry Nau, "Where Reaganomics Works," *Foreign Policy* 57 (winter 1984–1985): 27–28; Regan to Reagan and attachment, "The Search for Discipline," 31 March 1983, DDRS.

76. James Cronin, *Global Rules: America, Britain, and a Disordered World* (New Haven: Yale University Press, 2014), esp. 129. See also Reagan-Kohl MemCon, 2/19/1988, DDRS; Helleiner, *States and the Reemergence*, 140–44; Mark Gilbert, *European Integration: A Concise History* (Lanham, MD: Rowman & Littlefield, 2012), chaps. 6–7.

77. "International Monetary Policy—Next Steps: Strengthening the System of International Economic Policy Coordination," 4/15/1986, Box 96, Baker Papers. See also Shultz, Address at Princeton, 126–130; Economic Policy Council (EPC) to Reagan, 9/6/1985, CREST.

78. Reagan to Baker, 3/21/1986, Box 85, Baker Papers; Reagan, State of the Union Address, 2/4/1986, APP.

79. The distinctions between the G-5 and G-7 can be confusing. The G-7 had existed since the mid-1970s as the forum for annual economic summits. The G-5, however, remained the ministerial-level subgroup responsible for major policy coordination decisions. When Canada and Italy joined that group in 1986, the G-5 effectively merged with the G-7.

80. Statement to Congressional Summit, 11/12/1985, Box 147, Baker Papers; Robert Putnam and Nicholas Bayne, *Hanging Together: Cooperation and Conflict in the Seven-Power Summits* (Cambridge, MA: Harvard University Press, 1987), 205.

81. Peter Kilborn, "U.S. and 4 Allies Plan Move to Cut Value of Dollar," *New York Times,* 9/23/1985. The United States had acted to stabilize the dollar in the late 1970s, of course, but the Plaza agreements represented a more truly multilateral undertaking.

82. Statistics from Remarks to President's Export Council, 3/10/1986, Box 149, Baker Papers; Testimony to Joint Economic Committee, 1/30/1987, Box 80, Baker Papers.

83. Sam Gindin and Leo Panitch, *The Making of Global Capitalism* (New York: Verso, 2012), 210; Robert Gilpin, *The Political Economy of International Relations* (Princeton: Princeton University Press, 1987), 334; Michael Mastanduno, "System Maker and Privilege Taker: U.S. Power and the International Political Economy," *World Politics* 61, no. 1 (2009): esp. 141–42.

84. In Peter Kilborn, "U.S. and 4 Allies."

85. Putnam and Bayne, *Hanging Together,* 205. See also Funabashi, *Managing the Dollar,* 216; James Boughton, *Silent Revolution: The International Monetary Fund, 1979–1989* (Washington, DC: IMF, 2001), 203–9.

86. Statement of G6 Finance Ministers and Central Bank Governors, 2/22/1987, Thatcher MSS. The group meeting in France was known as the G-6 because Italy declined to participate in the accords.

87. Baker to Bush, 4/13/1987, Box 81, Baker Papers; Andrew Glyn, *Capitalism Unleashed: Finance, Globalization, and Welfare* (New York: Oxford University Press, 2006), 81.

88. Remarks to EMF Round Table, 5/14/1986, Box 149, Baker Papers. See also Remarks before Bretton Woods Committee, 1/22/1986, Box 148, Baker Papers.

89. Remarks to EMF Round Table, 5/14/1986; Putnam and Bayne, *Hanging Together,* 216–17; Remarks to Asia Society, 11/18/1986, Box 151, Baker Papers.

90. Remarks to Beijing American Chamber of Commerce, 5/9/1986, Box 149, Baker Papers.

91. Testimony to Senate Appropriations, 3/1/1988, Box 80, Baker Papers; McMinn to Wallis, 9/25/1987, DNSA; Webb, *Political Economy of Policy Coordination,* 227.

92. Nau, *Myth of America's Decline,* 283; Harold James, *International Monetary Cooperation since Bretton Woods* (New York: Oxford University Press, 1996), 456–59.

93. Reagan in State to NATO Capitals, 10/15/1988, DNSA.

94. IMF, *World Economic Outlook,* Oct. 1988 (Washington, DC: International Monetary Fund, 1988), 30.

95. MemCon between Reagan, de Mita, et al., 6/14/1988, DDRS; Webb, *Political Economy of Policy Coordination,* 227–28.

96. "Of course, sometimes the 'catcher' calls the signals," Nakasone added. Reagan-Nakasone MemCon, 5/27/1983, DNSA; Osgood to Rodman, in Rodman to Shultz, 7/23/1984, DNSA.

97. "Global Economic Forces," 1/22/1982, CREST; Funabashi, *Managing the Dollar,* 170.

98. "U.S.-Japan Trade Relations: A Proposed Negotiating Strategy," in Regan to SIG-IEP, 12/3/1984, DNSA.

99. INR, "The Nakasone Government: Prospects and Problems," 1/6/1983, DNSA.

100. Scope Paper, "U.S.-Japan Structural Dialogue," July 1986, DNSA. See also "U.S.-Japan Trade Relations: A Proposed Negotiating Strategy," in Regan to SIG-IEP, 12/3/1984, DNSA; Tokyo to State, 3/17/1982, DNSA.

101. Regan, Remarks at American Center in Tokyo, 3/24/1984, Regan Papers. See also Regan to Takeshita, 10/14/1983, Box 155, Regan Papers; "Talking Points on Japan for Use with President Reagan," 5/14/1984, Box 155, Regan Papers; Minutes of SIG-IEP, 12/5/1984, DNSA.

102. Jeffrey Frankel, *The Yen/Dollar Agreement: Liberalizing Japanese Capital Markets* (Washington, DC: Institute for International Economics, 1984), esp. 2–3.

103. On implementation, see Minutes of SIG-IEP, 12/5/1984, DNSA; "Talking Points on Japan for Use with President Reagan," 5/14/1984, Box 155, Regan Papers; Jeffrey Frankel, *And Now Won/Dollar Negotiations?: Lessons from the Yen/Dollar Agreement of 1984* (Washington, DC: Institute for International Economics, 1989), 1–4.

104. Destler and Henning, *Dollar Politics*, 29.

105. Hobart Rowen, "Reagan Seeks 'Internationalized' Yen," *Washington Post*, 11/10/1983; Frankel, *And Now Won/Dollar Negotiations?* 3–4.

106. Peter Kilborn, "Japan Invests Huge Sums Abroad, Much of It in U.S. Treasury Bonds," *New York Times*, 3/11/1985.

107. Gilpin, *Political Economy of International Relations*, 332. See also Joel Kotkin and Yoriko Kishimoto, *The Third Century: America's Resurgence in the Asian Era* (New York: Crown Publishers, 1988), 121–22.

108. McMinn to Clark, 10/13/1983, Box 8, CF, ESF, RRL.

109. Statement on Semiconductor Agreement, 7/31/1986, APP; Statement on Semiconductor Agreement, 3/27/1987, APP; State to Tokyo, 4/17/1987, DNSA.

110. NSDD-74, "Visit to the United States of Prime Minister Nakasone," 1/17/1983, DNSA.

111. Baldrige in Tokyo to State and Commerce, 8/2/1986, DNSA. See also "Ambassador Mike Mansfield's Off-the-Cuff Remarks," 7/27/1985, Box 83, Baker Papers; NSDD-154, "U.S.-Japan Trade Policy Relations," 12/31/1984, DNSA.

112. NSDD-74, "Visit to the United States of Prime Minister Nakasone."

113. On use of Section 301, see Reagan, Proclamation 5448, 3/16/1986, APP; Proclamation 5631, 4/17/1987, APP; "U.S.-Japan Trade Relations: A Proposed Negotiating Strategy," in Regan to SIG-IEP, 12/3/1984, DNSA; Michael P. Ryan, *Playing by the Rules: American Trade Power and Diplomacy in the Pacific* (Washington, DC: Georgetown University Press, 1995), 82–85. Section 301 refers to a provision of the 1974 trade bill. Section 301 was later succeeded by Super 301, which was part of the 1988 trade bill.

114. George Shultz, *Turmoil and Triumph: My Years as Secretary of State* (New York: Scribner, 1993), 190.

115. See, for instance, Wheeler to various, 1/13/1983, DNSA; "The Secretary's Trip to the Far East: Economic Briefing Book," July 1988, DNSA; Joan Spero, *The Politics of International Economic Relations*, 4th ed. (New York: St. Martin's Press, 1990), 82;

GAO, "U.S.-Japan Trade: Evaluation of the Market-Oriented Sector-Selective Talks," GAO/NSIAD-88-205, Washington, DC, July 1988, esp. 17–25.

116. State to Tokyo, 1/15/1986, DNSA. See also GAO, "U.S.-Japan Trade."

117. "The Secretary's Trip to the Far East: Economic Briefing Book," July 1988, DNSA; Briefing Book for Eagleburger Trip to China and Japan, Dec. 1989, DNSA.

118. Tokyo to State, 8/21/1986, DNSA; Interagency Group on Japan, "U.S.-Japan Economic Relations: Unresolved Policy Issues," 12/14/1984, DNSA.

119. On these issues, see Brock to Trade Policy Committee and Cabinet Council on Commerce and Trade and attachment, 12/7/1984, DNSA; Scope Paper, "U.S.-Japan Structural Dialogue," undated (1986), DNSA; Briefing Book, "U.S.-Japan Structural Adjustment: Tokyo, Japan," 3/3/1987, DNSA; State to Tokyo, 4/22/1985, DNSA.

120. Spero, *Politics of International Economic Relations* (1990 edition), 82.

121. Radio Address on Free and Fair Trade, 8/31/1985, APP.

122. Address by Deputy Undersecretary of State Morris, 11/16/1984, *AFP: CD,* 1984: 145.

123. "Governors' Speech," 8/5/1985, Box 147, Baker Papers; Reagan to Baker, 3/21/1986, Box 85, Baker Papers.

124. Reagan, Radio Address on Free and Fair Trade, 9/7/1985, APP; Remarks to Business and Trade Leaders, 9/23/1985, APP.

125. Baker, Statement to International Trade Subcommittee and International Finance and Monetary Policy Subcommittee, 5/13/1986, Box 149, Baker Papers; Remarks at Institute for International Economics, 9/14/1987, Box 154, Baker Papers; I. M. Destler, *American Trade Politics,* 4th ed. (Washington, DC: Institute for International Economics, 2005), 124.

126. EPC Minutes, 9/9/1985, CREST.

127. White House Briefing for Trade Association Representatives, 7/17/1986, APP.

128. Remarks to National Foreign Trade Council, 6/11/1986, Box 150, Baker Papers.

129. EPC Minutes, 9/9/1985, CREST.

130. Remarks to Canadian Club of Ottawa, 4/21/1988, Box 155, Baker Papers.

131. Alfred Eckes, "U.S. Trade History," in *U.S. Trade Policy: History, Theory and the WTO,* 2nd ed., edited by William Lovett, Alfred Eckes, and Richard Brinkman (London: M.E. Sharpe, 2004), 80; Michael Hart, *Decision at Midnight: Inside the Canada-U.S. Free Trade Negotiations* (Vancouver: University of British Columbia Press, 1994), esp. 21–22, 26–27, 44–45, 48–53, 93–94.

132. Baker, Statement to House Ways and Means, 2/9/1988, Box 80, Baker Papers.

133. Reagan, Address to Canadian Parliament, 4/6/1987, APP.

134. Regan to Reagan, 4/2/1986, Box 213, Regan Papers.

135. Destler, *American Trade Politics,* 83, 94–95, esp. 95; Edward Cohen, *The Politics of Globalization in the United States* (Washington, DC: Georgetown University Press, 2001), 98–100.

136. Quoted in State to NATO Capitals, 10/15/1988, DNSA.

137. Eckes, "U.S. Trade History," 83.

138. Testimony to Senate Appropriations, 3/1/1988, Box 80, Baker Papers.

139. Carla Hills Oral History, 1/6/2004, 22, POHP, Miller Center.

140. Andrew Brown, *Reluctant Partners: A History of Multilateral Trade Cooperation, 1950–2000* (Ann Arbor: University of Michigan Press, 2003), 158–66, esp. 166; Clayton Brown, *Globalization and America since 1945* (Wilmington, DE: Scholarly Resources, 2003), 35.

141. Reagan, *American Life,* 356; Briefing Paper, "Key Summit Economic Themes," May 1986, DNSA; Shultz and Baker to Reagan, May 1986, DNSA.

142. Reagan, Address from Venice Economic Summit, 6/5/1987, APP.

143. Jeffrey Sachs and Andrew Warner, "Economic Reform and the Process of Global Integration," *Brookings Papers on Economic Activity* 26, no. 1 (1995): 23.

144. Remarks at Annual Meeting of IMF and World Bank, 9/27/1989, APP.

145. William Clark Oral History, 10/5/1983, 19, World Bank Group Archives (WB).

146. Howard Handelman and Werner Baer, "The Economic and Political Costs of Austerity," in *Paying the Costs of Austerity in Latin America,* edited by Howard Handelman and Werner Baer (Boulder: Westview Press, 1989), 2.

147. External Finance Division, "Global External Debt Indicators for Developing Countries," 3/29/1982, in Bahram Nowzad to Various Recipients, 3/29/1982, Box 30, WHD Division Subject Files, IMF.

148. Development Committee Meeting Transcript, Morning Session, 9/5/1982, Folder 1791203, Development Committee Records (DC), WB; Secretary to Executive Board, 3/8/1983, "Fund Policies and External Debt Servicing Problems," SM/83/45, Executive Board Documents (EBD), IMF; Diane Kunz, *Butter and Guns: America's Cold War Economic Diplomacy* (New York: Free Press, 1997), 274–76.

149. Sebastian Edwards, *Crisis and Reform in Latin America: From Despair to Hope* (New York: Oxford University Press, 1995), 7; USAID, "Regional Strategic Plan for Latin America and the Caribbean," 12/1/1983, DNSA.

150. CIA, "Economic Forces for Change in the Third World," Dec. 1984, Box 1, Clark Files, RRL; Victor Bulmer-Thomas, *The Economic History of Latin America since Independence* (Cambridge, UK: Cambridge University Press, 2014), 296–309.

151. NSC Meeting, 11/18/1986, Box 91304, Meetings File, ESF, RRL.

152. CIA, "Trade Policy Formulation in Selected Developing Countries: Underlying Influences," 7/11/1986, CREST; Glen Biglaiser, "The Internationalization of Chicago's Economics in Latin America," *Economic Development and Cultural Change* 50, no. 2 (2002): 269–86.

153. Rosario Espinal, "The Right and the New Right in Latin America," in *The United States and Latin America in the 1990s: Beyond the Cold War,* edited by Jonathan Hartlyn, Lars Schoultz, and Augusto Varas (Chapel Hill: University of North Carolina Press, 1992), 86–99; Ernest Bartell and Leigh Payne, eds., *Business and Democracy in Latin America* (Pittsburgh: University of Pittsburgh Press, 1995).

154. Yergin and Stanislaw, *Commanding Heights,* 232–38, esp. 234.

155. Reagan, "State of the Union," 3/13/1980, 472.

156. Verbatim Report of Joint Development Committee, Afternoon Session, 9/27/1981, DC, WB.

157. Spero, *Politics of International Economic Relations* (1990 edition), 176; Regan in Development Committee Meeting, First Session, 5/22/1981, DC, WB.

158. Reagan, Statement at First Plenary Session of Cancun Summit, 10/22/1981, APP. See also Nau to NSC Staff, "Draft Strategy Paper for Cancun," 10/16/1981, APP; Leland to Regan, 9/29/1981, Box 140, Regan Papers.

159. McNamara to Executive Directors, "Lending for Structural Adjustment," 2/5/1980, WB.

160. De Larosière, Statement to IMF Board of Governors, 9/29/1981, Box 154, Regan Papers.

161. "The New and Strengthened Lending Policies of the International Monetary Fund," 1/19/1981, Box 154, Regan Papers.

162. Clyde Farnsworth, "U.S. Votes No at World Bank More Often under Reagan," *New York Times,* 11/26/1984. See also U.S. Treasury Department, *United States Participation;* "IMF Financing and Conditionality," Oct. 1981, CFOA 611, Meese Files, RRL; Art Pine, "IMF and World Bank Conclude Meeting, Prepare to Tighten Loan Requirements," *Wall Street Journal,* 10/5/1981.

163. Powell to Reagan, 6/9/1988, DDRS; Joseph Stiglitz, *Globalization and Its Discontents* (New York: W. W. Norton, 2002), 13.

164. State to Various Posts, undated (1982–1983), Box 1, Clark Files, RRL.

165. "Impact on U.S. Trade of the IMF Programs in Argentina, Brazil, Mexico," undated, Box 153, Regan Papers; SIG-IEP meeting, 12/14/1983, CREST; Statement to Senate Banking, Housing, and Urban Affairs, 2/14/1983, Box 93, Regan Papers; Clyde Farnsworth, "Third World Debts Mean Fewer Jobs for Peoria," *New York Times,* 12/11/1983.

166. Volcker to Baker, 10/25/1982, Box 63, Baker Papers.

167. USAID Latin America Bureau, "Regional Strategic Plan for Latin America and the Caribbean," 12/1/1983, DNSA.

168. "Is U.S. Foreign Economic Policy Bold Enough?" undated (1982), Box 9, Bailey Files, RRL.

169. Bailey to Clark, 3/14/1983, Box 2, Bailey Files, RRL; Casey to Buchanan, 6/18/1985, CREST; Draft of Presidential Address to World Bank and IMF, 9/24/1987, OA 18965, Robert Schmidt Files, RRL. See also CIA, "Economic Forces for Change in the Third World," Dec. 1984, Box 1, Clark Files, RRL.

170. "The International Debt Problem—The Need for Action," 10/23/1985, in Volcker to Baker, 10/25/1982, Box 63, Baker Papers; Maurice Ernst, "Conference on LDC Debt Problem," 5/19/1983, CREST; NIC, "Implications of the LDC Debt Problem," Oct. 1982, CREST.

171. Volcker to Baker, 10/25/1982, Box 63, Baker Papers; "Checklist of U.S. Actions in Support of Latin America," 6/14/1984, Box 102, Regan Papers; Regan, Statement to House Appropriations, 9/15/1983, Box 94, Regan Papers; Memorandum for the Files, 8/27/1982, Box 129, Western Hemisphere Department, WHDAI Country Files, IMF; Volcker and Gyohten, *Changing Fortunes,* 200–203; Ethan Kapstein, *Governing the Global Economy: International Finance and the State* (Cambridge MA: Harvard University Press, 1994), 88–89.

172. Richard McCormack Oral History, n.p., FAOHC; Roger Porter to Regan, 9/2/1982, Box 162, Regan Papers.

173. Remarks by Assistant Secretary of the Treasury David Mulford, 7/31/1984, *AFP: CD,* 1984: 979; Kunz, *Butter and Guns,* 277–78; Regan to Reagan, undated, Box 65, Regan Papers.

174. Regan, Statement to Senate Banking, Housing, and Urban Affairs, 2/14/1983, Box 93, Regan Papers. See also Development Committee Meeting, Morning Session, 4/28/1983, Folder 1791205, DC, WB.

175. James Boughton, "From Suez to Tequila: The IMF as Crisis Manager," *Economic Journal* 110, no. 460 (2000): 286–87; Volcker and Gyohten, *Changing Fortunes,* 206.

176. Scherer to Files, 12/4/1984, Folder 1774554, Argentina—Clausen Country Files—Correspondence—Vol. I, WB; Regan's Notes on Brazil, 12/9/1982, Box 151, Regan Papers; Regan to Reagan, 9/2/1983, Box 42, SF, ESF, RRL.

177. External Relations Department, "Ten Common Misconceptions about the IMF," May 1988, Box 12, WHDAI, SF, IMF. See also John Williamson, "What Washington Means by Policy Reform," in *Latin American Adjustment: How Much Has Happened?,* edited by John Williamson (Washington, DC: Institute for International Economics, 1990), 7–20.

178. De Larosière, Address to UN Conference on Trade and Development, 6/8/1983, Box 154, Regan Papers.

179. John Bushnell Oral History, 542, FAOHC.

180. Kinshasa to State et al., 7/16/1984, DDRS; Reagan to Mobutu, 1/27/1984, DDRS.

181. USAID Latin America Bureau, "Regional Strategic Plan."

182. R. T. McNamar, "The Inexorable Linkage: International Trade and Finance," 11/15/1982, CREST; Regan's Notes on Brazil, 12/9/1982, Box 151, Regan Papers.

183. USAID Administrator, FY1985 Country Development Strategy Statement, 10/29/1982, DDRS; William Robinson, *Transnational Conflicts: Central America, Social Change, and Globalization* (London: Verso, 2003), 90–93.

184. NIC, "Evolving LDC Debt Crisis," July 1983, CREST; Boughton, *Silent Revolution,* chaps. 7–9.

185. Reagan to Mobutu, 1/23/1985, DDRS; McFarlane, "Meeting with Zaire President Mobutu Sese Seko," 9/23/1984, Box 115, SF, ESF, RRL; John Mihevc, *The Market Tells Them So: The World Bank and Economic Fundamentalism in Africa* (London: Zed Books, 1995), 155–60.

186. De Larosière, Remarks to Association of Reserve City Bankers, 5/9/1983, Box 154, Regan Papers; de Larosière, "Adjustment Programs Supported by the Fund," *IMF Survey,* 2/6/1984, 46.

187. CIA, "The Current LDC Debt Situation: Rising Frustrations," Oct. 1985, CREST. See also World Bank, *World Development Report, 1990* (Washington, DC: World Bank, 1991), 115.

188. Dam, Remarks to World Affairs Council, 12/5/1984, *AFP: CD,* 1984: 990.

189. Kapstein, *Governing the Global Economy,* 97; Jesús Silva-Herzog, "Why the Baker Plan Isn't Enough," *Institutional Investor,* Mar. 1985, 25–26; Bulmer-Thomas, *Economic History,* 397–98.

190. SRE to Colombia, 5/22/1984, Exp. 7, Leg. 1, AHGE.

191. Schaeffer, *Understanding Globalization,* 95.

192. George De Lama, "Economic Storm Clouds Gather over Dominican Republic," *Chicago Tribune,* 8/5/1984; Daniel Sutherland, "Caribbean's Largest Democracy Staves Off Riots and Economic Slide," *Christian Science Monitor,* 9/5/1984.

193. "Message for Dr. K., from Minister Leitão de Abreu," 10/3/1983, Box 104, Regan Papers.

194. John Walton and David Seddon, *Free Markets and Food Riots: The Politics of Global Adjustment* (Cambridge, UK: Wiley-Blackwell, 1994), 39–41; NIE, "The Political Repercussions of the Debt Crisis in Major LDCs," Nov. 1984, CREST.

195. CIA, "Outlook for the International Debt Strategy," May 1984, CREST.

196. David Sheinen, *Argentina and the United States: An Alliance Contained* (Athens: University of Georgia Press, 2006), 191. See also Philip DuSault to Alton Keel, undated, Box 42, SF, ESF, RRL; Vinod Aggarwal, *Debt Games: Strategic Interaction in International Debt Rescheduling* (New York: Cambridge University Press, 1996), chaps. 12–14.

197. Mexico to State, 10/2/1985, Department of State FOIA.

198. Bailey to Robinson, 8/18/1983, Box 42, SF, ESF, RRL; Regan to Stockman, 9/28/1983, Box 104, Regan Papers; NIO-Economics to DCI and DDCI, 4/26/1984, CREST; Aggarwal, *Debt Games,* 417–18, 464, 474.

199. CIA, "South America: Struggling with Debt," Apr. 1984, CREST.

200. CIA, "The Current LDC Debt Situation: Rising Frustrations," Oct. 1985, CREST; Volcker to House Foreign Affairs, 8/8/1984, *AFP: CD,* 1984: 166.

201. Memorandum for Files, 6/7/1984, Box 130, WHDAI, CF, IMF. See also Executive Board Meeting 84/87, 6/6/1984, Executive Board Documents (EBD), IMF; Exchange and Trade Relations Department, "Financing for Countries with Payments Difficulties: Recent Experience and Possible Adaptations," 7/30/1987, Box 32, WHDAI, SF, IMF.

202. Baker, "A Program for Sustained Growth in the Developing Countries," 10/8/1985, *AFP: CD,* 1985: 153–59; Boughton, *Silent Revolution,* 418–20.

203. World Bank, *World Development Report, 1985* (Washington, DC: World Bank, 1985), iii.

204. De Larosière in "Baker Steers a New Course," *Time,* 10/21/1985, 62–63.

205. S. Karene Witcher, "Risky Medicine: Baker's Plan to Relieve Debt Crisis May Spur Future Ills, Critics Say," *Wall Street Journal,* 11/19/1985; Baker, "Program for Sustained Growth."

206. Baker, Testimony to Joint Economic Committee, 1/30/1987, Box 80, Baker Papers.

207. Bush to Reagan, 1/15/1987, Box 91710, LAAD, ESF, RRL. See also Christine Bogdanowicz-Bindert, "An Updated Look at the Debt Crisis," 11/24/1986, 13, Box 99, Part I, Robert McNamara Papers, LC.

208. Mulford, "The International Debt Situation: Toward Stronger Growth, Trade, and Financial Stability," 3/3/1987, Box 32, WHDAI Economic Subject Files, IMF; Jacob Frenkel, "Issues in the Debt Strategy," 1/12/1988, 2, EBS/88/5, EBD, IMF.

209. NSC Meeting, 8/11/1986, NSC 00135, NSC, NSPG MTG Minutes & Presidential MemCons, RRL; Report No. P-4954-ME, 5/22/1989, Folder 458171, WB.

210. "Volcker Warns of Debt-Crisis 'Fatigue,' Says Brazilian Growth Can Cover Loans," *Wall Street Journal,* 2/25/1987; William Cline, "The Baker Plan: Progress, Shortcomings, and Future," WPS 250, Aug. 1989, esp. 19–20, WB.

211. Baker, Remarks to Interim Committee of IMF, 4/9/1987, Box 153, Baker Papers; Stephen Haggard, "The Political Economy of the Philippine Debt Crisis," in *Economic Crisis and Policy Choice: The Politics of Adjustment in the Third World,* edited by Joan Nelson (Princeton: Princeton University Press, 1990), 248–53.

212. Barend de Vries in Morris Goldstein to MD and DMD, 3/31/1987, Box 31, WHDAI Subject Files, IMF; Cline, "Baker Plan," 5–7. Just how close the banks came to the Baker Plan targets is debated. See Boughton, *Silent Revolution,* 428n. 38.

213. Abrams, Remarks to Council of the Americas, 3/9/1988, *AFP: CD*, 1988: 699.

214. James, *International Monetary Cooperation since Bretton Woods*, 398. See also "Bretton Woods Committee's Colloquium on International Debt," 9/27/1987, Box 32, WHDAI, SF, IMF.

215. IMF, *World Economic Outlook, April 1989* (Washington, DC: IMF, 1989), 52; Charles McCoy, "Beyond the Dollars: Debt Crisis Is Inflicting a Heavy Human Toll in Dominican Republic," *Wall Street Journal*, 8/20/1987.

216. Jeffrey Ryser, "A Talk with Alfonsín: 'The Debt Cannot be Paid,'" *Business Week*, 6/22/1987, 66; Judith Evans, "Alfonsín Attacks IMF, Outlines Debt Offensive," *Wall Street Journal*, 9/11/1987.

217. Charles McCoy and Peter Truell, "Lending Imbroglio: Worries Deepen Again on Third World Debt as Brazil Stops Paying," *Wall Street Journal*, 3/3/1987; CIA, "International Financial Situation Report," 12/17/1987, DNSA; Laura Tedesco, *Democracy in Argentina: Hope and Disillusion* (London: Frank Cass, 1999), 134.

218. Negroponte-Nkema Liloo MemCon, 2/19/1988, DDRS; Ringdahl to Poindexter, 2/18/1986, DDRS; Kinshasa to State, 5/12/1986, DDRS.

219. Rainer Steckhan to Various Officials, 12/30/1988, Folder 1779794, Mexico—Country Files—Correspondence—Vol. 1, WB.

220. Camdessus, "Strengthening the Debt Strategy: The Role of the IMF and of the Banks," 5/31/1989, EBD, IMF; Abrams Remarks to Council of the Americas, 3/9/1988, *AFP: CD*, 1988: 699–700.

221. Alan Riding, "Brazil Seeks to Mend Rift with Lenders," *New York Times*, 2/15/1988; Aggarwal, *Debt Games*, 441–42, 485–88, 400–401; "Argentina: Background Papers Approved by Western Hemisphere Department," 3/19/1992, SM/92/66, EBD, IMF; Hardy to Managing Director and Deputy Managing Director, 11/23/1988, Box 157, WHDAI, CF, IMF.

222. Edwards, *Crisis and Reform in Latin America*, 48–56.

223. Hernando de Soto, *The Other Path: The Economic Answer to Terrorism* (New York: Harper & Row, 1989 [first printing 1987]), xv, xxi, 13, 245, 255, 258.

224. Peter Truell, "Since '87 Loss Reserves, Latin Debt Crisis Has Grown," *Wall Street Journal*, 5/19/1988. Ironically, the short-term effect of the Citicorp decision was to exacerbate concerns about the debt crisis by raising the prospect that the commercial banks, now less vulnerable to default, might simply opt out of the debt strategy.

225. Danzansky to Powell, 2/19/1988, DDRS; Flower to Sorzano, 1/5/1988, DDRS; Peter Truell, "Third World Creditors Give Debt-Equity Swaps a Try," *Wall Street Journal*, 6/11/1987.

226. Development Committee Meeting, Morning Session, 4/4/1989, Folder 1791252, DC, WB.

227. Brady, "Strengthening the International Debt Strategy," 3/10/1989, *AFP: CD*, 1989: 90–93.

228. Statistics from Brady's Statement of 3/22/1990, *AFP: CD*, 1990: 109; quotation from Chris Carvounis and Brinda Carvounis, *United States Trade and Investment in Latin America: Opportunities for Business in the 1990s* (Westport, CT: Quorum Books, 1992), 35.

229. Development Committee Meeting, Morning Session, 5/8/1990, Folder 1791254, DC, WB; Michael Reid, *Forgotten Continent: The Battle for Latin America's Soul* (New Haven: Yale University Press, 2007), 136.

230. Lima to State, 9/19/1992, DNSA.

231. Patrice Franko, *The Puzzle of Latin American Development,* 3rd ed. (Lanham, MD: Rowman & Littlefield, 2007), 243; Edwards, *Crisis and Reform in Latin America,* esp. 160.

232. Melvyn Westlake, "Latin America's Silent Revolution," *Guardian,* 6/25/1991.

233. NSC Meeting, 8/15/1986, NSC 00136, NSC, NSPG MTG Minutes & Presidential MemCons, RRL; IMF News Brief 94/7, 3/16/1994, EBD, IMF; Riordan Roett, *Brazil: Politics in a Patrimonial Society,* 5th ed. (Westport, CT: Praeger, 1999), 162–74.

234. Bush-Salinas TelCon, 3/8/1990, Presidential TelCons, GHWBL; Brady, Remarks to Bretton Woods Committee, 7/12/1991, EBD/91/215, IMF. See also Frederick Mayer, *Interpreting NAFTA: The Science and Art of Political Analysis* (New York: Columbia University Press, 1998), esp. 31–66.

235. Development Committee Meeting, Morning Session, 5/8/1990, Folder 1791254, DC, WB.

236. Brady, Remarks to Bretton Woods Committee, 7/12/1991, EBD/91/215, IMF.

237. Paul R. Krugman, Thomas Enders, and William R. Rhodes, "LDC Debt Policy," in *American Economic Policy in the 1980s,* edited by Martin Feldstein (Chicago: University of Chicago Press, 1994), 725.

238. JAB Meeting Notes, 3/2/1992, Box 111, Baker Papers; "Trade in Goods with Mexico," http://www.census.gov/foreign-trade/balance/c2010.html (accessed 5/28/2014).

239. William Rhodes, "Perspective on Latin America: Do-It-Yourself Recovery," *Los Angeles Times,* 2/7/1992. On investment treaties, see Gindin and Panitch, *Making of Global Capitalism,* 231.

240. A good survey is Will Martin and L. Alan Winters, *The Uruguay Round and the Developing Countries* (Cambridge, UK: Cambridge University Press, 1996).

241. Barbara Stallings and Wilson Peres, *Growth, Employment, and Equity: The Impact of the Economic Reforms in Latin America and the Caribbean* (Washington, DC: Brookings Institution Press, 2000), 20, 26, 107, 121; Bulmer-Thomas, *Economic History,* 432; Reid, *Forgotten Continent,* 124–58, esp. 151; "The Restoration of Latin America's Access to Voluntary Capital Market Financing—Developments and Prospects," Aug. 1991, WP/91/74, IMF.

242. James Brookes, "Big Latin Debtors Find That Lacking Austerity, Relief Is Not Coming Soon," *New York Times,* 7/26/1989.

243. Reid, *Forgotten Continent,* esp. 138–39.

244. Author's interview with Cresencio Arcos, 6/14/2007; Evelyn Huber and Fred Solt, "Successes and Failures of Neoliberalism," *Latin American Research Review* 39, no. 3 (2004): esp. 156–57.

245. Lima to State, 9/19/1992, DNSA.

246. "Targeted Programs for the Poor during Structural Adjustment: A Summary of a Symposium on Poverty and Adjustment," Apr. 1988, 1, WB; Michel Chossudovsky, "Under the Tutelage of IMF: The Case of Peru," *Economic and Political Weekly* 27, no. 2 (2/15/1992), 341; World Bank, *World Development Report, 1990,* 103.

247. World Bank Development Brief, "Unorthodox Reform Fails the Poor in Peru," Dec. 1992, 5–6, 15–17, WB; Edward Jaycox to Conable, 6/27/1990, Folder 1779841, Peru—Country Files—Correspondence—Vol. 1, WB.

248. Report No. 8643-BO, "Bolivia Poverty Report," 10/3/1990, 36, Latin America and the Caribbean Region, Country Operations Division, WB.

249. Eugene Rotberg, "An Outline of Remarks: 'Financing Development: The Real World,'" 2/24/1986, Box 99, Part I, McNamara Papers, LC.

250. Felix Moses Edoho, "Overview: Africa in the Age of Globalization and the New World Order," in *Globalization and the New World Order*, edited by Felix Moses Edoho (Westport, CT: Praeger, 1997), 14.

251. "Proposed Agenda for Meeting with the President," 4/10/1992, Box 115, Baker Papers.

252. Subcomandante Marcos, *Our Word Is Our Weapon: Selected Writings*, edited by Juana Ponce de León (New York: Seven Stories Press, 2001), 419.

253. Armacost, "China's Economic Reforms: Implications for the United States," 7/9/1985, *AFP: CD*, 1985: 702.

254. David Harvey, *A Brief History of Neoliberalism* (New York: Oxford University Press, 2007), 120–51; Ezra Vogel, *Deng Xiaoping and the Transformation of China* (Cambridge, MA: Harvard University Press, 2011), chaps. 7–16.

255. "Meeting with Vice-Premier Deng Xiaoping," 4/15/1980, Box 99, Part I, McNamara Papers.

256. Angus Maddison, *The World Economy: Historical Statistics* (Paris: OECD, 2003), 174, 184.

257. Odd Arne Westad, "The Great Transformation: China in the Long 1970s," in *The Shock of the Global: The 1970s in Perspective*, edited by Niall Ferguson, Charles S. Maier, Erez Manela, and Daniel Sargent (Cambridge, MA: Belknap Press, 2010), 77; Bob Bergland to Carter, 11/22/1978, DDRS.

258. Carter, Remarks at Signing Ceremony, 9/17/1980, APP; statistics in Commerce Dept. Briefing Book, "First Session: U.S.-China Joint Commission on Commerce and Trade," 5/23–5/25/1983, DNSA. See also Briefing Book for Visit of Secretary of Commerce Juanita Kreps to the People's Republic of China, May 1979, DNSA; PD/NSC-43, "U.S.-China Scientific and Technological Relationships," 11/3/1978, DNSA.

259. Shultz, Remarks to World Affairs Council of San Francisco, 3/5/1983, *AFP: CD*, 1983: 923.

260. Gregg Brazinsky, *Nation Building in South Korea: Koreans, Americans, and the Making of a Democracy* (Chapel Hill: University of North Carolina Press, 2007), 245–46.

261. Richard Solomon, "U.S.-China Relations since the Onset of Normalization: A Relationship in Search of a Rationale," RAND Corporation, Sept. 1984, 14, DNSA. See also Patrick Tyler, *A Great Wall: Six Presidents and China* (New York: PublicAffairs, 2007), 290–94.

262. Assistant Secretary of State John Holdridge, "U.S. Relations with China," 7/16/1981, *AFP: CD*, 1981: 960; McFarlane to Reagan, 4/7/1984, DDRS; J-5 Report to JCS, JSC/2118/292–2, 4/17/1981, Department of Defense FOIA.

263. Wolfowitz, "U.S. Trade with China," 5/31/1984, *AFP: CD*, 1984: 688.

264. NSDD-120, "Visit to the United States of Premier Zhao Ziyang," 1/9/1984, DNSA; "The Trip of President Reagan to the People's Republic of China," Apr. 1984, DNSA.

265. INR, "China's View of the U.S. and the USSR," 3/27/1984, DNSA.

266. See, for instance, "Working Group on the Exchange of Economic Information," undated (1981), Box 155, Regan Papers; "Summary of Discussions in Finance and Investment Working Group," undated (1981), Box 155, Regan Papers; Leland to Regan, 8/19/1981, Box 131, Regan Papers; Wolfowitz to Shultz, 1/26/1983, DNSA; NSDD-140, "The President's Visit to the People's Republic of China," 4/21/1984, EBB 19, NSArch.

267. Reagan, Remarks at Welcoming Ceremony for Premier Zhao Ziyang, 1/10/1984, APP.

268. Wolfowitz to Shultz, 1/27/1983 and 1/26/1983, DNSA.

269. Wolfowitz to Shultz, 1/27/1983, DNSA; Baldrige to Weinberger, 8/10/1983, DNSA; Clark to State, Defense, et al., "Implementation of Export Control Changes for China," 8/30/1983, Department of Defense FOIA.

270. Armacost, "China's Economic Reforms," 703; "U.S. Export Controls and Technology Transfer to China," July 1986, DNSA.

271. See "The Trip of President Reagan to the People's Republic of China," Apr. 1984, DNSA; Wolfowitz to Shultz, 1/26/1983 and 1/27/1983, DNSA; Summary of Discussions in Finance and Investment Working Group, undated (1981), Box 155, Regan Papers; Shultz, Address at Dalian Management Training Center, 3/3/1987, *AFP: CD*, 1987: 533–34.

272. USDEL Sec in Korea to Washington, 7/17/1988, DNSA; INR, "China's Open Door Policy: New Pressures and Opportunities," 6/20/1984, DNSA.

273. "Secretary's Message to Agricultural Secretary Block," 6/16/1981, DNSA; USDEL Sec in Korea to Washington, 7/17/1988, DNSA; INR, "China's View of the U.S. and the USSR," 3/27/1984, DNSA.

274. Defense Intelligence Agency (DIA), "China's Import of Foreign Technology, Survey and Chronology: 1 January–31 December 1984," Aug. 1985, DNSA.

275. Odd Arne Westad, *Restless Empire: China and the World since 1750* (New York: Basic Books, 2012), 377–78.

276. Harvey, *Brief History of Neoliberalism*, 135.

277. Statistics for 1977, 1982, and 1985–1986 from Commerce Dept. Briefing Book, "First Session: U.S.-China Joint Commission on Commerce and Trade"; Shultz, Address to Dalian Management Training Center, 533. Statistics for 1991 from Census Bureau, "Trade in Goods with China," http://www.census.gov/foreign-trade/balance/c5700.html (accessed 5/20/2014).

278. Holdridge, "Assessment of U.S. Relations with China," 12/13/1982, *AFP: CD*, 1982: 1056.

279. Shultz, "New Realities," 711.

280. Reagan, Remarks at Moscow State University, 5/31/1988, APP.

281. Address from Venice Economic Summit, 6/5/1987, APP. See also Shultz, *Turmoil and Triumph*, 396.

282. Chen Jian, "China and the Cold War after Mao," in *Cambridge History of the Cold War, Vol. 3: Endings,* edited by Odd Arne Westad and Melvyn Leffler (New York: Cambridge University Press, 2010), 195–97; INR, "China: Two Monographs on Social Reform," 6/13/1985, DNSA.

283. Fox Butterfield, "Deng Is Said to Link Force to Safety of Party," *New York Times,* 6/17/1989.

284. Memorandum for Secretary of Defense, "Technology Transfer to China," 5/6/1983, Department of Defense FOIA; DIA, "Implications of U.S. Assistance to China's Military Modernization for Non-Communist Regional Powers," Apr. 1985, DNSA.

285. Baker, Testimony to House Ways and Means Subcommittee on Trade, 2/10/1987, Box 80, Baker Papers.

286. Williamson, "What Washington Means by Policy Reform."

287. Address by Undersecretary of State for Economic and Agricultural Affairs, 10/30/1989, *AFP: CD,* 1989: 81.

288. Reagan, Farewell Address, 1/11/1989, APP. See also Bush, Remarks to Annual Meeting of IMF and World Bank, 9/25/1990, APP.

5. Structure versus Strategy in the Greater Middle East

1. I define the *greater Middle East* as the area from Muslim North Africa, to Turkey and the Levant, to the Persian Gulf (including Iraq and Iran), to Afghanistan and Pakistan. For convenience, I use *Middle East* and *greater Middle East* interchangeably.

2. Foreign Broadcast Information Service (FBIS) Daily Report, "Khomeyni on Hostages," 9/12/1980, FBIS-SAS-80-180.

3. PRC Meeting, 6/21–6/22/1979, NLC-31-11-12-4-8, JCL; Robert Art, *A Grand Strategy for America* (Ithaca: Cornell University Press, 2003), 62.

4. Brzezinski to Carter, 12/2/1978, Box 29, SF, Plains File, JCL.

5. Douglas Little, *American Orientalism: The United States and the Middle East since 1945* (Chapel Hill: University of North Carolina Press, 2008), 145–46; Roham Alvandi, "Nixon, Kissinger, and the Shah: The Origins of Iranian Primacy in the Persian Gulf," *Diplomatic History* 36, no. 2 (2012): 337–72.

6. Ford-Kissinger-Scowcroft MemCom, 8/17/1974, Box 5, MemCons, NSA, GFL.

7. Brzezinski to Carter, 12/26/1979, Box 17, GF, ZBDM, JCL.

8. Bruce Laingen Oral History, 83, FAOHC.

9. Christin Marschall, *Iran's Persian Gulf Policy: From Khomeini to Khatami* (New York: Routledge, 2003), 26–27, also 25–38.

10. Discussion Paper, "U.S. Relations with Arab States of Persian Gulf," undated, NLC-132-109-7-2-5, JCL.

11. Olav Njolstad, "Shifting Priorities: The Persian Gulf in U.S. Strategic Planning in the Carter Years," *Cold War History* 4, no. 3 (2004): 30; William Odom, "The Cold War Origins of the U.S. Central Command," *Journal of Cold War Studies* 8, no. 2 (2006): esp. 54–68.

12. SCC Meeting, 1/14/1980, NLC-128-10-6-14-8, JCL.

13. "President Carter Phone Call to MT," 12/28/1979, MTF; Brzezinski to Carter, 1/3/1980, DDRS; "Soviet Union and Southwest Asia," in Turner memo, 1/15/1980, DDRS.

14. Carter, State of the Union Address, 1/23/1980, APP.

15. Brzezinski to Carter, 3/28/1980, NLC-128-10-3-11-3, JCL; Brzezinski to Carter, 1/30/1980, NLC-25-99-16-7-0, JCL.

16. NFAC, "The Resurgence of Islam," Mar. 1979, DDRS. As background, see also William E. Griffith, "The Revival of Islamic Fundamentalism: The Case of Iran," 4/23/1979, DNSA; INR, "The New Islamic Fundamentalism," Feb. 1979, NLC-25-47-7-3-3, JCL; CIA, "Resurgent Islamic Nationalism in the Middle East," 3/12/1981, CREST; John Esposito, Unholy War: Terror in the Name of Islam (New York: Oxford University Press, 2003); Beverley Milton-Edwards, Islamic Fundamentalism since 1945, 2nd ed. (New York: Routledge, 2014), esp. 1–94.

17. NFAC, "The Resurgence of Islam," Mar. 1979, DDRS; National Intelligence Daily, 2/13/1979, CIA FOIA. On the revolution and Islam, see also Karen Armstrong, The Battle for God: A History of Fundamentalism (New York: Ballantine Books, 2001), 299–309; Vanessa Martin, Creating an Islamic State: Khomeini and the Making of a New Iran (London: I. B. Tauris, 2007).

18. "Khomeyni Addresses Representatives of Liberation Movements," FBIS-SAS-80-156, 8/9/1980.

19. Brzezinski to Carter, 2/2/1979, in Woodrow Wilson Center, The Carter Administration and the 'Arc of Crisis' 1977–1981: Declassified Documents Prepared for a Critical Oral History Conference, Washington, DC, 2005; Bruce Laingen Oral History, 82–83, FAOHC.

20. CIA, "Iran: At War with the U.S.," undated (1980–1981), CREST; NFAC, "Iran: Khomeini Aims to Defeat President Carter," 4/18/1980, CREST; Ray Takeyh, Guardians of the Revolution: Iran and the World in the Age of the Ayatollahs (New York: Oxford University Press, 2009), 18–20, 36–46.

21. Takeyh, Guardians of the Revolution, 18; CIA, "Iran: Outlook for the Islamic Republic," 5/24/1983, CREST.

22. Douglas Brinkley, ed., The Reagan Diaries Unabridged: Vol. I (New York: HarperCollins, 2009),72.

23. Khartoum to State, 12/5/1979, DDRS; Cairo to State, 1/23/1979, DNSA.

24. CIA, "Resurgent Islamic Nationalism in the Middle East," 3/12/1981, CREST.

25. This definition is drawn from Bruce Hoffman, Inside Terrorism (New York: Columbia University Press, 2006), esp. 40–41.

26. Brian Michael Jenkins, "Terrorism in the 1980's," RAND Corporation, Dec. 1980, DNSA; Statement by Sayre to Subcommittee of House Appropriations Committee, 3/18/1982, AFP: CD, 1982: 399; CIA, "Political Perspectives on Key Global Issues," Mar. 1977, NLC-132-64-1-1-2, JCL.

27. See Paul Thomas Chamberlin, The Global Offensive: The United States, the Palestine Liberation Organization, and the Making of the Post-Cold War Order (New York: Oxford University Press, 2012); Barry Rubin, Revolution until Victory?: The Politics and History of the PLO (Cambridge, MA: Harvard University Press, 1994), esp. chap. 2.

28. Odom to Brzezinski, 8/30/1977, NLC-17-29-4-7-1 JCL; Timothy Naftali, Blind Spot: The Secret History of American Counterterrorism (New York: Basic Books, 2005), chaps. 2–5, esp. 68, 107. For greater concern, see Heck to Vance, 2/3/1977, NLC-132-45-4-4-7, JCL; NFAC, "International Issues Review," 9/27/1978, NLC-17-139-3-1-6, JCL.

29. "International Terrorism: A Compendium," Vol. II—Middle East, 12/31/1984, DNSA.

30. "Report of the Department of Defense Commission on Beirut International Airport Terrorist Act," 12/20/1983, *AFP: CD,* 1983: 349; Department of State, *Patterns of Global Terrorism: 1984,* 2, DNSA. See also Hoffman, *Inside Terrorism,* 63–80, 89–93; Esposito, *Unholy War;* CIA, "The Supporters of International Terrorism," 1/29/1981, CREST.

31. David Farber, *Taken Hostage: The Iran Hostage Crisis and America's First Encounter with Radical Islam* (Princeton: Princeton University Press, 2006).

32. NFAC, "Iran: The Seizure of the Embassy in Retrospect," Nov. 1981, CREST.

33. Gary Sick, *All Fall Down: America's Tragic Encounter with Iran* (New York: Random House, 1986), 245.

34. NFAC, "Iran: The Seizure of the Embassy."

35. "Iran: At War with the US," undated, CREST. See also "Iran: Outlook for the Islamic Republic," 5/24/1983, CREST; CIA, "Special Feature—Iran: Spreading Islam and Terrorism," 3/1/1984, DDRS.

36. NFAC, "Patterns of International Terrorism: 1980," June 1981, DNSA. See also Takeyh, *Guardians of the Revolution,* 69–74; Hoffman, *Inside Terrorism,* 89–91.

37. Casey to NIC Chairman, 9/17/1981, CREST; "International Terrorism: A Compendium," Vol. II—Middle East, 12/31/1984, DNSA.

38. "Global Terrorism in 1983," in McFarlane to Meese, 8/15/1984, DNSA.

39. NSC Meeting, 1/2/1980, NLC-25-98-31-6-7, JCL; PS/NSC-63, "Persian Gulf Security Framework," 1/15/1981, Box 36, Odom Papers, LC.

40. "A Security Framework for Southwest Asia: Background for a Strategic Dialogue," 3/13/1980, Box 6, Lake Records, RG 59, NARA.

41. Carter to Brown, 2/9/1979, Box 30, SF, ZBDM, JCL; "Draft Speech on the Security Framework for the Persian Gulf Region," 9/7/1980, NLC-12-12-6-25-2, JCL; SCC Meeting on Persian Gulf Security Framework, 9/5/1980, GF, ZBDM, JCL; SCC Meeting, 9/27/1980, NLC-25-45-9-5-8, JCL; Jim Hoagland, "U.S. Gives Saudi Leaders Reassurances of Support," *Washington Post,* 4/27/1979; Carter, State of the Union Address, 1/23/1980, APP; Steve Yetiv, *America and the Persian Gulf: The Third Party Dimension in World Politics* (Westport, CT: Praeger, 1995), 37–38.

42. Brzezinski to Carter, 1/3/1980, GF, ZBDM, JCL; Brown to Carter, 2/12/1980, NLC-15-75-4-8-1, JCL.

43. "Military Presence in the Middle East/ Persian Gulf," in Christine Dodson memo, 6/18/1979, NLC-20-24-2-1-0, JCL; Brzezinski to Carter, 6/22/1979, Box 29, SF, Plains File, JCL; "Security Framework for Southwest Asia (A DoD Viewpoint)," 2/27/1980, Box 36, Odom Papers, LC; PS/NSC-63, "Persian Gulf Security Framework."

44. Thompson and Utgoff to Brzezinski, 7/8/1977, SF, ZBDM, JCL.

45. Aaron to Brzezinski, 12/27/1979, Box 15, GF, ZBDM, JCL; Memo to Harold Brown, 6/30/1980, Box 36, Odom Papers, LC. The precise structure of the RDF and later CENTCOM would shift over time.

46. Brzezinski to Carter, 9/2/1980, NLC-7-32-9-12-7, JCL; "Report of the State/Defense Team on U.S. Access to Military Facilities in the Persian Gulf/Indian Ocean," Jan. 1980, Box 31, SF, ZBDM, JCL; Odom to Brzezinski, 7/30/1980, DDRS; Yetiv, *America and the Persian Gulf,* 59.

47. Brzezinski to various, 11/5/1980, Box 36, Odom Papers, LC; Odom, "Cold War Origins," 72–75.

48. Hal Brands, "Why Did Saddam Invade Iran? New Evidence on Motives, Complexity, and the Israel Factor," *Journal of Military History* 75, no. 3 (2011): 861–85; F. Gregory Gause, "Iraq's Decisions to Go to War, 1980 and 1990," *Middle East Journal* 56, no. 1 (2002): esp. 62–69.

49. General Military Intelligence Directorate (GMID), Intelligence Report on Political, Military, and Economic Conditions in Iran, 7/1/1980 (approximately), SH-GMID-D-000-842, Conflict Records Research Center (CRRC).

50. Meeting between Saddam Hussein and High-Ranking Officials, 9/16/1980, SH-SHTP-A-000-835, CRRC.

51. Ray Takeyh, "The Iran-Iraq War: A Reassessment," *Middle East Journal* 64, no. 3 (2010): 366.

52. James G. Blight, Janet M. Lang, Hussein Banai, Malcolm Byrne, and John Tirman, eds., *Becoming Enemies: U.S.-Iran Relations and the Iran-Iraq War, 1979–1988* (Lanham, MD: Rowman & Littlefield, 2012), 95. The best military history is Kevin Woods and Williamson Murray, *The Iran-Iraq War: A Strategic and Military Analysis* (Cambridge, UK: Cambridge University Press, 2014).

53. Hal Brands, "Saddam Hussein, the United States, and the Invasion of Iran: Was There a Green Light?" *Cold War History* 12, no. 2 (2012): 319–44.

54. Author's phone interview with Wayne White, 6/7/2010; author's phone interview with Gary Sick, 8/26/2010.

55. Department of State cable to Muscat, undated (Sept./Oct. 1980), NLC-25-45-8-4-3, JCL. See also NSC Meeting, 9/24/1980, NLC-128-12-3-8-6, JCL.

56. Nicholas Veliotes Oral History, 98, FAOHC; Haig to Various Posts, 2/16/1981, EBB 82, NSArch; SCC Meeting, 9/27/1980, NLC-25-45-9-5-8, JCL. Ironically, Brzezinski briefly considered tilting toward *Iran* as the conflict began, hoping to trade weapons for the release of the hostages.

57. On Saddam's prospects, see SNIE, "Implications of Iran's Victory over Iraq," June 1982, EBB 167, NSArch; SNIE, "Prospects for Iraq," 7/19/1983, EBB 167, NSArch.

58. Rowen Memo, "The Iranian Threat to American Interests in the Persian Gulf," 7/20/1982, DDRS.

59. CIA, "Iran-Iraq: Consequences of an Iranian Breakthrough at al Basrah," 3/23/1984, CIA FOIA.

60. Douglas Brinkley, ed. *The Reagan Diaries* (New York: HarperCollins, 2007), 25.

61. McFarlane to Reagan, May 1984, Box 91689, Near East and South Asia Affairs (NESAA), ESF, RRL.

62. Talking Points for Rumsfeld Meeting with Aziz and Hussein, 12/14/1983, EBB 82, NSArch. See also GAO, *Iraq's Participation in the Commodity Credit Corporation's GSM-102/103 Export Credit Guarantee Program* (Washington, DC, 1991), 14; Stockholm International Peace Research Institute (SIPRI), "TIV of Arms Imports to Iraq, 1980–1988," http://armstrade.sipri.org/armstrade/html/export_values.php (accessed 7/6/2014); Stephen Rock, *Appeasement in International Politics* (Lexington: University of Kentucky Press, 2000), 104–6; Bruce Jentleson, *With Friends like These: Reagan, Bush, and Saddam, 1982–1990* (New York: W. W. Norton, 1994), 33–56; Steve Yetiv, *The Absence of Grand Strategy: The United States in the Persian Gulf, 1972–2005* (Baltimore: Johns Hopkins University Press, 2008), 51–54.

63. George Shultz, *Turmoil and Triumph: My Years as Secretary of State* (New York: Scribner, 1993), 237.

64. "Declaration of Howard Teicher," undated, in *The Origins, Conduct, and Impact of the Iran-Iraq War, 1980–1988: A Cold War International History Project Document Reader* (Washington, DC: Woodrow Wilson International Center for Scholars, 2004) [hereafter CWIHP-NSArch]; Seymour Hersh, "U.S. Secretly Gave Aid to Iraq Early in Its War against Iran," *New York Times,* 1/26/1992.

65. Memorandum for the Record, 3/26/1984, Box 91681–91682, Howard Teicher Files, RRL; Howe and Veliotes to Eagleburger, 10/7/1983, EBB 82, NSArch; author's phone interview with Wayne White; Jeffrey Richelson, *The U.S. Intelligence Community,* 6th ed. (Boulder: Westview Press, 2012), 438–39.

66. Ronald St. Martin to Poindexter, 10/16/1986, Box 91681–91682, Teicher Files, RRL; William Cokell, "Iran Game Plan," 11/21/1986, DNSA.

67. Reagan in Weinberger to Prince Sultan bin Abd al-Aziz, 7/26/1982, DDRS.

68. Statement by General George B. Crist, 3/12/1986, DNSA. See also "The Secretary's Welcoming Remarks" at GCC Luncheon, 10/1/1986, DNSA; Noel Koch to Deputy Assistant for National Security Affairs, 2/22/1984, DDRS.

69. NSPG Meeting, 5/17/1984, Box 91305, NSPG Meetings, ESF, RRL; CIA, "Saudi Air Force Modernization: The Emergence of a Regional Power," May 1985, CREST; Muscat to State, 2/13/1982, DDRS; Reagan News Conference, 10/1/1981, APP; Bruce Kuniholm, "The Carter Doctrine, the Reagan Corollary, and Prospects for United States Policy in Southwest Asia," *International Journal* 41, no. 2 (1986): 345–46.

70. NSDD-139, "Measures to Improve United States Posture and Readiness to Respond to Developments in the Iran-Iraq War," 4/5/1984, EBB 82, NSArch.

71. LG Robert Kingston, "United States Central Command," Jan. 1983, DNSA; U.S. CENTCOM, "CINC Policy and Strategy Book," Vol. I, 1984, DNSA.

72. LG Robert Kingston, "From RDF to CENTCOM: New Challenges?" *RUSI Journal,* 3/1/1984, 16–17; Yetiv, *America and the Persian Gulf,* 83–85; U.S. CENTCOM, "CINC Policy and Strategy Book," Vol. I, esp. 38–41; Department of State, "U.S. Peacetime Presence in Southwest Asia," 2/28/1983, DDRS; Rachel Bronson, *Thicker than Oil: America's Uneasy Partnership with Saudi Arabia* (New York: Oxford University Press, 2008), 162.

73. The estimate of $30–40 billion may be low; by one count, this was the total just for 1981–1982. Marschall, *Iran's Persian Gulf Policy,* 71.

74. *Developments in the Middle East, March 1988: Hearing before the Subcommittee on Europe and the Middle East of the Committee on Foreign Affairs, House of Representatives, 15 March 1988* (Washington, DC, 1988), 13–14.

75. Kemp, Memorandum for the Record, 3/26/1984, Boxes 91681–91682, Teicher Files, RRL; "Declaration of Howard Teicher"; Jentleson, *With Friends like These,* 46; Dilip Hiro, *The Longest War: The Iran-Iraq Military Conflict* (New York: Routledge, 1991), 160.

76. GMID Study, 5/12/1987, SH-GMID-D-000-265, CRRC; London to State, 5/14/1984, Box 91689, ESF, RRL.

77. Murphy to Armacost, July 1986, Box 7, Richard Murphy Papers, LC.

78. "Threat Analysis," appendix of "Military Presence in the Middle East/ Persian Gulf," in Dodson memo, 6/18/1979, NLC-20-24-2-1-0, JCL.

79. "A Politically Sensitive Approach to Military Cooperation with the Key Arab States in the Persian Gulf," in Dur to Poindexter, 5/18/1984, Box 91695, NESAA, ESF, RRL; Dhahran to State, 2/8/1982, DDRS.

80. "Summary of CPPG Review: Iran-Iraq War," 3/29/1984, Box 91307, NSPG, ESF, RRL.

81. Author's phone interview with Barbara Bodine, 8/25/2010.

82. Bernard Gwertzman, "Iraq Gets Reports from U.S. for Use in War with Iran," *New York Times,* 12/16/1986; Reagan to Saulnier, undated (1983–1984), NSDD 138–147 Files, NSDDs, ESF, RRL.

83. Author's phone interview with Bodine; Hill to McFarlane, 3/7/1984, NSDD 114, NSDDs, ESF, RRL.

84. CIA, "State Support for Terrorism, 1985," May 1986, Box 91690–91629, NESAA, ESF, RRL; McNeil to Shultz, 7/1/1986, DNSA; Patrick Tyler, *A World of Trouble: The White House and the Middle East—from the Cold War to the War on Terror* (New York: Farrar, Straus and Giroux, 2009), 326–27.

85. Saddam in Armed Forces General Command memoranda, various dates, SH-AFGC-D-000-094, CRRC.

86. Howe to Shultz, 11/1/1983, EBB 82, NSArch.

87. Interagency Intelligence Memorandum, "Impact and Implications of Chemical Weapons Use in the Iran-Iraq War," Apr. 1988, CIA FOIA; CIA, "The Iraqi Chemical Weapons Program in Perspective," Jan. 1985, CREST; *Comprehensive Report of the Special Advisor to the DCI on Iraq's WMD* (Washington, DC, 2004), Vol. III: 5. This report put Iraqi chemical weapons use at over 100,000 munitions, which included a comparatively small number used during internal revolts in 1991.

88. David Newton Oral History, 77, FAOHC.

89. Shultz to Amman, 4/6/1984, EBB 82, NSArch; State to Amman, 3/18/1984, CWIHP-NSArch; State to Geneva, 3/14/1984, EBB 82, NSArch; Joost Hiltermann, *A Poisonous Affair: America, Iraq, and the Gassing of Halabja* (Cambridge, UK: Cambridge University Press, 2007), 43–56.

90. Reagan, Remarks at Welcoming Ceremony for Freed Hostages, 1/27/1981, APP; Reagan-Emilio Colombo MemCon, 2/12/1981, NSC, NSPG MTG Minutes & Presidential MemCons, RRL.

91. Haig to Reagan, 3/25/1981, DDRS; Department of State, "A Public Affairs Strategy for Actions against Libya," 11/17/1981, DDRS; Michael Ledeen to McFarlane, 10/27/1981, RAC Box 5, Kemp Files, RRL; CIA, "Libya: Aims and Vulnerabilities," 1/30/1981, CIA FOIA; Ronald Bruce St. John, "Terrorism and Libyan Foreign Policy, 1981–1986," *World Today* 42, no. 7 (1986), esp. 111–12.

92. Richard Allen, "National Security Council Meeting," 5/22/1981, DDRS; McFarlane Memo, 10/14/1981, DDRS; Ronald Bruce St. John, *Libya and the United States: Two Centuries of Strife* (Philadelphia: University of Pennsylvania Press, 2002), 123–27; Joseph Stanik, *El Dorado Canyon: Reagan's Undeclared War with Qaddafi* (Annapolis: U.S. Naval Institute Press, 2003), 44, 64.

93. NSC Meeting, 7/31/1981, Box 91282, NSC Meetings, ESF, RRL.

94. NSC Meeting, 12/8/1981, NSC, NSPG MTG Minutes & Presidential MemCons, RRL.

95. Interagency Intelligence Assessment, "Implications of Planned U.S. Naval Exercise in the Gulf of Sidra, 18–20 August 1981," 8/10/1981, DDRS.

96. "Discussion Paper for February 18 NSC Meeting: Next Steps on Libya," 2/18/1982, DDRS.

97. CIA, "Growing Terrorist Danger for Americans," 12/23/1981, DDRS; Brinkley, *Reagan Diaries,* 50–51, 53–54; Bob Woodward, *Veil: The Secret Wars of the CIA* (New York: Simon & Schuster, 1987), 167, 181–83; David Martin and John Walcott, *Best Laid Plans: The Inside Story of America's War against Terrorism* (New York: HarperCollins, 1988), 80–81.

98. Casey, Remarks to Society of the Four Arts, Palm Beach, 2/23/1982, CREST.

99. "Discussion Paper for February 18 NSC Meeting."

100. Waterman to DCI and DDCI, 1/31/1982, CREST; Tanter to Allen, 11/13/1981, DDRS; Haig to Reagan, 3/25/1981, DDRS.

101. NSC Summary of State Paper for 2/4/1982 NSC Meeting, "Next Steps on Libya," CREST; Washington to NATO Capitals, 3/2/1982, DDRS; James Nance, "Meeting with Congressional Leadership," 12/10/1981, DDRS.

102. Stanik, *El Dorado Canyon,* 79–80; "Countering the Threat from Libya," undated (late 1981), CREST; Wolfowitz to Clark, 11/24/1981, DDRS.

103. Shultz, *Turmoil and Triumph,* 677.

104. NSC Meeting, 1/21/1982, NSC 00038, NSC, NSPG MTG Minutes & Presidential MemCons, RRL; INR, "Libya: Qadhafi on a Binge," 3/20/1984, DDRS.

105. Department of State, "Libya Sanctions," 1/8/1986, DNSA; Department of State, *Patterns of Global Terrorism: 1985* (Washington, DC, 1986), esp. 4–5; CIA, "Libyan-Sponsored Terrorism and Subversion," 6/13/1985, DDRS; Brian L. Davis, *Qaddafi, Terrorism, and the Origins of the U.S. Attack on Libya* (New York: Praeger, 1990), 65–69.

106. Fortier to McFarlane, 3/22/1984, DDRS.

107. There were actually two U.S.-led multinational interventions in Lebanon from 1982–1984, first a very brief one in mid-1982, and then the longer one from late 1982 to early 1984. For U.S. goals and policy, see NSDD-64, "Next Steps in Lebanon," 10/28/1982, DNSA; Lawrence Freedman, *A Choice of Enemies: America Confronts the Middle East* (New York: PublicAffairs, 2008), 122–49.

108. On these dynamics, see McFarlane to Reagan, 2/7/1983, DDRS; Weinberger to Reagan, 12/20/1983, Box 44, CF, ESF, RRL; *Report of the Department of Defense Commission on Beirut International Airport Terrorist Act, October 23, 1983* (Washington, DC, 1983), 40–41.

109. "International Terrorism—A Compendium," Vol. II—Middle East, 31 December 1984, DNSA. See also CIA, "Lebanon: The Hizb Allah," 9/27/1984, DNSA; Department of State, *Patterns of Global Terrorism: 1984,* DNSA, esp. 7; Ronen Bergman, *The Secret War with Iran: The 30-Year Clandestine Struggle against the World's Most Dangerous Terrorist Power* (New York: Free Press, 2011), 59–71.

110. "Remarks by General P. X. Kelley, USMC, SASC, 31 October 1983," NSDD 111, NSDDs, ESF, RRL.

111. Ibid.

112. Reagan, Address to the Nation, 10/27/1983, APP.

113. Teicher to McFarlane, 10/26/1983, NSDD 111, NSDDs, ESF, RRL; Brinkley, *Reagan Diaries,* 194. See also David Crist, *The Twilight War: The Secret History of America's Thirty-Year Conflict with Iran* (New York: Penguin, 2012), 140–44.

114. "A U.S. Policy for Lebanon," undated, RAC Box 7, Donald Fortier Files, RRL; Shultz, *Turmoil and Triumph,* 230; Naftali, *Blind Spot,* 132.

115. "A U.S. Policy for Lebanon." See also "Summary of CPPG Review: Iran-Iraq War," 3/29/1984, Box 91307, NSPG, ESF, RRL; CIA, "Impact of U.S. Attacks on Iran," 1/24/1985, CREST; David C. Wills, *The First War on Terrorism: Counter-Terrorism Policy during the Reagan Administration* (Lanham, MD: Rowman & Littlefield, 2003), 64; Nathan Thrall, "How the Reagan Administration Taught Iran the Wrong Lessons," *Middle Eastern Review of International Affairs* 11, no. 2 (2007), http://www.rubincenter.org/2007/06/thrall-2007-06-05/ (accessed 6/12/2014).

116. NSPG Meeting, 10/3/1984, DNSA.

117. See Caspar Weinberger, *Fighting for Peace: Seven Critical Years in the Pentagon* (New York: Grand Central Publishing, 1990), esp. 159–60, 167–68.

118. There remains some confusion over how and when this decision was made. See Crist, *Twilight War*, 144–48. The administration did later launch minor, and almost completely ineffectual, airstrikes following Syrian attacks on U.S. reconnaissance planes.

119. Transcript of *The MacNeil/Lehrer News Hour*, 2/23/1984.

120. CIA, "Lebanon: The Hizb Allah," 9/27/1984, DNSA.

121. State to Beirut, 2/9/1984, OA 91136, NESAA, ESF, RRL.

122. Some Hezbollah attacks were claimed by Islamic Jihad, a shadow organization under the control of Hezbollah.

123. Statement by Secretary of Defense, 6/5/1986, *AFP: CD*, 1986: 212. See also Department of State, *Patterns of Global Terrorism: 1985*; CIA, "Middle East Terrorism: Threat and Possible U.S. Responses," 2/15/1985, Box 34, North Files, RRL.

124. Casey, Remarks to American Jewish Committee, 5/15/1986, DNSA.

125. Shultz, "Terrorism and the World Order," 10/25/1984, OA/ID CF01573, Richard Canas Files, NSC, GHWBL; Bernard Gwertzman, "U.S. Backs Raid, Regrets Deaths," *New York Times*, 11/25/1985.

126. Shultz, "Terrorism and the World Order."

127. Shultz, Address to American Society for Industrial Security, 2/4/1985, *AFP: CD*, 1985: 276.

128. Bernard Gwertzman, "Shultz's Address Touches Off Stir in Administration," *New York Times*, 10/27/1984.

129. Statement by Secretary of Defense Weinberger, 6/5/1986, *AFP: CD*, 1986: 215. See also "The Uses of Military Power," Nov. 1984, Part III: Box 53, Weinberger Papers, LC.

130. Michael M. Gunter, "Countering Terrorism: The Reagan Record," *Conflict Quarterly* 14, no. 2 (1994): 10.

131. NSPG Meeting, 10/3/1984, DNSA; CIA, "Middle East Terrorism: The Threat and Possible U.S. Responses," 2/15/1985, CREST.

132. Brian Michael Jenkins, "Combatting Terrorism Becomes a War," RAND Corporation, May 1985, 1.

133. Department of State, *Report of the Secretary of State's Advisory Panel on Overseas Security*, June 1985, OA/ID 19849, Gregg Files, GHWBL.

134. NSPG Meeting, 3/2/1984, NPSG 0086, NSC, NSPG MTG Minutes & Presidential MemCons, RRL.

135. Allan Nanes, "International Terrorism," CRS Report, 6/26/1985, DNSA.

136. NSDD-138, "Combatting Terrorism," 4/3/1984, Box 1, NSDDs 1–220, Research Room Files, RRL.

137. Oakley Oral History, 118, FAOHC; Lou Cannon, "Antiterrorist Policy a Casualty," *Washington Post,* 6/24/1985.

138. NSPG Meeting, 10/3/1984, DNSA.

139. DCI Security Committee Minutes, 5/8/1985, CREST. See also statistics in Wills, *First War on Terrorism,* 6; Naftali, *Blind Spot,* 140–55, 171–75.

140. CIA, "Middle East: Terrorist Violence," 8/6/1985, DNSA; DCI Security Committee Minutes, 5/8/1985, CREST.

141. Background information attached to Menarchik and Gregg to Bush, 1/10/1986, DNSA.

142. Oakley, "Combating International Terrorism," 3/5/1985, OA/ID CF01573, Canas Files, NSC, GHWBL.

143. Casey, Address to Fletcher School of Law and Diplomacy, 4/17/1985, *AFP: CD,* 1985: 279.

144. Holloway to Fuller and Menarchik, 9/18/1985, OA/ID 19850, Gregg Files, GHWBL.

145. Menarchik to Gregg, 12/10/1985, OA/ID 19850, Gregg Files, GHWBL.

146. Department of State, "Report to the Congress on the Anti-Terrorism Assistance Program," 2/19/1986, OA/ID 19851, Gregg Files, GHWBL; Department of State, *Patterns of Global Terrorism: 1989,* iv, Department of Defense FOIA; *United States Special Operations Command History,* 2007, 5–8, http://fas.org/irp/agency/dod/socom/2007history.pdf (accessed 7/20/2014).

147. NSDD-207, "The National Program for Combating Terrorism," 1/20/1986, Carolyn Stettner Files, OA/ID CF01523-004, NSC Files, GHWBL; "Possible Topics to Be Introduced by Task Force Principals during Discussion at 18 September Task Force Meeting," undated, Box 32, North Files, RRL; "Text of State's Report on U.S.-Israel Anti-Terrorism Cooperation," undated, Box 32, North Files, RRL; Bush to Reagan, 6/2/1987, OA/ID 19849, Gregg Files, RRL.

148. NSDD-207, "National Program for Combatting Terrorism"; Poindexter to Reagan, 1/17/1985, DNSA; NSPG Meeting, 1/18/1985, DNSA.

149. Douglas Little, "To the Shores of Tripoli: America, Qaddafi, and Libyan Revolution, 1969–89," *International History Review* 35, no. 1 (2013): 87–89; Bob Woodward, "CIA Anti-Qaddafi Plan Backed," *Washington Post,* 11/3/1985.

150. State to OECD Capitals, 1/8/1986, DDRS; Brinkley, *Reagan Diaries,* 381.

151. Brinkley, *Reagan Diaries,* 381.

152. On the raid, see Stanik, *El Dorado Canyon,* 146–205; Weinberger, *Fighting for Peace,* 187–99; "Results of U.S. Military Operations against Libya on 15 April," 5/8/1986, DNSA.

153. Reagan to Chirac, 4/10/1986, DDRS.

154. Reagan to Mulroney, in Confidential White House Cable, 4/15/1986, DDRS.

155. "Next Steps with Libya," undated, Box 30, North Files, RRL. See also CIA, "Qadhafi's Political Position since the Airstrike," 7/17/1986, DDRS.

156. NSPG Meeting, 7/16/1986, Box 91308, NSPGs, ESF, RRL; Davis, *Qaddafi,* 161–62; Robert Gates, *From the Shadows: The Ultimate Insider's Story of Five Presidents and How They Won the Cold War* (New York: Simon & Schuster, 1996), 405–6; Bob Woodward, "Gadhafi Target of Secret U.S. Deception Plan," *Washington Post,* 10/2/1986.

157. Bruce Jentleson, "The Reagan Administration and Coercive Diplomacy: Restraining More than Remaking Governments," *Political Science Quarterly* 106, no. 1 (1991): 64; William Webster Oral History, 8/21/2002, 34–35, POHP.

158. Statement by Secretary of Defense, 1/21/1987, *AFP: CD*, 1987: 230; Prepared Statement by Ambassador at Large for Counter-Terrorism, 2/9/1989, *AFP: CD*, 1989: 242.

159. CIA, *Terrorism Review*, 10/6/1988, CIA FOIA.

160. Whitehead's comments in NSPG Meeting, 2/24/1987, NSC, NSPG MTG Minutes and Presidential MemCons, RRL. See also Department of State, *Patterns of Global Terrorism: 1989*, Department of Defense FOIA, iii–iv; Bush to Reagan, 6/2/1987, OA/ID 19849, Gregg Files, RRL; Naftali, *Blind Spot*, 194–200.

161. Reagan, Radio Address to the Nation, 5/31/1986, APP.

162. NSPG Meeting, 2/24/1987.

163. Oakley to Powell, 8/8/1988, Box 91843, William Burns Files, RRL; Naftali, *Blind Spot*, 186–87, 206–7, 219–21; CIA, *Terrorism Review*, 3/10/1988, CIA FOIA.

164. NSPG Meeting, 2/24/1987.

165. CIA, "Iran: Khomeini's Prospects and Views," 1/19/1979, DNSA.

166. Department of State, "The New Islamic Fundamentalism," Feb. 1979, NLC-25-47-7-3-3, JCL.

167. "Iran: The Crescent of Crisis," *Time*, 1/15/1979, http://content.time.com/time/archive/ (accessed 5/14/2014).

168. On these issues and Islamist anti-Sovietism more broadly, see Odd Arne Westad, *The Global Cold War: Third World Interventions and the Making of Our Times* (Cambridge, UK: Cambridge University Press, 2006), esp. 288–330; Seth Jones, *In the Graveyard of Empires: America's War in Afghanistan* (New York: W. W. Norton, 2009), 72; David B. Edwards, *Before Taliban: Genealogies of the Afghan Jihad* (Berkeley: University of California Press, 2002); Islamabad to State, 6/28/1981, DNSA.

169. Alexandre Benningsen, "The Soviet Union and Muslim Guerrilla Wars, 1920–1981: Lessons for Afghanistan," RAND Corporation, Aug. 1981, 15, DNSA.

170. NSDD-75, "U.S. Relations with the USSR," 1/17/1983, Box 91287, ESF, RRL.

171. Gates, *From the Shadows*, 131–32.

172. Larrabee to Brzezinski, 12/31/1979, DDRS.

173. SCC Meeting, 1/17/1980, Box 32, SF, ZBDM, JCL.

174. Artemy Kalinovsky, *A Long Goodbye: The Soviet Withdrawal from Afghanistan* (Cambridge, MA: Harvard University Press, 2011), 49–50; Dilip Hiro, *Apocalyptic Realm: Jihadists in South Asia* (New Haven: Yale University Press, 2012), 62. See also Westad, *Global Cold War*, 355; Bronson, *Thicker than Oil*, 169–77.

175. Gromyko, Andropov, Ustinov and Ponomarev to CC CPSU, 1/28/1980, Carter-Brezhnev Project, NSArch.

176. Shultz to Reagan, 11/29/1982, DDRS.

177. Husain Haqqani, *Magnificent Delusions: Pakistan, the United States, and an Epic History of Misunderstanding* (New York: PublicAffairs, 2013), 257–64; Arthur Hummel Oral History, 145–46, FAOHC; Statement by James Buckley of USAID, 11/12/1981, DNSA.

178. CIA, "Afghanistan: Limits to U.S. Pressure for Resistance Unity," 9/17/1985, CREST.

179. CIA, "Zia-ul-Haq: A Political Portrait," 9/27/1980, CREST. See also CIA, "Pakistan: Prospects for the Zia Government," Feb. 1981, CREST.

180. Islamabad to State, 6/28/1981, DNSA.

181. Edmund McWilliams Oral History, 74, FAOHC.

182. Haqqani, *Magnificent Delusions,* 269. See also Steve Coll, *Ghost Wars: The Secret History of the CIA, Afghanistan, and bin Laden, from the Soviet Invasion to September 10, 2001* (New York: Penguin, 2004), 62–68; Jones, *In the Graveyard of Empires,* 32–34; Bronson, *Thicker than Oil,* 170, 172–74.

183. INR, "Afghanistan: 18 Months of Occupation," Aug. 1981, DNSA; Francis Fukuyama, "The New Marxist-Leninist States in the Third World," RAND Corporation, Sept. 1984, 33, DNSA.

184. "Afghanistan: Status, U.S. Role, and Implications of a Soviet Withdrawal," CRS Report, 4/20/1988, 6, DNSA.

185. Andrew Hartman, "The Red Template: U.S. Policy in Soviet-Occupied Afghanistan," *Third World Quarterly* 23, no. 3 (2002), 480; Lawrence Wright, *The Looming Tower: Al-Qaeda and the Road to 9/11* (New York: Knopf, 2006), 109–50.

186. Remarks to CPAC, 3/1/1985, APP.

187. Charles Naseem (Pentagon consultant), "Proposed Sale of U.S. Military Weapons and Aid to Pakistan to Counter Soviet Military Threat," 9/29/1981, DDRS; briefing papers in Shultz to Reagan, 11/29/1982, DDRS.

188. Mary Anne Weaver, *Pakistan: In the Shadow of Jihad and Afghanistan* (New York: Farrar, Straus and Giroux, 2002), 79–80; Coll, *Ghost Wars,* 120.

189. Wright, *Looming Tower,* 54.

190. The reliance on Pakistan is evident in Shultz to Reagan, 11/26/1982, EBB 377, NSArch; Islamabad to State, 10/13/1982, DDRS.

191. John McCarthy Oral History, 76, FAOHC.

192. Tom Hundley, "U.S. Had Hand in Creating an Implacable Foe," *Chicago Tribune,* 9/17/2001.

193. Brinkley, *Reagan Diaries,* 619; Ahmed Rashid, *Descent into Chaos: The U.S. and the Disaster in Pakistan, Afghanistan, and Central Asia* (New York: Penguin, 2009), esp. 38–39.

194. Oakley Oral History, 153.

195. Gates, *From the Shadows,* 561; Coll, *Ghost Wars,* 128–29; Wright, *Looming Tower,* 162–66, 173–74; Alan Kuperman, "The Stinger Missile and U.S. Intervention in Afghanistan," *Political Science Quarterly* 114, no. 2 (1999): 232, 253–55.

196. *Hearings before the Select Committee on Intelligence of the United States Senate: Nomination of Robert M. Gates, to be Director of Central Intelligence,* Exec. Report 102-19, 49, http://www.intelligence.senate.gov/sites/default/files/publications/10219.pdf (accessed 6/5/2015); cable recounting U.S. mission to Tehran from 5/25–5/28/1986, DNSA. See also CIA Information Cable, 1/25/1986, CWIHP-NSArch.

197. On Iran-Contra, see Theodore Draper, *A Very Thin Line: The Iran-Contra Affair* (New York: Hill and Wang, 1991); *The Tower Commission Report: The Full Text of the President's Special Review Board* (New York: Bantam Books, 1987).

198. Frank Carlucci Oral History, 8/28/2001, 34–35, POHP.

199. Weinberger Notes, 12/7/1985, EBB 210, NSArch; President's Special Review Board, Interview of Donald T. Regan, 1/7/1987, 15, Box 211, Regan Papers. See also "Chronology of Iranian Events," 12/23/1986, CFOA 1130, Arthur Culvahouse Files, RRL.

200. Poindexter to Reagan, 1/17/1986, CWIHP-NSArch.

201. See Roche to McFarlane, undated, Box 6, Fortier Files, RRL; Charles Fairbanks to Fortier, 8/30/1984, Box 6, Fortier Files, RRL; "Strategic Recommendations: Iran," 4/9/1985, Box 6, Fortier Files, RRL; Casey to McFarlane, 7/18/1985, DNSA.

202. Fuller to DCI and DDCI, 5/17/1985, DNSA; Teicher, "U.S. Policy toward Iran," 5/24/1985, Box 91682, Teicher Files, RRL.

203. Casey to McFarlane, 7/18/1985, DNSA.

204. Poindexter to Reagan, 1/17/1986, CWIHP-NSArch; Draft NSDD, "U.S. Policy toward Iran," undated, DNSA.

205. "U.S. Policy toward Iran," 5/24/1985, Box 91682, Teicher Files, RRL.

206. Fuller to DCI and DDCI, 5/17/1985, DNSA; Fortier to McFarlane, 10/18/1983, Box 91306, NSPGs, ESF, RRL.

207. "Objectives of the Program," undated (1986), DNSA.

208. "DCI's Iran Testimony for HPSCI and SSCI," 11/21/1986, CFOA 1130, Culvahouse Files, RRL.

209. MemCon between U.S., Israeli, and Iranian Representatives, 5/26/1986, DNSA. See also Account of U.S. Mission to Tehran, May 1986, CWIHP-NSArch.

210. Weinberger in Powell to USD(P) and ASD(ISA), 6/19/1985, DNSA.

211. Shultz in Untitled Talking Points, 12/7/1985, DNSA. See also Shultz to McFarlane, 6/29/1985, DNSA.

212. Shultz, *Turmoil and Triumph*, 785; *Tower Commission Report*; Account of U.S. Mission to Tehran, 5/25–5/28/1986, DNSA; MemCon between U.S. and Iranian Representatives, 9/19–9/20/1986, DNSA; Lou Cannon, *President Reagan: The Role of a Lifetime* (New York: Simon & Schuster, 1991), 589–703.

213. Oakley and Kelly to Carlucci, 3/16/1987, DNSA; Department of State, "Iran's Use of International Terrorism," 10/27/1987, DNSA; CIA, *Terrorism Review*, 2/25/1988, CIA FOIA.

214. John H. Kelly Oral History, 137, FAOHC; Donette Murray, *U.S. Foreign Policy and Iran: American-Iranian Relations since the Islamic Revolution* (New York: Routledge, 2010), 177n. 95.

215. Marlin Fitzwater to Mark McIntyre, 1/14/1987, DNSA. See also Bush, Remarks to International Conference on Terrorism, 1/20/1987, OA/ID 19850, Gregg Files, GHWBL.

216. On these issues, see Draper, *Very Thin Line*, esp. 151–55, 455–56; Takeyh, *Guardians of the Revolution*, 54.

217. Poindexter Memo, 11/21/1986, DNSA. See also Oakley to Carlucci, 3/24/1987, DDRS; Kenneth Pollack, *The Persian Puzzle: The Conflict between Iran and America* (New York: Random House, 2005), 214–16.

218. Shultz's Untitled Talking Points, 12/7/1985, DNSA; Wayne White Oral History, 60, FAOHC; Nigel Ashton, *King Hussein of Jordan: A Political Life* (New Haven: Yale University Press, 2008), 223–225.

219. Oakley to Carlucci, 3/24/1987, DDRS.

220. London to State, 12/21/1983, EBB 82, NSArch.

221. Hussein's Meeting with Cabinet Ministers, early 1987, SH-SHTP-D-000-609, CRRC; Meeting with Senior Officials to Discuss a Speech by President Reagan, SH-SHTP-A-000-638, CRRC. See also Meeting regarding the Iran-Iraq War,

mid-November 1986, SH-SHTP-A-000-556, CRRC; Meeting with Revolutionary Command Council, 11/15/1986, SH-SHTP-A-000-555, CRRC.

222. Baghdad to State, 1/13/1987, Boxes 91981–91983, NESAA, ESF, RRL.

223. *Comprehensive Report,* Vol. I: 31. See also Hal Brands, "Inside the Iraqi State Records: Saddam Hussein, 'Irangate,' and the United States," *Journal of Strategic Studies* 34, no. 1 (2011): 105–15.

224. "Draft Presidential Speech on Iran," 11/13/1986, Box 295, Speechwriting Files, RRL.

225. Draft of Bush to Reagan, 5/7/1987, OA/ID 19849, Gregg Files, GHWBL; Bush to Reagan, 6/2/1987, OA/ID 19849, Gregg Files, GHWBL.

226. Ross to Powell, 1/21/1987, Boxes 91834/91840/91843, Burns Files, RRL; Weinberger in Powell Notes of NSC Meeting, 1/21/1987, CWIHP-NSArch.

227. Export-Import Bank Memorandum, 9/3/1987, DNSA; GAO, *Iraq's Participation,* 14.

228. Jentleson, *With Friends like These,* 62–67, 88; author's phone interview with Richard Perle, 12/17/2010.

229. Author's phone interview with Rick Francona, 8/24/2010; Rick Francona email to author, 8/24/2010; Patrick Tyler, "Officers Say U.S. Aided Iraq in War Despite Use of Gas," *New York Times,* 8/18/2002.

230. State to Baghdad and Other Posts, 2/25/1987, Boxes 91981–91983, NESAA, ESF, RRL; Lou Cannon and David Ottoway, "Reagan Plans to Ban Trade with Iran," *Washington Post,* 10/24/1987.

231. Geneva to State, 7/6/1987, DDRS. See also State to Baghdad, 7/11/1987, Boxes 91981–91983, NESAA, ESF, RRL; Powell-Aziz MemCon, 12/6/1987, Box 91849, Burns Files, RRL; Shultz-Shevardnadze MemCon, 4/21/1988, DDRS; David Malone, *The International Struggle over Iraq: Politics in the UN Security Council* (New York: Oxford University Press, 2007), 32–39.

232. CIA, "Iraq-Iran: The War Moves into the Gulf," 5/17/1984, CREST; Morton Abramowitz to Shultz, 5/18/1987, DNSA; Platt to Carlucci, 1/22/1987, DDRS; Little, *American Orientalism,* 250; Weinberger, *Fighting for Peace,* 387–88.

233. CIA, "Increasing Danger to Persian Gulf Shipping," 5/9/1987, CWIHP-NSArch.

234. Author's phone interview with W. Nathaniel Howell, 8/30/2010; Weinberger, "A Report to the Congress on Security Arrangements in the Persian Gulf," 6/15/1987, Department of Defense FOIA, esp. ii–iii, 9–10.

235. Geneva to State, 7/7/1987, DDRS; Edward Marolda and Robert John Schneller, *Shield and Sword: The United States Navy and the Persian Gulf War* (Annapolis: U.S. Naval Institute Press, 2001), 33–35.

236. "Ambassador to U.S. Nizar Hamdun on Gulf War," 10/20/1987, FBIS-NES-87-202.

237. Carlucci in Steven Hurst, *The United States and Iraq since 1979: Hegemony, Oil, and War* (Edinburgh: Edinburgh University Press, 2009), 65. See also Michael Palmer, *Guardians of the Gulf: A History of America's Expanding Role in the Persian Gulf, 1833–1992* (New York: Free Press, 1992), 128–49.

238. Weinberger, "Security Arrangements in the Persian Gulf," Department of Defense FOIA, i.

239. See Kenneth Pollack, *Arabs at War: Military Effectiveness, 1948–1991* (Lincoln: University of Nebraska Press, 2002), 225–32; Steven Ward, *Immortal: A History of Iran and Its Armed Forces* (Washington, DC: Georgetown University Press, 2009), 289–95.

240. Takeyh, "Iran-Iraq War," 381. On Iranian terrorism in 1987, see CIA, *Terrorism Review*, 2/25/1988, CIA FOIA; F. Gregory Gause, *The International Relations of the Persian Gulf* (New York: Cambridge University Press, 2010), 77; Shultz-Shevardnadze MemCon, 4/21/1988, DDRS.

241. MemCon between U.S. and Soviet Officials, 8/2/1988, DDRS.

242. Author's phone interview with Barbara Bodine, 12/21/2010.

243. NIC, Response to NSR-10, "Persian Gulf," 3/3/1989, CWIHP-NSArch; NSD-26, "U.S. Policy toward the Persian Gulf," 10/2/1989, NSD Files, GHWBL.

244. NIC, Response to NSR-10, "Persian Gulf." On Iranian grievances, see Hiro, *Longest War*, 244; Blight et al., *Becoming Enemies*, 334–35.

245. Department of State, *Patterns of Global Terrorism: 1993*, Apr. 1994, http://dosfan.lib.uic.edu/ERC/arms/PGT_report/1993PGT.html (accessed 8/5/2014); *U.S. Policy toward Iran: Hearing before the Committee on International Relations, House of Representatives, One Hundred Fourth Congress, First Session, November 9, 1995* (Washington, DC, 1996), 10.

246. CIA, "Iraq's National Security Goals," Dec. 1988, EBB 80, NSArch; Morris Mottale, *The Origins of the Gulf Wars* (Lanham, MD: University Press of America, 2001), 124.

247. Islamabad to State, 8/30/1988, NLC Database, JCL; Riesz to Goldthwait, 10/28/1988, DNSA. See also CIA, "Iraq: No End in Sight to Debt Burden," 4/12/1990, CIA FOIA.

248. Transition Paper, "Guidelines for U.S.-Iraq Policy," 1/20/1989, DNSA; Baghdad to State, 6/29/1989, DNSA; Murphy to Armacost, 9/19/1988, DNSA.

249. NSD-26, "U.S. Policy toward the Persian Gulf"; Memo to Baker, 11/9/1989, Box 10, William Otis Files, GHWBL.

250. Author's interview with Joseph McGhee, 6/4/2010; John Kelly Oral History, 181, FAOHC.

251. Murphy et al. to Shultz, 12/29/1988, DNSA; Richard L. Russell, "Iraq's Chemical Weapons Legacy: What Others Might Learn from Saddam," *Middle East Journal* 59, no. 2 (2005): esp. 198.

252. See CIA, "Iraq's Missile Program," undated (Nov. 1988), CIA FOIA; CIA, "Chemical and Biological Weapons: The Poor Man's Atomic Bomb," Dec. 1988, DNSA; "Recommendations to Strengthen U.S. Nuclear Nonproliferation Policy," 4/17/1989, DNSA. U.S. intelligence did, however, underestimate precisely how much progress Iraq had made toward a crude nuclear capability at the time of the 1990–1991 Persian Gulf conflict.

253. Meeting between Saddam Hussein and senior officials, 9/17/1988, SH-SHTP-A-000-554, CRRC.

254. "Collection of Security and Political Reports Addressed to Saddam Hussein's Office," various dates, SH-MISC-D-000-615, CRRC. See also Hal Brands and David Palkki, "Conspiring Bastards: Saddam Hussein's Strategic View of the United States," *Diplomatic History* 36, no. 3 (2012): esp. 640–54.

6. The Dawn of the Unipolar Moment

1. For such criticism, see Zbigniew Brzezinski, *Second Chance: Three Presidents and the Crisis of American Superpower* (New York: Basic Books, 2007), 45–82; Andrew Bacevich, *American Empire: The Realities and Consequences of U.S. Diplomacy* (Cambridge, MA: Harvard University Press, 2002), esp. 55–78.

2. Excerpts from Soviet Transcript of Malta Summit, 12/2–12/3/1989, EBB 296, NSArch.

3. Robert Gates, *From the Shadows: The Ultimate Insider's Story of Five Presidents and How They Won the Cold War* (New York: Simon & Schuster, 1996), 449.

4. James Baker, *The Politics of Diplomacy: Revolution, War, and Peace, 1989–1992* (New York: Putnam, 1995), 40.

5. Ross to Baker, 12/16/1988, Box 1, Zelikow-Rice (Z-R) Files, Hoover.

6. "Mary Finch Notes of Interview," 1/18/1995, Box 1, Z-R Files, Hoover.

7. Robert Gates Oral History, 7/23–7/24/2000, esp. 17, POHP; Brent Scowcroft Oral History, 11/12–11/13/ 1999, esp. 27–41, POHP.

8. David Rothkopf, *Running the World: The Inside Story of the National Security Council and the Architects of American Power* (New York: PublicAffairs, 2005), 260–302; Bartholomew Sparrow, *The Strategist: Brent Scowcroft and the Call of National Security* (New York: PublicAffairs, 2015), 265–91; George Bush and Brent Scowcroft, *A World Transformed* (New York: Vintage, 1999), esp. 16–40.

9. Andrew Rosenthal, "Differing Views of America's Global Role," *New York Times,* 11/2/1988.

10. "Bush: 'Our Work Is Not Done; Our Force Is Not Spent,'" *Washington Post,* 8/19/1988.

11. Bush, Inaugural Address, 1/20/1989, APP.

12. Bush, Address to UN General Assembly, 9/25/1989, APP; Baker, Address at Center for Strategic and International Studies, 5/4/1989, Box 158, Baker Papers. See also Bush-Robert Hawke MemCon, 6/27/1989, Presidential MemCons/TelCons, GHWBL. Unless otherwise noted, all Bush-era MemCons and TelCons cited are from this collection.

13. Baker, Testimony to House Foreign Affairs Committee, 6/22/1989, Box 158, Baker Papers; NSR-3, "Comprehensive Review of U.S.-Soviet Relations," 2/15/ 1989, NSR File, GHWBL.

14. Bush-Ciriaco de Mita MemCon, 5/27/1989, GHWBL.

15. Reported in Ross to Baker, 12/16/1988, Box 1, Z-R Files, Hoover.

16. In Michael Beschloss and Strobe Talbott, *At the Highest Levels: The Inside Story of the End of the Cold War* (Boston: Little, Brown, 1993), 17.

17. Bush, Remarks at U.S. Coast Guard Academy, 5/24/1989, APP.

18. Jeffrey Engel, "A Better World . . . but Don't Get Carried Away: The Foreign Policy of George H.W. Bush Twenty Years On," *Diplomatic History* 34, no. 1 (2010): 29.

19. *National Security Strategy of the United States* (Washington, DC, 1990), 5.

20. See, for instance, NSR-12, "Review of National Defense Strategy," 3/3/1989, NSR Files, GHWBL; David Broder, "Bush and the Fateful First Few Months," *Washington Post,* 12/14/1988; "JAB Personal Notes from 2/10/89 mtg. w/ POTUS & Canada PM Mulroney," Box 108, Baker Papers.

21. Bush, Address to Joint Session of Congress, 2/9/1989, APP; Bush, Remarks to Polish National Assembly, 7/10/1989, APP; Bush-Hurd MemCon, 1/29/1990, GHWBL.

22. "Even in foreign policy," one *Washington Post* retrospective noted, "Bush was accused of being reactive, too cautious, too unwilling to move in untested waters." Ann Devroy, "The Nation Changed, but Bush Did Not," *Washington Post,* 1/17/1993.

23. Zoellick, "Foreign Policy Overview Points: Managing Change," 10/17/1989, Box 108, Baker Papers.

24. "Record of Conversation with U.S. Ambassador to the USSR, J. Matlock," 12/24/1989, CWIHP.

25. Soviet Foreign Ministry, "The Political Processes in the European Socialist Countries, and the Proposals for Our Practical Steps Considering the Situation Which Has Arisen in Them," 2/24/1989, CWIHP. See also "Memorandum to Alexander Yakoklev from the Bogomolov Commission," Feb. 1989, CWIHP; Charles Maier, *Dissolution: The Crisis of Communism and the End of East Germany* (Princeton: Princeton University Press, 1997), esp. 3–166.

26. Gorbachev-Karoly Grosz Meeting, 3/23–3/24/1989, CWIHP.

27. On Gorbachev's role, see Jacques Levesque, *The Enigma of 1989: The USSR and the Liberation of Eastern Europe* (Berkeley: University of California Press, 1997); Mark Kramer, "The Collapse of East European Communism and the Repercussions within the Soviet Union (Part 1)," *Journal of Cold War Studies* 5, no. 4 (2003): 184–201; Archie Brown, *The Rise and Fall of Communism* (London: Bodley Head, 2009), 524–27, 536–37.

28. Gorbachev's Meeting with Soviet Ambassadors, 3/3/1989, in *Masterpieces of History: The Peaceful End of the Cold War in Europe, 1989,* edited by Svetlana Savranskaya, Thomas Blanton, and Vladislav Zubok (Budapest: Central European University Press, 2010), 417.

29. Chernyaev Diary, 10/5/1989, CWIHP.

30. Chernyaev Diary, 11/10/1989, CWIHP.

31. Scowcroft to Bush, 12/22/1989, Box 10, OA/ID 91116, Chron Files, German Unification Files (GUF), Brent Scowcroft Collection (BSC), GHWBL.

32. Scowcroft to Rice and Zelikow, 2/27/1995, Box 1, Z-R Files, Hoover; Scowcroft Oral History, 73; Ross to Baker, 2/21/1989, Box 1, Z-R Files, Hoover; "JAB Note from February 1989 re: U.S.-USSR Relations," Box 108, Baker Papers.

33. Gates, "Gorbachev and Critical Change in the Soviet Union," 4/1/1989, CF00719, Condoleezza Rice Files, GHWBL.

34. Bush-Woerner MemCon, 4/12/1989, GHWBL.

35. NSD-23, "U.S. Relations with the Soviet Union," 9/22/1989, NSD Files, GHWBL; "Press Points—Shevardnadze," 3/7/1989, Box 108, Baker Papers. See also "Key Impressions from the Trip," Mar. 1989, Box 108, Baker Papers; NIE, "Soviet Policy toward the West: The Gorbachev Challenge," Apr. 1989, CIA FOIA; Zelikow to Scowcroft, 5/17/1989, OA/ID CF01076, Nancy Bearg Dyke Files, GHWBL. NSD-23 was signed in September, but had been substantively completed by mid-spring.

36. Bush, Remarks at Texas A&M University, 5/12/1989, APP; NSD-23, "U.S. Relations with the Soviet Union."

37. "Talking Points on 'Beyond Containment,'" undated, in Hughes to Roy, OA/ID 30545, Blackwill Chron, GHWBL.

38. NSR-4, "Comprehensive Review of U.S.-East European Relations," 2/15/1989, NSR Files, GHWBL; "JAB Personal Notes from 2/10/89 mtg."

39. Bush, Remarks in Mainz, West Germany, 5/31/1989, APP; Bush, Remarks on Arrival at NATO Summit, 5/28/1989, APP.

40. Hal Brands, *From Berlin to Baghdad: America's Search for Purpose in the Post-Cold War World* (Lexington: University of Kentucky Press, 2008), 23; Bush to Mulroney, 5/25/1989, Box 15, OA/ID 91121, CFE, USSR Chron, BSC, GHWBL.

41. Bush-Momper MemCon, 4/19/1989, GHBWL. See also Bush-Jaruzelski MemCon, 7/10/1989, GHWBL; Remarks at Karl Marx University, 7/12/1989, APP. U.S. caution is stressed in Gregory Domber, "Skepticism and Stability: Reevaluating U.S. Policy during Poland's Democratic Transformation in 1989," *Journal of Cold War Studies* 13, no. 3 (2011): 52–82.

42. Bush, Remarks at the Solidarity Workers Monument, 7/11/1989, APP.

43. Philip Zelikow and Condoleezza Rice, *Germany Unified and Europe Transformed: A Study in Statecraft* (Cambridge, MA: Harvard University Press, 1995), 28; Bush-Kohl TelCon, 10/23/1989, GHWBL; "Early Steps in German Reunification: 1989," Box 174, Baker Papers.

44. Bush, Remarks in Mainz, 5/31/1989, APP.

45. Robert Hutchings, *American Diplomacy and the End of the Cold War: An Insider's Account of U.S. Policy in Europe, 1989–1992* (Baltimore: Johns Hopkins University Press, 1997), 52, 66–67.

46. Zoellick, "NATO Summit—Possible Initiatives," 5/15/1989, Box 1, Z-R Files, Hoover.

47. Notes on "White House Press Briefing," 7/12/1989, Box 108, Baker Papers; Bush-Woerner MemCon, 10/11/1989, GHWBL.

48. Bush, Remarks and Question-and-Answer Session, 11/9/1989, APP.

49. Bush, Remarks at Welcoming Ceremony in Brussels, 12/3/1989, APP.

50. Bush-Kohl TelCon, 11/10/1989, GHWBL; Mallaby to Hurd, 11/29/1989, Doc. 61, Vol. 7, Series III, *Documents on British Policy Overseas (DBPO)*, http://dbpo.chadwyck.com/home.do. See also James Sheehan, "The Transformation of Europe and the End of the Cold War," in *The Fall of the Berlin Wall: The Revolutionary Legacy of 1989*, edited by Jeffrey Engel (New York: Oxford University Press, 2009), 57–60.

51. Gorbachev-Mitterrand TelCon, 11/14/1989, EBB 293, NSArch. See also Powell to Wall, 1/20/1990, Doc. 103, *DPBO*.

52. Thatcher-Gorbachev Conversation, 9/23/1989, EBB 293, NSArch. See also Powell to Wall, 3/25/1990, Doc. 3, *DBPO*.

53. Meeting between Kohl and Walesa, 11/9/1989, CWIHP. See also Chernyaev Diary, 10/9/1989, EBB 275, NSArch.

54. Jonathan Haslam, *Russia's Cold War: From the October Revolution to the Fall of the Wall* (New Haven: Yale University Press, 2011), 385; Brown, *Rise and Fall of Communism*, 527.

55. "Verbal Message from Gorbachev to Mitterrand, Thatcher, and Bush," 11/10/1989, CWIHP; Melvyn Leffler, *For the Soul of Mankind: The United States, the Soviet Union, and the Cold War* (New York: Hill and Wang, 2007), 438.

56. State-DoD Group, "GDR Crisis Contingencies," 11/6/1989, CF00182, Blackwill Files, GHWBL.

57. Bush-Mulroney TelCon, 11/17/1989, GHWBL.

58. See Dobbins to Baker, 11/10/1989, CF01414-008 to CF01414-101, Robert Hutchings Files, GHWBL; Hutchings to Scowcroft, 11/20/1989, Box 10, OA/ID 91116, Chron, GUF, BSC, GHWBL; Zelikow and Rice, *Germany Unified and Europe Transformed,* 111–14; Hutchings, *American Diplomacy,* 97–98.

59. Scowcroft Oral History, 82; Excerpts from Soviet Transcript of Malta Summit, 12/2–12/3/1989, EBB 296, NSArch.

60. Bush, News Conference in Brussels, 12/4/1989, APP; "President's Afternoon Intervention on the Future of Europe," 12/6/1989, Box 18, FOIA 2000-0950-F, GHWBL.

61. Douglas Hurd Oral History, 3/17/2009, esp. 10, Box 7, Baker Oral History Collection, Mudd; Frederic Bozo, *Mitterrand, the End of the Cold War, and German Unification,* translated by Susan Emanuel (New York: Berghahn, 2009), esp. 123.

62. Bush-Kohl TelCon, 10/23/1989, GHWBL; Jeffrey Engel, "Bush, Germany and the Power of Time: How History Makes History," *Diplomatic History* 37, no. 4 (2013): 639–63.

63. Scowcroft to Bush, undated, Box 10, OA/ID 91116, Chron, GUF, BSC, GHWBL; "Points to Be Made for Telephone Conversation with Chancellor Kohl," undated, Box 10, OA/ID 91116, Chron, GUF, BSC, GHWBL.

64. Scowcroft to Bush, undated (late 1989), Box 10, OA/ID 91116, Chron, GUF, BSC, GHWBL.

65. Scowcroft to Bush, 11/29/1989, Box 10, OA/ID 91116, Chron, GUF, BSC, GHWBL. On German power and the Cold War, see Marc Trachtenberg, *A Constructed Peace: The Making of the European Settlement, 1945–1963* (Princeton: Princeton University Press, 1999).

66. Bush and Scowcroft, *World Transformed,* 230; Bush to Kohl, undated, CF00717, Rice Files, GHWBL.

67. Scowcroft to Bush, 12/22/1989, Box 10, OA/ID 91116, Chron, GUF, BSC, GHWBL; Bush-Woerner MemCon, 2/24/1990, GWHBL.

68. Baker in Bush-Kohl MemCon, 2/24/1990, GHWBL.

69. Blackwill to Scowcroft, 2/7/1990, CF00182, Blackwill Files, GHWBL.

70. Bush-Kohl TelCon, 3/20/1990, GHWBL; Bush-Thatcher MemCon, 11/24/1989, GHBWL; Mary Sarotte, "Perpetuating U.S. Preeminence: The 1990 Deals to 'Bribe the Soviets Out' and Move NATO In," *International Security* 35, no. 1 (2010): 110–37.

71. Michael Cox and Steven Hurst, "His Finest Hour? George Bush and the Diplomacy of German Unification," *Diplomacy & Statecraft* 13, no. 4 (2002): 135.

72. Kohl, for instance, believed that reunification might take five years. Mallaby to Hurd, 1/25/1990, Doc. 105, *DBPO.*

73. Outline of Remarks at NATO Headquarters, 12/4/1989, APP; Baker, Address to Berlin Press Club, 12/12/1989, Box 161, Baker Papers.

74. "First Restricted Bilateral Session," 12/2/1989, CF00769, Arnold Kanter Files, GHWBL; Bush-Kohl MemCon, 12/3/1989, GHWBL. See also Bush-Genscher MemCon, 11/21/1989, GHWBL.

75. Tebbit to Synott, 12/14/1989, Doc. 76, *DBPO*.

76. Bush-Kohl TelCon, 1/26/1990, GHWBL.

77. Maier, *Dissolution,* 234, 245–46, 255; Mary Sarotte, *1989: The Struggle to Create Post-Cold War Europe* (Princeton: Princeton University Press, 2009), 85–86, 99–100.

78. Gorbachev-Mitterrand Meeting, 12/6/1989, in *Masterpieces of History,* edited by Savranskaya, Blanton, and Zubok, 659; "Shevardnadze's Remarks at Central Committee Plenum, February 6," Box 108, Baker Papers.

79. Acland to FCO, 1/30/1990, Doc. 109, *DBPO*; Scowcroft to Bush, undated, OA/ID CF01414, Hutchings Files, GHWBL; Hutchings to Scowcroft, 1/26/1990, CF00182, Blackwill Files, GHWBL.

80. Scowcroft to Bush, undated, CF00182, Blackwill Files, GHWBL; "Two-Plus-Four Preparatory Paper: An Overall Strategy for Two-Plus-Four," undated, OA/ID CF00721, Rice Files, GHWBL.

81. Bush to Scowcroft, undated (Feb. 1990), CF00182, Blackwill Files, GHWBL; Bush and Scowcroft, *World Transformed,* 233.

82. Scowcroft to Bush, Feb. 1990, CF00182, Blackwill Files, GHWBL.

83. Letter with Scowcroft to Bush, undated, CF00182, Blackwill Files, GHWBL; Zelikow and Rice, *Germany Unified and Europe Transformed,* 186.

84. Bush-Kohl TelCon, 2/13/1990, GHWBL.

85. Kristina Spohr, "Precluded or Precedent Setting? The NATO Enlargement Question in the Triangular Bonn-Washington-Moscow Diplomacy of 1990–1991," *Journal of Cold War Studies* 14, no. 4 (2012): 13–14.

86. Scowcroft, "Meetings with German Chancellor Helmut Kohl," Feb. 1990, Box 10, OA/ID 91116, Chron, GUF, BSC, GHWBL; Bush-Kohl MemCon, 2/24/1990, GHWBL; Bush-Thatcher TelCon, 2/24/1990, GHWBL.

87. Bush-Kohl News Conference, 2/25/1990, APP.

88. Bush in Powell to Wall, 2/24/1990, Doc. 155, *DBPO*; White House to Elysée, 4/17/1990, Box 10, OA/ID 91116, Chron, GUF, BSC, GWHBL.

89. Bush-Hurd MemCon, 1/29/1990, GHWBL.

90. White House to Elysée, 4/17/1990, Box 10, OA/ID 91116, Chron, GUF, BSC, GWHBL; Bush-Mitterrand MemCon, 4/19/1990, GHWBL; Hutchings, *American Diplomacy,* 122–23; Michael Baun, "The Maastricht Treaty as High Politics: Germany, France, and European Integration," *Political Science Quarterly* 110, no. 4 (1995–1996): 605–24.

91. "Our Objectives for Chancellor Kohl's Visit," Feb. 1990, CF00182, Blackwill Files, GHWBL.

92. Bush-Havel MemCon, 2/20/1990, GHWBL; Talking Points for Meeting with Czech Leaders, Jan. 1990, Box 108, Baker Papers; Hutchings, *American Diplomacy,* 115–16, 123.

93. Bush-Mitterrand News Conference, 4/19/1990, APP.

94. Scowcroft to Bush, Feb. 1990, CF00182, Blackwill Files, GHWBL.

95. Bush-Woerner MemCon, 5/7/1990, GHBWL; Scowcroft, "Meetings with German Chancellor Helmut Kohl," Feb. 1990, Box 10, OA/ID 91116, GUF, BSC, GHWBL; Angela Stent, *Russia and Germany Reborn: Unification, the Soviet Collapse, and the New Europe* (Princeton: Princeton University Press, 1998), 114, 123–24.

96. Bush–Kohl MemCon, 2/25/1990, GHWBL.

97. Bush and Scowcroft, *World Transformed,* 253; "Interview of Bob Zoellick," 12/4/1990, Box 3, 9–10, Oberdorfer Papers; Scowcroft to Bush, undated, CF00182, Robert Blackwill Files, GHWBL.

98. Bush in Powell to Wall, 2/24/1990, Doc. 155, *DBPO;* "Interview with Bob Zoellick," 2.

99. Sicherman to Ross and Zoellick, 3/12/1990, Box 176, Baker Papers. See also Bush–Kohl MemCon, 2/25/1990, GHWBL; Bush and Scowcroft, *World Transformed,* 234–35; Baker, *Politics of Diplomacy,* 197–99.

100. Chernyaev Diary, 1/28/1990, EBB 317, NSArch.

101. Gorbachev–Baker Meeting, 2/9/1990, and Baker to Kohl, 2/10/1990, in *Masterpieces of History,* edited by Savranskaya, Blanton, and Zubok, 675–87; Baker's notes, "Germany," 2/8/1990, Box 108, Baker Papers.

102. The controversy centered on whether Baker's assurance covered all of Eastern Europe or simply the GDR, and whether it represented an ironclad pledge or simply a negotiating position. In retrospect, Baker was clearly referring to the GDR and not all of Eastern Europe, and the U.S. government did not believe that it had foreclosed NATO expansion. As Sarotte stresses, however, the Russians believed that they *had* received some sort of assurance. Mark Kramer, "The Myth of a No-NATO-Enlargement Pledge to Russia," *Washington Quarterly* 32, no. 2 (2009): 39–61; Mary Sarotte, "Not One Inch Eastward? Bush, Baker, Kohl, Genscher, Gorbachev, and the Origin of Russian Resentment toward NATO Enlargement in February 1990," *Diplomatic History* 34, no. 1 (2010): 119–40.

103. Gorbachev–Baker Meeting, 683; Gates, *From the Shadows,* 490.

104. Sarotte, *1989,* 112–13.

105. Jeffrey Legro, "Trip Report: Admiral Crowe's Visit to the Soviet Union," RAND/UCLA Center for Soviet Studies, Mar. 1990, 3. See also "Directives for the Negotiations of the USSR Foreign Minister with the U.S. President G. Bush and State Secretary J. Baker," 4/4–4/6/1990, Box 3, Z-R Files, Hoover; Mikhail Gorbachev, *Memoirs* (New York: Doubleday, 1995), 532.

106. G. John Ikenberry, "German Unification, Western Order, and the Post-Cold War Restructuring of the International System," in *German Unification: Expectations and Outcomes,* edited by Peter Caldwell and Robert Shandley (New York: Palgrave Macmillan, 2011), 26. See also Excerpt from Minutes of CC CPSU Politburo Session, 5/16/1990, EBB 320, NSArch.

107. "Evolving Soviet Position on Germany," 6/13/1990, CF01010 to CF01010-009, European and Soviet Directorate, NSC Files, GHWBL. See also Maier, *Dissolution,* 211–13, 271–72; Stent, *Russia and Germany Reborn,* 114, 122–24; Vladislav Zubok, *A Failed Empire: The Soviet Union in the Cold War from Stalin to Gorbachev* (Chapel Hill: University of North Carolina Press, 2007), 307–8.

108. "The Future of Europe: Germany, NATO, CFE, and CSCE," undated, Box 1, CF01308, Nicholas Burns Subject Files, GHWBL; Raymond Garthoff, *The Great Transition: American-Soviet Relations and the End of the Cold War* (Washington, DC: Brookings Institution Press, 1994), 427; USDEL Secretary to White House, 5/5/1990, OA/ID CF01354, Zelikow Files, GHWBL.

109. Bush–Shevardnadze MemCon, 4/6/1990, GHWBL; Baker to Gorbachev, 3/28/1990, Box 108, Baker Papers.

110. Baker, *Politics of Diplomacy,* 248; Scowcroft to Bush, "Meeting with NSC Principals on Lithuania," 4/23/1990, CF00719, Rice Files, GHWBL; Gorbachev to Bush, 5/2/1990, Box 109, Baker Papers; Jack Matlock, *Autopsy on an Empire: The American Ambassador's Account of the Collapse of the Soviet Union* (New York: Random House, 1995), 340, 355, 380–82.

111. Chernyaev Diary, 5/5/1990, EBB 317, NSArch.

112. Gorbachev-Baker Meeting, 683; USDEL Secretary Namibia to State, 3/20/1990, Department of State FOIA.

113. On warnings, see "One-on-One Talking Points (for Responding to Gorbachev's Opening Presentation)," CF01308-01 to CF01308-013, Burns Files, GHWBL; Department of State, "Theme Paper: German Unification," 5/23/1990, Department of State FOIA.

114. "Excerpt from the Second Conversation between M.S. Gorbachev and G. Bush," 5/31/1990, EBB 320, NSArch; "Excerpts from Conversation between M.S. Gorbachev and G. Bush," 5/31/1990, EBB 320, NSArch; Bush-Kohl TelCon, 6/1/1990, GHWBL.

115. Baker to Bush, 6/23/1990, Box 109, Baker Papers; "2+4 Min.," 6/22/1990, Box 1, Z-R Files, Hoover.

116. "Evolving Soviet Position on Germany," 6/13/1990, CF01010 to CF01010-009, European and Soviet Directorate, NSC, GHWBL.

117. Gates, *From the Shadows,* 492.

118. Bush-Kohl MemCon, 2/24/1990, GHWBL; Department of State, "German Unification," 5/23/1990, Department of State FOIA.

119. Sarotte, *1989,* 159, 170; Maier, *Dissolution,* 281; Levesque, *Enigma of 1989,* 235.

120. "7/2/90—Briefing of Pres. on NATO Summit," Box 109, Baker Papers.

121. Bush-Gorbachev TelCon, 7/17/1990, GHWBL; Bush News Conference in London, 7/6/1990, APP. See also London to Various Posts, 7/6/1990, CF01333, Susan Koch Files, GHWBL; "President's Intervention on the Transformation of the North Atlantic Alliance," July 1990, CF00290, Heather Wilson Files, GHWBL.

122. Quoted in Hurd to Alexander, 7/18/1990, Doc. 219, *DBPO.*

123. Zelikow and Rice, *Germany Unified and Europe Transformed,* 300–301, 329–31, 338–42.

124. Bush, Address to German People, 10/2/1990, APP.

125. By 1990–1991, Warsaw Pact countries were starting to seek NATO membership. Sicherman to Ross and Zoellick, 3/12/1990, Box 176, Baker Papers; "Summit Intervention Statement," undated (1991), Box 3, CF01693, Summit Briefing Books, NSC, GHWBL.

126. Zoellick, "Proposed Agenda for Meeting with the President," 1/24/1990, Box 115, Baker Papers.

127. Bozo, *Mitterrand,* 123, 175–76; Hurd Oral History, esp. 10; Anatoly Dobrynin, *In Confidence: Moscow's Ambassador to Six Cold War Presidents* (New York: Random House, 1995), 629–31, 635; Elizabeth Pond, *Beyond the Wall: Germany's Road to Unification* (Washington, DC: Brookings Institution, 1993), 185–86.

128. Bush-Kohl MemCon, 11/7/1991, GHWBL.

129. Statistics from Steve Yetiv, *The Absence of Grand Strategy: The United States in the Persian Gulf, 1972–2005* (Baltimore: Johns Hopkins University Press, 2008), 80.

The literature on the Gulf War is massive. As introductions, see Kevin Woods, *The Mother of All Battles: Saddam Hussein's Strategic Plan for the Persian Gulf War* (Annapolis: U.S. Naval Institute Press, 2008); Lawrence Freedman and Efraim Karsh, *The Gulf Conflict, 1990–1991: Diplomacy and War in the New World Order* (Princeton: Princeton University Press, 1993); Andrew Bacevich and Efraim Inbar, eds., *The Gulf War of 1991 Reconsidered* (London: Frank Cass, 2003); Christian Alfonsi, *Circle in the Sand: Why We Went Back to Iraq* (New York: Doubleday, 2006); Steve Yetiv, *Explaining Foreign Policy: U.S. Decision-Making in the Gulf Wars* (Baltimore: Johns Hopkins University Press, 2011); Michael Gordon and Bernard Trainor, *The Generals' War: The Inside Story of the Conflict in the Gulf* (Boston: Little Brown, 1995); Kevin Woods and Mark Stout, "Saddam's Perceptions and Misperceptions: The Case of 'Desert Storm,'" *Journal of Strategic Studies* 33, no. 1 (2010): 5–41.

130. "INA Reports President's Remarks," 4/2/1990, FBIS-NES-90-064; "Aziz Assails Kuwait, UAE in Letter to Klibi," 7/18/1990, FBIS-NES-40-138.

131. Barry Rubin and Judith Colp Rubin, *Anti-American Terrorism and the Middle East: A Documentary Reader* (New York: Oxford University Press, 2002), 122.

132. "Saddam Speech Marks Revolution's 22nd Anniversary," 7/17/1990, FBIS-NES-90-137. See also Baghdad to State, 4/24/1990, FOIA 1998-0099-F, GHWBL; GMID Intelligence Report Regarding the Strategic Intelligence Situation, May 1990, SH-PDWN-D-000-546, CRRC.

133. Meeting between Saddam and Soviet Delegation, 10/6/1990, SH-PDWN-D-000-533, CRRC. This interpretation builds on Hal Brands and David Palkki, "Conspiring Bastards: Saddam Hussein's Strategic View of the United States," *Diplomatic History* 36, no. 3 (2012), 647–57; Janice Gross Stein, "Deterrence and Compellence in the Gulf 1990–91: A Failed or Impossible Task?" *International Security* 17, no. 2 (1992): 147–79.

134. "Meeting between President Saddam Hussein and the American Ambassador in Baghdad," 7/25/1990, DNSA.

135. Ibid.; Baghdad to State, 7/26/1990, Richard Haass Files, Box 41, FOIA 1998-0099-F, GHWBL; Meeting between Saddam and Iraqi Government Officials, 7/17/1990, SH-SHTP-A-000-894, CRRC.

136. Richard Haass, *War of Necessity, War of Choice: A Memoir of Two Iraq Wars* (New York: Simon & Schuster, 2009), 60. See also Kelly to Kimmitt, 5/26/1990, DNSA; "PCC on Protection of U.S. Interests in the Persian Gulf," 7/26/1990, DNSA; Joint Staff to Various Posts, 7/25/1990, DNSA; State to Baghdad, 7/28/1990, Haass Files, FOIA 1998-0099-F; Alfonsi, *Circle in the Sand,* chaps. 1–2; Norman Schwarzkopf, *It Doesn't Take a Hero* (New York: Bantam Books, 1992), 286–92.

137. "Worldwide Proven Oil Reserves," undated, Virginia Lampley Subject File, FOIA 1998-0099-F, GHWBL.

138. NSC Meeting, 8/3/1990, Haass Files, Box 42, FOIA 1998-0099-F, GHWBL.

139. For figures, see W. Henson Moore to Gates, undated, OA/ID 90009, NSC/DC Meetings, GHWBL; Weinberger, *Report to the Congress on Security Arrangements in the Persian Gulf,* 6/15/1987, i, 5–6; Department of Defense FOIA, Haass, *War of Necessity, War of Choice,* 75–76.

140. "U.S. Security Relations, Commitments, and Interests in the Persian Gulf," 7/24/1990, OA/ID CF01937 to CF01478, Haass Files, Box 43, FOIA 1998-0099-F, GHWBL.

141. NSC Meeting, 8/3/1990, Haass Files, Box 42, FOIA 1998-0099-F, GHWBL; Presidential Remarks to Congressional Leaders, undated, Box 43, FOIA 1998-0099-F, GHWBL; Haass, *War of Necessity, War of Choice,* 62. See also Scowcroft to Bush, 8/6/1990, OA/ID CF01939 to CF01937, Haass Files, Box 42, FOIA 1998-0099-F, GHWBL.

142. Bush, Address to Joint Session of Congress, 9/11/1990, APP.

143. "Gulf Policy Themes," 12/14/1990, Box 17, SF, Marlin Fitzwater Files, Press Office Files, GHBWL.

144. Bush-Kaifu TelCon, 8/3/1990, GHWBL; Bush-Fahd TelCon, 8/4/1990, GHWBL.

145. Remarks and Exchange with Reporters, 8/5/1990, APP.

146. NSC Meeting, 8/4/1990, OA/ID CF01478 to CF01584, Haass Files, Box 44, FOIA 1998-0099-F, GHWBL. See also Bush-Fahd TelCon, 8/4/1990, GHWBL; Haass, *War of Necessity, War of Choice,* 66–67; William Webster Oral History, 8/21/2002, esp. 60, POHP.

147. Yetiv, *Explaining Foreign Policy,* 44; figures from Colin Powell, *My American Journey* (New York: Random House, 1995), 469; Max Boot, *War Made New: Technology, Warfare, and the Course of History, 1500 to Today* (New York: Penguin, 2006), 337–38.

148. Powell, *My American Journey,* 487.

149. See the compendium, "The New World Order: An Analysis and Document Collection," undated (1991), CO1473, Dyke Files, GHWBL; Bush, Address to UN General Assembly, 10/1/1990, APP.

150. Bush and Scowcroft, *World Transformed,* 491, 400.

151. "Talking Points" for Bush's meeting, undated, Box 1, CF00946, Robert Gates Files, GHWBL. See also "Executive Summary," 8/27/1990, Box 1, CF00946, Gates Files, GHWBL; James Baker Oral History, 3/17/2011, esp. 21–22, POHP.

152. This paragraph draws on Bush-Mubarak TelCon, 9/1/1990, GHWBL; Bush-Kaifu TelCon, 8/29/1990, GHWBL; Bush-Ozal TelCon, 8/3/1990, GHWBL; "Talking Points for Secretary Brady's Trip on Gulf Crisis Assistance: London," 9/2/1990, Box 1, CF00946, Gates Files, GHWBL; Baker, *Politics of Diplomacy,* 1–16, 275–99.

153. "Sharing of Responsibility for the Coalition Effort in the Persian Gulf (Feb 8 Update)," OA/ID CF01110 to CF01362, Lampley Files, Box 53, FOIA 1998-0099-F, GHWBL; OMB, "United States Costs in the Persian Gulf Conflict and Foreign Contributions to Offset Such Costs," Report #20, Oct. 1992, in Darman to Bush, 10/15/1992, Department of Defense FOIA. Other sources put the number of countries that eventually contributed military forces as high as thirty-six.

154. "Presidential Remarks to Congressional Leaders," 8/29/1990, OA/ID CF01937 to CF01478, Haass Files, Box 43, FOIA-1998-0099-F, GHWBL.

155. In Norman Kempster, "Baker Says Iraqi Threat Calls for Defense Alliance," *Los Angeles Times,* 9/5/1990. See also "Disproportionate U.S. Share of Troops," 11/27/1990, Box 165, Baker Papers.

156. Bush-Kaifu MemCon, 9/29/1990, GHWBL.

157. "Remarks by President on Gulf Crisis to Cabinet," 9/4/1990, OA/ID CF01478 to CF01584, Haass Files, Box 44, FOIA 1998-0099-F, GHWBL.

158. "The Gulf Crisis: Possible Futures," 10/30/1990, Box 1, CF00946, Gates Files, GHWBL.

159. "Themes for Call to PM Thatcher," OA/ID CF01478 to CF01584, Haass Files, Box 44, FOIA 1998-0099-F, GHWBL; Scowcroft to Bush, 10/30/1990, Box 1, CF00946, Gates Files, GHWBL. See also Riyadh to State, 10/29/1990, Haass Files, FOIA 1998-0099-F, GHBWL.

160. Haass, "The Gulf Crisis: Thoughts, Scenarios, & Options," 8/19/1990, Box 1, CF00946, Gates Files, GHWBL. See also USMISSION UN to State, 8/30/1990, OA/ID CF01937 to CF01478, Haass Files, Box 43, FOIA 1998-0099-F, GHWBL.

161. NSC Meeting, 8/6/1990, Haass Files, Box 43, FOIA 1998-0099-F, GHWBL.

162. DIA, "Iraq's Armed Forces after the Gulf Crisis: Implications of a Major Conflict," Defense Intelligence Memorandum (DIM) 22-91, Jan. 1991, OA/ID CF01584, Haass Files, FOIA 1998-0099-F, GWHBL; Untitled Discussion Paper, 1/11/1991, FOIA 98-0099-F, GHWBL.

163. Bush-Shamir MemCon, 12/11/1990, OA/ID CF01584, Haass Files, FOIA 1998-0099-F, GHWBL. See also Freedman and Karsh, *Gulf Conflict, 1990–1991,* 204–5; Robert H. Scales, *Certain Victory: The U.S. Army in the Gulf War* (Washington, DC: Office of the Chief of Staff, U.S. Army, 1993), 103–54; Keith Shimko, *The Iraq Wars and America's Military Revolution* (New York: Cambridge University Press, 2010), 56–63.

164. Baker to Bush, undated (Nov. 1990), Haass Files, Box 43, FOIA-1998-0099-F, GHWBL; Baker to Bush, 11/6, 11/8, and 11/10/1990, Haass Files, Box 43, FOIA-1998-0099-F, GHWBL.

165. Baker Oral History, 22; USDEL Sec USSR to State, 11/9/1990, OA/ID 91128, Gorbachev Files, Special Separate USSR Notes Files, BSC, GHWBL.

166. *U.S. Policy in the Persian Gulf: Hearings before the Committee on Foreign Relations* (Washington, DC, 1990), 9.

167. See Bush, Address to Joint Session of Congress, 9/11/1990, APP. See also Bush, Address to the Nation, 8/8/1990, APP; Baker's Notes of Meeting with Senators and Representatives, Oct. 1990, Box 109, Baker Papers.

168. Gordon Black/*USA Today* poll, 12/2/1990, USGBUSA.903227.R007, iPoll Database.

169. "Bush Applies Pressure for Gulf War Resolution," *Philadelphia Inquirer,* 1/12/1991; Brands, *From Berlin to Baghdad,* 58; Yetiv, *Explaining Foreign Policy,* 27–28. A good overview of the domestic debate is Gary Hess, *Presidential Decisions for War: Korea, Vietnam, the Persian Gulf, and Iraq,* 2nd ed. (Baltimore: Johns Hopkins University Press, 2009), 183–95.

170. "Points for Cabinet Room Meeting with Congressional Leaders," Jan. 1991, OA/ID CF01584, Haass Files, FOIA 1998-0099-F, GHWBL. See also Radio Address to the Nation, 1/5/1991, APP.

171. Baker-Aziz MemCon, 1/9/1991, Box 109, Baker Papers; "Excerpt from JABIII/T. Aziz Geneva 01/9/91 Mtg.," Box 104, Baker Papers.

172. NSD-54, "Responding to Iraqi Aggression in the Gulf," 1/15/1991, Box 2, CF00946, Gates Files, GHWBL.

173. Boot, *War Made New,* 318–22, 325–28. See also Thomas Keaney and Eliot Cohen, *Gulf War Air Power Survey: Summary Report* (Washington, DC: U.S. Government Printing Office, 1993), esp. 56–64 [hereafter *GWAPS*]; Shimko, *Iraq Wars,* 63–70; Allan R. Millett, Peter Maslowski, and William Feis, *For the Common Defense:*

A Military History of the United States from 1607 to 2012, 3rd ed. (New York: Free Press, 2012), 601–2.

174. Gates Meeting Notes, 2/22/1991, Box 2, CF00946, Gates Files, GHWBL; Nicolas Kerton-Johnson, *Justifying America's Wars: The Conduct and Practice of U.S. Military Intervention* (New York: Routledge, 2011), 35. See also Keaney and Cohen, *GWAPS,* 21–22, 66–83, 97–16, 24–227; Freedman and Karsh, *Gulf Conflict, 1990–1991,* 312–29. U.S. forces actually used a greater number of guided munitions in Vietnam, but the proportion of total munitions used was lower in that conflict than in the Gulf.

175. For skepticism, see Daryl Press, "The Myth of Air Power in the Persian Gulf War and the Future of Warfare," *International Security* 26, no. 2 (2001): 5–44.

176. Kenneth Pollack, *Arabs at War: Military Effectiveness, 1948-1991* (Lincoln: University of Nebraska Press, 2002), 243–46; Woods, *Mother of All Battles,* 14–27, esp. 22, 26.

177. Bush-Arens MemCon, 2/11/1991, Haass Files, OA/ID CF01584, FOIA 1998-0099-F, GHWBL. See also "Points for Jan 21 Phone Call to PM Shamir," Haass Files, OA/ID CF01584, Box 45, FOIA 1998-0099-F, GHWBL; Efraim Inbar, "Israel and the Gulf War," in *The Gulf War of 1991 Reconsidered,* edited by Andrew Bacevich and Efraim Inbar (London: Frank Cass, 2003), esp. 75–81.

178. See Keaney and Cohen, *GWAPS,* 83–87; Scales, *Certain Victory,* 184–86; Theodore Postol, "Lessons of the Gulf War Experience with Patriot," *International Security* 16, no. 3 (1991–1992): 119–71.

179. Bush to Shamir, 1/23/1991, OA/ID CF01584, Haass Files, Box 45, FOIA 1998-0099-F, GHWBL. See also Bush-Arens MemCon, 2/11/1991, OA/ID CF01584, Haass Files, Box 46, FOIA 1998-0099-F, GHWBL; White House to Jerusalem, 1/24/1991, Box 2, CF00946, Gates Files, GHWBL.

180. Bush-Gorbachev TelCon, 1/18/1991, GHWBL.

181. Chernyaev Diary, 2/22/1991, EBB 345, NSArch; Bush-Gorbachev Tel-Con, 2/21/1991, GHWBL; Gorbachev, *Memoirs,* 558–65.

182. Gates Meeting Notes, 2/22/1991, Box 2, CF00946, Gates Files, GHWBL.

183. Bush to Gorbachev, 2/21/1991, Box 109, Baker Papers.

184. "Points for Calls on Gulf State of Play," Feb. 1991, OA/ID CF01584 to CF01585, Haass Files, Box 47, FOIA 1998-0099-F, GHWBL; Bush-Mulroney TelCon, 2/19/1991, GHWBL. See also State to Various Posts, 2/22/1991, OA/ID CF00703, Papadiuk Files, Box 56, FOIA 1998-0099-F, GHWBL; Bush-Gorbachev TelCon, 2/23/1991, GHBWL.

185. Chernyaev Diary, 2/25/1991, EBB 345, NSArch.

186. Keaney and Cohen, *GWAPS,* ix. See also Scales, *Certain Victory,* 103–320; Lawrence Freedman and Efraim Karsh, "How Kuwait Was Won: Strategy in the Gulf War," *International Security* 16, no. 2 (1991): esp. 33–35; Shimko, *Iraq Wars,* 73–76; Department of Defense, *Conduct of the Persian Gulf War: Final Report to Congress,* Apr. 1992, 83–116, 311–416, Department of Defense FOIA.

187. Stephen Biddle, "Victory Misunderstood: What the Gulf War Tells Us about the Future of Conflict," *International Security* 21, no. 2 (1996): 139–79.

188. William Perry, "Desert Storm and Deterrence," *Foreign Affairs* 70, no. 4 (1991): esp. 66–67; Scales, *Certain Victory,* 361–78; Department of Defense, *Conduct of the Persian Gulf War,* esp. xii–xvi.

189. Bush-Dumas MemCon, 2/28/1991, GHWBL.

190. Herbert Parmet, *George Bush: The Life of a Lone Star Yankee* (New Brunswick, NJ: Transaction Publishers, 2001), 483. See also Gates Oral History, 59; Richard Cheney Oral History, 6/21/2006, esp. 27, Box 7, Baker Oral History Collection, Mudd; Alfonsi, *Circle in the Sand,* 172–76.

191. Gordon and Trainor, *Generals' War,* 416–29, 444–46; Thomas Mahnken, "A Squandered Opportunity? The Decision to End the Gulf War," in *The Gulf War of 1991 Reconsidered,* edited by Andrew Bacevich and Efraim Inbar (London: Frank Cass, 2003), 121–48.

192. Gates Oral History, 59.

193. Dennis Ross Oral History, 8/2/2001, 42–43, POHP; CIA, "Implications of Insurrection and Prospects for Saddam's Survival," 3/16/1991, EBB 167, NSArch.

194. Bush-Ozal TelCon, 4/15/1991, GHWBL.

195. Statement of Assistant Secretary of Defense Henry S. Rowen to SFRC, 6/6/1991, CF01391, Lampley Files, GHWBL.

196. Bush-Santer-Delors MemCon, 4/11/1991, GHWBL.

197. *1992 Joint Military Net Assessment* (Washington, DC, 1992), 1–2; "Iraq: Continuing to Hide Illicit Weapons," 4/27/1992, CIA FOIA; Steven Metz, *Iraq and the Evolution of American Strategy* (Washington, DC: Potomac Books, 2008), 41.

198. "Post-war Security Structures in the Gulf," 2/8/1991, in Kimmitt to various, 2/9/1991, Haass Files, Box 45, FOIA 1998-0099-F, GHWBL.

199. Karen DeYoung and Walter Pincus, "Despite Obstacles to War, White House Forges Ahead," *Washington Post,* 3/2/2003; Thomas Lippman, *Inside the Mirage: America's Fragile Partnership with Saudi Arabia* (Boulder: Westview Press, 2004), 308–24.

200. Cheney, Remarks to American Business Council Conference, 4/9/1991, Federal News Service Transcript (FNS).

201. Gates, "American Leadership in a New World Order," 5/7/1991, in "The New World Order: An Analysis and Document Collection," C01473, Dyke Files, NSC, GHWBL.

202. "America's Postwar Agenda in Europe," Mar. 1991, CF01468, Zelikow Files, GHWBL; Bush-Andreotti MemCon, 3/24/1991, GHWBL.

203. Tokyo to State and other posts, 3/14/1991, EBB 175, NSArch.

204. Bush Diary, 9/7/1990, in George H. W. Bush, *All the Best, George Bush: My Life in Letters and Other Writings* (New York: Scribner, 1999), 479.

205. The historiography on the Soviet collapse is immense. My account draws on Anatoly Chernyaev, *My Six Years with Gorbachev* (University Park: Penn State University Press, 2000); Stephen Kotkin, *Armageddon Averted: The Soviet Collapse, 1970–2000* (Oxford: Oxford University Press, 2008); Brown, *Rise and Fall of Communism;* Mark Kramer, "The Collapse of East European Communism and the Repercussions within the Soviet Union (Part 2)," *Journal of Cold War Studies* 6, no. 4 (2004): 3–64; Mark Kramer, "The Collapse of East European Communism and the Repercussions within the Soviet Union (Part 3)" *Journal of Cold War Studies* 7, no. 1 (2005): 3–96; Steven Solnick, *Stealing the State: Control and Collapse in Soviet Institutions* (Cambridge, MA: Harvard University Press, 1998); Graeme Gill, *The Collapse of a Single-Party System: The Disintegration of the Communist Party of the Soviet Union* (Cambridge, UK: Cambridge University Press, 1994); Matlock, *Autopsy on an Empire.*

206. Chernyaev Diary, 11/15/1990, EBB 317, NSArch; Brooks and Wohlforth, "Power, Globalization, and the End of the Cold War," 32.

207. Moscow to State, 5/11/1990, EBB 320, NSArch.

208. Chernyaev Diary, 1/2/1991, EBB 345, NSArch.

209. NIE 11-18-90, "The Deepening Crisis in the USSR: Prospects for the Next Year," Nov. 1990, CIA FOIA.

210. Gorbachev-Jaruzelski Meeting, 4/13/1990, EBB 504, NSArch.

211. Bush-Gorbachev TelCon, 12/25/1991, GHWBL.

212. Cheney Oral History, 35, Box 7, Baker Oral History Collection, Mudd.

213. Bush-Mitterrand MemCon, 3/14/1991, GHWBL. See also Bush-Mulroney MemCon, 3/13/1991, GHWBL; Scowcroft Oral History, 75; James Goldgeier and Michael McFaul, *Power and Purpose: U.S. Policy toward Russia after the Cold War* (Washington, DC: Brookings Institution Press, 2003), 21–34, 41–43.

214. Bush-Gorbachev TelCon, 6/21/1991, GHWBL. See also Scowcroft to Bush, undated (mid-1991), CF01308-001 to CF01308-013, Burns Subject Files, GHWBL; Chernyaev Diary, 6/21/1991, EBB 345, NSArch.

215. "Meeting on U.S.-Soviet Economic Relations," 6/3/1991, OA/ID CF01407-004 to CF01407-010, Box 1, Burns and Hewlett Chron, GHWBL; Chernyaev Diary, 7/23/1991, EBB 345, NSArch; Rachel Bronson, *Thicker than Oil: America's Uneasy Partnership with Saudi Arabia* (New York: Oxford University Press, 2008), 197.

216. Remarks in Kiev, 8/1/1991, APP. See also Gates, *From the Shadows,* esp. 525–31; Bush to Gorbachev, 1/23/1991, in Bush, *All the Best, George Bush,* 507–9.

217. See, for instance, William Safire, "After the Fall," *New York Times,* 8/29/1991.

218. Bush and Scowcroft, *World Transformed,* 518–61, esp. 542–43. See also Excerpts from Baker Intervention at North Atlantic Council, 8/21/1991, Box 2, CF01526, Barry Lowenkron Files, GHWBL; MemCon between Bush and Baltic Presidents, 9/17/1991, GHWBL; Bush-Kohl MemCon, 11/7/1991, GHWBL; Bush-Yeltsin TelCon, 11/30/1991, GHWBL.

219. Notes for talk with Gorbachev, 12/16/1991, Box 110, Baker Papers; Bush-Gorbachev TelCon, 11/30/1991, GHWBL.

220. Goldgeier and McFaul, *Power and Purpose,* 50.

221. Bush and Scowcroft, *World Transformed,* 564.

222. Gates, "American Leadership in a New World Order," 5/7/1991; U.S.-Japan comparison in Michael Boskin, "The United States and Japan in a Changing Economic World," 11/30/1990, OA/ID 08061, Boskin Files, CEA Files, GHWBL; defense figures in William Wohlforth, "The Stability of a Unipolar World," *International Security* 24, no. 1 (1999), 12.

223. Charles Krauthammer, "The Unipolar Moment," *America and the World 1990,* special issue of *Foreign Affairs* 70, no. 1, (1990/1991), 29, 32.

224. Don Oberdorfer, "Democrats Offer Broad Themes for U.S. Role in Post-Cold War Era," *Washington Post,* 3/15/1992; Jeane Kirkpatrick, "A Normal Country in a Normal Time," *National Interest* 21 (1990): 40–44; Patrick Buchanan, "America First—and Second, and Third," *National Interest* 19 (1990): 77–82. See also Paul Kennedy, *The Rise and Fall of the Great Powers: Economic Change and Military Conflict from 1500 to 2000* (New York: Random House, 1987).

225. Cheney, Remarks to American Society of Newspaper Editors, 4/4/1990, FNS; *National Security Strategy of the United States* (Washington, DC, 1991), esp. v.

226. Baker, Remarks to Executive Council of Foreign Diplomats, 4/26/1990, Box 162, Baker Papers.

227. Baker, Testimony to SFRC, 2/5/1992, Box 168, Baker Papers.

228. Bush, News Conference in Rome, 11/8/1991, APP; Powell in Tokyo to State, 11/29/1991, DSNA. See also "Defense Planning for Theater Forces," undated, OA/ID CF00293, Heather Wilson Subject Files, GHWBL; NSD-70, "U.S. Nonproliferation Policy," 7/10/1992, NSD File, GHWBL.

229. Diary entry, 7/2/1991, in Bush, *All the Best, George Bush,* 527; Bush-Woerner MemCon, 6/25/1991, GHWBL.

230. *National Security Strategy* (1990), 2.

231. Ibid., 23. See also "Defense Planning for Theater Forces," undated, OA/ID CF00293, Heather Wilson Subject Files, GHWBL.

232. Cheney, Remarks at National War College, 6/13/1990, Public Statements of Richard Cheney, Secretary of Defense, GHWBL. See also Powell at National Press Club, 6/22/1990, FNS.

233. Lorna Jaffe, *The Development of the Base Force, 1989–1992* (Washington, DC: Joint History Office of the Chairman of the Joint Chiefs of Staff, 1993). See also Paul Wolfowitz, "Shaping the Future: Planning at the Pentagon, 1989–1993," in *In Uncertain Times: American Policy after the Berlin Wall and 9/11,* edited by Melvyn P. Leffler and Jeffrey W. Legro (Ithaca: Cornell University Press, 2011), 48–54.

234. Remarks in Aspen, Colorado, 8/2/1990, APP.

235. Alexandra Homolar, "How to Last Alone at the Top: U.S. Strategic Planning for the Unipolar Era," *Journal of Strategic Studies* 34, no. 2 (2011), esp. 198–201; Metz, *Iraq and the Evolution,* 34–36.

236. Special Defense Department Briefing by Cheney, 1/29/1990, FNS; Department of Defense, "A Strategic Framework for the Asia Pacific Rim," 4/18/1990, in *AFP: CD,* 1990: 649.

237. Baker, *Politics of Diplomacy,* 340.

238. State of the Union Address, 1/31/1990, APP.

239. Baker, Address to World Affairs Council of Dallas, Mar. 1990, Box 162, Baker Papers.

240. Baker, "Summons to Leadership," 4/2/1992, Box 169, Baker Papers. See also Baker, "A Sound Investment in Freedom's Future," 4/25/1990, Box 162, Baker Papers; Tony Smith, *America's Mission: The United States and the Worldwide Struggle for Democracy in the Twentieth Century* (Princeton: Princeton University Press, 1994), 312–26; Hutchings, *American Diplomacy,* 54–56, 63–66, 190–203, 222. As in earlier eras, of course, this support for democratization was selective—Bush offered little response to the Tiananmen Square massacre in June 1989, for instance.

241. See Zoellick, "U.S. Engagement with Asia," 7/22/1991, in *AFP: CD,* 1991: 670–72; Bush, Remarks on Enterprise for the Americas Initiative, 6/27/1990, APP; G. John Ikenberry, *After Victory: Institutions, Strategic Restraint, and the Rebuilding of Order after Major Wars* (Princeton: Princeton University Press, 2002), 233–34, 239–46.

242. Baker, "A New Pacific Partnership," 6/26/1989, *AFP: CD,* 1989: 477.

243. "Core Points for PRC Meetings, 11/15/91," Box 111, Baker Papers.

244. Remarks in Aspen, Colorado, 8/2/1990, APP.

245. Bush, Remarks to American Society of Newspaper Editors, 4/9/1992, APP.

246. Gates, Remarks to Oklahoma Press Association, 2/21/1992, FNS.

247. Baker, Remarks to Chicago Council on Foreign Relations, 4/2/1992, Box 169, Baker Papers.

248. Quotes from Draft of FY 94-99 Defense Planning Guidance (DPG), in Vesser to Secretaries of Military Departments, CJCS, et al., 2/18/1992, EBB 245, NSArch. See also Barton Gellman, "Keeping the U.S. First; Pentagon Would Preclude a Rival Superpower," *Washington Post*, 3/11/1992. For background and context, see Paul Wolfowitz, "Shaping the Future"; and Eric Edelman, "The Strange Career of the 1992 Defense Planning Guidance," both in *In Uncertain Times: American Policy after the Berlin Wall and 9/11*, edited by Melvyn P. Leffler and Jeffrey W. Legro (Ithaca: Cornell University Press, 2011), chaps. 3-4. Please note that the version of the DPG quoted here consists of the text that was released through the FOIA process, as well as the text that became available through media leaks. The archivists of the National Security Archive have overlaid the two texts to form a more complete version of the February draft.

249. Draft of FY 94-99 DPG; Cheney, Remarks to Senate Budget Committee, 2/3/1992, FNS.

250. Draft of FY 94-99 DPG.

251. Ibid.

252. Ibid.

253. See Eugene Jarecki, *The American War of War: Guided Missiles, Misguided Men, and A Republic in Peril* (New York: Free Press, 2008), esp. 12; Joan Hoff, *A Faustian Foreign Policy from Woodrow Wilson to George W. Bush: Dreams of Perfectibility* (New York: Cambridge University Press, 2007), 138.

254. Draft of FY 94-99 DPG; Patrick Tyler, "U.S. Strategy Plan Calls for Insuring No Rivals Develop," *New York Times*, 3/8/1992.

255. Dale Vesser to Libby, 9/3/1991, EBB 245, NSArch.

256. Draft of FY 94-99 DPG.

257. Barton Gellman, "Aim of Defense Plan Supported by Bush: But President Says He Has Not Read Memo," *Washington Post*, 3/12/1992; "The New Pentagon Paper," *Washington Post*, 5/27/1992; Barton Gellman, "Pentagon War Scenario Spotlights Russia," *Washington Post*, 2/20/1992.

258. Scowcroft, "Meeting with Chancellor Kohl of Germany," 3/19/1992, OA/ID CF01414, Hutchings Country Files, GHWBL.

259. Patrick Tyler, "Pentagon Drops Goal of Blocking New Superpowers," *New York Times*, 5/24/1992; "Pentagon Abandons Goal of Thwarting U.S. Rivals," *Washington Post*, 5/24/1992; Memo to Cheney, 3/26/1992, EBB 245, NSArch; "Issues in the Policy and Strategy Section," 4/14/1992, EBB 245, NSArch.

260. *The Future of U.S. Foreign Policy in the Post-Cold War Era: Hearings before the Committee on Foreign Affairs, House of Representatives* (Washington, DC, 1992), 367; Cheney and Powell Remarks to Senate Budget Committee, 2/3/1992, FNS.

261. Bush note to speechwriters, 3/14/1992, in Bush, *All the Best, George Bush*, 551; Gellman, "Aim of Defense Plan."

262. Baker, "Summons to Leadership," 4/2/1992, Box 169, Baker Papers.

263. Patrick Tyler, "Lone Superpower Plan: Ammunition for Critics," *New York Times*, 3/10/1992.

264. Dick Cheney, *Defense Strategy for the 1990s: The Regional Defense Strategy*, Jan. 1993, EBB 245, NSArch. See also Wolfowitz to Cheney, 5/5 and 5/13/1992, EBB 245, NSArch; Memo from Don Pulling, 4/23/1992, EBB 245, NSArch.

265. Remarks at Texas A&M University, 12/15/1992, APP; Remarks at West Point, 1/5/1993, APP.

266. *National Security Strategy of the United States* (Washington, DC, 1993), 1.

267. This is not to say that there was only one administration perspective on post–Cold War policy. As other scholars have noted, in January 1993 Eagleburger wrote a long memo that in some ways reads as a rejoinder to the DPG. That memo placed greater stress on economics than military matters, it focused more on nontraditional security threats—from AIDS to the fragmentation of states themselves—than on the danger of traditional interstate aggression, and it emphasized the need for new partnerships with increasingly assertive players such as Japan and Europe. So there were indeed nontrivial differences when it came to viewing the post–Cold War world. But one should not make too much of these, because the similarities were also striking. Eagleburger's memo stressed the absence of a peer competitor, the need to combat nuclear proliferation, and the imperative of spreading markets and democracy. It reiterated the goal of "preventing the emergence of hostile, non-democratic regional hegemons." Above all, it affirmed the need for unmatched U.S. leadership in guiding post–Cold War affairs. "No one else can play that role," Eagleburger wrote. "The bottom line is that in this time of uncertainty, the United States has a unique role to play—as a provider of reassurance and architect of new security arrangements; as an aggressive proponent of economic openness; as an exemplar and advocate of democratic values; and as a builder and leader of coalitions to deal with the problems of a chaotic post-Cold War world." In short, this was a more polite call for U.S. primacy, but it was not a rejection of the primacist ethos. See Eagleburger to Christopher, 1/5/1993, FOIA (in author's possession). I thank James Goldgeier for sharing this document with me.

268. On Clinton's critique, see Derek Chollet and James Goldgeier, *America between the Wars: From 11/9 to 9/11: The Misunderstood Years between the Fall of the Berlin Wall and the Start of the War on Terror* (New York: PublicAffairs, 2008), esp. 37–43. On budget pressures, see Melvyn Leffler, "Dreams of Freedom, Temptations of Power," in *The Fall of the Berlin Wall: The Revolutionary Legacy of 1989,* edited by Jeffrey Engel (New York: Oxford University Press, 2009), 145.

269. Joint Chiefs of Staff, *Joint Vision 2010,* 1996, esp. 2, http://www.dtic.mil/jv2010/jv2010.pdf (accessed 12/10/2014); Homolar, "How to Last," 202–12.

270. *Report of the Quadrennial Defense Review*, May 1997, Section 3, "Defense Strategy," http://www.dod.gov/pubs/qdr/sec3.html (accessed 11/18/2014).

271. Barry Posen, *Restraint: A New Foundation for U.S. Grand Strategy* (Ithaca: Cornell University Press, 2014), 27. On continuity in post-Cold War strategy, see Leffler, "Dreams of Freedom, Temptations of Power," 132–69; Bacevich, *American Empire*; Peter Feaver and Stephen Biddle, "Assessing Strategic Choices in the War on Terror," in *How 9/11 Changed Our Ways of War,* edited by James Burk (Stanford: Stanford University Press, 2014), esp. 29–31.

272. Anthony Lake, "From Containment to Enlargement," 9/21/1993, http://fas.org/news/usa/1993/usa-930921.htm (accessed 5/2/2015).

Conclusion

1. William Fox, *The Super-Powers: The United States, Britain, and the Soviet Union; Their Responsibility for Peace* (New York: Harcourt and Brace, 1944).

2. Peregrine Worsthorne, "The Bush Doctrine," *Sunday Telegraph*, 3/3/1991.

3. On the prestige of socialism after World War II, see John Lewis Gaddis, *We Now Know: Rethinking Cold War History* (New York: Oxford University Press, 1997), 32–33.

4. Reagan, "SALT and the Search for Peace," undated (1979–1980), Box 435, CPD Papers, Hoover.

5. On these "waves" of pessimism, see Josef Joffe, *The Myth of America's Decline: Politics, Economics, and a Half Century of False Prophecies* (New York: Liveright, 2013).

6. This was the somewhat pejorative label coined by Samuel Huntington, "The U.S.—Decline or Renewal?" *Foreign Affairs* 67, no. 2 (1988–1989): 76–96.

7. Paul Kennedy, "The Eagle Has Landed," *Financial Times*, 2/2/2002.

8. Christopher Layne, "The Unipolar Illusion: Why New Great Powers Will Rise," *International Security* 17, no. 4 (1993): 5n. 2; Nuno Monteiro, "Unrest Assured: Why Unipolarity Is Not Peaceful," *International Security* 36, no. 3 (2011–2012): 13.

9. Stephen Brooks and William Wohlforth, "American Primacy in Perspective," *Foreign Affairs* 81, no. 4 (2002), 21. By the time of this article, the U.S. military lead was even greater than it had been in the mid-1990s.

10. This phrase is from Thomas Wright, "The Rise and Fall of the Unipolar Concert," *Washington Quarterly* 37, no. 4 (2015): 7–24.

11. Statistics from Freedom House, *Freedom in the World 2013: Democratic Break-throughs in the Balance*, 2013, 29, https://www.freedomhouse.org/sites/default/files/FIW%202013%20Booklet.pdf (accessed 3/9/2015); Larry Diamond, *Developing Democracy: Toward Consolidation* (Baltimore: Johns Hopkins University Press, 1999), 25.

12. Joseph Nye, "Soft Power," *Foreign Policy* 80 (1990): esp. 170.

13. Nuno Monteiro, *Theory of Unipolar Politics* (New York: Cambridge University Press, 2014), 58; Michael Hunt, *The American Ascendancy: How the United States Gained and Wielded Global Dominance* (Chapel Hill: University of North Carolina Press, 2007), esp. 257–64. See also Mary Sarotte, *1989: The Struggle to Create Post-Cold War Europe* (Princeton: Princeton University Press, 2009); Mary Sarotte, *The Collapse: The Accidental Opening of the Berlin Wall* (New York: Basic Books, 2014).

14. For a harsh critique of Reagan's statecraft, see Raymond Garthoff, *The Great Transition: American-Soviet Relations and the End of the Cold War* (Washington, DC: Brookings Institution Press, 1994), esp. 757–78. For high praise, see John Lewis Gaddis, *The Cold War: A New History* (New York: Penguin, 2005), 217–18, 222–36. The range of opinions on these matters can be traced in the sources cited in chapters 2, 3, and 4 of the present book.

15. Henry Kissinger, *Does America Need a Foreign Policy?: Toward a Diplomacy for the 21st Century* (New York: Simon & Schuster, 2001), 285.

16. The most insightful version of this flawed argument is put forward in James Graham Wilson, *The Triumph of Improvisation: Gorbachev's Adaptability, Reagan's Engagement, and the End of the Cold War* (Ithaca: Cornell University Press, 2014).

17. The basic point is made in Hal Brands, *What Good Is Grand Strategy?: Power and Purpose in American Statecraft from Harry S. Truman to George W. Bush* (Ithaca: Cornell

University Press, 2014). See also Charles Edel, *Nation Builder: John Quincy Adams and the Grand Strategy of the Republic* (Cambridge, MA: Harvard University Press, 2014).

18. For a critique of Cold War triumphalism, see Ellen Schrecker, ed., *Cold War Triumphalism: The Misuse of History after the Fall of Communism* (New York: New Press, 2004).

19. For a book that verges on this approach, see Robert Dreyfuss, *Devil's Game: How the United States Helped Unleash Fundamentalist Islam* (New York: Metropolitan Books, 2006). For a far more sober, balanced account, see Bruce Riedel, *What We Won: America's Secret War in Afghanistan, 1979–89* (Washington, DC: Brookings Institution Press, 2014).

20. The term *blowback* was popularized by Chalmers Johnson, *Blowback: The Costs and Consequences of American Empire* (New York: Henry Holt, 2000).

21. James Baker, *The Politics of Diplomacy: Revolution, War, and Peace, 1989–1992* (New York: Putnam, 1995), 84.

22. *National Security Strategy of the United States* (Washington, DC, 1991), v.

23. Quotation is from the preface to *A National Security Strategy for a New Century* (Washington, DC, 1997). See also Ronald Asmus, *Opening NATO's Door: How the Alliance Remade Itself for a New Era* (New York: Columbia University Press, 2002); James Goldgeier, *Not Whether but When: The U.S. Decision to Enlarge NATO* (Washington, DC: Brookings Institution Press, 1999).

24. *A National Security Strategy of Engagement and Enlargement* (Washington, DC, 1995), iii. See also Paul Miller, "American Grand Strategy and the Democratic Peace," *Survival*, 52, no. 2 (2012): 49–76; John Dumbrell, *Clinton's Foreign Policy: Between the Bushes, 1992–2000* (New York: Routledge, 2009), 41–61; *National Security Strategy of the United States of America* (Washington, DC, 2006), 25–34.

25. *Report of the Quadrennial Defense Review*, May 1997, Section 3, "Defense Strategy," http://www.dod.gov/pubs/qdr/sec3.html (accessed 11/18/2014).

26. Anthony Lake, "Confronting Backlash States," *Foreign Affairs* 73, no. 2 (1994): 45–55, esp. 55. See also Robert Litwak, *Rogue States and U.S. Foreign Policy: Containment after the Cold War* (Baltimore: Johns Hopkins University Press, 2000). *Rogue state* and *backlash state* were sometimes used interchangeably in the 1990s.

27. Colin Powell, *My American Journey* (New York: Random House, 1995), 576.

28. Remarks to Kosovo International Security Force Troops, 6/22/1999, APP. This was not, of course, a uniform doctrine. Most notoriously, the Clinton administration—stung by Somalia—failed to act during the Rwandan genocide in 1994.

29. For one critique, see Michael Mandelbaum, "Foreign Policy as Social Work," *Foreign Affairs* 75, no. 1 (1996): 16–32.

30. Freedom House, *Freedom in the World 2013*, 29.

31. Brooks and Wohlforth, "American Primacy in Perspective," 21. See also Stockholm International Peace Research Institute, *SIPRI Yearbook 2003: Armaments, Disarmament, and International Security*, esp. 305, http://www.sipri.org/yearbook/2003/10 (accessed 6/12/2015).

32. See year-by-year data in U.S. Department of Agriculture, Economic Research Service, "International Macroeconomic Data Set," "GDP Shares by Country and Regional Historical," http://www.ers.usda.gov/data-products/international-macro economic-data-set.aspx (accessed 10/14/2014).

33. John J. Mearsheimer, "Why We Will Soon Miss the Cold War," *Atlantic Monthly*, Aug. 1990, 35–50, esp. 35–36; John J. Mearsheimer, "Back to the Future: Instability in Europe after the Cold War," *International Security* 15, no. 1 (1990): 5–56; Aaron Friedberg, "Ripe for Rivalry: Prospects for Peace in Multipolar Asia," *International Security* 18, no. 3 (1993–1994): 5–33.

34. See G. John Ikenberry, *After Victory: Institutions, Strategic Restraint, and the Rebuilding of Order after Major Wars* (Princeton: Princeton University Press, 2002), 246–53.

35. Clinton, Address to the Nation, 3/24/1999, APP.

36. The term, ironically, comes from John J. Mearsheimer, "Why Is Europe Peaceful Today?" *European Political Science* 9, no. 3 (2010): 387–97. On these issues, see also Cheng Guan Ang, *Lee Kwan Yew's Strategic Thought* (New York: Routledge, 2013), 73, 80, 86; Mark Kramer, "Neorealism, Nuclear Proliferation, and East-Central European Strategies," in *Unipolar Politics: Realism and State Strategies after the Cold War*, edited by Ethan Kapstein and Michael Mastanduno (New York: Columbia University Press, 1999), 385–463; Ashton Carter and William Perry, *Preventive Defense: A New Security Strategy for America* (Washington, DC: Brookings Institution Press, 2000), 3–7, 65–91; Stephen Brooks, G. John Ikenberry, and William Wohlforth, "Don't Come Home, America: The Case against Retrenchment," *International Security* 37, no. 3 (2012–2013): 7–51.

37. Kenneth Waltz, "The Emerging Structure of International Politics," *International Security* 18, no. 2 (1993): 44–79; Layne, "Unipolar Illusion."

38. William Wohlforth, "The Stability of a Unipolar World," *International Security* 24, no. 1 (1999): 5–41; Charles Krauthammer, "The Unipolar Moment Revisited," *National Interest* 70 (2002–2003): 5–17, esp. 17.

39. Clinton, Remarks at George Washington University, 8/5/1996, APP. See also John Lewis Gaddis, *Strategies of Containment: A Critical Appraisal of American National Security Policy during the Cold War*, 2nd ed. (New York: Oxford University Press, 2005), 393; data from World Bank, "Military Expenditure (% of GDP)," http://data.worldbank.org/indicator/MS.MIL.XPND.GD.ZS?page=3 (accessed 3/9/2015).

40. Dani Rodrik, *Has Globalization Gone Too Far?* (Washington, DC: Institute for International Economics, 1997), 2.

41. Derek Chollet and James Goldgeier, *America between the Wars: From 11/9 to 9/11: The Misunderstood Years between the Fall of the Berlin Wall and the Start of the War on Terror* (New York: PublicAffairs, 2008), 163–69, 248–52. Of the $50 billion organized for Mexico, the United States contributed $20 billion directly. See David Sanger, "Emergency Power: International Package of Aid Could Reach about $50 Billion," *New York Times*, 2/1/1995.

42. Joan Spero, "The Challenges of Globalization," 9/26/1996, http://www.state.gov/www/issues/economic/960926.html (accessed 7/23/2015).

43. Martin Wolf, "In Defence of Global Capitalism," *Financial Times*, 12/8/1999. See also Rodrik, *Has Globalization Gone Too Far?*; Joseph Stiglitz, *Globalization and Its Discontents* (New York: W. W. Norton, 2002).

44. "Preface" to *A National Security Strategy for a Global Age* (Washington, DC, 2000). Russia would later be expelled from the G-8 in 2014.

45. Steven Erlanger, "Russia Warns NATO on Expanding East," *New York Times*, 11/26/1993. See also James Goldgeier and Michael McFaul, *Power and Purpose: U.S. Policy toward Russia after the Cold War* (Washington, DC: Brookings Institution Press,

2003), 181–210; Angela Stent, *The Limits of Partnership: U.S.-Russian Relations in the Twenty-First Century* (Princeton: Princeton University Press, 2014), 35–45.

46. Steven Mufson, "China Blasts U.S. for Dispatching Warship Groups," *Washington Post,* 3/20/1996. See also Aaron Friedberg, "The Struggle for Mastery in Asia," *Commentary,* November 2000, 17–26; Robert Suettinger, *Beyond Tiananmen: The Politics of U.S.-China Relations, 1989–2000* (Washington, DC: Brookings Institution Press, 2003), 243–63.

47. World Islamic Front Statement, "Jihad against Jews and Crusaders," 2/23/1998, fas.org/irp/world/para/docs/980223-fatwa.htm (accessed 12/29/2014); Mary Habeck, *Knowing the Enemy: Jihadist Ideology and the War on Terror* (New Haven: Yale University Press, 2007).

48. Richard Betts, "The Soft Underbelly of American Primacy: Tactical Advantages of Terror," *Political Science Quarterly* 117, no. 1 (2002), esp. 19.

49. John Lewis Gaddis, *Surprise, Security, and the American Experience* (Cambridge, MA: Harvard University Press, 2004).

50. Address at West Point, 6/1/2002, APP; Stockholm International Peace Research Institute, "Background Paper on SIPRI Military Expenditure Data, 2010," 4/11/2011, http://www.sipri.org/research/armaments/milex/factsheet2010 (accessed 7/13/2012). Copy of page now available at http://npsglobal.org/eng/news/34-conventional-arms/1018-background-paper-sipri-military-expenditure-2010.html.

51. "Introduction" to *National Security Strategy of the United States of America* (Washington, DC, 2002). See also Brands, *What Good Is Grand Strategy?* esp. 159–64.

52. On this model, see Stephen Biddle, "Afghanistan and the Future of Warfare," *Foreign Affairs* 82, no. 2 (2003): 31–46.

53. Rumsfeld, Notes for Briefing with Franks, 11/27/2001, EBB 326, NSA.

54. Remarks at Boeing F-18 Production Facility, 4/16/2003, APP. See also Williamson Murray and Robert Scales, *The Iraq War: A Military History* (Cambridge, MA: Harvard University Press, 2003). A good guide to troop levels is Amy Belasco, *Troop Levels in the Afghan and Iraq Wars, FY2001–FY2012: Costs and Other Potential Issues*, CRS Report R40682 (Washington, DC: Congressional Research Service, July 2009), esp. 35, 64–65.

55. A good contemporary study is Terry Anderson, *Bush's Wars* (New York: Oxford University Press, 2011).

56. "Spiegel Interview: America Had No Verdun," *Der Spiegel,* 3/24/2003, http://www.nytimes.com/2003/03/24/international/europe/24SPIEGEL.html (accessed 3/8/2015).

57. On these issues, see Brands, *What Good Is Grand Strategy?* 171–73, 181–88; F. Gregory Gause, *The International Relations of the Persian Gulf* (New York: Cambridge University Press, 2010), 168, 171–74; Frederic Wehrey, Dalia Dassa Kaye, Jessica Watkins, Jeffrey Martini, and Robert A. Guffey, *The Iraq Effect: The Middle East after the Iraq War* (Santa Monica: RAND Corporation, 2010); Dana Priest, "Iraq New Terror Breeding Ground," *Washington Post,* 1/14/2005; "Iraq Body Count," database, https://www.iraqbodycount.org/database/ (accessed 6/26//2015).

58. On the Georgia war and its implications, see Ronald Asmus, *A Little War That Shook the World: Georgia, Russia, and the Future of the West* (New York: St. Martin's Press, 2010).

59. For varying perspectives on these issues, see Daniel Drezner, *The System Worked: How the World Stopped Another Great Depression* (New York: Oxford University Press, 2014); Jonathan Kirshner, *American Power after the Financial Crisis* (Ithaca: Cornell University Press, 2014). Global losses are from Henry C. K. Liu, "The Crisis of Wealth Destruction," *Asia Times*, 4/13/2010, http://www.atimes.com/atimes/Global_Economy/LD13Dj05.html (accessed 3/25/2015).

60. MemCon between Ford, Kissinger, et al., 9/8/1975, Box 15, MemCons, NSA File, GFL.

61. The annual growth rate data for China are subject to some debate. This figure is from Wayne Morrison, *China's Economic Rise: History, Trends, Challenges, and Implications for the United States*, CRS Report RL33534 (Washington, DC: Congressional Research Service, Oct. 2014), 1.

62. Jonathan Holslag, *Trapped Giant: China's Military Rise* (London: International Institute for Strategic Studies, 2010), 7. Military spending figures calculated from Stockholm International Peace Research Institute, "SIPRI Milex Data 1988–2013," http://www.sipri.org/research/armaments/milex/milex_database (accessed 3/2/2015).

63. Fareed Zakaria, *The Post-American World* (New York: W. W. Norton, 2008); Stephen Walt, "The End of the American Era," *National Interest* 116 (2011): 6–17; Christopher Layne, "The Unipolar Illusion Revisited: The Coming End of the United States' Unipolar Moment," *International Security* 31, no. 2 (2006): 7–41.

64. Mike Lillis, "Most Voters Say the U.S. is in Decline," *The Hill*, 10/24/2011, http://thehill.com/polls/189273-the-hill-poll-most-voters-say-the-us-is-in-decline (accessed 10/24/2015).

65. Robert Kagan, *The World America Made* (New York: Knopf, 2012), 7; Brooks, Ikenberry, and Wohlforth, "Don't Come Home, America."

66. Glenn Kessler, "Secretary of State Clinton Says U.S. Must Partner with 'A Great Number of Actors,'" *Washington Post*, 7/16/2009.

67. On the debate over whether a "democratic recession" had begun, see Marc Plattner, "Is Democracy in Decline?" *Journal of Democracy* 26, no. 1 (2015): 5–10. See also Joshua Kurlantzick, *Democracy in Retreat: The Revolt of the Middle Class and the Worldwide Decline of Representative Government* (New Haven: Yale University Press, 2013).

68. On the military balance, see Office of the Secretary of Defense, *Annual Report to Congress: Military and Security Developments Involving the People's Republic of China 2014*, http://www.defense.gov/pubs/2014_DoD_China_Report.pdf (accessed 2/25/2015); James Dobbins, David C. Gompert, David A. Shlapak, and Andrew Scobell, *Conflict with China: Prospects, Consequences, and Strategies for Deterrence* (Santa Monica: RAND Corporation, 2011).

69. See 2014 data (the most recent available at this writing) at World Bank, "GDP (Current US$)," http://data.worldbank.org/indicator/NY.GDP.MKTP.CD (accessed 7/21/2015). Much was made in late 2014 of news that China's GDP had passed that of the United States at purchasing power parity. As numerous reports made clear, however, that statistic was often considerably overstated as a measure of overall economic strength and geopolitical capability.

70. See 2014 data at World Bank, "GDP per Capita, PPP (Current International $)," http://data.worldbank.org/indicator/NY.GDP.PCAP.PP.CD?order=wbapi_data_value_2013+wbapi_data_value+wbapi_data_value-last&sort=desc (accessed 7/21/2015).

71. Stockholm International Peace Research Institute, SIPRI Military Expenditure Database, "SIPRI Milex Data 1988–2014," http://www.sipri.org/research/armaments/milex/milex_database (accessed 7/21/2015).

72. By early 2015, there were hints that the slowdown was occurring. See Mark Magnier, Lingling Wei, and Ian Talley, "China Economic Growth Is Slowest in Decades," *Wall Street Journal,* 1/19/2015. See also Neil Gough, "Cooling of China's Stock Market Dents Major Drive of Economic Growth," *International New York Times,* 7/15/2015.

73. For bullish assessments of U.S. prospects, see Joffe, *Myth of America's Decline;* Robert Lieber, *Power and Willpower in the American Future: Why the United States Is Not Destined to Decline* (New York: Cambridge University Press, 2012); Michael Beckley, "China's Century? Why America's Edge Will Endure," *International Security* 36, no. 3 (2011–2012): 41–78.

INDEX

Page numbers followed by n indicate notes.